Lecture Notes in Computer Science   13913

The series Lecture Notes in Computer Science (LNCS), including its subseries Lecture Notes in Artificial Intelligence (LNAI) and Lecture Notes in Bioinformatics (LNBI), has established itself as a medium for the publication of new developments in computer science and information technology research, teaching, and education.

LNCS enjoys close cooperation with the computer science R & D community, the series counts many renowned academics among its volume editors and paper authors, and collaborates with prestigious societies. Its mission is to serve this international community by providing an invaluable service, mainly focused on the publication of conference and workshop proceedings and postproceedings. LNCS commenced publication in 1973.

Elisabeth Métais · Farid Meziane ·
Vijayan Sugumaran · Warren Manning ·
Stephan Reiff-Marganiec
Editors

Natural Language Processing and Information Systems

28th International Conference on Applications
of Natural Language to Information Systems, NLDB 2023
Derby, UK, June 21–23, 2023
Proceedings

Springer

Editors
Elisabeth Métais (ID)
Conservatoire National des Arts et Métiers
Paris, France

Vijayan Sugumaran (ID)
Oakland University
Rochester, NY, USA

Stephan Reiff-Marganiec (ID)
University of Derby
Derby, UK

Farid Meziane (ID)
University of Derby
Derby, UK

Warren Manning (ID)
University of Derby
Derby, UK

ISSN 0302-9743   ISSN 1611-3349 (electronic)
Lecture Notes in Computer Science
ISBN 978-3-031-35319-2   ISBN 978-3-031-35320-8 (eBook)
https://doi.org/10.1007/978-3-031-35320-8

This Springer imprint is published by the registered company Springer Nature Switzerland AG
The registered company address is: Gewerbestrasse 11, 6330 Cham, Switzerland

Preface

This volume contains the papers presented at NLDB 2023, the 28th International Conference on Applications of Natural Language to Information Systems, held during June 21–23, 2023 at the University of Derby, United Kingdom. The good on-site participation at last year's conference encouraged this year's organisers to resume with the traditional face-to-face organisation of the conference as it was also the wish of many authors. In exceptional circumstances, we allowed online presentations.

The conference was managed and administered through the EasyChair conference management system as in the previous years. We received 89 submissions for the conference. Each paper was assigned to at least three reviewers for single-blind review, considering preferences expressed by the Program Committee members as much as possible. After the review deadline, Program Committee members were asked to complete missing reviews. In addition, the Program Committee and the General Chairs acted as meta-reviewers, completing missing reviews, writing additional reviews for borderline papers, and acting as moderators for submissions with considerably conflicting reviews. At the end of the process, each paper had received at least three reviews.

To ensure transparency and fairness, all PC members were asked to declare any conflicts of interest through the conference management system. Furthermore, PC members were asked to not submit more than two papers, closely following the publisher's guidelines.

On the basis of these reviews, the Program Chairs decided to accept papers with an average score of approximately 1.0 or above as full papers and papers with scores above 0 but below 1.0 as short papers. The confidence score indicated by the reviewers played a role in deciding borderline cases, as well as the content of the reviews and the topic of the papers with respect to the conference scope. We have not accepted any poster papers this year as we had a good number of papers that scored high to satisfy both the conference acceptance rate and the publisher's required proportions of papers. We accepted 31 Long papers and 14 Short papers.

On the advice given by the publisher, long papers can have up to 15 pages and short papers between 8 and 11 pages. This turned out to be very popular among authors as they did not have to remove large portions of their work when their papers were accepted as short papers. Similarly, the authors of long papers were allowed to include more results and discussions. We have not considered any paper below 8 pages.

The NLDB conference continues to attract high-quality and state-of-the-art research and follows closely the developments of the application of natural language to databases and information systems in the wider meaning of the term. A well-established conference, NLDB is now attracting participants from all over the world. It has evolved from the early years, when most of the submitted papers where in the areas of Natural Language, Databases and Information Systems, to encompass more recent developments in the data- and language-engineering fields. The content of the current proceedings reflects these advancements. The conference also supports submissions on studies related to languages that have not been well supported in the early years, such as Arabic, Romanian and Scandinavian languages.

We would like to thank all the reviewers for their time and effort, and for completing their assignments on time despite tight deadlines. Many thanks go to the authors for their contributions.

June 2023

Elisabeth Métais
Farid Meziane
Vijayan Sugumaran
Warren Manning
Stephan Reiff-Marganiec

Organization

Conference Chairs

Elisabeth Métais   Conservatoire National des Arts et Metiérs, France
Farid Meziane   University of Derby, UK
Warren Manning   University of Derby, UK

Programme Committee Chairs

Stephan Reiff-Marganiec   University of Derby, UK
Vijay Sugumaran   Oakland University Rochester, USA

Programme Committee

Muhammad Aamir   University of Derby, UK
Asad Abdi   University of Derby, UK
Jacky Akoka   CNAM & TEM, France
Alaa AlZoubi   University of Derby, UK
Luca Anselma   University of Turin, Italy
Ahsaas Bajaj   University of Massachusetts Amherst, USA
Mithun Balakrishna   Morgan Stanley, USA
Somnath Banerjee   University of Tartu, Estonia
Valerio Basile   University of Turin, Italy
Imene Bensalem   University of Constantine 2, Algeria
Martin Braschler   ZHAW School of Engineering, Switzerland
Davide Buscaldi   Université Sorbonne Paris Nord, France
Elena Cabrio   Université Côte d'Azur, Inria, CNRS, I3S, France
Raja Chiky   3DS Outscale, France
Luis Chiruzzo   Universidad de la República, Uruguay
Philipp Cimiano   Bielefeld University, Germany
Danilo Croce   University of Rome "Tor Vergata", Italy
Mohsen Farid   University of Derby, UK
Elisabetta Fersini   University of Milano-Bicocca, Italy
Komal Florio   University of Turin, Italy
Vladimir Fomichov   Moscow Aviation Institute, Russia

Fouzi Harrag	University Ferhat Abbas of Setif, Algeria
Flavius Frasincar	Erasmus University Rotterdam, The Netherlands
Imane Guellil	University of Edinburgh, UK
Jon Atla Gulla	Norwegian University of Science and Technology, Norway
Yaakov HaCohen-Kerner	Jerusalem College of Technology, Israel
Helmut Horacek	DFKI, Germany
Ashwin Ittoo	University of Liège, Belgium
Sowmya Kamath S.	National Institute of Technology Karnataka, Surathkal, India
Epaminondas Kapetanios	University of Hertfordshire, UK
Zoubida Kedad	UVSQ, France
Christian Kop	University of Klagenfurt, Austria
Anna Koufakou	Florida Gulf Coast University, USA
Rim Laatar	University of Sfax, Tunisia
Chaya Liebeskind	Jerusalem College of Technology, Israel
Cédric Lopez	Emvista, France
Natalia Loukachevitch	Moscow State University, Russia
Aaisha Makkar	University of Derby, UK
Thomas Mandl	University of Hildesheim, Germany
Manjula D	Vellore Institute of Technology, Chennai, India
Paloma Martínez Fernández	Universidad Carlos III de Madrid, Spain
Patricio Martínez-Barco	Universidad de Alicante, Spain
Raquel Martínez Unanue	Universidad Nacional de Educación a Distancia, Spain
Abir Masmoudi	University of Le Mans, France
Alessandro Mazzei	University of Turin, Italy
Elisabeth Métais	Conservatoire des Arts et Métiers, France
Farid Meziane	University of Derby, UK
Luisa Mich	University of Trento, Italy
Nada Mimouni	Conservatoire des Arts et Métiers, France
Jelena Mitrović	University of Passau, Germany
Soto Montalvo	Universidad Rey Juan Carlos, Spain
Dror Mughaz	Bar-Ilan University, Israel
Rafael Muñoz	Universidad de Alicante, Spain
Lucia Passaro	University of Pisa, Italy
Davide Picca	University of Lausanne, Switzerland
Francisco Rangel	Symanto, Germany
Mathieu Roche	Cirad = TETIS, France
Paolo Rosso	Universitat Politècnica de València, Spain
Flora Sakketou	Philipps University of Marburg, Germany
Khaled Shaalan	British University in Dubai, UAE

Contents

Short papers

Full Papers

Large Language Models in the Workplace: A Case Study on Prompt Engineering for Job Type Classification

Benjamin Clavié[1(✉)], Alexandru Ciceu[2], Frederick Naylor[1], Guillaume Soulié[1], and Thomas Brightwell[1]

[1] Bright Network, Edinburgh, UK
{ben.clavie,frederick.naylor,guillaume.soulie,
thomas.brightwell}@brightnetwork.co.uk
[2] Silicon Grove, Edinburgh, UK
alex@silicongrove.co

Abstract. This case study investigates the task of job classification in a real-world setting, where the goal is to determine whether an English-language is appropriate for a graduate or entry-level position. We explore multiple approaches to text classification, including supervised approaches such as traditional models like Support Vector Machines (SVMs) and state-of-the-art deep learning methods such as DEBERTA. We compare them with Large Language Models (LLMs) used in both few-shot and zero-shot classification settings. To accomplish this task, we employ prompt engineering, a technique that involves designing prompts to guide the LLMs towards the desired output. Specifically, we evaluate the performance of two commercially available state-of-the-art GPT-3.5-based language models, TEXT-DAVINCI-003 and GPT-3.5-TURBO. We also conduct a detailed analysis of the impact of different aspects of prompt engineering on the model's performance.

Our results show that, with a well-designed prompt, a zero-shot GPT-3.5-TURBOclassifier outperforms all other models, achieving a 6% increase in Precision@95% Recall compared to the best supervised approach. Furthermore, we observe that the wording of the prompt is a critical factor in eliciting the appropriate "reasoning" in the model, and that seemingly minor aspects of the prompt significantly affect the model's performance.

Keywords: Large Language Models · Text Classification · Natural Language Processing · Industrial Applications · Prompt Engineering

1 Introduction

The combination of broadened access to higher education and rapid technological advancement with the mass-adoption of computing has resulted in a number of phenomena. The need for computational tools to support the delivery of quality education at scale has been frequently highlighted, even allowing for the development of an active academic subfield [27]. At the other end of the pipeline,

E. Métais et al. (Eds.): NLDB 2023, LNCS 13913, pp. 3–17, 2023.
https://doi.org/10.1007/978-3-031-35320-8_1

technological advances have caused massive changes in the skills required for a large amount of jobs [35], with some researchers also highlighting a potential mismatch between these required sets of skills and the skills possessed by the workforce [16]. These issues lead to a phenomenon known as the "education-job mismatch", which can lead to negative effects on lifetime income [30].

Due in part to these factors, the modern employment landscape can be difficult to enter for recent graduates, with recent LinkedIn surveys showing that over a third of "entry-level" positions require multiple years of experience, and more than half of such positions requiring 3 years experience in certain fields or extremely specific skills [1]. As a result, it has been noted that entering the job market is an increasingly difficult task, now demanding considerable time and effort [20]. While computational advances are now commonly used to support education and to assist workers in their everyday work, there is a lack of similarly mature technological solutions to alleviate the issues presented by exiting education to enter the workplace. We believe that the rapid development of machine learning presents a powerful opportunity to help ease this transition.

The case study at the core of this paper focuses on one of the important tasks to build towards this objective: Graduate Job Classification. Given a job posting containing its title and description, our aim is to be able to automatically identify whether or not the job is a position fit for a recent graduate or not, either because it requires considerable experience or because it doesn't require a higher education qualification. In light of the information presented above, as well as the sheer volume of job postings created every day, this classification offers an important curation. This would allow graduates to focus their efforts on relevant positions, rather than spending a considerable amount of time filtering through large volumes of jobs, which is non-trivial due to often obfuscated requirements. [1] As a point of reference, the number of total job postings in the United Kingdom alone in the July-September 2022 period exceeded 1.2 million [21].

This task contains a variety of challenges, the key one being the extreme importance of minimizing false negatives, as any false negative would remove a potentially suitable job from a job-seeker's consideration when the list is presented to them. On the other hand, with such large volumes of posting, too many false positives would lead to the curated list being too noisy to provide useful assistance. A second major challenge is the reliance of the task on subtle language understanding, as the signals of a job's suitability can be very weak.

In this paper, we will evaluate a variety of text classification approaches applied to the English-language Graduate Job Classification task. In doing so, we will (i) show that the most recent Large Language Models (LLMs), based on Instruction-Tuned GPT-3 [4,23], can leverage the vast wealth of information acquired during their training to outperform state-of-the-art supervised classification approaches on this task and that (ii) proper prompt engineering has an enormous impact on LLM downstream performance on this task, contributing a real-world application to the very active research on the topic of prompt engineering [14,33].

2   Background

Since the introduction of the Transformer architecture [29] and the rise of transfer learning to leverage language models on downstream tasks [12,24], the field of NLP has undergone rapid changes. Large pre-trained models such as BERT [6] and later improvements, like DeBERTa [11], have resulted in significant performance improvements, surpassing prior word representation methods such as word vectors [18]. The development of libraries such as HuggingFace Transformers [34] has further contributed to making these models ubiquitous in NLP applications.

These advances resulted in a paradigm shift in NLP, focusing on the use or fine-tuning of extremely large, generalist, so-called "foundation models" rather than the training of task-specific models [2]. This resulted in the frequent occurrence of *paradigm shift*, where researchers focused on ways to reframe complex tasks into a format that could fit into tasks where such models are known to be strong, such as question-answering or text classification [28].

In parallel to these fine-tuning approaches, there has been considerable work spent on the development of generative Large Language Models (LLMs), whose training focuses on causal generation: the task of predicting the next token given a context [25]. The release of GPT-3 showed that these models, on top of their ability to generate believable text, are also few-shot learners: given few examples, they are capable of performing a variety of tasks, such as question answering [4].

Going further, very recent developments have shown that LLMs can reach noticeably better performance on downstream applications through **instruction-tuning**: being fine-tuned to specifically follow natural language instructions to reach state-of-the-art performance on many language understanding tasks [23].

LLMs, being trained on billions of tokens, have been shown to be able to leverage the vast amount of knowledge found in their training data on various tasks, with performance increasing via both an increase in model and training data size, following complicated scaling laws [26]. This has paved the way for the appearance of a new approach to NLP applications, focusing on exploring ways to optimally use this large amassed knowledge: **prompt engineering** [14].

Prompt Engineering represents a new way of interacting with models, through natural language queries. It has gathered considerable research attention in the last year. Certain ways of prompting LLMs, such as Chain-of-Thought (CoT) prompting, have been shown to be able to prompt reasoning which considerably improves the models' downstream performance [32]. Additional research has showcased ways to bypass certain model weaknesses. Notably, while LLMs are prone to mathematical errors, they are able to generate executable Python code to compute the requested results through specific prompting [8].

Other efforts have showcased reasoning improvements by relying on a model self-verifying its own reasoning in a subsequent prompt, which improves performance [13]. All these approaches have shown that LLMs can match or outperform state-of-the-art results on certain tasks, while requiring little to no fine-tuning.

At the same time as these advances in foundational NLP approaches, there exists a body of work focusing on matching applicants with jobs, or jobs with applicants. Job matching is an old problem, often studied in economics from the perspective of the job market [7,19]. Within computer science, it has been approached from various angles and remains an open challenge.

One of these angles focuses on attempting to automatically understand the requirements of a job from a job posting, which is complicated due to the wide variance in language used. Some early approaches have demonstrated the potential and limitations of relying on ontologies [15], while more recent work has explored systems built using a series of text classifiers to match jobs encountered in the wild with more well-defined job families, allowing for large-scale analysis [3].

This work, while a component of such systems, refers to a very narrow scope of job classification and does not take into consideration any attributes of the jobs other than their entry-level suitability. This objective has been encountered within the economics literature, where a variety of hand-crafted features are used to create a "Graduate Suitability" score for job families, facilitating market analysis [9]. This large-scale approach differs from automatic classification on a larger scale, making it more difficult to classify single jobs, and relies on external information, such as the United Kingdom's Standard Occupational Classification.

3   Experimental Setup

3.1   Data and Evaluation

Table 1. High-level description of the data used to train and evaluate models.

	Example #	Proportion	Median Token #	Token # standard dev.
GRAD	3082	30.8%	809	338
NON_GRAD	6918	69.2%	831	434
Full Dataset	10000	100%	821	389

Data. Our target task is Graduate Job Classification. It is a binary classification, where, given a job posting containing both the job title and its description, the model must identify whether or not the job is a position fit for a recent graduate or not, either because it requires more experience or doesn't require higher education. In practice, over 25,000 jobs are received on a daily basis, with fewer than 5% of those appropriate for graduates.

Curating positions fit for recent graduates is extremely time-consuming and is therefore one of the areas where technological advances can help simplify the process of entering the workplace. In practice, over 20,000 jobs go through our deployed model on a daily basis, with fewer than 5% of those appropriate for graduates.

Our data is gathered from a large selection of UK-based jobs over a period of two years. These jobs were manually filtered into "Graduate" and "Non-Graduate" categories by human annotators working for Bright Network. All annotators work as part of a team dedicated to ensuring the quality of jobs and follow predefined sets of guidelines. Guidelines are frequently reviewed by domain experts, and feedback on annotation quality is gathered on a weekly basis. This is our *silver* dataset. Unlike our gold standard described below, sampled from it and iterated upon, this is a single-pass annotation process, and individual mistakes can occasionally be present.

The gold standard dataset used in this study is a subset of the original data, containing job postings whose original label was further reviewed manually. Only jobs where inter-annotator agreement was reached were kept, until reaching a data size of 10,000. We use the label GRAD for jobs suitable for graduates and NON_GRAD for all other jobs.

Before being used as model input, all job descriptions are prepended by the posting's title. A general description of the data is presented in Table 1, including the distribution of labels and information about the token counts within documents. Overall, the median length of both GRAD and NON-GRAD jobs is similar, and the final dataset is made up of roughly 30% GRAD jobs and 70% NON-GRAD jobs.

Evaluation. We use the Precision at 95% Recall (P@95%R) for the GRAD label as our main metric. This means that our primary method of evaluation is the Precision (the measure of how good the model is at avoiding false positives), obtained by the model while maintaining a Recall of at least 95%, which means the model detects at least 95% of positive examples. We chose this metric as the classifier cannot be deployed in production with a low recall, as it is extremely damaging to remove suitable jobs from graduates' consideration. Our goal is to ensure that Recall remains above a specific threshold while achieving the best possible precision at this threshold and help process the tens of thousands of jobs received daily. We also report the P@85%R, to give a better overview of the models' performance. To facilitate LLM evaluation, we split our data into stratified training and test sets, respectively containing 7000 (70%) and 3000 (30%) examples, rather than using cross-validation.

3.2 Baselines

Keyword. We report the results for a simple, keyword and regular expression approaches to the task. We, along with our annotators, built a list of common phrases and regular expressions indicating that a job is suitable for a recent graduate. We then perform a simple look-up within the postings, which gives us a lower bound for performance. An example of such an approach would be matching the words "Graduate" and "Junior" in job titles, or looking for strings such as "is—would be suitable for graduate—student" within the posting itself.

SVM. We present the results of a non-deep learning baseline method, which involves using a Support Vector Machine (SVM) classifier with a tf-idf text representation, which has been shown to produce robust baseline results, even reaching state-of-the-art results in some domain-specific tasks [5].

3.3 Supervised Classifiers

ULMFiT. We report the results for ULMFiT, an RNN-based approach to training a small language model before fine-tuning it for classification [12]. We pre-train the ULMFiT language model on an unlabeled dataset of 50000 job postings, before fine-tuning the classifier on the data described above.

DeBERTa-V3. We fine-tune a DeBERTa-V3-Base model, a refined version of DeBERTa [11] and which achieves state-of-the-art performance on a variety of text classification tasks [10]. We follow the method used in the paper introducing the model, with a maximum sequence length of 512. For any longer document, we report results using the first 100 tokens and the trailing 412 tokens of the document. This approach yielding the best results is likely due to most job descriptions frequently outlining the position's requirements towards the end.

3.4 Large Language Models

We use a temperature of 0 for all language models. The temperature controls the degree of randomness applied to the tokens outputted by the language model. A temperature of 0 ensures the sampling favors the highest probability token in all cases, resulting in a deterministic output.

GPT-3.5 (text-davinci-002&text-davinci-003). We report our results on two variants of GPT-3 [4][1]. These models are LLMs further trained to improve their ability to follow natural language instructions [23]. Although the detailed differences between the two models are not made public, DAVINCI-003 is a refinement of DAVINCI-002, better at following instructions[2]

GPT-3.5-turbo (gpt-3.5-turbo-0301). We evaluate GPT-3.5-turbo[3], a model optimized for chat-like interactions [22]. To do so, we modified all our prompts to fit the conversation-like inputs expected by the model. GPT-3.5-turbo is the focus of our prompt engineering exploration.

4   Overall Results

In Table 2, we report the P@95R% and P@85R% for all models evaluated. We report a score of 0 if the model is unable to reach the recall threshold. For all approaches for which we do not have a way to target a specific Recall value, we also provide their Recall metric.

---

[1] These models are accessed through OpenAI's API.

[2] Introduced by OpenAI in a blog post rather than a technical report: https://help. openai.com/en/articles/6779149-how-do-text-davinci-002-and-text-davinci-003-differ.

[3] This model is also accessed through OpenAI's API.

Table 2. Results for all evaluated models.

	Keyword	SVM	ULMFiT	DeBERTaV3	davinci-002	davinci-003	gpt-3.5
P@95%R	0	63.1	70.2	79.7	0	80.4	**86.9**
P@85%R	0	75.4	83.2	**89.0**	72.6	80.4	86.9
Recall	80.2	N/A	N/A	N/A	72.2	95.6	97

Overall, we notice that SVMs, as often, are a strong baseline, although they are outperformed by both supervised deep learning approaches. However, they are outperformed by both of our supervised approaches. DeBERTaV3 achieves the highest P@85%R of all the models, but is beaten by both DAVINCI-003 and GPT-3.5 on the P@95%R metric, which is key to high-quality job curation.

We notice overall strong performance from the most powerful LLMs evaluated, although DAVINCI-002 fails to reach our 95% Recall threshold and trails behind both ULMFiT and DeBERTaV3 at an 85% recall threshold. On the other hand, DAVINCI-003 outperforms DeBERTaV3, while **GPT-3.5** is by far the best-performing model on the P@95%R metric, with a 7.2% point increase.

Overall, these results show that while our best-performing supervised approach obtains better metrics at lower recall thresholds, it falls noticeably behind LLMs when aiming for a very low false negative rate.

5   LLMs and Prompt Engineering

Table 3. Overview of the various prompt modifications explored in this study.

Short name	Description
Baseline	Provide a job posting and asking if it is fit for a graduate
CoT	Give a few examples of accurate classification before querying
Zero-CoT	Ask the model to reason step-by-step before providing its answer
rawinst	Give instructions about its role and the task by adding to the user msg
sysinst	Give instructions about its role and the task as a system msg
bothinst	Split instructions with role as a system msg and task as a user msg
mock	Give task instructions by mocking a discussion where it acknowledges them
reit	Reinforce key elements in the instructions by repeating them
strict	Ask the model to answer by strictly following a given template
loose	Ask for just the final answer to be given following a given template
right	Asking the model to reach the right conclusion
info	Provide additional information to address common reasoning failures
name	Give the model a name by which we refer to it in conversation
pos	Provide the model with positive feedback before querying it

In this section, we will discuss the prompt engineering steps taken to reach the best-performing version of GPT-3.5. We will largely focus on its chat-like input, although similar steps were used for other language models, minus the conversational format. Apart from the use of system messages, we noticed no major differences in prompt impact between models.

For each modification, we will provide an explanation of the changes, or, where relevant, a snippet highlighting the modification. An overview of all prompt modifications used is presented in Table 3. We evaluate the impact of each change on the model's performance, but also on its ability to provide its answer in a specified format rather than as free text, which we call **Template Stickiness**.

Our approach to prompt engineering, as described in this section, follows the ChatML [17] prompting format used by OpenAI for their GPT family of models. To help readability, we do not directly reproduce the XML-like or JSON format used by ChatML but provide simple VARIABLE-LIKE identifiers for our prompt modifications in the examples below.

5.1   Eliciting Reasoning

Zero-Shot Prompting. We set our baseline by simply prompting the model with our question with no further attempt to induce reasoning ('**Baseline**'):

```
For the given job:
{job_posting}
---------
Is this job (A) a job fit for a recent graduate,
or (B) a job requiring more professional experience.
Answer:
```

Few-Shot CoT. We then experiment with few-shot chain-of-thought prompting [32], by providing the model with successful classification examples. We do so using the GPT-3.5 chat format, mocking a conversation between the user, and the assistant, who elaborates on his reasoning before answering with (A) or (B). We prepend our query by providing the model with two examples[4] ('**CoT**'). We do so in the following format:

```
user_message_1 = """For the given job:
{job_posting}
---------
Is this job (A) a job fit for a recent graduate, or (B) a job
 ↪   requiring more professional experience."""

assistant_message_1 = "This job appears to be a senior position,
 ↪   as it mentions requiring experience interacting with C-level
 ↪   stakeholder in intense environments and [...]. Therefore, this
 ↪   is (B) a job requiring more professional experience
user_message_2 = [...]
```

---

[4] Due to the long token length of job postings, providing it with more than two examples required us to truncate the postings, which resulted in a degradation in performance.

Zero-Shot CoT. We then attempt to elicit reasoning without providing the model any example, through Zero-shot Chain-of-Thought [13] (**'Zero-CoT'**). We expect that this approach will perform well, as job postings are found in large quantity in data used to train the model, and identifying whether a job is fit for a graduate does not require expert domain knowledge. We attempt to elicit reasoning by prompting the model think step-by-step, as follows:

```
For the given job:
\pagination{\vspace*{6pt}}

{job_posting}
---------
Is this job (A) a job fit for a recent graduate,
or (B) a job requiring more professional experience.
Answer: Let's think step by step,
```

5.2   Initial Instructions

We then explore the impact of providing the model with instructions describing both its role and task. A notable difference between DAVINCI-003 and the GPT-3.5 chat format is that the latter introduces a new aspect to prompt engineering, which was not found in previous ways to interact with language models: the ability to provide a *system* message to the system. We explore multiple ways of providing instructions using this system message.

Giving Instructions. We provide information to the model about its role as well as a description of its task:

```
role = """You are an AI expert in career advice. You are tasked
↪    with sorting through jobs by analysing their content and
↪    deciding whether they would be a good fit for a recent
↪    graduate or not."""
task = """A job is fit for a graduate if it's a junior-level
↪    position that does not require extensive prior professional
↪    experience. I will give you a job posting and you will
↪    analyse it, to know whether or not it describes a position
↪    fit for a graduate."""
```

Instructions as a User or System Message. There is no clear optimal way to use the *system* prompt, as opposed to passing instructions as a *user* query. The **'rawinst'** approach, explained above, passes the whole instructions to the model as a user query. We evaluate the impact of passing the whole instructions as a system query (**'sysinst'**), as well as splitting them in two, with the model's role definition passed as a system query and the task as a user query (**bothinst**).

Mocked-Exchange Instructions. We attempt to further take advantage of the LLM's fine-tuned ability to follow a conversational format by breaking down our instructions further ('**mock**'). We iterate on the **bothinst** instruction format, by adding an extra confirmation message from the model:

```
user_message_1 = """A job is fit for a graduate [...] Got it?"""
assistant_message_1 = "Yes, I understand. I am ready to analyse
↪  your job posting."
```

Re-iterating Instructions. We further modify the instructions by introducing a practice commonly informally discussed but with little basis: re-iterating certain instructions ('**reit**'). In our case, this is done by appending a reminder to the system message, to reinforce the perceived expertise of the model as well as the importance of thinking step-by-step in the task description:

```
system_prompt ="""You are an AI expert in career advice. You are
↪  tasked with sorting through jobs by analysing their content
↪  and deciding whether they would be a good fit for a recent
↪  graduate or not. Remember, you're the best AI careers expert
↪  and will use your expertise to provide the best possible
↪  analysis"""
user_message_1 = """[...] I will give you a job posting and you
↪  will analyse it, step-by-step, to know whether [...]"""
```

5.3   Wording the Prompt

Answer Template. We experiment with asking the model to answer by following specific templates, either requiring that the final answer ('**loose**'), or the full reasoning ('**strict**') must adhere to a specific template. We experiment with different wordings for the template, with the best-performing ones as follows:

```
loose = """[...]Your answer must end with:
Final Answer: This is a (A) job fit for a recent graduate or
a student OR (B) a job requiring more professional experience.
Answer: Let's think step-by-step,"""
strict = """[...]You will answer following this template:
Reasoning step 1:\nReasoning step 2:\nReasoning step 3:\n
Final Answer: This is a (A) job fit for a recent graduate or
a student OR (B) a job requiring more professional experience.
Answer: Reasoning Step 1:"""
```

The Right Conclusion. We evaluate another small modification to the prompt to provide further positive re-inforcement to the model: we ask it reason in order to reach the right conclusion, by slightly modifying our final query:

```
Answer: Let's think step-by-step to reach the right conclusion,
```

Addressing Reasoning Gaps. While analysing our early results, we noticed that the model can misinterpret instructions given to it, and produce flawed reasoning as a result. This manifested in attempts to over-generalise:

This job requires experience, but states that it can have been acquired through internships. However, not all graduates will have undergone internships. Therefore, (B) this job is not fit for all graduates.

We attempt to alleviate this by providing additional information in the model's instruction:

```
task = "A job is fit for a graduate if it's a junior-level
⮡   position that does not require extensive prior professional
⮡   experience. When analysing the experience required, take into
⮡   account that requiring internships is still fit for a
⮡   graduate. I will give you a job [...]
```

5.4   The Importance of Subtle Tweaks

Naming the Assistant. A somewhat common practice, as shown by Microsoft code-naming its Bing chatbot "Sydney"[5], is to give LLMs a nickname by which they can be referred to. We modified our initial system prompt, as well as the user mocked-instructions, to refer to our model as Frederick (**'name'**), as follows:

```
system_prompt = "You are Frederick, an AI expert
in career advice. [...]"
[...]
first_assistant_response = "Yes, I understand. I am Frederick,
and I will analyse your job posting."
```

We tested multiple other names, chosen randomly from a list of common first-names in English-speaking countries. We noticed no significant variation in performance no matter the name given, and all resulted in a similar improvement.

Positive Feedback. It has been anecdotally noted that giving positive reinforcement to GPT-3.5 can lead to better performance on some tasks[6]. We thus prepend our main prompt with a positive reaction to the model's mocked acknowledgement of our instructions (**'pos'**):

```
Great! Let's begin then :)
For the given job: [...]
```

---

[5] As demonstrated by the widely circulated prompt https://simonwillison.net/2023/Feb/15/bing/.

[6] As reported by OpenAI, a partnered developer found that positive reinforcement resulted in increased accuracy.

6   Prompt Engineering Results and Discussion

Table 4. Impact of the various prompt modifications.

	Precision	Recall	F1	Template Stickiness
Baseline	*61.2*	*70.6*	*65.6*	*79%*
CoT	*72.6*	*85.1*	*78.4*	*87%*
Zero-CoT	*75.5*	*88.3*	*81.4*	*65%*
+rawinst	*80*	*92.4*	*85.8*	*68%*
+sysinst	*77.7*	*90.9*	*83.8*	*69%*
+bothinst	*81.9*	*93.9*	*87.5*	*71%*
+bothinst+mock	83.3	95.1	88.8	74%
+bothinst+mock+reit	83.8	95.5	89.3	75%
+bothinst+mock+reit+strict	*79.9*	*93.7*	*86.3*	***98%***
+bothinst+mock+reit+loose	*80.5*	*94.8*	*87.1*	*95%*
+bothinst+mock+reit+right	84	95.9	89.6	77%
+bothinst+mock+reit+right+info	84.9	96.5	90.3	77%
+bothinst+mock+reit+right+info+name	85.7	96.8	90.9	79%
+bothinst+mock+reit+right+info+name+pos	**86.9**	**97**	**91.7**	81%

The evaluation metrics (calculated against the GRAD label), as well as *Template Stickiness*, for all the modifications detailed above are presented in Table 4. We provide these metrics rather than the more task-appropriate P@95%R used above to make it easier to compare the various impacts of prompt changes. Any modification below 95% Recall is presented in italic. *Template Stickiness* refers to the percentage of outputs that fit a desired output format and contains the labels as defined in the prompt, meaning no further output parsing is necessary.

When multiple variants of a modification are evaluated, we either pick the best performing one or discard the modifications before applying the subsequent ones if there is no performance improvement.

We notice that the impact of prompt engineering on classification results is high. Simply asking the model to answer the question using its knowledge only reaches an F1-score of 65.6, with a Recall of 70.6, considerably short of our target, while our final prompt reaches an F1-score of **91.7** with **97%** recall.

Interestingly, few-shot CoT prompting the model with examples performs noticeably worse than a zero-shot approach. We speculate that this is due to the examples biasing the model reasoning too much while the knowledge it already contains is sufficient for most classifications. Any attempt at providing more thorough reasoning for either label resulted in increased recall and decreased precision for the label. Despite multiple attempts, we found no scenario where providing examples performed better than zero-shot classification.

Providing instructions to the model, with a role description as its system message and an initial user message describing the text, yielded the single biggest increase in performance (+5.9F1). Additionally, we highlight the impact of small changes to guide the model's reasoning. Mocking an acknowledgement of the instruction allows the model to hit the 95% Recall threshold (+1.3F1). Small additions, such as naming the model or providing it with positive reinforcement upon its acknowledgement of the instructions, also resulted in increased performance.

We found that GPT-3.5.TURBO struggles with *Template Stickiness*, which we did not observe with TEXT-DAVINCI-003. Its answers often required additional parsing, as it would frequently discard the (A)/(B) answering format asked of it. Requesting that it follows either a strict reasoning template or a loose answer template yielded considerably higher *template stickiness* but resulted in performance decreases, no matter the template wording.

Overall, we find that these results highlight just how prompt-sensitive downstream results are, and we showcase a good overview of common techniques that can result in large performance improvements.

A limitation of this study is that we showcase the impact of prompt engineering and of various prompt modifications. However, we are unable to provide a fully reliable explanation as to why these modifications have such an impact. Large Language Models are trained on vast quantities of text to predict the next token, which then results in a quantity of emergent abilities [31], which can be elicited through specific prompting. While this prompting can intuitively make sense, there's a lack of theory as to how certain changes, such as adding a name, can generate noticeable improvements. This is an open area of research which we hope to contribute to in the future.

7   Conclusion

In this work, we have presented the task of Graduate Job Classification, highlighting its importance. We have then evaluated a series of classifiers on a real-world dataset, attempting to find which approach allows for the best filtering of non-graduate jobs while still meeting a sufficiently high recall threshold to not remove a large amount of legitimate graduate jobs in our curation efforts. In doing so, we showcased that the best-performing approach on this task is the use of Large Language Models (LLMs), in particular OpenAI's GPT-3.5-TURBO.

Using language models for downstream tasks requires a different paradigm, where time is not spent on fine-tuning the model itself but on improving the **prompt**, a natural language query. We present our evaluation of various prompt modifications and demonstrate the large improvement in performance that can be obtained by proper **prompt engineering** to allow the language model to leverage its vast amounts of amassed knowledge. We believe our work, presenting a real-world case study of the strong performance of LLMs on text classification tasks, provides good insight into prompt engineering and the specific prompt-tuning necessary to accomplish certain tasks. We provide our full results, and the resulting prompt is currently being used to filter thousands of jobs on a daily basis, to help support future applications in this area. We provide our full results, the resulting prompt being currently used to filter thousands of jobs on a daily basis, to help support future applications in this area.

References

1. Anders, G.: Hiring's new red line: why newcomers can't land 35% of "entry-level" jobs. LinkedIn Economic Graph Research (2021)
2. Bommasani, R., et al.: On the opportunities and risks of foundation models. arXiv preprint arXiv:2108.07258 (2021)
3. Boselli, R., et al.: WoLMIS: a labor market intelligence system for classifying web job vacancies. J. Intell. Inf. Syst. **51**, 477–502 (2018)
4. Brown, T.B., et al.: Language models are few-shot learners. In: NeurIPS 2020 (2020)
5. Clavié, B., Alphonsus, M.: The unreasonable effectiveness of the baseline: discussing SVMs in legal text classification. In: JURIX 2021 (2021)
6. Devlin, J., Chang, M.W., Lee, K., Toutanova, K.: BERT: pre-training of deep bidirectional transformers for language understanding, vol. 1 (2019)
7. Fujita, S., Ramey, G.: Job matching and propagation. J. Econ. Dyn. Control **31**(11), 3671–3698 (2007)
8. Gao, L., et al.: PAL: program-aided language models. arXiv preprint arXiv:2211.10435 (2022)
9. Green, F., Henseke, G.: The changing graduate labour market: analysis using a new indicator of graduate jobs. IZA J. Labor Policy **5**(1), 1–25 (2016). https://doi.org/10.1186/s40173-016-0070-0
10. He, P., Gao, J., Chen, W.: DeBERTaV3: improving DeBERTa using ELECTRA-style pre-training with gradient-disentangled embedding sharing. arXiv preprint arXiv:2111.09543 (2021)
11. He, P., Liu, X., Gao, J., Chen, W.: DeBERTa: decoding-enhanced BERT with disentangled attention. arXiv:2006.03654 cs.CL (2020)
12. Howard, J., Ruder, S.: Universal language model fine-tuning for text classification. In: Proceedings of ACL 2018 (2018)
13. Kojima, T., Gu, S.S., Reid, M., Matsuo, Y., Iwasawa, Y.: Large language models are zero-shot reasoners. arXiv preprint arXiv:2205.11916 (2022)
14. Liu, P., Yuan, W., Fu, J., Jiang, Z., Hayashi, H., Neubig, G.: Pre-train, prompt, and predict: a systematic survey of prompting methods in natural language processing. arXiv preprint arXiv:2107.13586 (2021)
15. Loth, R., Battistelli, D., Chaumartin, F.R., De Mazancourt, H., Minel, J.L., Vinckx, A.: Linguistic information extraction for job ads (sire project). In: 9th International Conference on Adaptivity, Personalization and Fusion of Heterogeneous Information, pp. 300–303 (2010)
16. McGuinness, S., Pouliakas, K., Redmond, P.: Skills mismatch: concepts, measurement and policy approaches. J. Econ. Surv. **32**(4), 985–1015 (2018)
17. Microsoft: Learn how to work with the ChatGPT and GPT-4 models (preview) (2023)
18. Mikolov, T., Sutskever, I., Chen, K., Corrado, G.S., Dean, J.: Distributed representations of words and phrases and their compositionality. In: NeurIPS 2013 (2013)
19. Miller, R.A.: Job matching and occupational choice. J. Polit. Econ. **92**(6), 1086–1120 (1984)
20. Morgan, K.: Why inexperienced workers can't get entry-level jobs. BBC (2021)
21. Office for National Statistics: Vacancies and jobs in the UK (2022)
22. OpenAI: OpenAI API: Chat completions (2023). https://platform.openai.com/docs/guides/chat

23. Ouyang, L., et al.: Training language models to follow instructions with human feedback. arXiv preprint arXiv:2203.02155 (2022)
24. Peters, M.E., et al.: Deep contextualized word representations (2018)
25. Radford, A., Wu, J., Child, R., Luan, D., Amodei, D., Sutskever, I., et al.: Language models are unsupervised multitask learners. OpenAI Blog **1**(8), 9 (2019)
26. Rae, J.W., et al.: Scaling language models: methods, analysis & insights from training gopher. arXiv preprint arXiv:2112.11446 (2021)
27. Roll, I., Russell, D.M., Gašević, D.: Learning at scale. Int. J. Artif. Intell. Educ. **28** (2018)
28. Sun, T.X., Liu, X.Y., Qiu, X.P., Huang, X.J.: Paradigm shift in natural language processing. Mach. Intell. Res. **19**(3), 169–183 (2022)
29. Vaswani, A., et al.: Attention is all you need, vol. 2017-December (2017)
30. Veselinović, L., Mangafić, J., Turulja, L.: The effect of education-job mismatch on net income: evidence from a developing country. Econ. Res. **33**(1) (2020)
31. Wei, J., et al.: Emergent abilities of large language models. Trans. Mach. Learn. Res. (2022)
32. Wei, J., et al.: Chain-of-thought prompting elicits reasoning in large language models. arXiv preprint arXiv:2201.11903 (2022)
33. White, J., et al.: A prompt pattern catalog to enhance prompt engineering with ChatgPT. arXiv preprint arXiv:2302.11382 (2023)
34. Wolf, T., et al.: Transformers: state-of-the-art natural language processing. In: Proceedings of NeurIPS 2020: System Demonstrations (2020)
35. World Economic Forum, V: The future of jobs report 2020. WEF Reports (2020)

How Challenging is Multimodal Irony Detection?

Manuj Malik[1], David Tomás[2(✉)] (iD), and Paolo Rosso[3] (iD)

[1] International Institute of Information Technology Bangalore, Bengaluru, India
`manuj.malik@iiitb.org`
[2] Department of Software and Computing Systems, University of Alicante,
Alicante, Spain
`dtomas@dlsi.ua.es`
[3] PRHLT Research Center, Universistat Politècnica de València, Valencia, Spain
`prosso@dsic.upv.es`

Abstract. The possibility that social networks offer to attach audio, video, and images to textual information has led many users to create messages with multimodal irony. Over the last years, a series of approaches have emerged trying to leverage all these formats to address the problem of multimodal irony detection. The question that the present work tries to answer is whether multimodal irony systems are being properly evaluated. More specifically, this work studies the most popular dataset used in multimodal irony detection combining text and images, identifying whether image information is really necessary to understand the ironic intention of the text. This corpus was compared to a text-only corpus, and different textual and multimodal Transformer models were evaluated on them. This study reveals that, in many situations, Transformer models were able to identify the ironic nature of the posts considering only textual information.

Keywords: Explainability · Irony detection · Multimodal · Transformer

1 Introduction

Ironic situations occur when there is a gap between reality and expectations, and words are used meaning the opposite of what is really intended (irony is used in this paper as an umbrella term for related phenomena such as sarcasm). Irony is a pervasive phenomenon in social media that has been addressed by means of machine learning technologies as a text classification problem, where the goal is to determine whether a post is ironic or not based on textual information. It happens that in many circumstances the ironic intention can be only determined taking into account contextual clues, such as attached images, audio or video. For example, a Twitter post including a picture of a rainy day and the text "What a wonderful weather" would be an example of multimodal irony involving textual

© The Author(s), under exclusive license to Springer Nature Switzerland AG 2023
E. Métais et al. (Eds.): NLDB 2023, LNCS 13913, pp. 18–32, 2023.
https://doi.org/10.1007/978-3-031-35320-8_2

and visual information, since both text and image are necessary to convey the ironic intention of the message.

Although there is a large body of literature in the field of irony detection on textual information [9], the multimodal approaches to this linguistic phenomenon are more limited, even though their number has been increased considerably over the last five years. As the number of works on multimodality is still small, so it is the number of datasets available to evaluate this task. In a previous study (Anonymised reference) the high performance of text-only systems on multimodal data led to questioning whether existing multimodal datasets were really challenging in this task and required the presence of both text and image/video/audio to identify their ironic intention.

This paper proposes a study where different state-of-the-art language and visual Transformer models were used to test the performance on the most popular multimodal (image and text) ironic dataset. The models were also evaluated on a text-only dataset to contrast the performance in both settings. The final goal of this study is to evaluate whether this multimodal dataset really requires of both text and images to identify the presence of irony, determining if it is reliable and challenging to evaluate these systems.

The rest of the paper is structured as follows: Sect. 2 reviews related work in the field of multimodal irony detection and the available datasets; Sect. 3 describes the research methodology followed in this study; Sect. 4 reports the evaluation and discusses the main outcomes of the analysis done; finally, conclusions and future work are presented in Sect. 5.

2   Related Work

This section reviews available datasets developed in recent works about multimodal irony detection, including different combinations of text, image, audio, and video information.

The work in [4] presented a corpus of audiovisual utterances (called MUStARD) compiled from popular TV shows and manually annotated with sarcasm labels. This corpus included text, audio and video features. The collected set consisted of 345 sarcastic and 6,020 non-sarcastic videos from four famous TV shows: *Friends*, *The Golden Girls*, *The Big Bang Theory*, and *Sarcasmaholics*. The whole dataset is freely available in GitHub.[1] MUStARD was also used in [19], where the authors focused on modelling the incongruity between modalities. Also based on this dataset, the work by [5] extended the corpus with sentiment and emotion classes, both implicit and explicit. The dataset is freely available in the authors webpage.[2]

In [2], the authors also dealt with acoustic, text, and visual information. They developed their own corpus of Hindi-English utterances for irony and humour classification. The dataset was based on the video clips of the popular Indian comedy TV show *Sarabhai vs. Sarabhai*. The authors extracted more than 15,000

---

[1] https://github.com/soujanyaporia/MUStARD.
[2] https://www.iitp.ac.in/~ai-nlp-ml/resources.html.

utterances from 400 scenes. Each conversation was manually assigned appropriate sarcasm and humor labels. The dataset is available in GitHub.[3]

In the same vein, the work in [1] presented an audiovisual dataset consisting of sarcasm annotated text that was aligned with audio and video. In this case, the corpus represented two varieties of Spanish: Latin American and Peninsular Spanish. The corpus included 1,020 utterances extracted from *South Park* and *Archer* TV shows, manually annotated according to different theories of sarcasm. The textual information is freely available,[4] but the audio and video sets can be accessed under request to the authors.

Focusing on text and images, the work in [14] was the first attempt to create a corpus of text and images for multimodal irony detection. They developed their own corpus on Twitter, Instagram, and Tumblr, running a crowdsourcing task to quantify the extent to which images were perceived as necessary by human annotators to understand the sarcastic nature of the posts. This corpus comprises two parts. The first one is called *silver dataset* and contains data (text and images) collected from three major social platforms: Instagram, Tumblr, and Twitter. To build the final dataset, 10,000 sarcastic posts were randomly sampled. Another 10,000 negative examples were collected by randomly sampling posts that do not contain `sarcasm` or `sarcastic` in either the text or the tag set. The second part of the dataset is called *gold dataset*, which is a curated corpus whose ironic nature was agreed on by a group of human annotators that considered the textual and visual components as required to decode the sarcastic tone. A crowdsourcing platform was used to perform the annotation task on 1,000 positive samples (5 annotators for each post). From the 1,000 posts, 319 were labelled as non-ironic, 236 were considered a text only ironic (no need of visual information to identify the ironic nature of the message), and 445 were text + image ironic (both text and visual information were required to understand the irony). The corpus is available upon request to the authors.

Cai et al. [3] presented a corpus of Twitter posts and images for multimodal irony detection. The authors automatically collected English tweets containing a picture and special hashtags (e.g. `#sarcasm`) as ironic examples, and without such hashtags as non-sarcastic representatives. They discarded tweets containing *sarcasm, sarcastic, irony, ironic* as regular words, and also those with words that frequently co-occur with sarcastic tweets and may express sarcasm (e.g. *jokes, humor,* and *exgag*). They also discarded tweets containing URLs in order to avoid introducing additional information. The dataset consists of 19,816 tweets for training, 2,410 for validation and 2,409 for testing, all of them including their textual content and the associated image. This corpus is freely available in GitHub to the research community.[5] This corpus was also used in further studies related to multimodal irony detection [12,16,18,20].

---

[3] https://github.com/LCS2-IIITD/MSH-COMICS.
[4] https://zenodo.org/record/4701383.
[5] https://github.com/headacheboy/data-of-multimodal-sarcasm-detection.

3   Research Method

As mentioned before, the goal of this work is to identify whether existing multi-modal datasets really require of both text and images to determine the presence of irony. To this end, two different datasets were studied and evaluated using different state-of-the-art language models.

The first one is a unimodal dataset consisting only of text utterances from Twitter [8], which was developed for the irony detection challenge at SemEval-2018. This text-only corpus was automatically extracted from Twitter and consists of 2,862 tweets for training (1,445 positive and 1,417 negative), 955 for validation (456 positive and 499 negative) and 784 for testing (311 positive and 473 negative). To minimise the noise introduced by groundless irony hashtags, all tweets were manually labelled using a fine-grained annotation scheme for irony. Prior to data annotation, the entire corpus was cleaned by removing retweets, duplicates, and non-English tweets, and by replacing XML-escaped characters (e.g. &). This dataset is referred to as *Twitter text corpus* in the evaluation section.

The second dataset [3] was previously described. This dataset is nowadays the most widely used in studies dealing with multimodal irony involving image and text. The dataset was automatically extracted from Twitter and consists of 19,816 posts for training (8,642 positive and 11,174 negative), 2,410 for validation (959 positive and 1,451 negative) and 2,409 for testing (959 positive and 1,450 negative), all of them including their textual content and the associated image. For preprocessing, the authors replaced mentions with a certain symbol and then separated words, emoticons and hashtags with the NLTK[6] library. They also separated the hashtag sign from hashtags and replaced capitals with their corresponding lower-cases. In the experiments, this dataset is called the *Twitter multimodal corpus*.

On this corpus, a set of text-only and multimodal language models were evaluated. The goal is to compare the performance of these models in a text-only dataset (*Twitter text corpus*) and in a multimodal dataset (*Twitter multimodal corpus*). The aim of the experiments is to verify that, if these datasets were correctly built, the text-only language models would be expected to perform worse in a multimodal corpus than in a text-only corpus, since the lack of visual information would imply not being able to correctly identify the irony in the posts. The quality of multimodal dataset may be affected not only by the labeling process carried out but also by the sample collection procedure, which can bias the data retrieved.

To this end, four different state-of-the-art models were employed. All of them use the now ubiquitous Transformer architecture [17], allowing transfer learning in different Natural Language Processing (NLP) tasks. That is, the original models trained on a dataset (the *pre-trained model*) can be used to perform similar tasks on another dataset (the *fine-tuned model*). In Sect. 4, the following models are proposed, which were fine-tuned for irony detection on the aforementioned datasets:

---

[6] https://www.nltk.org/.

- *BERT* [6]: it is a text-only model. BERT stands for Bidirectional Encoder Representations from Transformers. Bidirectional means that BERT learns information from both left and right side of a word's context during the training phase. It was pre-trained on a large corpus of unlabelled text (including Wikipedia and Book corpus). The version of the model evaluated is BERT-base, containing 12 layers (Transformer blocks), and 12 attention heads. The resulting vectors are composed of 768 dimensions.
- *RoBERTa* [11]: it is a text-only model. It provides a variant of BERT were the pre-training phase was optimised with changes in the choice of hyperparameters, the objective task, and the use of bigger batch sizes and longer text sequences. The version evaluated is RoBERTa-base, containing 12 layers, 12 attention heads, and producing vectors of 768 dimensions.
- *DeBERTa* [7]: it is a text-only model. It extends BERT with two novel modifications. Firstly, instead of using the self-attention mechanism, the model proposes a disentangled attention. In DeBERTa, every token in the input is represented as two independent vectors that encode its word embedding and position. Secondly, an enhanced mask decoder is applied to predict the masked tokens during the pre-training phase. The version evaluated contains 12 layers, 12 attention heads, and produces vectors of 768 dimensions.
- *VisualBERT* [10]: it is a multimodal model that combines text and image. It consists of a stack of Transformer layers that implicitly align elements of an input text and regions in an associated input image with self-attention. The experiments showed that this model could ground elements of language to image regions without any explicit supervision. The version evaluated is based on BERT-base, containing 12 layers, 12 attention heads, and producing vectors of 768 dimensions.

In the *Twitter multimodal corpus*, the text-only models (BERT, RoBERTa, and DeBERTa) were fine-tuned taking into account only the textual content, whereas VisualBERT also incorporated image information.

In addition to this evaluation, different quantitative and qualitative characteristics of the corpora were analysed. The most frequent n-grams in each dataset were obtained to have a broad overview of the vocabulary used. The Polarized Weirdness Index [13] was calculated to complement the results of the n-gram analysis. Also the most influential words in the identification of irony were obtained by using χ^2 for feature selection. Additionally, different characteristics of the textual posts were studied in both corpora, such as the presence of punctuation marks, slang words or hashtags.

Finally, a random subset of the multimodal dataset was manually reviewed. The goal was to determine, in the eyes of human reviewers, whether these samples actually required from images and text to identify the ironic intention of the user. This subset was further analysed using explainability techniques to highlight the words that Transformer models are paying attention to for identifying the ironic nature of the utterances.

4   Experiments

This section summarises the experimental results and the analysis carried out with the different datasets and models. First, the data preprocessing procedure is described. The performance obtained by the models on the selected corpora is then shown. Subsequently, a quantitative analysis of the datasets is presented, concluding with a manual analysis of a subset of samples.

4.1   Data Preprocessing

Before the language models can be trained, it is necessary to carry out a series of preprocessing tasks to adapt the data to the expected input format. To this end, the NLTK library was used to lowercase all the texts, removing usernames, links, punctuation marks, and special characters (e.g. #, $, %). Finally, the text was lemmatised to reduce the size of the vocabulary. In addition, stopwords were removed in the corpora analysis carried out in Sect. 4.4.

To discard possible outliers in the text (e.g., unusually long sequences that could exceed the maximum input length of the models), a threshold was established corresponding to the 99th percentile of posts' lengths. Text sequences exceeding this length were truncated. In the *Twitter text corpus*, this threshold corresponds to 24 words, with an average of 13.60 words per post, a median of 13 and a standard deviation of 6.69. In the *Twitter multimodal corpus*, the 99th percentile corresponds to 35 words, with an average of 15.70, a median of 17, and a standard deviation of 7.97. Figure 1 shows the frequencies of posts' lengths in the (a) text-only and the (b) multimodal dataset. These histograms reflect that the most frequent post length in the textual dataset is around 9 words, whereas in the multimodal dataset this value is around 15 words. In the latter, there are proportionally more short messages than in the textual corpus. The presence of visual information may lead to the need for less textual content to express the ironic intent of the message.

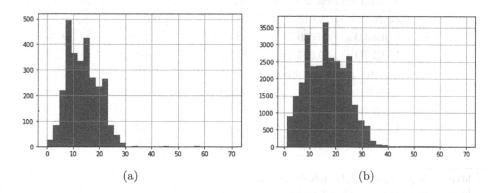

(a)   (b)

Fig. 1. Histogram of posts' lengths (number of words) in the (a) *Twitter text corpus* and in the (b) *Twitter multimodal corpus*.

Regarding visual information in the *Twitter multimodal corpus*, images were scaled and resized to 224×224 pixels and then passed through the VGG Net [15] and an average pooling layer to extract visual tokens. The outcome of this process is a vector of size 4096 that was further reduced using Principal Component Analysis (PCA) to make it suitable as an input for VisualBERT.

4.2 Experimental Setup

The four Transformer models proposed (BERT, RoBERTa, DeBERTa, and VisualBERT) were fine-tuned on the training subsets of the text-only and multimodal corpora. The hyperparameters were fixed using the validation subsets and, finally, the test subsets were used for the evaluation. All the experiments used Adam optimiser and ran for 10 epochs, except VisualBERT that was trained for 2 epochs because of limited computational resources.

The models versions used in the experiments were BERT-base,[7] RoBERTa-base,[8] DeBERTa-base,[9] and VisualBERT pre-trained on COCO,[10] a large-scale object detection, segmentation, and captioning dataset comprising 330K images, 1.5 million object instances, 80 object categories and 91 stuff categories.

4.3 Results

Table 1 shows the training loss, validation loss and accuracy of the four models in the two datasets studied. In both experiments RoBERTa obtained the best results, achieving an accuracy of up to 0.910 in the multimodal corpus. As a reference, previous works on this corpus achieved the following accuracy values: 0.834 [3], 0.840 [20], 0.885 [18], 0.888 [12] and 0.940 [16].

Table 1. Training loss, validation loss and accuracy of the models in both corpora.

Model	Training loss	Validation loss	Accuracy
Twitter text corpus			
BERT	0.619	0.625	0.660
RoBERTa	0.639	0.665	**0.750**
DeBERTa	0.697	0.696	0.600
Twitter multimodal corpus			
BERT	0.459	0.520	0.750
RoBERTa	0.241	0.305	**0.910**
DeBERTa	0.694	0.684	0.600
VisualBERT	0.339	0.486	0.810

---

[7] https://huggingface.co/bert-base-uncased.
[8] https://huggingface.co/roberta-base.
[9] https://huggingface.co/microsoft/deberta-base.
[10] https://huggingface.co/uclanlp/visualbert-vqa-coco-pre.

The most interesting finding in these results is the performance obtained by the text-only models on the *Twitter multimodal corpus*. BERT and RoBERTa performed significantly better on this dataset than in the text-only corpus, whereas DeBERTa obtained the same accuracy in both.

These results seem to confirm the initial hypothesis that this multimodal corpus does not really pose a challenge that involves leveraging textual and visual information, so that text-only models can achieve a good performance.

Regarding the results of VisualBERT, this model achieved 0.810 accuracy, surpassing DeBERTa (0.600) and BERT (0.750), but the best model was RoBERTa (0.910), which demonstrates the high performance that a text-only model can achieve in the multimodal dataset used.

4.4 Corpora Analysis

This section presents an analysis of the corpora used in the previous experiments to provide a better understanding of their nature.

N-Gram Frequency Count. The first task consisted of extracting n-grams of words from both datasets (taking into account training, validation, and test splits). Specifically, unigrams and bigrams were identified for further analysis. Then, a straightforward count of the frequencies of n-grams in ironic posts was carried out. Table 2 shows the 50 most frequent n-grams for each corpus. Most of them are unigrams, along with a few bigrams, as would be expected in a list based on frequencies.

Table 2. List of 50 most frequent n-grams for each corpus.

Twitter text corpus
user, user user, love, day, people, work, time, one, thank, today, great, oh, really, good, know, christmas, fun, u, going, well, see, make, new, lol, go, morning, thing, think, got, wait, back, want, look, feel, right, say, need, life, much, hour, someone, yay, school, week, getting, way, still, yeah, final, guy

Twitter multimodal corpus
user, user user, love, emoji_15 emoji_15, num, day, funny, know, one, really, thank, look, today, new, people, u, time, life, great, well, good, right, guy, work, got, need, think, best, see, make, oh, never, much, sure, say, friend, happy, going, wow, want, go, thing, way, trump, fun funny, back, lol lolsarcasm, true, always, lolsarcasm lolsarcasms

These two lists reflect that there are n-grams common to both datasets that are frequently repeated and that give an idea of the ironic nature of the texts.

Such is the case of fun/funny and lol. In the case of the *Twitter multimodal corpus*, there are more frequent n-grams that could be intuitively associated with ironic comments, such as lolsarcasm, which indeed contains the word sarcasm in it. The presence of emojis is also frequent in this corpus (e.g. emoji_15).[11] These language clues in the *Twitter multimodal corpus* may be one of the reasons for the good performance of the text-only models in this dataset.

Polarized Weirdness Index. In addition to the n-gram frequency count, an analysis was carried out by computing the Polarized Weirdness Index (PWI) [13] of the unigrams in both corpora in order to extract the most characteristic words of each one. The PWI is a variant of WI, which is a metric to retrieve word characteristics of a special language with respect to their common use in general language. The intuition behind WI is that a word is highly weird in a specific corpus if it occurs significantly more often in that context than in a general language corpus. Given a specialist and a general corpus, the metric can be described as the ratio of its relative frequencies in the respective corpora. In the case of PWI, the metric compares the relative frequencies of a word as it occurs in the subset of a labeled corpus by one value of the label against its complement. In the present work, the PWI is used to compare the prevalence of words in ironic and non ironic utterances.

Table 3 shows the top 20 unigrams extracted from the ironic and the non-ironic samples in both corpora based on the PWI metric. It is interesting to note that the unigrams extracted from the text-only corpus offer no clues about the ironic nature of the posts, since none of the tokens listed in the "Ironic" column of this corpus seems to be specifically related to the vocabulary expected in ironic messages.

On the contrary, the "Ironic" column of the multimodal corpus contain many n-grams that could be intuitively associated with ironic messages, including humor, funnyquotes, jokes, funnysayings, lolsarcasm, hilariousquotes, funny, funniest quotes, hilarious sayings and even irony, which reflects that the corpus might not be properly cleaned up. This confirms the findings of the previous frequency analysis, but in this case reflecting more clearly the differences between ironic and non-ironic samples in both corpora. Thus, the occurrence of this vocabulary in the ironic samples of the *Twitter multimodal corpus* can be a reason for the good performance of the text-only models.

Feature Selection. A feature selection procedure using χ^2 was applied to identify what unigrams were considered as most relevant in order to differentiate between ironic and non-ironic posts. Before applying χ^2 it is necessary to transform every post into a numerical vector. The TF-IDF weighting schema was used to obtain a number representing the frequency of the token in the post (TF) and its prevalence in the dataset (IDF). The number of dimensions of each post

---

[11] The numbering corresponding to each emoji was assigned by the authors of the corpus and does not match any known standard.

Table 3. List of 20 most relevant unigrams based on PWI for the ironic and non-ironic samples in the *Twitter text corpus* and the *Twitter multimodal corpus*.

Twitter text corpus		Twitter multimodal corpus	
Ironic	Non-ironic	Ironic	Non-ironic
another	please	mug	emoji623
saying	email	humor	carpet
pakistan	high	jokes	emoji1495
driving	remember	num	falcons
ironyuser	least	funnyquotes	emoji744
job	2015	relatable	former
emoji	watch	lolsarcasm	de
phone	cute	hilariousquotes	awards
nice	tweets	lolsarcasms	emoji682
wait	girl	quotes	rts
seems	anyone	satire	riseup
sick	side	funnysayings	announce
glad	beautiful	reposting	emoji2
straight	must	irony	emoji958
hair	via	lnyhbt	bestfanarmy
gotta	wonder	ccot	emoji245
state	stuff	graphic	allstar
rights	act	snappy	jan
traffic	seriously	sayings	emoji238
gay	mum	funny	marching
hindu	change	tshirt	overall
took	past	tshirts	womensmarch

vector is equal to the length of the vocabulary of the corpus, i.e., each dimension corresponds to one token. The value of the dimension is the TF-IDF weight if the token exists in the post or 0 otherwise. In the *Twitter text corpus* the length of the vocabulary was 10,150, wheres the length in the multimmodal corpus was 32,249. Texts were preprocessed in advance as in the previous analysis.

Table 4 shows the 50 best unigrams in order to differentiate ironic from non-ironic posts according to χ^2.

This analysis reveals again what was perceived previously: there are many clues in the text of *Twitter multimodal corpus* that intuitively can reveal the ironic nature of the post without requiring visual information. Tokens such as funny, lol, fun, and meme, together with three emoji symbols (emoji_15, emoji_623, and emoji_238), are among the top 10 most relevant tokens identified by χ^2. Indeed, there are fourteen emojis in the top 50 list. It is not the case

Table 4. List of 50 most relevant unigrams for each corpus according to χ^2.

Twitter text corpus
great, user, love, fun, yay, hour, waking, check, via, morning, monday, thanks, work, test, nice, oh, awesome, follow, joy, day, glad, understand, start, wonderful, working, teacher, wow, final, sick, co, customer, wait, ugly, notcies, calling, 2015, monstermmorpg, fix, seen, driver, exam, helpful, sleep, throwing, gamergate, lovely, fantastic
Twitter multimodal corpus
emoji_15, funny, num, lol, quote, fun, emoji_623, emoji_238, meme, womensmarch, goldenglobes, funnyquotes, lolsarcasm, lolsarcasms, thanks, funnysayings, funnypics, prlife, pr_roast, prworld, comedy, emoji_156, well, emoji_8, 2017, really, prlove, emoji_2, yay, iheartawards, yeah, blessed, oh, job, emoji_1930, emoji_32, university, great, inauguration, pr, emoji_549, glad, emoji_131, emoji_75, emoji_590, emoji_1495, tonight, emoji_92, service, fail

of the *Twitter text corpus*, where most relevant tokens are not as clearly related to irony or humorous situations (the only exception being fun).

Textual Characteristics. In addition to this word analysis, a set of textual characteristics were analysed in both corpora: (i) the presence of punctuation marks (with special attention to questions and exclamations); (ii) the use of hashtags (#); (iii) the use of cuss words;[12] and (iv) the use of slang words.[13]

Table 5. Characteristics of the *Twitter text corpus*. Column *Average* indicates the average number of characteristics found per post (4,601 samples). Median and standard deviation are also provided.

Column	Total count	Average	Median	Std. dev.
Question marks	626	0.1361	0.0	0.4474
Exclamations	1,311	0.2849	0.0	0.8702
Punctuation marks	21,058	4.5768	4.0	3.5612
Cuss words	136	0.0296	0.0	0.1794
Slang words	252	0.0548	0.0	0.2520
Hashtags	5,145	1.1182	0.0	2.0223

---

[12] https://en.wiktionary.org/wiki/Category:English_swear_words.
[13] https://bit.ly/3Hv4avo.

Table 6. Characteristics of the *Twitter multimodal corpus*. Column *Average* indicates the average number of characteristics found per post (24,635 samples). Median and standard deviation are also provided.

Column	Total count	Average	Median	Std. dev.
Question marks	2,575	0.1045	0.0	0.4398
Exclamations	8,685	0.3525	0.0	1.011
Punctuation marks	116,179	4.7160	4.0	3.93
Cuss words	430	0.0175	0.0	0.1328
Slang words	1,909	0.0775	0.0	0.3066
Hashtags	27,950	1.1346	0.0	1.8860

Table 5 and Table 6 show the result of this analysis. Both corpora are similar attending to the average occurrence of the characteristics studied. The only significant variations are in the use of cuss words and slang words: the first are more prevalent in the *Twitter text corpus*, whereas the latter occur more often in the *Twitter multimodal corpus*. Nevertheless, these differences do not offer an evidence that both datasets present significant variations at this level.

Reassessing the Corpora. A manual analysis was carried out by two annotators (both experts researchers in the field of irony identification) in a random sample of 100 ironic comments of the *Twitter multimodal corpus*. A third annotator would make the final decision in the case of disagreement. The goal was to test whether the post was really ironic and, in that case, if the image attached to the text was indeed necessary to identify its ironic condition.

This analysis revealed that 14% of the samples were considered as non-ironic, and 37% were deemed not to require the attached image to identify the post as ironic. A similar analysis was performed on the *Twitter text corpus*, but in this case the assessment consisted of just identifying whether the text was ironic or not, as there are no images attached in this dataset. In this case, 23% of the samples reviewed were considered as non-ironic.

A further analysis was done on a set of examples from the *Twitter multimodal corpus* using the Captum[14] library for eXplainable Artificial Intelligence (XAI), which provides tools for model interpretability. Figure 2 shows the contribution of each token to irony identification using RoBERTa on the textual part of the post. Green colour indicates positive contribution of tokens towards the predicted class, whereas red shows tokens contributing negatively. The intensity of the colour indicates the magnitude of the contribution. All these examples were correctly classified by RoBERTa as ironic.

The first example in Fig. 2 highlights how emojis strongly contribute to identify that the post is ironic. In the other examples, the presence of "lol" and "funny" is also a strong indication of irony, as might be expected. However, the

---

[14] https://captum.ai/.

#s wow how sweet emoji _ 19 emoji _ 19 emoji _ 19 emoji _ 417 emoji _ 417 #/s

#s mini ? are you f * * * * * k idd in ' me ? ! ? ! died for a second ! # funny # heart attack # stairs # pay att ention #/s

#s when your friend is about to do something stupid but you kinda wanna see what ' s gonna happen # funny #/s

#s me in a nutshell . like if you agree too . # lol # l ols arc asm # l ols arc asms # fun # funny # funny p ics #/s

#s my life : / # lol # l ols arc asm # l ols arc asms # fun # funny # funny p ics #/s

#s when your friend gives you a major confidence boost #/s

Fig. 2. Contribution of each token to identify the ironic intention of the text. (Color figure online)

most interesting thing that this analysis shows is the role of expressions such as "when your friend", "my life" or "me in a nutshell". These utterances are usually followed by an image that shows the implicit ironic intention of the user. The textual Transformers can learn this type of linguistic patterns in text, making unnecessary the presence of an image to correctly classify them as ironic, and therefore justifying the high accuracy of the text-only models.

5   Conclusion and Future Work

This work presented a study on the most popular corpus for multimodal irony detection [3]. In this corpus, both image information and text information are supposed to be required to identify the ironic nature of the messages. Otherwise, the corpus would not pose a real challenge to multimodal systems.

In order to test the suitability of this dataset, different Transformer models (textual and multimodal) were tested, comparing the results with a text-only dataset. The results showed that a text-only model such as RoBERTa performed surprisingly well on the multimodal dataset, revealing that text information provides clues in many cases to identify the ironic intention of the message without requiring the presence of visual information.

A further analysis was done to compare the textual and multimodal datasets, where it was found that text in multimodal messages was proportionally shorter than in textual corpus, suggesting that the presence of visual information may lead to the need for less textual content to express the ironic intent of the message. Moreover, different textual features gave clues to the ironic nature of the messages, which could justify the high accuracy of the text-only Transformer models in the multimodal setting. Tokens such as fun, lol, and meme, together with emoji symbols, were among the top most relevant tokens identified by the features selection procedure carried out. That was not the case of the text-only corpus, where most relevant tokens were not as clearly related to irony or humorous situations. The PWI metric provided similar findings, since n-grams such as humor, lolsarcasm, funniest quotes and even irony where on the top ranked list of the ironic samples in the multimodal corpus.

Finally, a manual reassessing of a random set of samples of both datasets was carried out, revealing that a percentage of the samples in the multimodal corpus (over 30%) were not considered to require the image as a hint to identify the irony. The interpretability analysis performed using the XAI Captum library identified that some expressions, such as "when your friend" or "my life", are identified by Transformers as relevant to classify a text as ironic. Indeed, these are typical social media utterances that are accompanied by an image that completes the ironic intention of the message.

Although it is the most widely used dataset in multimodal irony detection, these results suggest that the corpus used does not present a significant challenge when it comes to assessing the capacity of current multimodal systems to effectively merge textual and visual data.

As a future work, the analysis carried out can be extrapolated to other corpora mentioned in the bibliography. Also, additional machine learning models, including other Transformer architectures and traditional algorithms, can be studied. Finally, a remarkable contribution to the field would be the development of a really challenging dataset for multimodal irony identification, where there is a human supervision that guarantees the necessity of both image and text to convey the ironic sense of the samples.

Acknowledgements. The work of Paolo Rosso was in the framework of "FairTransNLP-Stereotypes" research project (PID2021-124361OB-C31), funded by MCIN/AEI/10.13039/ 501100011033 and by ERDF, EU A way of making Europe. The work of David Tomás was developed in the framework of "Technological Resources for Intelligent VIral AnaLysis through NLP (TRIVIAL)" (PID2021-122263OB-C22), funded by MCIN/AEI/ 10.13039/501100011033 and by the European Union Next-GenerationEU/PRTR.

References

1. Alnajjar, K., Hämäläinen, M.: ¡Qué maravilla! multimodal sarcasm detection in Spanish: a dataset and a baseline. In: Proceedings of the Third Workshop on Multimodal Artificial Intelligence, Mexico City, Mexico, pp. 63–68. Association for Computational Linguistics (2021). https://doi.org/10.18653/v1/2021.maiworkshop-1.9
2. Bedi, M., Kumar, S., Akhtar, M.S., Chakraborty, T.: Multi-modal sarcasm detection and humor classification in code-mixed conversations. IEEE Trans. Affect. Comput. 1–13 (2021). https://doi.org/10.1109/TAFFC.2021.3083522
3. Cai, Y., Cai, H., Wan, X.: Multi-modal sarcasm detection in Twitter with hierarchical fusion model. In: Proceedings of the 57th Annual Meeting of the ACL, pp. 2506–2515. Association for Computational Linguistics (2019). https://doi.org/10.18653/v1/P19-1239
4. Castro, S., Hazarika, D., Pérez-Rosas, V., Zimmermann, R., Mihalcea, R., Poria, S.: Towards multimodal sarcasm detection (an obviously perfect paper). In: Proceedings of the 57th Annual Meeting of the Association for Computational Linguistics, pp. 4619–4629. Association for Computational Linguistics (2019). https://doi.org/10.18653/v1/P19-1455
5. Chauhan, D.S., Dhanush, S.R., Ekbal, A., Bhattacharyya, P.: Sentiment and emotion help sarcasm? A multi-task learning framework for multi-modal sarcasm, sentiment and emotion analysis. In: Proceedings of the 58th Annual Meeting of the Association for Computational Linguistics, pp. 4351–4360. Association for Computational Linguistics (2020). https://doi.org/10.18653/v1/2020.acl-main.401

6. Devlin, J., Chang, M.W., Lee, K., Toutanova, K.: BERT: pre-training of deep bidirectional transformers for language understanding. In: Proceedings of the 2019 Conference of the North American Chapter of the Association for Computational Linguistics, Minneapolis, MN, USA, pp. 4171–4186. Association for Computational Linguistics (2019). https://doi.org/10.18653/v1/N19-1423

7. He, P., Liu, X., Gao, J., Chen, W.: DeBERTa: decoding-enhanced BERT with disentangled attention. CoRR abs/2006.03654 (2020)

8. Hee, C.V., Lefever, E., Hoste, V.: SemEval-2018 task 3: irony detection in English tweets. In: Proceedings of the 12th International Workshop on Semantic Evaluation, New Orleans, Louisiana, pp. 39–50. Association for Computational Linguistics (2018). https://doi.org/10.18653/v1/S18-1005

9. Joshi, A., Bhattacharyya, P., Carman, M.J.: Automatic sarcasm detection: a survey. ACM Comput. Surv. **50**(5), 1–22 (2017). https://doi.org/10.1145/3124420

10. Li, L.H., Yatskar, M., Yin, D., Hsieh, C., Chang, K.: VisualBERT: a simple and performant baseline for vision and language. CoRR abs/1908.03557 (2019)

11. Liu, Y., et al.: RoBERTa: a robustly optimized BERT pretraining approach. CoRR abs/1907.11692 (2019)

12. Pan, H., Lin, Z., Fu, P., Qi, Y., Wang, W.: Modeling intra and inter-modality incongruity for multi-modal sarcasm detection. In: Findings of the Association for Computational Linguistics: EMNLP 2020, pp. 1383–1392. Association for Computational Linguistics (2020). https://doi.org/10.18653/v1/2020.findings-emnlp.124

13. Poletto, F., Basile, V., Sanguinetti, M., Bosco, C., Patti, V.: Resources and benchmark corpora for hate speech detection: a systematic review. Lang. Resour. Eval. **55**(2), 477–523 (2020). https://doi.org/10.1007/s10579-020-09502-8

14. Schifanella, R., de Juan, P., Tetreault, J., Cao, L.: Detecting sarcasm in multimodal social platforms. In: Proceedings of the 24th ACM International Conference on Multimedia, MM 2016, pp. 1136–1145. Association for Computing Machinery, New York (2016). https://doi.org/10.1145/2964284.2964321

15. Simonyan, K., Zisserman, A.: Very deep convolutional networks for large-scale image recognition. In: Bengio, Y., LeCun, Y. (eds.) 3rd International Conference on Learning Representations, ICLR, San Diego, CA, USA (2015)

16. Tomás, D., Ortega-Bueno, R., Zhang, G., Rosso, P., Schifanella, R.: Transformer-based models for multimodal irony detection. J. Ambient Intell. Hum. Comput. 1–12 (2022). https://doi.org/10.1007/s12652-022-04447-y

17. Vaswani, A., et al.: Attention is all you need. In: Advances in Neural Information Processing Systems, Long Beach, CA, USA, vol. 30, pp. 5998–6008. Curran Associates Inc. (2017)

18. Wang, X., Sun, X., Yang, T., Wang, H.: Building a bridge: a method for image-text sarcasm detection without pretraining on image-text data. In: Proceedings of the First International Workshop on Natural Language Processing Beyond Text, pp. 19–29. Association for Computational Linguistics (2020). https://doi.org/10.18653/v1/2020.nlpbt-1.3

19. Wu, Y., et al.: Modeling incongruity between modalities for multimodal sarcasm detection. IEEE Multimed. **28**(2), 86–95 (2021). https://doi.org/10.1109/MMUL.2021.3069097

20. Xu, N., Zeng, Z., Mao, W.: Reasoning with multimodal sarcastic tweets via modeling cross-modality contrast and semantic association. In: Proceedings of the 58th Annual Meeting of the Association for Computational Linguistics, pp. 3777–3786. Association for Computational Linguistics (2020). https://doi.org/10.18653/v1/2020.acl-main.349

Less is More: A Prototypical Framework for Efficient Few-Shot Named Entity Recognition

Yue Zhang[1,2(✉)] and Hui Fang[1,2]

[1] Department of Electrical and Computer Engineering, University of Delaware, Newark, USA
{zhangyue,hfang}@udel.edu
[2] Center for Plastics Innovation, University of Delaware, Newark, USA

Abstract. Few-shot named entity recognition (NER) aims to leverage a small number of labeled examples to extract novel-class named entities from unstructured text. Although existing few-shot NER methods, such as ESD and DecomposedMetaNER, are effective, they are quite complex and not efficient, which makes them unsuitable for real-world applications when the prediction time is a critical factor. In this paper, we propose a simple span-based prototypical framework that follows the metric-based meta-learning paradigm and does not require time-consuming fine-tuning. In addition, the BERT encoding process in our model can be pre-computed and cached, making the final inference process even faster. Experiment results show that, compared with the state-of-the-art models, the proposed framework can achieve comparable effectiveness with much better efficiency.

Keywords: Few-shot NER · Metric-learning · Efficiency

1 Introduction

Named Entity Recognition (NER) is an important natural language understanding task, which aims to extract certain types of named entities (e.g., locations) from unstructured text. Most neural NER models follow the supervised learning paradigm and require a large amount of annotated data for training. These models have impressive performance in extracting existing entity types. However, in practice, we want a NER model to rapidly adapt to novel entity types so that we can test the prototype NER systems and get feedback for future improvement. As a result, few-shot NER [5,7], which can learn to extract novel types of entities based on a few training examples for each class, has gotten a lot of attention recently.

The focus of existing few-shot NER research is mainly on optimizing accuracy over very little training data. However, for real applications, improving accuracy will not help if the benefits it brings become outweighed by the inconvenience caused by increasing prediction latency. As it is well known that the more training data you have, the better performance you get, using few-shot models may

© The Author(s), under exclusive license to Springer Nature Switzerland AG 2023
E. Métais et al. (Eds.): NLDB 2023, LNCS 13913, pp. 33–46, 2023.
https://doi.org/10.1007/978-3-031-35320-8_3

become less attractive if the time taken to generate predictions is too long. In such cases, people may just annotate more data and use a traditional supervised NER instead. For example, in scientific literature mining, researchers often want to extract entities from thousands of research articles to compose a knowledge base and mine patterns [13,29]. However, based on our preliminary results, existing few-shot NER methods can only finish predicting several articles per second, making the entire waiting time uncomfortably long. In this case, domain experts may give up using few-shot models as a prototype development tool. Therefore for practical applications, we need to focus on optimizing not only accuracy but also prediction latency.

The state-of-the-art few-shot NER methods often utilize pre-trained language models (e.g. BERT [4]) to get the prior knowledge of human language and train their model on existing entities to learn NER specific prior knowledge. DecomposedMetaNER [17] and CONTaiNER [3], additionally followed the transfer learning paradigm and fine-tuned their models on a few examples of novel entities for better adaptation. However, this fine-tuning process forces the whole prediction process to be carried out online since the model's parameters may change as the user provides different examples. As a result, the state-of-the-art few-shot NER models are not very efficient, making them impractical to be used in applications requiring shorter prediction time.

On the contrary, metric-based meta-learning models can accelerate the prediction process through pre-computing and caching part of the model's computation result. These models project samples into an embedding space, where similar and dissimilar samples can be easily discriminated by non-parametric methods. For example, for each class, prototypical network [20] takes the mean vector of all embedded same class examples as the prototype representation for that class. It then classifies each test example to the class of its nearest prototype based on Euclidean distance. In this case, the similarity part needs to be computed online, but the time-consuming encoding part can be done offline. Clearly, this approach seems to shed a light towards efficient few-shot NER methods.

In this work, we propose a **S**imple **S**pan-base **P**rototypical framework (SSP) for few-shot NER. SSP follows the metric-based meta-learning paradigm and does not require fine-tuning. Specifically, our model leverages Layer Normalization [1] to transform the span representation, which ensures the representation of nice geometric properties and is beneficial for the subsequent non-parametric classification process. We also incorporate the attention mechanism into the metric-based meta-learning process to dynamically focus on closely related examples and better handle outliers in the labeled examples. Additionally, we pre-train SSP on supervised NER tasks before training it on meta-learning tasks in order to enhance its span representation capability. The simple structure of our model, combined with pre-computing the BERT representation, makes our inference speed significantly faster than existing models. The contributions of our work can be summarized as follows: (1) We conduct a comparative study to compare the efficiency of existing state-of-the-art (SoTA) methods and find their prediction efficiency is not satisfying. (2) We propose a lightweight few-shot NER model, which is as accurate as previous SoTA models but much more efficient.

2   Related Work

Meta-learning has become a popular method for tackling the few-shot learning problem. Especially, metric-based meta-learning methods have become the mainstream methods for few-shot image classification [20–22] and have also been widely adapted to other NLP tasks such as relation extraction [9]. Our model follows the same nearest class prototype classification idea and generalizes the mean pooling to attention pooling. Compared with ESD [23], which uses four types of attention, our model has a much simpler attention module and is equally effective.

Early few-shot NER methods are typically based on token-level classification [7,12]. Such token-level models tend to make single-token errors, where one of the words inside a multi-word entity is misclassified due to the lack of training examples. StructShot [27], CONTaiNER [3] and L-TapNet+CDT [11] added a label-agnostic conditional random field (CRF) for modeling label dependency between tokens. But a lot of valuable similarity information between tokens has already been lost before CRF because the CRF only takes a single scalar to represent the label distribution. In practice, the transition matrix needs to be learned from existing entities, making it prone to the domain-shift problem if the span length distribution changes greatly. Alternatively, Proto+Reptile [15] used a neural network to predict the transition probability. Recently, span-based few-shot NER methods, such as ESD [23], DecomposedMetaNER [17], and SpanNER [25], have been proposed to explicitly model phrasal representation and ensure the integrity of the phrase. Our model also uses span embedding to model phrases directly.

Moreover, prompt-learning [2] and language modeling [16] were also adapted to solve the few-shot NER problem. However, they needed either a large validation set to choose the template [2] or external lexical annotation to select label word [16]. Similarly, another work [12] uses noisy-supervised pre-training for few-shot NER, but an additional large-scale noisy NER dataset is not always available. So these works does not align well with the meta-learning set up of our work. So we do not compare our model against these methods and leave the exploration of using external resources for future work.

3   Task Formulation

NER aims to identify each named entity correctly and classify it into the corresponding categories. We follow the idea of previous meta-learning studies [5,11] and formalize the few-shot NER problem as solving a list of N-way K-shot NER tasks.

Each task, namely the episode, mimics a real-world few-shot learning challenge. The set of all known examples in an episode is denoted as the **support set S**, and the set of all unknown examples is denoted as the **query set Q**. **N** denotes the number of entity types in the task, and **K** denotes the number of annotated examples for each entity type in the support set. For each task, the model encounters a set of novel entities and needs to extract entities in Q only using the examples in S. Figure 1 shows an example of a 2-way 2-shot task.

This process needs to be repeated multiple times for the model to learn how to adapt to a new task quickly with a few examples. Therefore, in practice, we randomly sample the annotated sentences to construct episodes according to the N-way K-shot constraints. And the testing set comes from a domain that is different from the training set and has non-intersecting label spaces in order to truly test the model's capability of generalizing to unseen types of entities.

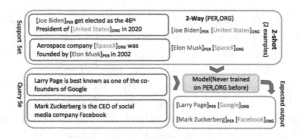

Fig. 1. A 2-way 2-shot task for Person(PER) and Organization(ORG) entity.

4   Simple Span-Based Prototypical (SSP) Framework

We propose a simple span-based prototypical (SSP) framework to tackle the few-shot NER problem. The proposed model consists of four parts: (1) span representation and normalization, where we model and normalize the span embedding; (2) metric based meta-learning with attention, where we generate class centers using an attention mechanism and classify spans accordingly; (3) whole classification pre-training, where we pre-train our model on supervised NER tasks before meta-learning; and (4) post-processing, where we resolve overlapping conflicts in span predictions.

Span Representation and Normalization. Our method formulates the few-shot NER as a span classification problem instead of a token classification problem since token-based models tend to recognize only part of multi-token entities and produce many false positive predictions. For every possible span (i.e. continuous piece of text) in the sentence, our model classifies it into either one of the predefined categories or the special category **O** (i.e. ordinary spans). For instance, given the sentence "Aerospace company SpaceX was founded by Elon Musk in 2002", "SpaceX" and "Elon Musk" will be classified as Person and Organization span while "founded" and "in 2002" will be identified as type O spans. Spans that are partially overlapped with ground truth, like "Aerospace company SpaceX", are not treated as correct spans during evaluation and will be used to construct the prototype for type O spans.

We take BERT [4] as our backbone sentence encoder and follow the standard head-tail concatenation way to compose the span embedding [8,14,18,23]. The last output layer of BERT is used as the contextual representation for tokens in the sentence. We take the first subword of the span's starting and ending words to form its initial span representation $[\mathbf{h_{start}}, \mathbf{h_{end}}]$. Here $\mathbf{h}$ denotes the BERT encoder's output for each subword. To incorporate the length information into the span representation, following the same methodology proposed in the previous study [8], we add word length embedding $\mathbf{WL}$ and subword length embedding $\mathbf{TL}$ to the initial span representation.

After that, the span representation is projected into the desired dimension with linear transformation and normalized using **Layer Normalization** (LN) [1]

$$\tilde{\mathbf{s}} = \text{LN}\left(\mathbf{W}\left([\mathbf{h_{start}}, \mathbf{h_{end}}] + \mathbf{WL} + \mathbf{TL}\right)\right) \in \mathbb{R}^D \tag{1}$$

Here $\tilde{\mathbf{s}}$ denotes the output of our span embedding module, D denotes the span embedding size, and it is set to 768 in our model. Layer Normalization aims to first zero-center and standardize the embedding, and then re-scale and re-center the embedding with parameter γ and $\beta \in \mathbb{R}^D$.

$$LN(\tilde{\mathbf{s}}) = \left(\frac{\tilde{\mathbf{s}} - mean(\tilde{\mathbf{s}})}{\sqrt{var(\tilde{\mathbf{s}})}}\right) * \gamma + \beta \tag{2}$$

An inspection of the trained weights reveals that $\gamma \approx \mathbf{1}, \beta \approx \mathbf{0}$. Thus, the mean of each normalized embedding is around $\mathbf{0}$ and the L2 norm is around $\sqrt{D}$. The Euclidean distance metric that we use to calculate embedding similarity could then be further deduced to

$$|\tilde{\mathbf{s}}_1 - \tilde{\mathbf{s}}_2|_2^2 = |\tilde{\mathbf{s}}_1|_2^2 + |\tilde{\mathbf{s}}_1|_2^2 - 2\tilde{\mathbf{s}}_1 \cdot \tilde{\mathbf{s}}_2 = 2D - 2D\cos(\tilde{\mathbf{s}}_1, \tilde{\mathbf{s}}_2) \propto \cos(\tilde{\mathbf{s}}_1, \tilde{\mathbf{s}}_2), \tag{3}$$

which is proportional to a cosine distance with a $2D$ scale factor. In this way, we can see that our span normalization method is a special case for the widely adapted scaled cosine similarity. This also explains why we need to use a higher-than-usual(for supervised span-based NER, a typical value is 256 [14] or 150 [28]) embedding size as a theoretical analysis shows increasing size help reduce false positive rate [19] for cosine distance based representation learning. Our experiment analysis later shows both normalization and embedding size plays an important role in the model's good performance.

Metric-Based Meta-Learning with Attention. Given an N-way K-shot task $(\mathbf{S}, \mathbf{Q})$ with entity label space $\mathbf{Y}$, our model first enumerates every possible span in each sentence of $\mathbf{S}$ and $\mathbf{Q}$ and encodes them into corresponding span representation collection $\mathbf{R_S}$ and $\mathbf{R_Q}$. Similar to prototypical network [20], our model predicts the span label y_m based on the distance between the span representation $\tilde{\mathbf{s}}_m$ and each class center $\tilde{\mathbf{c}}_k$. More specifically, we assign y_m to the label of class center $\tilde{\mathbf{c}}_k$, in which it is nearest to $\tilde{\mathbf{s}}_m$ based on the squared Euclidean distance metric.

$$y_m^* = \underset{k \in \mathbf{Y} \cup \{O\}}{argmin} |\tilde{\mathbf{s}}_m - \tilde{\mathbf{c}}_k|_2^2 \tag{4}$$

We denote the set of support span representations having label k as $\mathbf{Z_k} = \{\tilde{\mathbf{s}}_n : \tilde{\mathbf{s}}_n \in \mathbf{R_S}$ and $y_n = k\}$. The original prototypical network computes the mean pooling of $\mathbf{Z_k}$ as the class center $\tilde{\mathbf{c}}_k$, which can be viewed as a special case of attention mechanism where the weight is fixed to **1**. Like ESD [23] and HATT [9], we use **query-support attention** (QSA) to let the class center representation bias towards similar support span representations and be more robust to outliers.

$$\tilde{\mathbf{c}}_k^m = \sum_i \frac{e^{\tilde{\mathbf{s}}_m \cdot \mathbf{Z}_k^i}}{\sum_i e^{\tilde{\mathbf{s}}_m \cdot \mathbf{Z}_k^i}} \mathbf{Z}_k^i \tag{5}$$

Here $\cdot$ denotes the dot product operation, $\mathbf{Z}_k^i$ is the i_{th} member of $\mathbf{Z_k}$, $\tilde{\mathbf{c}}_k^m$ is the type k class center for query span $\tilde{\mathbf{s}}_m$. Figure 2 summarizes the entire span representation and meta-learning process.

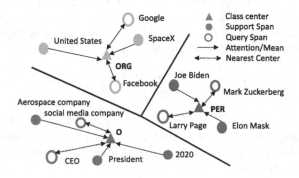

Fig. 2. The span-based prototypical meta-learning framework

The model parameters are updated using gradient descent, and the negative log-likelihood is minimized over a batch of randomly sampled N-way K-shot tasks:

$$-\log \sum_{(\mathbf{S},\mathbf{Q})} \sum_{(\tilde{\mathbf{s}}_m, y_m) \in \mathbf{Q}} \frac{e^{|\tilde{\mathbf{s}}_m - \tilde{\mathbf{c}}_k^m|_2^2}}{\sum_{k \in \mathbf{Y} \cup \{O\}} e^{|\tilde{\mathbf{s}}_m - \tilde{\mathbf{c}}_k|_2^2}}. \tag{6}$$

Whole Classification Pre-training. Instead of training our span encoder directly on N-way K-shot episodes, we find pre-training the encoder on the same training set in a supervised NER manner helps the model learn better span representation. Compared with training on N-way K-shot tasks, where the model only optimizes loss on a subset of entity types each time, whole classification pre-training optimizes for the whole label space.

In classification pre-training, the class center $\tilde{\mathbf{c}}_k$ is not generated based on the support set but becomes a learnable parameter. We also use the standard dot product instead of squared Euclidean distance as our distance metric. And the loss function is also computed on the sentence level instead of the task level.

Post-processing. The raw output of our model cannot be used directly because there might be overlapping conflicts inside span predictions. For example, two overlapped spans might be both predicted as Non-O entities, which is not allowed for flat NER. We use a greedy pruning algorithm, which adapts the Non-maximum Suppression algorithm for NER scenario [28], to decode a set of valid span predictions from the raw output. The algorithm sorts all Non-O span predictions based on their confidence scores and then iterates over them, keeping the highest-scoring span and suppressing any overlapping span with a lower score.

5   Experiments

5.1   Experiment Setup

Datasets: *Few-NERD* [5] is a large-scale few-shot NER dataset with a hierarchy of 8 coarse-grained entity types (e.g., Person, Organization) and 66 fine-grained entity types (e.g., Person-Politician, Person-Actor, Organization-Company). There are two different train/valid/test data splitting settings: (1) *Few-NERD Intra*: data are split based on the coarse-grained label of entities (e.g., the train split has all Person entities while the test split has all Organization entities) (2) *Few-NERD Inter*: data are split based on the fine-grained label of entities and the hierarchy relationship is ignored. (e.g. the train split has all Person-Politician entities while the test split has all Person-Actor, this is not allowed in *Few-NERD Intra* because of sharing the same coarse-grained label "Person").

As there is no other few-shot NER dataset available, we pick *SNIPS* as our second benchmark to evaluate if our methods can be generalized to other structure prediction tasks. *SNIPS* is an intent detection and slot-filling dataset with crowdsourced queries expressing seven kinds of user intents. The slot-filling task and NER task both need to make structure predictions on text, but slot-filling is more specific to dialog circumstances. We use the few-shot slot-filling dataset sampled by Hou [11]. It is constructed using the "leaving-one-out" cross-validation strategy. Each time one user intent is used for sampling testing episodes, another intent for validation, and the remaining five intents for training.

Implementation Details: We use *bert-base-cased* as our backbone encoder because some entities, like Music and Movie, would be hard to identify if converted to lowercase. But we also have a variant using *bert-base-uncased* since our baselines use uncased BERT. The *Few-NERD Inter/Intra* training set each has 36/35 fine-grained entity types, which is much bigger than the number of entity types in sampled 5-way/10-way episodes, meaning only a subset of entity types is used in each training step. Therefore, we apply the whole class pre-training for this dataset. In *SNIPS*, we only use uncased BERT since all its sentences are in lowercase. We also do not use whole class pre-training for *SNIPS* since the episodes sampled from each domain are already constructed with their entire label space. We make our codes public at https://github.com/nsndimt/SSP.

Baselines: We compare our model against three state-of-the-art few-shot NER methods and also re-implement three token-based few-shot NER methods originally implemented by *Few-NERD* [5]. In our experiments, we found the three token-based methods (i.e., **ProtoBERT** [20], **NNShot** and **StructShot** [27]) have shown comparable performance to more complicated methods, especially after careful re-implementation and hyperparameter tuning. We find that, in their original implementation, the dropout regularization(with dropout probability set to 0.5) that is directly applied to the final token embedding significantly decreases their performance on *Few-NERD*. In our re-implementation, we set the dropout probability to 0. **CONTaiNER** [3], **ESD** [23], and **DecomposedMetaNER** [17] are three recently proposed few-shot NER models and should represent the state-of-the-art methods on *Few-NERD* dataset. Among them, **CONTaiNER** is token-based while the other two are span-based Also, **ESD** [23] reach state-of-the-art performance on *SNIPS*. Additionally, we include **L-TapNet+CDT** [11] as the state-of-the-art token-based approach for *SNIPS*.

5.2   Efficiency Comparison

We conduct experiments to evaluate the efficiency of our model and the three state-of-art models on *Few-NERD*. The results are shown in the left plot of Fig. 3 (Note. we cannot measure CONTaiNER's prediction time in the 10-shot scenario since it causes Out-of-Memory error on GPU). It is clear the proposed SSP model is much faster than three state-of-art baselines.

To better understand which system components take more time in each model, we also break down the prediction time into three categories, i.e., fine-tuning, encoding, and inference, and report the results in the right part of Fig. 3.

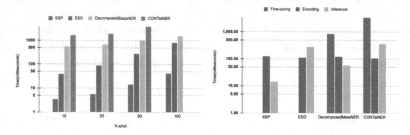

Fig. 3. Left: Prediction time on a single 10-way **K**-shot episode; Right: Prediction time breakdown on a single 10-way 5-shot episode; All tested on a 3090 GPU

The fine-tuning time measures the amount of time CONTaiNER and DecomposedMetaNER are fine-tuned on the support set while SSP and ESD do not have this step. The encoding time consists of both the BERT encoding time and the span/token representation extraction time. The inference time includes the class center/nearest neighbor construction time and distance calculation time. For ESD and our model, the encoding time can be saved by pre-computing the representation offline. And only the inference time is needed for deploying the model. But for CONTaiNER and DecomposedMetaNER, since fine-tuning would update model parameters, the total prediction time would be the sum of fine-tuning, encoding, and inference time. As shown in Fig. 3, the fine-tuning time is the largest source of latency for models that have it. All models have similar encoding latency because they all use BERT. And our model has the lowest inference time thanks to its simplified structure. Fine-tuning is slow since it runs BERT forward and backward process multiple times while encoding only runs the forward process once. Our model has the lowest inference time since we avoid adding complicated attention mechanisms (used in ESD [23]) or CRF Viterbi decoding (used in CONTaiNER [3] and DecomposedMetaNER [17]) to our model.

5.3 Effectiveness Comparison

Table 1. Performance (F1 percent) on *Few-NERD*. †means we report the result in the original paper; ‡ means we run testing by use using provided checkpoint; cased and uncased denotes whether the backbone BERT is cased. Note: all baselines use uncased

Models	Intra				Inter			
	1 Shot		5 Shot		1 Shot		5 Shot	
	5 way	10 way	5 way	10 way	5 way	10 way	5 way	10 way
ProtoBERT	38.03 ± 0.29	31.43 ± 0.37	53.13 ± 1.03	46.07 ± 0.69	58.08 ± 0.26	52.00 ± 0.59	65.29 ± 0.51	60.54 ± 0.55
NNShot	37.89 ± 0.83	31.56 ± 0.39	50.90 ± 0.48	43.76 ± 0.41	55.62 ± 0.46	50.22 ± 0.34	63.50 ± 0.23	59.70 ± 0.21
StructShot	42.25 ± 0.55	35.25 ± 0.61	51.13 ± 0.26	44.98 ± 0.32	58.81 ± 0.34	53.62 ± 0.46	64.20 ± 0.26	60.22 ± 0.39
CONTaiNER‡	38.48	31.76	53.58	47.10	49.75	44.68	61.74	57.17
ESD†	36.08 ± 1.60	30.00 ± 0.70	52.14 ± 1.50	42.15 ± 2.60	59.29 ± 1.25	52.16 ± 0.79	69.06 ± 0.80	64.00 ± 0.43
DecomposedMetaNER†	49.48 ± 0.85	42.84 ± 0.46	62.92 ± 0.57	57.31 ± 0.25	64.75 ± 0.35	58.65 ± 0.43	71.49 ± 0.47	68.11 ± 0.05
SSP (uncased)	45.30 ± 0.53	38.34 ± 0.34	63.91 ± 0.18	57.99 ± 0.23	64.38 ± 0.11	58.88 ± 0.18	73.75 ± 0.08	70.56 ± 0.06
SSP (cased)	47.50 ± 0.36	39.79 ± 0.19	66.16 ± 0.18	59.66 ± 0.14	65.98 ± 0.20	59.93 ± 0.18	75.09 ± 0.16	71.61 ± 0.12

Previous experiment results show the SSP model is more efficient. We also conduct experiments to evaluate its effectiveness. Table 1 shows effectiveness comparison on the *Few-NERD* data. The SSP model consistently outperforms all baseline models in the 1-shot and 5-shot setting of *Few-NERD Inter* and the 5-shot setting of *Few-NERD Intra*. In the 1-shot setting of *Few-NERD Intra*, SSP performs slightly worse than DecomposedMetaNER, but performs slightly better than DecomposedMetaNER in the 1-shot setting of *Few-NERD Inter*. DecomposedMetaNER is a two-stage pipeline consisting of separate span detection and classification model. Therefore, we additionally calculate the span detection F1 score of our cased model(i.e. span type can be wrong, as long as it is not classified as O). It turns out that our model's span detection F1 score is 8–10% lower than DecomposedMetaNER in the 1-shot setting of *Few-NERD Intra*. This may indicate having separate span detection and classification is a possible improvement direction for our model.

Moreover, the three re-implemented token-based baselines can outperform more complicated SoTA methods in certain settings, highlighting the importance of properly implementing and tuning the baseline. Our re-implementation avoids applying dropout regularization directly on the token embedding. Moreover, we find if we apply dropout regularization(even with a drop probability of 0.1) to the span embedding in our SSP model, the performance also drops noticeably. This may indicate that the token/span embedding is highly correlated between different dimensions and applying dropout regularization would break such correlation. We find that implementation decisions are important, and simple models such as SSP, when implemented in the correct way, can achieve superior performance than existing complicated models.

Table 2. Performance (F1 percent) of baselines and our methods on *SNIPS*. †denotes the result reported in their paper. We report all seven cross-validation results, each time testing one user intent: Weather (We), Music (Mu), PlayList (Pl), Book (Bo), Search Screen (Se), Restaurant (Re), and Creative Work (Cr).

Models	We	Mu	Pl	Bo	Se	Re	Cr	Avg
ProtoBERT	78.58 ± 1.04	67.27 ± 0.32	79.07 ± 1.18	**90.30 ± 1.08**	82.43 ± 0.52	76.74 ± 1.31	73.91 ± 2.67	78.33
NNShot	80.18 ± 0.74	68.93 ± 1.20	74.24 ± 1.64	84.49 ± 1.17	83.24 ± 1.10	79.50 ± 0.52	73.51 ± 3.61	77.73
StructShot	83.26 ± 1.63	74.27 ± 0.68	77.94 ± 0.98	86.26 ± 1.16	85.89 ± 0.87	81.92 ± 0.30	72.83 ± 4.13	80.34
L-TapNet+CDT†	71.64 ± 3.62	67.16 ± 2.97	75.88 ± 1.51	84.38 ± 2.81	82.58 ± 2.12	70.05 ± 1.61	73.41 ± 2.61	75.01
ESD †	84.50 ± 1.06	66.61 ± 2.00	79.69 ± 1.35	82.57 ± 1.37	82.22 ± 0.81	80.44 ± 0.80	**81.13 ± 1.84**	79.59
SSP	**85.70 ± 2.56**	**74.28 ± 1.85**	**84.15 ± 0.48**	87.23 ± 0.73	**88.65 ± 0.73**	**82.83 ± 0.51**	78.83 ± 0.60	**83.09**

Table 2 reports the experiment result on *SNIPS*. On average, our model can outperform all our baselines in the 5-shot setting. This demonstrates our model's potential to be adapted as a few-shot slot-filling model. This is promising for scientific text mining because the slot-filling method has been successfully adapted to extract solid oxide fuel cell information [6] and chemical reaction information [10].

5.4   Additional Analysis

Span vs Token Representations: We conduct a detailed analysis to explore why span-based methods can outperform token-based ones. ProtoBERT is used to represent the token-based models. A simple version of our model that does not use whole class pre-training or Query-Support Attention, and uses uncased BERT is used to represent the span-based models for a fair comparison. All comparisons are carried out on the 5-way 5-shot setting of Few-NERD Inter.

First, we break the evaluation metric by different span lengths, as shown in Fig. 4 Left. Compared with the token-based model, the span-based model has significantly higher precision for single-word entities while having a slight advantage in both the precision and recall for multi-word entities. We hypothesize that the token-based model breaks multi-word entities into small spans more frequently and therefore causes a lot of false-positive single-word entities.

Therefore, we dig deeper and concentrate on two groups of entities: single-word prediction and multi-word ground truth. The analyzing result is demonstrated in Fig. 4 Mid and Right. For single-word prediction, we classified the error into three cases: (1) "Inside", denoting it is inside a ground truth entity that has the same label as the prediction (2) "Misclassified", denoting it has a wrong label; (3) "Outside", denoting it is not part of any ground truth entities. Clearly, the span-based method makes much fewer Inside errors. For multi-word ground truth, we classified the error into three cases: (1) "All O", denoting all the words inside the ground truth are misclassified as O; (2) "Partial O", denoting part of the words are misclassified as O; (3) Other, denoting the rest occasions. Here, we can see that the token base method makes more "Partial O" errors, indicating that the token base method breaks a lot of multi-word entities by misclassifying one of its tokens as O.

Ablation Studies: We also conduct ablation studies to explore the contribution of different components in our SSP model. Due to the huge number of possible variants, we split our ablation studies into two parts. We start with a simplified version and gradually add or modify some components until it is the same as the SSP model reported in Table 1. Both studies are carried out on *Few-NERD* and we report the averaged F1 score in percentage across all eight settings (i.e $5/10\,way \times 1/5\,shot \times Inter/Intra\,split$).

The first part focuses on studying the effect of span representation size and different representation normalization techniques as mentioned in Sect. 4. We do not use attention or pre-training in our model and we use uncased BERT in order to control the number of variables and also make SSP comparable to other span-based methods. We introduce the following variants of SSP, each with a different normalization strategy: (1) *No-Norm*, which removes the Layer Normalization layer; (2) *L2-Norm*, in which we not only remove Layer Normalization but also replaces the Euclidean distance with cosine distance $Tcosine(\tilde{s}_m \cdot \tilde{c}_k)$; Here T is a temperature paramcter and $T = 40$; (3) *LayerNorm**, which is a variation of LayerNorm by removing the re-scaling and re-centering part. The results of these three variations together with the original SSP, when the span embedding dimension is 768, are reported at the top part in the left plot of Fig. 5. The results

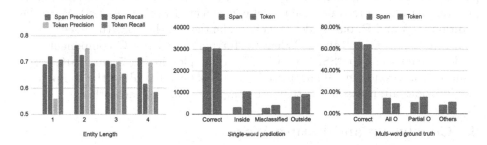

Fig. 4. Left: Evaluation metric breakdown by entity length; Mid: Single-word prediction breakdown Right: Multi-word ground truth breakdown

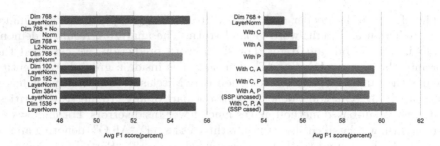

Fig. 5. Left: Ablations on Layer Normalization and representation dimension; Right: Ablations on different model components, where C denotes cased BERT, A denotes Query Support attention, and P denotes Whole class pre-training. The last two configurations is the same as SSP (cased/uncased) reported in Table 1

of SSP with the original LN but with different span embedding dimensions (i.e., 100, 192, 384, 1538) are shown at the lower part in the same plot.

The plot shows that having Layer Normalization on span representation greatly improves our model's performance over *No-Norm*. And the LayerNorm* result confirms our observation on trained γ and β, indicating that the affine projection which is applied after the re-scaling and re-centering operation makes little difference. Moreover, the L2-Norm result proves that just re-scaling is not enough, and re-centering also plays an important role here. Moreover, we can see that the span representation capacity (aka the embedding dimensions) also makes a huge difference. The bigger the span representation, the better the few-shot learning performance. This discovery is also in line with other studies in metric-learning [24]. We choose to fix the dimension to 768 for all other experiments since this is also the hidden size of *bert-base* and should make our model comparable to other token-based models(including DecomposedMetaNER which use the average of in-span token embedding as span representation).

In the second part of ablation studies, we start with the "Dim 768 + Layer-Norm" configuration in the first part and gradually add or change some model components, including (1) **C** - Cased BERT encoder which replaces the uncased BERT (Sect. 5.1); (2) **A** - Query support Attention which replaces the mean pooling in the class center construction process (Sect. 4); (3) **P** - Whole class pre-training which pre-trains the model before mete-learning (Sect. 4). With the addition of **A** and **P**, our model variant is identical to the "SSP(uncased)" configuration reported in Table 1. When we further added the **C** component, our model is equivalent to "SSP(cased)". The right plot in Fig. 5 summarizes the result of our second part ablation study, which shows that all of the component modifications are necessary as they are complementary to each other.

6   Conclusion and Future Work

In this work, we present a simple span-based prototypical framework (SSP) for few-shot NER. Compared with the token-based models, SSP makes fewer single-token errors and can better extract multi-word entities. We discovered that techniques such as layer normalization, query-support attention, and whole-class pre-training are beneficial for boosting model performance. Additionally, experimental results indicate that certain implementation details, such as dropout and span representation size, require careful consideration and tuning. Experiments on *Few-NERD* and *SNIPS* datasets show that SSP is significantly faster than existing state-of-the-art methods with comparable effectiveness.

Our work sheds a light on how to make few-shot NER suitable for domain applications, where there exists a large corpus to be analyzed within a limited amount of prediction time (e.g. scientific text mining [10,13,26,29]). Also, the problem we find can help construct future few-shot NER benchmarks to consider more real word influence factors. Additionally, our model can be combined with active learning to help accelerate annotation. Two potential use cases include (1) prioritizing the annotation of difficult examples and (2) saving search time by filtering rare entities out of a big corpus.

Acknowledgements. We greatly thanks all reviewers for their constructive comments. The research was supported as part of the Center for Plastics Innovation, an Energy Frontier Research Center, funded by the U.S. Department of Energy (DOE), Office of Science, Basic Energy Sciences (BES), under Award Number DE-SC0021166. The research was also supported in part through the use of DARWIN computing system: DARWIN - A Resource for Computational and Data-intensive Research at the University of Delaware and in the Delaware Region, Rudolf Eigenmann, Benjamin E. Bagozzi, Arthi Jayaraman, William Totten, and Cathy H. Wu, University of Delaware, 2021, URL: https://udspace.udel.edu/handle/19716/29071.

References

1. Ba, J., Kiros, J.R., Hinton, G.E.: Layer normalization. arXiv e-print archive (2016)
2. Cui, L., Wu, Y., Liu, J., Yang, S., Zhang, Y.: Template-based named entity recognition using BART. In: ACL-IJCNLP (2021)
3. Das, S.S.S., Katiyar, A., Passonneau, R., Zhang, R.: CONTaiNER: few-shot named entity recognition via contrastive learning. In: ACL (2022)
4. Devlin, J., Chang, M.W., Lee, K., Toutanova, K.: BERT: pre-training of deep bidirectional transformers for language understanding. In: NAACL (2019)
5. Ding, N., et al.: Few-NERD: a few-shot named entity recognition dataset. In: ACL-IJCNLP (2021)
6. Friedrich, A., et al.: The SOFC-exp corpus and neural approaches to information extraction in the materials science domain. In: ACL (2020)
7. Fritzler, A., Logacheva, V., Kretov, M.: Few-shot classification in named entity recognition task. In: SAC (2019)
8. Fu, J., Huang, X., Liu, P.: SpanNER: named entity re-/recognition as span prediction. In: ACL-IJCNLP (2021)
9. Gao, T., Han, X., Liu, Z., Sun, M.: Hybrid attention-based prototypical networks for noisy few-shot relation classification. In: AAAI (2019)
10. Guo, J., et al.: Automated chemical reaction extraction from scientific literature. J. Chem. Inf. Model. **62**(9), 2035–2045 (2021)

11. Hou, Y., et al.: Few-shot slot tagging with collapsed dependency transfer and label-enhanced task-adaptive projection network. In: ACL (2020)
12. Huang, J., et al.: Few-shot named entity recognition: an empirical baseline study. In: EMNLP (2021)
13. Kononova, O., et al.: Text-mined dataset of inorganic materials synthesis recipes. Sci. Data **6**(1), 1–11 (2019)
14. Li, Y., Liu, L., Shi, S.: Empirical analysis of unlabeled entity problem in named entity recognition. In: ICLR (2021)
15. de Lichy, C., Glaude, H., Campbell, W.: Meta-learning for few-shot named entity recognition. In: 1st Workshop on Meta Learning and Its Applications to Natural Language Processing (2021)
16. Ma, R., Zhou, X., Gui, T., Tan, Y.C., Zhang, Q., Huang, X.: Template-free prompt tuning for few-shot NER. In: NAACL (2022)
17. Ma, T., Jiang, H., Wu, Q., Zhao, T., Lin, C.Y.: Decomposed meta-learning for few-shot named entity recognition. In: ACL (2022)
18. Ouchi, H., et al.: Instance-based learning of span representations: a case study through named entity recognition. In: ACL (2020)
19. Reimers, N., Gurevych, I.: The curse of dense low-dimensional information retrieval for large index sizes. In: ACL (2021)
20. Snell, J., Swersky, K., Zemel, R.S.: Prototypical networks for few-shot learning. In: NIPS (2017)
21. Sung, F., Yang, Y., Zhang, L., Xiang, T., Torr, P.H.S., Hospedales, T.M.: Learning to compare: relation network for few-shot learning. In: CVPR (2018)
22. Vinyals, O., Blundell, C., Lillicrap, T., Kavukcuoglu, K., Wierstra, D.: Matching networks for one shot learning. In: NISP (2016)
23. Wang, P., et al.: An enhanced span-based decomposition method for few-shot sequence labeling. In: NAACL (2022)
24. Wang, X., Han, X., Huang, W., Dong, D., Scott, M.R.: Multi-similarity loss with general pair weighting for deep metric learning. In: CVPR (2019)
25. Wang, Y., Chu, H., Zhang, C., Gao, J.: Learning from language description: low-shot named entity recognition via decomposed framework. In: EMNLP (2021)
26. Weston, L., et al.: Named entity recognition and normalization applied to large-scale information extraction from the materials science literature. J. Chem. Inf. Model. **59**(9), 3692–3702 (2019)
27. Yang, Y., Katiyar, A.: Simple and effective few-shot named entity recognition with structured nearest neighbor learning. In: EMNLP (2020)
28. Yu, J., Bohnet, B., Poesio, M.: Named entity recognition as dependency parsing. In: ACL (2020)
29. Zhang, Y., Wang, C., Soukaseum, M., Vlachos, D.G., Fang, H.: Unleashing the power of knowledge extraction from scientific literature in catalysis. J. Chem. Inf. Model. **62**(14), 3316–3330 (2022)

Don't Lose the Message While Paraphrasing: A Study on Content Preserving Style Transfer

Nikolay Babakov[1], David Dale[3], Ilya Gusev[3], Irina Krotova[4],
and Alexander Panchenko[2,5]([✉])

[1] Centro Singular de Investigación en Tecnoloxías Intelixentes (CiTIUS),
Universidade de Santiago de Compostela, Santiago de Compostela, Spain
[2] Skolkovo Institute of Science and Technology (Skoltech), Moscow, Russia
a.panchenko@skol.tech
[3] Moscow, Russia
[4] Mobile TeleSystems (MTS), Moscow, Russia
[5] Artificial Intelligence Research Institute (AIRI), Moscow, Russia

Abstract. Text style transfer techniques are gaining popularity in natural language processing allowing paraphrasing text in the required form: from toxic to neural, from formal to informal, from old to the modern English language, etc. Solving the task is not sufficient to generate *some* neural/informal/modern text, but it is important to preserve the original content unchanged. This requirement becomes even more critical in some applications such as style transfer of goal-oriented dialogues where the factual information shall be kept to preserve the original message, e.g. ordering a certain type of pizza to a certain address at a certain time. The aspect of content preservation is critical for real-world applications of style transfer studies, but it has received little attention. To bridge this gap we perform a comparison of various style transfer models on the example of the formality transfer domain. To perform a study of the content preservation abilities of various style transfer methods we create a parallel dataset of formal vs. informal task-oriented dialogues. The key difference between our dataset and the existing ones like GYAFC [17] is the presence of goal-oriented dialogues with predefined semantic slots essential to be kept during paraphrasing, e.g. named entities. This additional annotation allowed us to conduct a precise comparative study of several state-of-the-art techniques for style transfer. Another result of our study is a modification of the unsupervised method LEWIS [19] which yields a substantial improvement over the original method and all evaluated baselines on the proposed task.

Keywords: text style transfer · formality transfer · content preservation

N. Babakov and D. Dale—Work mostly has been done while at Skoltech.
D. Dale and I. Gusev—Independent Researcher.

E. Métais et al. (Eds.): NLDB 2023, LNCS 13913, pp. 47–61, 2023.
https://doi.org/10.1007/978-3-031-35320-8_4

1   Introduction

Text style transfer (**TST**) systems are designed to change the style of the original text to an alternative one, such as more positive [12], more informal [17], or even more Shakespearean [8]. Such systems are becoming very popular in the NLP. They could be applied to many purposes: from assistance in writing to diversifying responses of dialogue agents and creating artificial personalities.

Task-oriented dialogue agents are one of the possible applications of TST. In such dialogues, it is crucial to preserve important information such as product names, addresses, time, etc. Consider the task of making the source sentence from dialogue agent *Do you want to order a pizza to your office at 1760 Polk Street?* more informal to improve the user experience with the agent. This text contains named entities (*pizza, 1760 Polk Street*) that are critical to understanding the meaning of the query and following the correct scenario and that could be easily lost or corrupted during standard beam search-based generation even if the model is trained on parallel data [1]. At the same time, there are several words in this sentence that could be changed to make the style more informal. For example, a target sentence such as *do u wanna order a pizza 2 ur office at 1760 Polk Street?* requires only small edition of some words not related to the important entities. This suggests that it could be better to keep the important entities intact and train the model to fill the gaps between them.

In this work, we focus on text formality transfer, or, more precisely, transferring text style from formal to informal with an additional requirement to preserve the predefined important slots. We assume that the transfer task is supervised, which means that a parallel corpus of the text pairs in the source and target style is available (we use the GYAFC dataset [17]).

A similar intuition has been used in the unsupervised TST domain in LEWIS [19], where the authors created a pseudo-parallel corpus, trained a RoBERTa [30] tagger to identify coarse-grain Levenshtein edit types for each token of the original text, and finally used a BART [10] masked language model to infill the final edits. With the increasing interest in the TST field, several large parallel datasets have been collected for the most popular TST directions, such as formality transfer [17]. Thus, it became possible to use the advantage of parallel data to address the specific task of content preservation.

The contributions of our work are three-fold:

1. We present *PreserveDialogue*: the first dataset for evaluating the content-preserving formality transfer model in the task-oriented dialogue domain.
2. We perform a study of strong supervised style transfer methods, based on transformer models, such as GPT2 and T5 (as well as simpler baselines), showing that methods based on Levenstein edit distance such as LEWIS [10] are outperforming them if content shall be strictly preserved.
3. We introduce LEWIT, an improved version of the original LEWIS model based on T5 encoder-decoder trained on parallel data which yields the best results across all tested methods.

We open-source the resulting dataset and the experimental code[1]. Additionally, we release the best-performing pre-trained model LEWIT for content preserving formality transfer on HugingFace model hub.[2]

2 Related Works

In this section, we briefly introduce the existing approaches to text generation with an emphasis on preserving certain content.

Constrained Beam Search. The standard approach to text generation is beam search which iteratively generates possible next tokens, and the sequence yielding the highest conditional probability is selected as the best candidate after each iteration. There are several methods to constraint the beam search process which can be roughly divided into two broad categories: hard and soft constraints. In the hard constrained category, all constraints are ensured to appear in the output sentence, which is generally achieved by the modified type of beam search, allowing to directly specify the tokens to be preserved [7]. Opposite to hard-constrained approaches, soft-constrained approaches modify the model's training process by using the constraints as an auxiliary signal. Such signal is often either marked with special tags [11] or simply replaced with delexicalized tokens [5] during the training process and inference.

Edit Based Generation. Beam search is not the only existing approach to text generation. One popular substitution is Levenstein transformer [6]—a partially autoregressive encoder-decoder framework based on Transformer architecture [23] devised for more flexible and amenable sequence generation. Its decoder models a Markov Decision Process (MDP) that iteratively refines the generated tokens by alternating between the insertion and deletion operations via three classifiers that run sequentially: deletion, a placeholder (predicting the number of tokens to be inserted), and a token classifier.

Content Preservation in Text Style Transfer. Content preservation in text style transfer has mostly been addressed in the unsupervised domain. These methods mostly rely on text-editing performed in two steps: using one model to identify the tokens to delete and another model to infill the deleted text slots [26]. LEWIS [19] approach first constructs pseudo parallel corpus using an attention-based detector of style words and two style-specific BART [10] models, then trains a RoBERTa-tagger [30] to label the tokens (insert, replace, delete, keep), and finally fine-tunes style-specific BART masked language models to fill in the slots in the target style. LEWIT extrapolates this idea to a supervised setting. The main features of this work are that the token tagger is trained on tags obtained from parallel data, and the slots are filled with a T5 model [16], by taking advantage of its initial training task of slot filling.

---

[1] https://github.com/s-nlp/lewit-informal.
[2] https://huggingface.co/s-nlp/lewit-informal.

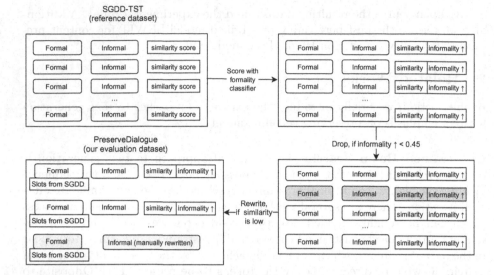

Fig. 1. The pipeline of collecting the PreserveDialogue dataset. The reference SGDD-TST dataset consists of formal-informal sentence pairs annotated with semantic similarity scores. The pairs are scored with the formality classifier model and the pairs with insignificant informality increase are dropped. The pairs with significant formality increase that have low semantic similarity scores are manually rewritten to be semantically similar. Finally, the important slots related to the formal sentence are extracted from the SGDD dataset.

3   Datasets

In this section, we describe the parallel training dataset and the evaluation dataset used respectively for tuning and evaluating the content-preserving formality transfer methods.

3.1   Parallel Training Dataset: GYAFC

In terms of our work, we assume the availability of parallel data. We also focus our experiments on the transfer of formal text to a more informal form. Grammarly's Yahoo Answers Formality Corpus (GYAFC) containing over 110K informal/formal sentence pairs fits well to this task. The main topics of the sentences in this dataset are related to either entertainment and music or family and relationships, both of these topics take almost equal part in the dataset [17].

3.2   Parallel Evaluation Dataset: PreserveDialogue

We create a special evaluation dataset denoted as *PreserveDialogue*. It is based on SGDD-TST [1][3]. SGDD-TST consists of sentence pairs in a formal and informal style with human annotation of semantic similarity. Its formal phrases were

---

[3] https://github.com/s-nlp/SGDD-TST.

Table 1. Examples of texts from the PreserveDialogue dataset used for evaluation.

Source formal text	Important slots	Target informal rewrite
Red Joan sounds great	Red Joan	red joan is cool
What do I have scheduled Tuesday next week?	Tuesday next week	what stuff do i have to do on tuesday next week?
I am looking for a unisex salon in SFO	SFO	i wanna find a unisex salon in SFO
Please confirm this: play Are You Ready on TV	Are You Ready	plz confirm this: play Are You Ready on TV
Where do you want to pick it up at?	–	where do u wanna pick it up at?

obtained from SGDD [18] and informal ones were generated by a large T5-based model tuned on the GYAFC dataset. Some of the generated paraphrases were annotated as semantically different, which is why SGDD-TST in its original form is not appropriate for evaluating content-preserving style transfer. Thus we create PreserveDialogue as a derivative from SGDD-TST. Figure 1 shows the main steps of the PreserveDialogue collection process. These steps are also described in more details below:

1. **Selecting sentences with significant informality increase.** We score all sentence pairs of SGDD-TST with a formality classifier (described in Sect. 4) and leave only 1100 pairs with an informality increase (namely, the difference between formality classifier scores of formal and informal sentences) greater than the empirically selected threshold of 0.45.
2. **Rewriting paraphrases with the corrupted sense.** Within the 1100 pairs, 369 are not semantically equal to each other (according to the similarity score available in the reference SGDD-TST dataset). Such pairs are rewritten by the members of our team according to the common intuition of informal style. After the messages are rewritten their informality is verified with the similar formality classifier used in the previous step.
3. **Extracting important slots.** The SGDD dataset [18] (the source of formal phrases of SGDD-TST) contains task-oriented dialogues with predefined named entities. We use them as important slots for the sentences in a formal style in PreserveDialogue.

Finally, the PreserveDialogue dataset consists of 1100 sentence pairs of formal and informal phrases. By the steps described above we make sure that these pairs have the equivalent sense and significantly differ in terms of informality. Moreover, each pair has a set of entity slots extracted from SGDD [18] (predecessor of SGDD-TST). These slots are related to the first sentence in the pair and are considered significant information which should be kept during formality transfer. A sample from the dataset can be found in Table 1.

4   Evaluation

In this section, we describe the methods of automatic evaluation of the formality transfer models.

In most TST papers (e.g. [13, 22, 28]) the methods are evaluated with the combination of the measures that score the basic TST properties: style accuracy, content preservation, and fluency. Our work is dedicated to formality transfer with an additional task to preserve particular slots. That is why we have to use an additional evaluation method: slot preservation. All of these measures evaluate TST quality from significantly different points of view, thus to reveal the TST method that performs best we aggregate them by *multiplying the four measures for each sentence and then averaging the products over the dataset*, following the logic of [9]. More details about each measure are provided in the following paragraphs. The code of measures calculations is also open-sourced in our repository.

Content Preservation. To score the general similarity between the generated text and the reference informal text we use Mutual Implication Score[4], a measure of content preservation based on predictions of NLI models in two directions. This measure has been compared [2] to a large number of SOTA content similarity measures and it was shown that it demonstrates one of the highest correlations with human judgments in the formality transfer domain: Spearman correlation between 0.62 and 0.77 depending on the dataset.

Slots Preservation. The key point of content preservation, especially in task-oriented dialogues, is keeping the important entities from a source sentence (see Sect. 3.2). Thus, we check whether these entities exist in the generated sentence. Most entities could have at least two different forms, which could be considered correct (e.g. "fourteen" and "14"). To ensure that the entity is not considered lost even if it is generated in an alternative form, we normalize the important slots and generated text in the following way. All text tokens are lowercased and lemmatized. The state names (e.g. "Los Angeles"—"LA"), numbers (e.g. "six"—"6"), and time values (e.g. "9am"—"9a.m."—"nine in the morning") are adjusted to a standard form using a set of rules. Some frequent abbreviations (geographic entity types, currencies) are expanded. The slots that still were not matched exactly are matched to the n-gram of the new sentence with the highest ChrF score [15]. The final slots preservation score is calculated as the ratio of the preserved slots in a new sentence (with ChrF scores as weights for the slots that were matched approximately) to the total number of slots in a source sentence. This ratio calculation takes into account both original and standardized forms of the tokens. This approach uses the idea similar to copy success rate calculation used for scoring constraints preservation in machine translation [4].

Style Accuracy. To ensure that the generated text corresponds to the target style we use a RoBERTA-based formality ranker[5]. The ranker was trained on two formality datasets: GYAFC [17] and P&T [14]. We verified the quality of

---

[4] https://huggingface.co/s-nlp/Mutual-Implication-Score.
[5] https://huggingface.co/s-nlp/roberta-base-formality-ranker.

this ranker by calculating the Spearman correlation of its score on the test split of GYAFC and P&T, which was 0.82 and 0.76 correspondingly.

Fluency. The generated text should look natural, grammatical and fluent. Fluency is often evaluated as the perplexity of a large language model, but to make the results more interpretable, we use a RoBERTA-based classifier trained on the Corpus of Linguistic Acceptability (CoLA) [24]. It is a diverse dataset of English sentences annotated in a binary way, as grammatically acceptable or not. A detailed justification of using a CoLA-based classifier for fluency evaluation is presented in [9]. We use an opensource RoBERTA-based classifier[6] trained on CoLA for 5 epochs with a batch size of 32, a learning rate of 2e-05, and a maximum sequence length of 128. Its scores range from 0 to 1 with greater values meaning higher quality, just like all the other metrics we use for evaluation. The reported accuracy of this model on the CoLA validation set is 0.85.

5   Supervised Style Transfer Methods

In this section, we describe the baseline methods used in our computational study dedicated to finding the best approach to content-preserving formality transfer. All models requiring tuning described in this section are tuned on the GYAFC parallel dataset (see Sect. 3.1).

5.1   Naive Baselines

We use two naive baselines. In *copy-paste*, we simply copying the source text, and in *only-slots*, the target string is simply a list of important slots separated by commas. The motivation of these methods is the sanity check of the proposed evaluation pipeline (see Sect. 4). The joint score (multiplication of four measures) is supposed to place the naive methods at the bottom of the leaderboard, which could be treated as a necessary condition of acceptance of the proposed evaluation method.

5.2   Sequence-to-Sequence Approaches

As the setting of our work assumes the availability of parallel data, it is natural to try standard sequence-to-sequence models (seq2seq), both "as is" and with some modifications related to the task of content and slots preservation.

Standard Seq2Seq. We tune the following models in the standard seq2seq approach: pure T5-base (*seq2seq-t5*) and T5-base pre-tuned on a paraphrasing datasets[7] (*seq2seq-t5-para*). We also experiment with using a template generated from the target sentence as a text pair for the training of the T5 model (*seq2seq-t5-template*).

---

[6] https://huggingface.co/textattack/roberta-base-CoLA.
[7] https://huggingface.co/ceshine/t5-paraphrase-paws-msrp-opinosis.

Seq2Seq with Hard Lexical Constraints. The models trained in the standard seq2seq approach can be inferenced with lexically constrained beam search (*seq2seq-t5-para-constr*, *seq2seq-t5-constr*) which is implemented in the Hugging-Face library mainly based on dynamic beam allocation[8] [7].

Re-ranking Beam Search Outputs with a Neural Textual Similarity Metric. We experiment with re-ranking beam search outputs with neural textual similarity metric. The hypothesis obtained after the beam search could be re-ranked w.r.t. some content preservation measure. To avoid overfitting, we should not rerank with the same measure (MIS) that we use for evaluation. In [2], the authors show that apart from MIS, BLEURT [21] also demonstrates reasonable performance in the formality transfer domain. We use a mean of BLEURT-score and conditional probability to perform a final re-ranking of the hypothesis generated after the beam search. This approach is used in combination with seq2seq-para-constr (*rerank-BLEURT-constr*) and with seq2seq-para (*rerank-BLEURT*).

Learning to Preserve Slots with Tags. Finally, we try to embed the task of content preservation into the seq2seq training. One of the possible ways to do that is to embed a signal in the training data indicating that a certain slot should be preserved. We use two different types of such signals. First, similarly to the idea presented in [27] we put special `<tag>` tokens around the slots to be preserved (*slot-tags*). Second, we replace the whole slot with a placeholder token and train model to re-generate this placeholder, which is then filled with the value from the original sentence [5] (*delex*).

5.3   Language Models Inference

There exists some evidence of the possibility to use the large pre-trained language models (LM) in zero- and few-shot way [3]. The LM can also be slightly fine-tuned on the parallel data to be capable of performing the desired task.

Similarly to the idea of [20], we construct a prompt for the language model to make it generate more informal text: *"Here is a text, which is formal: <formal text>. Here is a rewrite of the text which contains <slot 1>, <slot 2> and is more informal"* and train GPT2-medium[9] on parallel data to continue this prompt. We use two variations of such approach: with (*GPT2-tuned-constr*) and without (*GPT2-tuned*) the information about constraints in the prompt.

5.4   LEWIS and Its Modifications

An intuitively straightforward approach for a human to generate an informal paraphrase is to apply some slight modifications to the formal source text.

---

[8] https://github.com/huggingface/transformers/issues/14081.
[9] https://huggingface.co/gpt2-medium.

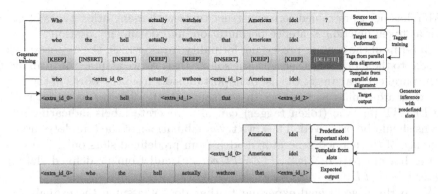

Fig. 2. LEWIT model workflow: The edit tags are obtained from the alignment of source formal and target informal texts. These tags are used to train the token tagger. These edit tags are also used to create a template used to train a T5-generator model, which fills the slots between the preserved tokens.

This group of approaches is named "edit-based". Most of these approaches use numerous models to perform separate edition actions for generating a new text: deletion, insertion, placeholder, infiller models [29]. We experimented with the LEWIS model [19] representing this kind of methods.

LEWIS was designed in the unsupervised domain, so the authors first created a pseudo-parallel corpus, then trained a RoBERTa tagger to identify coarse-grain Levenshtein edit types for each token from the original text, and finally used a BART masked language model to infill the final edits. We use LEWIS in a parallel data setting by tuning BART on our parallel dataset and using it either with known constraints (*LEWIS-constr*) or with the labels inferred from the RoBERTa tagger trained on the edits from parallel data (*LEWIS-tag*).

We also test a modified version of LEWIS denoted as LEWIT (T5-based LEWIS): similarly to LEWIS architecture it involves a token tagger trained on Levenshtein edits obtained from the alignment of the parallel data, but its infiller model (i.e. the model inserting the tokens between other tokens) is based on T5 that was originally trained with the specific task of infilling gaps of several tokens. The LEWIT model consists of two steps as illustrated in Fig. 2. First, the RoBERTa token tagger is trained on the tags from the GYAFC dataset (see Sect. 3.1) which are directly computed from edits required to transform the source texts into the target texts. Second, the T5-based[10] generator model is trained on the templates from parallel data that was also generated from the GYAFC dataset sentence pairs. The model receives the concatenation of the source sentence and the template constructed w.r.t. the edit tokens and is expected to generate the words masked from the target sentence.

LEWIT inherits the general logic of LEWIS. Its distinguishing feature is that its generator model is T5-based. The choice of this model seems more suitable for this task, because gap filling is the main pre-training objective of T5, whereas

---

10 https://huggingface.co/t5-base.

BART has been pretrained to reconstruct texts with many other types of noise, such as token deletion, sentence permutation, and document rotation.

In terms of the content preserving formality transfer task, the important slots are sent to the model together with the source text. As we assume the availability of the parallel data, we get the list of important slots from the words of the target text that are similar to the ones in the source text. However, the first part of the LEWIT pipeline (token tagger) can also generate labels indicating which tokens should be preserved. Thus, we try combinations of the templates used for inference of the trained generator model: from predefined slots only, like shown on the bottom part of Fig. 2, (*LEWIT-constr*) and from predefined slots and tagger labels (*LEWIT-constr-tag*).

We perform additional experiments that do not assume the availability of predefined slots. The templates for these approaches are obtained from the afore-mentioned RoBERTa-based tagger labels (*LEWIT-tag*) and third-party NER-tagger (*LEWIT-NER*). A significant part of the tags generated with the tagger within the test set was either "replace" (46,7%) or "equal" (50%). "Delete" and "insert" took 3% and 0.3% correspondingly. This proportion corresponds to the general intuition of small-edits-based paraphrasing of formal texts into more informal style by keeping the most important content intact and either slightly altering or sometimes deleting less important parts.

6   Results

The results are grouped according to the availability of the predefined important slots or constraints in the inference time and are shown in Table 2. We can see that both naive approaches are pushed to the bottom of the tables and their joint measure value is substantially less than the closest non-naive approach. We can also see that the LEWIT approach outperforms all strong baselines in both settings of the experiments.

Case 1: the slots are not known in the inference time. Both NER-tagger and edits-tagger-based approaches perform similarly by the joint measure outperforming the baseline methods. The edits-tagger approach yields better content and slots preservation but worse style transfer accuracy. The examples of the generated paraphrases are shown in Table 3.

Case 2: the slots are known in the inference time. Different varia-tions of LEWIT also outperform the baseline methods. We can see that if the important slots are known, their combination with the edits token tagger can increase content preservation, however, this yields a decrease in style accuracy. The examples of the generated paraphrases are shown in Table 4.

The examples suggest that pure seq2seq models (such as *seq2seq-t5-para*) occasionally change the overall intent or specific slots in undesirable ways, and simple approaches to slot preservation (such as *delex*) sometimes result in unnat-ural outputs. Edit-based methods seem to avoid these problems in most cases.

LEWIS-based models demonstrate top performance within the baselines, however, LEWIT still performs better according to the joint score. This is most

Table 2. Results with and without the usage of the predefined important slots. "Joint" is the average product of all four measures. The values **in bold** show the highest value of the metric with the significance level of $\alpha = 0.05$ (by Wilcoxon signed-rank test). The values with an insignificant difference between LEWIT and other methods are marked with a "*" sign. The highest value for the slot preservation for the methods with known constraints is not indicated because in most cases all constraints are preserved by the design of the methods from this group.

Method	Style Accuracy	Content Preservation	Slot Preservation	Fluency	Joint
Without known constraints					
LEWIT-tag (T5)	0.69	0.85	0.98	0.75*	**0.43**
LEWIT-NER (T5)	0.82	0.74	0.94	0.74	0.42
LEWIS-tag [19] (BART)	0.77	0.69	0.99	0.72	0.38
seq2seq-t5-para	0.60	0.82	0.95	0.74	0.34
seq2seq-t5	0.54	0.87	0.98	0.73	0.33
rerank-BLEURT	0.46	0.84	0.97	0.75*	0.28
GPT2-tuned [20]	**0.91**	0.57	0.76	0.69	0.27
copy-paste	0.03	**0.90**	**1.00**	**0.83**	0.02
With known constraints					
LEWIT-constr (T5)	0.80	0.76	1.00	0.76*	**0.46**
LEWIT-constr-tag (T5)	0.73	**0.83**	1.00	0.74	0.45
LEWIS-constr [19] (BART)	0.81	0.68	1.00	0.75	0.41
delex [5]	0.69	0.75	0.98	0.78*	0.40
seq2seq-t5-template	0.49	0.83	0.97	0.78*	0.31
seq2seq-t5-constr [7]	0.71	0.71	1.00	0.61	0.31
slot-tags [27]	0.56	0.74	0.97	0.76	0.31
seq2seq-t5-para-constr	0.64	0.74	1.00	0.61	0.29
rerank-BLEURT-constr	0.54	0.77	1.00	0.64	0.27
GPT2-tuned-constr [20]	**0.91**	0.41	0.82	0.68	0.21
only-slots	0.73	0.21	1.00	**0.81**	0.12

probably an evidence that T5 fits better than the BART model for the specific task of gap filling.

Results in Table 2 pass Wilcoxon signed-rank test [25] with a significance threshold of 0.05. We tested the hypothesis of the significance of the difference between the best-performing LEWIT method within each group and all baseline methods. The test was performed by splitting the test set into 30 random parts of 900 samples and calculating the significance over the mean of the measurement values from the selected samples.

Certainly, LEWIT has its limitations. The most notable one is that sticking to the structure of the source sentence limits the ability of the TST model to alter its syntactical structure. Moreover, in some contexts, a text may look more natural if rewritten from scratch.

We see the main use-case of LEWIT in applications where exact preservation of content is crucial, such as goal-oriented dialogue systems (e.g. pizza ordering), where communication goals cannot be compromised for better fluency.

Table 3. Examples of samples generated by top performing formality transfer systems with known constraints.

Formal source text	Important slots	Informal rewrite	System
SAN International Airport is the location of flight departure	SAN International Airport	SAN International Airport is where the flight departs	LEWIT-constr
		SAN International Airport International airport is the place of flight departure	LEWIS-constr
		SAN International Airport is the start of your flight	delex
How will the weather be in Delhi, India on the tomorrow?	Delhi; India; tomorrow	whats the weather like in Delhi, India for tomorrow	LEWIT-constr
		Will the weather be in india on the next day?	LEWIS-constr
		i'm not sure, but it's going to be cool in Delhi, India on tomorrow	delex
Your destination will be at Sacramento Valley Station	Sacramento Valley Station	go to Sacramento Valley Station !	LEWIT-constr
		destination will be at Sacramento Valley Station	LEWIS-constr
		Sacramento Valley Station	delex

Table 4. Examples of samples generated by top performing formality transfer systems without known constraints.

Formal source text	Informal rewrite	System
No I am leaving on the 3rd from Seattle, WA	No I 'm leaving on the 3rd from Seattle, WA	LEWIT-tag
	No I leaving on the 3rd from Seattle, WA	LEWIS-tag
	No I'm leaving on the 3rd from Seattle WA	seq2seq-t5-para
Do you have any preference in city and type of events, for example, music or Sports something like that?	do you like city or music or Sports something like that?	LEWIT-tag
	u like city and sports like that music or sports something like that?	LEWIS-tag
	Do you like city and type of things, like music or sports?	seq2seq-t5-para
I will be returning Tuesday next week	I 'll be back Tuesday next week !	LEWIT-tag
	I l be back tUESDAY next week	LEWIS-tag
	I'll be back on Tuesday next week	seq2seq-t5-para
I would like to leave tomorrow from Atlanta	I 'm leaving tomorrow from Atlanta	LEWIT-tag
	I to get away from Atlanta.tomorrow	LEWIS-tag
	i want to leave tomorrow from atlanta	seq2seq-t5-para

7   Conclusions

In this paper, we study the ways of supervised transfer of formal text to more informal paraphrases with special attention to preserving the content. In this task, the content of the source text is supposed to have a set of predefined important slots that should be kept in the generated text in either their original or slightly changed form but without a change of their meaning. To evaluate various methods for this task we collect a dataset of parallel formal-informal texts all of which have a set of predefined important slots. Using the new dataset we perform a computational study of modern approaches to supervised style transfer in two settings: with and without information about the predefined important slots provided at the inference time.

Results of our study show that if content preservation is a crucial goal, methods that do not rewrite the text completely are preferable. In this setting, it is better to use a token tagger marking spans with key information to be kept (named entities, etc.) from everything else which can be rewritten more freely with a separate generator that rephrases the rest. We show that the LEWIS [10] approach operating in this way outperforms strong baselines trained on parallel data by a large margin. We also show the original model can be substantially further improved if the T5-based generator is used.

Acknowledgements. This work was supported by the MTS-Skoltech laboratory on AI, the European Union's Horizon 2020 research and innovation program under the Marie Skodowska-Curie grant agreement No 860621, and the Galician Ministry of Culture, Education, Professional Training, and University and the European Regional Development Fund (ERDF/FEDER program) under grant ED431G2019/04.

References

1. Babakov, N., Dale, D., Logacheva, V., Krotova, I., Panchenko, A.: Studying the role of named entities for content preservation in text style transfer. In: Rosso, P., Basile, V., Martínez, R., Métais, E., Meziane, F. (eds.) NLDB 2022. LNCS, vol. 13286, pp. 437–448. Springer, Cham (2022). https://doi.org/10.1007/978-3-031-08473-7_40
2. Babakov, N., Dale, D., Logacheva, V., Panchenko, A.: A large-scale computational study of content preservation measures for text style transfer and paraphrase generation. In: Proceedings of the 60th Annual Meeting of the Association for Computational Linguistics: Student Research Workshop, Dublin, Ireland, pp. 300–321. Association for Computational Linguistics (2022)
3. Brown, T., et al.: Language models are few-shot learners. In: Advances in Neural Information Processing Systems, vol. 33, pp. 1877–1901 (2020)
4. Chen, G., Chen, Y., Wang, Y., Li, V.O.: Lexical-constraint-aware neural machine translation via data augmentation. In: Bessiere, C. (ed.) Proceedings of the Twenty-Ninth International Joint Conference on Artificial Intelligence, IJCAI 2020, pp. 3587–3593. International Joint Conferences on Artificial Intelligence Organization (2020). Main track

5. Cui, R., Agrawal, G., Ramnath, R.: Constraint-embedded paraphrase generation for commercial tweets. In: Proceedings of the 2021 IEEE/ACM International Conference on Advances in Social Networks Analysis and Mining, ASONAM 2021, pp. 369–376. Association for Computing Machinery, New York (2021)
6. Gu, J., Wang, C., Junbo, J.Z.: Levenshtein Transformer. Curran Associates Inc., Red Hook (2019)
7. Hu, J.E., et al.: Improved lexically constrained decoding for translation and monolingual rewriting. In: Proceedings of the 2019 Conference of the North American Chapter of the Association for Computational Linguistics: Human Language Technologies, Minneapolis, Minnesota (Volume 1: Long and Short Papers), pp. 839–850. Association for Computational Linguistics (2019)
8. Jhamtani, H., Gangal, V., Hovy, E., Nyberg, E.: Shakespearizing modern language using copy-enriched sequence to sequence models. In: Proceedings of the Workshop on Stylistic Variation, Copenhagen, Denmark, pp. 10–19. Association for Computational Linguistics (2017)
9. Krishna, K., Wieting, J., Iyyer, M.: Reformulating unsupervised style transfer as paraphrase generation. In: Proceedings of the 2020 Conference on Empirical Methods in Natural Language Processing (EMNLP), pp. 737–762. Association for Computational Linguistics, Online (2020). https://doi.org/10.18653/v1/2020.emnlp-main.55
10. Lewis, M., et al.: BART: denoising sequence-to-sequence pre-training for natural language generation, translation, and comprehension. In: Proceedings of the 58th Annual Meeting of the Association for Computational Linguistics, pp. 7871–7880. Association for Computational Linguistics, Online (2020)
11. Li, H., Huang, G., Cai, D., Liu, L.: Neural machine translation with noisy lexical constraints. IEEE/ACM Trans. Audio Speech Lang. Process. **28**, 1864–1874 (2020). https://doi.org/10.1109/TASLP.2020.2999724
12. Luo, F., et al.: Towards fine-grained text sentiment transfer. In: Proceedings of the 57th Annual Meeting of the Association for Computational Linguistics, Florence, Italy, pp. 2013–2022. Association for Computational Linguistics (2019)
13. Moskovskiy, D., Dementieva, D., Panchenko, A.: Exploring cross-lingual text detoxification with large multilingual language models. In: Proceedings of the 60th Annual Meeting of the Association for Computational Linguistics: Student Research Workshop, Dublin, Ireland, pp. 346–354. Association for Computational Linguistics (2022)
14. Pavlick, E., Tetreault, J.: An empirical analysis of formality in online communication. Trans. Assoc. Comput. Linguist. **4**, 61–74 (2016)
15. Popović, M.: chrF: character n-gram F-score for automatic MT evaluation. In: Proceedings of the Tenth Workshop on Statistical Machine Translation, Lisbon, Portugal, pp. 392–395. Association for Computational Linguistics (2015). https://doi.org/10.18653/v1/W15-3049
16. Raffel, C., et al.: Exploring the limits of transfer learning with a unified text-to-text transformer. J. Mach. Learn. Res. **21**(1) (2020)
17. Rao, S., Tetreault, J.: Dear sir or madam, may I introduce the GYAFC dataset: corpus, benchmarks and metrics for formality style transfer. In: Proceedings of the 2018 Conference of the North American Chapter of the Association for Computational Linguistics: Human Language Technologies, New Orleans, Louisiana (Volume 1: Long Papers), pp. 129–140. Association for Computational Linguistics (2018)

18. Rastogi, A., Zang, X., Sunkara, S., Gupta, R., Khaitan, P.: Towards scalable multi-domain conversational agents: the schema-guided dialogue dataset. In: Proceedings of the AAAI Conference on Artificial Intelligence, vol. 34, pp. 8689–8696 (2020)
19. Reid, M., Zhong, V.: LEWIS: Levenshtein editing for unsupervised text style transfer. In: Findings of the Association for Computational Linguistics: ACL-IJCNLP 2021, pp. 3932–3944. Association for Computational Linguistics, Online (2021)
20. Reif, E., Ippolito, D., Yuan, A., Coenen, A., Callison-Burch, C., Wei, J.: A recipe for arbitrary text style transfer with large language models. In: Proceedings of the 60th Annual Meeting of the Association for Computational Linguistics, Dublin, Ireland (Volume 2: Short Papers), pp. 837–848. Association for Computational Linguistics (2022)
21. Sellam, T., Das, D., Parikh, A.: BLEURT: learning robust metrics for text generation. In: Proceedings of the 58th Annual Meeting of the Association for Computational Linguistics, pp. 7881–7892. Association for Computational Linguistics, Online (2020)
22. Shen, T., Lei, T., Barzilay, R., Jaakkola, T.: Style transfer from non-parallel text by cross-alignment. In: Guyon, I., et al. (eds.) Advances in Neural Information Processing Systems, vol. 30. Curran Associates, Inc. (2017)
23. Vaswani, A., et al.: Attention is all you need (2017)
24. Warstadt, A., Singh, A., Bowman, S.R.: Neural network acceptability judgments. arXiv preprint arXiv:1805.12471 (2018)
25. Wilcoxon, F.: Individual comparisons by ranking methods. Biometrics Bull. 1(6), 80–83 (1945)
26. Wu, X., Zhang, T., Zang, L., Han, J., Hu, S.: Mask and infill: applying masked language model for sentiment transfer. In: Proceedings of the Twenty-Eighth International Joint Conference on Artificial Intelligence, IJCAI 2019, pp. 5271–5277. International Joint Conferences on Artificial Intelligence Organization (2019)
27. Zhang, M., et al.: Don't change me! user-controllable selective paraphrase generation. In: Proceedings of the 16th Conference of the European Chapter of the Association for Computational Linguistics: Main Volume, pp. 3522–3527. Association for Computational Linguistics, Online (2021)
28. Zhang, Y., Ge, T., Sun, X.: Parallel data augmentation for formality style transfer. In: Proceedings of the 58th Annual Meeting of the Association for Computational Linguistics, pp. 3221–3228. Association for Computational Linguistics, Online (2020)
29. Zhang, Y., Wang, G., Li, C., Gan, Z., Brockett, C., Dolan, B.: POINTER: constrained progressive text generation via insertion-based generative pre-training. In: Proceedings of the 2020 Conference on Empirical Methods in Natural Language Processing (EMNLP), pp. 8649–8670. Association for Computational Linguistics, Online (2020)
30. Zhuang, L., Wayne, L., Ya, S., Jun, Z.: A robustly optimized BERT pre-training approach with post-training. In: Proceedings of the 20th Chinese National Conference on Computational Linguistics, Huhhot, China, pp. 1218–1227. Chinese Information Processing Society of China (2021)

A Review of Parallel Corpora for Automatic Text Simplification. Key Challenges Moving Forward

Tania Josephine Martin[1,2]([envelope]) [ORCID], José Ignacio Abreu Salas[2] [ORCID],
and Paloma Moreda Pozo[3] [ORCID]

[1] Department of English Philology, University of Alicante,
03690 Alicante, Spain
[2] University Institute for Computing Research, University of Alicante,
03690 Alicante, Spain
{tania.martin,ji.abreu}@ua.es
[3] Department of Computing and Information Systems, University of Alicante,
03690 Alicante, Spain
moreda@dlsi.ua.es

Abstract. This review of parallel corpora for automatic text simplification (ATS) involves an analysis of forty-nine papers wherein the corpora are presented, focusing on corpora in the Indo-European languages of Western Europe. We improve on recent corpora reviews by reporting on the target audience of the ATS, the language and domain of the source text, and other metadata for each corpus, such as alignment level, annotation strategy, and the transformation applied to the simplified text. The key findings of the review are: 1) the lack of resources that address ATS aimed at domains which are important for social inclusion, such as health and public administration; 2) the lack of resources aimed at audiences with mild cognitive impairment; 3) the scarcity of experiments where the target audience was directly involved in the development of the corpus; 4) more than half the proposals do not include any extra annotation, thereby lacking detail on how the simplification was done, or the linguistic phenomenon tackled by the simplification; 5) other types of annotation, such as the type and frequency of the transformation applied could identify the most frequent simplification strategies; and, 6) future strategies to advance the field of ATS could leverage automatic procedures to make the annotation process more agile and efficient.

Keywords: Automatic Text Simplification (ATS) · Parallel Corpora for Text Simplification · Review of European corpora for ATS

1 Introduction

This paper reviews the state of the art for parallel corpora created for automatic text simplification (ATS), focusing on those that present a holistic approach to

E. Métais et al. (Eds.): NLDB 2023, LNCS 13913, pp. 62–78, 2023.
https://doi.org/10.1007/978-3-031-35320-8_5

text simplification as well as those sourced from the Indo-European languages of Western Europe. This review reports on the corpus language, source domain, alignment level, annotation strategy used, and the transformation applied as well as the target audience for whom the simplification is carried out.

Parallel corpora for ATS present simplified versions of an original text in the same language. The corpora can be aligned sentence-by-sentence, or in some cases at a document level. They are widely used in natural language processing (NLP) to train language models for ATS.

ATS aims to make the text more accessible and easier to understand. Some approaches to ATS focus on, for example, removing or substituting long sentences and specialised jargon via, lexical substitution and sentence splitting. However, these approaches are not within the scope of this work, as they are designed to address related but specific tasks, such as text compression [41], complex word identification [63], readability assessment [59] and benchmarking lexical simplification [24]. Our review targets parallel corpora for ATS and includes the papers wherein the corpora are presented and is not limited to a specific simplification operation.

Research in ATS has been propelled by two main initiatives at European Union (EU) Level to facilitate the plain language and the Easy-to-Read Movement. The EU has demonstrated a commitment to eliminate barriers that prevent persons with disabilities from participating in society on an equal basis. It sets out actions to be taken in several priority areas, including accessibility of information and communications technologies and systems, and assistive devices for people with disabilities [23]. Furthermore, the recommendation for a European standard for digital accessibility supports the provision of easy-to-read texts on public authority websites, for instance, to assist those with learning or language difficulties [32].

Data driven ATS solutions need the design of suitable corpora that address the needs of intended audiences. As acknowledged in the literature, existing datasets are not necessarily suitable for approaches aimed at a specific domain or user profile [21,29,46,49,64].

The present review of the corpora for ATS indicates the state of the art for addressing text simplification in Indo-European languages located in the Western European region. Moreover, what sets this review apart from, for example, recent corpora reviews for text simplification such as [2] and [14] is that it includes far more data for each corpus, thereby providing a more robust and fine-grained analysis that can pinpoint precisely where the research opportunities exist for developing new parallel corpora for ATS. The review explores and analyses the following data, where available: the source domain; the target audience for whom the simplification is intended; the language of the corpus; alignment level; whether the corpus was annotated; and, the transformation applied to the parallel simplified text. We expect the corpora review to be of value to the ATS research community as it will provide an easy reference point as to the domains, audience profiles, and languages where resources are presently lacking. This deficit could potentially hamper social inclusion strategies.

The paper is organised into three further sections. Section 2 describes the steps involved in searching and selecting the papers to be included in the corpora review. Section 3 reviews the relevant proposals on corpora for automatic text simplification and reports on the following: corpus name; content language; domains covered; corpus size in terms of the approximated number of pairs of original/simplified content; the target audience; the alignment level of the corpus; and, other available metadata. Section 4 highlights the main conclusions of the corpora review for ATS and some research opportunities.

2   Methodology

The corpora review was driven by a methodology that involved the following 4 steps:

(i) Definition of the research scope. To identify parallel corpora developed for ATS that present a holistic approach to text simplification. Thus, we did not consider other related papers dedicated to specific tasks, i.e., complex word identification, substitute generation, and substitute ranking as defined in [45], paraphrasing, or sentence compression. Also, no limit was set for the time frame.

(ii) Querying the bibliographic databases. Our search terms were "text simplification" AND ("dataset" OR "corpora" OR "corpus" OR "corpuses"). We searched within the title, abstract and keywords in Web of Science[1] (103 results) and Scopus[2] (249 results).

(iii) Fine-grained filtering of the materials found. We verified that the papers describe a new parallel corpus for text simplification. In our case, proposals such as [31,37] were discarded since they focused on languages outside our scope, or are not parallel corpora. After this step, we obtained 31 papers.

(iv) Analysis of the materials collected considering the language, domain, the intended audience of the simplified content. Also, analysis of the alignment level, the language phenomenon considered, as well as other metadata included in the corpus. The aim was to discover commonalities between the different proposals as well as highlight research opportunities.

During step (iv) new proposals may be discovered and incorporated into the review if they meet the set selection criteria. We found 18 additional papers, bringing the total to 49.

3   Parallel Corpora for Text Simplification

In this section, we review the relevant proposals for text simplification corpora. Table 1 shows an overview of the materials. In Sect. A we complement this information with references to the data. We include the name used to identify the

---

[1] https://www.webofscience.com.
[2] https://www.scopus.com.

corpus in the literature, the language of the content, and an overview of the domains covered by the different corpora. Also the size in terms of the approximated number of pairs of original/simplified content, the target audience, the alignment level of the corpus, and other metadata available. They represent requirements or decisions which drive the corpus creation process.

3.1 Corpora Language

This section comments on trends in so far as the language of the ATS corpora. The aim is to highlight research opportunities related to the creation of resources and tools for languages where they are presently lacking.

Data in column **Language** in Table 1 indicate that the majority of the corpora in the area of ATS have been produced for the English language. However, other Indo-European languages such as French, Danish, Dutch, German, Italian, Portuguese, and Spanish are also generating interest among the research community, albeit on a smaller scale. Work has also been conducted using the Basque language, which is the only non Indo-European language in Western Europe [58].

To tackle low-resource setups, [17,38] proposed the use of automatically translated corpora. This opens interesting questions on the suitability of an approach that exploits existing simplified versions in one language to build ATS or corpora in another.

3.2 Corpora Domain

A pattern is also manifest in terms of the domains from which the texts were sourced. In column **Domain** of Table 1, we can corroborate that the vast majority of the corpora analysed were from general information sources such as Wikipedia or news media.

An important outcome from the data is the limited number of corpora related to domains with arguably a great impact on society, such as health or public administration [16,28,39,49,51,57]. Content that is difficult to understand may pose an exclusion barrier for people with diverse cognitive levels, depriving them of information they have the right to access.

Table 1. Corpora for Automatic Text Simplification Indo-European Languages

No	Year	Reference & Corpus	Lang.[a]	Domain[b]	Audience[c]	Alignment[d]	Size[e]	Metadata[f]
1	2003	no-name [7]	ENG	general (ency)	children	doc (M) sent (A)	doc: 103 sent: 601 8K non-aligned	1 SL
2	2007	no-name [44]	ENG	general (news)	non-native	doc (M) sent (M)	doc: 104 sent: 2.5K	1 SL; simplification operations (manually)
3	2009	no-name [3]	ENG	general (news)	non-native	doc (M)	doc: 243	3 SL (elementary, intermediate, advanced)
4	2009	no-name [18]	POR	general (news) science	children	doc (M) sent (M)	doc: 104 sent: 2K	2 SL; annotation guide; per document: (1) origin, (2) logical division, (3) sentence boundaries, (4) tokens, (5) PoS tags, (6) phrases, (7) sentence alignment, (8) simplification operations
5	2010	PWKP(Wiki-Small) [67]	ENG	general (ency)	SW	sent (A)	sent: 63.1K	1 SL
6	2011	no-name [10]	SPA	general (news)	SL;ER	doc (M) sent (A)	doc: 200	1 SL
7	2011	no-name [19]	ENG	general (ency)	SW	sent	sent: 137K	1 SL
8	2011	no-name [60]	ENG	general (ency)	SW	doc (A) sent (A)	doc: 15K sent: 14.8K	1 SL
9	2012	no-name [20]	ENG	general (news)	non-native	doc (M)	doc: 100	1 SL 3 simplifications
10	2012	DSim [36]	DAN	general (news)	CI non-native	doc (M) sent (A)	doc: 3.7K sent: 48.1K	1 SL
11	2013	no-name [34]	ENG	general (ency)	SW	doc (M) sent (A)	doc: 60K sent:150K	1 SL
12	2013	no-name [35]	GER	general (web)	SL;ER	doc (M) sent (A)	doc: 256 sent: 7K	1 SL
13	2013	FIRST Simplext [53]	SPA	general (news)	SL;ER	doc (M) sent (A)	doc: 225 sent: 1.4K	1 SL
14	2014	no-name [11]	SPA	general (news)	SL;ER	doc (M) sent (M)	doc: 200	1 SL
15	2014	no-name [12]	FRE	general (ency) literature	Vikidia non-native	doc (M) sent (M, A)	doc: 36 sent: 155	1 SL
16	2014	no-name [40]	SPA	general (news)	SL;ER	doc (M)	doc: 10	1 SL; simplification operations

(continued)

Table 1. (*continued*)

No	Year	Reference & Corpus	Lang.ᵃ	Domainᵇ	Audienceᶜ	Alignmentᵈ	Sizeᵉ	Metadataᶠ
17	2014	no-name [43]	ENG	public adm miscellaneous	SL|ER	sent (M)	sent: 200	1 SL; 10 simplifications
18	2015	Automatic Noticias Fácil [52]	SPA	general (news)	SL|ER	doc (M)	doc: 300	1 SL
19	2015	Terence & Teacher [15]	ITA	literature education	children non-native	doc (M) sent (M)	doc: 50 sent: 1.3K	1 SL; simplification operations
20	2015	Newsela [61]	ENG SPA	general (news)	children	doc (M)	doc: 1.1K	4 SL
21	2016	PaCCSSIT [13]	ITA	general (web)	SL|ER	sent (A)	sent: 63K	1 SL; readability scores
22	2016	SSCorpus [33]	ENG	general (ency)	SW	sent (A)	doc: 126.7K sent: 492.9K	1 SL; similarity score
23	2016	SIMPITIKI [57]	ITA	general (ency) public adm	SL|ER	sent (M)	sent: 1K	1 SL; annotated simplification operations
24	2016	TurkCorpus [62]	ENG	general (ency)	SL|ER	sent (M)	sent: 2.3K	1 SL; 8 simplifications
25	2017	WikiLarge [66]	ENG	general (ency)	SW	sent (A)	sent: 296K	1 SL
26	2018	CBST [27]	EUS	science	SL|ER	doc (M) sent (M)	sent: 227	2 SL; simplification operations
27	2018	CLEAR [30]	FRE	health science	children SL|ER	doc (M) sent (M)	doc: 16.1K sent: 4.5K	1 SL
28	2018	SimPA [49]	ENG	public adm	SL|ER	sent (M)	sent: 1.1K	1 SL; 4 simplifications 3 lexical and 1 syntactic
29	2018	One-Stop English [1]	ENG	general (news)	non-native	doc (M) sent (A)	doc: 189 sent: 6.8K	3 SL (elementary, intermediate, advanced)
30	2019	no-name [54]	SPA	general (news)	SL|ER	sent (M)	sent: 764	1 SL; simplification operations
31	2019	no-name [9]	ENG	health	children	sent (M, A)	sent: 9.2K	1 SL
32	2020	ASSET [4]	ENG	general (ency)	non-native	sent (M)	sent: 2.3K	1 SL; 10 simplifications
33	2020	WikiLarge FR [8]	GER	general (web)	SL|ER	doc (A) sent (A)	doc: 378 sent: 17.1K	1 SL; document structure and metadata
34	2020	WikiLarge FR [17]	FRE	general (ency)	non-native	sent (A)	sent: 296K	1 SL
35	2020	Alector [25]	FRE	literature science	children poor-readers	doc (M)	doc: 79	4 SL; simplification operations; reading errors

(*continued*)

Table 1. (*continued*)

No	Year	Reference & Corpus	Lang.[a]	Domain[b]	Audience[c]	Alignment[d]	Size[e]	Metadata[f]
36	2020	no-name [48]	GER	general (news)	non-native	sent (A)	sent: 3.6K	2 SL
37	2020	no-name [65]	ENG	science	SL|ER	doc (A)	doc: 5.2K	1 SL
38	2021	Simplicity-DA [5]	ENG	general (ency)	SL|ER	sent (M)	sent: 600	1 SL; human evaluation on simplicity
39	2021	20m [26]	GER	general (news)	SL|ER	doc (M)	doc: 18.3K	1 SL
40	2021	Newsela Translated [38]	ITA	general (news)	children	doc (M) sent (A)	doc: 1.1K sent: 9.4K	4 SL
41	2021	no-name [42]	ENG	philosophy	SL|ER	doc (M) para (A) sent (A)	doc: 15 para: 1.6K sent: 8.4K	1 SL
42	2021	D-Wikipedia [55]	ENG	general (ency)	children	doc (A)	doc: 143.5K	1 SL
43	2022	Klexikon [6]	GER	general (ency)	children	doc (A)	doc: 2.8K	1 SL
44	2022	CLARA-MED [16]	SPA	health	non experts	doc (M) sent (M)	doc: 24.2K sent: 3.8K	1 SL
45	2022	Web & APA & Wikipedia & Capito [6]	GER	general (ency) SL|ER	children	doc (M, A) sent (M, A)	doc: 111.2K sent: 1.4M	3 SL
46	2022	IrekiaLF [28]	SPA	public adm	SL|ER	doc (M) sent (M)	doc: 288 sent: 705	1 SL; complex words + definition at document level
47	2022	Admin-It [39]	ITA	public adm	SL|ER	sent (M)	sent: 736	3 simplifications
48	2022	SIMPLETICO-19 [51]	ENG SPA	health	children	sent (M)	sent: 6K	1 SL; simplification operations (automatically)
49	2022	no-name [56]	GER	general (web)	CI SL|ER	doc (M) sent (A)	doc: 708 sent: 5.9K	1 SL

[a] Language: Basque (EUS), Danish (DAN), English (ENG), French (FRE), German (GER), Italian (ITA), Portuguese (POR), Spanish (SPA)

[b] Domain: Wikipedia or Britannica (general (ency)), public administration (public adm)

[c] Audience: Simple Wikpedia (SW), simple language|easy-to-read (SL|ER), cognitive impaired (CI)

[d] Alignment: automatically (A), manually aligned (M)

[e] Size: In pairs of document (doc), paragraphs (par) or sentences (sent). This is an approximated size due to many-to-many correspondences.

[f] Metadata: simplification levels (SL)

3.3 Intended Audience of the Simplified Text

As pointed out in [49] and [4] among others, a given simplification strategy may not work for all audiences. Thus, knowing the target audience is crucial to develop solutions that are tailored to their specific needs. In Table 1, column **Audience**, we can see the different target audiences. When no explicit mention of the audience was included, we used simple language/easy-to-read. We also decided to keep SimpleWikipedia for the proposals using this source, despite its intended audience being children and language learners. This is to signal the large portion of papers using this source. When a proposal targeted more than one audience, we counted each one separately for the statistics.

Children and language learners/non-native speakers are the most frequent audiences for the simplified content, with 28 proposals in this group. Within this group, 10 proposals used Simple Wikipedia, Vikidia or Klexikon as the source for the simplified content, following the earlier work of [67].

Another large set of 23 proposals seems not to have a particular target profile. In this case, simplified content was created following general simplification guidelines, such as in [39, 62] or [28].

The takeaway from this analysis is twofold. Firstly, is the lack of corpora specialised in simplifications for people with cognitive impairments with the exception being for Danish [36] and German [56]. Secondly, is the scarcity of experiments where the target audience was directly involved in the development of the corpus. Except for examples such as the Alector corpus [25], in most cases, human evaluators outside the target group gauged the simplified material. This is not necessarily a problem, but we hypothesise that direct assessment that involves the target audience for whom the simplification is being done would not only benefit the quality of the corpus but also the development of tailored systems.

3.4 Alignment Level

The alignment between original and simplified content may benefit the development of ATS systems. For example, text-to-text models like [66] may use simplified content as a target to drive language model learning. Also, researchers may leverage this information to better understand the simplification process, introducing this knowledge into their systems so as to enhance the learning process, such as in [47]. The alignment can occur at the document, phrase, sentence, or word level, providing coarse (document level) or more fine-grained (sentence level) information.

Table 1, column **Alignment** shows that most corpora are aligned at sentence level except for Alector [25], which, to our knowledge, is aligned at the document level.

There are two other important questions related to the alignment, namely (i) the cardinality and, (ii) how the alignment was performed. A many-to-many cardinality may be desirable since it better captures the simplification process. For example, a sentence in the simplified text may come from one or more sentences in the original content or vice-versa. Most works reported 1:1 alignment, with a few exceptions such as [1, 18, 36, 49, 67] mentioning 1:N alignment at sentence level.

The other issue is the nature of the procedure involved in building the alignment. A manually aligned corpus would provide more precise information since qualified human evaluators may be the ultimate judge of the quality of the alignment. This approach has the drawback of being resource-consuming, which explains why only a few authors such as [4, 15, 16, 28] report on having conducted manually aligned sentences. Moreover, the approach seems to be more common when the simplified version is built from scratch. It is also worth mentioning the use of crowd-sourcing for the simplification [62] or the selection of sentences that are the best simplifications [4].

To improve efficiency, automatic alignment speeds up corpus construction, but at the cost of some noise. Most of the works analysed rely on automatic alignment. Moreover, early proposals such as [7] focused on alignment, and are included here as they worked with original-simplified content. The quality of the alignment algorithm becomes central in works that heavily rely on automatic alignment such as [10]. The simplified version did not come from a parallel version but from a huge collection of texts where potential simplifications are discovered.

3.5   Corpora Size

Concerning size, except for the corpora using Wikipedia, most of them include only a few hundred documents or sentences, see field **Size** in Table 1. This small number may be related to the alignment procedure and the simplification process. Producing a simplified aligned corpus is a resource-consuming task. However, small-sized corpora may hinder the development of data-driven solutions as acknowledged by [47], in particular in non-general domains such as public administration.

3.6   Annotations and Other Metadata

Besides the alignment level, other annotations may provide valuable insights into the simplification process. For example, knowledge about the type and frequency of the transformation applied could highlight simplification strategies as in the case of [11].

One possible handicap evidenced by Table 1, column **Metadata** is that more than half the proposals do not include any extra annotation or metadata. This can be explained by the fact that most of them are works using content available beforehand. Therefore, how the simplification was done is not well documented.

In other cases, [49] and [39] provide simplification guidelines that help to document, at least at the general level, the simplification procedure applied to the sentences. However, information about the linguistic phenomena solved by the simplification process is scarce. Only a few authors, such as [57] included detailed annotations about the transformation and where the change was done. Annotation guides with a typology of the possible transformation were also described in [15, 27, 50].

Illustrating the wide range of metadata that could be included, in [28] the authors also annotated complex words plus definitions. In the case of [66], Named Entity Recognition was performed, replacing occurrences with markers, thereby keeping track of them. The work of [25] documented reading errors by children with dyslexia and [5] included human evaluations about the simplicity.

In general, most corpora included only one simplification level. Among the exceptions are the Newsela [61], One-Stop [1] and Alector [25] corpora. They provided content with different degrees of simplification. For example, in [1] they have different simplified versions for elementary, intermediate, and advanced level students of English as a foreign language. In the other cases, there are different simplifications of the content targeting the same target audience, as in the case of the TurkCorpus [62] with 8 simplified versions of the original content.

Arguably, opportunities in this research field could be related to optimising the annotation strategies. Despite the research community making available the simplification instructions or annotation guidelines, the time required to do this manually is likely to be prohibitive. Moreover, when performing complex simplification it may be difficult to simultaneously map the procedure to a list of transformation types. Thus, automatic procedures could be leveraged or proposed to make the annotation process more agile, such as in [51].

Figure 1 shows an overview of the time distribution of the proposed corpora, as well the language, domains and audience.

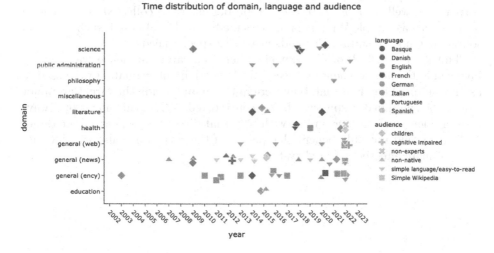

Fig. 1. Overview of time distribution in terms of corpora domains, language and target audience. Proposals dealing with multiple options appear as separate points.

4   Conclusions and Future Research

The overall conclusion of this review of forty-nine papers that present parallel corpora for ATS for European languages is that despite there being 24 official languages of the European Union[3], we only encountered seven of them with papers that present ATS parallel corpora at the time of conducting the review. Surprisingly, for German and French, both procedural languages of the European Union, our search identified 7 and 4 text simplification resources, respectively. Moreover, these resources were not specifically produced for cognitive accessibility to aid collectives with cognitive impairment. They were produced for non-native speakers, children, or as simple language generally that was not tailored to meet the needs of distinctive collectives, as indicated in Table 1. Moreover, most of the corpora in the seven official EU languages represented, apart from English, include only a few hundred documents, which hinder the development of data-driven solutions. The only exceptions are very few corpora whose sources were encyclopaedias, such as Wikipedia, or general news or health science sources.

There are four other main conclusions that stem from the corpora review in relation to the criteria assessed in Table 1. Firstly, is the lack of resources that address ATS aimed at domains that are important for social inclusion such as health and public administration. On a positive note, the few corpora in these specific domains of health and public administration have been proposed within the last five years. Indeed, almost 51% of all the reviewed corpora are from the last five years, highlighting growing interest in the field.

Secondly, is a scarcity of parallel corpora whose intended audience is people with mild-to-moderate cognitive impairment with only two identified corpora in Danish [36] and German [56]. However, a potential drawback is that these corpora, as well as most of the other proposals, were collected from general sources such as Simple Wikipedia or news media. As [4, 43] noted, such a general source may not be suitable for audiences with special needs.

Thirdly, is the lack of experiments where the target audience was directly involved in the development of the corpus. When human evaluators were used to assess the simplified material, they were in the main outside the target group for whom the simplified corpus was being constructed. While this may not always be a problem, we consider, in line with [29], that direct assessment by the target audience would not only benefit the quality of the corpus but also the development of more effective tailored systems.

---

[3] https://european-union.europa.eu/principles-countries-history/languages_en.

Fourthly, more than half of the proposals do not include any extra annotation, thereby lacking in terms of adequately documenting how the simplification was done, or the linguistic phenomenon tackled by the simplification.

Reflecting on other types of annotations that were not included in the vast majority of the corpora reviewed may provide valuable insights into the simplification process. For example, knowledge about the type and frequency of the transformation applied could identify the most frequent simplification strategies such as in the work of [11]. Moreover, an opportunity exists in this research field related to optimising annotation strategies as the time involved in manually annotating corpora lacks resource efficiency. Thus, future strategies to advance the field of ATS could leverage automatic procedures to make the annotation process more agile, such as in the work of [51].

Finally, the present corpora review indicates that we need to develop more datasets for languages that are poorly resourced in the field of corpora for ATS, like Spanish, French, and Italian, as well as many other languages of the EU. Moreover, to aid cognitive accessibility across Europe, and thereby social inclusion, resources should be deployed towards constructing large corpora sourced from domains, such as public administration and public health, that are highly relevant for social inclusion.

Acknowledgements. This research was conducted as part of the CLEAR.TEXT project (TED2021-130707B-I00), funded by MCIN/AEI/10.13039/501100011033 and European Union NextGenerationEU/PRTR, and the R&D project CORTEX: Conscious Natural Text Generation (PID2021-123956OB-I00), funded by MCIN/ AEI/10.13039/501100011033/ and by "ERDF A way of making Europe". Moreover, it has been also partially funded by the Generalitat Valenciana through the project "NL4DISMIS: Natural Language Technologies for dealing with dis- and misinformation with grant reference (CIPROM/2021/21)".

A Appendix

(See Table 2).

Table 2. Corpora Availability details on accessed date

No	Source	Source	Accessed Date
1	[7]	http://www.cs.columbia.edu/~noemie/alignment	2023-03-01
2	[44]	not publicly available to our knowledge	2023-03-01
3	[3]	not publicly available to our knowledge	2023-03-01
4	[18]	https://github.com/sidleal/porsimplessent	2023-03-01
5	[67]	https://tudatalib.ulb.tu-darmstadt.de/handle/tudatalib/2447	2023-03-01
6	[10]	not publicly available to our knowledge	2023-03-01
7	[19]	https://cs.pomona.edu/~dkauchak/simplification	2023-03-01
8	[60]	https://homepages.inf.ed.ac.uk/mlap/index.php?page=resources (broken link)	2023-03-01
9	[36]	not publicly available to our knowledge	2023-03-01
10	[20]	not publicly available to our knowledge	2023-03-01
11	[34]	https://cs.pomona.edu/~dkauchak/simplification	2023-03-01
12	[35]	not publicly available to our knowledge	2023-03-01
13	[53]	not publicly available to our knowledge	2023-03-01
14	[11]	not publicly available to our knowledge	2023-03-01
15	[12]	not publicly available to our knowledge	2023-03-01
16	[40]	not publicly available to our knowledge	2023-03-01
17	[43]	https://dialrc.org/simplification/data.html (broken link)	2023-03-01
18	[52]	not publicly available to our knowledge	2023-03-01
19	[15]	http://www.italianlp.it/resources/terence-and-teacher	2023-03-01
20	[61]	https://newsela.com/data	2023-03-01
21	[13]	https://www.cnr.it/en/institutes-databases/database/1027/paccss-it-parallel-corpus-of-complex-simple-sentences-for-italian	2023-03-01
22	[33]	https://github.com/tmu-nlp/sscorpus	2023-03-01
23	[57]	https://github.com/dhfbk/simpitiki	2023-03-01
24	[62]	https://github.com/cocoxu/simplification	2023-03-01
25	[66]	https://github.com/xingxingzhang/dress	2023-03-01
26	[27]	http://ixa2.si.ehu.es/cbst/etsc_cbst.zip	2023-03-01
27	[30]	http://natalia.grabar.free.fr/resources.php	2023-03-01
28	[49]	https://github.com/simpaticoproject/simpa	2023-03-01
29	[1]	https://zenodo.org/record/1219041	2023-03-01
30	[54]	not publicly available to our knowledge	2023-03-01
31	[9]	https://research.mytomorrows.com/datasets	2023-03-01
32	[4]	https://github.com/facebookresearch/asset	2023-03-01
33	[8]	not publicly available to our knowledge	2023-03-01
34	[17]	http://natalia.grabar.free.fr/resources.php	2023-03-01
35	[25]	https://corpusalector.huma-num.fr	2023-03-01
36	[48]	not publicly available to our knowledge	2023-03-01
37	[65]	https://github.com/slab-itu/HTSS	2023-03-01
38	[5]	https://github.com/feralvam/metaeval-simplification	2023-03-01
39	[26]	https://github.com/ZurichNLP/20Minuten	2023-03-01
40	[38]	not publicly available to our knowledge	2023-03-01
41	[42]	https://github.com/stefanpaun/massalign	2023-03-01
42	[55]	https://github.com/RLSNLP/Document-level-text-simplification	2023-03-01
43	[6]	https://github.com/dennlinger/klexikon	2023-03-01
44	[16]	https://github.com/lcampillos/clara-med	2023-03-01
45	[22]	https://zenodo.org/record/5148163	2023-03-01
46	[28]	https://github.com/itziargd/irekialf	2023-03-01
47	[39]	https://github.com/unipisa/admin-it	2023-03-01
48	[51]	https://github.com/mmu-tdmlab/simpletico19 (broken link)	2023-03-01
49	[56]	https://github.com/mlai-bonn/simple-german-corpus	2023-03-01

References

1. ACL (ed.): OneStopEnglish corpus: a new corpus for automatic readability assessment and text simplification (2018)
2. Al-Thanyyan, S.S., Azmi, A.M.: Automated text simplification: a survey. ACM Comput. Surv. (CSUR) **54**(2), 1–36 (2021)
3. Allen, D.: A study of the role of relative clauses in the simplification of news texts for learners of English. System **37**(4), 585–599 (2009)
4. Alva-Manchego, F., Martin, L., Bordes, A., Scarton, C., Sagot, B., Specia, L.: Asset: a dataset for tuning and evaluation of sentence simplification models with multiple rewriting transformations. arXiv preprint arXiv:2005.00481 (2020)
5. Alva-Manchego, F., Scarton, C., Specia, L.: The (un) suitability of automatic evaluation metrics for text simplification. Comput. Linguist. **47**(4), 861–889 (2021)
6. Aumiller, D., Gertz, M.: Klexikon: a German dataset for joint summarization and simplification. In: Proceedings of the Thirteenth Language Resources and Evaluation Conference, pp. 2693–2701 (2022)
7. Barzilay, R., Elhadad, N.: Sentence alignment for monolingual comparable corpora. In: Proceedings of the 2003 Conference on Empirical Methods in Natural Language Processing, pp. 25–32 (2003)
8. Battisti, A., Pfütze, D., Säuberli, A., Kostrzewa, M., Ebling, S.: A corpus for automatic readability assessment and text simplification of German. In: Proceedings of the Twelfth Language Resources and Evaluation Conference, pp. 3302–3311 (2020)
9. Van den Bercken, L., Sips, R.J., Lofi, C.: Evaluating neural text simplification in the medical domain. In: The World Wide Web Conference, pp. 3286–3292 (2019)
10. Bott, S., Saggion, H.: An unsupervised alignment algorithm for text simplification corpus construction. In: Proceedings of the Workshop on Monolingual Text-To-Text Generation, pp. 20–26 (2011)
11. Bott, S., Saggion, H.: Text simplification resources for Spanish. Lang. Resour. Eval. **48**(1), 93–120 (2014)
12. Brouwers, L., Bernhard, D., Ligozat, A.L., François, T.: Syntactic sentence simplification for French. In: Proceedings of the 3rd Workshop on Predicting and Improving Text Readability for Target Reader Populations (PITR)@ EACL 2014, pp. 47–56 (2014)
13. Brunato, D., Cimino, A., Dell'Orletta, F., Venturi, G.: Paccss-it: a parallel corpus of complex-simple sentences for automatic text simplification. In: Proceedings of the 2016 Conference on Empirical Methods in Natural Language Processing, pp. 351–361 (2016)
14. Brunato, D., Dell'Orletta, F., Venturi, G.: Linguistically-based comparison of different approaches to building corpora for text simplification: a case study on Italian. Front. Psychol. **13**, 97 (2022)
15. Brunato, D., Dell'Orletta, F., Venturi, G., Montemagni, S.: Design and annotation of the first Italian corpus for text simplification. In: Proceedings of the 9th Linguistic Annotation Workshop, pp. 31–41 (2015)
16. Campillos-Llanos, L., Reinares, A.R.T., Puig, S.Z., Valverde-Mateos, A., Capllonch-Carrión, A.: Building a comparable corpus and a benchmark for Spanish medical text simplification. Procesamiento del Lenguaje Nat. **69**, 189–196 (2022)
17. Cardon, R., Grabar, N.: French biomedical text simplification: when small and precise helps. In: Proceedings of the 28th International Conference on Computational Linguistics, pp. 710–716 (2020)

18. Caseli, H.M., Pereira, T.F., Specia, L., Pardo, T.A., Gasperin, C., Aluísio, S.M.: Building a Brazilian Portuguese parallel corpus of original and simplified texts. Adv. Comput. Linguist. Res. Comput. Sci. **41**, 59–70 (2009)
19. Coster, W., Kauchak, D.: Simple English Wikipedia: a new text simplification task. In: Proceedings of the 49th Annual Meeting of the Association for Computational Linguistics: Human Language Technologies, pp. 665–669 (2011)
20. Crossley, S.A., Allen, D., McNamara, D.S.: Text simplification and comprehensible input: a case for an intuitive approach. Lang. Teach. Res. **16**(1), 89–108 (2012)
21. De Belder, J., Moens, M.F.: Text simplification for children. In: Proceedings of the SIGIR Workshop on Accessible Search Systems, pp. 19–26. ACM, New York (2010)
22. Ebling, S., et al.: Automatic text simplification for German. Front. Commun. **7**, 15 (2022)
23. European Parliament, C.o.t.E.U.: Directive (EU) 2016/2102 of the European parliament and of the council of 26 October 2016 on the accessibility of the websites and mobile applications of public sector bodies (2016)
24. Ferrés, D., Saggion, H.: Alexsis: a dataset for lexical simplification in Spanish. In: Proceedings of the Thirteenth Language Resources and Evaluation Conference, pp. 3582–3594 (2022)
25. Gala, N., Tack, A., Javourey-Drevet, L., François, T., Ziegler, J.C.: Alector: a parallel corpus of simplified French texts with alignments of misreadings by poor and dyslexic readers. In: Proceedings of the 12th Language Resources and Evaluation Conference, pp. 1353–1361 (2020)
26. Gonzales, A.R., et al.: A new dataset and efficient baselines for document-level text simplification in German. In: Proceedings of the Third Workshop on New Frontiers in Summarization, pp. 152–161 (2021)
27. Gonzalez-Dios, I., Aranzabe, M.J., Díaz de Ilarraza, A.: The corpus of basque simplified texts (CBST). Lang. Resour. Eval. **52**(1), 217–247 (2018)
28. Gonzalez-Dios, I., Gutiérrez-Fandiño, I., Cumbicus-Pineda, O.M., Soroa, A.: IrekiaLFes: a new open benchmark and baseline systems for Spanish automatic text simplification. In: Proceedings of the Workshop on Text Simplification, Accessibility, and Readability (TSAR 2022), pp. 86–97 (2022)
29. Gooding, S.: On the ethical considerations of text simplification. arXiv preprint arXiv:2204.09565 (2022)
30. Grabar, N., Cardon, R.: Clear-simple corpus for medical French. In: Proceedings of the 1st Workshop on Automatic Text Adaptation (ATA), pp. 3–9 (2018)
31. Hauser, R., Vamvas, J., Ebling, S., Volk, M.: A multilingual simplified language news corpus. In: Proceedings of the 2nd Workshop on Tools and Resources to Empower People with REAding DIfficulties (READI) within the 13th Language Resources and Evaluation Conference, pp. 25–30 (2022)
32. ETS Institute: Accessibility requirements for ICT products and services - EN 301 549 (v3.2.1) (2021)
33. Kajiwara, T., Komachi, M.: Building a monolingual parallel corpus for text simplification using sentence similarity based on alignment between word embeddings. In: Proceedings of COLING 2016, the 26th International Conference on Computational Linguistics: Technical Papers, pp. 1147–1158 (2016)
34. Kauchak, D.: Improving text simplification language modeling using unsimplified text data. In: Proceedings of the 51st Annual Meeting of the Association for Computational Linguistics (Volume 1: Long papers), pp. 1537–1546 (2013)
35. Klaper, D., Ebling, S., Volk, M.: Building a German/simple German parallel corpus for automatic text simplification. In: ACL 2013, p. 11 (2013)

36. Klerke, S., Søgaard, A.: DSim, a Danish parallel corpus for text simplification. In: LREC, pp. 4015–4018 (2012)
37. Maruyama, T., Yamamoto, K.: Simplified corpus with core vocabulary. In: Proceedings of the Eleventh International Conference on Language Resources and Evaluation (LREC 2018) (2018)
38. Megna, A.L., Schicchi, D., Bosco, G.L., Pilato, G.: A controllable text simplification system for the Italian language. In: 2021 IEEE 15th International Conference on Semantic Computing (ICSC), pp. 191–194. IEEE (2021)
39. Miliani, M., Auriemma, S., Alva-Manchego, F., Lenci, A.: Neural readability pairwise ranking for sentences in Italian administrative language. In: Proceedings of the 2nd Conference of the Asia-Pacific Chapter of the Association for Computational Linguistics and the 12th International Joint Conference on Natural Language Processing, pp. 849–866 (2022)
40. Mitkov, R., Štajner, S.: The fewer, the better? A contrastive study about ways to simplify. In: Proceedings of the Workshop on Automatic Text Simplification-Methods and Applications in the Multilingual Society (ATS-MA 2014), pp. 30–40 (2014)
41. Nomoto, T.: A comparison of model free versus model intensive approaches to sentence compression. In: Proceedings of the 2009 Conference on Empirical Methods in Natural Language Processing, pp. 391–399 (2009)
42. Paun, S.: Parallel text alignment and monolingual parallel corpus creation from philosophical texts for text simplification. In: Proceedings of the 2021 Conference of the North American Chapter of the Association for Computational Linguistics: Student Research Workshop, pp. 40–46 (2021)
43. Pellow, D., Eskenazi, M.: An open corpus of everyday documents for simplification tasks. In: Proceedings of the 3rd Workshop on Predicting and Improving Text Readability for Target Reader Populations (PITR), pp. 84–93 (2014)
44. Petersen, S.E., Ostendorf, M.: Text simplification for language learners: a corpus analysis. In: Workshop on Speech and Language Technology in Education. Citeseer (2007)
45. Qiang, J., Li, Y., Zhu, Y., Yuan, Y., Shi, Y., Wu, X.: LSBERT: lexical simplification based on BERT. IEEE/ACM Trans. Audio Speech Lang. Process. **29**, 3064–3076 (2021)
46. Rello, L., Baeza-Yates, R., Bott, S., Saggion, H.: Simplify or help? Text simplification strategies for people with dyslexia. In: Proceedings of the 10th International Cross-Disciplinary Conference on Web Accessibility, pp. 1–10 (2013)
47. Saggion, H., Štajner, S., Bott, S., Mille, S., Rello, L., Drndarevic, B.: Making it simplext: implementation and evaluation of a text simplification system for Spanish. ACM Trans. Accessible Comput. (TACCESS) **6**(4), 1–36 (2015)
48. Säuberli, A., Ebling, S., Volk, M.: Benchmarking data-driven automatic text simplification for German. In: Proceedings of the 1st Workshop on Tools and Resources to Empower People with Reading Difficulties (READI), pp. 41–48 (2020)
49. Scarton, C., Paetzold, G., Specia, L.: Simpa: a sentence-level simplification corpus for the public administration domain. In: Proceedings of the Eleventh International Conference on Language Resources and Evaluation (LREC 2018), Miyazaki, Japan (2018)
50. Shardlow, M.: A survey of automated text simplification. Int. J. Adv. Comput. Sci. Appl. **4**(1), 58–70 (2014)
51. Shardlow, M., Alva-Manchego, F.: Simple TICO-19: a dataset for joint translation and simplification of Covid-19 texts. In: Proceedings of the Thirteenth Language Resources and Evaluation Conference, pp. 3093–3102 (2022)

52. Štajner, S., Mitkov, R., Corpas Pastor, G.: Simple or not simple? A readability question. In: Gala, N., Rapp, R., Bel-Enguix, G. (eds.) Language Production, Cognition, and the Lexicon. TSLT, vol. 48, pp. 379–398. Springer, Cham (2015). https://doi.org/10.1007/978-3-319-08043-7_22

53. Stajner, S., Saggion, H.: Adapting text simplification decisions to different text genres and target users. Procesamiento del Lenguaje Nat. **51**, 135–142 (2013)

54. Štajner, S., Saggion, H., Ponzetto, S.P.: Improving lexical coverage of text simplification systems for Spanish. Expert Syst. Appl. **118**, 80–91 (2019)

55. Sun, R., Jin, H., Wan, X.: Document-level text simplification: dataset, criteria and baseline. In: Proceedings of the 2021 Conference on Empirical Methods in Natural Language Processing, pp. 7997–8013 (2021)

56. Toborek, V., Busch, M., Boßert, M., Welke, P., Bauckhage, C.: A new aligned simple German corpus. arXiv preprint arXiv:2209.01106 (2022)

57. Tonelli, S., Aprosio, A.P., Saltori, F.: SIMPITIKI: a simplification corpus for Italian. In: CLiC-it/EVALITA, pp. 4333–4338 (2016)

58. Trask, R.L.: Origins and relatives of the Basque language: review of the evidence. In: Amsterdam Studies in the Theory and History of Linguistic Science Series, vol. 4, pp. 65–100 (1995)

59. Vajjala, S., Meurers, D.: On the applicability of readability models to web texts. In: Proceedings of the Second Workshop on Predicting and Improving Text Readability for Target Reader Populations, pp. 59–68 (2013)

60. Woodsend, K., Lapata, M.: Learning to simplify sentences with quasi-synchronous grammar and integer programming. In: Proceedings of the 2011 Conference on Empirical Methods in Natural Language Processing, pp. 409–420 (2011)

61. Xu, W., Callison-Burch, C., Napoles, C.: Problems in current text simplification research: new data can help. Trans. Assoc. Comput. Linguist. **3**, 283–297 (2015)

62. Xu, W., Napoles, C., Pavlick, E., Chen, Q., Callison-Burch, C.: Optimizing statistical machine translation for text simplification. Trans. Assoc. Comput. Linguist. **4**, 401–415 (2016)

63. Yimam, S.M., et al.: A report on the complex word identification shared task 2018. arXiv preprint arXiv:1804.09132 (2018)

64. Young, D.N.: Linguistic simplification of SL reading material: effective instructional practice? Mod. Lang. J. **83**(3), 350–366 (1999)

65. Zaman, F., Shardlow, M., Hassan, S.U., Aljohani, N.R., Nawaz, R.: HTSS: a novel hybrid text summarisation and simplification architecture. Inf. Process. Manag. **57**(6), 102351 (2020)

66. Zhang, X., Lapata, M.: Sentence simplification with deep reinforcement learning. arXiv preprint arXiv:1703.10931 (2017)

67. Zhu, Z., Bernhard, D., Gurevych, I.: A monolingual tree-based translation model for sentence simplification. In: Proceedings of the 23rd International Conference on Computational Linguistics (Coling 2010), pp. 1353–1361 (2010)

Explaining a Deep Learning Model for Aspect-Based Sentiment Classification Using Post-hoc Local Classifiers

Vlad Miron[1], Flavius Frasincar[1]($\boxtimes$)(iD), and Maria Mihaela Truşcă[2]

[1] Erasmus University Rotterdam, Burgemeester Oudlaan 50,
3062 PA Rotterdam, The Netherlands
`frasincar@ese.eur.nl`
[2] Bucharest University of Economic Studies, 010374 Bucharest, Romania
`maria.trusca@csie.ase.ro`

Abstract. Aspect-Based Sentiment Classification (ABSC) models are increasingly utilised given the surge in opinionated text displayed on the Web. This paper aims to explain the outcome of a black box state-of-the-art deep learning model used for ABSC, LCR-Rot-hop++. We compare two sampling methods that feed an interpretability algorithm which is based on local linear approximations (LIME). One of the sampling methods, SS, swaps out different words from the original sentence with other similar words to create neighbours to the original sentence. The second method, SSb, uses SS and then filters its neighbourhood to better balance the sentiment proportions in the localities created. We use a 2016 restaurant reviews dataset for ternary classification and we judge the interpretability algorithms based on their hit rate and fidelity. We find that SSb can improve neighbourhood sentiment balance compared to SS, reducing bias for the majority class, while simultaneously increasing the performance of LIME.

Keywords: aspect-based sentiment classification · explainable artificial intelligence · sampling methods

1 Introduction

In today's world, the amount of opinionated text shared on the Web is growing at unprecedented speeds. All of this text can be very valuable in gauging the public's perception of a given topic and thus allowing a brand to learn more about their customers to improve an existing product or service [3]. Sentiment analysis [6] has also been shown to be useful for consumers trying to make more informed decisions, allowing them to evaluate a given product or service more holistically, based on the aggregated opinions of many past customers [17]. A subfield of sentiment analysis is Aspect-Based Sentiment Analysis (ABSA) where the sentiment is computed with respect to aspects of the entity of interest [15]. ABSA comprises two steps: Aspect Detection (AD), which determines the

E. Métais et al. (Eds.): NLDB 2023, LNCS 13913, pp. 79–93, 2023.
https://doi.org/10.1007/978-3-031-35320-8_6

aspects [18], and Aspect-Based Sentiment Classification (ABSC), which determines the sentiment related to the previously discovered aspects [1]. We focus on ABSC. The main downfall of deep learning models for ABSC is their black box nature. Interpretability algorithms aim to solve this issue.

This paper aims to explore a state-of-the-art deep learning model, used for ABSC using one interpretability technique and two sampling methods on a restaurant reviews dataset. [19] introduces the Hybrid Approach for ABSA using BERT embeddings (HAABSA++), which is the basis of our work through its back up algorithm, LCR-Rot-hop++ (Left-Centre-Right separated neural network with Rotatory attention repeated for a number of iterations). We focus on LCR-Rot-hop++ due to its good performance.

We group interpretability algorithms by the taxonomy proposed by [9]. We split the algorithms into intrinsic or post-hoc, and local or global. We analyse post-hoc algorithms because an intrinsically interpretable Deep Neural Network (DNN) would suffer greatly in terms of accuracy. Then, we aim for local interpretability algorithms as our main goal is to explain to an individual the result produced by the model. In use cases such as these, a global approach may offer an interpretation which is too vague or even not applicable to the individual requesting an explanation. Thus, we employ post-hoc, local interpretability algorithms.

Furthermore, the chosen interpretability algorithm should require creating a local neighbourhood of instances around the prediction it aims to explain. This allows it to cater better to the instances explained locally, as methods that do not use a local neighbourhood have difficulties in gaining valuable insight in individual outcomes. Additionally, the sampling methods should feed the interpretability algorithm with roughly equal proportions of class instances, in our case, negative, neutral, and positive sentiment opinions. This is important as otherwise, the DNN becomes biased towards the majority class. Therefore, using a local neighbourhood and making sure to balance the sentiment proportions of its instances should increase the performance of the interpretability algorithm.

The central research question is thus *"Which sampling method and post-hoc, local classifier configuration is best suited to increase the interpretability of LCR-Rot-hop++?"*.

We consider one interpretability technique that satisfies our desired properties: Local Interpretable Model-Agnostic Explanations (LIME) [12]. We introduce two sampling methods that are used by the interpretability algorithm: Similarity-based Sampling (SS), which is similar to the method introduced by [12], and Similarity-based Sampling with balanced sentiment (SSb), which is an extension of SS. Our goal in this paper is to Sample and Interpret LCR-Rot-hop++ (SI-LCR-Rot-hop++), in order to gain insight into the model predictions.

SS works by changing a given percentage of the words in the initial sentence x with other words in the embedding space that are similar (i.e., words between which the distance in the embedding space is relatively small). SSb filters the neighbours of x based on the sentiment they show when being fed into

LCR-Rot-hop++, aiming to get as close as possible to creating neighbourhoods that are of equal size for each of the three labels.

Our first contribution stands in increasing the class balance using SSb and a tuned version of SSb. The second contribution stands in improving the performance of LIME, especially as we perform sensitivity analysis on a key hyperparameter of our sampling methods. We gain a better understanding of what factors have a positive impact on LIME, allowing us to optimise its results, simultaneously improving its neighbourhood class balance and performance. The code for our paper is written in Python 3.6.5 and made publicly available on GitHub, https://github.com/VladMiron00/SI-ABSA.

This paper is structured as follows. Section 2 discusses the development of our base model, as well as our interpretability technique, positioning them in the literature. Section 3 shows the characteristics of our data. Section 4 presents in more detail the base deep learning model, sampling approaches, interpretability algorithm, and evaluation measures used. Section 5 discusses the results obtained by our sampling approaches, interpretability algorithm, and performs sensitivity analysis on an influential hyperparameter of our sampling methods to improve the class balance and performance of our interpretability algorithm. Lastly, Sect. 6 gives our conclusion and suggestions for future work.

2   Related Works

This section showcases the latest developments regarding the topics researched. Subsection 2.1 reviews the current literature surrounding ABSC. Subsection 2.2 presents adjacent work regarding the black box interpretability algorithms used.

2.1   Aspect-Based Sentiment Classification

Aspect-Based Sentiment Analysis (ABSA) aims to capture the sentiment of aspects discussed in text [15]. It includes the steps of Aspect Detection (AD) responsible for finding the discussed aspects [18] and Aspect-Based Sentiment Classification (ABSC) responsible for determining the sentiment concerning the previously discussed aspects [1]. We focus on ABSC and assume the aspect to be given.

In previous work, [16] took an ontology approach to ABSC. Observing how the ontological approach failed from time to time in detecting the sentiment, researchers proposed using a deep learning model as a backup, employing a hybrid approach to solve the shortcomings of ABSC, also known as the Hybrid Approach for ABSA (HAABSA) [20]. The first version of what would become the backup DNN of HAABSA was introduced by [21] under the name of LCR-Rot, which stands for Left-Centre-Right separated neural network with Rotatory attention. This DNN splits the sentence into the target (which is the centre or the aspect) and its left and right contexts, assigning weights to the words in the different parts of the sentence based on how important they are with regard to the target.

Then, [20] applied an improved version of LCR-Rot, LCR-Rot-hop, which iterates over the rotatory mechanism of LCR-Rot multiple times to ensure consistency. The latest HAABSA extension is presented by [19] as LCR-Rot-hop++, which improves LCR-Rot-hop by adding a hierarchical attention layer to DNN. Furthermore, LCR-Rot-hop++ changes the context-independent word embeddings of LCR-Rot-hop to the context-dependent BERT embeddings. This allows LCR-Rot-hop++ to better deal with word polysemy.

2.2 Black Box Interpretability Algorithms

Based on the current literature we note that the interpretability of deep learning attention models for ABSC has not been studied to a large extent [2,4,14].

That said, diagnostic classification has been tried on HAABSA, namely with the contribution of [8]. This implementation used LCR-Rot-hop as the backup for the ontological approach. Its findings show that context representation is the main factor in determining the relations between the target and other words in the sentence. Furthermore, the performance of the model determining the sentiment value shown concerning the target does not greatly vary along with the 10 iterations (hops) that were implemented. [5] conducts a similar study and obtain comparable results, using LCR-Rot-hop++ instead of LCR-Rot-hop.

An interpretability algorithm which satisfies our desired characteristics is the Local Agnostic attribute Contribution Explanation (LACE) [10]. This rule-based algorithm brings interpretability to a prediction by analyzing the joint effect of subsets of features that can be formed out of the initial feature pool on the model outcome. This model is local because the prediction to be explained is in the vicinity of the feature value subsets chosen. We eliminate LACE from our analysis because it uses an ad-hoc method to generate its classifiers.

Another interpretability algorithm that fits our desired properties was introduced by [13], being named Anchor. Anchor is a rule-based method that works by selecting a set of instances in the neighbourhood of the instance we want to explain. It assesses which features in the set of local instances are most influential. We eliminate Anchor from our analysis because of its slow convergence.

[7] proposes SHAP, a method that works using the principles of cooperative game theory. SHAP calculates a coefficient that shows how important a feature is for each subset of features it can be included in and then averages out the importance coefficient over all possible subsets. We exclude this approach from our analysis because it does not make use of a neighbourhood sampling method.

3 Data

The data used in this paper follows the preprocessing rules and manipulations of [19], using the same *SemEval 2016 Task 5 Subtask 1 Slot 3* dataset [11].

The descriptive statistics of the sentences remaining after preprocessing are presented in Table 1, where train and test data represent the basis of our analysis. The sentences which could not be classified by the ontology approach are

Table 1. Sentiment labels within the filtered SemEval 2016 datasets.

Dataset	Negative		Neutral		Positive		Total	
	Freq.	%	Freq.	%	Freq.	%	Freq.	%
Train data	489	26	72	3.8	1319	70.2	1880	100
Test data	135	20.8	32	4.9	483	74.3	650	100
Rem. test data	82	33	22	8.9	144	58.1	248	100
Used test data	8	32	2	8	15	60	25	100

collected in *"remaining test data"*, which is the dataset that LCR-Rot-hop++ should run on as a backup for the ontology. To avoid long run times (as each instance requires its own local model) we create a smaller dataset that emulates *"remaining test data"*. Thus, *"used test data"* aims to have similar sentiment proportions to *"remaining test data"*, while trimming down the number of instances from 248 to 25. The dataset *"used test data"* is fed in all LCR-Rot-hop++ runs.

As the positive class is present in a clear majority of instances, it causes the ontological approach to disproportionately classify incorrectly the neutral and negative instances within the test sample. This created bias for the majority class explains why neutral and negative sentiment sentences increase in proportion within *"remaining test data"*.

4 Methodology

In this section, we present the methods behind the analysed ABSC model. Subsection 4.1 presents this paper's chosen model for ABSC, LCR-Rot-hop++. We explore LCR-Rot-hop++ using different sampling methods applied on the interpretability algorithm. Subsection 4.2 shows the sampling methods used by our interpretability algorithm. Subsection 4.3 discusses the used interpretability algorithm. Lastly, Subsect. 4.4 presents evaluation measures for the sampling methods and interpretability algorithm.

4.1 LCR-Rot-hop++

As [19] describes, LCR-Rot-hop++ splits the input (a sentence), into three parts: the left context, the centre, and the right context. The centre is the aspect target value of the sentence, having T words, where T may be larger or equal to 1. A sentence may look like *"this restaurant is amazing"*, where *"this"* is the left context, *"restaurant"* is the target, and *"is amazing"* is the right context. These words are then embedded using BERT, a method based on transformers.

Next, three Bidirectional Long Short-Term Memory (Bi-LSTM) models are used, each Bi-LSTM corresponding to a different part of the sentence. The system consists of four parts: the left and right contexts which are used to obtain one target representation for the left context and another target representation for the right context, and the two target representations which are used to produce the left and right context representations. The rotatory attention mechanism is continuously used to change the representation of the different parts of the sentence for the hierarchical attention mechanism, which takes them as input and weights them. After attaining these four weighted representations, LCR-Rot-hop++ proceeds to feed them back into the rotatory attention mechanism and weigh them again using the hierarchical attention mechanism for the desired number of iterations.

After the last rotation, the final representations of the four parts are used as input for the Multi-Layer Perceptron (MLP). The MLP uses a softmax function to output the aspect-level sentiment predictions.

4.2 Sampling Methods

As the "S" in SI-LCR-Rot-hop++ suggests, the sampling methods are a key part of our paper. Their existence is required for the approach of LIME, as it is based on creating a local neighbourhood around the prediction $x \in X$ (X is the set of instances) that it aims to explain. The neighbourhood it creates is denoted as Z_x, where $z \in Z_x$ is a perturbed sample, being similar to x in many regards, except for a couple of features which are changed. The feature changes refer to swapping one or more words f from the original sentence x with other words that are similar out of the set of F features which compose the used *SemEval-2016* restaurant reviews datasets. We create local neighbours by changing words (features) only in the left or the right context of the original sentence x.

Since a sentence x is originally represented as a sequence of word embeddings, we change its format to input it into our algorithms. We achieve this by using the modified x' instances, which are a binary representation of x indicating which features $f \in F$ are contained within the sentence x, $x' \in \{0,1\}^{|F|}$.

Algorithm 1 shows how interpretability algorithm m_x (in our case LIME) functions for any given instance $x \in X$. The explanation that algorithm m_x provides for x is denoted $\xi_m(x)$. The neighbourhood size Z_x is denoted as n_x.

Algorithm 1. Using m_x to explain prediction of $b(x)$

Arguments of method: Black box model b, interpretation model m_x, instance $x \in X$, desired neighbourhood size n_x

$Z'_x \leftarrow \emptyset$
for $i \in \{1, 2, ..., n_x\}$ **do**
    $z'_i \leftarrow apply\_sampling\_method\_on(x)$
    $Z'_x \leftarrow Z'_x \cup z'_i$
end for
$\xi_m(x) \leftarrow m_x(Z'_x, b)$
return $\xi_m(x)$

The size of the neighbourhoods created by the Similarity-based Sampling method (SS) and the Similarity-based Sampling method with balanced sentiment (SSb) differ, as SS creates neighbourhoods of 5000 local instances, while SSb trims down the initial, larger, neighbourhood created by SS to a balanced neighbourhood of 150 perturbations for each instance x.

4.2.1 Similarity-Based Sampling Method

LIME needs to have a neighbourhood of local instances generated around an input instance. The Similarity-based Sampling (SS) method is similar to that of [12]. It works by analysing the embedding space for each word w_1 in sentence x and finding another similar word. The first step in this task is assigning a POS tag to the elements of set F, consisting of all the different words in the *SemEval-2016* datasets. The possible tags are noun, verb, adjective, adverb, adposition, and determiner. Assuming the same POS tag for w_1 and w_2, the distance between the 2 words is calculated by the formula:

$$D(w_1, w_2) = 1 - \frac{w_1 \cdot w_2}{||w_1||||w_2||}. \tag{1}$$

Algorithm 2 generates a local instance z' for any $x \in X$ via SS. We transform the local instance z to attain the binary representation of the instance, z'.

Algorithm 2. Using SS to generate a local instance z' for instance x $(apply\_SS(x))$

Arguments of method: instance $x \in X$
$z \leftarrow \emptyset$
for $w_1 \in x$ **do**
    $change\_boolean \leftarrow change\_function(change\_probability)$
    if $change\_boolean$ is $True$ **then**
        $distances \leftarrow \emptyset$
        for $w_2 \in F$ **do**
            $distances \leftarrow distances \cup D(w_1, w_2)$
        end for
        $top\_n\_words \leftarrow pick\_top\_n\_words(distances)$
        $z \leftarrow z \cup picking\_algorithm(top\_n\_words)$
    else
        $z \leftarrow z \cup w_1$
    end if
end for
$z' \leftarrow transform(z)$
return z'

Algorithm 2 changes the words in the left and the right contexts of the original instance x with other words in the dataset which are similar. It iterates through each word $w_1 \in x$, deciding if it has to replace said word or not.

A higher *change_probability* suggests that more words in any given sentence x are going to be replaced with other words from the dataset. If the decision is to not change the current word in the sentence, the perturbed instance z receives the original word w_1. If the decision is to change the current word, we start this process by calculating the distances between word w_1 and all of the other words in its embedding space, words contained in F. Note that the original word w_1 is included in the pool of words which may be chosen for its replacement, meaning that a *change_probability* of 100% does not guarantee that all words in all perturbations are different to the ones in the original instance.

Next, we create the ranking *top_n_words*, where words that are closer to w_1 rank higher. We need to pick out one word from *top_n_words*. This ranking shows which words are closest to w_1, assigning a probability to each word.

Said probability is decided by the *picking_algorithm*, which is set for a weighted pick. The weight is given based on the ranking, where words closer to the first position in the ranking receive a higher weight and are thus more likely to be picked. We consider the word chosen a suitable replacement for w_1 in sentence x as it is contextually similar and grammatically identical to w_1.

After iterating through the words in x we attain the perturbed sentence z, which we transform into binary format and return as z', that is output.

4.2.2   Similarity-Based Sampling Method with Balanced Sentiment

Similarity-based Sampling method with balanced sentiment (SSb) builds on top of SS by aiming to solve its main issue. Because SS creates local instances for $x \in X$ by replacing words in x with other similar words, the created neighbours are bound to be similar to x, and thus to get the same label as the original instance. Since the original dataset contains a clear majority of positive labelled instances, this sentiment distribution is likely to carry over to the local instances that SS creates, possibly affecting the performance of the interpretability algorithms due to the bias that class imbalance creates for the majority class.

SSb aims to solve this issue and provide LIME with a more balanced set of instances to train on, achieving this by taking into account the sentiment of the neighbours created when choosing whether to keep them or not (Algorithm 3).

Algorithm 3. Using SSb for LIME to create a balanced neighbourhood $Z_x^{b\prime}$ for instance x

---
Arguments of method: instance $x \in X$
$Z_x \leftarrow \emptyset$
$Z_x^b \leftarrow \emptyset$
$M \leftarrow 0$
$SS\_neigh\_size \leftarrow 5000$
$SSb\_neigh\_size \leftarrow 150$
while $M < SS\_neigh\_size$ **do**
    $z' \leftarrow apply\_SS(x)$
    $z \leftarrow transform(z')$
    $Z_x \leftarrow Z_x \cup z$
    $M \leftarrow M + 1$
end while
$neighs\_sentiments \leftarrow get\_sentiments(Z_x)$
$chosen\_perturb \leftarrow get\_balanced\_perturb(neighs\_sentiments, SSb\_neigh\_size)$
for $z \in Z_x$ **do**
    if $z \in chosen\_perturb$ **then**
        $Z_x^b \leftarrow Z_x^b \cup z$
    end if
end for
$Z_x^{b\prime} \leftarrow transform(Z_x^b)$
return $Z_x^{b\prime}$

Z_x^b is the balanced neighbourhood of instance x. This neighbourhood is obtained by filtering the original, larger, neighbourhood of Z_x. Z_x is created using Algorithm 2 (called by $apply\_SS(x)$) and it contains SS_neigh_size

(5000 in this paper) perturbations. In SSb, we trimmed down the neighbour-hood size of SS to a balanced, smaller, neighbourhood of SSb_neigh_size (150) perturbations.

We obtain the unbalanced neighbourhood of SS_neigh_size instances by iteratively applying the SS algorithm and saving its output. Then, we run LCR-Rot-hop++ to obtain the sentiment predictions for each perturbation created for instance x, using the function $get\_sentiments(Z_x)$. We store the results in a counter vector, $neighs\_sentiments$, which shows how many perturbations of each sentiment correspond to an instance x. This vector is then fed into the $get\_balanced\_perturb()$ function along with the balanced neighbourhood size to determine how many perturbations of each sentiment we should keep. Ideally, for an original neighbourhood of 5000 instances and a balanced neighbourhood of 150 instances, we should have at least 50 perturbations of each of the three sentiments in the original neighbourhood. This would allow us to obtain a balanced neighbourhood of roughly 33.3% of each sentiment.

Last, we iterate through the original set of perturbations Z_x and pick out based on the indexes saved in $chosen\_perturb$ the local instances that we add to the balanced set Z_x^b. We return this set of neighbours in binary format.

4.3 LIME

This section discusses the second component of SI-LCR-Rot-hop++, our interpretability method, namely LIME [12]. LIME is a popular model-agnostic interpretability algorithm which samples instances in the neighbourhood of x and applies a linear approximation to said instances to attain a model that performs similarly on a local level to the original black box.

For our paper, we are dealing with a ternary classification problem with the classes $K = \{-1, 0, 1\}$, corresponding to negative, neutral, and positive sentiments, respectively. The underlying interpretable model g is log-linear, as the method used is the multinominal logistic regression. It works by training 3 ($|K|$) binary classification models $g^{(k)}(x)$ for each instance $x \in X$, corresponding to the 3 combinations possible when you consider one of the $|K|$ classes, k, as the benchmark and you group the other 2 classes under k^c. Its formula is:

$$g^{(k)}(x') = ln(Pr[b(x) = k|x]) = \beta_0^{(k)} + \sum_{j \in F} \beta_j^{(k)} x_j' - ln(L). \qquad (2)$$

The binary form representation of the instance we aim to explain is x'. The interpretable model computes the natural logarithm of the probability that the black box model classifies x as the sentiment k ($k \in K$). $\beta_j^{(k)}$ with $j \in F$ represents the marginal effect of feature j on the binary sentiment classification of x. L is the normalization term, explicited as $\sum_{k \in K} e^{\beta^{(k)} x'}$ with $\beta^{(k)}$ denoting the vector that contains the set of all coefficients $\beta_j^{(k)}$ with $j = \{0, 1, ..., |F|\}$.

We can draw interpretability insight from these marginal effects, with the mention of keeping the number of marginal effects chosen limited. We select a maximum of S features with the highest influence to be included in the interpretability model. The influence of feature j (e_j) is calculated as the sum of the absolute marginal effects of feature j on classes $k \in K$, $e_j = \sum_k |\beta_j^{(k)}|$ with $k = 1, 2, 3$.

The interpretation brought by LIME stands in the set S of marginal effects, corresponding to the top $|S|$ out of $|F_x|$ most influential features of F_x (F_x being the set of words in sentence x). To determine this set of marginal effects we apply a weighted multinominal logistic regression trained on Z_x according to Eq. 2. The neighbourhood of x, Z_x, is generated via SS or SSb and the weights attributed to the local instances included in the neighbourhood depend on the proximity of the perturbations z' to x, π_x, which is defined by an exponential kernel, $\pi_x(z) = exp(-D(x,z)^2/\sigma^2)$. σ is the width of the kernel and $D(x,z)$ is the distance function applied on the word embeddings of instances x and z.

4.4   Performance Evaluation

Subsubsection 4.4.1 presents an instance evaluation measure for the sampling methods picked and Subsubsect. 4.4.2 shows evaluation measures for LIME.

4.4.1   Measure for the Sampling Methods

As previously discussed, achieving balanced labels within the neighbourhoods created using SS and SSb is important in training an unbiased model.

One way to quantify the degree of overall balance within our neighbourhoods is by computing the entropy, calculated as follows:

$$Entropy = -\sum_k p(k) \log_2 p(k), \tag{3}$$

where $p(k)$ is the proportion of sentences labelled as $k \in K$. The higher the entropy, the better the balance of sentiments, as the highest entropy value is achieved when roughly 33.3% of the sentences are of each sentiment.

4.4.2   Measures for LIME

The first performance measure is the *hit rate*, which shows how often the interpretable model m_x, trained in the neighbourhood of instance x, and the black box model b give the same prediction for a given instance $x \in X$. It is calculated as the number of times b and m_x match their predictions for $x \in X$ over the cardinality of X (X being the set of sentences we create neighbourhoods for). This indicates that a larger hit rate is better.

Another quantitative performance measure is the *fidelity*, which shows how often the interpretable model m_x and the black box model b give the same prediction for a local instance in Z_x. It is calculated as the number of times b and m_x match their predictions for all instances x and their perturbations over the cardinality $|Z_x| * |X|$. A larger fidelity value is better.

A high value is needed for both the hit rate and fidelity to ensure that the interpretability model is true to the original black box. To judge the balance

Table 2. Sentiment proportions given the sampling methods.

SI Comb.	Negative		Neutral		Positive		Entropy Value
	Freq.	%	Freq.	%	Freq.	%	
SS for LIME	42737	34.2	410	0.3	81853	65.5	0.95
SSb for LIME	1219	32.5	221	5.9	2310	61.6	**1.2**

between the hit rate and the fidelity we propose to use the harmonic mean of the two. This measure is used as a proxy for the overall performance of the configuration ran, with a higher value being better. The formula for the harmonic mean in our case is:

$$Harmonic\ Mean = \frac{2}{\frac{1}{Hit\ Rate} + \frac{1}{Fidelity}}. \tag{4}$$

5   Results

In this section we present the results of our proposed method evaluation. Subsection 5.1 evaluates our proposed sampling methods with regards to the sentiment proportions created. Subsection 5.2 compares the hit rate and fidelity achieved by LIME under different sampling methods. Subsection 5.3 performs sensitivity analysis on a key hyperparameter of our sampling methods to improve the tuning of SSb and the performance of LIME using SSb.

5.1   Sampling Methods

The results in Table 2 correspond to LCR-Rot-hop++ classification aggregated over the 25 instances $x \in X$ from *"used test data"* and their respective neighbours. The sampling methods need to be run for LIME, which gets fed 5000 local instances for each sentence x for SS and 150 local instances for SSb. The *change_probability* is set to 50%.

Table 2 shows how SSb impacted the proportions of sentiment labels for LIME compared to SS. The number of negative and positive labelled sentences gets marginally decreased, while the neutral category is increased almost twenty times in frequency (from 0.3% to 5.9%). Thus, the entropy increases from 0.95 under SS to 1.2 under SSb, showing the overall improvement in label balance.

5.2   Interpretability Algorithms

To find the best sampling method configuration for LIME, we measure the hit rate and fidelity, as shown in Table 3. We calculate the harmonic mean to judge the overall performance of a given configuration.

Looking at the harmonic mean of the hit rate and the fidelity, we notice SSb performing better than SS. The reduced sample used, containing 25 out of the 248 sentences, may be the reason for values of 100% for the hit rate.

Table 3. Hit rate and fidelity of LIME given the sampling methods.

SI Combination	Hit Rate %	Fidelity %	Harmonic Mean %
LIME with SS	100	90.1	94.8
LIME with SSb	100	91.1	**95.4**

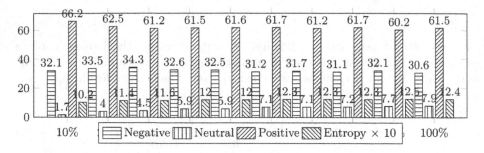

Fig. 1. Sensitivity analysis of SSb for the sentiment distribution under LIME, x-axis shows the value of *change_probability* in presented run.

5.3 Sensitivity Analysis

In the previous sections, we find that SSb is a useful extension, being able to improve both the class balance, measured by the entropy, and the hit rate and fidelity judged jointly using the harmonic mean. We are now interested if we are able to bring a further beneficial effect to our interpretability algorithm by iteratively altering an influential hyperparameter, *change_probability*, with the intent of finding out what value brings the best results. We use *change_probability* with values from 10% to 100% with 10% increments for LIME with SSb. We do not perform this analysis for SS because we have observed how it underperforms both in terms of class balance and performance measures compared to SSb.

Figure 1 shows an increasing trend for the class balance of LIME as the *change_probability* shifts from 10% to 90%, where it achieves its peak entropy of 1.25. The results up to the run using a 90% *change_probability* show that altering the original sentence x to a larger extent leads to neighbouring sentences that are more likely to receive labels different from the label of x (more diverse).

The unexpected result is in the last run, using a probability of changing the words of 100%, where we notice a slight decrease in the balance of sentiments compared to the run using 90%, as entropy drops from 1.25 to 1.24. It seems that as the hyperparameter of interest reaches high values, the balance of sentiments becomes a matter of chance. Therefore, it is possible that as the *change_probability* exceeds 90%, the impact on the balance of sentiments becomes unpredictable, as it may improve or not across runs or datasets.

Figure 2 shows the impact of the varying *change_probability* on the fidelity and hit rate of LIME, measures which are summed up using the harmonic mean. There is a clear up trend in the performance of the models as the mentioned

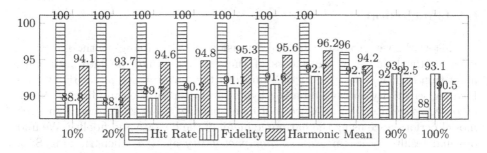

Fig. 2. Sensitivity analysis of SSb for the quantitative measures of LIME, x-axis shows the value of *change_probability* in presented run.

hyperparameter increases in value. Thus, a more diverse neighbourhood improves performance. A peak harmonic mean of 96.2% is reached for a *change_probability* of 70%.

One interesting observation regarding Fig. 2 concerns the fact that a trade off between the hit rate and the fidelity appears as the probability to change a feature increases. This is to be expected as higher probabilities of changing a word imply a more diverse set of neighbours in terms of the range of vocabulary. Thus, as the sentences in the neighbourhood Z_x start to differ more from x, LIME gets less trained to recognize and correctly classify x, reducing the hit rate. At the same time, LIME gets used to training on a broader range of neighbours, recognizing the varying sentiments they have, leading to an increase in fidelity.

Another interesting observation about Fig. 2 is that the benefit of increasing the word replacement probability ceases to exist as the probability to change a word reaches or exceeds 80%. Although more word replacements create more diverse sentences and more balanced label proportions, from about 80% word replacement probability onward, the perturbed sentences start to not make as much grammatical or contextual sense as before.

For example, given a word replacement probability of 100%, the sentence *"the owner is belligerent to guests that have a complaint."* (where *"owner"* is the target) turned in one of the perturbations into *"an owner was belligerent about drinks which use the disappointment."*. In contrast, for a change probability of 50%, one perturbation looked like *"this owner is belligerent to people that make a request."*. This is just an anecdote, but it goes to show that using high feature changing probabilities risks creating neighbours which are not representative of a real review left by a customer, reducing the performance obtained by the interpretability algorithm.

To conclude on our results concerning LIME, it seems that in our runs a *change_probability* of 70% is optimal, as it reaches the best value for the harmonic mean, while drastically improving sentiment balance compared to SS. To be exact, the class balance measured by the entropy increases from 0.95 under SS to 1.23 under tuned SSb. Further, the harmonic mean of the hit rate and the fidelity increases from 94.8% under SS to 96.2% under tuned SSb.

6 Conclusion

In this work, we propose SSb, an extension of a sampling method (SS) to improve the balance of sentiments of the sentences that the interpretability algorithm (LIME) uses. We further improve the performance of LIME by performing sensitivity analysis on a key hyperparameter for the sampling methods, *change_probability*. We measure sentiment balance using the entropy and the model performance using the harmonic mean of the hit rate and fidelity. We find optimal results by setting the *change_probability* at 70% when running SSb. This configuration yields an increase in the entropy (and thus in the class balance) from a value of 0.95 under SS to 1.23 under tuned SSb. The harmonic mean increases from 94.8% under SS to 96.2% under tuned SSb. Thus, we manage to find a configuration that improves both the class balance and the model performance simultaneously for LIME.

A possible future research opportunity lies in further improving the method of balancing sentiment proportions of the perturbations. This may be achieved by using both BERT embeddings and sentiment-aware BERT embeddings. The sampling method may replace a word in sentence x only with another word that is close in the BERT embedding space (being a contextually feasible replacement) and far in the sentiment-aware BERT embedding space (increasing the chance that the replacement will change the original sentiment label attributed to the sentence). This way, we will build on purpose rather than by chance perturbations which are not only suitable neighbours given the context but also diverse in sentiment.

References

1. Brauwers, G., Frasincar, F.: A survey on aspect-based sentiment classification. ACM Comput. Surv. 55(4), 65:1–65:37 (2023)
2. Du, M., Liu, N., Hu, X.: Techniques for interpretable machine learning. arXiv preprint arXiv:1808.00033 (2018)
3. Godbole, S., Roy, S.: Text classification, business intelligence, and interactivity: automating C-SAT analysis for services industry. In: 14th ACM SIGKDD International Conference on Knowledge Discovery and Data Mining (KDD 2008), pp. 911–919. ACM (2008)
4. Guidotti, R., Monreale, A., Ruggieri, S., Turini, F., Pedreschi, D., Giannotti, F.: A survey of methods for explaining black box models. arXiv preprint arXiv:1802.01933 (2018)
5. Kunal, G., Frasincar, F., Trușcă, M.M.: Explaining a deep neural model with hierarchical attention for aspect-based sentiment classification. In: Di Noia, T., Ko, I.Y., Schedl, M., Ardito, C. (eds.) ICWE 2022. LNCS, vol. 13362, pp. 268–282. Springer, Cham (2022). https://doi.org/10.1007/978-3-031-09917-5_18
6. Liu, B.: Sentiment Analysis: Mining Opinions, Sentiments, and Emotions, 2nd edn. Cambridge University Press, Cambridge (2020)
7. Lundberg, S.M., Lee, S.I.: A unified approach to interpreting model predictions. In: 31st Annual Conference on Neural Information Processing Systems (NIPS 2017), vol. 30, pp. 4765–4774 (2017)

8. Meijer, L., Frasincar, F., Truşcă, M.M.: Explaining a neural attention model for aspect-based sentiment classification using diagnostic classification. In: 36th ACM/SIGAPP Symposium on Applied Computing (SAC 2021), pp. 821–827. ACM (2021)
9. Molnar, C.: Interpretable machine learning. In: Second International Workshop in eXplainable Knowledge Discovery in Data Mining (XKDD 2020). CCIS, vol. 1323, p. 414. Springer, Cham (2020)
10. Pastor, E., Baralis, E.: Explaining black box models by means of local rules. In: 34th ACM/SIGAPP Symposium on Applied Computing (SAC 2019), pp. 510–517. ACM (2019)
11. Pontiki, M., et al.: SemEval-2016 task 5: aspect based sentiment analysis. In: 10th International Workshop on Semantic Evaluation (SemEval 2016), pp. 19–30. ACL (2016)
12. Ribeiro, M.T., Singh, S., Guestrin, C.: "Why should I trust you?": explaining the predictions of any classifier. In: 22nd ACM SIGKDD International Conference on Knowledge Discovery and Data Mining (KDD 2016), pp. 1135–1144. ACM (2016)
13. Ribeiro, M.T., Singh, S., Guestrin, C.: Anchors: high-precision model-agnostic explanations. In: Thirty-Second AAAI Conference on Artificial Intelligence (AAAI 2018), vol. 32, pp. 1527–1535. AAAI Press (2018)
14. Rudin, C., Chen, C., Chen, Z., Huang, H., Semenova, L., Zhong, C.: Interpretable machine learning: fundamental principles and 10 grand challenges. Stat. Surv. **16**, 1–85 (2022)
15. Schouten, K., Frasincar, F.: Survey on aspect-level sentiment analysis. IEEE Trans. Knowl. Data Eng. **28**(3), 813–830 (2016)
16. Schouten, K., Frasincar, F., de Jong, F.: Ontology-enhanced aspect-based sentiment analysis. In: Cabot, J., De Virgilio, R., Torlone, R. (eds.) ICWE 2017. LNCS, vol. 10360, pp. 302–320. Springer, Cham (2017). https://doi.org/10.1007/978-3-319-60131-1_17
17. Singla, Z., Randhawa, S., Jain, S.: Statistical and sentiment analysis of consumer product reviews. In: 8th International Conference on Computing, Communication and Networking Technologies (ICCCNT 2017), pp. 1–6. IEEE (2017)
18. Truşcă, M.M., Frasincar, F.: Survey on aspect detection for aspect-based sentiment analysis. Artif. Intell. Rev. **56**(5), 3797–3846 (2023)
19. Truşcă, M.M., Wassenberg, D., Frasincar, F., Dekker, R.: A hybrid approach for aspect-based sentiment analysis using deep contextual word embeddings and hierarchical attention. In: Bielikova, M., Mikkonen, T., Pautasso, C. (eds.) ICWE 2020. LNCS, vol. 12128, pp. 365–380. Springer, Cham (2020). https://doi.org/10.1007/978-3-030-50578-3_25
20. Wallaart, O., Frasincar, F.: A hybrid approach for aspect-based sentiment analysis using a lexicalized domain ontology and attentional neural models. In: Hitzler, P., et al. (eds.) ESWC 2019. LNCS, vol. 11503, pp. 363–378. Springer, Cham (2019). https://doi.org/10.1007/978-3-030-21348-0_24
21. Zheng, S., Xia, R.: Left-center-right separated neural network for aspect-based sentiment analysis with rotatory attention. arXiv preprint arXiv:1802.00892 (2018)

Arabic Privacy Policy Corpus and Classification

Malak Mashaabi[✉], Ghadi Al-Yahya, Raghad Alnashwan, and Hend Al-Khalifa

Information Technology Department, College of Computer and Information Sciences, King
Saud University, Riyadh, Saudi Arabia
{444203610,442202932,444203361}@student.ksu.edu.sa,
hendk@ksu.edu.sa

Abstract. Privacy policies are the main sources of information for Internet users
on how organizations gather, use, and share personal data. However, most consumers find it difficult to read and become unaware of the content. To simplify it
for consumers, an automatic technique verifies whether websites and applications
comply with the established privacy and data protection laws in companies worldwide. The implementation of the Personal Data Protection Law (PDPL) in the
Kingdom of Saudi Arabia (KSA) was effective on March 23, 2022. To the best of
our knowledge, checking the compliance of Saudi websites with the PDPL has not
yet been addressed. Hence, this project aims to automatically analyze the compliance of KSA privacy policies with PDPL using Machine Learning and Deep Learning techniques. We manually extracted and annotated a dataset of privacy policies
from 1000 Saudi websites belonging to seven sectors. The Logistic Regression
technique was used as the baseline model to train the dataset along with other
classifiers, including Naïve Bayes, Support Vector Machine, Long Short-Term
Memory (LSTM), Feed-Forward Neural Network (FFNN), ARABERT, MAR-
BERT, and CamelBERT. The results show that both MARBERT and CamelBERT
models achieved the best performance with a micro-average F1 score of 0.93,
compared to the baseline approach and other models.

Keywords: Privacy policies · Personal Data Protection Law · Corpus Analysis ·
Saudi websites · Text Classification

1 Introduction

The rapid increase in data volume has introduced a continuous excess in the collection
of personal data required by websites, leading companies worldwide to prioritize data
protection. Personal data are any information that relates to a person and can directly or
indirectly identify them, including the individual's name, date of birth, email address, etc.
(Javed et al. 2020). Any organization that collects the personal information of individuals must have a privacy policy that states how they gather and process this information
(Wilson et al. 2016). Privacy policies are required by privacy regulations and tend to be
lengthy legal documents that are often difficult for users to understand (Bannihatti Kumar
et al. 2020). There are many well-known data protection regulations in the world, such
as the General Data Protection Regulation (GDPR)[1] of the European Union. In addition,

---

[1] https://gdpr.eu/what-is-gdpr/ [Date Accessed 20/3/2023].

E. Métais et al. (Eds.): NLDB 2023, LNCS 13913, pp. 94–108, 2023.
https://doi.org/10.1007/978-3-031-35320-8_7

Canada's federal data protection law is the Personal Information Protection and Electronic Documents Act (PIPEDA) (Xu 2021). As well as China's Personal Information Protection Law (PIPL) and many other international regulations regulate how businesses collect, process, and store personal data in a legally compliant manner.

The Personal Data Protection Law (PDPL) was the first data protection law in the Kingdom of Saudi Arabia (KSA). The features of PDPL are consistent with the principles of GPDR and other international data protection laws and differ in some unique aspects, such as taxes, notifications, data transfer, and other restrictions (Kablawi 2022). The main objectives of the PDPL are to protect individual privacy, control data sharing, and stop misuse of personal information in accordance with the Kingdom's Vision 2030 objectives of creating a digital infrastructure and encouraging innovation to create a digital economy. On the other hand, companies that process individuals' personal data must comply with the requirements of PDPL data regulations; otherwise, they will face severe penalties.

The implementation of PDPL in the KSA has only recently been effective since March 23, 2022. To the best of our knowledge, no studies have verified whether websites and applications in KSA comply with the established privacy and data protection laws in PDPL. In this study, we aim to automate the process of identifying the compliance of Saudi websites' privacy policy statements with the PDPL law. We trained our dataset of 1000 privacy policy websites collected from seven sectors (Finance, Government, Healthcare, Education, News, E-Commerce, and Others) using multiple Machine Learning (ML) models, namely: Logistic Regression (LR), Naïve Bayes (NB), and Support Vector Machine (SVM). As well as Deep Learning models include Long Short-Term Memory (LSTM), Feed-Forward Neural Network (FFNN), and Transformer-based models such as ARABERT, MARBERT, and CamelBERT. The results of the study revealed that CamelBERT and MARBERT were the best-performing models, surpassing all other models in terms of their micro-average F1 scores, which were recorded at 0.933. In comparison, the ARABERT model had similar performance, with a micro-average F1 score of 0.932.

The main objectives of this study are summarized as follows:

(1) Construct an annotation of an Arabic corpus of privacy policies for Saudi websites.
(2) Automate the process of checking Saudi websites' compliance with PDPL principles.

The rest of the paper is structured as follows: Sect. 2 describes the background of the PDPL. Section 3 presents related work on privacy-policy classifications. Section 4 provides all corpus details from the data collection to the annotation process. Section 5 presents the results of the different classifier comparisons. Section 6 presents the experimental results. Finally, Sect. 7 provides an outlook for future work.

2 Background: The Personal Data Protection Law (PDPL)

On September 24, 2021, the KSA published the PDPL and put it into effect on March 23, 2022. The PDPL applies to any entity (including public and private companies) that processes the personal data of Saudi residents and provides services to them, whether these entities are inside or outside Saudi Arabia (Kablawi 2022). Therefore, the PDPL was established to be compatible with GDPR, one of the most comprehensive data regulations worldwide. The PDPL has 43 articles that cover definitions, the law's scope of application, how it interacts with other laws' provisions, who is entitled to use personal data, how to file complaints, and the consequences of breaking the law. A summary of PDPL principles is presented below:

1. **User Consent:** Outlines that a user's personal information may not be processed, modified, or published—whether manually or automatically—without his/her consent, unless it is necessary to provide essential services or is done for legal purposes. In addition, the controller should notify any other party in case of any modifications to the transferred data.
2. **Data Collection and Processing:** Outlines that the data controller shall define the purpose for data collection, the method of data collection, and the content of the data. Unless the data is being gathered for security reasons, the user should be informed of the identity of the company collecting the data. The data shall be used only for the purposes it was initially collected for.
3. **Data Retention:** The controller must destroy the personal data as soon as the purpose of its collection ends unless certain cases allow the controller to retain the personal data.
4. **Data Protection:** Outline that personal data storage should be kept safe. The controller must protect the user's personal data when transferring them from one place to another for processing.
5. **Data Sharing:** The controller should not share, transfer, or disclose personal data to other parties, except in special circumstances allowed in the kingdom system. The data should not be disclosed or access should not be enabled to any person except in special cases allowed in the Kingdom system.
6. **Data Rectification:** The user holds the right to rectify the data held by the controller.
7. **Data Destruction:** Outlines that a user has the right to request the destruction of his/her Personal Data if it is no longer required.
8. **Data Access:** The user has the right to view and obtain a copy of the data collected by the controller.
9. **Advertisements:** The controller may not use the personal means of communication - including postal and electronic addresses - of the user to send promotional or educational materials, except if the user approves, and there is a mechanism for the user to express his/her desire to stop sending the materials to him/her.
10. **Breach Notification:** The controller must notify the competent authority and data owner as soon as it becomes aware of leakage, corruption, or illegal access to personal data.
11. **Responsibility:** Organizations are accountable for how they process data and comply with the PDPL.

3 Related Work

Privacy policies are often difficult for people to understand. Most people tend not to read it and become unaware of the many options it offers. Several studies are required to analyze privacy policies across different sectors and assess their compliance with regional laws and other criteria. Some of the studies presented below are briefly discussed.

In 2016, (Wilson et al. 2016) automated the extraction of the main details from privacy policy text. They developed a web-based annotation tool to analyze the privacy policies of websites. Subsequently, they applied machine-learning approaches and used Precision, Recall, and F1 measures to evaluate this privacy policy. They created a corpus called OPP-115, which was later used by many studies, such as (Wilson et al. 2019) and (Alabduljabbar et al. 2021).

Some studies have used specific metrics to evaluate privacy-policy compliance. (Liu et al. 2022) proposed three evaluation metrics for app privacy policy compliance: integrity, accuracy, and privacy of data collected before user consent. They created a topic-candidate title table by manually extracting some of the titles in privacy policies. They then used BERT to calculate the features of the candidate titles and privacy policy titles to be tested. After that, they designed an automatic detection scheme to dynamically analyze the app and found that from 2000 apps, 274 apps had poor privacy policies, 268 apps started to collect users' privacy data before obtaining the user's agreement, and 1131 apps did not fulfill the obligation of the consent solicitation. In addition, (Javed et al. 2020) performed a qualitative assessment of website privacy policies using a dataset of 284 websites from 10 different sectors in India, Pakistan, and Bangladesh. To check how accessible, readable, and compliant their privacy statements are with the 11 privacy principles of the GDPR. Their overall results show that the accessibility and compliance with privacy statements from the three countries are low, especially in the education, healthcare, and government sectors, with the exception of e-commerce and finance. As for readability, it appears to be quite low for websites in all 10 sectors of the three countries.

Another study analyzed the compliance of websites' privacy policies with data protection laws. (Asif et al. 2021) automated the analysis of compliance of Pakistani websites' privacy policies with the GDPR and Pakistan Data Protection Act (PPDA). They used the Privacy Checktool to analyze the privacy policy of the website. Subsequently, they applied four machine learning approaches and used accuracy measures to evaluate compliance with GDPR and PPDA, and found that the Support Vector Machine (SVM) approach had the highest accuracy, which was equal to 97.7% in determining compliance with GDPR and Pakistan Data Protection Act.

To determine whether a certain data processing agreement (DPA) complies with the GDPR, (Amaral et al. 2022) suggested an automated solution. They developed two artifacts in close collaboration with legal professionals, including a glossary table, clarifying the legal terms used in the requirements and "shall" requirements taken directly from GDPR laws that are relevant to DPA compliance. Subsequently, using natural language processing technology, they created an automated system to assess a specific DPA's compliance with the "shall" requirements. This method specifically develops automatic phrasal-level representations of the DPA's textual content and compares them to predetermined representations of the "shall" criteria. In addition to determining whether the DPA complies with the GDPR, this technique compares these two representations and provides recommendations for any information that is still missing.

Meanwhile, other studies explored the instructions of privacy-policy text and used specific approaches for labeling its content to be more readable for the user. (Bannihatti Kumar et al. 2020) developed a web browser extension called "Opt-Out Easy" to automatically detect Opt-Out choices in privacy-policy text. Opt-Out offers in privacy policies that allow users to exclude themselves from data practices such as tracking by advertising networks. They used the LR approach on a corpus of 236 websites in the United States to determine the existence of a privacy policy. In addition, to extract websites, Opt-Out hyperlinks use anchor tags and check if they have non-zero false-negative rates. Their approach achieved a precision of 0.93 and a recall of 0.9. Their results showed that the number of Opt-Out choices found in privacy policies is relatively small, and more popular websites have more Opt-Out on average. Furthermore, they conducted a usability evaluation and confirmed that Opt-Out Easy helps users easily find and access available Opt-Out choices in privacy policies and enables them to make use of these choices more effectively.

Privacy policies are important, but often not read, because of time constraints. As a result, (Wilson et al. 2019) addressed this issue by automating the annotation process with Crowdworkers and trained annotators. They found that highlighting relevant paragraphs could speed up the process without affecting accuracy. They used binary classifiers to label policy segments with information related to data practices, with results at segment level of precision 0.80, recall 0.77, and micro-F1 of 0.78 with SVMs. The results at the sentence level were slightly lower than those at the segment level.

Additionally, to facilitate the reading and understanding of privacy policies. (Alabduljabbar et al. 2021) introduced TLDR, which organizes the contents of privacy policies into nine labeled categories. The classification and labeling system makes it easier for users to concentrate on key passages and spot privacy policies' missing details. The authors intend to improve the accuracy because the previous literature falls short of high accuracy. They automated the selection of paragraphs that highlighted relevant topics and used the OPP-115 corpus. They also conducted a case study on the privacy policies of the top 10,000 websites according to Alexa and expanded their work by conducting a user study that illustrates the advantages of the policy-highlighting mechanism for the average user in terms of information reduction, reading time, and policy knowledge. The results show that TDLR reduces reading time by 39.14% and increases the understanding of privacy policies by 18.84%. Moreover, (Oltramari et al. 2018) introduced PrivOnto, a framework for the semantic web that facilitates knowledge elicitation and expresses data practices in privacy rules. This is a solution that semi-automatically extracts key phrases from privacy regulations, models their content using ontology-based representations, and then uses semantic web technologies to explore the resulting knowledge structures. The authors converted policy elements into descriptive logic statements, as it made it easier to identify contradictions and inconsistencies in privacy policies. Annotation disagreement among Crowdworkers also aids in spotting any ambiguities in the policy. The authors also intend to provide website owners with the findings of the analysis to enhance their privacy practices.

In conclusion, the ML classifier was employed in most studies, with the LR and SVM approaches demonstrating good accuracy in evaluating compliance with international data privacy rules. Additionally, they assessed how well they complied with the privacy laws of the other sectors. To the best of our knowledge, no corpus exists for Saudi websites' privacy policies, written in Arabic. Additionally, no previous study has examined Saudi websites' adherence to PDPL. Therefore, in this study, we built a corpus for Saudi website privacy policies across different sectors and evaluated their compliance with the PDPL.

4 Corpus

4.1 Corpus Collection

Privacy policies vary in length and complexity, as well as in the language used based on the category of the organization. For example, the language used in the privacy policies of government websites differs from that used in E-commerce websites. To reflect this variation, we ensured that our search covered different organizational categories. We divided the categories into seven categories that include: Government, E-commerce, Education, Healthcare, Finance, News, and Others. The Others category represents any website that does not belong to the remaining categories.

In accordance with the categories we chose, we gathered our data from a variety of sources, including the Saudi Central Bank[2] for websites related to finance, the Saudi Arabia National United Platform[3] for websites related to government, and the Council of Health Insurance[4] for websites related to healthcare. We also used Google and Wikipedia to search for general websites in Saudi Arabia. Searching by classification on Wikipedia helped us find websites and companies owned by Saudi Arabia more easily. While choosing privacy policy websites, we found that there was much irrelevant information on each webpage. Therefore, we decided to manually extract the required information. We considered collecting only the first webpage of the privacy policy on each website and discarded the following: any privacy policy written in a PDF file, any links in websites that indicated more privacy policy content, and any website where copy-text functionality was disabled.

4.2 Corpus Description

The dataset was collected in December 2022. The total number of privacy policy files collected was 1036. However, owing to certain websites' downtime and others' incorrectly stated privacy policies, we had to exclude some privacy policy websites. The final number of extracted privacy policies was 1000 files. Table 1 illustrates the category description and number of webpages collected for each category.

The final dataset consisted of 4638 lines of text. Each line was labeled with an appropriate PDPL category that is defined as shown in Fig. 1. The number of tokens was 775,370, and the size of the corpus was 8,353 KB.

---

[2] https://www.sama.gov.sa/en-us/licenseentities/pages/licensedbanks.aspx [Date Accessed 20/3/2023].

[3] https://www.my.gov.sa/wps/portal/snp/agencies/!ut/p/z0/04_Sj9CPykssy0xPLMnMz0vMAfI jo8zivQIsTAwdDQz9_d29TAwCnQ1DjUy9wgwMgk31g1Pz9AuyHRUBX96rjw!!/ [Date Accessed 20/3/2023].

[4] https://chi.gov.sa/en/insurancecompanies/pages/default.aspx [Date Accessed 20/3/2023].

Table 1. Category Description and number of websites for each category

Category	Description	File Number
News	Contains News, Magazines, etc.	19
Healthcare	Contains Hospitals, Charites, Clinics, etc.	27
Educational	Contains Collages, Institutes, Universities, etc.	42
Finance	Contains Banks and anything related to finance	52
Government	Contains Government entities and anything related to this aspect with (gov) extension	80
Other	Contains any website that does not belong to the remaining categories	155
E-commerce	Contains anything related to commercial transactions	625
Total		**1000**

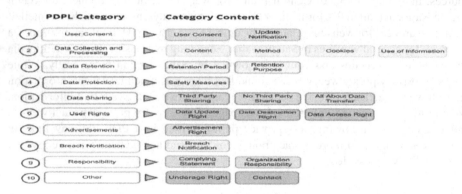

Fig. 1. Annotation Category

4.3 Corpus Annotation

The PDPL principles were summarized into 10 categories numbered from 1–10 for annotation purposes. An explanation of the annotation categories is shown in Fig. 1. Each category represents a PDPL principle we defined in our summary; however, category 10 represents principles mentioned on the collected websites but are not included in our summary, such as contact information and underage rights. Right next to the PDPL categories are the category content specified for each category. We used Microsoft Excel as our annotation tool to annotate the policy text with the policy number assigned to it and saved it in a CSV file format.

4.3.1 Annotation Recruitment Criteria

To ensure the reliability of the findings, the annotation procedure was carried out by the authors, who hold Bachelor's degrees in the field of Information Technology, with a native Arabic language background, and a strong understanding of privacy policies. Each annotator annotated 333 policies by assigning the appropriate label to each sentence or paragraph. To ensure annotation accuracy, all authors participated in the process, adhering to a comprehensive set of guidelines with examples. A two-step validation, involving double-checking by another author and group discussion, resolved discrepancies and reached a consensus on the final annotation.

4.3.2 Annotation Quality

Annotation Quality The distribution of work was carried out among the annotators in such a way that each one was assigned specific websites to annotate. Table 2 shows the intersection files between every two annotators. The total number of intersectional files was 302. They were used to compute the Inter Annotator Agreement (IAA) to measure the understanding between the annotators and how well their annotations were consistent. Cohen's kappa is a commonly used measure of inter-annotator agreement (IAA) that takes into account the possibility of agreement occurring by chance. It is often used to evaluate the quality of annotations in natural language processing and machine learning tasks (Cohen 1960).

Table 2. Annotation Files Distribution

Intersection	Annotator1	Annotator2	Annotator3
Intersection 1 (103)	Finance (1–52) E-Commerce (1–51)		
Intersection 2 (96)		Government (1–50) Healthcare (1–27) News (1–19)	
Intersection 3 (103)	Educational (1–23) Other (1–80)		Educational (1–23) Other (1–80)

Table 3 illustrates the results of IAA, Cohen Kappa has been used to measure the agreement between each two annotators. The results showed almost perfect agreement between every two annotators, Annotator-1 & Annotator-2, Annotator-1 & Annotator-3, and Annotator-2 & Annotator-3, with an average of 95%, 96%, and 95%, respectively.

Table 3. Cohen Kappa Result

Category	Annotators Agreement		
	Annotator1 & Annotator2	Annotator1 & Annotator3	Annotator2 & Annotator3
Finance	0.96		
E-commerce	0.94		
Government		0.92	
News		0.98	
Healthcare		0.98	
Educational			0.94
Other			0.97
Average	0.95	0.96	0.95

4.4 Corpus Preprocessing

4.4.1 Data Cleaning

To prepare the text for analysis, we followed a series of steps. First, we manually extracted the relevant information from the text file while eliminating any unnecessary details such as introductions and contact information. Additionally, we removed hyperlinks through a copy/paste operation.

Then, we combined all privacy policy files into a single CSV file and began cleaning the data. For each line in the policy, we manually removed Arabic numbers using the following sequence:

اولا, ثانيا, ثالثا, رابعا, خامسا, سادسا, سابعا, ثامنا, تاسعا, عاشرا, حادي عشر, ثاني عشر, ثالث عشر,)
رابع عشر), as well as the numbers (١, ٢, ٣, ٤, ٥, ٦, ٧, ٨, ٩).

To further clean the data, we used regular expressions in Python to remove Arabic diacritics and extracted any English letters, symbols, and numbers. Finally, we removed any blank lines, blank rows, and multiple spaces within each cell.

4.4.2 Data Normalization

To obtain a homogeneous format, we performed the following processes on the dataset:

(1) Normalization: we normalized the following:

   i.   [إ آ أ ا] ⟶ [ا]

   ii. [ؤ و] ⟶ [و]

   iii. [ئ ى] ⟶ [ي]

   iv. [ة] ⟶ [ه]

   v.   Tashkeel removal

   vi. Tatweel removal

(2) Tokenization: The words in each policy line were separated into different tokens based on whitespaces using a Whitespace Tokenizer.

We investigated the use of stop word removal. However, we found that this removes the negation letters in Arabic, which in turn changes the context of the privacy-policy text and loses its significant meaning. Therefore, we decided not to use stop word removal in this study. As a result, we found that the corpus contained 775,370 tokens. The size of the corpus equals 8,353 KB.

5 Experimental Results

Our project classifies the content of privacy policies into a multiclass classification of 10 categories to determine whether it complies with the PDPL principles. To accomplish this, we trained different classification models on our multiclass corpus, which had an unequal distribution of categories data. In the process of training the models, the dataset was divided into two parts: the first 80% was used for training and the remaining 20% was used for testing. Accordingly, our corpus of size 4638 was split into subsets of 3710 for training and 928 for testing. In our situation where data is imbalanced, the micro-average F1 score is a suitable evaluation metric as it consolidates the performance of each class, giving greater emphasis to the performance of the minority classes. This is particularly necessary in cases where the dataset exhibits a significant imbalance in the distribution of its categories.

5.1 Model Selection

Although some studies have suggested that Naive Bayes (NB) can be a good starting point for text classification problems because of its ease of use and effectiveness in handling smaller datasets, we found that LR performed better in our case. Some studies have also used LR as a baseline for text classification problems, such as (Wilson et al. 2019), (Bannihatti Kumar et al. 2020) and (Wilson et al. 2016). Hence, we decided to choose LR to be our baseline model. In addition, a range of ML and DL models including NB, SVM, FFNN, and LSTM were used in our experiments. Furthermore, the BERT-based models: ARABERT, MARBERT, and CamelBERT were also used. These three models are based on the BERT architecture but are adapted to the specific characteristics and challenges of the Arabic language and its varieties. They are trained on large collections of Arabic text from different sources and domains and achieve state-of-the-art results on various Arabic natural language understanding tasks.

5.2 Corpus Evaluation

We evaluated the results of using TF-IDF and Word2Vec for Word Embedding before applying ML classifiers and used Tokenizer along with One Hot Encoding for LSTM. We also used TF-IDF for FFNN and applied One Hot Encoding to only (y) label data, to solve the issue of one-to-one mapping between (x) and (y) that could not be established while computing the neural network. Additionally, according to (Mikolov et al. 2013), the SkipGram approach in the Word2Vec model demonstrates good results when applied to smaller corpora compared to the Common Bag of Words (CBOW). Consequently, we decided to utilize the SkipGram method to attain better performance with our small corpus, which has only 4638 privacy policy lines.

Next, to prevent overfitting during the evaluation and validation phases, the initial dataset was divided into two parts: 80% for training and 20% for testing, with a random state value of 62 for ML modes and a value of 52 for DL models. To assess the performance of each classifier, we used a confusion matrix to display a summary of the correct and incorrect predictions. Afterward, we computed various evaluation metrics to measure the quality of the model, including the micro-average of Recall, Precision, and F1 score. We organized our analysis results into three parts: Summary of All Classifiers Comparison, ML Comparison with TF-IDF & Word2Vec, and Deep Learning Comparison.

5.2.1 Summary of All Classifier

Table 4 presents a summary of the results of all models across various vectorizers. The evaluation metrics used for the analysis included micro-average Recall, Precision, and F1 score. When comparing the ML models, both the LR and SVM models showed similar performance when using both vectorizers. However, the NB model outperformed the Word2Vec Vectorizer with a score of 0.82 for all metrics, while the TF-IDF Vectorizer had a score of 0.72. In general, Word2Vec produced better results for most ML models. Furthermore, the SVM model had the highest micro-average score 0.91 for all metrics when using Word2Vec. In the Neural Network comparison, the FFNN model performed better than the LSTM model in all metrics. In contrast, the ARABERT, MARBERT, and CamelBERT models demonstrated better performance than both the LTSM and FFNN models in all metrics except for precision, where the FFNN had a score of 0.96 and the BERT models had a score of 0.93.

Table 4. Classifiers Comparison

Classifier	Vectorizer	Model	F1-score	Recall	Precision
Machine Learning	TF-IDF	NB	0.72	0.72	0.72
		LR	0.90	0.90	0.90
		SVM	0.90	0.90	0.90
	Word2Vec	NB	0.82	0.82	0.82
		LR	0.89	0.89	0.89
		SVM	0.91	0.91	0.91
Neural Network	TF-IDF	FFNN	0.90	0.85	0.96
	Tokenizer & One Hot Encoding	LSTM	0.80	0.76	0.85
Transformers	Tokenizer	ARABERT	0.93	0.932	0.93
		MARBERT	0.93	0.933	0.93
		CamelBERT	0.93	0.933	0.93

5.2.2 ML Comparison with TF-IDF and Word2Vec

Figure 3 shows the Confusion Matrix for the three ML models (Naive Bayes, Logistic Regression, and SVM) using both TF-IDF and Word2Vec vectorizers. The x-axis represents the actual correct PDPL categories, whereas the y-axis represents all the predicted PDPL categories. The numbers along the diagonal show the accurate True values for each PDPL category. As shown in Fig. 3, the majority of the data in all models using both vectorizers (TF-IDF and Word2Vec) were located along the diagonal, indicating that the values were correctly predicted, while the number of errors or incorrect predictions was low.

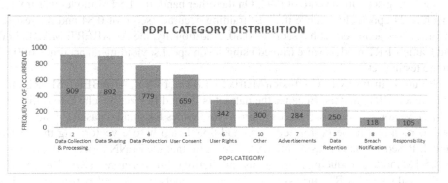

Fig. 2. PDPL Categories Distribution

Among the models tested, the Naïve-based model had the highest level of confusion. This model produced the poorest outcome when using the TF-IDF vectorizer and was the only model that did not consider all the PDPL categories in the test set, where the value of category 8 on the diagonal was zero because of the imbalanced data, as demonstrated in Fig. 2.

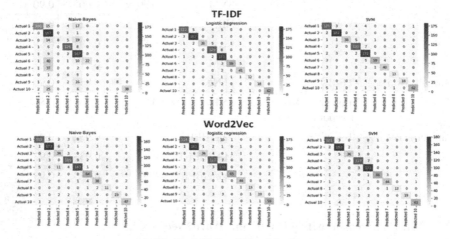

Fig. 3. ML Confusion Matrix

5.2.3 Deep Learning Comparison

We trained the dataset on five Deep Learning models: LSTM, FFNN, ARABERT, MAR-BERT, and CamelBERT. The model was trained with FFNN using seven epochs, achieving high accuracy on the training set with a score of 0.98, and achieving high accuracy on the testing set with a score of 0.92. On the other hand, the LSTM model was trained for up to 24 epochs to achieve the best training accuracy score of 0.84 and the test set accuracy was achieved with a score of 0.80. Additionally, the ARABERT, MARBERT, and CamelBERT models were trained using seven epochs, yielding an accuracy of 0.93 on the testing set.

Figure 4 illustrates the Confusion Matrix for LSTM, FFNN, ARABERT, MARBERT, and CamelBERT models. Because the dataset is limited in size, we chose to utilize the TF-IDF vectorizer because it yields improved outcomes for small datasets. Nonetheless, tokenization had to be performed as an additional step before vectorizing the LSTM model. Based on the confusion matrix, it is evident that the FFNN model outperformed the LSTM model, producing more precise predictions. Furthermore, ARABERT, MAR-BERT, and CamelBERT surpassed all the other models in terms of performance. The performance of the three variants of BERT was quite similar. However, CamelBERT and MARBERT performed slightly better than the other models. It should be noted that the FFNN had difficulty predicting classes 8 and 9, which can be attributed to imbalanced data, as demonstrated in Fig. 2.

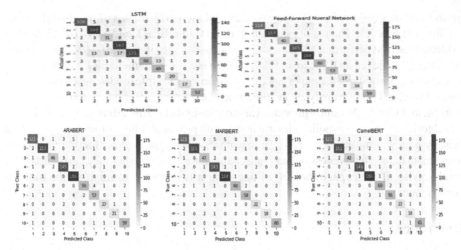

Fig. 4. LSTM, FFNN, ARABERT, MARBERT and CamelBERT models Confusion Matrix

6 Discussion

We compared the use of two word embedding (TF-IDF and Word2Vec) techniques with ML models and concluded that the Word2Vec technique had better results, particularly with SVM. Furthermore, we evaluated five different DL models, namely FFNN, LSTM, ARABERT, MARBERT, and CamelBERT, and found that CamelBERT and MARBERT performed better than the other models. Based on our analysis, we conclude that transformers trained specifically in Modern Standard Arabic (MSA) are more suitable for our dataset. The CamelBERT and MARBERT models achieved the highest score among the neural networks, with a micro-average F1 score of 0.933, indicating that they are the most appropriate models for our data. The ARABERT model exhibited a similar performance, with a micro-average F1 score of 0.932. Hence, we can conclude that BERT models are suitable for our problem due to their comparable performance.

All models had a low number of test samples in categories 8 and 9, as indicated by the confusion matrix in the previous section because our dataset was imbalanced, that is, the categories in the dataset were not distributed equally. The number of records in each category also impacted the Confusion Matrix results for all classifiers. Specifically, the Data Collection & Processing category contained 909 records, while the Responsibility category had only 105 records. As a result, the Confusion Matrix indicated that the Data Detection & Processing and Data Sharing categories were the most compliant with the PDPL.

7 Conclusion

In conclusion, we propose the task of categorizing privacy policies into ten categories based on PDPL principles. We manually extracted a dataset of 1000 Saudi websites from seven sectors and annotated them. After that, we trained eight different models belonging to ML, DL, and Transformers classifiers on a multiclass dataset consisting of 4638 privacy policy lines. Then, we evaluated the performance of the models based on different metrics. The results showed that the CamelBERT and MARBERT models exhibited the best performance, achieving a micro-average F1 score of 0.933. In addition, ARABERT achieved an F1 score of 0.932, which is close to CamelBERT's performance. These findings highlight the importance of considering multiple models when conducting multiclass classification analyses and the value of exploring different approaches to solve a problem. Overall, this study provides valuable insights into the effective use of ML and DL algorithms in privacy policy classification, with practical implications for automating privacy policy compliance analysis. In the future, we might explore alternative models to evaluate their effectiveness on our dataset and determine whether they can yield better results. Also, if we expand the size of our data, it is expected to improve the model's performance.

References

Alabduljabbar, A., Abusnaina, A., Meteriz-Yildiran, Ü., Mohaisen, D.: TLDR: deep learning-based automated privacy policy annotation with key policy highlights. In: Proceedings of the 20th Workshop on Workshop on Privacy in the Electronic Society, pp. 103–118 (2021). https://doi.org/10.1145/3463676.3485608

Amaral, O., Azeem, M.I., Abualhaija, S., Briand, L.C.: NLP-based automated compliance checking of data processing agreements against GDPR. arXiv http://arxiv.org/abs/2209.09722 (2022)

Asif, M., Javed, Y., Hussain, M.: Automated analysis of Pakistani websites' compliance with GDPR and Pakistan data protection act. In: 2021 International Conference on Frontiers of Information Technology (FIT), pp. 234–239 (2021). https://doi.org/10.1109/FIT53504.2021.00051

Bannihatti Kumar, V., et al.: Finding a choice in a haystack: automatic extraction of opt-out statements from privacy policy text. In: Proceedings of the Web Conference, pp. 1943–1954 (2020). https://doi.org/10.1145/3366423.3380262

Cohen, J.: A coefficient of agreement for nominal scales. Educ. Psychol. Measur. 20(1), 37–46 (1960). https://doi.org/10.1177/001316446002000104

Javed, Y., Salehin, K.M., Shehab, M.: A study of south asian websites on privacy compliance. IEEE Access 8, 156067–156083 (2020). https://doi.org/10.1109/ACCESS.2020.3019334

Kablawi, B.: Preparing Organizations for Saudi Arabia's New Data Protection Law. ISACA Industry News, pp. 1–5 (2022)

Liu, K., Xu, G., Zhang, X., Xu, G., Zhao, Z.: Evaluating the privacy policy of Android apps: a privacy policy compliance study for popular apps in China and Europe. Sci. Program. 2022, e2508690 (2022). https://doi.org/10.1155/2022/2508690

Mikolov, T., Sutskever, I., Chen, K., Corrado, G., Dean, J.: Distributed Representations of Words and Phrases and their Compositionality (2013). https://doi.org/10.48550/arXiv.1310.4546

Oltramari, A., et al.: PrivOnto: a semantic framework for the analysis of privacy policies. Semant. Web 9(2), 185–203 (2018). https://doi.org/10.3233/SW-170283

Wilson, S., et al.: The creation and analysis of a website privacy policy corpus. In: Proceedings of the 54th Annual Meeting of the Association for Computational Linguistics (Volume 1: Long Papers), pp. 1330–1340 (2016). https://doi.org/10.18653/v1/P16-1126

Wilson, S., et al.: Analyzing privacy policies at scale: from crowdsourcing to automated annotations. ACM Trans. Web 13(1), 1–29 (2019). https://doi.org/10.1145/3230665

Xu, L.: PIPEDA: Personal Information Protection and Electronic Documents Act. Termly (2021). https://termly.io/resources/articles/pipeda/

SmartEDU: Accelerating Slide Deck Production with Natural Language Processing

Maria João Costa[1]([✉])[iD], Hugo Amaro[1][iD], and Hugo Gonçalo Oliveira[2][iD]

[1] LIS, Instituto Pedro Nunes, Coimbra, Portugal
{mcosta,hamaro}@ipn.pt
[2] CISUC, DEI, University of Coimbra, Coimbra, Portugal
hroliv@dei.uc.pt

Abstract. Slide decks are a common medium for presenting a topic. To reduce the time required for their preparation, we present SmartEDU, a platform for drafting slides for a textual document, and the research that lead to its development. Drafts are Powerpoint files generated in three steps: pre-processing, for acquiring or discovering section titles; summarization, for compressing the contents of each section; slide composition, for organizing the summaries into slides. The resulting file may be further edited by the user. Several summarization methods were experimented in public datasets of presentations and in Wikipedia articles. Based on automatic evaluation measures and collected human opinions, we conclude that a Distillbart model is preferred to unsupervised summarization, especially when it comes to overall draft quality.

Keywords: Slide Generation · Automatic Summarization · Applied Natural Language Processing

1 Introduction

Slide decks are a widespread means for presenting information while supporting, for instance, oral presentations on any topic and in a variety of contexts (e.g., conferences, classrooms). While there is a good, widely used selection of tools to create slideshows, like Microsoft PowerPoint[1], Prezi[2], etc., they only help in making aesthetically appealing slides with the use of themes or templates, whereas adding contents is up to the author of the presentation. On the other hand, tools for the automatic generation of the slides' textual content are still in their infancy, also due to the task's complexity. In fact, accurately condensing and summarizing textual information while preserving key details and ensuring a coherent flow within the slides remains a significant challenge.

This paper presents SmartEDU, a platform for accelerating the process of producing slide decks, which leverages on Natural Language Processing (NLP)

---

[1] https://www.microsoft.com/microsoft-365/powerpoint.
[2] https://prezi.com.

© The Author(s), under exclusive license to Springer Nature Switzerland AG 2023
E. Métais et al. (Eds.): NLDB 2023, LNCS 13913, pp. 109–123, 2023.
https://doi.org/10.1007/978-3-031-35320-8_8

for creating presentation drafts. Besides being heavily based on automatic summarization, the platform further exploits methods for section discovery, title generation, and keyword extraction. The work was developed in collaboration with MindFlow[3], a company specialized in organizational and human resource development, behavioral and professional training. Given that slide decks are a key medium for the previous actions, optimizing the time required for their preparation is of uttermost importance for the company.

Powerpoint drafts are created from textual documents, either unstructured or organized in sections. Text is summarized and resulting sentences are distributed to different slides, according to their sections in the original document. The resulting draft can be used as the starting point of a presentation, hopefully saving much time. This process, however, does not dismiss the human role when it comes to finalizing the presentation, which may involve reviewing the slides, making necessary adaptations, and adding additional components, like images. For this manual part of the process, SmartEDU further suggests relevant images, either taken from the original document or retrieved from the Web.

Besides an overview of SmartEDU, experiments are reported, for conclusions on available options for summarization and on the value of the resulting drafts. Several methods for automatic summarization were assessed in the context of slide generation, covering two types of summarization (extractive and abstractive) and different approaches, namely: unsupervised, rarely used in this context; supervised in similar data as the testing data; and state-of-the-art methods based on transformers, fine-tuned in well-known summarization datasets.

The most promising methods, including two unsupervised (TextRank, QueSTS) and one based on transformers (Distillbart) were then used for producing drafts for Wikipedia articles, later were assessed by human judges. The main conclusions were that the generated drafts capture relevant information, which is well organized, and can indeed be a good starting point for creating slide decks. However, the overall quality of the drafts based on Distillbart was better than those by unsupervised methods.

The remainder of this paper is structured as follows: Sect. 2 reviews previous work on slide generation; Sect. 3 overviews the adopted approach; Sect. 4 describes the performed experiments; Sect. 5 concludes the paper.

2   Related Work

In order to create presentation slides, most researchers follow two main steps: automatic summarization and slide generation. The former is often the primary focus, and generally applies extractive summarization. Moreover, most researchers test the proposed techniques in scientific articles and their slides.

Initial approaches [8,25,30] relied on discourse structures in the source text for organizing information in slides. Slides were created for discovered topics and included related sentences [30].

---

[3] https://mindflow.pt/.

Document structures were represented as graphs of sentences of the source document [27,28], or of textual and image components [8], linked according to their semantic similarity. An alternative was to use ontologies [15,18], which allowed to score sentences according to their position, centrality, number of noun phrases, number of keywords, and semantic links between their keywords and keywords in other sentences.

Slides are often organized in bullet points [11,15,18,25], with the main topics [25] or key phrases [11,21] in the top level, and other relevant sentences in the second level. The discourse structure may help when grouping components in slides [8]. Highest ranking sentences can be converted to a Subject-Verb-Object format and, based on used keywords, further organized into Definition, Types, Examples, Advantages and Disadvantages [15].

When available, section titles in the source document can be used as slide titles [11,28]. Alternatively, slide titles may be obtained from nouns with most semantic connections to other used nouns [15] or from domain concepts [18].

The QueSTS system [27,28] summarizes text based on queries (i.e., key phrases) that will return the relevant information from a graph. When creating slides from a source scientific paper, different queries are used for different sections. For instance, for the Introduction, similarities are computed between each sentence and sentences in the abstract, whereas for the Related work, it is computed between sentences in the Introduction and cite tags.

In the scope of slide generation, a common approach for summarization is supervised machine learning, in particular with Support Vector Regression (SVR). Support Vector Regression (SVR) [1,11,24]. From source documents and reference slide decks, a model is learned for scoring sentences in the source text according to their importance, considering a broad range features (e.g., position, length, word overlap) [11] or just word overlap and sentence position [24].

The previous methods focus on summarizing the whole document at once. An alternative [13] is to define a set of common topics in scientific papers (e.g., contributions, model design, experimentation, future work) and search the source document for the most relevant sentences for each. Each topic and its respective sentences result in a slide.

A limitation of extractive summarization is that it is not possible to derail from the sentences in the source document. A shortcut to avoid the previous is to run a paraphraser on the extractive summary, hopefully resulting in different words than in the original text [6]. But the alternative is to explore abstractive summarization, which has also been used for slide generation [29]. Initially, the user provides slide titles, for which relevant sections of the source document are retrieved. The title is then transformed to a question and given to a question answering model, which returns an answer used as the slide context.

3   Approach

The goal of SmartEDU is to reduce the necessary time for producing slide decks from any textual document. Slide drafts are generated in three steps, as depicted in Fig. 1: Pre-processing, Automatic Summarization, and Slide Composition.

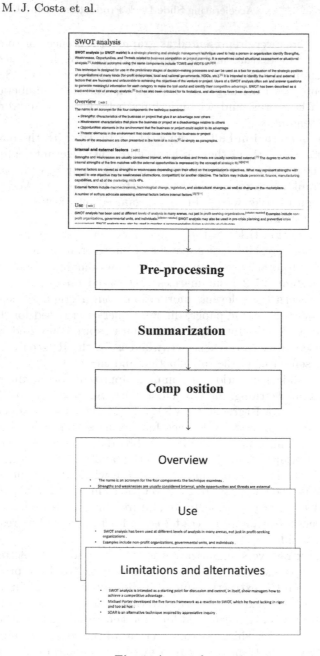

Fig. 1. Approach overview.

The source document can be in raw text or PDF, and structured or not. For the later, no preprocessing is required before the Summarization step. But, when possible, the main title, section titles and images are extracted from structured documents, due to their utility for the slide creation process.

If documents are in PDF, text needs to be first extracted. The document is first converted to XML-TEI, where all the sections are represented, separated by their respective headers. GROBID[4], a library for parsing and re-structuring documents, is used for this. It suits better for English scientific papers, but can be used for transforming any PDF, regardless of its type or language. Once the document is in TEI, titles and text are extracted. Images are extracted with two additional libraries: PyMuPDF[5] and Pillow[6]. The former is for extracting images from PDFs, and the latter for processing and and storing them.

As the name suggests, the goal of the Summarization step is to reduce the text of the document to its most relevant parts. Summarization can either be extractive (i.e., by selecting the most relevant sentences without adding new words or changing the phrase structure), or abstractive (i.e., the source text can be paraphrased). In addition to the types of summarization, methods can be unsupervised (i.e., no training is required), or supervised (i.e., training in datasets of documents and their summaries is required). Despite not completely adapted to the goal, unsupervised methods can be advantageous, since they allow us to summarize any text, regardless of the type or language. Nevertheless, when data is not available, supervised models, even if trained other types of text, can also be tested at a low cost.

The Composition step completes the pipeline by organizing the sentences of the summaries into slides. Two methods were tested for this: one for structured and another for unstructured documents.

For structured documents, section titles are used as slide titles. For unstructured text, possible sections for each sentence are discovered with topic modeling. This is performed with Latent Dirichlet Allocation (LDA) [2], with n topics (empirically set as $n = 5\%$ of the number of tokens). Since discovered sections will not have titles, a model can be trained for that, e.g., using sections of scientific or Wikipedia articles and their sections.

If sentences are organized in sections, sections can be summarized independently, with each summary added to its respective slide.

The result of SmartEDU is the draft of a presentation, which, in most cases, will not be completely ready. After the automatic pipeline, the draft can be manually edited by the user, who may additionally add non-textual components, such as images. When the input is structured, its original images are made available for inclusion anywhere in the presentation. Moreover, a tool was included for searching the Web for images potentially related to the content of the slides. It relies on keywords and named entities extracted from each slide, respectively with the help of KeyBERT [7] and of spaCy[7]. For each keyword, images are retrieved with the Bing crawler[8], and the top public domain images are suggested.

---

[4] https://github.com/kermitt2/grobid.
[5] https://github.com/pymupdf/PyMuPDF.
[6] https://python-pillow.org/.
[7] https://spacy.io/.
[8] https://github.com/kermitt2/grobid.

4   Experimentation

Different summarization methods and approaches for slide composition fit the proposed approach. This section reports on experiments performed in order to take conclusions on the suitability of the previous, hopefully reducing the number of options.

4.1   Summarization

Several options were compared for summarization, namely: unsupervised extractive methods (LexRank [5], TextRank [16], TF-IDF weighting, QueSTS [27], LSA [4], Lexical Chains (LC) [23] using the Open Multilingual WordNet [3]); a supervised extractive method (SVR [11]); and supervised methods for abstractive summarization, all based on the transformer architecture (Distillbart [26], Pegasus [31], Multilingual-T5 [9]). QueSTS, TF-IDF, and SVR were selected due to their previous utilization in automatic slide generation [1,11,27]. The others were included due to their popularity in the context of automatic text summarization.

The only parameter of the unsupervised methods was a compression rate or equivalent, which we empirically set to 10%. SVR was trained on the used datasets and the transformer-based models were used from HuggingFace. Distillbart[9] and Pegasus[10] are fine-tuned on the CNN/DailyMail dataset [10,19], which covers news stories and their summaries. For non-English languages, the Multilingual-T5 (mT5)[11] was used instead. It is pretrained on a variant of the C4 dataset [17] (mC4, available in 101 languages), and then fine-tuned in the XLSum [9] dataset, which has article-summary pairs from BBC, in 45 different languages.

Even though transformers achieve the state-of-the-art in several NLP tasks, they are only able to summarize short texts (e.g., as in the CNN/DailyMail dataset). When input text is too large, it has to be trimmed, and only the first part is summarized. To avoid this, when using these models, each section or topic is summarized individually, and then concatenated to form the final summary.

Summarizing Scientific Papers. Most of the explored methods have been extensively used in automatic summarization tasks, but not so much for slide generation. To test them in this specific use case, we identified two datasets of scientific papers, in English, and their slides, produced by humans, namely PS5K [20] and SciDuet [29]. Included papers are in the fields of Computer and Information Science, Machine Learning, Neural Information Processing Systems, and Computational Linguistics. SciDuet has 952-55-81 paper-slide pairs in the Train-Dev-Test split, while PS5K has 4000-250-250.

In the first experiment, the text of each paper was summarized with each method, and the text of the resulting summaries was evaluated against the text

---

[9] https://huggingface.co/sshleifer/distilbart-cnn-12-6.
[10] https://huggingface.co/google/pegasus-cnn_dailymail.
[11] https://huggingface.co/csebuetnlp/mT5_multilingual_XLSum.

of the slides of the paper, using typical metrics for evaluating computer-generated summaries, namely: three variations of ROUGE [14] (1, 2, and Longest Common Subsequence); BERTScore [32], and BLEURT [22]. The latter are motivated by the underlying limitation of ROUGE, which only considers overlaps in the surface text (n-grams), whereas BERTScore and BLEURT consider semantic similarity, computed with the help of a BERT model[12].

Tables 1 and 2 report the performance of the tested methods in the two datasets, respectively PS5K and SciDuet.

Table 1. Evaluation scores in PS5K.

Method	ROUGE-1	ROUGE-2	ROUGE-L	BERTScore	BLEURT
TF-IDF	0.233	0.052	0.212	−0.231	0.254
TextRank	0.255	**0.062**	**0.247**	**−0.202**	**0.287**
QueSTS	0.246	0.048	0.227	−0.236	0.268
LexRank	0.253	0.060	0.233	−0.218	0.286
LSA	0.260	0.049	0.235	−0.227	0.272
LC	0.236	**0.062**	0.220	−0.208	0.283
SVR	0.260	0.054	0.237	−0.232	0.247
Pegasus	**0.262**	0.052	0.239	−0.247	0.244
Distilbart	0.249	0.054	0.227	−0.252	0.239

Table 2. Evaluation scores in SciDuet.

Method	ROUGE-1	ROUGE-2	ROUGE-L	BERTScore	BLEURT
TF-IDF	0.196	0.020	0.181	−0.306	0.203
TextRank	0.192	0.018	0.177	−0.361	0.221
QueSTS	0.194	0.022	0.182	−0.305	0.220
LexRank	0.195	0.019	0.181	−0.312	0.222
LSA	0.185	0.013	0.168	−0.298	0.202
LC	0.182	0.020	0.170	−0.294	0.213
SVR	0.185	0.016	0.169	−0.315	0.196
Pegasus	0.308	0.075	**0.276**	−0.174	0.217
Distilbart	**0.310**	**0.078**	**0.276**	**−0.167**	**0.227**

Even if TextRank performs best in four out of five metrics in PS5K, differences between methods are low in this dataset. ROUGE-1 and 2 scores are all below the best supervised method reported for PS5K in related work [20], respectively 0.48 and 0.12. For ROUGE-L, however, the best score was 0.238, in line with our SVR (0.237) and LSA (0.235), and outperformed by TextRank (0.247) and Pegasus (0.239).

---

[12] For English, `roberta-large`; for other languages, `bert-base-multilingual-cased`.

The situation is much different in SciDuet, where the best performing methods are clearly the abstractive, specifically Distillbart. This happens despite the used transformers being fine-tuned in shorter texts in a different domain (news), but may benefit from the option of summarizing each section individually. Otherwise, these models would not be useful, because scientific papers are much longer than the maximum input size for transformers. In related work [29], the best reported ROUGE-1, ROUGE-2, ROUGE-L scores are respectively 0.20, 0.05, 0.19, which Distillbart and Pegasus improve.

Overall, results are inconclusive. Scores in PS5K suggest that all methods would lead to similar results, but performance in SciDuet was clearly improved with more recent methods. This shows that the selection of the best method is highly dependent on the data, which adds to the underlying subjectivity of evaluating summaries. Furthermore, even though these datasets provided valuable resources for evaluating the methods, the limited number of datasets used in this study is a notable constraint. It is crucial to expand the availability of diverse datasets to facilitate more comprehensive evaluations and enable the development of more robust and generalizable slide generation techniques. Next section describes a more restricted evaluation in a different kind of data, Wikipedia articles.

Summarizing Wikipedia Articles. The previous experiment targeted scientific papers because we could not find other datasets of documents and their slides. However, scientific papers are a very specific kind of text, on which our evaluation should not rely exclusively.

Therefore, in addition to PS5K and SciDuet, we created a small dataset with the English and the Portuguese versions of ten Wikipedia articles[13]. These were split into: gold summary (initial section) and text (remainder of the article). Besides enabling experimentation in other languages, our intuition is that Wikipedia articles are more straightforward to read, and possibly closer to most documents of the company we are collaborating with.

Tables 3 and 4 show the scores of the algorithms, respectively for English and Portuguese. SVR was not tested because training would require the collection of additional articles; and we recall that, for Portuguese, mT5 was used instead of Distillbart and Pegasus. We stress the low effort of applying unsupervised algorithms to different languages.

In line with the results of SciDuet, Distillbart was again the best performing method for English. LC was the best unsupervised method. For Portuguese, however, results are inconclusive. LSA has the best ROUGE-1 and L, LexRank the best ROUGE-2, QueSTS the best BERTScore, and mT5 the best BLEURT. Despite being the most recent method, mT5 might have suffered from being multilingual, also suggesting that unsupervised methods are preferable when no language-specific supervised model is available. Results suggest that, in the tested scenario, LSA is a suitable option.

---

[13] Carnation_Revolution, Cristiano_Ronaldo, Coimbra, Europe, Luís_de_Camões, Programming_language, Pythagorean_theorem, University_of_Coimbra, Queen_ (band), Star_Wars.

Table 3. Evaluation scores in the English Wikipedia dataset.

Method	ROUGE-1	ROUGE-2	ROUGE-L	BERTScore	BLEURT
TF-IDF	0.189	0.056	0.118	−0.092	0.293
TextRank	0.184	0.059	0.117	−0.097	0.307
QueSTS	0.309	0.076	0.199	−0.089	0.315
LexRank	0.230	0.067	0.143	−0.080	0.307
LSA	0.291	0.056	0.170	−0.113	0.291
LC	0.243	**0.111**	0.174	−0.080	**0.320**
Pegasus	0.329	0.083	0.209	−0.074	0.264
Distillbart	**0.344**	0.087	**0.212**	**−0.070**	0.263

Table 4. Evaluation scores in the Portuguese Wikipedia.

Method	ROUGE-1	ROUGE-2	ROUGE-L	BERTScore	BLEURT
TF-IDF	0.266	0.062	0.155	0.144	−0.134
TextRank	0.278	0.074	0.160	0.159	−0.101
QueSTS	0.299	0.071	0.179	**0.195**	−0.122
LexRank	0.313	**0.080**	0.181	−0.105	−0.126
LSA	**0.333**	0.058	**0.185**	0.131	−0.131
LC	0.208	0.050	0.151	0.050	−0.107
Multilingual	0.236	0.064	0.174	0.062	**−0.052**

4.2   Slide Composition

The previous sections reported on the automatic evaluation of summaries, even if some were used slides as the reference. This helped reducing the range of available options, but our final goal is to produce slide presentations, which are even more subjective to evaluate. For the final evaluation, we resorted to human opinions on the drafts generated in the Slide Composition step.

We focused on English, for being the highest-resourced language, where summarization results were better, and selected six Wikipedia articles on topics well-known to the group of volunteers involved in the evaluation ("Coimbra", "Europe", "Queen", "Carnation Revolution", "Cristiano Ronaldo", and "Star Wars"). For each article, slide drafts were produced with three different summarization methods (TextRank, QueSTS, Distillbart). In Appendix A, Fig. 5 has a draft made with TextRank for the "Europe" article.

A questionnaire was created for each article and included the three drafts and a set of five questions for each. A link to the source article was provided, but the method for producing each draft was not revealed. The selection of questions aimed at evaluating the application and covered five relevant aspects: quantity (*I am satisfied with the amount of information*), relevance (*I am satisfied with the relevance of the information*), organization (*I am satisfied with how information is organized*); overall quality (*I am satisfied with overall quality of the presentation*), starting point (*The draft is a good starting point for preparing the presentation*). Each question was answered with the following scale: strongly disagree (SD), disagree (D), agree (A), and strongly agree (SA).

We collected the opinions of 30 volunteers on the drafts of each article, which is relatively small. While their feedback provided valuable insights, the limited sample size may not fully represent the diversity of perspectives and preferences that exist among potential users or audiences.

Table 5 has the distribution of the participants answers, followed by the statistical mode (Mo).

Table 5. Compendium of all the human evaluation results.

Method	Quantity					Relevance					Organization				
	SD	D	A	SA	Mo	SD	D	A	SA	Mo	SD	D	A	SA	Mo
TextRank	1	10	12	7	A	2	9	10	9	A	2	4	13	11	SA
QueSTS	5	15	8	2	D	1	9	18	2	A	0	8	8	14	SA
Distillbart	0	6	17	7	A	0	4	15	11	A	0	0	9	21	SA

Method	Quality					Starting Point				
	SD	D	A	Mo	SA	SD	D	A	SA	Mo
TextRank	1	14	7	8	D	1	6	11	12	SA
QueSTS	3	14	8	5	D	1	10	15	4	A
Distillbart	1	6	15	8	A	0	2	13	15	SA

In line with the results of the Summarization step, the best opinions were on drafts by Distillbart. TextRank follows, but is especially worse when it comes to the overall quality. The preference of Distillbart over TextRank might be due to its shorter sentences, which are more suitable for slides. QueSTS as shorter summaries, which might result from a significant cut on relevant information. In Appendix A, Fig. 3 has a draft by Distillbart.

All evaluated drafts took advantage of the section titles in the source articles. When structure is not available, sections are discovered with topic modelling. This was not evaluated but, in Appendix A, Fig. 4 has another draft by Distillbart, this time not considering the original document structure. Slide titles were generated with mT5, fine-tuned with sections in Wikipedia articles and their titles.

5 Conclusion

We have presented SmartEDU, a platform for generating slide presentation drafts, and reported on some experiments performed during its development.

Drafts can be produced from either plain unstructured texts, or documents structured in sections. Figure 2 shows SmartEDU's interface for slide generation from uploaded text, which includes a button for generating and another for downloading the presentation. In the process, the input is summarized, so multiple methods for automatic summarization was tested, for producing slide decks from English scientific papers, and for summarizing Wikipedia articles, in English and in Portuguese. Conclusions were not very strong, but methods based on transformers performed better in most scenarios. This is confirmed by human opinions on presentation drafts produced by three summarization methods.

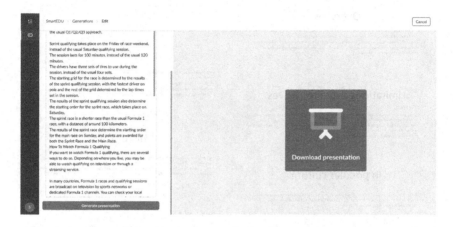

Fig. 2. Interface for Slide Generation.

Transformers are the state-of-the-art architecture for NLP and, even when data or computer power is not available for training them, many related models are available and straightforward to use. We recall that the transformers used were fine-tuned in news data but tested in other types of text, and also that they were used for summarizing each section of a document independently. So, results could possibly be improved if fine-tuning was performed in the same type of text, in this case, scientific papers. However, SmartEDU aims to be used with different types of text, for which large quantities are not always available, making it difficult to take more general conclusions.

In any case, human opinions on produced drafts were mostly positive, and we are sure that SmartEDU will have a positive impact on the time required for preparing slide decks. This will be beneficial for the partner company and to their customers, which will be able to invest more time in other aspects, like delivering, and in other tasks, such as research and development.

Despite this, there is much room for improvement, and we will keep on improving SmartEDU, not only by testing other supervised methods for slide generation, but also by including other features in the platform, such as a question generation [12] module for accelerating the production of tests on the same topics for which presentations are created.

Acknowledgements. This work was funded by: project SmartEDU (CENTRO-01-0247-FEDER-072620), co-financed by FEDER, through PT2020, and by the Regional Operational Programme Centro 2020; and through the FCT – Foundation for Science and Technology, I.P., within the scope of the project CISUC – UID/CEC/00326/2020 and by the European Social Fund, through the Regional Operational Program Centro 2020.

A   Appendix: Example Drafts

Fig. 3. Presentation draft generated with Distillbart for the Wikipedia article "SWOT analysis" (https://en.wikipedia.org/wiki/SWOT_analysis), as of June 2022, considering the section titles. Read from left to right.

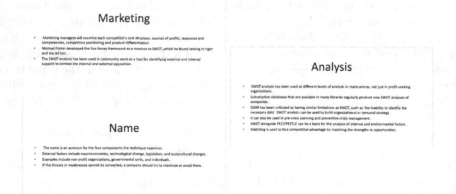

Fig. 4. Presentation draft generated with Distillbart for the Wikipedia article "SWOT analysis" (https://en.wikipedia.org/wiki/SWOT_analysis), as of June 2022, with sections discovered automatically and generated titles. Read from left to right.

Definition

- Europe is taken to be bounded by large bodies of water to the north, west and south; Europe's limits to the east and north-east are usually taken to be the Ural Mountains, the Ural River and the Caspian Sea; to the south-east, the Caucasus Mountains, the Black Sea and the waterways connecting the Black Sea to the Mediterranean Sea.
- Prior to the adoption of the current convention that includes mountain divides, the border between Europe and Asia had been redefined several times since its first conception in classical antiquity, but always as a series of rivers, seas and straits that were believed to extend an unknown distance east and north from the Mediterranean Sea without the inclusion of any mountain ranges.
- Anaximander placed the boundary between Asia and Europe along the Phasis River (the modern Rioni River on the territory of Georgia) in the Caucasus, a convention still followed by Herodotus in the 5th century BCE.

- The Book of Jubilees described the continents as the lands given by Noah to his three sons; Europe was defined as stretching from the Pillars of Hercules at the Strait of Gibraltar, separating it from Northwest Africa, to the Don, separating it from Asia.The convention received by the Middle Ages and surviving into modern usage is that of the Roman era used by Roman-era authors such as Posidonius, Strabo and Ptolemy, who took the Tanais (the modern Don River) as the boundary.
- A cultural definition of Europe as the lands of Latin Christendom coalesced in the 8th century, signifying the new cultural condominium created through the confluence of Germanic traditions and Christian-Latin culture, defined partly in contrast with Byzantium and Islam, and limited to northern Iberia, the British Isles, France, Christianised western Germany, the Alpine regions and northern and central Italy.
- Throughout the Middle Ages and into the 18th century, the traditional division of the landmass of Eurasia into two continents, Europe and Asia, followed Ptolemy, with the boundary following the Turkish Straits, the Black Sea, the Kerch Strait, the Sea of Azov and the Don (ancient Tanais).

- Around 1715, Herman Moll produced a map showing the northern part of the Ob River and the Irtysh River, a major tributary of the Ob, as components of a series of partly-joined waterways taking the boundary between Europe and Asia from the Turkish Straits, and the Don River all the way to the Arctic Ocean.
- He drew a new line along the Volga, following the Volga north until the Samara Bend, along Obshchy Syrt (the drainage divide between the Volga and Ural Rivers), then north and east along the latter waterway to its source in the Ural Mountains.
- By the mid-19th century, there were three main conventions, one following the Don, the Volga–Don Canal and the Volga, the other following the Kuma–Manych Depression to the Caspian and then the Ural River, and the third abandoning the Don altogether, following the Greater Caucasus watershed to the Caspian.

- The question was still treated as a "controversy" in geographical literature of the 1860s, with Douglas Freshfield advocating the Caucasus crest boundary as the "best possible", citing support from various "modern geographers".In Russia and the Soviet Union, the boundary along the Kuma–Manych Depression was the most commonly used as early as 1906.
- In 1958, the Soviet Geographical Society formally recommended that the boundary between the Europe and Asia be drawn in textbooks from Baydaratskaya Bay, on the Kara Sea, along the eastern foot of Ural Mountains, then following the Ural River until the Mugodzhar Hills, and then the Emba River; and Kuma–Manych Depression, thus placing the Caucasus entirely in Asia and the Urals entirely in Europe.
- However, most geographers in the Soviet Union favoured the boundary along the Caucasus crest, and this became the common convention in the later 20th century, although the Kuma–Manych boundary remained in use in some 20th-century maps.

Geography

- Its maritime borders consist of the Arctic Ocean to the north, the Atlantic Ocean to the west and the Mediterranean, Black and Caspian Seas to the south.
- The water of the Mediterranean extends from the Sahara desert to the Alpine arc in its northernmost part of the Adriatic Sea near Trieste.In general, Europe is not just colder towards the north compared to the south, but it also gets colder from the west towards the east.
- The geological history of Europe traces back to the formation of the Baltic Shield (Fennoscandia) and the Sarmatian craton, both around 2.25 billion years ago, followed by the Volgo–Uralia shield, the three together leading to the East European craton (≈ Baltica) which became a part of the supercontinent Columbia.
- Europe's present shape dates to the late Tertiary period about five million years ago.The geology of Europe is hugely varied and complex and gives rise to the wide variety of landscapes found across the continent, from the Scottish Highlands to the rolling plains of Hungary.

- Although over half of Europe's original forests disappeared through the centuries of deforestation, Europe still has over one quarter of its land area as forest, such as the broadleaf and mixed forests, taiga of Scandinavia and Russia, mixed rainforests of the Caucasus and the Cork oak forests in the western Mediterranean.
- A number of insects, such as the small tortoiseshell butterfly, add to the biodiversity.The extinction of the dwarf hippos and dwarf elephants has been linked to the earliest arrival of humans on the islands of the Mediterranean.Sea creatures are also an important part of European flora and fauna.

Economy

- The richer states tend to be in the West, followed by Central Europeans, while some of the Eastern Europe economies are still emerging from the collapse of the Soviet Union and the breakup of Yugoslavia.
- The majority of Central and Eastern European states came under the control of the Soviet Union and thus were members of the Council for Mutual Economic Assistance (COMECON).The states which retained a free-market system were given a large amount of aid by the United States under the Marshall Plan.

Culture

- The boundaries of Europe were historically understood as those of Christendom (or more specifically Latin Christendom), as established or defended throughout the medieval and early modern history of Europe, especially against Islam, as in the Reconquista and the Ottoman wars in Europe.This shared cultural heritage is combined by overlapping indigenous national cultures and folklores, roughly divided into Slavic, Latin (Romance) and Germanic, but with several components not part of either of these group (notably Greek, Basque and Celtic).
- Different cultural events are organized in Europe, with the aim of bringing different cultures closer together and raising awareness of their importance, such as the European Capital of Culture, the European Region of Gastronomy, the European Youth Capital and the European Capital of Sport.

Fig. 5. Slides generated with TextRank for the article "Europe", in the English Wikipedia, as of June, 19, 2022. Read from left to right. Article Link: https://en.wikipedia.org/wiki/Europe

References

1. Bhandare, A.A., Awati, C.J., Kharade, S.: Automatic era: presentation slides from academic paper. In: 2016 International Conference on Automatic Control and Dynamic Optimization Techniques (ICACDOT), pp. 809–814 (2016)
2. Blei, D.M., Ng, A.Y., Jordan, M.I.: Latent Dirichlet allocation. J. Mach. Learn. Res. **3**(Jan), 993–1022 (2003)
3. Bond, F., Paik, K.: A survey of wordnets and their licenses. Small **8**(4), 5 (2012)

4. Deerwester, S.C., Dumais, S.T., Furnas, G.W., Landauer, T.K., Harshman, R.A.: Indexing by latent semantic analysis. J. Am. Soc. Inf. Sci. **41**, 391–407 (1990)
5. Erkan, G., Radev, D.R.: LexRank: graph-based lexical centrality as salience in text summarization. J. Artif. Int. Res. **22**(1), 457–479 (2004)
6. Fu, T.J., Wang, W.Y., McDuff, D.J., Song, Y.: DOC2PPT: automatic presentation slides generation from scientific documents. ArXiv abs/2101.11796 (2021)
7. Grootendorst, M.: KeyBERT: minimal keyword extraction with BERT (2020). https://doi.org/10.5281/zenodo.4461265
8. Hanaue, K., Ishiguro, Y., Watanabe, T.: Composition method of presentation slides using diagrammatic representation of discourse structure. Int. J. Knowl. Web Intell. **3**, 237–255 (2012)
9. Hasan, T., et al.: XL-sum: large-scale multilingual abstractive summarization for 44 languages. In: Findings of the Association for Computational Linguistics: ACL-IJCNLP 2021, pp. 4693–4703. ACL (2021)
10. Hermann, K.M., et al.: Teaching machines to read and comprehend. In: Advances in Neural Information Processing Systems, pp. 1693–1701 (2015)
11. Hu, Y., Wan, X.: PPSGen: learning to generate presentation slides for academic papers. In: Proceedings of 23rd International Joint Conference on Artificial Intelligence (IJCAI) (2013)
12. Kurdi, G., Leo, J., Parsia, B., Sattler, U., Al-Emari, S.: A systematic review of automatic question generation for educational purposes. Int. J. Artif. Intell. Educ. **30**, 121–204 (2020)
13. Li, D.W., Huang, D., Ma, T., Lin, C.Y.: Towards topic-aware slide generation for academic papers with unsupervised mutual learning. In: Proceedings of AAAI Conference on Artificial Intelligence. AAAI (2021)
14. Lin, C.Y.: ROUGE: a package for automatic evaluation of summaries. In: Text Summarization Branches Out, pp. 74–81. ACL, Barcelona (2004)
15. Mathivanan, H., Jayaprakasam, M., Prasad, K.G., Geetha, T.V.: Document summarization and information extraction for generation of presentation slides. In: 2009 International Conference on Advances in Recent Technologies in Communication and Computing, pp. 126–128 (2009)
16. Mihalcea, R., Tarau, P.: TextRank: bringing order into text. In: Proceedings of 2004 Conference on Empirical Methods in Natural Language Processing, pp. 404–411. ACL, Barcelona (2004)
17. Raffel, C., et al.: Exploring the limits of transfer learning with a unified text-to-text transformer. J. Mach. Learn. Res. **21**(1), 5485–5551 (2020)
18. Sathiyamurthy, K., Geetha, T.V.: Automatic organization and generation of presentation slides for e-learning. Int. J. Dist. Educ. Technol. **10**, 35–52 (2012)
19. See, A., Liu, P.J., Manning, C.D.: Get to the point: summarization with pointer-generator networks. CoRR (2017). http://arxiv.org/abs/1704.04368
20. Sefid, A., Mitra, P., Wu, J., Giles, C.L.: Extractive research slide generation using windowed labeling ranking. In: Proceedings of 2nd Workshop on Scholarly Document Processing, pp. 91–96. ACL (2021)
21. Sefid, A., Wu, J.: Automatic slide generation for scientific papers. In: 3rd International Workshop on Capturing Scientific Knowledge Co-located with K-CAP 2019, SciKnow@ K-CAP 2019 (2019)
22. Sellam, T., Das, D., Parikh, A.: BLEURT: learning robust metrics for text generation. In: Proceedings of 58th Annual Meeting of the Association for Computational Linguistics, pp. 7881–7892. ACL (2020)

23. Sethi, P., Sonawane, S.S., Khanwalker, S., Keskar, R.B.: Automatic text summarization of news articles. In: 2017 International Conference on Big Data, IoT and Data Science (BID), pp. 23–29 (2017)
24. Shaikh, P.J., Deshmukh, R.A.: Automatic slide generation for academic paper using PPSGen method. In: International Journal of Technical Research and Applications, pp. 199–203 (2016)
25. Shibata, T., Kurohashi, S.: Automatic slide generation based on discourse structure analysis. In: Dale, R., Wong, K.-F., Su, J., Kwong, O.Y. (eds.) IJCNLP 2005. LNCS (LNAI), vol. 3651, pp. 754–766. Springer, Heidelberg (2005). https://doi.org/10.1007/11562214_66
26. Shleifer, S., Rush, A.M.: Pre-trained summarization distillation. CoRR abs/2010.13002 (2020). https://arxiv.org/abs/2010.13002
27. Sravanthi, M., Chowdary, C.R., Kumar, P.S.: QueSTS: a query specific text summarization system. In: Proceedings of 21st International Florida Artificial Intelligence Research Society Conference (FLAIRS) (2008)
28. Sravanthi, M., Chowdary, C.R., Kumar, P.S.: SlidesGen: automatic generation of presentation slides for a technical paper using summarization. In: Proceedings of 22nd International Florida Artificial Intelligence Research Society Conference (FLAIRS) (2009)
29. Sun, E., Hou, Y., Wang, D., Zhang, Y., Wang, N.X.R.: D2S: document-to-slide generation via query-based text summarization. In: Proceedings of 2021 Conference of North American Chapter of the Association for Computational Linguistics: Human Language Technologies, pp. 1405–1418. ACL (2021)
30. Utiyama, M., Hasida, K.: Automatic slide presentation from semantically annotated documents. In: Proceedings of Workshop on Coreference and Its Applications (COREF@ACL). ACL (1999)
31. Zhang, J., Zhao, Y., Saleh, M., Liu, P.: PEGASUS: pre-training with extracted gap-sentences for abstractive summarization. In: International Conference on Machine Learning, pp. 11328–11339. PMLR (2020)
32. Zhang, T., Kishore, V., Wu, F., Weinberger, K.Q., Artzi, Y.: BERTScore: evaluating text generation with BERT (2020). https://arxiv.org/abs/1904.09675

Explainable Integration of Knowledge Graphs Using Large Language Models

Abdullah Fathi Ahmed[1] , Asep Fajar Firmansyah[1,2](✉) ,
Mohamed Ahmed Sherif[1] , Diego Moussallem[1,3] ,
and Axel-Cyrille Ngonga Ngomo[1]

[1] Paderborn University, Warburger Str. 100, 33098 Paderborn, Germany
`{afaahmed,mohamed.sherif,diego.moussallem,axel.ngonga}@upb.de`
[2] The State Islamic University Syarif Hidayatullah Jakarta, Jakarta, Indonesia
`asep.fajar.firmansyah@upb.de, asep.airlangga@uinjkt.ac.id`
[3] Jusbrasil, Salvador, Brazil

Abstract. Linked knowledge graphs build the backbone of many data-driven applications such as search engines, conversational agents and e-commerce solutions. Declarative link discovery frameworks use complex link specifications to express the conditions under which a link between two resources can be deemed to exist. However, understanding such complex link specifications is a challenging task for non-expert users of link discovery frameworks. In this paper, we address this drawback by devising NMV-LS, a language model-based verbalization approach for translating complex link specifications into natural language. NMV-LS relies on the results of rule-based link specification verbalization to apply continuous training on T5, a large language model based on the Transformer architecture. We evaluated NMV-LS on English and German datasets using well-known machine translation metrics such as BLUE, METEOR, ChrF++ and TER. Our results suggest that our approach achieves a verbalization performance close to that of humans and outperforms state of the art approaches. Our source code and datasets are publicly available at https://github.com/dice-group/NMV-LS.

Keywords: KG Integration · Neural Machine Verbalization · Explainable AI · Semantic Web · Machine Learning Applications · Large Language Models

1 Introduction

Heterogeneous knowledge graphs that obey the principles of linked data are increasing in number. However, relatively few heterogeneous knowledge graphs

Abdullah Fathi Ahmed and Asep Fajar Firmansyah contributed equally to this research.

are actually linked. The current Linked Open Data (LOD) statistic[1] shows that there are 1301 knowledge graphs having 395.12 billion triples and only 2.72 billion links. Therefore, discovering links among these knowledge graphs is a major challenge to achieving the LOD vision[2]. Moreover, the linked knowledge graphs build the backbone of various data-driven applications, including information retrieval, recommender systems, search engines, question answering systems and digital assistants.

Declarative link discovery (LD) frameworks are used to link entities among knowledge graphs. These frameworks use complex link specifications (LSs) to express the conditions required to declare a link between two resources. For instance, state-of-the-art LD frameworks such as LIMES [15] and SILK [10] adopt a property-based computation of links between entities. For configuring link discovery frameworks, the user can either (1) manually enter a LS or (2) use machine learning for automatic generation of LSs. In both cases, a domain expert must manually write LS or set the configuration of machine learning algorithms that are used to generate LS. Furthermore, LD experts can easily understand the LS produced by such algorithms and modify it if needed. However, most lay users lack the expertise to proficiently interpret those LSs. Due to this lack of expertise, these users have difficulty when they i) check the correctness of the generated LS, ii) customize their LS, or iii) decide between possible interpretations of their input in an informed manner.

The aforementioned challenges can be seen as a bottleneck problem which degrade the effort and potential for ML algorithms to create such LSs automatically. Thus, addressing the explainability of link discovery-based artificial intelligence has become increasingly popular. For instance, the authors from [2] introduced a bilingual rule-based approach to verbalize the LS thus addressing the explainability of LD. In addition, Ahmed et al. [1] extended the previous approach and devised a multilingual rule-based approach including English, German, and Spanish. They also presented a first attempt for creating neural architecture, which is a bidirectional RNN-LSTM 2 layers encoder-decoder model with an attention mechanism [14]. However, their neural model failed to generalize as the vocabulary was very small and not diverse.

In this work, we alleviate the vocabulary problem found in Ahmed et al. [1] by proposing a language-based LS approach, named NMV-LS. To this end, we propose a pipeline architecture consisting of two stages. The first stage is a rule-based verbalizer to generate the necessary data to feed the second stage. The second stage relies on a few-shot learning approach by fine-tuning a large language model (LLM), in our case, T5. The underlying idea of using a language model is to verbalize LS from different types of systems only by using few examples. For example, LSs from LIMES [15] differ from the ones used in SILK [10]. In addition, the second stage contains a standard seq2seq 2 layers encoder-decoder architecture using different RNN cells such as GRU, LSTM, BiLSTM,

---

[1] Release: 05.05.2021, accessed 24.11.2021 https://lod-cloud.net/#about, retrieved using https://github.com/lod-cloud/lod-cloud-draw/blob/master/scripts/count-data.py.

[2] https://www.w3.org/DesignIssues/LinkedData.html.

and transformer trained with more diverse data. Figure 2 depicts the proposed architecture.

To evaluate NMV-LS, we designed two settings. In the first setting, we used two datasets for assessing the first part of our approach (i.e., standard encoder-decoder architectures). The first dataset contains 107 thousand English pairs and the second dataset contains 73 thousand German pairs. It should be noted that each pair is nothing but an LS and its verbalization. In the second setting, we used human annotated data for evaluating our second part of our approach (i.e., few-shot learning using T5 model). We created a human annotated data from LIMES with only 100 pairs, human annotated manipulated data from LIMES with only 8 pairs, and human annotated data from SILK with only 8 pairs. It is important to note that we evaluated our second part only on English.

Our main contributions are as follows:

- We present NMV-LS, a language model-based LS verbalization approach which relies on a few-shot learning strategy.
- We propose an approach which is capable of verbalizing different types of LS thus mitigating the high efforts for creating linguistic rules to each system.
- We propose an approach which is easily extensible to other languages.

The rest of this paper is structured as follows: First, we introduce our basic notation in Sect. 2. Then we give an overview of our approach underlying neural machine verbalization LS in Sect. 3, followed by the evaluation of our approach with respect to the automatic evaluation standard metrics BLEU, METEOR, ChrF++, and TER. We used BENG [12] to automatically measure the performance of our approach in Sect. 4. After a brief review of related work in Sect. 5, we conclude with some final remarks in Sect. 6.

2   Preliminaries

2.1   Link Specification LS

LS consists of two types of atomic components: *similarity measures* m, which are used to compare the property values of input resources, and *operators* ω that are used to combine these similarities into more complex specifications. We define a similarity measure m as a function $m : S \times T \rightarrow [0, 1]$, where S and T are the sets of source and target resources, respectively. We use *mappings* $M \subseteq S \times T$ to store the results of the application of a similarity function m to $S \times T$.

We also define a *filter* as a function $f(m, \theta)$. A specification is named *atomic LS* when it consists of exactly one filtering function. Although a complex specification (*complex LS*) can be obtained by merging two specifications L_1 and L_2 through an *operator* ω that combines the results of L_1 and L_2, here we use the operators $\sqcap$, $\sqcup$ and $\setminus$ as they are complete and frequently used to define LS [20]. A graphical representation of a complex LS is given in Fig. 1. We define the semantics $[[L]]_M$ of an LS L w.r.t. a mapping M as given in Table 1. The mapping $[[L]]$ of an LS L with respect to $S \times T$ contains the links that will be generated by L.

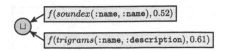

Fig. 1. A complex LS. The filter nodes are rectangles while the operator node is a circle.

Table 1. Link Specification Syntax and Semantics.

LS	$[[LS]]_M$
$f(m, \theta)$	$\{(s,t)|(s,t) \in M \wedge m(s,t) \geq \theta\}$
$L_1 \sqcap L_2$	$\{(s,t)|(s,t) \in [[L_1]]_M \wedge (s,t) \in [[L_2]]_M\}$
$L_1 \sqcup L_2$	$\{(s,t)|(s,t) \in [[L_1]]_M \vee (s,t) \in [[L_2]]_M\}$
$L_1 \backslash L_2$	$\{(s,t)|(s,t) \in [[L_1]]_M \wedge (s,t) \notin [[L_2]]_M\}$

2.2 Neural Machine Verbalization

Given a source sentence $\mathbf{x}$ and a target sentence $\mathbf{y}$, verbalization is tasked with finding $\mathbf{y}$ that maximizes the conditional probability of $\mathbf{y}$ (i.e., $\arg\max_{\mathbf{y}} p(\mathbf{y} \mid \mathbf{x})$). In neural machine verbalization, an encoder-decoder model with a set of parameters is trained to maximize the conditional probability of sentence pairs using a parallel training dataset. Accordingly, a verbalization model that learned the conditional distribution can generate a corresponding verbalization of a given sentence by searching for the sentence that maximizes the conditional probability.

3 Approach

NMV-LS consists of two stages. The first stage is rule-based verbalizer introduced in [1] to generate silver data for the second stage, blue colored background in Fig. 2 . The second stage is with green colored background in Fig. 2. The second stage contains two independent parts. The first part of stage 2 is based on standard encoder-decoder architectures such as two layers seq2seq with GRU, LSTM and BiLSTM, and transformer. The second part of stage 2 applies the concept of few-shot learning and is based on T5 model. In Fig. 2, ① means that the data is from LIMES silver data, ② means that the training data is a combination of LIMES silver data and human annotated LIMES silver data, ③ is a combination of ② and humane annotated manipulated LIMES LS, and ④ is a combination of ③ and humane annotated SILK LS. In ②, the human annotation is applied only on the verbalization of LS without changing LS. Manipulated LIMES LS means that we altered the structure of LIMES LS. Listing 1.1 shows an example of LIMES silver data, Listing 1.2 is an example of LIMES human annotated data, Listing 1.3 is an example of LIMES human annotated manipulated data, and Listing 1.4 is an example of SILK human annotated data.

3.1 Rule-Based Verbalizer

The rule-based verbalizer in [1] is based on Reiter & Dale NLG architecture [19]. In [1], real datasets (knowledge graphs) are used to generate LSs using WOMBAT [20]. Since the number of properties used in [1] is limited, it results in less diverse LSs. Our goal is to add more proprieties into each generated LSs. Therefore, in this work we create 10 templates to generate LSs relying on the

```
1   Source =
2   OR(mongeElkan(x.title,y.title)|0.45,
3       cosine(x.title,y.streetName)|0.37)
4
5   Target =
6   A link will be generated if
7   - the titles of the source and the target have a Mongeelkan similarity of
            45% or
8   - the title of the source and the streetName of the target have a Cosine
            similarity of 37%.
```

Listing 1.1. LIMES silver data: A pair that contains an LS and its verbalization
in English.

```
1   Source=
2   AND(AND(ratcliff(x.givenName,y.givenName)|0.0,AND(OR(jaroWinkler(x.
            givenName,y.authors)|0.37,cosine(x.givenName,y.givenName)|0.0)|0.0,
            ratcliff(x.givenName,y.givenName)|0.37)|0.37)|0.0,jaroWinkler(x.
            givenName,y.givenName)|0.37)
3
4   Target= a link will be produced supposing that the givenNames of the
            source and the target have a Ratcliff similarity of 0% or the
            givenName of the source and the author of the target have a
            Jarowinkler similarity of 37% or the givenNames of the source and the
            target have a Cosine similarity of 0% and a Ratcliff similarity and
            a Jarowinkler similarity of a 37%
```

Listing 1.2. LIMES human annotated data: A pair that contains an LS and its
verbalization in English.

rules defined in WOMBAT. The complexity of an LS is formally defined as the
number of the combined atomic LS so that an LS is more complex when it contains a higher number of the combined atomic LS. For example, the template
$(A_1 \sqcup A_2) \sqcap (A_3 \sqcup A_4)$ is less complex than $(A_1 \sqcup A_2) \sqcap (A_3 \sqcup A_4) \sqcap (A_5 \sqcup A_6)$,
where A_i is atomic LS.

3.2   Standard Encoder-Decoder Architectures

As we can see in Fig. 2, the first part of the second stage in our approach deploys
a set of standard encoder-decoder architectures. Our first part of the second stage
is motivated by the advance in sequence-to-sequence neural translation, which
belongs to a family of encoder-decoder architecture [22]. The encoder neural
network reads and encodes a source sentence into a vector. The decoder trans-
lates from the encoded vectors to a sequence of symbols (i.e., words). The goal
here is to maximize the probability of a correct translation by jointly training the whole encoder-decoder system using source sentences. We rely on a
Recurrent Neural Network (RNN) for both encoding and decoding [7], with the
attention mechanism introduced in [3]. We deploy RNN-GRU-2 layer and RNN-
Bi/LSTM-2 layer architectures to perform the verbalization. The first architecture is based on Long Short-Term Memory (LSTM) [9], while the second
architecture is based on Gated Recurrent Unit (GRU) [7]. Given a sequence of

```
1  Source=
2  trigrams(x.givenName, y.name)|0.8 AND cosine(x.title, y.label)|0.7 Or
        levenshtein(x.streetAdress, y.locationAdress)|0.9
3
4  Target=
5  The link will be generated when the givenname of the source and the name
        of the target have a trigrams similarity of 80% and the title of the
        source and the label of the target have a cosine similarity of 70% or
        the streetAdressenname of the source and the locationAdress of the
        target have a levenshtein similarity of 90%
```

Listing 1.3. LIMES human annotated manipulated data: A pair that contains an LS and its verbalization in English.

```
1  Source=
2   min( mongeelkanSimilarity(?x/p:producer, ?y/p:producer),
        ratclifDisitance(x/p:city,y/p:city))
3
4  Target=
5   The link will be generated if the labels of the source and the target
        have minimum mongeelkan similarity or the cities of the source and
        the target have minimum ratclif distance
```

Listing 1.4. SILK human annotated data: A pair that contains an LS and its verbalization in English.

tokens (i.e., words) $\mathbf{x} = (x_1, \cdots, x_T)$ as input at time step t and a sequence of tokens $\mathbf{y} = (y_1, \ldots, y_T)$ as output, our encoder-decoder is jointly trained to maximize the probability of a correct verbalization.Where $\mathbf{x}$ is the representation of LS and $\mathbf{y}$ is the representation of natural text verbalized by a trained decoder. The length of $\mathbf{x}$ may differ from the length of $\mathbf{y}$. For our proposed NMV-LS (i.e., part one of stage two), we use additive attention (as in [3]) with the conditional probability $p(y_i|y_1, \ldots, y_{i-1}, \mathbf{x}) = g(y_{i-1}, s_i, \mathbf{c}_i)$, where s_i is an RNN decoder's hidden state at time i. Formally, $s_i = f(s_{i-1}, y_{i-1}, \mathbf{c}_i)$ (see [7] for more details). In this part of our approach, we also deploy transformer. Transformer is a sequence-to-sequence architecture that relies entirely on the attention mechanism to transform one sequence into another with the help of two parts encoder and decoder without implying any recurrent networks (GRU, LSTM, etc). The architecture consists of multiple identical encoders and decoders stacked on top of each other (more details in [25]). We use our rule-based verbalizer to generate silver data to train our models. However, before feeding these data, we need to apply some preprocessing techniques.

3.3 Few-Shot Learning Using T5 Model

As depicted in Fig. 2, the second part of the second stage in our approach is based on a few-shot learning strategy that involves fine-tuning a large language model (LLM).

To address the vocabulary issue in Ahmed et al. [1], we base our approach on a few-shot learning approach by fine-tuning a large language model (LLM) such

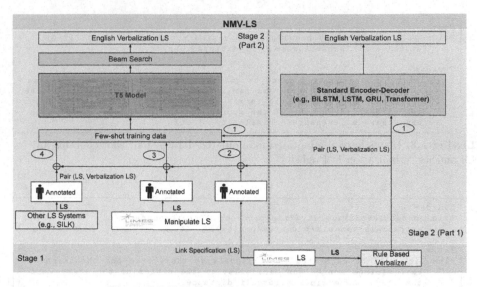

Fig. 2. LS Neural Machine Verbalization System

T5 model [18]. T5 is a pre-trained model for text-to-text generative multitasking based on transformer encoder-decoder and it is pre-treained on a large pre-training dataset (C4) [18]. Using T5 pre-trained model allows the model to learn the structure and pattern of natural language from a vast quantity of diverse, real-world text data. This can assist the model in learning to comprehend and generate high-quality, human-like text, which is useful for a variety of natural language processing tasks. In addition, T5 pre-trained model can frequently be fine-tuned for specific tasks, particularly in our case to learn the complexity of LS and generate verbalizations of LS with additional data and training time.

To use the T5 pre-trained model for few-shot learning in our model, as shown in Fig. 2, we fine-tune it on four different small training datasets, as detailed in Sect. 4.3, where those datasets were designed based on the LSs of LIMES. The model's goal is to generalize the verbalization of a wide range of LSs. Given a sequence LS tokens as input represented by $ls = \{w_1, w_2, ..., w_N\}$ and mapped into sequence embeddings before being fed into the encoder of T5, which outputs a sequence of embedding vectors. Furthermore, the decoder of T5 accepts as inputs both encoder outputs and previously generated tokens from the decoder during the auto-regressive decoding. Moreover, linear transformation and softmax functions are applied to the decoder outputs. In addition, beam search decoding [23] is utilized to generate the verbalization LS from the model outputs.

4   Evaluation

4.1   Data

Since there are no gold standard datasets for an NM verbalization task to translate link specification to natural languages, we generated silver standard datasets

Table 2. Statistics about our datasets used in the experiments, where V_{max} is the maximum verbalization length (in words) and V is the verbalization length.

Data	# Records	$V < 50$	$51 < V < 100$	$V > 100$
EN	107424	3744 (3.49%)	88320 (82.22%)	15360 (14.30%)
DE	73008	3888 (5.33%)	48384 (66.27%)	20736 (28.40%)

using the rule-based approach introduced in [2] and [1]. For evaluating the standard encoder-decoder architecture, we generated three datasets with the following sizes: 107k pairs (English) and 73k pairs (German). Table 2 shows statistical information about the data. For evaluating the fine-tuning of T5, we combined 10k pairs (English) from 107k pairs (English) with 100 pairs human annotated data from LIMES, 8 pairs human annotated manipulated data from LIMES, and only 8 pairs human annotated data from SILK.

4.2   Evaluation Metrics

To ensure consistent and clear evaluation, we evaluate our approach with respect to the automatic evaluation standard metrics BLEU [16], METEOR [4], ChrF++ [17] and TER [21].

We used BENG [12] to evaluate our approach automatically. BENG is an evaluation tool for text generation that abides by the FAIR principles and is built upon the successful benchmarking platform GERBIL [24].

4.3   Experimental Setup

As we can see in Fig. 2, our approach consists of two stages. The first stage is the rule-based verbalizer and the second stage contains two parts. The first part is based on standard encoder-decoder architectures and the second part is based on few-shot learning method by fine-tuning a large language model (LLM) such T5. However, the first stage feeds the two parts of the second stage. For instance, ① means that the data is from LIMES silver data generated by the first stage of NMV-LS which is the rule-based verblizer. ① feeds the both two parts of the second stage in our pipeline architecture. For evaluating our first part of the second stage in our approach (i.e., standard encoder-decoder architectures), we conducted three sets of experiments for both English and German to answer the following research question:

Q_1. Does the complexity of LS impact the performance of our NMV-LS in case of training standard encoder-decoder architectures?

For evaluating our second part of the second stage in our approach (i.e., few-shot learning using T5 model), we conducted one set of experiments for English to answer the following research questions:

Q_2. Does fine-tuning a LLM improve the verbalization of our NMV-LS system?

Q_3. Does fine-tuning a LLM help to the generalization of different LS for verbalization.

Q_4 How large is the impact of using human annotated data on the quality of verbalization in comparison with using silver data?

Experiment Set 1, English Language (107k ***Dataset).*** We evaluated a GRU/LSTM/BiLSTM-2 layers encoder-decoder on an English dataset consisting of 107k pairs (each pair contains an LS and its verbalization in English or German), split into 70% for training, 20% for validation, and 10% for testing. For all experiments, we set the parameters as follows: The learning rate is {0.1, 0.01, and 1}, the dropout is 0.1, the embedding dimensionality is 256, the epochs number is {100, 1000, and 10000}, the clipping value is 0.25, SGD optimizer with negative log-likelihood loss function, and the max length of a sentence is {107 and 187 tokens}. The max length of a sentence means that model can filter out all the pairs that have a length greater than the max length. For LSTM/BiLSTM, the batch size is 256. The selection of parameters is manually tuned. We run all GRU on colab and LSTM/BiLSTM on a local server with 1 GPU, 16 CPUs and 32 GB of memory. We use `Pytorch` library to implement our model. The results are listed in Table 3. For these results, we set the learning rate to 0.01 in case for using GRU and to 0.1 in case with using LSTM/BiLSTM. We conducted additional experiments with the learning rate set to 1 to study the impact of learning rate on the results using LSTM/BiLSTM. The results are provided in the Table 5.

Experiment Set 2, German Language. We evaluated the GRU/LSTM/-BiLSTM-2 layers encoder-decoder on the German dataset containing only 73k pairs. LSs are also complex in terms of atomic LSs. For instance, an LS can contain up to 6 atomic LSs A_i combined using operators ⊔ and ⊓. The results of the experiments are shown in the Table 4. The results in Table 4 are obtained with the learning rate set to 0.01 for GRU and to 0.1 for LSTM/BiLSTM with a batch size of 265. We ran more experiments with the learning rate set to 1 to study the impact of learning rate on the results. The results are presented in Table 6.

Table 3. BLEU, METEOR, ChrF++, and TER scores for the English language, evaluated on the 107k dataset; the learning rate is 0.01 for GRU and 0.1 for LSTM/BIlSTM.

Model	Length	Iter.	BLEU	BLEU-NLTK	METEOR	ChrF++	TER
GRU	107	100	35.92	0.36	0.36	0.66	0.69
GRU	187	100	21.73	0.22	0.33	0.58	1.69
GRU	107	1000	41.05	0.41	0.39	0.71	0.63
GRU	187	1000	22.07	0.22	0.22	0.44	0.56
GRU	107	10000	**99.22**	**0.99**	**0.78**	**0.99**	**0.01**
GRU	187	10000	88.81	0.89	0.60	0.93	0.05
LSTM	107	100	82.61	0.83	0.65	0.92	0.27
LSTM	187	100	77.31	0.77	0.58	0.87	0.40
BiLSTM	107	100	85.37	0.85	0.64	0.91	0.26
BiLSTM	187	100	79.23	0.79	0.59	0.89	0.34

Table 4. BLEU, METEOR, ChrF++, and TER scores for the German language evaluated on the 73K dataset. The learning rate is 0.01 for GRU and 0.10 for LSTM/BiLSTM.

Model	Length	Iter.	BLEU	BLEU-NLTK	METEOR	ChrF++	TER
GRU	107	100	41.84	0.42	0.43	0.74	0.66
GRU	187	100	28.67	0.29	0.4	0.67	1.41
GRU	107	1000	49.75	0.50	0.47	0.79	0.59
GRU	187	1000	54.01	0.54	0.40	0.71	0.38
GRU	107	10000	**99.98**	**1.00**	**0.90**	**1.00**	**0.00**
GRU	187	10000	79.52	0.80	0.54	0.84	0.32
LSTM	107	100	60.40	0.60	0.44	0.70	0.45
LSTM	187	100	76.67	0.77	0.63	0.86	0.49
BiLSTM	107	100	81.90	0.82	0.59	0.86	0.21
BiLSTM	187	100	81.30	0.81	0.59	0.85	0.30

Table 5. BLEU, METEOR, ChrF++, and TER scores for English language evaluated on the 107K dataset with learning rate set to 1.00.

Model	length	Iter.	BLEU	BLEU-NLTK	METEOR	ChrF++	TER
LSTM	107	100	83.01	0.83	0.61	0.86	0.22
LSTM	187	100	68.06	0.68	0.67	0.89	0.55
BiLSTM	107	100	**94.45**	**0.94**	**0.70**	**0.96**	**0.08**
BiLSTM	187	100	86.18	0.86	0.66	0.89	0.16

Experiment Set 3, Transformer. We implemented our transformer model using the `Pytorch` framework with the default parameters, i.e., the number of epochs is 30, the batch size is 256, and the max sentence length is {107, 187}. The results are listed in Table 7.

Experiment Set 4, Few-Shot Learning on T5. To address the issues raised by employing conventional architectures, such as overfitting and limited vocabulary size as we have seen in previous experiments, we implemented few-shot learning of text generation on the T5 model with a small number of training samples. This experiment is designed with four distinct sets of few-shot training data and three distinct sets of testing data, as shown in Table 8. In the first experiment, we fine-tuned the T5 model using a training dataset of 10k pairs,

Table 6. BLEU and METEOR, ChrF++, and TER scores for the German language evaluated on the 73K pairs dataset with learning rate set to 1.

Model	Length	Iter.	BLEU	BLEU-NLTK	METEOR	ChrF++	TER
LSTM	107	100	87.19	0.87	0.66	0.90	0.13
LSTM	187	100	96.67	0.97	0.82	0.99	0.06
BiLSTM	107	100	91.74	0.92	0.71	0.93	0.07
BiLSTM	187	100	**99.58**	**1.00**	**0.85**	**1.00**	**0**

Table 7. BLEU, METEOR, ChrF++, and TER scores for German and English evaluated on the 73K and 107K pairs datasets using Transformers.

Data	Length	Iter.	BLEU	BLEU-NLTK	METEOR	ChrF++	TER
107K (En)	107	30	90.89	**0.91**	**0.67**	**0.98**	**0.12**
107K (En)	187	30	**90.92**	**0.91**	**0.67**	**0.98**	**0.12**
73K (De)	107	30	89.98	0.90	0.66	0.97	0.15
73K (De)	187	30	79.11	0.79	0.60	0.93	0.29

Table 8. BLEU, METEOR, ChrF++, and TER scores for English language using Fine-tuned T5 model leveraging few-shot learning.

Train set	Test set	BLEU	BLEU-NLTK	METEOR	ChrF++	TER
①	LIMES original LS	76.27	0.76	0.54	0.87	0.15
①	SILK LS	34.26	0.35	0.26	0.54	0.71
②	LIMES original LS	77.91	0.78	0.54	0.89	0.13
②	LIMES Manipulated LS	45.76	0.46	0.37	0.68	0.55
③	LIMES Manipulated LS	63.64	0.64	0.43	0.80	0.48
③	SILK LS	34.93	0.35	0.27	0.54	0.67
④	SILK LS	36.58	0.37	0.34	0.59	0.62

each consisting of a LS and its English verbalization from LIMES silver data ①.
In the second experiment, we fine-tuned T5 using the previous training dataset
in combination with 70 pairs of LS and their human-annotated verbalizations
from the LIMES silver data ②. In the third experiment, the training dataset
from the second experiment is combined with human-annotated manipulated
LIMES LS ③. By modifying the formula, the manipulated LIMES LS is defined
differently than the previous LS. In addition, we fine-tuned the T5 model on the
training dataset in an effort to determine whether the model can improve the
verbalization of manipulated LIMES LS. In the last experiment, we fine-tuned
the T5 model using the training data from the previous experiment in combination with SILK LS ④. All experiments are built using the Pytorch lightning
framework, with following hyper-parameters: We set the number of epochs to
five and the learning rate to 3e−45 and use beam search decoding to generate
verbalization LS with the parameters *max length* = 256, *num beams* = 15, *no
repeat ngram size* = 6. In addition, *t5-base* is utilized as a pre-trained model. All
models based on few-shot learning are evaluated using Table 8's test set, which is
designed to investigate the effect of each training dataset on the model's ability
to improve the generalization quality of LS verbalization.

4.4   Results and Analysis

To answer Q_1, we set the maximum length of a sentence to be either 107 words
(tokens) or 187 words (tokens) based on the statistics in Table 2. This means we
filtered out all verbalized sentences that have a length greater than 107 words
for experiments where the maximum length of a sentence is set to 107 words.
We also removed all verbalized sentences that exceed 125 words for experiments
where the maximum sentence length is set to 125 words. In Table 3, we can
observe that NMV-LS using GRU achieves a better BLEU score, up to 99.22
(see Table 3). In Table 4, we can observe that the BLEU score is up to 99.98
obtained from our model using GRU when the length of a verbalized sentence is
also less than or equal to 107. In Table 5, the BLEU score is 94.45 using BiLSTM
with a max length of 107. Furthermore, Table 4 and 6 show that the NMV-LS
model achieves better scores when the length of a verbalized sentence is 187. For
instance, the BLEU score on the 73k German dataset is 76.67 using LSTM and
99.58 using BiLSTM (see Table 4 and 6). The reason is that the 73k German
dataset contains complex LSs and 28.40% of their verbalizations have sentence
lengths greater than 100 words, and these sentences are filtered out, which in
turn affects the training process. Especially since the size of the dataset is only
73k pairs, resulting in a decreased performance. From all these observations, we
conclude that the complexity of LS plays a crucial role in the performance of
our NMV-LS model. Furthermore, GRU is more sensitive to the complexity of
LS than LSMT/BiLSTM. LSMT/BiLSTM can handle very complex LSs and
improve performance.

   To answer Q_2, we analysed the results in Table 8. First, LIMES original LS
(i.e., it means that LS generated by LIMES) is used to evaluate the second part of

NMV-LS. Our findings indicate that our technique is capable of generating verbalization at the human level and outperforms earlier approaches. For instance, BLUE score is 76.27, ChrF++ is 0.87, and METEOR is 0.54. Note that we fine-tuned our model with only ①. In another word, we only used LIMES silver data generated by the first stage of NMV-LS (i.e., rule-based verbalizer) to fine-tune our model. This answers Q_2.

To answer Q_3, we deployed the fine-tuned model on ① LIMES silver data and evaluated on SILK LS as extremest case because LIMES & SILK have different rules and grammars to build their LSs. The goal is to study to which extent our model can be generalized to verbalize LSs in different formats and from different systems (e.g., SILK). The results in Table 8 show that our model achieves BLUE score of 34.26. Another case is that we fine-tuned NMV-LS using ② and tested on LIMES manipulated LSs. In this case, NMV-LS scores 45.76 BLUE, 0.68 ChrF++, and 0.37. Another case is fine-tuning our model on training data ③ and evaluating on SILK. From the results, there is no improvement comparing with the result generated by the model fine-tuned on ① and tested on SILK. This can be justified that both ① and ③ do not contain any information about SILK. To investigate this further, we added few samples of SILK LSs to create ④. To this end, we used ④ for fine-tuning NMV-LS and then evaluated on SILK. This improved the performance by 1.65%. We see these results, in all cases, as a big milestone toward generalizing our approach to verbalize LSs produced by other systems.

To answer Q_4, we implemented a couple of cases. In first case, we fine-tuned NMV-LS using ② and evaluated on LIMES original LSs. The results in Table 8 indicates that human annotated verbalization of a LS improves the verbalization very slightly. For instance, BLUE score is 77.91 and it is 1.65% higher than BLUE score produced using ①. In the second case, we fine-tuned NMV-LS applying ③ and evaluated on LIMES manipulated LSs. This improved the performance by 17.88 in BLUE score. We believe that the improvement is lead by including LIMES manipulated LSs in the training data ③. This answer Q_4.

5   Related Work

Explainable artificial intelligence (XAI) is widely acknowledged as a crucial feature for the practical use of AI models. Thus, there is an emerging need for understanding the results achieved by such models. With this comes the need for *the verbalization of semantic data (i.e., translation to natural text)* involved with such approaches (e.g., LD and LS systems which are our focus here). For instance, the authors of [5] have surveyed (XAI) as new field of research and covered many aspects of it. While in the work [8], the authors used a convolutional neural network (CNN) model combined with a BiLSTM model as encoder to extract video features and then feed these features to an LSTM decoder to generate textual descriptions. This work [8] and our work both fall under post-hoc explainability approaches such as text explanations(see [5]). In last years, the neural machine translation has achieved a notable momentum [3,7,11,22]

[6]. These papers have proposed the use of neural networks to directly learn this conditional distribution that reads a sentence and outputs a correct translation (from a natural language to another natural language, e.g., English to French or English to German).

Recently,transfer learning, where a model is initially pre-trained on a data-rich task before being fine-tuned on a downstream task, has emerged as a potent method in natural language processing (NLP). Applying few-shot learning by fine-tuning LLM such as T5 on a range of English-based NLP tasks, including as sentiment analysis, question answering, and document summarizing achieves state-of-the-art results [18]. However, few works have addressed the link specification verbalization (i.e., translation to natural languages). Recently, the authors addressed the readability of LS and proposed a generic rule-based approach to produce natural text from LS [2]. Their approach is motivated by the pipeline architecture for natural language generation (NLG) systems performed by systems such as those introduced by Reiter & Dale [19]. While in this work [1], they proposed a multilingual rule-based approach, including English, German, and Spanish, to produce natural text from LS. They also have presented a neural architecture which is a bidirectional RNN-LSTM 2 layers encoder-decoder model with an attention mechanism [13]. We used [2] and [1] to generate our silver dataset.

6   Conclusion and Future Work

In this paper, we present NMV-LS, a language-based LS verbalization system that is able to translate (verbalize) LS into natural language. our approach consists of two independent parts. The first part is based on standard encoder-decoder architectures such as two layers seq2seq with GRU, LSTM and BiLSTM, and transformer. The second part applies the concept of few-shot learning and is based on T5 model. The first part of our approach is multilingual in nature, where we tested it to generate both English and German verbalization. The second part is evaluated on English. In future work, we plan to evaluate the second part of the second stage in NMV-LS on more languages such as German, French, and Spanish. In addition, we will integrate our model into the LS learning algorithms, e.g., WOMBAT and EAGLE for generating on-the-fly multilingual verbalization of the learned LS.

Acknowledgements. We acknowledge the support of the German Federal Ministry for Economic Affairs and Climate Action (BMWK) within project SPEAKER (01MK20011U), the German Federal Ministry of Education and Research (BMBF) within the EuroStars project PORQUE (01QE2056C), the German Research Foundation (DFG) within the project INGRID (NG 105/7-3), the Ministry of Culture and Science of North Rhine-Westphalia (MKW NRW) within the project SAIL (NW21-059D), the European Union's Horizon Europe research and innovation programme within project ENEXA (101070305), and Mora Scholarship from the Ministry of Religious Affairs, Republic of Indonesia.

138   A. F. Ahmed et al.

References

1. Ahmed, A.F., Sherif, M.A., Moussallem, D., Ngonga Ngomo, A.C.: Multilingual verbalization and summarization for explainable link discovery. Data Knowl. Eng. **133**, 101874 (2021). https://doi.org/10.1016/j.datak.2021.101874
2. Ahmed, A.F., Sherif, M.A., Ngomo, A.-C.N.: LSVS: link specification verbalization and summarization. In: Métais, E., Meziane, F., Vadera, S., Sugumaran, V., Saraee, M. (eds.) NLDB 2019. LNCS, vol. 11608, pp. 66–78. Springer, Cham (2019). https://doi.org/10.1007/978-3-030-23281-8_6
3. Bahdanau, D., Cho, K., Bengio, Y.: Neural machine translation by jointly learning to align and translate (2016)
4. Banerjee, S., Lavie, A.: Meteor: An automatic metric for MT evaluation with improved correlation with human judgments. In: Proceedings of the ACL Workshop on Intrinsic and Extrinsic Evaluation Measures for MT and/or Summarization, pp. 65–72. ACL (2005)
5. Barredo Arrieta, A., et al.: Explainable artificial intelligence (XAI): concepts, taxonomies, opportunities and challenges toward responsible AI. Inf. Fusion **58**, 82–115 (2020). https://doi.org/10.1016/j.inffus.2019.12.012
6. Cho, K., van Merrienboer, B., Bahdanau, D., Bengio, Y.: On the properties of neural machine translation: Encoder-decoder approaches (2014)
7. Cho, K., et al.: Learning phrase representations using rnn encoder-decoder for statistical machine translation (2014)
8. Dong, Y., Su, H., Zhu, J., Zhang, B.: Improving interpretability of deep neural networks with semantic information (2017)
9. Hochreiter, S., Schmidhuber, J.: Long short-term memory. Neural Comput. **9**(8), 1735–1780 (1997). https://doi.org/10.1162/neco.1997.9.8.1735
10. Isele, R., Jentzsch, A., Bizer, C.: Efficient multidimensional blocking for link discovery without losing recall. In: WebDB (2011)
11. Kalchbrenner, N., Blunsom, P.: Recurrent continuous translation models. In: Proceedings of the 2013 Conference on Empirical Methods in Natural Language Processing, pp. 1700–1709. Association for Computational Linguistics, Seattle (2013). https://www.aclweb.org/anthology/D13-1176
12. Moussallem, D., et al.: A general benchmarking framework for text generation, pp. 27–33 (2020). International Workshop on Natural Language Generation from the Semantic Web 2020, WebNLG+; Conference date: 18-12-2020 Through 18-12-2020
13. Moussallem, D., Ngonga Ngomo, A.C., Buitelaar, P., Arcan, M.: Utilizing knowledge graphs for neural machine translation augmentation. In: Proceedings of the 10th International Conference on Knowledge Capture, pp. 139–146 (2019)
14. Moussallem, D., Wauer, M., Ngomo, A.C.N.: Machine translation using semantic web technologies: a survey. J. Web Semant. **51**, 1–19 (2018). https://doi.org/10.1016/j.websem.2018.07.001
15. Ngonga Ngomo, A.C., et al.: LIMES - a framework for link discovery on the semantic web. KI-Künstliche Intell. German J. Artif. Intell. Organ des Fachbereichs "Künstliche Intelligenz" der Gesellschaft für Informatik e.V. (2021). https://papers.dice-research.org/2021/KI_LIMES/public.pdf
16. Papineni, K., Roukos, S., Ward, T., Zhu, W.J.: BLEU: a method for automatic evaluation of machine translation. In: Proceedings of the 40th Annual Meeting on Association for Computational Linguistics (2002)
17. Popović, M.: chrF++: words helping character n-grams. In: Proceedings of the Second Conference on Machine Translation, pp. 612–618 (2017)

18. Raffel, C., et al.: Exploring the limits of transfer learning with a unified text-to-text transformer. J. Mach. Learn. Res. **21**, 140:1–140:67 (2020). http://jmlr.org/papers/v21/20-074.html
19. Reiter, E., Dale, R.: Building Natural Language Generation Systems. Cambridge University Press, New York (2000)
20. Sherif, M.A., Ngonga Ngomo, A.-C., Lehmann, J.: WOMBAT – a generalization approach for automatic link discovery. In: Blomqvist, E., Maynard, D., Gangemi, A., Hoekstra, R., Hitzler, P., Hartig, O. (eds.) ESWC 2017. LNCS, vol. 10249, pp. 103–119. Springer, Cham (2017). https://doi.org/10.1007/978-3-319-58068-5_7
21. Snover, M., Dorr, B., Schwartz, R., Micciulla, L.: A study of translation edit rate with targeted human annotation (2006)
22. Sutskever, I., Vinyals, O., Le, Q.V.: Sequence to sequence learning with neural networks (2014)
23. Sutskever, I., Vinyals, O., Le, Q.V.: Sequence to sequence learning with neural networks. In: Ghahramani, Z., Welling, M., Cortes, C., Lawrence, N.D., Weinberger, K.Q. (eds.) Advances in Neural Information Processing Systems 27: Annual Conference on Neural Information Processing Systems 2014, 8–13 December 2014, Montreal, Quebec, Canada, pp. 3104–3112 (2014). https://proceedings.neurips.cc/paper/2014/hash/a14ac55a4f27472c5d894ec1c3c743d2-Abstract.html
24. Usbeck, R., et al.: GERBIL: general entity annotator benchmarking framework. In: Proceedings of the 24th International Conference on World Wide Web, WWW 2015, pp. 1133–1143. International World Wide Web Conferences Steering Committee, Republic and Canton of Geneva, CHE (2015). https://doi.org/10.1145/2736277.2741626
25. Vaswani, A., et al.: Attention is all you need (2017)

Cross-Domain and Cross-Language Irony Detection: The Impact of Bias on Models' Generalization

Reynier Ortega-Bueno[1]([⊠]) (iD), Paolo Rosso[1] (iD), and Elisabetta Fersini[2] (iD)

[1] PRHLT Research Center, Universitat Politècnica de València,
Camí de Vera S/N, Valencia, Spain
rortega@prhlt.upv.es
[2] Università degli Studi di MILANO-BICOCCA, Milan, Italy

Abstract. Irony is a complex linguistic phenomenon that has been extensively studied in computational linguistics across many languages. Existing research has relied heavily on annotated corpora, which are inherently biased due to their creation process. This study focuses on the problem of bias in cross-domain and cross-language irony detection and aims to identify the extent of topic bias in benchmark corpora and how it affects the generalization of models across domains and languages (English, Spanish, and Italian). Our findings offer a first insight into this issue and showed that mitigating the topic bias in these corpora improves the generalization of models beyond their training data. These results have important implications for the development of robust models in the analysis of ironic language.

Keywords: Irony · Bias · Cross-Domain · Cross-Language · Bias Mitigation

1 Irony in Languages

Several theories have been developed in Western countries to explain the concept of irony, including Irony as Opposition [27], Irony as Echo [45,49], Irony as Pretense [14] and Irony as Negation [25]. These theories suggest that irony is a universal phenomenon, with no evidence indicating any culture completely lacks the capacity to produce and understand it. While socio-cultural and individual aspects impact irony comprehension [16], studies have confirmed that verbal irony exists across different languages.

Computational Linguistics tried to explain irony by mingling language theories and empirical evidence found in linguistic corpora using computational models. Pioneer works [9,47] focused on analysing the phenomenon from a monolingual perspective, and mainly for English. However, there have been efforts to propose new corpora and study irony in other languages such as: Czech [38], French [5], Italian [11], Portuguese [9], Spanish [35], and Arabic [23]. These works confirm the idea that verbal irony is realized in distinct languages, but

E. Métais et al. (Eds.): NLDB 2023, LNCS 13913, pp. 140–155, 2023.
https://doi.org/10.1007/978-3-031-35320-8_10

they do not provide insights on how their findings can be generalized across different languages, even among those closed-related language. In this sense, [29] introduced and validated a fine-grained annotation schema in tweets and a multilingual corpus-based study for measuring the impact of pragmatic phenomena on the understanding of irony. The authors proved that the schema is reliable for French and that it is portable to English and Italian, observing relatively the same tendencies in terms of irony categories and linguistic markers. Similarly, in [10] the authors, investigated irony in English and Arabic, and discovered that both languages share similarities in the rhetorical usage of irony. This fact suggests that there is a common-ground in the underlying features of how irony is used and comprehended in distinct languages. However, minimal works have considered the fact to investigate the problem of irony in cross-domain, cross-variant and cross-language scenarios. The work in [24] was the first to address irony taking advantages of multiple languages for training and validating a computational model. Although the results indicate that computational models can capture common pragmatic and linguistic knowledge in cross-lingual scenarios, further efforts are needed to uncover the reasons for their generalization. Specifically, studying the narrow and biased nature of the corpora and its impact on generalization during the learning process, in both cross-domain and cross-language contexts, is a crucial issue in computational irony. This work provides insights into how irony is used across domains and languages. It can also help identify common patterns in the use of irony across different domains and language that can help to improve the generalization of the irony detection.

Bias is nothing new in machine learning [1,22]. Special attention has been paid to unconscious and stereotypical bias because of the harm it causes to people and minority groups [31,44]. However, bias may come from diverse ways and in distinct forms like activity, data, sampling, algorithm, interaction, annotators, etc [1]. One interesting bias derived from the data and sampling is the topic bias [36]. This kind of bias refers to the presence of a systematic preference for words associated to certain topics in a dataset, often resulting from the sources from which the data is collected or the way in which it is sampled. This bias can lead to unequal representation of different topics or perspectives, which can impact the algorithms' inductive learning process, the fairness of the model, and the generalization out of domains. In this paper we address the following research questions:

RQ1. Are the benchmark corpora used for computational irony detection biased?

RQ2. How can bias be mitigated in irony corpora in order to increase the models' generalization capability across domains and languages?

RQ3. Is the knowledge about irony, learned from one domain or one language, helpful to predict irony in other languages, and how does the bias mitigation impact it?

The rest of this paper is organized as follows. Section 2 introduces related work on multilingual and cross-lingual irony detection, and some results in the field of bias mitigation. The proposed methodology is presented in Sect. 3. In this section, we describe the used measures for quantifying the biased words. Moreover, we describe the transformer-based models used for detecting irony; we relied on these models because they have shown high performance in several Natural Language Processing (NLP) tasks. Also, we propose a method for debiasing the datasets. Section 4 describes the experimental settings and the irony corpora. Specifically, the experimental settings and results of the monolingual, cross-lingual and the impact of bias mitigation on cross-lingual experiments in the irony corpora. Also, it discusses the results and findings obtained. Finally, Section 5 includes conclusive remarks and ideas for future work.

2   Related Works

In this section, we review recent literature on computational irony detection. We focus on those works that address the problem from multilingual, cross-domain and cross-lingual perspectives. Irony has captured the attention of the NLP and Machine Learning research communities [17,29]. In [47] the authors go beyond the literal matches of user queries enriched information retrieval systems with new operators to enable the non-literal retrieval of creative expressions. Sentiment analysis systems' performances drastically drop when applied to ironic texts [20,30]. Irony as language provides a mechanism that can subtly mask language of hatred, offence and discrimination towards specific individuals or social groups [21].

In interpersonal communication, it was introduced the problem of irony bias [6]. The authors investigated the role of verbal irony in the communication and maintenance of social stereotypes. They observed that irony is found more appropriated in situations in which stereotypes are violated than in situations in which social stereotypes are confirmed. A shared task on profiling authors that spread stereotyped content using irony was recently organized [34].

A vast amount of works addressed irony in English [20,26,39,46] with some efforts in French [29], Portuguese [9], Italian [11], Spanish variants [35] and Arabic [23]. One of the main issues is the lack of computational approaches that address the problem in a multilingual or cross-lingual perspectives. A bilingual approach with one model per language has been explored for English-Czech [38]. Going a step towards a more elaborating linguistic approach, a fine-grained annotation schema was introduced in [29]. The authors proposed a multilevel annotation schema to determine whether or not tweets are ironic, the type of irony involved (explicit/implicit), the category of irony used, and the linguistic cues revealing the existence of irony (such as emoticons, punctuation and opinion words). The proposed schema was evaluated for French, Italian and English showing that it is relevant for Italian and English which present the same tendencies as French. Moreover, the authors showed the portability of the schema to the Arabic language. The work [12] addressed computational irony from a multilingual perspective. It introduced a syntax-aware irony detection system in for English, Spanish, French and Italian. For that the authors investigated the impact of different sources of syntactic information when used on top of Recurrent Neural Networks (RNNs) and Transformer models. It is the first attempt to show the invariant of some syntax- and dependency-based features across languages, however it lacks the portability of these features in a cross-language scenario. In [24] the authors were pioneer in addressing the problem of irony detection from a cross-lingual (French, English and Arabic) and cross-cultural (Indo-European languages) perspective. For that, the authors used Random Forest (RF) models with surface features, which seem to be language independent, to verify which pair of the three languages has similar ironic pragmatic devices, and uses similar text-based patterns in the writing. Moreover, a Convolutional Neural Network (CNN) architecture with bilingual embedding was tested. Results showed that despite of the language and cultural differences (e.g. between Arabic/French), deep learnig model obtained a high performance comparing to the other languages pairs when the model was trained on each of these two languages and tested on the other one. This fact supports the idea that irony has certain similarity among the languages despite the cultural differences. In [19] explored the effectiveness of different models in detecting sarcasm and irony in text. They utilized an ensemble of models trained on various text features to better capture the nuanced patterns of these linguistic devices. Results showed that the models are quite robust even when considering more variance in the training data. Prior research has overlooked the issue of bias in the training data and its detrimental effects on the generalization of irony detection models across different domains and languages.

3   Methodology

The first step to create the scenario for evaluating the impact of bias in cross-domain and cross-language settings consists of collecting the corpora necessary for this aim. Fortunately, benchmark collections released for automatic irony classification cover several languages (e.g. IroSvA19 for Spanish [35], SemEval 2018 Task 3 [46] for English, IronITA2018 [11] for Italian, etc.). We focuses on three European languages: English, Spanish and Italian. The second step is the selection of the learning models used for detecting irony. In this sense, we rely on transformer-based language models. They have proven to be especially effective for many NLP tasks [21, 26]. We considered models trained on a single language for monolingual and cross-domain settings, whereas we used a multilingual model for cross-language analysis. Crucial aspects for discovering and evaluating the impact of bias on irony detection are: a measure to assess how biased the words are in the corpora, and a strategy to mitigate the bias on the data. For that, we used the measure proposed in [36] and evaluated a simple mitigation strategy. Particularly, the mitigation relies on masking the most biased term in each corpus according to different schemas. It is important to note that our aim is not to outperform the current state of the art on cross-domains and cross-languages irony detection but to investigate if irony detection can benefit from analysing and mitigating bias in the corpora.

3.1 Corpora

Many corpora have been proposed for irony detection. They differ in sources, genres, the strategy used to retrieve texts, domains, size, time period, annotation schema, etc. Mainly, they have been created from social media data, being Twitter the most used source. Twitter's search engine provided a keyword-based retrieval method (e.g., #irony, #ironic, #sarcasm, #sarcastic and #not). This strategy can inject a sort of bias in the corpora, often a bias related to the author's personality, the topics discussed, the ranking in which the queries are resolved by the search engine, the time covered by data, etc. These concerns impact on how widely, narrow and biased the data represent the phenomenon. In Table 1 is showed statistics about the corpora used in this work. It is important to notice that we did not perform any change on the corpora.

English Corpora. TwRiloff13 Corpus [39] is a manually annotated corpus from Twitter, including 3200 tweets. They followed a mixed approach for developing a corpus of samples, including ironic and non-ironic tweets. Firstly, a set of 1600 tweets tagged with the #sarcasm and #sarcastic hashtags and 1600 tweets from a random stream were retrieved and presented to the annotators. TwMohammad15 Corpus [32] contains a set of tweets with a multi-layer annotation concerning different aspects: sentiment, emotions, purpose, and style (simple statement, sarcasm, exaggeration or hyperbole, understatement). It is essential to highlight that only 23.01% of the tweets were labelled with a style tag pertinent to the expression of irony. The tweets labelled with hashtags pertaining to the 2012 US presidential elections were collected. TwSemEval18 Corpus in the Task 3 of SemEval 2018 [46] two different subtasks were presented. The first subtask addresses irony detection as a binary classification problem. In contrast, in the second subtask, the participants should distinguish among three different types of irony: verbal irony realised through a polarity contrast, verbal irony without such a polarity contrast, and descriptions of situational irony. The tweets were manually annotated using a fine-grained annotation schema.

Spanish Corpora. We use the corpus proposed in the *IroSvA'19* shared task [35]. Three sub-corpora with short messages from Spain, Mexico and Cuba were proposed to explore how irony changes in Spanish variants. In particular, the Castilian (*TwIroSvA19es*) and Mexican (*TwIroSvA19mx)* sub-corpora consist of ironic tweets about ten controversial topics for Spanish and Mexican users. In the case of the Cuban sub-corpus (*NewsIroSvA19cu*), it consists of ironic news comments which were extracted from controversial news concerning the Cuban people. We considered each corpus as isolated in the cross-domains scenario, and we mixed them into a single corpus for cross-languages analyis. Hereafter we refer to this full corpus as *IroSvA19Full*.

Italian Corpora. *TwIronITA18 Corpus* has tweets annotated for irony and sarcasm in the Italian language [11]. The tweets come from different sources:

Hate Speech Corpus (HSC) [43] and Twittirò corpus [13], which is composed
of tweets from LaBuonaScuola (TW-BS), Sentipolc (TW-SPOL), Spinoza (TW-
SPINO) [2]. Only in the test set some tweets been added from the TWITA collection [2]. This multi-source composition allows us to split the corpus for investigating irony in distinct domains. With this aim, we separate the tweets from
TW-BS, TW-SPINO and TW-SPOL in a single corpus (henceforth *TwIroni-
taTwittiro18*) and the tweets in the TWITA and HSC as another corpus (henceforth *TwIronItaOther18*).

Table 1. Distribution for ironic and non-ironic classes in the corpora

Corpus	Training			Testing		
	Non-iro	Iro	Total	Non-iro	Iron	Total
TwRiloff13	–	–	–	1687	474	2161
TwSemEva18	1916	1901	3817	473	311	784
TwMohammad15	1397	532	1929	–	–	–
TwIroSvA19es	1600	800	2400	400	200	600
TwIroSvA19mx	1600	800	2400	401	199	600
NewsIroSvA19cu	1600	800	2400	400	200	600
IroSvA19Full	4800	2400	7200	1200	600	1800
TwIronItaTwittiro18	1271	1270	2541	161	184	345
TwIronItaOther18	683	753	1436	276	251	527
TwIronITA18	1954	2023	3977	437	435	872

3.2 Transformer-Based Models

We used BERTweet for English, BETO for Spanish, ALBERTo for Italian and
mBERT in the multilingual case.

BERTweet [33] is the first public large-scale model trained on English tweets.
It has the same architecture as BERT [18], but was trained using the RoBERTa
pre-training procedure [50]. Regarding the parameters, the model kept the same
configuration as BERT, 12 Transformer layers (L = 12), 768 hidden neurons (H
= 768), 12 heads of attention (A = 12) and 110M parameters. The model is
publicly available on GitHub[1].

BETO [7] is a recent BERT-based model trained on Spanish corpora. It was
trained using all the data from Wikipedia, and all of the sources of the OPUS
Project that had text in Spanish. BETO has 12 Transformer layers (L = 12) with
16 attention heads (A = 16) each and 1024 as hidden sizes (H = 1024). It has
been compared with multilingual models obtaining better or competitive results
in several language processing tasks [7]. It is publicly available on Github[2].

---
[1] https://github.com/VinAIResearch/BERTweet.
[2] https://huggingface.co/dccuchile/bert-base-spanish-wwm-cased.

ALBERTo [37] aimed to develop a tool for understanding the Italian language used on social media platforms, particularly on Twitter. ALBERTo is based on the BERT architecture and uses a similar learning strategy. The model was trained on TWITA [4], a large dataset collecting Italian tweets from 2012 to 2015. The model was trained on 200 million tweets. Regarding the parameters, the model uses 12 Transformer layers (L = 12), with 12 attention heads (A = 12), a size of 768 neurons (H = 768) and 128 tokens as max_seq_len. It is publicy available on GitHub[3].

mBERT The transformer-based neural network architectures paved the way for training robust and contextual-aware language models in an unsupervised manner. The use of these pre-trained contextualized models have been widely spread through BERT [18] and BERT's family architectures. BERT model relies on bidirectional representation from transformers and achieves the state of the art for contextual language modelling and contextual pre-trained embeddings. We use the pre-trained multilingual versions of BERT[4] (mBERT, henceforth) that is pre-trained on the concatenation of monolingual Wikipedia datasets from 104 languages.

3.3   Quantifiying the Lexical Bias

Quantifying bias is difficult in the symbolic level, however from statistical point of view it is possible to get insights about the usage of words in a corpus or even among the classes in which the corpus is structured. The works [36,48] computed statistical scores to determine the correlation between the words and hate speech labels. Findigs shown that the corpora contain a certain extent of bias, with negative implications during the learning process: a supervised system could learn that words related to the domain or topic are indicative of the surveyed phenomenon. Instead of using Point Mutual Information like in [48], the work [36] performs a similar analysis of the lexical content in the corpora, but this time by using of the *Weiredness Index* (WI) and the *Polarized Wierdness Index* (PWI). Distinctly, PWI compares the relative frequencies of a word w as it occurs in the subset of a labeled corpus identified by one class against its complement. The WI is the ratio of the relative frequencies between the specific corpus ζ_ρ and the background corpus ζ_β. Let us define w_ρ and t_ρ as the frequency of the word w and the total words in the specific corpus; w_β and t_β as the frequency of the word w and the total words in the background corpus. The WI is computed as:

$$WI(w) = \frac{w_\rho/t_\rho}{w_\beta/t_\beta} \tag{1}$$

The PWI respects to the positive label is the ratio of the relative frequency of w in the subset $\zeta_1 = \{e_i \in \zeta : l_i = 1\}$ over the relative frequency of w in the subset

---

[3] https://huggingface.co/m-polignano-uniba/bert_uncased_L-12_H-768_A-12_italian_alb3rt0.

[4] https://huggingface.co/bert-base-multilingual-uncased.

$\zeta_0 = \{e_i \in \zeta : l_i = 0\}$. Where $\zeta = \{(e_1, l_1), (e_2, l_2), ..., (e_n, l_n)\}$ a labeled corpus, $e_i = \{w_{i1}, w_{i2}, ..., w_{im}\}$ is a labeled instance of the text, $w_i m$ is the mth word in the instance e_i and $l_i \in \{0, 1\}$ is the label of e_i (1 means the positive class and 0 is the negative class). w_{ζ_1} and t_{ζ_1} are w_β and t_β the frequency of the word w and the total words in the positive class; and w_{ζ_0} and t_{ζ_0} the frequency of the word w and the total words in the negative one. The PWI is computed as:

$$PWI(w, \zeta_1, \zeta_0) = \frac{w_{\zeta_1}/t_{\zeta_1}}{w_{\zeta_0}/t_{\zeta_0}} \qquad (2)$$

Words with highest PWI value give a strong indication of the most characteristic words to distinguish the class (e.g., irony) from its complement (e.g., no-irony).

The WI measure required a background corpus to obtain the words' frequency in general language. We compute the word frequencies from the British National Corpus [15] for English, from the ItWaC corpus [3] for Italian, and we used Billion Word corpus [8] for Spanish. We only carried out a light preprocessing involving tokenization and ignoring cases. Moreover, we do not apply any smoothing schema. We considered that every word in the specialized corpus is present in the background corpus, and simply set $WI = 0$ when this is not the case.

3.4   Bias Mitigation

One way to mitigate bias relies on investigating what features (words in our case) are biased in the corpus considering the task we try to solve. In this sense, the masking technique becomes an interesting way for exploring the impact of removing biased word to increase the model's performance in out of domain and out of language scenarios. Masking has been effectively applied to other NLP tasks to improve the preformance of the classification models [40–42], however it has not been applied from a bias mitigation perspective in irony detection. Due to its capabilities to deliver good and human-understandable results, few masking schemas have been investigated. This is motivated by two main reasons: i) its computational simplicity, and ii) it is easy to evaluate and to a certain degree explains the impact of bias on the learning process. Depending on the way that biased words are masked, some information can be kept or discarded. In this work we evaluate three distinct masking schemas. Given a text $e_i = w_{i1}, w_i 2, ..., w_{im}$ where w_{ij} is the word in the position j in the text e_i, and ξ the set of biased words,

i *SimpleMask*: Replacing each word w_i in the sequence e by the mask if $w_i \in \xi$.
ii *LengthMask*: Replacing each word w_i in the sequence e by the wildcard mark (*) if $w_i \in \xi$. This time the mark takes into account the length of the biased terms to be masked. It is to say, if w_i is a biased word with length five it should be replaced by (*****).
iii *PoSMask*: Aiming to keep some morph-syntactic aspect associated to the biased words, this strategy replace each word w_i in the sequence e by its Part of Speech (PoS) tag if $w_i \in \xi$.

4   Experiment and Results

In this section we describe our experiments and present the main results obtained. We aimed to investigate whether mitigating bias in a corpus could improve the generalization of transformer models for detecting irony across domains and languages. Firstly we applied the proposed measures for identifying biased words in each corpora. After having the biased words, we conducted two experiments: i) fine-tuning monolingual transformers models with and without bias mitigation in a cross-domain scenario, and evaluating the strategy of bias mitigation in a cross-language scenario using a multilingual model. The results of our study have important implications for improving the accuracy and robustness of NLP models in real-world applications.

In our experiments, we fine-tuned the BERT-based model on our corpora using a binary classification approach, where the task was to identify whether a given sentence is ironic or not. We used the Adam optimizer, and all weights were learned together. Specifically, the strategy adopted was that proposed in ULM-FiT [28] for tuning pre-trained models in a gradual unfreezing-discriminative fashion. In an intent to prevent overfitting in the training step, no fixed number of *epochs* was defined. Instead, the process relied on the *early stopping* criterion, setting the value of *patience* to 15 and the maximum number of epochs to 50. The *maximum lenght* of the sequence was fixed to 50 and the *batch size* equal to 32. We reported the metric Macro F1-score. All experiments were carried out using the PyTorch deep learning library on a GPU-enabled computing environment. Table 2 shows the top ten biased words in each English corpus according to WI and PWI measures. As can be observed, WI prioritizes those words related to the writing style of Twitter, even when identifying domain-dependent words. Besides, PWI highlights words related to ironic lexica (e.g., #great, asleep, waking, friday_morning, #irony, wonderful, fantastic) in the *TwSemEval18* and *TwRiloff13* corpora. Whereas, for *TwMohammad15*, PWI pinpoints words about controversial political topics *(e.g., rape, control, promises, favor, control, shitty)*. This because the former captures domain-dependent and source-dependent infor-

Table 2. The biased words in the English corpora

Corpus	WI	PWI
TwSemEval18	wanna, obama, tweeting, dont, nigga, idk, lol, haha, hahaha, cuz	yay, waking, test, fix, teacher, #irony, coin, wonderful, busy, soo
TwRiloff13	wanna, nigga, dont, tweeting, thats, haha, lol, yay, aww, soo	#not, #great, asleep, waking, friday_morning, nothing, fantastic, entire, #fml, yay
TwMohammad15	obama, mitt, wanna, niggas, nigga, romney, gop, dont, thats, dnc	rape, small, king, control, seem, shitty, promises, food, favor, half

mation. Additional information for the top ten biased words in Spanish and Italian can be found in Appendix[5].

Table 3. Cross-domain irony detection *(EN)*

Train/Test	TwSemEval18	TwRiloff13	TwMohammad15
BERTweet			
TwSemEval18	×	0.655	0.561
TwRiloff13	**0.613**	×	**0.472**
TwMohammad15	0.451	0.499	×
Masking + BERTweet			
TwSemEval18	×	**0.733**	**0.575**
TwRiloff13	*0.582*	×	*0.429*
TwMohammad15	**0.463**	**0.520**	×

After highlighting the most biased words using the two measures, we separately applied the masking techniques on the most 100 biased words in each corpus. We conducted experiments on all possible combinations of both measures (WI and PWI) and the three mitigation schemas, but we only report the best results.

In the first experiment, we fine-tuned BERTweet for the irony detection task on each English corpus, and we validated it on the two remaining corpora. In Table 3, the results in a cross-domain scenario can be observed when the *LengthMask* masking is applied. The best results, in terms of average, were obtained using WI and masking 100 biased terms for English. The masking strategy was *LengthMask*. Analizing the results shown in Table 3, can be observed that mitigating bias helps the model's generalization for *TwSemEval18* and

Table 4. Cross-domain irony detection *(ES)*

Train/Test	TwIroSvA19es	TwIroSvA19mx	NewsIroSvA19cu
BETO			
TwIroSvA19es	×	0.552	0.523
TwIroSvA19mx	**0.553**	×	0.582
NewsIroSvA19cu	0.527	0.577	×
Masking + BETO			
TwIroSvA19es	×	**0.579**	**0.580**
TwIroSvA19mx	*0.545*	×	**0.589**
NewsIroSvA19cu	**0.543**	0.577	×

---

[5] https://github.com/reynierortegabueno86/NLDB2023-Irony-Paper.

TwMohammad15. However, for *TwRiloff13*, a drop in the performance was obtained. The best results are in bold, and those that decrease their performance are in italic. The Spanish and Italian procedures are identical, but BETO and ALBERTo were fine-tuned. The results are shown in Table 4 and Table 5. Spanish cross-domain results highlight that WI and the masking strategy *PoS-Mask* were the best setting. When the bias is mitigated on *TwIroSvA19es* and *NewsIroSvA19cu* a positive impact on the model generalization is observed. Conversely, we obtained a slight drop in the performance of the model trained on *TwIroSvA19mx* and validated on *TwIroSvA19es*. Bias mitigation on the Italian corpora shows the best performance w.r.t the other results. Specifically the model's generalization is improved on both corpora. These results were achieved using PWI as bias measure and the *PoSMask* masking strategy.

Table 5. Cross-domain irony detection *(IT)*

Train/Test	*TwIronItaTwittiro18*	*TwIronItaOther18*
ALBERTo		
TwIronItaTwittiro18	×	0.604
TwIronItaOther18	0.686	×
Masking + ALBERTo		
TwIronItaTwittiro18	×	**0.705**
TwIronItaOther18	**0.700**	×

In the second experiment, we extend our idea of bias mitigation to the cross-language scenario. For that, we fine-tuned mBERT on *TwSemEval18*, *TwIronIta-Full18*, and *MixIroSvA19Full* independently; for validation, we used the two remaining corpora. We fine-tuned the mBERT for each corpus without bias mitigation and applied the mitigation strategy. The results are shown in Table 6. It can be easily note that in four out of six experiments mitigating bias increases the model's performance (see Table 6). We noticed that training in Italian or Spanish and validating in Spanish and Italian are the best pair of languages. In the case of training the model on English when tested in Spanish its performance decreases. Similarly, results decrease when the model is trained on Italian and validated on English. This can be because the kind of irony covered in TwSemEval18 is situational and common usage of irony, whereas, in Italian and Spanish corpora, irony is about controversial topics such as *Mexican government*, *flat earthers, politician Pablo Iglesias*, etc. for Spanish and; *immigrants, school reform*, etc. for Italian. These results were obtained using WI as bias measure and the *PoSMask* masking strategy.

Table 6. Cross-language irony detection

Train/Test	MixIroSvA19Full	TwSemEval18	TwIronItaFull18
mBERT			
MixIroSvA19Full	×	0.461	0.557
TwSemEval18	**0.486**	×	0.498
TwIronItaFull18	0.498	**0.516**	×
Masking + mBERT			
MixIroSvA19Full	×	**0.469**	**0.572**
TwSemEval18	*0.463*	×	**0.533**
TwIronItaFull18	**0.521**	*0.513*	×

This work has different limitations, and we are aware that WI and PWI measures are dependent on the background corpora used to calculate the ratio of the frequencies of terms. The writing style of the background corpus is different from the ironic corpora which were built from Twitter. PWI and WI also do not analyze the commonality and differences among ironic corpora which help to find domain- and language independent ironic patterns.

5 Conclusion

In conclusion, our study provides insights into the impact of lexical bias on cross-domain and cross-language irony detection. The results show that irony corpora are biased and this bias affects the performance of BERT-based models for irony detection. The WI measure was able to identify a set of biased terms in each corpus (**RQ1**). Instead, the use of simple bias mitigation methods show an improvement in the generalization of these models in an out of domain scenario (**RQ2**). Moreover, it was observed that reducing the bias impacts positively in the generalization across languages (**RQ3**). These findings suggest the need for continued efforts to develop unbiased irony corpora and to explore further methods to mitigate bias to ensure that these models can be applied across different domains and languages.

Based on our findings, there are several avenues for future work in the field of irony detection. Firstly, we plan to extend our analysis to a broader range of languages and domains to evaluate the generalizability of our approach. Secondly, we aim to develop more robust measures to identify biased words in irony corpora, by not only considering the ratio between word frequencies in the corpus and the background, but also contrasting terms across corpora to identify invariant and domain-dependent terms. Furthermore, future research could explore social bias in ironic language and investigate ways to address it.

Acknowledgement. The work of Ortega-Bueno and Rosso was in the framework of the FairTransNLP research project (PID2021-124361OB-C31) funded by MCIN/AEI/10.13039/501100011033 and by ERDF, EU A way of making Europe.

References

1. Baeza-Yates, R.: Bias on the web. Commun. ACM **61**(6), 54–61 (2018)
2. Barbieri, F., Basile, V., Croce, D., Nissim, M., Novielli, N., Patti, V.: Overview of the Evalita 2016 SENTIment POLarity classification task. In: Proceedings of Third Italian Conference on Computational Linguistics (CLiC-it 2016) & Fifth Evaluation Campaign of Natural Language Processing and Speech Tools for Italian. Final Workshop (EVALITA 2016) (2016)
3. Baroni, M., Bernardini, S., Ferraresi, A., Zanchetta, E.: The WaCky wide web: a collection of very large linguistically processed web-crawled corpora. Lang. Resour. Eval. **43**(3), 209–226 (2009)
4. Basile, V., Lai, M., Sanguinetti, M.: Long-term social media data collection at the university of Turin. In: Fifth Italian Conference on Computational Linguistics (CLiC-it 2018), pp. 1–6. CEUR-WS (2018)
5. Benamara, F., Grouin, C., Karoui, J., Moriceau, V., Robba, I.: Analyse d'Opinion et langage figuratif dans des tweets: présentation et Résultats du défi fouille de textes DEFT2017. In: Actes de l'atelier DEFT2017 Associé à la Conférence TALN. Orléans, France (2017)
6. Beukeboom, C.J., Burgers, C.: Seeing bias in irony: how recipients infer speakers' stereotypes from their ironic remarks about social-category members. Group Process. Intergroup Relat. **23**(7), 1085–1102 (2020)
7. Cañete, J., Chaperon, G., Fuentes, R., Ho, J.H., Kang, H., Pérez, J.: Spanish pretrained BERT model and evaluation data. In: PML4DC at ICLR 2020 (2020)
8. Cardellino, C.: Spanish billion words corpus and embeddings (2016). https://crscardellino.me/SBWCE/, https://crscardellino.me/SBWCE/. Accessed 14 Mar 2023
9. Carvalho, P., Sarmento, L., Silva, M.J., De Oliveira, E.: Clues for detecting irony in user-generated contents: oh...!! it's "so easy";-. In: Proceedings of the 1st International CIKM Workshop on Topic-Sentiment Analysis for Mass Opinion, pp. 53–56 (2009)
10. Chakhachiro, R.: Translating irony in political commentary texts from English into Arabic. Babel **53**(3), 216 (2007)
11. Cignarella, A.C., et al.: Overview of the Evalita 2018 task on irony detection in Italian tweets (IronITA). In: Proceedings of the 6th evaluation campaign of Natural Language Processing and Speech tools for Italian (EVALITA'18). CEUR.org, Turin (2018)
12. Cignarella, A.T., Basile, V., Sanguinetti, M., Bosco, C., Rosso, P., Benamara, F.: Multilingual irony detection with dependency syntax and neural models. In: 28th International Conference on Computational Linguistics, pp. 1346–1358. Association for Computational Linguistics (ACL) (2020)
13. Cignarella, A.T., Bosco, C., Patti, V., Lai, M.: Twittirò: an Italian twitter corpus with a multi-layered annotation for irony. IJCoL. Ital. J. Comput. Linguist. **4**(4–2), 25–43 (2018)
14. Clark, H.H., Gerrig, R.J.: On the pretense theory of irony. J. Exp. Psychol. Gener. **113**(1), 121–126 (1984)
15. Clear, J.H.: The British national corpus. In: The Digital World, pp. 163–187 (1993)
16. Colston, H.L.: Irony as indirectness cross-linguistically: on the scope of generic mechanisms. In: Capone, A., García-Carpintero, M., Falzone, A. (eds.) Indirect Reports and Pragmatics in the World Languages. PPPP, vol. 19, pp. 109–131. Springer, Cham (2019). https://doi.org/10.1007/978-3-319-78771-8_6

17. del Pilar Salas-Zárate, M., Alor-Hernández, G., Sánchez-Cervantes, J.L., Paredes-Valverde, M.A., García-Alcaraz, J.L., Valencia-García, R.: Review of English literature on figurative language applied to social networks. Knowl. Inf. Syst. **62**(6), 2105–2137 (2020)

18. Devlin, J., Chang, M.W., Lee, K., Toutanova, C.: BERT: pre-training of deep bidirectional transformers for language understanding. In: Proceedings of the 2019 Conference of the NAACL: HLT, Volume 1 (Long and Short Papers), pp. 4171–4186. ACL, Minneapolis (2019)

19. Famiglini, L., Fersini, E., Rosso, P.: On the generalization of figurative language detection: the case of irony and sarcasm. In: Métais, E., Meziane, F., Horacek, H., Kapetanios, E. (eds.) NLDB 2021. LNCS, vol. 12801, pp. 178–186. Springer, Cham (2021). https://doi.org/10.1007/978-3-030-80599-9_16

20. Farías, D.I.H., Patti, V., Rosso, P.: Irony detection in Twitter: the role of Affective content. ACM Trans. Internet Technol. **16**(3), 1–24 (2016)

21. Frenda, S., Cignarella, A.T., Basile, V., Bosco, C., Patti, V., Rosso, P.: The unbearable hurtfulness of sarcasm. Expert Syst. Appl. **193**, 116398 (2022)

22. Garrido-Muñoz, I., Montejo-Ráez, A., Martínez-Santiago, F., Ureña-López, L.A.: A survey on bias in deep NLP. Appl. Sci. (Switz.) **11**(7), 3184 (2021)

23. Ghanem, B., Karoui, J., Benamara, F., Moriceau, V., Rosso, P.: IDAT at FIRE2019: overview of the track on irony detection in Arabic tweets. In: Proceedings of the 11th Forum for Information Retrieval Evaluation, pp. 10–13 (2019)

24. Ghanem, Bilal, Karoui, Jihen, Benamara, Farah, Rosso, Paolo, Moriceau, Véronique.: Irony detection in a multilingual context. In: Jose, J.M., et al. (eds.) ECIR 2020. LNCS, vol. 12036, pp. 141–149. Springer, Cham (2020). https://doi.org/10.1007/978-3-030-45442-5_18

25. Giora, R.: On irony and negation. Discour. Process. **19**(2), 239–264 (1995)

26. González, J.Á., Hurtado, L.F., Pla, F.: Transformer based contextualization of pre-trained word embeddings for irony detection in Twitter. Inf. Process. Manage. **57**, 1–15 (2020)

27. Grice, H.P.: Logic and conversation. In: Cole, P., Morgan., J. (eds.) Syntax and Semantics 3: Speech Acts, pp. 41–58. Academic Press, New York (1975)

28. Howard, J., Ruder, S.: Universal language model fine-tuning for text classification. In: Proceedings of the 56th Annual Meeting of the ACL, pp. 328–339. Association for Computational Linguistics (2018)

29. Karoui, J., Benamara, F., Moriceau, V.: Automatic Detection of Irony, 1st edn. Wiley, Hoboken (2019)

30. Maynard, D., Greenwood, M.A.: Who cares about sarcastic tweets? Investigating the impact of sarcasm on sentiment Analysis. In: Proceedings of the Ninth International Conference on Language Resources and Evaluation (LREC 2014). European Language Resources Association (2014)

31. Mehrabi, N., Morstatter, F., Saxena, N., Lerman, K., Galstyan, A.: A survey on bias and fairness in machine learning. ACM Comput. Surv. **54**(6), 1–35 (2021). https://doi.org/10.1145/3457607

32. Mohammad, S.M., Zhu, X., Kiritchenko, S., Martin, J.: Sentiment, emotion, purpose, and style in electoral tweets. Inf. Process. Manage. **51**(4), 480–499 (2015)

33. Nguyen, D.Q., Vu, T., Tuan Nguyen, A.: BERTweet: a pre-trained language model for English tweets. In: Proceedings of the 2020 Conference on Empirical Methods in Natural Language Processing: System Demonstrations, pp. 9–14. Association for Computational Linguistics (2020)

34. Ortega-Bueno, R., Chulvi, B., Rangel, F., Paolo, R., Fersini, E.: Profiling irony and stereotype spreaders on twitter (IROSTEREO) at PAN 2022. CEUR-WS. org (2022)

35. Ortega-Bueno, R., Rangel, F., Hernández Farías, D., Rosso, P., Montes-y Gómez, M., Medina Pagola, J.E.: Overview of the task on irony detection in Spanish variants. In: Proceedings of the Iberian Languages Evaluation Forum (IberLEF 2019), Co-located with 34th Conference of the Spanish Society for Natural Language Processing (SEPLN 2019), vol. 2421, pp. 229–256. CEUR-WS. org (2019)

36. Poletto, F., Basile, V., Sanguinetti, M., Bosco, C., Patti, V.: Resources and benchmark corpora for hate speech detection: a systematic review. Lang. Resour. Eval. **55**, 1–47 (2020)

37. Polignano, M., Basile, V., Basile, P., de Gemmis, M., Semeraro, G.: ALBERTo: modeling Italian social media language with BERT. IJCoL. Ital. J. Comput. Linguist. **5**(5–2), 11–31 (2019)

38. Ptáček, T., Habernal, I., Hong, J.: Sarcasm detection on Czech and English Twitter. In: Proceedings of COLING 2014, the 25th International Conference on Computational Linguistics, pp. 213–223. Dublin City University and Association for Computational Linguistics, Dublin (2014)

39. Riloff, E., Qadir, A., Surve, P., De Silva, L., Gilbert, N., Huang, R.: Sarcasm as contrast between a positive sentiment and negative situation. In: Conference on Empirical Methods in Natural Language Processing (EMNLP 2013), pp. 704–714 (2013)

40. Sánchez-Junquera, J., Rosso, P., Montes, M., Chulvi, B., et al.: Masking and BERT-based models for stereotype identication. Procesamiento Lenguaje Nat. **67**, 83–94 (2021)

41. Sánchez-Junquera, J., Rosso, P., Montes, M., Ponzetto, S.P.: Masking and transformer-based models for hyperpartisanship detection in news. In: Proceedings of the International Conference on Recent Advances in Natural Language Processing (RANLP 2021), pp. 1244–1251 (2021)

42. Sánchez-Junquera, J., Villaseñor-Pineda, L., Montes-y Gómez, M., Rosso, P., Stamatatos, E.: Masking domain-specific information for cross-domain deception detection. Pattern Recogn. Lett. **135**, 122–130 (2020)

43. Sanguinetti, M., Poletto, F., Bosco, C., Patti, V., Stranisci, M.: An Italian twitter corpus of hate speech against immigrants. In: Proceedings of the Eleventh International Conference on Language Resources and Evaluation (LREC 2018) (2018)

44. Sap, M.: Positive AI with social commonsense models. Ph.D. thesis (2021)

45. Sperber, D., Wilson, D.: Irony and the use-mention distinction. In: Cole, P. (ed.) Radical Pragmatics, pp. 295–318. Academic Press, New York (1981)

46. Van Hee, C., Lefever, E., Hoste, V.: SemEval-2018 task 3: irony detection in English tweets. In: Proceedings of The 12th International Workshop on Semantic Evaluation, pp. 39–50. Association for Computational Linguistics, New Orleans (2018)

47. Veale, T.: Creative language retrieval: a robust hybrid of information retrieval and linguistic creativity. In: Proceedings of the 49th Annual Meeting of the Association for Computational Linguistics: Human Language Technologies, pp. 278–287. Association for Computational Linguistics, Portland (2011)

48. Wiegand, M., Ruppenhofer, J., Kleinbauer, T.: Detection of abusive language: the problem of biased datasets. In: Proceedings of the 2019 Conference of the North American Chapter of the Association for Computational Linguistics: Human Language Technologies, Volume 1 (Long and Short Papers), pp. 602–608. Association for Computational Linguistics, Minneapolis (2019)

49. Wilson, D., Sperber, D.: On verbal irony. Lingua **87**, 53–76 (1992)
50. Zhuang, L., Wayne, L., Ya, S., Jun, Z.: A robustly optimized BERT pre-training approach with post-training. In: Proceedings of the 20th Chinese National Conference on Computational Linguistics, pp. 1218–1227. Chinese Information Processing Society of China (2021)

Prompt and Instruction-Based Tuning for Response Generation in Conversational Question Answering

Yujie Xing[(✉)] and Peng Liu[ID]

Norwegian University of Science and Technology, Trondheim, Norway
{yujie.xing,peng.liu}@ntnu.no

Abstract. In recent years, prompt-based tuning and instruction-based tuning have emerged as popular approaches for natural language processing. In this paper, we investigate the application of prompt and instruction-based tuning approaches for response generation in conversational question answering. We approach this task from both extractive and generative angles, where we adopt prompt-based tuning for the extractive angle and instruction-based tuning for the generative angle. Additionally, we utilize multi-task learning to integrate these two angles. To evaluate the performance of our proposed approaches, we conduct experiments on the GPT-2 model. The results show that the approaches improve performance by 18% on F1 score over the baseline. We share our codes and data for reproducibility. (https://github.com/yujie-xing/Multi-Turn_QA_Prompt).

Keywords: Prompt · Instruction · Pre-Trained Language Model · Response Generation · Conversational Question Answering

1 Introduction

Conversational Question Answering (CQA) is a QA dialogue system that can answer user questions based on a given document. CQA is an extension of traditional QA systems to a conversational setting and engages in multi-turn conversation to satisfy a user's information needs. According to the types of QA, CQA is studied in two settings: extractive and generative. In the extractive setting, the answer is marked as a span in the text paragraph, whereas in the generative setting, i.e. response generation in CQA, the answer is free-form text generated by autoregressively predicting tokens.

With the rapid development of language modeling techniques, a lot of pre-trained language models have been successfully applied to extractive CQA [3, 20], generative CQA [7,27] and unified systems that solve various CQA tasks through a single model [10,24]. Recently, Gekhman et al. [5] have conducted a comprehensive robustness study of history modeling approaches for CQA and propose a prompt-based history highlighting method to improve robustness while

© The Author(s), under exclusive license to Springer Nature Switzerland AG 2023
E. Métais et al. (Eds.): NLDB 2023, LNCS 13913, pp. 156–169, 2023.
https://doi.org/10.1007/978-3-031-35320-8_11

maintaining overall high performance. However, prompts are generally short and do not generalize well to reformulations and new tasks.

Instruction tuning is an emergent paradigm where models are trained on a variety of tasks with natural language instructions. Instructions of natural language formats are easy for questioners to ask questions, and are proven to achieve a good performance due to the nature of the language model [6]. To the best of our knowledge, we are the first to apply instruction tuning for response generation on conversational question answering. Our paper proposes approaches for enhancing the response generation of conversational question answering by integrating prompt-based and instruction-based tuning. We adopt the prompt-based tuning method introduced by Gekhman et al. [5] to improve from the extractive angle on the multi-turn scenario. Additionally, we propose an instruction-based tuning method to enhance from the generative angle, based on the work of Zhong et al. [29] and Gupta et al. [6]. Furthermore, we investigate the integration of these two angles through multi-task learning.

In our experiments, we verify the influence of prompt-based tuning, instruction-based tuning, and multi-task learning for the task. We evaluate the performance of various settings, including prompt-based tuning with or without multi-task learning, prompt-based with or without instruction-based tuning, and prompt-based tuning with both multi-task learning and instruction-based tuning. We conduct the experiments on GPT-2 and evaluate the results on F1 score with 2 modes: the decoding mode and the evaluation mode. Additionally, we assess the extractive question answering part of the settings with a GPT-2 fine-tuned on the extractive question answering task.

The results show that our prompt-based tuning together with other approaches has improved the performance by about 18% on F1 score over the baseline, and the instruction-based tuning and multi-task learning settings have improved further at about 1% compared to pure prompt-based tuning approach.

The main contributions of this work are:

- To the best of our knowledge, we are the first to incorporate instruction tuning in conversational question answering.
- We investigate tuning approaches based on prompt and instruction for the response generation task on conversational question answering. The approaches are simple and easy to be adapted to other models.
- We conduct comprehensive experiments on the influence of instruction-based tuning, prompt-based tuning and multi-task learning for this task. The results show that the best approach improves about 18% on F1 score than the baseline.

The paper is organized as follows: we summarize related works in Sect. 2. We define our task and introduce the approaches used in our research in Sect. 3. In Sect. 4 we describe the setups of our experiments, and in Sect. 5 we present our results. We conclude and describe future works in Sect. 6.

2   Related Work

2.1   Conversational Question Answering with Prompts

In earlier times, recurrent neural networks (RNN) and attention variations were used to model conversation histories of QA [21,30]. Modern approaches leverage transformer-based pre-trained language models for QA by fine-tuning the models on massive annotated data from downstream QA tasks [8,11]. Recently, some works proposed to effectively adapt the pre-trained LMs to the downstream QA with only a handful of annotated data [2,20]. For instance, Chada et al. [2] proposed to cast QA as a text-generation problem by designing a prompt of a concatenation of the question and a special mask token representing the answer span. Similarly, Chen et al. [3] proposed to use Masked Language Model on entities to enhance few-shot QA learning. However, none of the abovementioned research works adopt instructions in prompt tuning for QA tasks. Considering the various QA tasks, some works explore multi-task learning QA by jointly training a single encoder to enhance the sharing of knowledge across tasks [4,22]. However, these works may suffer from poor scalability and flexibility when facing new types of QA tasks due to the requirement of deploying distinct prediction heads for different tasks.

2.2   Response Generation on Question Answering Task

Generative QA models [7,10,12,19] have shown remarkable performance, where the goal is to generate answers by autoregressively predicting tokens. Generative methods are more often used in open-domain [7,12,19,27] and unified settings [10,24]. Roberts et al. [19] proposed to use large pre-trained generative models, without using additional knowledge, for open-domain question answering. Lewis et al. [12] introduced retrieval-augmented generative models for open-domain question answering. Khashabi et al. [10] and Tafjord et al. [24] proposed to learn various QA formats in a unified way to alleviate the manual effort of task-specific design. Different from them, our work focuses on conversational answer generation with passages from the given task and investigates the influence of instruction tuning, prompt tuning and multi-task learning for conversational QA.

2.3   Instruction Tuning

Instruction tuning is a paradigm where models are trained on a variety of tasks with natural language instructions. Recent literature has been motivated by building models that are generalizable across a variety of NLP tasks when prompted with a few examples [1,13,14] or language definitions and constraints [26,28] introduced natural language instructions to improve the performance of LMs such as BART and GPT-3 for cross-task. Followed by this, FLAN [25] has been proposed, which uses instructions to achieve generalization across unseen tasks. Recently, Mishra et al. [9] have shown reframing instructional prompts can boost both few-shot and zero-shot model performance. The InstructGPT model is proposed, which is fine-tuned with human feedback [15]. Puri et al. [18] introduced instruction augmentation to improve model performance in task-specific, multi-task and cross-task learning paradigms. Prasad et al. [17] introduced Gradient-free Instructional Prompt Search (GrIPS) to improve task instructions for large language models. Motivated by the effectiveness of instruction tuning, in this work, we explore the potential application of instructional prompts for conversational question-answering response generation.

3   Methodology

In this section, we first define the tasks of conversational question answering and response generation, and we introduce how these tasks are realized under GPT-2. After that, we explain the proposed multi-task learning, prompt tuning, and instruction tuning in detail.

3.1   Conversational Question Answering

The task of conversational question answering is to predict the answer span (start position, end position) in a passage for the given question and the previous questions and answer spans. The question answering task can be transferred to two classification tasks: one for the start position, and the other for the end position. Given a question Q and a passage X, the tasks are to calculate the probability of the t-th token in the passage X is the start position $P_{x_t=\text{start}}$ and is the end position $P_{x_t=\text{end}}$:

$$P(x_t = \text{start} \mid Q, X) \tag{1}$$
$$P(x_t = \text{end} \mid Q, X), \tag{2}$$

where $Q = q_1, \ldots, q_k$, $X = x_1, \ldots, x_m$ are sequences of tokens.

The difference between the task of conversational question answering with regular question answering is that there are conversation histories, i.e. multiple turns of questions and answer spans.

The question answering task is dealt with the GPT-2 model as follows. First, a hidden vector that is to be input to the transformer block is calculated as:

$$h_0 = E(Q, X) + (E_0, E_1) + W_p, \tag{3}$$

where $E(Q, X)$ is the sub-word embedding for question Q and passage X. E_0 and E_1 are state embeddings, where E_0 is assigned to the question, and E_1 is assigned to the passage. W_p is a pre-trained position embedding. Then, the probability of the subword t to be the start or end position is calculated as:

$$h_X = transformer\_block(h_0)[X] \tag{4}$$
$$P(x_t = start) = softmax(A \cdot h_X)[t] \tag{5}$$
$$P(x_t = end) = softmax(B \cdot h_X)[t], \tag{6}$$

where $A \in \mathbb{R}^{1 \times \dim(h)}$ and $B \in \mathbb{R}^{1 \times \dim(h)}$, h_X denotes for slice of the passage X part in the hidden vector, and $[t]$ denotes for the t-th subword token in the passage X. We simplify the structure of the transformer block as $transformer\_block$. In the block, a mask bans past words from attending to future words. Equation 5 and Eq. 6 transfer $h_X \in \mathbb{R}^{\dim(h) \times |X|}$ into sequences of probabilities for each subword token in X, where the probability of a subword t being the start position or the end position can be obtained.

3.2   Response Generation

The task of response generation is to predict the next token given the past and current tokens of the context and response, and to make the generated response as similar to the original response as possible. In the scale of the conversational question answering task, the response generation task can be described as follows. Probability of answer Y given a question Q and a passage X is predicted as:

$$P(Y \mid Q, X) = \prod_{t=1}^{n} P(y_t | y_1, \ldots, y_{t-1}, Q, X), \tag{7}$$

where $Q = q_1, \ldots, q_k$, $X = x_1, \ldots, x_m$ and $Y = y_1, \ldots, y_n$ are sequences of tokens. (Q,X,Y) is a question-passage-answer tuple.

The response generation task is dealt with the GPT-2 model as follows. First, a hidden vector that is to be input to the transformer block is calculated as:

$$h_{0[t]} = E(Q, X, Y_{[1:t]}) + (E_0, E_0, E_1) + W_p, \tag{8}$$

where $Y_{[1:t]}$ is $(y_1, \ldots, y_t)$, $E(Q, X, Y_{[1:t]})$ is the sub-word embedding for question Q, passage X and answer $Y_{[1:t]}$. E_0 and E_1 are state embeddings, where E_0 is assigned to the question and passage, and E_1 is assigned to the answer. W_p is a pre-trained position embedding. Then, the probability of the subword to generate is calculated as:

$$h_{[t]} = transformer\_block(h_{0[t]}) \tag{9}$$

$$P(y)_{t+1} = softmax(E^{\top}(h_{[t]})), \tag{10}$$

where $y \in V$, and V stands for the sub-word vocabulary. We simplify the structure of the transformer block as $transformer\_block$. The hidden vector of t_{th} sub-word is used to generate the probability distribution for the vocabulary $(P(y), y \in V)$ for $(t+1)_{\text{th}}$ sub-word. $E^{\top}$ means that the model uses the sub-word embeddings in calculating sub-word probabilities for generation.

3.3   Prompt-Based Tuning

Following Gekhman et al. [5], we add prompts to the passage for the conversational question answering task, where the prompts indicate the answers to the previous questions. For any turn i, all the answer spans of the previous turns (S_j, A_j) $(j \in [1, \ldots, i-1])$ are marked in the passage X with the prompts $<j>$. Examples of prompt-based tuning can be found in the following Table 1:

Table 1. An example of prompt-based tuning

Turn	Question	Text of Answer Span	Prompted Passage
1	What color was Cotton?	a little white kitten named Cotton	Once upon a time, in a barn near a farm house, there lived a little white kitten named Cotton. Cotton lived high up...
2	Where did she live?	in a barn near a farm house, there lived a little white kitten	Once upon a time, in a barn near a farm house, there lived <1> a little white kitten named Cotton <1>. Cotton lived high up...
3	Did she live alone?	Cotton wasn't alone	Once upon a time, <2> in a barn near a farm house, there lived <1> a little white kitten <2> named Cotton <1>. Cotton lived high up...

Note that for any turn j that does not have an answer span, there is not a prompt $<j>$ for it.

3.4 Instruction-Based Tuning

Furthermore, following Zhong et al. [29] and Gupta et al. [6], we add instructions to the inputs. We use two kinds of instructions: an *instruction* at the beginning of the input, and several *guidances* among the sections that constitute the input. The instruction at the beginning of the input is word-based, and it introduces what the task is about. The guidances are word-based with symbols, such as "[Instruction]:", "[Question]:", "[Passage]:" and "[Answer]:", which separate each section and clarify what each section is. We denote an instruction as a sequence of tokens: $I = I_1, \ldots, I_j$, and guidances for each section as $G_{\text{Section 1}}, G_{\text{Section 2}}, \cdots$. The instruction and the guidances are inserted into the original input as follows:

$$[G_{\text{instruction}}, I, G_{\text{question}}, Q, G_{\text{passage}}, X, G_{\text{answer}}, Y], \tag{11}$$

where Q is the question, X is the passage, and Y is the answer. Q, X and Y are all sequences of tokens, and in Eq. 11 they are concatenated. We denote $X_I = [G_{\text{instruction}}, I, G_{\text{question}}, Q, G_{\text{passage}}, X, G_{\text{answer}}]$, then the hidden vector to be input to the transformer block is calculated as:

$$h_{0[t]} = E(X_I, Y_{[1:t]}) + (E_0, E_1) + W_p, \tag{12}$$

3.5 Multi-task Learning

To fully leverage the extractive question answering task, we employ a multi-task learning approach to integrate it with the response generation task. Specifically, we use the same hidden vector as described in Eq. 7 as input to the transformer block, which is then used for calculating the probability distribution of the vocabulary for the next token, as well as the probability of the start and end position for each token in the passage. The multi-task learning approach optimizes both answer span extraction and response generation simultaneously. The loss is then integrated as:

$$\mathcal{L}_{QA} = \frac{\mathcal{L}_{\text{start position}} + \mathcal{L}_{\text{end position}}}{2} \tag{13}$$

$$\mathcal{L} = \mathcal{L}_{QA} + \mathcal{L}_{\text{response generation}}. \tag{14}$$

4   Experimental Setup

4.1   Dataset

We employ the CoQA (Conversational Question Answering) dataset [21] for our research. The CoQA dataset is a collection of conversational question answering instances spanning a broad range of domains, such as literature, news, and Wikipedia articles. The dataset is conversational because it includes conversational histories, i.e., the previous turns in a conversation leading up to the current question-answer pair. The answers in the dataset include both answer spans for extractive question answering and human-written free-form answers for generative question answering.

4.2   Model and Tuning

In the experiments, we will evaluate 5 models:

(1) Response generation (baseline)
(2) Response generation with prompt-based tuning (`prompt`)
(3) Response generation with prompt-based tuning & instruction-based tuning (`w instruct`)
(4) Response generation with prompt-based tuning & multi-task learning (`w multi-task`)
(5) Response generation with prompt-based tuning & instruction-based tuning & multi-task learning (`w multi-task & w instruct`)

We have excluded three other settings, namely response generation with instruction-based tuning, response generation with multi-task learning, and response generation with instruction-based tuning & multi-task learning, since prompts are necessary indicators for multi-turns. Our task–the conversational question answering–is based on multi-turns, so any model without prompt-based tuning, other than the baseline, is considered not relevant to the task.

The instructions and prompts that we used in the prompt-based tuning and instruction-based tuning are described in the following Table 2:

Table 2. An example for prompt and instruction based tuning

	Prompt-Based Tuning	Instruction-Based Tuning
Instruction	\	[Instruction]: Answer the question based on the given passage
Question	Where did she live?	[Question]: Where did she live?
Passage	Once upon a time, in a barn near a farm house, there lived <1> a little white kitten named Cotton <1>. Cotton lived high up...	[Passage]: Once upon a time, in a barn near a farm house, there lived a little white kitten named Cotton. Cotton lived high up...
Answer	in a barn	[Answer]: in a barn

4.3 Training

Our implementation makes use of Pytorch [16] and the HuggingFace Transformers[1]. We adopted GPT-2 basic[2] which has 12 layers and 12 heads with a dimension of 768. The training procedure was with a batch size of 16, 10 epochs, a learning rate of $3 \cdot 10^{-5}$, a weight decay of 0.01, cross-entropy loss and AdamW. The input sequences are 1024 tokens.

4.4 Evaluation

We evaluate the similarity between the human input answers and the generated answers using the F1 score. We compare the performance of five models, namely the baseline, `prompt`, `w instruct`, `w multi-task`, and `w multi-task & w instruct`, using the official dev dataset for evaluation. We compare the latter 4 models with the baseline and the latter 3 models with the prompt model. To ensure consistency, we limit the maximum output length to 64 tokens. We use two different evaluation modes, decoding mode and evaluation mode, to assess the performance of the models.

In decoding mode, models are not provided with any information about the previous turns and are required to use the predicted answer spans from the previous turn as prompts for generating responses. Only models with multi-task learning can generate answers under this mode. In contrast, the evaluation mode provides the correct information on previous turns to the models. This mode enables pure generation models to handle multi-turns with prompts, thus making them more accurate in generating responses. We employ prompt-tuning in the evaluation mode, whereby the correct information on the previous answers is prompted in the same way as introduced in Sect. 3.3.

---

[1] https://huggingface.co/.
[2] https://huggingface.co/gpt2.

By default, the evaluation mode generates better results than the decoding mode, given the correct information on previous turns. We provide results for both the evaluation mode and decoding mode to ensure a comprehensive evaluation. In many real-life scenarios, we cannot assume that we have access to the correct answer spans for previous questions, which makes evaluation using the evaluation mode impractical. Therefore, by including decoding mode results, we can provide a more realistic evaluation of our approach that reflects the real-life scenarios.

We also evaluate the performance of the extractive QA part of the two models with multi-task learning (w multi-task and w multi-task & w instruct) and compare them with an GPT-2 model fine-tuned on extractive question answering task. We measure the similarity between the predicted answer span text and the original answer span text using the F1 score.

We show which mode is applied for each model in the following Table 3:

Table 3. Models and modes

	Decoding Mode	Evaluation Mode
baseline	✗	✓
prompt	✗	✓
w instruct	✗	✓
w multi-task	✓	✓
w multi-task & w instruct	✓	✓

5 Results

5.1 Automatic Results

Table 4 and Table 5 summarize the response generation performance of five models w.r.t. F1 score and its improvements. Since only models with multi-task learning can generate answers in the decoding mode, we use backslash '\' to denote this setting is not applicable to the first three models.

Table 4. F1 results for different models. Numbers in the brackets state F1 improvements compared to the baseline under evaluation mode.

	F1 (decoding mode)	F1 (evaluation mode)
baseline	\	53.8
prompt	\	63.0 (+17.1)
w instruct	\	63.7 (+18.4)
w multi-task	61.6 (+14.4)	63.9 (+18.7)
w multi-task & w instruct	56.5 (+5.0)	57.8 (+7.4)

Table 5. F1 improvement compared to prompt (evaluation mode)

	F1 (decoding mode)	F1 (evaluation mode)
w instruct	\	+1.1
w multi-task	−2.2	+1.4
w multi-task & w instruct	−10.3	−8.2

From the results, we have the following observations:

1) As shown in all the tables, the performance of the evaluation mode is better than decoding mode. This is because the evaluation mode can provide the correct answer spans from previous turns to the models for prompt-tuning.
2) In Table 4, prompt-based tuning outperforms baseline by a large margin, demonstrating that prompt can encode valuable information about the answers from previous conversation turns for model tuning. Besides, instruction-based tuning can further improve the response generation performance, which proves the usefulness of injecting task-specific guidance during fine-tuning. Apart from that, compared with the "prompt" model and the "w instruct" model, the "w multi-task" model achieves the best performance, from which we can find the conversational question answering task can significantly facilitate the response generation task.
3) The brackets of Table 4 show the F1 score improvements compared to the baseline under evaluation mode. As expected, all the models have certain performance improvements compared to the baseline. In particular, the "w multi-task" model has the highest performance improvement, which is 18.7% and 14.4% in the evaluation and decoding modes, respectively.
4) Table 5 shows the F1 score improvement compared to the "prompt" model (evaluation mode). We find that the performance of the "w multi-task" model drops by 2.2% in the decoding mode, suggesting that answer prediction errors from previous conversation turns can accumulate to have a large impact on the response generation task. Another interesting observation is that the performance of the "w multi-task & w instruct" model drops 10.3% and 8.2% in the decoding and evaluation modes, respectively. This is probably because the optimization of the multi-task learning and instruction-based tuning are conflicting with each other.

Table 6. F1 results and improvement for the extractive question answering part. Answer span texts instead of human answers are used for evaluation.

	F1 (decoding mode)	F1 (evaluation mode)
GPT-2 fine-tuned on extractive QA	63.9 (\)	64.7 (\)
w multi-task (QA part)	60.2 (−5.7)	65 (+0.4)
w multi-task & w instruct (QA part)	64.9 (+1.6)	70.1 (+8.3)

Table 6 reports the evaluation results of the extractive question answering part of a GPT-2 model fine-tuned on extractive question answering task and the two models with multi-task learning. Compared with the baseline (GPT-2 fine-tuned on extractive question answering), both multi-task learning models can improve the performance of question answering task, which demonstrates the effectiveness of prompt-based and instruction-based tuning and the boosting effect of the response generation task on the question answering task. We can also observe that the performance of the "w multi-task" model drops by 5.7% in the decoding mode, which is due to the accumulated answer prediction errors from previous turns.

5.2   Qualitative Results

Table 7. An example of the difference between extractive question answering and generated answers

Question	Gold Answer Span Text	Human	Extractive QA Answer	Generated
Is it a small city?	the most populated city in the state of Nevada	No	is the 28th-most populated city in the United States	No
Which state is it in?	Vegas, is the 28th-most populated city in the United States, the most populated city in the state of Nevada	Nevada	is the 28th-most populated city in the United States, the most populated city in the state of Nevada	Nevada
What is it famous for?	The city bills itself as The Entertainment Capital of the World, and is famous for its mega casino hotel	mega casino hotel	famous for its mega casino hotels and associated activities	gambling, shopping, fine dining, entertainment, and nightlife

Table 7 presents a comparative analysis between answer spans predicted by the question answering module and generated answers. The first question demonstrates that for yes/no questions, the generated answer provides a more direct response, whereas the extractive QA answer only provides the information required to answer the question without a simple yes or no. The second question highlights that in cases where there is no direct answer in the passage, the generated answer provides a better response as it directly addresses the question. However, the third question illustrates that in some cases, extractive QA answers are superior, as the given answer is fully grounded in the passage. The generated answer may be based on the passage and relevant to the question, but not necessarily grounded in the passage.

Table 8. An example of answers generated by different models

Question	Baseline	prompt	w instruct	w multi-task	w multi-task & w instruct
What is it famous for?	its the largest city within the greater Mojave Desert	its real things	its gambling, shopping, fine dining, entertainment, and nightlife	gambling, shopping, fine dining, entertainment, and nightlife	a guitar hotels and associated activities

Table 8 provides a comparative analysis of answers generated by different models. The baseline model generates answers that are not related to the question, while the "prompt" model generates answers that are related to the question but not grounded in the passage. In contrast, the "w instruct" and "w multi-task" models generate good quality answers that are grounded in the passage. The "w multi-task & w instruct" model generates an answer that is almost identical to the gold standard, however with a deviation in the form of "guitar hotels" instead of "mega casino hotels". Qualitatively, the "w instruct" and "w multi-task" models can generate better and more robust answers compared to the baseline and the "prompt" model.

6   Conclusion and Future Works

This study aimed to explore different tuning approaches for response generation in conversational question answering. Specifically, we experimented with the effectiveness of prompt tuning, instruction tuning, and multi-task learning on GPT-2, under both decoding mode and evaluation mode. The F1 results demonstrated that prompt-based tuning outperformed the baseline, while models with instruction-based tuning and multi-task learning yielded slightly better results than those with prompt-based tuning alone. In the future, we will explore more multi-task learning algorithms and test instruction-based tuning on a larger language model.

Acknowledgements. This paper is funded by the collaborative project of DNB ASA and Norwegian University of Science and Technology (NTNU). We also received assistance on computing resources from the IDUN cluster of NTNU [23]. We would like to thank Jon Atle Gulla for his helpful comments.

References

1. Bragg, J., Cohan, A., Lo, K., Beltagy, I.: FLEX: unifying evaluation for few-shot NLP. Adv. Neural. Inf. Process. Syst. **34**, 15787–15800 (2021)
2. Chada, R., Natarajan, P.: FewshotQA: a simple framework for few-shot learning of question answering tasks using pre-trained text-to-text models. In: Proceedings of the 2021 Conference on Empirical Methods in Natural Language Processing, pp. 6081–6090 (2021)
3. Chen, X., Zhang, Y., Deng, J., Jiang, J.Y., Wang, W.: Gotta: generative few-shot question answering by prompt-based cloze data augmentation. In: Proceedings of the 2023 SIAM International Conference on Data Mining (SDM) (2023)
4. Deng, Y., et al.: Multi-task learning with multi-view attention for answer selection and knowledge base question answering. In: Proceedings of the AAAI Conference on Artificial Intelligence, vol. 33, pp. 6318–6325 (2019)
5. Gekhman, Z., Oved, N., Keller, O., Szpektor, I., Reichart, R.: On the robustness of dialogue history representation in conversational question answering: a comprehensive study and a new prompt-based method. arXiv preprint arXiv:2206.14796 (2022)
6. Gupta, P., Jiao, C., Yeh, Y.T., Mehri, S., Eskenazi, M., Bigham, J.: InstructDial: improving zero and few-shot generalization in dialogue through instruction tuning. In: Proceedings of the 2022 Conference on Empirical Methods in Natural Language Processing, Abu Dhabi, UAE, pp. 505–525. Association for Computational Linguistics (2022). https://aclanthology.org/2022.emnlp-main.33
7. Izacard, G., Grave, É.: Leveraging passage retrieval with generative models for open domain question answering. In: Proceedings of the 16th Conference of the European Chapter of the Association for Computational Linguistics: Main Volume, pp. 874–880 (2021)
8. Joshi, M., Chen, D., Liu, Y., Weld, D.S., Zettlemoyer, L., Levy, O.: SpanBERT: improving pre-training by representing and predicting spans. Trans. Assoc. Comput. Linguist. **8**, 64–77 (2020)
9. Khashabi, D., Baral, C., Choi, Y., Hajishirzi, H.: Reframing instructional prompts to GPTk's language. In: Findings of the Association for Computational Linguistics: ACL 2022, pp. 589–612 (2022)
10. Khashabi, D., et al.: UnifiedQA: crossing format boundaries with a single QA system. In: Findings of the Association for Computational Linguistics: EMNLP 2020, pp. 1896–1907 (2020)
11. Lan, Z., Chen, M., Goodman, S., Gimpel, K., Sharma, P., Soricut, R.: ALBERT: a lite BERT for self-supervised learning of language representations. arXiv preprint arXiv:1909.11942 (2019)
12. Lewis, P., et al.: Retrieval-augmented generation for knowledge-intensive NLP tasks. Adv. Neural. Inf. Process. Syst. **33**, 9459–9474 (2020)
13. Min, S., Lewis, M., Zettlemoyer, L., Hajishirzi, H.: MetaICL: learning to learn in context. In: Proceedings of the 2022 Conference of the North American Chapter of the Association for Computational Linguistics: Human Language Technologies, pp. 2791–2809 (2022)
14. Min, S., et al.: Rethinking the role of demonstrations: what makes in-context learning work? arXiv preprint arXiv:2202.12837 (2022)
15. Ouyang, L., et al.: Training language models to follow instructions with human feedback. Adv. Neural. Inf. Process. Syst. **35**, 27730–27744 (2022)

16. Paszke, A., et al.: PyTorch: an imperative style, high-performance deep learning library. Advances Neural Inf. Process. Syst. **32** (2019)
17. Prasad, A., Hase, P., Zhou, X., Bansal, M.: GrIPS: gradient-free, edit-based instruction search for prompting large language models. arXiv preprint arXiv:2203.07281 (2022)
18. Puri, R.S., Mishra, S., Parmar, M., Baral, C.: How many data samples is an additional instruction worth? arXiv preprint arXiv:2203.09161 (2022)
19. Raffel, C., et al.: Exploring the limits of transfer learning with a unified text-to-text transformer. J. Mach. Learn. Res. **21**(1), 5485–5551 (2020)
20. Ram, O., Kirstain, Y., Berant, J., Globerson, A., Levy, O.: Few-shot question answering by pretraining span selection. In: Proceedings of the 59th Annual Meeting of the Association for Computational Linguistics and the 11th International Joint Conference on Natural Language Processing (Volume 1: Long Papers), pp. 3066–3079 (2021)
21. Reddy, S., Chen, D., Manning, C.D.: CoQA: a conversational question answering challenge. Trans. Assoc. Comput. Linguist. **7**, 249–266 (2019). https://aclanthology.org/Q19-1016
22. Shen, T., et al.: Multi-task learning for conversational question answering over a large-scale knowledge base. In: Proceedings of the 2019 Conference on Empirical Methods in Natural Language Processing and the 9th International Joint Conference on Natural Language Processing (EMNLP-IJCNLP), pp. 2442–2451 (2019)
23. Själander, M., Jahre, M., Tufte, G., Reissmann, N.: EPIC: an energy-efficient, high-performance GPGPU computing research infrastructure (2019)
24. Tafjord, O., Clark, P.: General-purpose question-answering with macaw. arXiv preprint arXiv:2109.02593 (2021)
25. Wei, J., et al.: Finetuned language models are zero-shot learners. In: International Conference on Learning Representations (2022)
26. Weller, O., Lourie, N., Gardner, M., Peters, M.E.: Learning from task descriptions. In: Proceedings of the 2020 Conference on Empirical Methods in Natural Language Processing (EMNLP), pp. 1361–1375 (2020)
27. Xiong, W., et al.: Answering complex open-domain questions with multi-hop dense retrieval. In: International Conference on Learning Representations (2021)
28. Xu, H., et al.: ZeroPrompt: scaling prompt-based pretraining to 1,000 tasks improves zero-shot generalization. arXiv preprint arXiv:2201.06910 (2022)
29. Zhong, W., et al.: ProQA: structural prompt-based pre-training for unified question answering. In: Proceedings of the 2022 Conference of the North American Chapter of the Association for Computational Linguistics: Human Language Technologies, Seattle, USA, pp. 4230–4243. Association for Computational Linguistics (2022). https://aclanthology.org/2022.naacl-main.313
30. Zhu, C., Zeng, M., Huang, X.: SDNet: contextualized attention-based deep network for conversational question answering. arXiv preprint arXiv:1812.03593 (2018)

IndQNER: Named Entity Recognition Benchmark Dataset from the Indonesian Translation of the Quran

Ria Hari Gusmita[1,2(✉)] ⓘ, Asep Fajar Firmansyah[1,2] ⓘ, Diego Moussallem[1,3] ⓘ, and Axel-Cyrille Ngonga Ngomo[1] ⓘ

[1] Paderborn University, Warburger Street 100, Paderborn, Germany
{ria.gusmita,asep.firmansyah,diego.moussallem,
axel.ngonga}@uni-paderborn.de
[2] The State Islamic University Syarif Hidayatullah Jakarta,
Ir. H. Juanda Street 95, Ciputat, South Tangerang, Banten, Indonesia
{ria.gusmita,asep.airlangga}@uinjkt.ac.id
[3] Jusbrasil, Salvador, Brazil
https://dice-research.org/team/

Abstract. Indonesian is classified as underrepresented in the Natural Language Processing (NLP) field, despite being the tenth most spoken language in the world with 198 million speakers. The paucity of datasets is recognized as the main reason for the slow advancements in NLP research for underrepresented languages. Significant attempts were made in 2020 to address this drawback for Indonesian. The Indonesian Natural Language Understanding (IndoNLU) benchmark was introduced alongside IndoBERT pre-trained language model. The second benchmark, Indonesian Language Evaluation Montage (IndoLEM), was presented in the same year. These benchmarks support several tasks, including Named Entity Recognition (NER). However, all NER datasets are in the public domain and do not contain domain-specific datasets. To alleviate this drawback, we introduce IndQNER, a manually annotated NER benchmark dataset in the religious domain that adheres to a meticulously designed annotation guideline. Since Indonesia has the world's largest Muslim population, we build the dataset from the Indonesian translation of the Quran. The dataset includes 2475 named entities representing 18 different classes. To assess the annotation quality of IndQNER, we perform experiments with BiLSTM and CRF-based NER, as well as IndoBERT fine-tuning. The results reveal that the first model outperforms the second model achieving 0.98 F1 points. This outcome indicates that IndQNER may be an acceptable evaluation metric for Indonesian NER tasks in the aforementioned domain, widening the research's domain range.

Keywords: NER benchmark dataset · Indonesian · Specific domain

E. Métais et al. (Eds.): NLDB 2023, LNCS 13913, pp. 170–185, 2023.
https://doi.org/10.1007/978-3-031-35320-8_12

1   Introduction

Despite being the world's tenth most spoken language, with 198 million speakers[1], Indonesian remains an underrepresented language in the Natural Language Processing (NLP) field. The key issue for the slow progress in NLP for underrepresented languages is frequently defined as a lack of datasets [1]. Fortunately, major efforts to address the problem have recently been initiated: in 2020, the first Indonesian natural language understanding benchmark, IndoNLU, was created [9]. It includes benchmarks for 12 different core NLP tasks, which are divided into four categories: a) single-sentence classification, b) single-sentence sequence-tagging, c) sentence-pair classification, and d) sentence-pair sequence labeling. IndoBERT, an Indonesian pre-trained language model, was also introduced to enable the development of contextual language models in Indonesian.[2] The Indonesian Language Evaluation Montage (IndoLEM) was introduced in the same year as a comprehensive dataset for seven NLP tasks grouped into morphosyntax and sequence labeling, semantics, and discourse coherence [4]. Another Indonesian pre-trained language model with the same name, IndoBERT, was also presented.[3] The most recent initiative (which is still ongoing at the time of writing) is to launch a joint-collaboration project named NusaCrowd.[4] The project's goal is to collect datasets written in Indonesian and its local languages and make them publicly available for reproducible research purposes.

Named Entity Recognition (NER) is one of the NLP tasks supported by the aforementioned benchmarks. NER is a fundamental task that identifies named entities (NEs) in unstructured or semi-structured text and assigns them to the appropriate classes. All the NER datasets were used to fine-tune IndoBERT. The results reveal that IndoBERT significantly increases the performance of the NER models. However, all datasets are intended for general use. This also applies to two versions of IndoBERT, as they were trained on formal and informal corpora from the general domain. In line with what has been done in [9] and [4], we propose IndQNER, an NER benchmark dataset for a specific domain, to help accelerate the advancement of NER research in Indonesian. Because Indonesia has the world's largest Muslim population[5], we choose the Indonesian translation of the Quran as a source for the dataset. This dataset is created using a meticulously designed annotation guideline, as well as the participation of Quran and Tafseer experts. It has 2475 NEs from 18 different classes. To properly measure the quality of the annotation, we conduct experiments in two different scenarios, including supervised and transfer learning. In the latter, we intend to discover how well IndoBERT can serve NER tasks in a specific domain. The evaluation results indicate that the dataset has the potential to significantly contribute to broadening the domain range of Indonesian NER tasks and hence help to

---

[1]   https://www.berlitz.com/blog/most-spoken-languages-world.
[2]   https://huggingface.co/indobenchmark/indobert-base-p1.
[3]   https://huggingface.co/indolem/indobert-base-uncased.
[4]   https://github.com/IndoNLP/nusa-crowd.
[5]   https://worldpopulationreview.com/country-rankings/muslim-population-by-country.

advance research development. IndQNER is now one of eight NER datasets that contribute to the NusaCrowd project.[6]

2   Related Work

Because there is no work on creating Indonesian NER datasets in a specific domain, we present the works in a general domain as follows.

The first attempt to create a NER dataset is described in [2]. This was motivated by the fact that the NER dataset generated by benefited Indonesian Wikipedia and DBpedia [6] contains numerous NEs with inaccurate labels. The main reason for this problem is the non-standard appearance of entities in DBpedia. Because the entity search applies exact matching, incomplete entities are disregarded and categorized as *Other*. To address this issue, a DBpedia entity expansion is proposed in order to produce a higher-quality dataset. All NEs are grouped into *Person, Location*, and *Organization* classes before performing name cleansing, normalization, expansion, and validation. The resultant NEs are evaluated using the Stanford NER library, and the obtained F1 score is more than twice that of [6].

Alfina et al. expanded the work in [2] to overcome incorrect assignments of NEs from the person class on Indonesian DBpedia. This issue contributed to the appearance of incorrect NEs and misplaced class members. Some rules from [2] are modified to correct *Person* entities to fix the problem. This produces a new set of entities known as MDEE (Modified DBpedia Entities Expansion). The changes to the rules include: 1) creating new rules for both removed and existing entries, and 2) revising existing rules. In addition, a new rule for the *Organization* class is added following a thorough analysis of its existing rules. Gazetteers are used to add country names and 100 city names to the MDEE after the Unicode-based names handling task obtains 500 new *Place* entities. All the rules and procedures result in over 6521 NEs for *Person*, and 2036 and 352 NEs for *Place* and *Organization*, respectively.

In 2020, [3] presented an Indonesian NER dataset that is claimed to be a more standardized Indonesian NER dataset.[7] The dataset is created by manually re-annotating an existing dataset, termed as S&N [8]. The annotation is performed by three native speakers. This is the first NER dataset created using an annotation guideline. The dataset is referred to as Idner-news-2k. The dataset consists of 2340 sentences and 5995 NEs from the *Person, Location*, and *Organization* classes.

3   The Indonesian Translation of the Quran

The Quran is the Muslim sacred book written in Arabic. It uses unique terms with distinct meanings. Furthermore, because the Quran is both rich in meaning and literary, translation into other languages becomes extremely difficult. We

---

[6] https://indonlp.github.io/nusa-catalogue/.
[7] https://github.com/khairunnisaor/idner-news-2k.

discuss the principles that were used to construct the Indonesian translation of the Quran in order to help readers understand the Quran easily. In particular, we examine the ideas from the NER viewpoint, i.e., how NEs, which are in the form of proper nouns, appear in the translation version. To acquire a clear understanding of the ideas, we contrast the Indonesian and English translations of the Quran.[8]

1. Some common nouns are provided with the corresponding proper nouns. In the English translation, this is accomplished by placing the article *the* before a common noun. In the Indonesian translation in Table 1, the proper noun *Sinai* was included in a bracket to indicate that the common noun *gunung* (mountain) refers to a mountain named Sinai.

Table 1. Some common nouns are presented along with their corresponding proper nouns in the Indonesian translation of the Quran.

Indonesian Translation	English Translation
Kami pun telah mengangkat gunung **(Sinai)** di atas mereka untuk (menguatkan) perjanjian mereka.182) Kami perintahkan kepada mereka, "Masukilah pintu gerbang (Baitulmaqdis) itu sambil bersujud". Kami perintahkan pula kepada mereka, "Janganlah melanggar (peraturan) pada hari Sabat." Kami telah mengambil dari mereka perjanjian yang kukuh	And We raised over them **the mount** for [refusal of] their covenant; and We said to them, "Enter the gate bowing humbly", and We said to them, "Do not transgress on the sabbath", and We took from them a solemn covenant

2. Non-popular proper nouns are paired with synonyms that are popular with readers. In Table 2, the proper noun *Ahmad* is a rare name, hence it is supplemented by its well-known synonym, *Nabi Muhammad* (Prophet Muhammad). In contrast, the English translation only mentions *Ahmad* and provides no further information.
3. Pronouns are supplemented by the proper nouns to which they refer. The proper nouns are written in brackets as additional information. The Indonesian translation in Table 3 contains a pronoun, i.e. *engkau* (you), followed by the proper noun it refers to, i.e. *Nabi Muhammad* (Prophet Muhammad). This is not the case in the English translation, as neither the proper noun nor the pronoun appear.

4   Methodology

4.1   Architecture and Workflow

IndQNER has a pipeline that includes 1) the definition of the initial classes and the corresponding NEs using the Quran concepts ontology (*Initials*), 2)

---

[8] All English translations are the sahih international version from https://corpus.quran.com/translation.jsp.

Table 2. How non-popular proper nouns are presented in the Indonesian translation of the Quran.

Indonesian Translation	English Translation
(Ingatlah) ketika Isa putra Maryam berkata, "Wahai Bani Israil, sesungguhnya aku adalah utusan Allah kepadamu untuk membenarkan kitab (yang turun) sebelumku, yaitu Taurat, dan memberi kabar gembira tentang seorang utusan Allah yang akan datang setelahku yang namanya **Ahmad** (Nabi Muhammad)". Akan tetapi, ketika utusan itu datang kepada mereka dengan membawa bukti-bukti yang nyata, mereka berkata, "Ini adalah sihir yang nyata"	And [mention] when Jesus, the son of Mary, said, "O children of Israel, indeed I am the messenger of Allah to you confirming what came before me of the Torah and bringing good tidings of a messenger to come after me, whose name is **Ahmad**". But when he came to them with clear evidences, they said, "This is obvious magic"

Table 3. How some pronouns are presented in the Indonesian translation of the Quran.

Indonesian Translation	English Translation
Kebenaran itu dari Tuhanmu. Maka, janganlah sekali-kali **engkau** (Nabi Muhammad) termasuk orang-orang yang ragu	The truth is from your Lord, so never be among the doubters

the definition of the comprehensive annotation guideline, 3) text annotation, 4) the modification of the annotation guideline during text annotation, 5) the verification of the class and NE candidates by involving experts, and finally 6) the annotation of new NEs before producing the final annotated dataset, as can be seen in Fig. 1.

4.2   Named Entities and Classes

Because the Quran is a holy book, we believed that the NEs and classes derived from it needed to be meticulously defined. Conveniently, there is a publicly available Arabic Quranic corpus with three levels of analysis required in computational linguistics tasks: morphological annotation, syntactic treebank, and semantic ontology.[9] The latter comprises Quranic main concepts, as well as instances of the lowest-level concepts.[10] Each instance is supplemented with a Quran verse in which it appears, so the reader can acquire a solid understanding of the instance in the Quran. We started defining NEs and classes for our dataset by examining the lowest-level concepts as well as the instances. If an instance is a proper noun, we set the corresponding name in the Indonesian translation of the Quran as an NE and the concept as the NE class. This resulted in the creation of initial NEs and classes for our dataset. We term them *Initials*, and

---

[9] https://corpus.quran.com/.

[10] https://corpus.quran.com/concept.jsp.

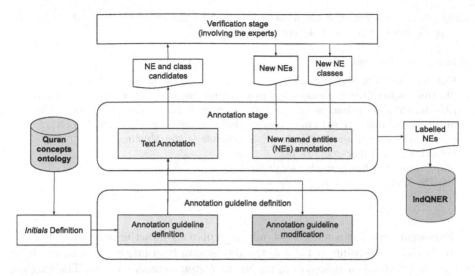

Fig. 1. The pipeline of IndQNER creation.

the classes include *Allah, Artifact, Astronomical body, Event, Holy book, Angel, Person, Location, Color,* and *Religion.* Following the trial annotation stage, we updated *Initials* to include more classes and NEs. The *Person* class is divided into three categories: *Messenger, Prophet,* and *Person.* The *Location* class is further classified into *Geographical location* and *Afterlife location.* We also added new classes, including *Allah's throne, False deity, Language,* and *Sentient.* We observed NEs that belong to two distinct classes: *Messenger* and *Prophet.* To address this, we transferred the NEs from the *Prophet* class to the *Messenger* class because while a messenger is certainly a prophet, not all prophets become messengers.

Since we discovered more NEs during the annotation stage, the number of NEs has increased (details are in Sect. 4.4). They are the synonyms of *Initials'* NEs, which typically appear in the following manners.

1. Synonyms appear as a name followed by an explanation in the form of an NE in *Initials.* The additional explanation is written in a pair of brackets. In Table 4, the Indonesian translation includes *Ruhulkudus* as a synonym of *Jibril* (an *Initials'* NE from the *Angel* class). The English translation just mentions *The Pure Spirit* instead of a name like *Jibril.*

Table 4. A synonym exists as a name followed by the corresponding NE in Initials that is written in a pair of brackets.

Indonesian Translation	English Translation
Katakanlah (Nabi Muhammad), "**Ruhulkudus** (Jibril) menurunkannya (Al-Qur'an) dari Tuhanmu dengan hak untuk meneguhkan (hati) orang-orang yang telah beriman dan menjadi petunjuk serta kabar gembira bagi orang-orang muslim (yang berserah diri kepada Allah)"	Say, [O Muhammad], "**The Pure Spirit** has brought it down from your Lord in truth to make firm those who believe and as guidance and good tidings to the Muslims"

2. Synonyms exist as a name without an explanation of the corresponding NE in *Initials*. According to Table 5, the Indonesian translation has a name, *fajar* (dawn), which is a synonym of an NE in *Initials*, *subuh* (dawn). The English version, by contrast, portrays *fajar* in a descriptive manner, i.e., *the white thread of morning distinguishes itself from the dark thread [of night]*.

Table 5. A synonym exists as a name without additional information in the Indonesian Translation of the Quran.

Indonesian Version	English Version
Dihalalkan bagimu pada malam puasa bercampur dengan istrimu. Mereka adalah pakaian bagimu dan kamu adalah pakaian bagi mereka. Allah mengetahui bahwa kamu tidak dapat menahan dirimu sendiri, tetapi Dia menerima tobatmu dan memaafkanmu. Maka, sekarang campurilah mereka dan carilah apa yang telah ditetapkan Allah bagimu. Makan dan minumlah hingga jelas bagimu (perbedaan) antara benang putih dan benang hitam, yaitu **fajar** ...	It has been made permissible for you the night preceding fasting to go to your wives [for sexual relations]. They are clothing for you and you are clothing for them. Allah knows that you used to deceive yourselves, so He accepted your repentance and forgave you. So now, have relations with them and seek that which Allah has decreed for you. And eat and drink until **the white thread of dawn becomes distinct to you from the black thread [of night]** ...

3. The synonyms of *Allah* are precisely defined. They must be among the 99 names for Allah known as Asmaul Husna.[11] *Yang Maha Pengasih* (The Most or Entirely Merciful) and *Yang Maha Penyayang* (The Bestower of Mercy) are examples of Asmaul Husna. In addition, we discovered names that possess characteristics of Allah's synonyms but do not appear in Asmaul Husna.

---

[11] We used the Asmaul Husna reference that can be seen at https://github.com/dice-group/IndQNER/blob/main/Asmaul_Husna_Reference.pdf.

In this case, we used the Arabic version of the names and verified that they appeared in the Asmaul Husna reference before deciding they were a valid synonym of Allah. For example, in the Asmaul Husna reference, *Maha Mengurus* appears as *Maha Pemelihara* (The Guardian, The Witness, The Overseer). Based on our analysis of all appearances of Allah's synonyms in the translation of the Quran, we defined three forms of their existence in the text as follows:

(a) One of Asmaul Husna's names that is preceded with word *Yang* (The). The appearance of *Yang Maha Pengasih* in this translation "*Sesungguhnya bagi orang-orang yang beriman dan beramal saleh, (Allah) Yang Maha Pengasih akan menanamkan rasa cinta (dalam hati) mereka.* (Indeed, those who have believed and done righteous deeds - the Most Merciful will appoint for them affection.)" is defined as a synonym of Allah.

(b) Two names of Asmaul Husa that are preceded with word *Yang* and connected with word *lagi* (also). For example, *Yang Mahahalus lagi Mahateliti* in a translation "*Dia tidak dapat dijangkau oleh penglihatan mata, sedangkan Dia dapat menjangkau segala penglihatan itu. Dialah Yang Mahahalus lagi Mahateliti.* (Vision perceives Him not, but He perceives [all] vision; and He is the Subtle, the Acquainted.)" is a synonym of Allah.

(c) One or two names of Asmaul Husna that is/are preceded with the phrase *Tuhan Yang* and connected with the word *lagi* (when two names exist). A phrase *Tuhan Yang Maha Penyayang* in "*(Ingatlah) Ayyub ketika dia berdoa kepada Tuhannya, "(Ya Tuhanku,) sesungguhnya aku telah ditimpa penyakit, padahal Engkau Tuhan Yang Maha Penyayang dari semua yang penyayang*". (And [mention] Job, when he called to his Lord, "Indeed, adversity has touched me, and you are the Most Merciful of the merciful.")" is defined as a synonym of Allah.

The annotation stage also produces candidates of NE and class. We consulted Quran and Tafseer experts to see if a candidate should be classified as an NE or a class (details are in Sect. 4.5).

4.3   Annotation Guideline

We designed the annotation guideline for IndQNER creation because there none existed for the domain. We had the preliminary version before the annotation. This version was updated during the annotation process based on findings in the Indonesian translation of the Quran (we refer to it as corpus) discovered during the annotation process. The guideline includes detailed instructions on how to annotate, what to annotate, and what information to collect during the annotation process. Each one is detailed in depth below.

How to do the Annotation. The annotation is performed using Tagtog, a web-based text annotation tool.[12] Each of the two annotators labels two different

---

[12] https://www.tagtog.com/.

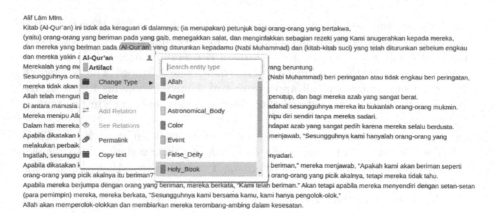

Fig. 2. The annotation process on Tagtog.

chapters of the Indonesian translation of the Quran. Labeling is conducted by first selecting an NE and then specifying the appropriate label, as shown in Fig. 2.

What to Annotate. In the beginning, we have a list of NEs as well as the corresponding classes, as mentioned in Sect. 4.2. The annotators must locate NEs in the corpus and assign appropriate labels to them. *Person, Messenger,* and *Prophet* NEs have an additional labeling rule that excludes the title of a name (if available). In this translation, for example, *"Kebenaran itu dari Tuhanmu. Maka, janganlah sekali-kali engkau (Nabi Muhammad) termasuk orang-orang yang ragu* (Because the truth comes from your Lord, never be among the doubters)", *Nabi Muhammad* is an NE from *Messenger.* Because it appears with a title, *Nabi* (Prophet), the annotators should merely label *Muhammad.* Since synonyms of NEs are regarded as NEs, annotators must ascertain if a name that does not appear in *Initials* is a synonym of an NE. This is done by acquiring more information about the name from Wikipedia, either in Indonesian[13] or in English.[14] To validate Allah's synonyms, annotators must first verify if a name with relevant criteria exists in the Asmaul Husna reference. If no acceptable name is found, they need to find the Arabic version of the name and then check to ensure that the Arabic name is in the reference.

Which Information to Capture During the Annotation Process. According to the trial annotation stage's output, we discovered several names that did not exist in *Initials.* Therefore, the annotators are required to record these names and the location of their appearance in the corpus (including the chapter and verse numbers). Those names are considered NE candidates. In addition, the annotators might suggest a class candidate for each of the NE candidates. We also observed the presence of NEs in the form of metonymy in the

---

[13] https://id.wikipedia.org/wiki/Halaman_Utama.
[14] https://en.wikipedia.org/wiki/Main_Page.

corpus.[15] The annotators not only log these NEs, but also provide information about the classes involved. The annotators must also be aware if an NE in *Initials* belongs to the correct class. Furthermore, they must identify those that are improperly classified and recommend the correct one (if it is possible). All of this information is confirmed in the verification stage (Sect. 4.5).

4.4 Annotation Process and Results

The annotation process was carried out by eight annotators who are third- and fourth-year students at the Informatics Engineering Department of the State Islamic University Syarif Hidayatullah Jakarta. It was conducted in two stages, trial and actual, and held in two months. The trial step aimed to determine if all annotators have a common understanding of the annotation guideline. This stage also enabled us to discover several facts about the Indonesian translation of the Quran, as detailed in Sects. 3 and 4.2. We used the Indonesian translation of the Quran that was released in 2019 by the Ministry of Religion Affairs of the Republic of Indonesia.[16] During the trial period, the annotators only annotated one chapter of the Quran, Al-Baqarah, with corresponding labels in *Initials*. We calculated the Inter-Annotator Agreement (IAA) among all annotators based on NE classes. *Color* class has the lowest number, with an IAA score of 3.7%. This is because two annotators labeled color names that do not appear in *Initials*. Those are actually intended to be NE candidates from the *Color* class. *Location* is the second class with an IAA score of less than 50%. This is because two annotators completely overlooked labeling location names.

To create IndQNER, we implemented the actual annotation step to annotate eight chapters in the Indonesian translation of the Quran. The Quran's chapters are classified as lengthy, medium, or short based on their number of words. We used seven lengthy chapters and one medium chapter. The lengthy chapters include *Chapter 2: Al-Baqarah* (l-baqarah), *Chapter 3: Ali-'Imran* (āl'im'rān), *Chapter 4: An-Nisā* (l-nisā), *Chapter 5: Al-Maidāh* (l-māidah), *Chapter 6: Al-An'ām* (l-an'ām), *Chapter 7: Al-A'rāf* (l-a'rāf), and *Chapter 10: Yūnus* (Yūnus). *Chapter 16: An-Nahl* (l-nahl) is a medium chapter. Each of the two annotators worked on two different chapters to conduct the annotation. Figure 3 shows the IAA scores obtained from annotation results across all chapters. NEs from *False Deity* and *Sentient* are nonexistent in all chapters. Meanwhile, the NEs from *Language*, *Afterlife Location*, and *Color* classes are each found in only one chapter, namely Chap. 16, Chap. 7, and Chap. 3, respectively. *Allah's Throne* and *Artifact* are two more classes whose NEs appear in less than half the number of chapters.

As mentioned in Sect. 4.3, annotators produce NE and class candidates in addition to the annotated corpus. We initially obtained 208 NE and three class candidates. After eliminating the duplicates, we had 142 NE and three class candidates left. We chose only NE candidates that are proper nouns to be checked

---

[15] https://en.wikipedia.org/wiki/Metonymy.

[16] https://lajnah.kemenag.go.id/unduhan/category/3-terjemah-al-qur-an-tahun-2019.

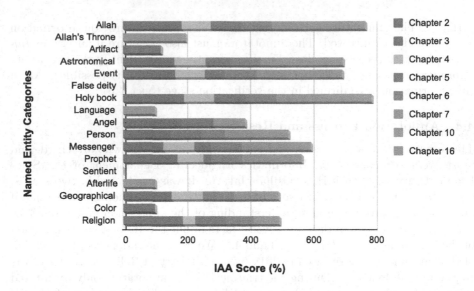

Fig. 3. Inter-annotator agreement (IAA) in the actual annotation stage.

in the next step. As a result, we had 59 NE and three class candidates. The majority of NE candidates were proposed as *Person*'s NEs. Furthermore, there are eight NE candidates whose proposed classes are still unknown. The names *Food* and *Fruit* were proposed for the two class candidates, but one class candidate's name remained unknown. The annotators also discovered one NE that was incorrectly classified, namely *Daud*. The annotators suggested *Messenger* as the correct class rather than keeping it as an NE from the *Prophet* class. The annotation results also assisted in locating NE synonyms in the corpus. We discovered 38 synonyms for *Allah* and eight synonyms for other NEs. The first appears in two forms, including being preceded by the phrases *Tuhan Yang* and *Yang*, which appear nine and 29 times, respectively.

4.5   Expert Curation

All NE and class candidates obtained through the annotation process were validated by three Quran and Tafseer experts. The experts are lecturers in the Quran and Tafseer Department of the State Islamic University Syarif Hidayatullah Jakarta. To facilitate the verification process, we provided at least one Quran verse in which the NE candidates appear. Each expert specifically verified if the proposed NE classes were correct. In the case of unknown or incorrectly proposed NE classes, the expert provided the appropriate ones. Furthermore, the experts examined if the new proposed classes and corresponding NE candidates were acceptable. To obtain the final results, we chose the majority of the verification results. If each expert had a different result, we would ask them to discuss and decide on the final result. All experts shared the same results on

56 NE candidates. Meanwhile, two experts concluded the same results on three candidates. At this point, we had three more NE classes and 54 new NEs from existing classes. *Food, Fruit,* and *the Book of Allah* are the new classes, with two NEs for each of *Food* and *Fruit,* and one NE for *the Book of Allah*. Table 6 lists all classes, including the description and sample of the corresponding NEs.

5 Evaluation

Goals. The purpose of the evaluation was to assess the annotation quality of IndQNER. In doing so, we acquired results from NER models testing, in which the models were trained on the dataset using two different settings. They were supervised learning and transfer learning, respectively. In the first setting, we used a combination of BiLSTM and CRF techniques [5] because it is the most commonly used approach in Indonesian NER tasks. An Indonesian pre-trained language model, IndoBERT,[17] was utilized to provide word embeddings. For the transfer learning setting, we used the IndoBERT which we fine-tuned and then tested. We were also interested in how much IndoBERT, which was trained on a large-scale general domain dataset, can support NER tasks in specific domains like the Indonesian translation of the Quran.

Experimental Setup. The IndQNER dataset was annotated using the BIO (Beginning-Inside-Outside) tagging format. It has 3117 sentences, 62,027 tokens, and 2475 NEs. A sentence is marked by the end of a dot character. Each line in the dataset consists of a token, a tab, and the corresponding NE label. Figure 4 depicts the distribution of NEs in the dataset by class. *False Deity* and *Sentient* are two classes with no NEs in the corpus. To enable the two experiment settings, we split the dataset into training, validation, and test sets.[18] The split was made with an 8:1:1 ratio [7], with 2494, 312, and 311 sentences in the training, validation, and test sets, respectively.

Evaluations both in supervised and transfer learning settings were conducted with the following parameters: learning rate of 2e-5, maximum sequence length $\in \{256, 512\}$, batch size of 16, and number of epochs $\in \{10, 20, 40, 100\}$.

Results. Table 7 provides evaluation results of IndQNER in two settings. The first NER model surprisingly outperforms the second on all setting parameters. The BiLSTM and CRF-based NER system obtains the highest F1 score of 0.98 and on other parameter settings, the numbers are consistently above 0.90. Meanwhile, the highest F1 score obtained from the fine-tuned IndoBERT model is 0.71. The results indicate that the existing Indonesian pre-trained language model is insufficient for supporting specific domain NER tasks, such as the Indonesian translation of the Quran. On the other hand, we believe that the annotation quality of the IndQNER dataset is satisfactory, as the learning

---

[17] https://huggingface.co/indobenchmark/indobert-base-p1.
[18] https://github.com/dice-group/IndQNER/tree/main/datasets.

Table 6. All classes, descriptions, and samples of the corresponding named entities. The descriptions are taken from https://corpus.quran.com/concept.jsp.

Classes	Description	Sample of Named Entities
Allah	Allah (God in Islam) and all Allah's names that are known as Asmaul Husna	Allah, Tuhan Yang Maha Esa (*The Unique, The Only One*), Yang Maha Pengasih (*The Most or Entirely Merciful*)
Allah's Throne	The seat of Allah's power and authority	'Arasy (*Allah's Throne*)
Artifact	Man-made constructions that are mentioned in the Quran	Ka'bah (*Kaaba*), Masjidilaqsa (*Al-Aqsa mosque*)
Astronomical body	Astronomical objects that are mentioned in the Quran	Bintang Syi'ra (*Sirius*), bumi (earth)
Event	Temporal events	hari kiamat (*Day of Resurrection*), subuh (*fajr*)
False deity	The Worship of false gods mentioned in the Quran	Al-'Uzza, Al-Lata (*al-Lat*)
Holy book	Holy books and other religious texts that are mentioned in the Quran	Al-Qur'an (*Qur'an*), Injil (*the Gospel*)
Language	The languages mentioned in the Quran	Bahasa Arab (*Arabic*)
Angel	The creations of Allah mentioned in the Quran known as angels	Malaikat maut (*The Angel of death*), Jibril (*Gabriel*)
Person	Individual human beings or groups of people mentioned in the Quran	Orang-orang Arab Badui (*The bedouins*), Azar (*Azar*)
Messenger	The messengers of Allah mentioned in the Quran	Ibrahim (*Abraham*), Muhammad (*Muhammad*)
Prophet	The prophets of Allah mentioned in the Quran	Harun (*Aaron*), Sulaiman (*Solomon*)
Sentient	The sentient creation mentioned in the Quran	makhluk bergerak dari bumi (*creature from the earth*)
Afterlife Location	Locations in the afterlife	Surga Firdaus (*The Gardens of Paradise*), Sidratulmuntaha (*The Lote Tree*)
Geographical location	Geographical locations mentioned in the Quran	Negeri Babilonia (*Babylon*), Makkah (*Makkah*)
Color	The different colors that are mentioned in the Quran	Hijau (*green*)
Religion	The major religions, or other systems of ancient belief, that are mentioned by name in the Quran	Islam (*Islam*), Nasrani (*Christianity*)
Food	The food mentioned in the Quran	Manna and Salwa
Fruit	The fruit mentioned in the Quran	Palm and Grave
The Book of Allah	The book of Allah mentioned in the Quran	Lauf Mahfuzh

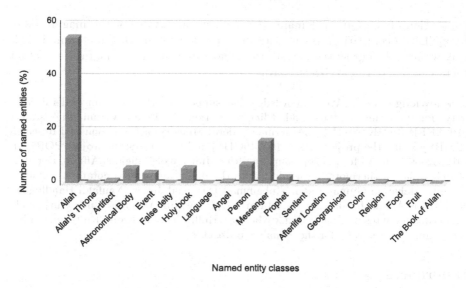

Named entity classes

Fig. 4. Distribution of named entities from each class in IndQNER.

process using a deep learning approach has been shown to successfully achieve a highly promising result.

Table 7. Evaluation results of IndQNER using supervised learning and transfer learning scenarios.

NER technique	e-poch 10			e-poch 20			e-poch 40			e-poch 100		
	P	R	F1	P	R	F1	P	R	F1	P	R	F1
Max. sequence length 256												
Supervised learning	0.94	0.92	0.93	0.99	0.97	0.98	0.96	0.96	0.96	0.97	0.96	0.96
Transfer learning	0.67	0.65	0.65	0.60	0.59	0.59	0.75	0.72	0.71	0.73	0.68	0.68
Max. sequence length 512												
Supervised learning	0.92	0.92	0.92	0.96	0.95	0.96	0.97	0.95	0.96	0.97	0.95	0.96
Transfer learning	0.72	0.62	0.64	0.62	0.57	0.58	0.72	0.66	0.67	0.68	0.68	0.67

6   Conclusion and Future Works

We presented IndQNER, a NER benchmark dataset in a specific domain, namely the Indonesian translation of the Quran. This dataset creation is part of an attempt to satisfy the need for publicly accessible datasets in order to accelerate the progress of NLP research in Indonesian. The evaluation findings show that IndQNER can be a suitable metric for NER task evaluation in the Indonesian translation of the Quran domain. However, we are aware of the magnitude of IndQNER in comparison to the total number of chapters in the Quran. This is why we intend to grow the dataset to include all chapters in the future, so that there will be even more benefits available.

Acknowledgements. We acknowledge the support of the German Federal Ministry for Economic Affairs and Climate Action (BMWK) within the project SPEAKER (01MK20011U), the German Federal Ministry of Education and Research (BMBF) within the project KIAM (02L19C115) and the EuroStars project PORQUE (01QE2056C), and Mora Scholarship from the Ministry of Religious Affairs, Republic of Indonesia. Furthermore, we would like to thank our amazing annotators, including Anggita Maharani Gumay Putri, Muhammad Destamal Junas, Naufaldi Hafidhigbal, Nur Kholis Azzam Ubaidillah, Puspitasari, Septiany Nur Anggita, Wilda Nurjannah, and William Santoso. We also thank Khodijah Hulliyah, Lilik Ummi Kultsum, Jauhar Azizy, and Eva Nugraha for the valuable feedback.

References

1. Aji, A.F., et al.: One Country, 700+ languages: NLP challenges for underrepresented languages and dialects in Indonesia. In: Proceedings of the 60th Annual Meeting of the Association for Computational Linguistics (Volume 1: Long Papers), Dublin, Ireland, pp. 7226–7249. Association for Computational Linguistics (2022). https://doi.org/10.18653/v1/2022.acl-long.500, https://aclanthology.org/2022.acl-long.500
2. Alfina, I., Manurung, R., Fanany, M.I.: DBpedia entities expansion in automatically building dataset for Indonesian NER. 2016 International Conference on Advanced Computer Science and Information Systems, ICACSIS 2016, pp. 335–340 (2017). https://doi.org/10.1109/ICACSIS.2016.7872784
3. Khairunnisa, S.O., Imankulova, A., Komachi, M.: Towards a standardized dataset on indonesian named entity recognition. In: Proceedings of the 1st Conference of the Asia-Pacific Chapter of the Association for Computational Linguistics and the 10th International Joint Conference on Natural Language Processing: Student Research Workshop, pp. 64–71. Association for Computational Linguistics (2020). https://www.tempo.co/, https://www.aclweb.org/anthology/2020.aacl-srw.10
4. Koto, F., Rahimi, A., Lau, J.H., Baldwin, T.: IndoLEM and IndoBERT: a benchmark dataset and pre-trained language model for indonesian NLP. In: Proceedings of the 28th International Conference on Computational Linguistics, Barcelona, Spain, pp. 757–770. International Committee on Computational Linguistics (2020). https://doi.org/10.18653/v1/2020.coling-main.66, https://www.aclweb.org/anthology/2020.coling-main.66
5. Lample, G., Ballesteros, M., Subramanian, S., Kawakami, K., Dyer, C.: Neural architectures for named entity recognition. In: Proceedings of the 2016 Conference of the North American Chapter of the Association for Computational Linguistics: Human Language Technologies, San Diego, California, pp. 260–270. Association for Computational Linguistics (2016). https://doi.org/10.18653/v1/N16-1030, https://aclanthology.org/N16-1030
6. Luthfi, A., Distiawan, B., Manurung, R.: Building an Indonesian named entity recognizer using Wikipedia and DBPedia. In: Proceedings of the International Conference on Asian Language Processing 2014, IALP 2014, pp. 19–22 (2014). https://doi.org/10.1109/IALP.2014.6973520

7. Martinez-Rodriguez, J.L., Hogan, A., Lopez-Arevalo, I.: Information extraction meets the semantic web: a survey (2020). https://doi.org/10.3233/SW-180333, http://prefix.cc
8. Syaifudin, Y., Nurwidyantoro, A.: Quotations identification from Indonesian online news using rule-based method. In: Proceeding - 2016 International Seminar on Intelligent Technology and Its Application, ISITIA 2016: Recent Trends in Intelligent Computational Technologies for Sustainable Energy, pp. 187–194 (2017). https://doi.org/10.1109/ISITIA.2016.7828656
9. Wilie, B., et al.: IndoNLU: benchmark and resources for evaluating Indonesian natural language understanding (2020). http://arxiv.org/abs/2009.05387

Comparing Object Recognition Models and Studying Hyperparameter Selection for the Detection of Bolts

Tom Bolton$^{(\boxtimes)}$ [iD], Julian Bass [iD], Tarek Gaber [iD], and Taha Mansouri [iD]

Department of Science, Engineering, and Environment, University of Salford,
The Crescent, Salford M5 4WT, UK
T.J.E.Bolton@edu.salford.ac.uk

Abstract. The commonly-used method of bolting, used to secure parts of apparatus together, relies on the bolts having a sufficient preload force in order to the ensure mechanical strength. Failing to secure bolted connections to a suitable torque rating can have dangerous consequences. As part of a wider system that might monitor the integrity of bolted connections using artificial intelligence techniques such as machine learning, it is necessary to first identify and isolate the location of the bolt. In this study, we make use of several contemporary machine learning-based object detection algorithms to address the problem of bolt recognition. We use the latest version of You Only Look Once (YOLO) and compare it with algorithms RetinaNet and Faster R-CNN. In doing so, we determine the optimum learning rate for use with a given dataset and make a comparison showing how this particular hyperparameter has a considerable effect on the accuracy of the trained model. We also observe the accuracy levels achievable using training data that has been lowered in resolution and had augmentation applied to simulate camera blurring and variable lighting conditions. We find that YOLO can achieve a test mean average precision of 71% on this data.

Keywords: Deep learning · Transfer learning · Continuous maintenance

1 Introduction

Bolts and bolting are commonly used as a method of securing parts of structures to one another. To ensure integrity of a connection, the bolts must be secured with a sufficient preload force in order to provide a rated level of mechanical security; this force can be measured in many ways, for example by the use of a mechanical torque wrench [11]. Ensuring the correct preload force of a bolted connection is essential: an incorrectly-installed blind flange, secured with bolts, was responsible for the Piper Alpha gas platform explosion in 1988 which resulted in the loss of 167 lives [2].

Supported by Add Energy.

In industrial settings, predictive maintenance techniques ranging from visual inspection to advanced signal processing analysis have been proven more accurate than time-based preventative methods in such safety critical situations as nuclear power plants [3]. However, visual inspections are far from foolproof and human error is a factor [1]. Signal analysis, whilst more accurate, cannot help if the faulty component is made from static parts that are unable to offer any measurement data.

Research has recently moved towards studying the use of artificial intelligence (AI)-based techniques such as machine learning to analyse images and video in order to identify degradation that might adversely affect equipment in an industrial setting [15]. Detecting a faulty bolted connection from a video using AI is complex [4,12]; however, the first task is to determine the presence of bolts within an image or frame of video.

Machine learning algorithms that are capable of performing object recognition tasks require training using data that has been annotated by a person - or 'oracle' - from which a model can learn. The NPU-BOLT dataset, assembled in order to train a bolt detection algorithm, offers us a solid basis from which to work [17]. The authors of NPU-BOLT used their dataset to train a number of object recognition algorithms; however, the authors used full-resolution images which are of high quality.

Potential sources of training data from continuous maintenance processes, such as fixed CCTV, might not be able to offer as high a resolution per image. Moreover, it is possible that images captured by a person performing a maintenance inspection, whether using a handheld or body-worn camera, may be susceptible to motion blurring and uncontrollable changes in lighting conditions.

One challenge in training a machine learning model is selecting the hyperparameters - those parameters whose values control the learning process - in order to allow the model to reach as great a level of accuracy as possible [5]. The value chosen for the learning rate hyperparameter, which dictates the size of the adjustment made each time the model's weights are updated during backpropagation, has a big effect on the model's performance; choosing the correct learning rate is not a straightforward task [14].

We summarise our contributions in this paper as follows: 1) we make an experimental comparison with the eighth and latest iteration of object recognition algorithm You Only Look Once (YOLO) for the detection of bolts, and systematically experiment with fixed and variable learning rates to find the optimum value for a given training dataset; 2) we compare these results with those achievable using other, current object detection algorithms; 3) we use a combination of resolution reduction and image augmentation in our training data to observe the accuracy levels achievable with a training set that simulates lower-quality training data.

The rest of this paper is organised as follows: Sect. 2 examines the background of the techniques used and existing research in the field; Sect. 3 contains the methodology and approaches used in the experiments; Sect. 4 outlines the experimental scenarios; and Sect. 5 shows the results of the experiments, discussion of the outcomes, avenues for future research, and concludes the paper.

2   Background and Related Work

The dataset used in this paper, NPU-BOLT, was constructed with the aim of training machine learning-based object recognition algorithms to identify four different classes of bolt [17]. The dataset comprises 337 images, annotated with 1275 individual bounding boxes in Pascal VOC format. The authors trained several algorithms - YOLO v5, Faster R-CNN, and CentreNet, achieving average precision scores of 97.38% and 91.88% for the two most prolific classes in the dataset using YOLO v5l. The authors trained the models using the full resolution of the images which offers the potential for a comparison with models that are trained using the images at a reduced size. The authors mentioned augmentation of the training dataset, but no detail was given - again, an interesting comparison might be made

Zhang et al. used an object detection algorithm - Faster R-CNN - to detect bolts in two states - tight and loose [16]. The authors compiled a dataset of images showing tightened bolts, in which none of the bolt's thread was visible, and loose bolts that were displaying an amount of visible thread. This was an interesting and comprehensive study that combined two tasks - the recognition of bolts, and the distinguishing of tight bolts and loose bolts. The authors' model demonstrated high accuracy levels: 85.59% average precision for tightened bolts, 99.60% for loose bolts.

Studies centred around the detection of bolts have also used older object detection techniques to good effect. As part of a study aiming to detect the rotational angle of bolts, Huynh et al. used an R-CNN model to detect and localise bolts within an image [4]. Claiming accuracy of between 90% and 100% on a test dataset, the authors found that the accuracy of their trained model began to fall as the camera's angle changed from the straight-ahead; with a horizontal distortion of 50°, the model accuracy fell to 19%. Wang et al. used a single-shot detector (SSD) as part of an interesting study that used a bolt's distinct marking to estimate the angle of the marking in relation to the head of the bolt, and therefore the rotational angle of the bolt itself [12].

From these studies we can see a selection of recent deep learning models selected by the authors. In order to better understand these models, and why the selection of models used in our study was chosen, we need to look at the background of deep learning and its use in object recognition.

2.1   Faster-RCNN

Faster R-CNN, first proposed at the 2015 Advances in Neural Information Processing Systems conference, is an object detection algorithm employing a region-based convolutional neural network, and is a progression from its predecessors R-CNN and Fast R-CNN [9]. Faster R-CNN is a two-stage object detection algorithm that firstly generates a sparse set of candidate object locations, and a second stage that classifies those locations. The paper proposing Faster R-CNN has, at the time of writing, attracted 56,082 citations, demonstrating its popularity in the research community. For the backbone used to generate feature maps, Faster R-CNN is capable of using different convolutional neural network architectures.

2.2 YOLO

Object detection algorithm You Only Look Once (YOLO) was first presented by Redmon et al. at the 2016 IEEE Conference on Computer Vision and Pattern Recognition [8]. YOLOv8 provides several architectures for use in object recognition tasks. YOLO is a single-stage algorithm, able to run object detection on an image in one forward pass of a convolutional neural network; this results in faster detection speeds with accuracy approaching that of two-stage detectors such as Faster R-CNN. Research interest in YOLO is considerable - the 2016 conference paper introducing YOLO has, at the time of writing, 14,954 citations. Since the authors of the NPU-BOLT included YOLO in their comparison of models, the algorithm has undergone three further major releases.

2.3 RetinaNet

Another single-stage object detection algorithm, RetinaNet, was proposed in 2020 and is claimed by its authors to offer speed similar to YOLO, whilst showing accuracy approaching that of more complex two-stage detectors such as Faster R-CNN [6]. RetinaNet would appear to have been used in few studies experimenting with bolt detection; as such, we felt it would make a good candidate for experimentation.

2.4 Transfer Learning and COCO

Transfer learning is a technique by which learning in one domain is improved by transferring information from another domain. The process has been likened to examples in the real world, comparing two people who would like to learn to play the piano; one person has no experience of playing music whilst the other has gained musical knowledge through playing the guitar. The person who plays the guitar will be able to learn the piano more efficiently by transferring the musical knowledge they have learned on another instrument [13].

As a baseline for this transfer of knowledge, there are several large, publicly available databases of annotated, categorised images with which researchers in computer vision can train models. Microsoft's Common Objects in Context (COCO) is a large, open source collection of annotated image data currently spanning 80 object categories [7]. Having a total of 330,000 images, COCO is a popular basis for experimentation in object recognition research [10].

3   Proposed Methodology

The methodology used in a series of experiments to determine the accuracy levels achievable, and the optimum learning rates to do so, in bolt detection is described here. The models compared were Yolov8n, Yolov8s, Yolov8m, Yolov8l, Yolov8x, and RetinaNet. The RetinaNet algorithm can use different backbones to perform feature extraction; two were tested here - ResNet-50, and ResNet-101. Faster R-CNN was tested with a ResNet-50 backbone.

3.1   Evaluation Metrics

To assess the effectiveness of each experiment, accuracy will be measured with the following evaluation metrics. These metrics use a combination of true positives (TP), false positives (FP), and false negatives (FN) to calculate precision, recall, and average precision.

Precision indicates the ratio of correctly predicted positives against the total number of positives for a given label.

$$Precision = \frac{TP}{TP + FP} \tag{1}$$

Recall is the ratio of correctly predicted positives against all positives for a given label.

$$Recall = \frac{TP}{TP + FN} \tag{2}$$

Average Precision (AP) is given as

$$AP = \sum_n (R_n - R_{n-1})P_n \tag{3}$$

where R_n and P_n are the precision and recall at the nth threshold. AP can also be regarded as the area under the precision-recall curve. Mean average precision (mAP) is the mean of AP for all class labels. In these experiments, AP and mAP are given with an intersection over union threshold of 0.5.

3.2   Dataset Description

The NPU-BOLT dataset is the result of a study by Zhao et al. in which the authors assembled a dataset of images, annotated with four classes [17]: Bolt Head, Bolt Nut, Bolt Side, and Blur Bolt.

Some of the images were photographed by the authors themselves, using an SLR camera, smartphone camera, and an unmanned aerial vehicle (drone). The remainder of the images were obtained from the internet. The files have a pixel resolution of between 500 × 500 and 6,000 × 4,000; the authors selected images depicting a variety of bolted structures and, in the images they themselves photographed, a range of angles and lighting conditions. A small number (17) of the images in the dataset were generated from a computer-aided design (CAD) model.

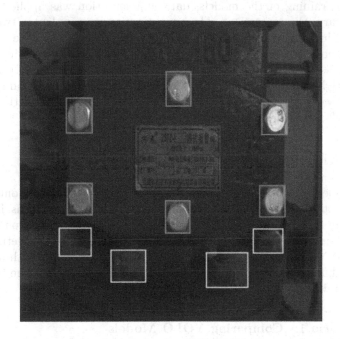

Fig. 1. A sample of training data from the NPU-BOLT dataset, depicting bounding boxes

Figure 1 shows an example taken from the NPU-BOLT training dataset complete with annotations; two classes are shown here, Bolt Head in orange, and Bolt Side in yellow. The dataset contains 337 images, having 1,275 annotations. The four classes are not equally represented; 'bolt nut' is the most prolific class, with 'bolt side' having fewest annotations.

The annotations are supplied in Pascal VOC format; this is an XML-based system for recording the dimensions and locations of the bounding boxes within the image files. To simplify the process of managing images and annotation formats for training all the models used here, whilst keeping a consistent dataset, cloud-based dataset management service Roboflow was used.

The dataset was split into three parts - training, validation, and testing. 70% of the total (236 images) comprised the training set, 20% (67 images) comprised the validation set, and the remaining 10% (34 images) was used as a test set. These splits were managed by Roboflow such that the selections were made randomly but, for each experiment, the same random selection was used. All images were resized to 640 × 640 pixels. Roboflow manages the adjustment of the samples' annotations such that the bounding boxes remain tightly defined around the regions of interest within each image.

3.3 Data Augmentation

During the training of the models, data augmentation was applied using the Python library Albumentations. The augmentation was applied in two sets: one of motion blur, median blur, or blur was applied to each sample to create a new and unique image. Another group of augmentations, consisting of one of either contrast limited adaptive histogram equalization (CLAHE) or random contrast/brightness adjustment was also used to generate new samples. Augmentations were only applied to the training dataset - the validation and test sets were left untouched.

4   Experiments

The experimentation we performed was split into discrete phases, outlined here as experimental scenarios. YOLO considers training phases as epochs, i.e. a single pass through every sample in the training dataset takes place before the model's weights are updated. The Detectron2 framework, with which the RetinaNet and Faster R-CNN models were tested, is more granular and works with iterations - 17,700 of which were necessary to make a fair comparison with the 300 epochs of YOLO training.

4.1   Scenario 1 - Comparing YOLO Models

Designed to find the optimal learning rate for training each of the five variations of YOLOv8 to as high an accuracy level as possible. Each of the five variations on the YOLO object detection architecture was trained on the NPU-BOLT dataset at learning rates of 0.01, 0.001, 0.0001, and 0.00001. After each training epoch, the model was evaluated on the evaluation dataset; the metrics outlined in Sect. 3.1 were observed, and the highest mean average precision values of each evaluation were noted.

4.2   Scenario 2 - Variable Learning Rate for YOLO

The experiments in Scenario 1 all used a fixed learning rate. Scenario 2 was designed to observe the effect on training YOLO with a cosine-decay learning rate, such that training starts at a higher learning rate and decays using a cosine function to a lower rate. After each training epoch, the model was evaluated on the evaluation dataset; the metrics were observed and the highest mean average precision values of each evaluation noted.

4.3 Scenario 3 - Comparing RetinaNet and Faster-RCNN Models

Designed to compare other object detection models with YOLO, again using different learning rates to attempt to find the rate at which each model reached its highest accuracy. RetinaNet was trained using two backbones - ResNet-50 and ResNet-101; Faster R-CNN was trained with a ResNet-50 backbone. Learning rates of 0.01, 0.001, 0.0001, and 0.00001 were used. After every 500 iterations, the model was evaluated on the evaluation dataset; the metrics outlined in Sect. 3.1 were observed, and the highest mean average precision values of each evaluation were noted.

5 Results and Discussion

In this section we train the convolutional neural networks outlined in Sect. 4 with the dataset outlined in Sect. 3 and observe the results. All models were trained starting from weights inferred by training on the COCO 2017 dataset; the transfer learning from the pretraining was retained by freezing the initial layers of the models' feature extractors such that only the classifier layers were trained.

5.1 Training the Models

Each of the models was implemented in code, using Python along with a variety of machine learning libraries. Discrete Python environments and their installed packages were managed with the Anaconda distribution of Python.

The computer used for training was equipped with an 11th generation Intel Core i7 CPU, 32 GB of RAM, and an RTX3080 GPU with 16 GB of VRAM.

5.2 Results - Scenario 1 (Comparing YOLO Models)

Table 1 shows the highest mean average precision values observed during 300 epochs of training of all five YOLOv8 object detection models at learning rates of 0.01, 0.001, 0.0001, and 0.00001.

Table 1. Results from training of five YOLOv8 models with fixed learning rates

	mAP at 0.01	mAP at 0.001	mAP at 0.0001	mAP at 0.00001
YOLOv8n	0.51422	0.44249	0.39862	0.20763
YOLOv8s	0.53069	0.54595	0.5094	0.30499
YOLOv8m	0.56655	0.62583	0.62789	0.42957
YOLOv8l	0.6013	0.70928	0.62535	0.45789
YOLOv8x	0.62183	0.68388	0.6042	0.38474

5.3   Results - Scenario 2 (Variable Learning Rate for YOLO)

Scenario 1 showed that the most accurate of the YOLO models was the Large (YOLOv8l) variation, trained at a learning rate of 0.001. Figure 1 shows the mean average precision of the YOLOv8l model graphed at different learning rates on the evaluation dataset after every epoch (Fig. 2).

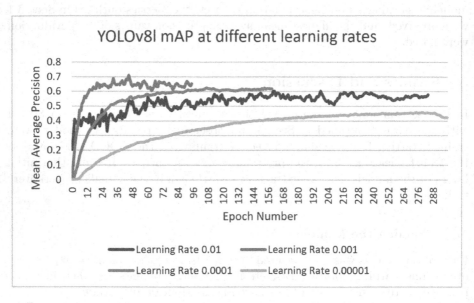

Fig. 2. mAP at IoU of 0.5 for each training epoch of YOLOv8l at different learning rates

From this graph, it can be seen that at the smallest learning rate tested - 0.00001 - the model failed to converge. The model's weights updated too slowly for it to reach the higher levels of accuracy that were possible with a faster rate within the 300 epochs of training. There was little point, therefore, in testing a cosine decay learning rate that began with a rate this small and decayed to an even smaller rate.

Table 2 shows the highest mean average precision value observed during 300 epochs of training each of the five YOLO models using a cosine decay learning rate, with values of 0.01 to 0.001, 0.001 to 0.0001, and 0.0001 to 0.00001.

Table 2. Results from training of five YOLOv8 models with variable learning rates

	mAP at 0.01–0.001	mAP at 0.001–0.0001	mAP at 0.0001–0.00001
YOLOv8n	0.46105	0.46295	0.3949
YOLOv8s	0.57001	0.55347	0.50117
YOLOv8m	0.5366	0.64278	0.61955
YOLOv8l	0.57806	0.68535	0.63791
YOLOv8x	0.60663	0.66593	0.60492

5.4   Results - Scenario 3 (Comparing RetinaNet and Faster R-CNN Models)

Table 3 shows the highest mean average precision values observed during the training of a RetinaNet model with two different backbones, as well as Faster R-CNN with a ResNet-50 backbone. The models were trained using the Detectron2 deep learning framework for 17,700 iterations. Inference was performed on the test dataset every 500 iterations. Learning rates of 0.01, 0.001, 0.0001, and 0.00001 were used.

Table 3. Results from training RetinaNet and Faster R-CNN with fixed learning rates

	mAP at 0.01	mAP at 0.001	mAP at 0.0001	mAP at 0.00001
RetinaNet (ResNet-50)	0.44665	0.46361	0.40877	0.36634
RetinaNet (ResNet-101)	0.44384	0.40333	0.39826	0.36511
Faster R-CNN	0.48204	0.39473	0.40913	0.37409

5.5   Discussion

Observing the results, it can be seen that the YOLO models generally were more accurate when trained with the NPU-BOLT dataset when compared with both RetinaNet and Faster R-CNN. YOLO has five different models that can be used for object detection, increasing in model size and complexity through Nano, Small, Medium, Large, and X-large. In our experiments, YOLOv8l performed most accurately of all the models tested in these experiments with a headline mean average precision of 0.71.

Table 4 shows the average precision for each of the class labels in the dataset using this model.

Table 4. Per-class average precision (AP) results for YOLOv8l

	AP - Bolt head	AP - Bolt nut	AP - Bolt side	AP - Blur bolt
YOLOv8l	0.879	0.925	0.253	0.648

The varied average precision values in Table 4 reflect the imbalance in the dataset - the Bolt side and Blur bolt labels were represented by fewer samples.

The latest version of YOLOv8 used in this study outperformed, by some margin, the other models tested - RetinaNet and Faster R-CNN when using the NPU-BOLT dataset as described in Sect. 3.2. They were less accurate than YOLO with a considerable difference in the achievable mAP of YOLOv8l (0.71) and Faster R-CNN (0.48).

Selecting a learning rate is a difficult task, and here we used experimentation to discover optimal values for each model. Different values were used to observe the points at which the rate was too big and the model oscillated, and too small such that the model was unable to reach convergance. The small, large, and x-large variants of YOLO reached the highest accuracy with a learning rate of 0.001, whilst the medium variant required a smaller rate of 0.0001. The nano variant was most accurate with a rate of 0.01. There is, in other words, no one-size-fits-all answer with selecting hyperparameters.

Our experiments with YOLO and evolving the learning rate throughout training using a cosine-decay adjustment, such that the learning begins quickly and slows down towards the end of training, showed that gains could be made in the eventual accuracy of the trained model using the small variant which showed a higher mAP of 0.57 using a variable (0.01–0.001) rate, compared with the mAP of 0.55 using a fixed (0.001) rate. The medium variant, likewise, recorded a higher mAP of 0.64 using a variable (0.001–0.0001) rate when compared with the maximum mAP of 0.63 using a fixed (0.0001) rate. The nano, large, and x-large variants made no gains, with better accuracy achieved via a fixed rate. There are, therefore, potential advantages to using a variable rate but not in every case.

As a wider system is developed that might observe degradation over time, these models will be used in such a way as to resemble a production environment. However, when testing on previously unseen data from the test dataset, it can be observed that even the YOLO8l model that achieved the highest validation accuracy during training has issues with generalisation. A model is said to generalise well when it is able to adapt to new data which it has not previously seen. The following examples depict what might happen when a model does not generalise.

Figure 3 shows the predictions made by the most accurate model in our experiments (YOLO v8l, trained at a learning rate of 0.001). It can be observed that the model has failed to predict one bolt head, clearly visible to the lower right of the image.

Figure 4 shows the same model making predictions on another image. Whilst the model has correctly predicted some components as bolts, one prediction is misclassified as a bolt when it is, in fact, the head of a Philips screw visible to the top right of the image.

A model's inability to generalise to new data can be caused by overfitting, a behaviour that occurs when a model has learned a set of training data too well. The outcome is that reasonably accurate predictions can be made for the training

Fig. 3. YOLO v8 predictions on unseen data - missing prediction

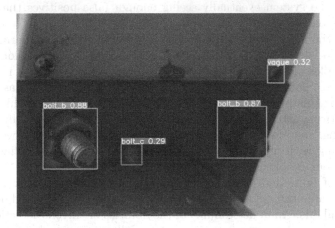

Fig. 4. YOLO v8 predictions on unseen data - incorrect classification

data but, when the model sees samples that are previously unseen, predictions become inaccurate. Overfitting can be caused by a number of factors such as data samples that lack variation, or samples containing a lot of noise. It is likely, however, that a contributing factor in this case was the small size of the training dataset. We trained our models on only a few hundred samples; whilst we felt that these images were reasonably representative of the images that the models might be asked to predict in a production scenario, it is likely that there simply was not enough data.

5.6   Conclusion

As part of a wider system that might be able to observe bolts and bolted connections over time in order to detect slowly-occurring and unwanted loosening, the initial detection of bolts is a first stage. We have found in this study that cutting-edge machine learning object detection algorithms offered by YOLO in its latest incarnation are capable of promising levels of accuracy when used to perform this task.

In collecting training data, it is possible that high quality and high resolution images might not always be obtainable; closed-circuit television (CCTV) systems are not always of the highest quality; moreover, images captured by body-worn cameras are susceptible to blurring and changing lighting conditions. Even when using training data augmentations and reducing the resolution of the images in this study, we were able to reach accuracy levels of over 70%.

We have observed issues with generalisation - the YOLOv8l model that reached the highest accuracy observed is still not capable of accurately identifying every instance of bolt. In a production system this is a problem - that missed bolt might be the one that is slowly working loose. Furthermore, too many mis-classified bolts that are not, in fact, bolts could lead to operator fatigue and the user of the system eventually seeing enough false positives that they lose trust in its abilities.

Despite the issues with generalisation, we feel that these experiments show promise for models trained on datasets that are small in size and contain lower-quality samples. The latest iteration of YOLO has shown that it is capable of achieving reasonable accuracy on only a few hundred data. YOLO has also shown accuracy, for this problem, that is markedly higher than that achievable with RetinaNet (from 2017) or Faster R-CNN (2015). This, perhaps, illustrates the pace of change in object detection research - and one lesson is that we must keep experimenting with newer and more sophisticated algorithms to find the most suitable for our problem.

Images of bolts and other specific industrial objects are hard to come by, expensive to annotate manually, and few (if any) already-annotated datasets are publicly available. An understanding of the abilities of current detection models, and the outcome when experimenting by manually tuning models for these cases where little data is available is, we feel, a useful insight.

5.7   Future Work

More experimentation needs to take place, particularly with regard to the selection of optimal training hyperparameters. All of the models tested here have hyperparameters besides the learning rate, and in reality it is common for machine leaning practitioners to use a method of automating hyperparameter selection. Previous versions of Ultralytics' YOLO distribution offered such a facility, whereby a model's training was performed many times and the metrics observed by the executing code; a genetic algorithm is used to refine the hyperparameters for each run. The user is left with optimal hyperparamters for use in training, taking the time-consuming guesswork out of the process.

Whilst this is an obvious limitation of the experiments, we intended to demonstrate how YOLO's hyperparameter evolution might compare with basic manual selection, giving us a clearer insight into how this variation might affect the accuracy achievable. We would, however, like to compare the results from training models with manually selected hyperparameters, and the accuracy achievable from using automation for selecting the values.

Given more time, we would like to have experimented by varying not only the learning rate, but other hyperparameters such the batch size and the type of optimiser. We performed our experiments on a laptop computer with a consumer-grade GPU and, as such, each round of training took many times longer than it would were the experiments carried out on more powerful hardware. As our experimentation moves closer to implementing these models as part of a wider system, we intend to fine-tune the hyperparameters to ensure we are achieving the highest accuracy possible with a given set of training data.

Acknowledgements. This research is supported by the University of Salford and Add Energy.

References

1. Liu, Y., Dhillon, B.S.: Human error in maintenance: a review. J. Qual. Maint. Eng. **12**, 21–36 (2006)
2. Drysdale, D.D., Sylvester-Evans, R.: The explosion and fire on the piper alpha platform, 6 July 1988. A case study. Philos. Trans.: Math. Phys. Eng. Sci. **356**(1748), 2929–2951 (1998). ISSN 1364503X. http://www.jstor.org/stable/55055. Accessed 13 Mar 2023
3. Hashemian, H.M.: State-of-the-art predictive maintenance techniques. IEEE Trans. Instr. Meas. **60**(1), 226–236 (2011)
4. Pham, H.C., et al.: Bolt-loosening monitoring framework using an image-based deep learning and graphical model. Sensors **20**, 3382 (2020). https://www.ncbi.nlm.nih.gov/pmc/articles/PMC7349298/
5. Li, Z., et al.: A survey of convolutional neural networks: analysis, applications, and prospects. IEEE Trans. Neural Netw. Learn. Syst. **33**(12), 6999–7019 (2022). https://doi.org/10.1109/TNNLS.2021.3084827
6. Lin, T.-Y., et al.: Focal loss for dense object detection. IEEE Trans. Pattern Anal. Mach. Intell. **42**(2), 318–327 (2020). https://doi.org/10.1109/TPAMI.2018.2858826
7. Lin, T.-Y., et al.: Microsoft COCO: common objects in context. In: Fleet, D., Pajdla, T., Schiele, B., Tuytelaars, T. (eds.) ECCV 2014. LNCS, vol. 8693, pp. 740–755. Springer, Cham (2014). https://doi.org/10.1007/978-3-319-10602-1_48
8. Redmon, J., et al.: You only look once: unified, real-time object detection. In: 2016 IEEE Conference on Computer Vision and Pattern Recognition (CVPR), pp. 779–788 (2016). https://doi.org/10.1109/CVPR.2016.91
9. Ren, S., et al.: Faster R-CNN: towards real-time object detection with region proposal networks. In: Cortes, C., Lawrence, N., Lee, D., Sugiyama, M., Garnett, R. (eds.) Advances in Neural Information Processing Systems, vol. 28. Curran Associates Inc. (2015). https://proceedings.neurips.cc/paper/2015/file/14bfa6bb14875e45bba028a21ed38046-Paper.pdf
10. Sohail, A., et al.: A systematic literature review on machine learning and deep learning methods for semantic segmentation. IEEE Access **10**, 134557–134570 (2022). https://doi.org/10.1109/ACCESS.2022.3230983

11. Wang, T., et al.: Review of bolted connection monitoring. Int. J. Distrib. Sens. Netw. **9**(12), 871213 (2013). https://doi.org/10.1155/2013/871213
12. Zhao, X., Zhang, Y., Wang, N.: Bolt loosening angle detection technology using deep learning. Struct. Control Health Monit. (2018). https://onlinelibrary.wiley.com/doi/full/10.1002/stc.2292?saml_referrer
13. Weiss, K., Khoshgoftaar, T., Wang, D.: A survey of transfer learning. J. Big Data **3**, 1–40 (2016)
14. Wen, L., et al.: Convolutional neural network with automatic learning rate scheduler for fault classification. IEEE Trans. Instrum. Meas. **70**, 1–12 (2021). https://doi.org/10.1109/TIM.2020.3048792
15. Yu, L., et al.: AMCD: an accurate deep learning-based metallic corrosion detector for MAV-based real-time visual inspection. Jo. Ambient Intell. Human. Comput. (2021)
16. Zhang, Y., et al.: Autonomous bolt loosening detection using deep learning. Struct. Health Monit. (2019). https://journals.sagepub.com/doi/full/10.1177/1475921719837509'
17. Zhao, Y., Yang, Z., Xu, C.: NPU-BOLT: a dataset for bolt object detection in natural scene images (2022). https://arxiv.org/abs/2205.11191

Morphosyntactic Evaluation for Text Summarization in Morphologically Rich Languages: A Case Study for Turkish

Batuhan Baykara[(✉)] and Tunga Güngör

Department of Computer Engineering, Boğaziçi University,
Bebek, 34342 Istanbul, Turkey
{batuhan.baykara,gungort}@boun.edu.tr

Abstract. The evaluation strategy used in text summarization is critical in assessing the relevancy between system summaries and reference summaries. Most of the current evaluation metrics such as ROUGE and METEOR are based on n-gram exact matching strategy. However, this strategy cannot capture the orthographical variations in abstractive summaries and is highly restrictive especially for languages with rich morphology that make use of affixation extensively. In this paper, we propose several variants of the evaluation metrics that take into account morphosyntactic properties of the words. We make a correlation analysis between each of the proposed approaches and the human judgments on a manually annotated dataset that we introduce in this study. The results show that using morphosyntactic tokenization in evaluation metrics outperforms the commonly used evaluation strategy in text summarization.

Keywords: Text summarization · Morphologically rich languages ·
Text summarization evaluation

1 Introduction

Large volumes of textual data have become available since the emergence of the Web. It becomes gradually more challenging to digest the vast amount of information that exists in sources such as websites, news, blogs, books, scientific papers, and social media. Hence, text summarization has emerged as a popular field of study in the past few decades which aims to simplify and make more efficient the process of obtaining relevant piece of information.

Text summarization can be defined as automatically obtaining brief, fluent, and salient piece of text from a much longer and more detailed input text. The two main approaches to text summarization are extractive text summarization and abstractive text summarization. Extractive summarization aims to summarize a given input by directly copying the most relevant sentences or phrases without any modification according to some criteria and ordering them. Abstractive summarization, on the other hand, aims to automatically generate

E. Métais et al. (Eds.): NLDB 2023, LNCS 13913, pp. 201–214, 2023.
https://doi.org/10.1007/978-3-031-35320-8_14

new phrases and sentences based on the given input and incorporate them in the output summary.

Evaluation of summarization methods is critical to assess and benchmark their performance. The main objective of evaluation is to observe how well the output summary is able to reflect the reference summaries. The commonly used evaluation methods in summarization such as ROUGE [17] and METEOR [3] are based on n-gram matching strategy. For instance, ROUGE computes the number of overlapping word n-grams between the reference and system summaries in their exact (surface) forms. While the exact matching strategy is not an issue for extractive summarization where the words are directly copied, it poses a problem for abstractive summarization where the generated summaries can contain words in different forms. In the abstractive case, this strategy is very strict especially for morphologically rich languages in which the words are subject to extensive affixation and thus carry syntactic features. It severely punishes the words that have even a slight change in their forms. Hence, taking the morphosyntactic structure of these morphologically rich languages into account is important for the evaluation of text summarization.

In this paper, we introduce several variants of the commonly used evaluation metrics that take into account the morphosyntactic properties of the language. As a case study for Turkish, we train state-of-the-art text summarization models mT5 [31] and BERTurk-cased [27] on the TR-News dataset [4]. The summaries generated by the models are evaluated with the proposed metrics using the reference summaries. In order to make comparisons between the evaluation metrics, we perform correlation analysis to see how well the score obtained with each metric correlates with the human score for each system summary-reference summary pair. Turkish is a low-resource language and it is challenging to find manually annotated data in text summarization. Hence, for correlation analysis, we annotate human relevancy judgements for a randomly sampled subset of the TR-News dataset and we make this data publicly available[1]. Correlation analysis is performed using the annotated human judgements to compare the performance of the proposed morphosyntactic evaluation methods as well as other popular evaluation methods.

2   Related Work

Text summarization studies in Turkish have been mostly limited to extractive approaches. A rule-based system is introduced by Altan [2] tailored to the economics domain. Çığır et al. [7] and Kartal and Kutlu [13] use classical sentence features such as position, term frequency, and title similarity to extract sentences and use these features in machine learning algorithms. Özsoy et al. [21] propose variations to the commonly applied latent semantic analysis (LSA) and Güran et al. [12] utilize non-negative matrix factorization method. Nuzumlalı and Özgür [19] study fixed-length word truncation and lemmatization for Turkish multi-document summarization.

---

[1] https://github.com/batubayk/news_datasets.

Recently, large-scale text summarization datasets such as MLSum [28] and TR-News [4] have been released which enabled research in abstractive summarization in Turkish. The abstractive studies are currently very limited and they mostly utilize sequence-to-sequence (Seq2Seq) architectures. Scialom et al. [28] make use of the commonly used pointer-generator model [29] and the unified pretrained language model (UniLM) proposed by Dong et al. [10]. Baykara and Güngör [4] follow a morphological adaptation of the pointer-generator algorithm and also experiment with Turkish specific BERT models following the strategy proposed by Liu and Lapata [18]. In a later study, Baykara and Güngör [5] use multilingual pretrained Seq2Seq models mBART and mT5 as well as several monolingual Turkish BERT models in a BERT2BERT architecture. They obtain state-of-the-art results in both TR-News and MLSum datasets.

Most of the evaluation methods used in text summarization and other NLP tasks are more suitable for well-studied languages such as English. ROUGE [17] is the most commonly applied evaluation method in text summarization which basically calculates the overlapping number of word n-grams. Although initially proposed for machine translation, METEOR [3] is also used in text summarization evaluation. METEOR follows the n-gram based matching strategy which builds upon the BLEU metric [22] by modifying the precision and recall computations and replacing them with a weighted F-score based on mapping unigrams and a penalty function for incorrect word order. Recently, neural evaluation methods have been introduced which aim to capture semantic relatedness. These metrics usually utilize embeddings at word level such as Word mover distance (WMD) [15] or sentence level such as Sentence mover distance (SMD) [8]. BERTScore [32] makes use of the BERT model [9] to compute a cosine similarity score between the given reference and system summaries.

There has been very limited research in summarization evaluation for Turkish which has different morphology and syntax compared to English. Most of the studies make use of common metrics such as ROUGE and METEOR [21,28]. Recently, Beken Fikri et al. [6] utilized various semantic similarity metrics including BERTScore to semantically evaluate Turkish summaries on the MLSum dataset. In another work [30], the BLEU+ metric was proposed as an extension to the BLEU metric by incorporating morphology and Wordnet into the evaluation process for machine translation.

3   Overview of Turkish Morphology

Turkish is an agglutinative language which makes use of suffixation extensively. A root word can take several suffixes in a predefined order as dictated by the morphotactics of the language. It is common to find words affixed with 5–6 suffixes. During the affixation process, the words are also subject to a number of morphophonemic rules such as vowel harmony, elisions, or insertions. There are two types of suffixes as inflectional suffixes and derivational suffixes. The inflectional suffixes do not alter the core meaning of a word whereas the derivational suffixes can change the meaning or the part-of-speech.

Table 1. Morphological analysis of an example sentence.

Input	Morphological Analysis
tutsağı	[tutsak:Noun] tutsağ:Noun+A3sg+ı:Acc
serbest	[serbest:Adj] serbest:Adj
bıraktılar	[bırakmak:Verb] bırak:Verb+tı:Past+lar:A3pl

Table 1 shows the disambiguated morphological analysis of the sentence *tutsağı serbest bıraktılar* (*they released the prisoner*) as an example. The square bracket shows the root and its part-of-speech, which is followed by the suffixes attached to the root and the morphological features employed during the derivation[2].

4   Methodology

In this section, we explain the proposed methods that are based on the morphosyntactic features of Turkish and the evaluation metrics used in the study.

4.1   Morphosyntactic Variations

While comparing a system summary and a reference summary, the evaluation metrics used in text summarization use either the surface forms or the lemma or stem forms of the words. As stated in Sect. 1, the former approach is too restrictive and misses matches of the inflected forms of the same words, whereas the latter approach is too flexible and allows matches of all derivations of the same root which causes semantically distant words to match. In this work, we propose and analyze several other alternatives in between these two extreme cases based on morphosyntactic properties of the language. The obtained system and reference summaries are preprocessed according to the details of each proposed method before being passed to the evaluation metrics (ROUGE, METEOR, etc.). The implementation of the evaluation metrics are not changed. The proposed methods can easily be adapted to other morphologically rich languages in the case of readily available morphological analyzer tools.

Table 2 gives the list of the methods used to process the words before applying the evaluation metrics and shows the result of each one for the example sentence depicted in Table 1. The Surface method leaves the words in their written forms, while the Lemma (Stem) method strips off the suffixes and takes the lemma (stem) forms of the words. The lemma and stem forms are obtained using the Zemberek library [1] which applies morphological analysis and disambiguation processes. For the Lemma and Stem methods, in addition to their bare forms,

---

[2] The morphological features used in the example are as follows: Acc = accusative, A3pl = third person plural number/person agreement, A3sg = third person singular number/person agreement, Past = past tense.

Table 2. Proposed methods based on morphosyntactic variations of words.

Method	Processed Text
Surface	tutsağı serbest bıraktılar
Lemma	tutsak serbest bırak
Stem	tutsağ serbest bırak
Lemma and all suffixes	tutsak ##ı serbest bırak ##tı ##lar
Lemma and combined suffixes	tutsak ##ı serbest bırak ##tılar
Lemma and last suffix	tutsak ##ı serbest bırak ##lar
Lemma and all suffixes with Surface	tutsağı##tutsak tutsağı##ı serbest##serbest bıraktılar##bırak bıraktılar##tı bıraktılar##lar
Lemma and combined suffixes with Surface	tutsağı##tutsak tutsağı##ı serbest##serbest bıraktılar##bırak bıraktılar##tılar
Lemma and last suffix with Surface	tutsağı##tutsak tutsağı##ı serbest##serbest bıraktılar##bırak bıraktılar##lar

six different variations based on different usages of the suffixes are employed. The suffixes used in these variations are also obtained from the morphological parse by the Zemberek library. Only the variations of the Lemma method are shown in the table to save space; the same forms are also applied to the Stem method. The methods are explained below.

Surface: The text is only lower-cased and punctuations are removed. All the other methods also perform the same cleaning and lower-casing operations. For Turkish, this is the default evaluation strategy for all the metrics.

Lemma: The text is lemmatized and the lemma forms of the words are used.

Stem: The text is stemmed and the stem forms of the words are used.

Lemma and all Suffixes: The text is lemmatized and the suffixes are extracted. The lemma and each suffix of a word are considered as separate tokens.

Lemma and Combined Suffixes: The text is lemmatized and the suffixes are extracted. The suffixes are concatenated as a single item. The lemma and the concatenated suffixes of a word are considered as separate tokens.

Lemma and Last Suffix: The text is lemmatized and the suffixes are extracted. The lemma and the last suffix of a word are considered as separate tokens.

The last three methods above split the lemma and the suffixes and use them as individual tokens. This may cause the same tokens obtained from different words to match mistakenly. For instance, if the system summary contains the word *tutsağı* (*the prisoner*) (the accusative form of *tutsak* (*prisoner*)) and the reference summary contains the word *gardiyanı* (*the guardian*) (the accusative form of *gardiyan* (*guardian*)), the morphological parse will output the suffix 'ı' for both of them. The evaluation metric (e.g. ROUGE-1) will match these two suffixes (tokens) although they belong to different words. To prevent such cases, we devise another variation of these three methods where the surface form of the word is prefixed to each token generated from the word as explained below.

Lemma and all Suffixes with Surface: The text is lemmatized and the suffixes are extracted. The surface form of a word is added as a prefix to the lemma and each of the suffixes of the word. The lemma and each suffix of the word are then considered as separate tokens.

Lemma and Combined Suffixes with Surface: The text is lemmatized and the suffixes are extracted. The suffixes are concatenated as a single item. The surface form of a word is added as a prefix to the lemma and the concatenated suffixes of the word. The lemma and the concatenated suffixes of the word are then considered as separate tokens.

Lemma and Last Suffix with Surface: The text is lemmatized and the suffixes are extracted. The surface form of a word is added as a prefix to the lemma and the last suffix of the word. The lemma and the last suffix of the word are then considered as separate tokens.

4.2   Evaluation Metrics

We use five different metrics for comparing system summaries and reference summaries. We apply the morphosyntactic variations to the summaries and then score the performance using these metrics. In this way, we make a detailed analysis related to which combinations of evaluation metrics and morphosyntactic tokenizations correlate well with human judgments. We explain below each metric briefly.

ROUGE [17] is a recall-oriented metric which is commonly used in text summarization evaluation. ROUGE-N computes the number of overlapping n-grams between the system and reference summaries while ROUGE-L considers the longest common sub-sequence matches.

METEOR [3] is another commonly used metric in text summarization [14, 28]. It is based on unigram matches and makes use of both unigram precision and unigram recall. Word order is also taken into account via the concept of chunk.

BLEU [22] is a precision-oriented metric originally proposed for machine translation evaluation. It uses a modified version of n-gram precision and takes into account both the common words in the summaries and also the word order by the use of higher order n-grams. Although not common as ROUGE, BLEU is also used in text summarization evaluation as an additional metric [11,23].

BERTScore [32] is a recent metric proposed to measure the performance of text generation systems. It extracts contextual embeddings of the words in the system and reference summaries using the BERT model and then computes pairwise cosine similarity between the words of the summaries.

chrF [24] is an evaluation metric initially proposed for machine translation. The F-score of character n-gram matches are calculated between system output and references. It takes into account the morphosyntax since the method is based on character n-grams.

In this work, we make use of the Huggingface's `evaluate` library[3] for all the metrics explained above. We use the monolingual BERTurk-cased [27] model for computing the BERTScore values.

5   Dataset, Models, and Annotations

In this section, we first explain the dataset and the models used for the text summarization experiments. We then give the details of the annotation process where the summaries output by the models are manually scored with respect to the reference summaries. The human judgment scores will be used in Sect. 6 to observe the goodness of the proposed morphosyntactic methods.

5.1   Dataset

We use the **TR-News** [4] dataset for the experiments. TR-News is a large-scale Turkish summarization dataset that consists of news articles. It contains 277,573, 14,610, and 15,379 articles, respectively, for train, validation, and test sets.

5.2   Models

In this work, we use two state-of-the-art abstractive Seq2Seq summarization models. The models are trained on the TR-News dataset and used to generate the system summaries of a sample set of documents to compare with the corresponding reference summaries.

mT5 [31] is the multilingual variant of the T5 model [25] and closely follows its model architecture with some minor modifications. The main idea behind the T5 model is to approach each text-related task as a text-to-text problem where the system receives a text sequence as input and outputs another text sequence.

BERTurk-cased [27] is a bidirectional transformer network pretrained on a large corpus. It is an encoder-only model used mostly for feature extraction. However, Rothe et al. [26] proposed constructing a Seq2Seq model by leveraging model checkpoints and initializing both the encoder and the decoder parts by making several modifications to the model structure. Consequently, we constructed a BERT2BERT model using BERTurk-cased and finetuned it on abstractive text summarization.

The maximum encoder length for mT5 and BERTurk-cased are set to, respectively, 768 and 512, whereas the maximum decoder length is set to 128. The learning rate for the mT5 model is 1e−3 and for the BERTurk-cased model 5e−5. An effective batch size of 32 is used for both models. The models are finetuned for a maximum of 10 epochs where early stopping with patience 2 is employed based on the validation loss.

---

[3] https://github.com/huggingface/evaluate.

Table 3. Average scores and inter-annotator agreement scores for the models. In the first row, the averages of the two annotators are separated by the/sign.

	BERTurk-cased	mT5
Avg. annotator score	5.86/6.22	6.00/5.88
Pearson correlation	0.85	0.88
Krippendorff's alpha	0.84	0.87
Cohen's Kappa coefficient	0.44	0.25

5.3 Human Judgment Annotations

In order to observe which morphosyntactic tokenizations and automatic summarization metrics perform well in evaluating the performance of text summarization systems for morphologically rich languages, we need a sample dataset consisting of documents, system summaries, reference summaries, and relevancy scores between the system and reference summaries. For this purpose, we randomly sampled 50 articles from the test set of the TR-news dataset. For each article, the system summary output by the model is given a manual score indicating its relevancy with the corresponding reference summary. This is done for the mT5 model and the BERTurk-cased model separately. The relevancy scores are annotated by two native Turkish speakers with graduate degrees. An annotator is shown the system summary and the reference summary for an article without showing the original document and is requested to give a score. We decided to keep the annotation process simple by giving a single score to each system summary-reference summary pair covering the overall semantic relevancy of the summaries instead of scoring different aspects (adequacy, fluency, style, etc.) separately. The scores range from 1 (completely irrelevant) to 10 (completely relevant).

Table 3 shows the average scores of the annotators and the inter-annotator agreement scores. The averages of the two annotators are close to each other for both models. The Pearson correlation and Krippendorf's alpha values being around 0.80–0.90 indicate that there is a strong agreement in the annotators' scores. We also present the Cohen's Kappa coefficient as a measure of agreement between the annotators. The values of 0.44 and 0.25 signal, respectively, moderate agreement and fair agreement between the scores [16]. Since the Cohen's Kappa coefficient is mostly suitable for measuring agreement in categorical values rather than quantitative values as in our case, the results should be approached with caution.

Table 4. Pearson correlation results of the morphosyntactic methods with prefix tokens for the BERTurk-cased summarization model. Bold and underline denote, respectively, the best score and the second-best score for a column.

BERTurk-cased	ROUGE-1	ROUGE-2	ROUGE-L	METEOR	BLEU	BERTScore	chrF
Surface	0.770	0.723	0.750	0.736	0.649	**0.800**	0.789
Lemma with Surface	**0.802**	**0.730**	**0.768**	**0.807**	**0.776**	0.766	**0.804**
Stem with Surface	0.792	0.728	0.759	0.802	0.773	0.763	0.801
Lemma and all suffixes with Surface	0.773	0.712	0.743	0.796	0.765	0.760	0.793
Stem and all suffixes with Surface	0.768	0.712	0.740	0.794	0.764	0.760	0.791
Lemma and combined suffixes with Surface	0.774	0.718	0.747	0.796	0.771	0.768	0.797
Stem and combined suffixes with Surface	0.767	0.718	0.741	0.794	0.770	0.767	0.794
Lemma and last suffix with Surface	0.781	0.718	0.749	0.798	**0.776**	0.766	0.795
Stem and last suffix with Surface	0.774	0.718	0.743	0.798	**0.776**	0.766	0.792

Table 5. Pearson correlation results of the morphosyntactic methods with prefix tokens for the mT5 summarization model. Bold and underline denote, respectively, the best score and the second-best score for a column.

mT5	ROUGE-1	ROUGE-2	ROUGE-L	METEOR	BLEU	BERTScore	chrF
Surface	0.682	0.648	0.693	0.697	0.591	0.693	0.718
Lemma with Surface	**0.701**	**0.669**	**0.709**	0.753	0.719	0.682	**0.739**
Stem with Surface	0.688	0.665	0.700	0.742	0.714	0.674	0.734
Lemma and all suffixes with Surface	0.699	0.658	0.700	**0.771**	**0.730**	**0.694**	0.733
Stem and all suffixes with Surface	0.693	0.658	0.698	0.767	0.728	0.690	0.731
Lemma and combined suffixes with Surface	0.685	0.653	0.693	0.750	0.714	0.690	0.738
Stem and combined suffixes with Surface	0.677	0.653	0.688	0.745	0.712	0.687	0.734
Lemma and last suffix with Surface	0.692	0.653	0.699	0.749	0.712	0.674	0.734
Stem and last suffix with Surface	0.684	0.653	0.693	0.743	0.710	0.671	0.730

6 Correlation Analysis

In this work, we mainly aim at observing the correlation between the human evaluations and the automatic evaluations for the system generated summaries. For each of the proposed morphosyntactic tokenization methods (Sect. 4.1), we first apply the method to the system and reference summaries of a document and obtain the tokenized forms of the words in the summaries. We then evaluate the similarity of the tokenized system and reference summaries with each of the standard metrics (Sect. 4.2). Finally, we compute the Pearson correlation between the human score (average of the two annotators) given to the reference summary-system summary pair (Sect. 5.3) and the metric score calculated based on that morphosyntactic tokenization.

In this way, we make a detailed analysis of the morphosyntactic tokenization method and text summarization metric combinations. The results are shown in Tables 4 and 5. For the ROUGE metric, we include the results for the ROUGE-1, ROUGE-2, and ROUGE-L variants that are commonly used in the literature. For the tokenization methods that include suffixes, we show only the results with the surface forms of the words prefixed to the tokens (*with Surface*). The results without the prefixed tokens are given in the Appendix. Interestingly, the methods that do not use the prefix forms correlate better with the human judgments, although they tend to produce incorrect matches as shown in Sect. 4.1.

We observe that the Lemma method mostly yields the best results for the summaries generated by the BERTurk-cased model. The Lemma method is followed by the Stem method. These results indicate that simply taking the root of the words in the form of lemma or stem before applying the evaluation metrics is sufficient instead of more complex tokenizations. One exception is the BERTScore metric which works best with the surface forms of the words. This may be regarded as an expected behavior since BERTScore is a semantically-oriented evaluation approach while the others are mostly syntactically-oriented metrics. Hence, when fed with the surface forms, BERTScore can capture the similarities between different orthographical forms of the words.

The summaries generated by the mT5 model follow a similar pattern in ROUGE evaluations. The Lemma method and the Stem method yield high correlations with human scores. On the other hand, the other three metrics correlate better with human judgments when suffixes are also incorporated as tokens into the evaluation process in addition to the lemma or stem form. The BERTScore metric again shows a good performance when used with the Surface method.

We observe a significant difference between the correlation scores of the BERTurk-cased model and the mT5 model. The higher correlation results of the BERTurk-cased model indicate that summaries with better quality are generated. This may be attributed to the fact that BERTurk-cased is a monolingual model unlike the multilingual mT5 model and this distinction might have enabled it to produce summaries with better and more relevant context.

The high correlation ratios obtained with the Lemma tokenization approach may partly be attributed to the success of the Zemberek morphological tool. Zemberek has a high performance in morphological analysis and morphological disambiguation for Turkish [1]. When the Lemma and Stem methods are compared, we see that the Lemma method outperforms the Stem method for both models and for all evaluation metrics. This is the case for both the bare forms of these two methods and their variations. The tokenization methods where the last suffixes are used follow the top-ranking Lemma and Stem methods in BERTurk-cased evaluations, whereas they fall behind the tokenization variations with all suffixes in mT5 evaluations. The motivation behind the last suffix strategy is that the last suffix is considered as one of the most informative morphemes in

Turkish [20]. We see that this simple strategy is on par with those that use information of all the suffixes.

Finally, comparing the five text summarization evaluation metrics shows that METEOR yields the best correlation results for both models followed by the chrF metric. Although the underlying tokenization method that yields the best performance is different in the two models (Lemma for BERTurk-cased and Lemma with all suffixes in mT5), we can conclude that the METEOR metric applied to lemmatized system and reference summaries seems as the best metric for text summarization evaluation. This is an interesting result considering that ROUGE is the most commonly used evaluation metric in text summarization.

It should be noted that the Surface method corresponds to the approach used in the evaluation tools for these metrics. That is, the ROUGE, METEOR, BLEU, chrF, and BERTScore tools used in the literature mostly follow a simple strategy and work on the surface forms of the words. However, Tables 4 and 5 show that other strategies such as using the lemma form or using the lemma form combined with the suffixes nearly always outperform this default strategy. This indicates that employing morphosyntactic tokenization processes during evaluation increases correlation with human judgments and thus contributes to the evaluation process.

7   Conclusion

In this study, we introduced various morphosyntactic methods that can be used in text summarization evaluation. We trained state-of-the-art text summarization models on the TR-News dataset. The models were used to generate the system summaries of a set of documents sampled from the test set of TR-News. The relevancy of the system summaries and the reference summaries were manually scored and correlation analysis was performed between the manual scores and the scores produced by the morphosyntactic methods. The correlation analysis revealed that making use of morphosyntactic methods in evaluation metrics outperforms the default strategy of using the surface form for Turkish. We make the manually annotated evaluation dataset publicly available to alleviate the resource scarcity problem in Turkish. We believe that this study will contribute to focus on the importance of preprocessing in evaluation in this area.

Appendix

The correlation results of the morphosyntactic tokenization methods without the prefix tokens are shown in Tables 6 and 7.

Table 6. Pearson correlation results of the morphosyntactic methods without prefix tokens for the BERTurk-cased summarization model. Bold and underline denote, respectively, the best score and the second-best score for a column.

BERTurk-cased	ROUGE-1	ROUGE-2	ROUGE-L	METEOR	BLEU	BERTScore	chrF
Surface	0.770	0.723	0.750	0.736	0.649	**0.800**	0.789
Lemma	**0.831**	**0.744**	**0.795**	**0.809**	0.671	<u>0.775</u>	<u>0.797</u>
Stem	<u>0.815</u>	<u>0.738</u>	<u>0.777</u>	<u>0.799</u>	0.668	0.768	0.791
Lemma and all suffixes	0.796	0.737	0.762	0.783	<u>0.768</u>	0.746	**0.798**
Stem and all suffixes	0.789	0.736	0.757	0.779	0.766	0.745	0.794
Lemma and combined suffixes	0.798	0.727	0.769	0.793	0.763	0.752	0.794
Stem and combined suffixes	0.789	0.725	0.758	0.789	0.759	0.753	0.789
Lemma and last suffix	0.807	0.733	0.769	0.789	**0.773**	0.756	0.793
Stem and last suffix	0.795	0.732	0.757	0.784	<u>0.768</u>	0.757	0.788

Table 7. Pearson correlation results of the morphosyntactic methods without prefix tokens for the mT5 summarization model. Bold and underline denote, respectively, the best score and the second-best score for a column.

mT5	ROUGE-1	ROUGE-2	ROUGE-L	METEOR	BLEU	BERTScore	chrF
Surface	0.682	0.648	0.693	0.697	0.591	**0.693**	0.718
Lemma	**0.713**	**0.677**	**0.708**	0.737	0.602	0.682	<u>0.723</u>
Stem	0.696	<u>0.659</u>	0.693	0.716	0.594	0.675	0.714
Lemma and all suffixes	<u>0.702</u>	0.648	0.691	0.730	**0.701**	0.671	0.719
Stem and all suffixes	0.693	0.642	0.688	0.721	<u>0.695</u>	0.666	0.714
Lemma and combined suffixes	0.691	0.652	0.690	**0.748**	0.678	0.687	**0.727**
Stem and combined suffixes	0.680	0.643	0.679	0.737	0.669	<u>0.690</u>	0.720
Lemma and last suffix	0.700	0.656	<u>0.702</u>	<u>0.741</u>	0.678	0.656	0.718
Stem and last suffix	0.688	0.647	0.690	0.730	0.669	0.652	0.710

References

1. Akın, A.A., Akın, M.D.: Zemberek, an open source NLP framework for Turkic languages. Structure **10**, 1–5 (2007)
2. Altan, Z.: A Turkish automatic text summarization system. In: IASTED International Conference on (2004)
3. Banerjee, S., Lavie, A.: METEOR: an automatic metric for MT evaluation with improved correlation with human judgments. In: Proceedings of the ACL Workshop on Intrinsic and Extrinsic Evaluation Measures for Machine Translation and/or Summarization, Ann Arbor, Michigan, pp. 65–72. Association for Computational Linguistics (2005)
4. Baykara, B., Güngör, T.: Abstractive text summarization and new large-scale datasets for agglutinative languages Turkish and Hungarian. Lang. Resour. Eval. **56**, 1–35 (2022)
5. Baykara, B., Güngör, T.: Turkish abstractive text summarization using pretrained sequence-to-sequence models. Nat. Lang. Eng. 1–30 (2022)

6. Beken Fikri, F., Oflazer, K., Yanikoglu, B.: Semantic similarity based evaluation for abstractive news summarization. In: Proceedings of the 1st Workshop on Natural Language Generation, Evaluation, and Metrics (GEM 2021). Association for Computational Linguistics, Online (2021)

7. Çığır, C., Kutlu, M., Çiçekli, İ.: Generic text summarization for Turkish. In: ISCIS, pp. 224–229. IEEE (2009)

8. Clark, E., Celikyilmaz, A., Smith, N.A.: Sentence mover's similarity: Automatic evaluation for multi-sentence texts. In: Proceedings of the 57th Annual Meeting of the Association for Computational Linguistics, Florence, Italy, pp. 2748–2760. Association for Computational Linguistics (2019)

9. Devlin, J., Chang, M.W., Lee, K., Toutanova, K.: BERT: pre-training of deep bidirectional transformers for language understanding. In: Proceedings of the 2019 Conference of the North American Chapter of the Association for Computational Linguistics: Human Language Technologies, Volume 1 (Long and Short Papers), Minneapolis, Minnesota, pp. 4171–4186. Association for Computational Linguistics (2019)

10. Dong, L., et al.: Unified language model pre-training for natural language understanding and generation. In: Wallach, H., Larochelle, H., Beygelzimer, A., d'Alché-Buc, F., Fox, E., Garnett, R. (eds.) Advances in Neural Information Processing Systems, vol. 32. Curran Associates, Inc. (2019)

11. Graham, Y.: Re-evaluating automatic summarization with BLEU and 192 shades of ROUGE. In: EMNLP (2015)

12. Güran, A., Bayazit, N.G., Bekar, E.: Automatic summarization of Turkish documents using non-negative matrix factorization. In: 2011 International Symposium on Innovations in Intelligent Systems and Applications, pp. 480–484. IEEE (2011)

13. Kartal, Y.S., Kutlu, M.: Machine learning based text summarization for Turkish news. In: 2020 28th Signal Processing and Communications Applications Conference (SIU), pp. 1–4. IEEE (2020)

14. Koupaee, M., Wang, W.Y.: WikiHow: a large scale text summarization dataset (2018)

15. Kusner, M., Sun, Y., Kolkin, N., Weinberger, K.: From word embeddings to document distances. In: Bach, F., Blei, D. (eds.) Proceedings of the 32nd International Conference on Machine Learning. Proceedings of Machine Learning Research, Lille, France, vol. 37, pp. 957–966. PMLR (2015)

16. Landis, J.R., Koch, G.G.: The measurement of observer agreement for categorical data. Biometrics **33**(1), 159–74 (1977)

17. Lin, C.Y.: ROUGE: a package for automatic evaluation of summaries. In: Text Summarization Branches Out, Barcelona, Spain, pp. 74–81. Association for Computational Linguistics (2004)

18. Liu, Y., Lapata, M.: Text summarization with pretrained encoders. In: Proceedings of the 2019 Conference on Empirical Methods in Natural Language Processing and the 9th International Joint Conference on Natural Language Processing (EMNLP-IJCNLP), Hong Kong, China, pp. 3730–3740. Association for Computational Linguistics (2019)

19. Nuzumlalı, M.Y., Özgür, A.: Analyzing stemming approaches for Turkish multi-document summarization. In: Proceedings of the 2014 Conference on Empirical Methods in Natural Language Processing (EMNLP), Doha, Qatar, pp. 702–706. Association for Computational Linguistics (2014)

20. Oflazer, K., Say, B., Hakkani-Tür, D.Z., Tür, G.: Building a Turkish Treebank. In: Abeillé, A. (ed.) Treebanks. Text, Speech and Language Technology, vol. 20, pp.

261–277. Springer, Dordrecht (2003). https://doi.org/10.1007/978-94-010-0201-1_15

21. Özsoy, M.G., Çiçekli, İ., Alpaslan, F.N.: Text summarization of Turkish texts using latent semantic analysis. In: Proceedings of the 23rd International Conference on Computational Linguistics, COLING 2010, pp. 869–876. Association for Computational Linguistics, USA (2010)

22. Papineni, K., Roukos, S., Ward, T., Zhu, W.J.: BLEU: a method for automatic evaluation of machine translation. In: Proceedings of the 40th Annual Meeting of the Association for Computational Linguistics, Philadelphia, Pennsylvania, USA, pp. 311–318. Association for Computational Linguistics (2002)

23. Parida, S., Motlícek, P.: Abstract text summarization: a low resource challenge. In: EMNLP (2019)

24. Popović, M.: chrF: character n-gram F-score for automatic MT evaluation. In: Proceedings of the Tenth Workshop on Statistical Machine Translation, Lisbon, Portugal, pp. 392–395. Association for Computational Linguistics (2015). https://doi.org/10.18653/v1/W15-3049, https://aclanthology.org/W15-3049

25. Raffel, C., et al.: Exploring the limits of transfer learning with a unified text-to-text transformer. J. Mach. Learn. Res. **21**(140), 1–67 (2020)

26. Rothe, S., Narayan, S., Severyn, A.: Leveraging pre-trained checkpoints for sequence generation tasks. Trans. Assoc. Comput. Linguist. **8**, 264–280 (2020)

27. Schweter, S.: BERTurk - BERT models for Turkish (2020). https://doi.org/10.5281/zenodo.3770924

28. Scialom, T., Dray, P.A., Lamprier, S., Piwowarski, B., Staiano, J.: MLSUM: the multilingual summarization corpus. In: Proceedings of the 2020 Conference on Empirical Methods in Natural Language Processing (EMNLP), pp. 8051–8067. Association for Computational Linguistics, Online (2020)

29. See, A., Liu, P.J., Manning, C.D.: Get to the point: Summarization with pointer-generator networks. In: Proceedings of the 55th Annual Meeting of the Association for Computational Linguistics (Volume 1: Long Papers), Vancouver, Canada, pp. 1073–1083. Association for Computational Linguistics (2017)

30. Tantuğ, A.C., Oflazer, K., El-Kahlout, I.D.: BLEU+: a tool for fine-grained BLEU computation. In: Proceedings of the Sixth International Conference on Language Resources and Evaluation (LREC 2008), Marrakech, Morocco. European Language Resources Association (ELRA) (2008)

31. Xue, L., et al.: mT5: a massively multilingual pre-trained text-to-text transformer. ArXiv abs/2010.11934 (2021)

32. Zhang, T., Kishore, V., Wu, F., Weinberger, K.Q., Artzi, Y.: BERTScore: evaluating text generation with BERT (2019)

Building Knowledge Graphs in Heliophysics and Astrophysics

Fech Scen Khoo[1]([⊠]) [iD], Megan Mark[2] [iD], Roelien C. Timmer[3] [iD],
Marcella Scoczynski Ribeiro Martins[4] [iD], Emily Foshee[5], Kaylin Bugbee[6] [iD],
Gregory Renard[7] [iD], and Anamaria Berea[8] [iD]

[1] University of Oldenburg, 26111 Oldenburg, Germany
`fech.scen.khoo@uni-oldenburg.de`
[2] Florida Institute of Technology, Melbourne, FL 32901, USA
`markm2012@my.fit.edu`
[3] University of New South Wales, Sydney, NSW 2052, Australia
`r.timmer@unsw.edu.au`
[4] Federal University of Technology, Ponta Grossa, PR 84017-220, Brazil
`marcella@utfpr.edu.br`
[5] University of Alabama, Huntsville, AL 35805, USA
`elf0005@uah.edu`
[6] NASA Marshall Space Flight Center, Huntsville, AL 35808, USA
`kaylin.m.bugbee@nasa.gov`
[7] The Applied AI Company (AAICO), Redwood City, CA 94062, USA
[8] George Mason University, Fairfax, VA 22030, USA
`aberea@gmu.edu`

Abstract. We propose a method to build a fully connected knowledge graph in the scientific domains of heliophysics and astrophysics, using word embeddings from BERT which are adaptively fine-tuned to these domains. We extract the scientific concepts automatically by a keyword extractor. The graph nodes representing these concepts are connected and weighed based on the cosine similarities computed from their fine-tuned embeddings. Our method is able to capture various meaningful scientific connections, and it incorporates the possibility to enable knowledge discovery.

Keywords: Knowledge graph · Knowledge discovery · Language models

1 Introduction

As we carry out our daily scientific work within our own expertise, the ever expanding knowledge web inevitably becomes unstructured in a way that it can be disconnected among concepts, let alone if there is a meaningful relation hidden between different domains. Within and across domains, the same scientific term can mean differently to the respective communities, for instance the term *radiation*: it could be related to X-ray observation for astronomers, or UV radiation effect to the skin for biologists. On the other hand, cross-disciplinary researches have become increasingly important, as scientific discoveries in modern days usually benefit from huge collaborative efforts.

Therefore, structuring the knowledge base can encourage more dialogues and make possible new discoveries across the domains. Most of all, it will save the researchers' time in sorting out the ingredients they need for their research, and efforts can be well invested into the thought processes, experiments and etc., shedding lights on numerous questions or mitigations from how does the Sun affect lives on earth, to what is the origin of the Universe, and so on.

In science, to accept or rule out a concept or theory it requires sufficient experiments, observations and etc., which take time. With this in mind, how could we build a knowledge graph (KG) that incorporates probable or even accelerates new discoveries as well? In this regard, we turn into the investigation of how strongly or distantly connected are the given concepts.

On the other hand, from the perspective of data, the challenge adds up as we do not have a labeled dataset to train on for a Named Entity Recognition (NER) task, nor a ground truth to validate against. Apart from that, we also do not have an ontology which is typically used as a foundation to build a knowledge graph. Therefore, to extract the relevant entities, we will be using an automatic keyword extractor, and we rely on human experts in our team for validation. A naive strategy for us would be to start from constructing a smaller-sized knowledge graph that can be well verified in the process.

In our approach, we mine the texts using a controlled set of terms. We will specify these controlled terms in our experiments. The extracted keywords from the texts are taken to be related, and are examined in more detail where they are found to carry higher cosine similarities of at least 0.5. As a result, we will present specifically several pairs of the scientific terms or concepts that we obtained to illuminate what our embedding-based method using the fine-tuned language models can accomplish. In particular, we work on the domains of heliophysics and astrophysics, as we have the related knowledge expertise, and these 2 domains are known to be closely connected.

Our contributions from the present work are:

- We created 4 fine-tuned language models in heliophysics and in astrophysics: helioBERT, hierarchical helio-astroBERT, large helioBERT, and large hierarchical helio-astroBERT.
- We propose a novel method to build a knowledge graph based on cosine similarities for heliophysics and astrophysics domains.

2 Related Work

Some recent techniques such as logical reasoning and post-processing operations have been applied as refinement methods for knowledge graphs (e.g. automatic

completion and error detection) [1]. Reasoning can deal with automatically deriv-
ing proofs for theorems, and for uncovering contradictions in a set of axioms. It
is widely adopted in the Semantic Web community, leading to the development
of a larger number of ontology reasoners. For example, if a person is defined to be
the capital of a state, this is a contradiction, since cities and persons are disjoint,
i.e., no entity can be a city and a person at the same time. Some approaches for
knowledge graph building have implemented reasoning when new axioms are to
be added (NELL dataset, PROSPERA).

To validate a KG, a naive but popular approach is to randomly sample triples
from the KG to annotate manually. A triple is considered correct if the corresponding relationship is consistent with the domain expertise [2], hence the KG
accuracy can be defined as the percentage of triples in the KG being correct
– a sampling approach. While in terms of the quality of the extracted entities
themselves, the most common approach is again human evaluation [3]. In general, the target entities can be extracted by a (fine-tuned) NER model through
e.g. flairNLP[1]. Also, the flairNLP text embedding library comes with its word
embeddings Flair, and options such as GloVe [4] and BERT [5], or a combination of different embeddings can be chosen. On the other hand, one can consider
some structure graph metrics such as the Structure Hamming Distance metric
[6], which can be applied to compare the built KG with a known ontology as a
reference graph.

There has been an increased interest in generating knowledge graphs for heliophysics and astrophysics domains, such as the NASA Heliophysics KNOWledge
Network project [7] and other initiatives [8,9]. We draw our inspiration from a
recent approach that proposes a language model for astronomy and astrophysics
known as astroBERT [10]. The language model astroBERT is found to outperform BERT on NER task on the data of astronomical content. Similarly, another
BERT variant, SciBERT [11] which was proposed earlier, has been fine-tuned
on scientific texts with 18% from computer science and 82% from biomedical
domains.

3   Methodology

Our methodology consists of two main components. It begins with data collection, followed by a knowledge graph construction which requires a fine-tuning
procedure of the language model BERT. We propose the following machine learning pipeline (Fig. 1):

First, to enrich our primary dataset from NASA's Science Mission Directorate
(SMD), we collected abstracts from arXiv from the year 2021. These abstracts
are more descriptive than SMD. They widen the knowledge spectrum in our
SMD dataset, as they contain research findings from a larger scientific community. Thus this data addition potentially provides multiple (new) connections
between knowledge entities. From this pool of abstracts from various research
fields that cover for instance *Astrophysics*, and *Condensed Matter*, to further

---

[1] https://github.com/flairNLP/flair.

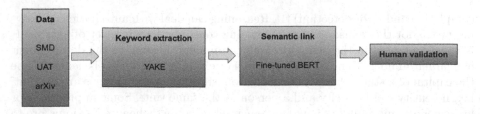

Fig. 1. Pipeline for building a knowledge graph.

align with the scientific context in our primary SMD dataset, we will narrow down our experiments to some specific research areas. For this, we define a number of different sets of scientific terms using two principal sources: SMD, and additionally Unified Astronomy Thesaurus (UAT), to extract only the relevant abstracts, by simply requiring that the set of terms (or any of them) form part of the abstract. With this, we have indirectly established to a certain degree a document similarity among the selected texts before we proceed to building the respective knowledge graph.

Next, we choose to extract only tri-grams out of our text data using YAKE [12]. Tri-gram turns out to be an optimal choice as it is sufficient to account for scientific terms such as *James Webb Space* (*James Webb Space Telescope* in full), and *Schwarzschild black holes* (a bi-gram *black holes* in general). YAKE which stands for Yet Another Keyword Extractor is an automatic keyword extractor, which includes readily the text pre-processing procedure that involves tokenization and stopword removal. The algorithm is succeeded by a statistical feature extraction then evaluated for a term score, followed by an n-gram (tri-gram in our case) keyword generation where its score is built out of the term score. The final step of the YAKE algorithm consists of data deduplication which further improves the ranking of the relevant keywords. For our purpose, we have chosen to extract a total of 20 keywords per text, ranked by the distance similarity metric, that is the Sequence Matcher (SEQM), implemented in YAKE. The lower the SEQM is, the more relevant or important the associated keyword is. These extracted keywords will serve as the nodes in our knowledge graph. These nodes are linked directly, that is, considered connected since these keywords come from a same pool of texts extracted using a particular set of terms (which represent a certain research topic) as explained before.

Now the question remains on how related the nodes are. We evaluate the strength of the connection or the semantic link between the nodes by computing cosine similarities based on the fine-tuned word embeddings from BERT. The threshold for cosine similarity value varies in each of our experiment, ranging from a minimum of 0.5 to 0.8 (1 being the highest), where below the set minimum value, we regard the pairs of entities as not strongly connected, and hence discard them for further analysis. We use the pre-trained transformer-based language model, BERT (BERTbase), and adaptively fine-tune the model on our datasets in order to shift BERT into our knowledge domains. Using the fine-tuned embeddings, we obtain a representation of our knowledge graph. For visualization, we use a package, igraph to create the graphs.

To effectively utilize the word embeddings, we propose the following 4 variations of BERT shown in Fig. 2, fine-tuned on a Masked Language Modeling (MLM) task using our datasets.[2] In an MLM task, a portion of the words in a sequence is masked and BERT learns to predict the masked tokens based on the context.

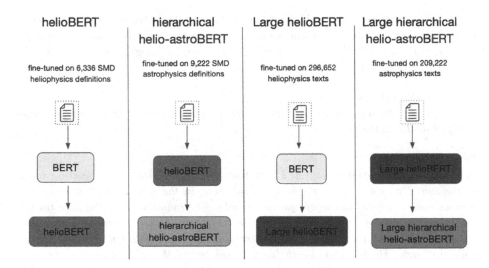

Fig. 2. BERT variations, differently fine-tuned on heliophysics and astrophysics texts.

Model I. helioBERT: BERT was trained on heliophysics texts.

Model II. Hierarchical helio-astroBERT: We froze the first 10 layers in *helioBERT*, and trained the embedding layer and the last 2 BERT layers on astrophysics texts. Research works in heliophysics and astrophysics share some common glossaries. Instead of collectively training with the texts from these 2 domains, we hierarchically trained the model where it has retained the prior knowledge of heliophysics and will then learn about astrophysics.

Model III. Large helioBERT: Compared to *helioBERT*, a larger amount of heliophysics texts from different sources was used in the training.

Model IV. Large hierarchical helio-astroBERT: We froze the first 10 layers in the *large helioBERT*, and trained the embedding layer and the last 2 BERT layers on a larger amount of astrophysics texts from different sources.

This work is a collaboration between domain scientists and computer scientists. We are able to manually identify meaningful or strong pairs of keywords as a validation of our knowledge graph in the respective scientific domain. As

---

[2] Impacts from fine-tuning on a Next Sentence Prediction task are left for future studies.

our knowledge graph is fully connected, we sample the results in duplet. We will discuss some of these examples in the result Sect. 5, at times citing the relevant research publications.

4   Experimental Setup

4.1   Data

Our primary data source is NASA's Science Mission Directorate (SMD) dataset, which contains mainly *terms* and *definitions* from 5 scientific domains: Astrophysics, Heliophysics, Planetary, Earth Science, and Biological & Physical Sciences. Examples of such data instances are:

Term: Big Bang theory
Definition: The theory that the Universe 'started' with an event that created time and space, about 13 billion years ago.

Term: Solar Flares
Definition: A great burst of light and radiation due to the release of magnetic energy on the sun. Flares are by far the biggest explosions in the solar system, with energy releases comparable to billions of hydrogen bombs. The radiation from the flare travels at the speed of light, and so reaches Earth within eight minutes. The energy is generally absorbed by Earth's atmosphere, which protects humans on Earth, however, the energy can cause radio blackouts on Earth for minutes or, in the worst cases, hours at a time. The radiation from a flare would also be harmful to astronauts outside of Earth's atmosphere. Some, but by no means all, flares have an associated coronal mass ejection (CME).

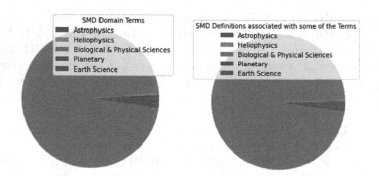

Fig. 3. Pie charts for the number of terms in the SMD dataset per domain (left), and for the number of definitions associated with the terms per domain (right).

Figure 3 shows an overview of our SMD dataset. There are a total of 9,291,463 terms, and 3,096,448 definitions. About 97% of the data come from Biological &

Physical Sciences, while other domains each contribute 0.3–1% of the data. In this work, we will focus on 2 domains: Heliophysics, Astrophysics.

The Unified Astronomy Thesaurus (UAT) data[3] is a table containing 2826 unique terms in the field of astronomy and astrophysics, categorized in 11 levels or hierarchies. For example, if one chooses a level 1 term *Astrophysical processes*, one of the level 2 terms that follows is *Astrophysical magnetism*, then there can be *Magnetic fields* at level 3, and *Primordial magnetic fields* at level 4, etc. The terms become more specific in the higher levels.

Furthermore, we find that there are SMD heliophysics terms which exist in UAT as well: 2% of a total of 29,846 SMD heliophysics terms are in the UAT table. We will refer to these overlapping SMD terms at each UAT level # as "SMD heliophysics level #". Therefore, although these terms are part of SMD heliophysics data, they are less heliophysics-apparent and can be more astrophysics-like. In another word, one can also view this as a shared vocabulary by the two domains.

Basically, the data is used in the following scenarios to: extract relevant arXiv abstract, fine-tune BERT, and extract keywords. The data involved for these purposes are not always the same. In particular, the data we used to fine-tune BERT are (number of texts):
(i) SMD heliophysics definitions (6,336), (ii) SMD astrophysics definitions (9,222), (iii) arXiv abstracts collected using some SMD heliophysics terms (290,316), and (iv) arXiv abstracts collected using some SMD astrophysics terms (200,000).
The data we used for keyword extractions are (number of texts):
(a) arXiv abstracts extracted using SMD heliophysics level 1 (14,227), (b) arXiv abstracts extracted using a particular hierarchy in UAT (5,963), (c) SMD heliophysics definitions (6,336), and (d) SMD astrophysics definitions (9,222).

4.2 Fine-Tuning on BERT: Setup

During the training, we have kept the BERT hyperparameters by default. Following are the specifics for each model training:

helioBERT: Trained on 6,336 SMD heliophysics definitions for 5 epochs.
Hierarchical helio-astroBERT: Trained on 9,222 SMD astrophysics definitions for 5 epochs.
Large helioBERT: Trained on 296,652 texts for 2 epochs. The texts comprise the prior 6,336 SMD heliophysics definitions, and 290,316 arXiv abstracts extracted using a random sample of 100 SMD heliophysics terms.
Large hierarchical helio-astroBERT: Trained on 209,222 texts for 2 epochs. The texts comprise the prior 9,222 SMD astrophysics definitions, and 200,000 arXiv abstracts randomly sampled from a pool of 626,388 arXiv abstracts extracted using a randomly sampled 50 SMD astrophysics terms.

---

[3] https://astrothesaurus.org, where the list of UAT terms we used are available at https://github.com/astrothesaurus/UAT/blob/master/UAT.csv.

4.3   Keyword Extraction: Setup

For the feasibility of analyzing the results by our domain scientists, for each experiment, we typically select 100 top keywords (tri-grams) extracted by YAKE with the lowest SEQM (i.e. the most relevant ones). As we have considered *a priori* that all the keywords extracted are related, for n keywords selected for further analysis, there will be $\frac{n(n-1)}{2}$ unique pairs of them. We compute the cosine similarities of all the pairs, where a higher cosine value indicates that the pair is more closely connected.

We highlight the following 3 experiments, under two contrasting elements: (i) data sources, and (ii) fine-tuned word embeddings considered.

Experiment I:
The data source is a collection of arXiv abstracts, extracted using a set of terms from a particular hierarchical branch from the UAT table, based on the level 1 term *Astrophysical processes*, level 2 term *Gravitation*, and level 3 term *General Relativity*, and all the terms which follow up to level 11. Hence, there exists a particular knowledge structure here in the data. From this pool of abstracts, we extracted the keywords using YAKE and analyzed the pairs formed out of the top 70 YAKE keywords. In the next section, we will show the comparison of the connections resulted using the embeddings from *hierarchical helio-astroBERT* against its *large* version.

Experiment II:
This experiment plans to show how BERT which has learned some heliophysics handles the more astrophysical data or the shared vocabularies between heliophysics and astrophysics domains. The data source is a collection of arXiv abstracts, extracted using a set of terms which we refer to as "SMD heliophysics level 1". This experiment compares the resulted graphs of scientific pairs using the word embeddings from *helioBERT* and *large helioBERT*. Top 89 YAKE keywords were selected.

Experiment III:
The data source is simply a collection of SMD heliophysics definitions and SMD astrophysics definitions. This is to examine the connectivity between the two scientific domains. Top 172 YAKE keywords were selected in this experiment.

We summarize the background details of the experiments in the following Table 1:

Table 1. Characteristics of the experiments. Shorthand for the model names: *lhhaB*: *large hierarchical helio-astroBERT*, *hhaB*: *hierarchical helio-astroBERT*, *lhb*: *large helioBERT*, *hb*: *helioBERT*, where their word embeddings are used.

Expt.	# unique keywords	# pairs	SEQM	Embedding	# pairs with cosine sim., α
I	70	2415	$(6.4\text{--}25)\times10^{-5}$	*hhaB*	203 ($\alpha > 0.6$)
I	70	2415	$(6.4\text{--}25)\times10^{-5}$	*lhhaB*	334 ($\alpha > 0.6$)
II	89	3916	$(1.0\text{--}9.9)\times10^{-4}$	*hB*	20 ($\alpha > 0.8$)
II	89	3916	$(1.0\text{--}9.9)\times10^{-4}$	*lhB*	41 ($\alpha > 0.8$)
III	172	14,706	$(1.0\text{--}9.9)\times10^{-4}$	*hhaB*	5751 ($\alpha > 0.5$)

5   Results

Our fully-connected knowledge graphs are massive even with under 200 key-words/nodes. As there is no ground truth to verify all the connections, it is useful that we could single out a number of interesting or true example pairs for discussions. We present these examples here and furthermore, we provide some relevant references accordingly (externally linked).

Result from Experiment I:
We compare the representations resulted from two word embeddings: *hierarchical helio-astroBERT* and its *large* version, focusing on the pairs whose cosine similarities α are higher than 0.6. By the *hierarchical helio-astroBERT* embeddings, we point out in particular in Table 2 some interesting example pairs.

Table 2. Example pairs highlighted from Experiment I (with *hhab* embeddings).

(*James Webb Space, Schwarzschild black hole*): $\alpha = 0.7112$
(*Generalized Uncertainty Principle, Einstein General Relativity*): $\alpha = 0.601$ (reference)

Although black hole of precisely Schwarzschild is rather too specific (theoretical), black holes can be connected with James Webb, as data from Webb can be used to study e.g. the growth rate of supermassive black holes (reference). Also, we find that the three physics journals (*Phys. Rev. Lett, Proc. Roy. Soc, Phys. Dark Univ.*) are connected to each other with a cosine similarity of more than 0.7. Table 3 shows a list of results with the highest cosine similarity.

Table 3. Top results from Experiment I (with *hhab* embeddings).

(*Phys. Rev. Lett., Laser Interferometer Gravitational-wave*): $\alpha = 0.8637$
(*polynomial curvature invariants, Gravitational Lensing Experiment*): $\alpha = 0.8703$
(*Small Magellanic Cloud, Large Magellanic Cloud*): $\alpha = 0.8815$
(*Counterpart All-sky Monitor, Laser Interferometer Gravitational-wave*): $\alpha = 0.9624$
(*Cosmic Microwave Background, Phys. Rev. Lett*): $\alpha = 0.9812$

While, by the *large hierarchical helio-astroBERT* embeddings, we point out in particular in Table 4:

Table 4. Example pairs highlighted from Experiment I (with *lhhab* embeddings).

(*James Webb Space, Cold Dark Matter*): $\alpha = 0.8701$
(*Cold Dark Matter, Webb Space Telescope*): $\alpha = 0.6076$
(*Event Horizon Telescope, Massive Black Hole*): $\alpha = 0.6124$

These are again convincing pairs. The data from James Webb will help to verify the existence of cold dark matter (reference). Note the changes in the cosine similarity α for the pair containing *Cold Dark Matter* when its partner is *James Webb Space* or *Webb Space Telescope*. Even though the keyword extraction by YAKE is not complete as in *James Webb Space Telescope* (as we had required for tri-gram), the associated cosine similarity is still high. Table 5 shows a list of results with the highest cosine similarity.

Table 5. Top results from Experiment I (with *lhhab* embeddings).

(Fourth Mexican School, Laser Interferometer Gravitational-wave): $\alpha = 0.8828$
(Gravitational Lens Astrophysics, Einstein General Relativity): $\alpha = 0.8864$
(Massive Black Hole, Extremely Compact Objects): $\alpha = 0.9388$
(Expansive Nondecelerative Universe, Field Dark Matter): $\alpha = 0.9489$
(Interferometer Space Antenna, Cosmological Gravitational Lensing): $\alpha = 0.9767$

By narrowing down our scope in the text corpus to gravity in general (built off a particular hierarchy in UAT), we are able to observe extremely informative pairs right from this research area.

Result from Experiment II:
We compare the representations resulted from two word embeddings: *helioBERT* and its *large* version, focusing on the pairs whose cosine similarities α are higher than 0.8. By the *helioBERT* embeddings, we point out in particular in Table 6 the example pairs found. Table 7 shows a list of results with the highest cosine similarity.

Table 6. Example pairs highlighted from Experiment II (with *hb* embeddings).

(Spitzer IRAC based, Big Bang theory): $\alpha = 1$ (reference)
(phantom divide line, quantum gravity community): $\alpha = 0.8373$ (reference)

Table 7. Top results from Experiment II (with *hb* embeddings).

(neutral massive fields, phantom divide line): $\alpha = 0.9494$
(main modern developments, CMB anisotropy data): $\alpha = 0.9609$
(GOYA Survey imaging, QSO absorption line): $\alpha = 0.9892$
(understanding current theories, Long Baseline Array): $\alpha = 1$
(spinning fluid embedded, Supernova Legacy Survey): $\alpha = 1$

While, by the *large helioBERT* embeddings, we point out in particular in Table 8 some example pairs.

Table 8. Example pairs highlighted from Experiment II (with *lhb* embeddings).

(*asymmetric dark matter, Standard Model imposed*): $\alpha = 1$
(*Hubble Volume N-body, Long Baseline Array*): $\alpha = 1$ (reference)
(*phantom divide line, main modern developments*): $\alpha = 0.9455$
(*phantom divide line, dark matter halo*): $\alpha = 0.8635$
(*main modern developments, dark matter halo*): $\alpha = 0.8633$

Although the keywords *asymmetric dark matter* and *Standard Model imposed* are paired with cosine similarity 1 (Table 8), it should not be taken literally, as we need to go beyond the *Standard Model* in order to explain dark matter. Table 9 shows a list of results with the highest cosine similarity.

Table 9. Top results from Experiment II (with *lhb* embeddings).

(*observed Velocity Dispersion, X-ray analyses lead*): $\alpha = 0.9513$
(*Cosmological General Relativity, cosmic microwave background*): $\alpha = 0.9891$
(*Hartle-Hawking No-Boundary Proposal, Density linear perturbations*): $\alpha = 1$

Interestingly, these highlighted examples show that BERT with only heliophysics knowledge is able to identify with a good indication of the strength of the relations on astrophysical contents such as *CMB*, *Big Bang theory*, to name a few.

Result from Experiment III:
By *hierarchical helio-astroBERT* embeddings, we find elements from the 2 domains connected with more than 0.5 cosine similarity, in particular in Table 10 we point out some example pairs.

Table 10. Example pairs highlighted from Experiment III (with *hhab* embeddings).

(*Martian satellite Phobos, Heliospheric Solar Magnetospheric*): $\alpha = 0.5349$
(*Measurements CME motion, Heliospheric Solar Magnetospheric*): $\alpha = 0.5284$ (reference)

There are indeed studies on interactions between solar wind and the Mars-Phobos (reference). Table 11 shows a list of results with the highest cosine similarity.

The cross-domain relations that we find are encouraging. The terms in SMD dataset are usually more technical, very specific to a smaller research community, as it involves for example names of instruments. Hence the connections established here are more technical than conceptual.

Table 11. Top results from Experiment III (with *hhab* embeddings), with $\alpha = 1$.

(*South Pacific Ocean, Synthetic Aperture Radar*) (reference)
(*Geocentric Equatorial Inertial, Lunar Reconnaissance Orbiter*)
(*SSA Space Weather, Explorer Mission satellite*)
(*Sciences Laboratory Facility, Polar Cap Indices*)
(*Naval Observatory Astronomical, Small Explorer Project*)

6   Discussions

In our approach, firstly, the strength of the cosine similarity is rather relative to the scope, and the size of the text corpus being considered during both the fine-tuning stage and keyword extraction. The scope of the corpus can be inferred from the set of terms we used to extract the relevant texts. It is non-trivial to determine exactly the relatedness of the entities, as the rank could change according to the depth and width of the respective research area, or its collection of research papers. On the other hand, one can see from Table 1 that a larger fine-tuned language model tends to produce a larger number of pairs at the same level of cosine similarity.

Secondly, there is not a clear best language model among those we proposed. The reason is related to the first point. Here we have looked at the aspect of hierarchical training, and also the results from using a different text size in fine-tuning. We do find interesting outputs from all the cases considered. Most importantly, the type of texts where the keyword extraction is performed plays a crucial role in producing some of the strongest relations: there is an implicit term hierarchy in the texts from Experiment I; shared scientific terms between the 2 domains from Experiment II; purely a combination of the technical terms from the 2 domains from Experiment III. Thus, we think that the models could as well complement each other in completing a knowledge graph. For more discussions about the related challenges, see e.g. [13].

7   Conclusions

We propose an embedding-based method to construct a knowledge graph in heliophysics and astrophysics domains, utilizing the cosine similarities computed from the word embeddings of the respective domain-specific BERT. Bypassing the need for a fine-tuned named entity extraction or such labeled training dataset, and out of a pool of texts selected based on a set of controlled scientific terms, our constructed knowledge graph is able to present many convincing relations of scientific concepts or terms in and across the domains. Moreover, our fine-tuned BERT models can also be used for other downstream tasks such as NER.

For future work, we plan to improve our validation method by using automatic metrics proposed in such as [14,15] which are based on declarative and mined rules, in addition to human-in-the-loop. We also plan to extend our method to study the synergies with the remaining scientific domains of planetary, earth science and biological & physical sciences.

In our fine-tuning of BERT and also in the arXiv abstract extraction (arXiv content to enrich our SMD dataset), scientific terms from the SMD dataset have been actively involved. Our ultimate goal is to develop our approach into a useful search tool for domain scientists to assist them in their research, and for integration into NASA's SMD data system.

Acknowledgements. This work has been enabled by the Frontier Development Lab (FDL) (https://frontierdevelopmentlab.org). FDL is a collaboration between SETI Institute and Trillium Technologies Inc., in partnership with NASA, Google Cloud, Intel, NVIDIA, and many other public and private partners. This material is based upon work supported by NASA under award No(s) NNX14AT27A. Any opinions, findings, conclusions, or recommendations expressed in this material are those of the authors and do not necessarily reflect the views of the National Aeronautics and Space Administration. The authors would like to thank the FDL organizers, the SETI institute, Trillium, the FDL partners and sponsors, and the reviewers for their constructive comments during the research sprint. The authors thank Sergi Blanco-Cuaresma and Felix Grezes for helpful discussions. Finally, the authors also thank Google for providing access to computational resources without which this project would not have been possible.

References

1. Paulheim, H.: Knowledge graph refinement: a survey of approaches and evaluation methods. Semant. Web **8**(3), 489–508 (2017)
2. Gao, J., Li, X., Xu, Y.E., et al.: Efficient knowledge graph accuracy evaluation. VLDB Endow. **12**, 1679–1691 (2019)
3. Mintz, M., Bills, S., Snow, R., et al.: Distant supervision for relation extraction without labeled data. In: Proceedings of the Joint Conference of the 47th Annual Meeting of the ACL and the 4th International Joint Conference on Natural Language Processing of the AFNLP, pp. 1003–1011 (2009)
4. Pennington, J., Socher, R., Manning, C.: GloVe: global vectors for word representation. In: Proceedings of the 2014 Conference on Empirical Methods in Natural Language Processing (EMNLP), pp. 1532–1543 (2014)
5. Devlin, J., Chang, M.-W., Lee, K., et al.: BERT: pre-training of deep bidirectional transformers for language understanding. In: Proceedings of the 2019 Conference of the North American Chapter of the Association for Computational Linguistics: Human Language Technologies, pp. 4171–4186 (2019)
6. de Jongh, M., Druzdzel, M.J.: A comparison of structural distance measures for causal Bayesian network models. In: Recent Advances in Intelligent Information Systems, Challenging Problems of Science, Computer Science Series, pp. 443–456 (2009)
7. McGranaghan, R., Klein, S.J., Cameron, A.: The NASA Heliophysics KNOWledge Network (Helio-KNOW) project (an essay for the Space Data Knowledge Commons)
8. Bentley, R., Brooke, J., Csillaghy, A., et al.: HELIO: discovery and analysis of data in heliophysics. Futur. Gener. Comput. Syst. **29**, 2157–2168 (2013)

9. Efthymiou, V.: CosmOntology: creating an ontology of the cosmos. In: DL4KG: Deep Learning for Knowledge Graphs Workshop (ISWC 2022) (2022)

10. Grezes, F., et al.: Building astroBERT, a language model for astronomy & astrophysics. arXiv preprint arXiv:2112.00590 (2021)

11. Beltagy, I., Lo, K., Cohan, A.: SciBERT: a pretrained language model for scientific text. In: Proceedings of the 2019 Conference on Empirical Methods in Natural Language Processing and the 9th International Joint Conference on Natural Language Processing (EMNLP-IJCNLP), pp. 3615–3620 (2019)

12. Campos, R., Mangaravite, V., Pasquali, A., et al.: YAKE! keyword extraction from single documents using multiple local features. Inf. Sci. **509**, 257–289 (2020)

13. Timmer, R.C., Mark, M., Khoo, F.S., et al.: NASA science mission directorate knowledge graph discovery. In: WWW 2023 Companion: Companion Proceedings of the ACM Web Conference 2023, pp. 795–799 (2023)

14. Ortona, S., Meduri, V.V., Papotti, P.: RuDiK: rule discovery in knowledge bases. In: Proceedings of the VLDB Endowment, pp. 1946–1949 (2018)

15. Tanon, T., Bourgaux, C., Suchanek, F.: Learning how to correct a knowledge base from the edit history. In: Proceedings of WWW 2019: The World Wide Web Conference, pp. 1465–1475 (2019)

Text to Image Synthesis Using Bridge Generative Adversarial Network and Char CNN Model

Sudhakaran Gajendran[1]($\boxtimes$) (iD), Ar. Arunarani[2] (iD), D. Manjula[3] (iD),
and Vijayan Sugumaran[4,5] (iD)

[1] School of Electronics Engineering, Vellore Institute of Technology, Chennai, India
sudhakaran.g@vit.ac.in
[2] Department of Computational Intelligence, School of Computing, SRM Institute of Science
and Technology, Kattankulathur, Chennai, India
arunaraa@srmist.edu.in
[3] School of Computer Science and Engineering, Vellore Institute of Technology, Chennai, India
manjula.d@vit.ac.in
[4] Center for Data Science and Big Data Analytics, Oakland University, Rochester, MI 48309,
USA
sugumara@oakland.edu
[5] Department of Decision and Information Sciences, School of Business Administration,
Oakland University, Rochester, MI, USA

Abstract. A content to picture production approach seeks to produce photorealistic images that are semantically coherent with the provided descriptions from text
descriptions. Applications for creating photorealistic visuals from text includes
photo editing and more. Strong neural network topologies, such as GANs (Generative Adversarial Networks) have been shown to produce effective outcomes in
recent years. Two very significant factors, visual reality and content consistency,
must be taken into consideration when creating images from text descriptions.
Recent substantial advancements in GAN have made it possible to produce images
with a high level of visual realism. However, generating images from text ensuring high content consistency between the text and the generated image is still
ambitious. To address the above two issues, a Bridge GAN model is proposed,
where the bridge is a transitional space containing meaningful representations of
the given text description. The proposed systems incorporate Bridge GAN and
char CNN – RNN model to generate the image in high content consistency and
the results shows that the proposed system outperformed the existing systems.

Keywords: Generative Adversarial Network · CNN · Text Encoder · Image
Synthesis

1 Introduction

Learning the mapping link between semantic text space and complicated RGB image
space is the fundamental step in text-to-image synthesis. A key issue in many applications, including art generation and computer-aided design, is the creation of visuals

E. Métais et al. (Eds.): NLDB 2023, LNCS 13913, pp. 229–242, 2023.
https://doi.org/10.1007/978-3-031-35320-8_16

from text descriptions [1]. An artist or graphic designer can create a realistic image of a mountain and a grassy field by simply describing the scenario in his mind; this will greatly increase productivity and make it simpler for those who are new to the industry. It has a big impact on how people and computers interact. One of the most active study topics in recent years, multimodal learning and inference across vision and language, is likewise fueled by it [2]. Moreover, people may forget the names of items but recall their descriptions.

Generative Adversarial Networks (GANs) are the foundation for the most recent text-to-image synthesis techniques that have been suggested. In order to generate images using a GAN, it is usual practice to encode the entire text description into a global phrase vector. Although the outstanding results that have been shown, the production of high-quality images is hindered by the lack of crucial fine-grained information at the word level when conditioning GAN exclusively on the global phrase vector. In their approach, Das et al. [14] created a game between two players (models), with the goal of the generator being to generate a distribution as near as feasible to the real data distribution reflected in the training data. The goal of the second player, known as the discriminator, is to be able to distinguish between examples taken from the real training data and fake examples produced by the other player, the generator. The discriminator is a relatively straightforward supervised model with only two classes, fake or real (0, 1). The police, who are responsible for telling fake money from genuine money, serve as the discriminator in this structure, and the counterfeiter receives feedback from the police that can aid in making counterfeit money look more realistic. This is a common approach to explain this framework. The fact that the generator only learns about the data distribution through the discriminator rather than having direct access to the training data is a key feature of this design, making the generator more resistant to over-fitting.

This is a very difficult process since there are two extremely essential considerations that must be made: visual reality and content consistency [3]. Due to significant advancements made in the field of GANs, creating visually realistic images is not that difficult [4, 5]. The goal of creating images from text is still to ensure high content consistency between the text and the resulting image. Images can be created with excellent content consistency by selecting the key elements from the text descriptions. A Bridge Generative Adversarial Network (Bridge-GAN) is suggested as a solution to this problem in order to attain visual reality and content consistency. The Bridge GAN creates an area of transition with comprehensible representations of the supplied text. Images can be created with excellent content consistency by selecting the key elements from the text descriptions.

The purpose of the study is to translate a scene description in prose to the image pixels that correspond to it. The model needs to be taught to uncover connections between text-based properties and various arrangements of pixels in an image, which makes the job extremely difficult. Due to the fact that a text description can correlate to a very large number of photos, this is particularly difficult. Due to the fact that generative adversarial networks learn the underlying distribution rather than converting a feature vector to an output directly, this attribute makes them the obvious choice. The research's main objective is to produce semantically coherent visuals from captions. To do this, the text embeddings from the input text are obtained using a Text encoder model (CNN-RNN) [15]. Then, to achieve content consistency, a Transitional mapping network (MLP model) is applied. Ultimately, an image is produced using the text embeddings obtained by a Generative Adversarial Network (GAN). The proposed system results are compared with the existing systems like Stack GAN++, DGatt GAN. The results obtained by the proposed framework is promising and outperformed the existing systems.

2 Related Work

A challenging task that combines computer vision and natural language processing (NLP) methods is used for the conversion of text descriptions into images. The objective is to produce an image that faithfully conveys the meaning of a given text description. Zhang et al. [6] study the task of creating photographic images based on semantic image descriptors. In order to regularize mid-level representations and aid generator training in capturing complicated image statistics, their method incorporates supplementary hierarchically nested adversarial objectives inside the network hierarchies. Using three open datasets, this work could produce high quality photographic photographs and outperform the state of the art by a wide margin. One disadvantage is that a very slight semantic consistency is also seen.

Jingcong et al. [7] presented a residual block feature pyramid attention generative adversarial network, or ResFPA-GAN. In order to produce the fine-grained image synthesis, they also introduced multi-scale feature fusion by embedding feature pyramid structure. Reed [8] introduced a novel model called the Generative Adversarial What-Where Network (GAWWN), which synthesizes images in response to commands indicating what to draw where. With the Caltech-UCSD Birds dataset, they demonstrate high-quality 128×128 image synthesis that is conditioned on both informal text descriptions and item placement.

The align DRAW model, which combines an alignment model over words and a recurrent variational autoencoder, was successful in producing images that match a given input caption. [10] introduces new techniques for enhancing the training of generative adversarial networks (GANs) for picture synthesis. They create a GAN variation that uses label conditioning to produce global coherent picture samples with a resolution of 128×128. They offer two brand-new methods for evaluating the variety and discriminability of samples derived from class-conditional image synthesis models. According to these analyses, high resolution samples offer class information that low resolution ones do not. Although some synthesized image classes have high Inception accuracy, the model's average Inception accuracy ($10.1\% \pm 2.0\%$) is still significantly lower than the 81% genuine training data.

[11] suggests using Stacked Generative Adversarial Networks (StackGAN) with Conditioning Augmentation to create photorealistic photos. The suggested approach breaks down text-to-image synthesis into a brand-new process of sketch-refinement. A Reinforced Cross-media Bidirectional Translation (RCBT) approach was put forth to carry out cross-media correlation learning as well as bidirectional translation between image and text [12]. Gregor et al. [13] describe the Deep Recurrent Attentive Writer (DRAW) neural network architecture for image production. A unique spatial attention

mechanism that replicates the foveation of the human eye and a framework for sequential variational auto-encoding that enables the repeated creation of complex visuals are combined in DRAW networks.

The fact that there is a huge gap between these two different modalities, and how advantageous it is to provide a transitional space for learning an interpretable representation, is ignored by these systems, which can use visual information from text description to generate visuals. Hence, the Bridge-GAN approach is suggested as a solution to this problem, which can significantly improve the visual realism and consistency of the content of synthetic images.

Because to the interpretable representation learning, the Bridge-GAN technique effectively learns the latent manifold of real data. The interpretable representation learning process is guided by a ternary mutual information objective in this method, which also improves the visual realism and content consistency of synthetic images. Since the interpretable representation contains more interpretable and consistent information with the synthetic picture and higher linear separability, the content consistency between conditioned text information and synthetic image can be improved using this subnetwork.

The generative adversarial subnetwork, made up of a generator G and a discriminator D, is then built. The visual reality of synthetic images is improved through a progressive training procedure that gradually develops both the generator and discriminator. The generator begins by synthesizing images at a low resolution, and then throughout the subsequent training phase, more layers are added to generate images at a high resolution. The objective is to produce photorealistic images with a high degree of visual realism and a high degree of content consistency by maximizing the mutual information between the given text descriptions, the interpretable representation, and the observations of synthetic images.

To translate the text descriptor into images, a number of methods have been suggested, including CNN-RNN models, ResFPA-GAN, GAWWN, align DRAW, and Stacked GANs, among others. These models, however, fail to take into account the necessity of a transitional area for acquiring an interpretable representation, which can greatly enhance the visual realism and content coherence of synthetic images. The Bridge-GAN approach, which employs a generative adversarial subnetwork and a progressive training procedure to create photorealistic images with a high level of visual realism and content consistency, is recommended as a solution to this problem. The approach uses interpretable representation learning that is driven by a ternary mutual information objective to enhance the content consistency between conditioned text information and synthetic images.

3 Proposed System

The overall system architecture is represented in Fig. 1. The system is primarily divided into 3 parts: the Encoder part, the Mapping subnetwork and the Generative adversarial network (GAN) part. In the text encoder, the text descriptions from the dataset (CUB_200_2011), which consists of text descriptions and the corresponding images for 200 bird classes and each class consisting of 60 images is encoded using the one hot encoding and the encoded text is fed to the char CNN RNN model. The proposed model is implemented using 2 models, one is the fixed_rnn model and the other is the fixed_gru model. From the better model, the text embeddings are obtained which are then fed to the mapping subnetwork.

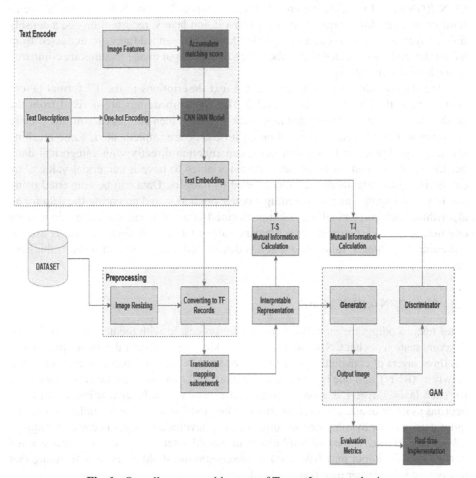

Fig. 1. Overall system architecture of Text to Image synthesis

Apart from this, the image features in the T7 format are compared with the text embeddings obtained from the CNN RNN model to get the matching score. The images from the dataset are resized to 256 × 256 and converted to tensor flow (TF) records. The text embeddings from the encoder part are also converted to TF records. Both these are then fed to the transitional mapping subnetwork which is a Multi-layer perceptron (MLP) model from which the interpretable representation is obtained. Finally, the interpretable representation is fed to the Generative Adversarial network which consists of the generator and discriminator that works on a loop process. The generator generates the image which is checked by the discriminator on a loop process to get the corresponding proper image. With the output image, the inception score is calculated.

3.1 Text Encoder

Using one-hot encoding, which generates new (binary) columns showing the presence of every conceivable value from the original data, the text descriptions are encoded. The CNN-RNN model receives the encoded text as input. The layers in this model are as follows: an embedding layer, a series of convolution layers, recurrent layers, a densely linked layer, and then an output projection layer. Text embeddings are extracted from the model, and the extracted text embeddings and the input image features are compared to see how closely they match.

One hot encoding is used to encode the text descriptions in the T7 format before being sent to the char CNN-RNN model. The text embeddings are derived from the model. To obtain the accumulated match score, this is then compared with the picture attributes in the T7 format. Depending on how they are implemented, some machine learning algorithms, such decision trees, can function directly with categorical data, but the majority need all input and output variables to have a numerical value. Any categorical data must therefore be converted to integers. Data can be converted using one hot encoding as a means of getting a better prediction and preparing the data for an algorithm. Each categorical value is transformed into a new categorical column using one-hot, and each column is given a binary value of 1 or 0. A binary vector is used to represent each integer value. The index is designated with 1, and all of the values are zero.

3.2 Char CNN – RNN Model

After text encoding, the embedded vectors are processed with the neural network with the combination of char CNN and RNN model. The proposed neural network framework has three layers of convolutional neural networks (CNNs), one layer of recurrent neural networks (RNN), and one layer of projection, as well as a max pool layer and threshold for each layer. Layer 1 is a one-dimensional convolutional layer that has 70 and 384 neurons as its input and output respectively. The model slides a 4×4 window across the input data in order to compute the output of the convolutional layer because it employs a 4×4 kernel size. The model's minimum threshold is set to 1×10^{-6}, the lowest value that a neuron's output may have, and its maximum threshold is set to 0, meaning that any output value larger than 0 is accepted.

Layer 1 is followed by the max pool layer, which has a striding and kernel size of 3 $\times$ 3 and 3×3 respectively. This layer reduces the output size while keeping the most crucial characteristics by taking the maximum value from each 3×3 block of the output from the preceding layer. Another one-dimensional convolutional layer, Layer 2, has 384 and 512 neurons as its input and output respectively from the previous max pool layer. Additionally, a 4×4 kernel size is used to compute the output of the convolutional layer while sliding across the input data. With a kernel size of 4×4, layer 3 is comparable to layer 2, having an input of 384 neurons, an output of 512 neurons, and a dimension of 4×4.

An RNN layer is utilized to capture the temporal dependencies in the input sequence after the convolutional layers. The RNN layer, which is composed of a series of recurrent cells with the ability to keep an internal state and analyze each input in succession, receives the output of the final convolutional layer. The output of the projection layer is applied to the RNN layer output to produce model's final output.

3.3 Mapping Subnetwork and GAN

The images from the dataset are resized to ensure that all images are of the same dimension. The text embeddings from the previous module and the resized images are converted to Tensor flow records that store data in the form of a binary representation. The TF-records are now given to the training network that consists of a transitional mapping subnetwork and a GAN that are trained progressively together. The output from the mapping network is sent to the GAN. The image batch is mapped to a value representing the score of visual reality and content consistency. These constraints help with training the model further. Finally, the training is stopped when the GAN generates images that are realistic and clear.

Text descriptions are passed to the trained model for generating the respective images for testing. Then the inception score is calculated. Finally, the Bridge-GAN's performance is compared with other similar models that synthesize text from images. The algorithm for mapping subnetwork and GAN is presented in Algorithm 1.

Algorithm 1: Mapping Subnetwork and GAN

Step 1: Load un-pickled text embeddings from pickle file into test_texts

Step 2: Call generate_img method with trained model path and test_texts

Step 3: test set_size = len(test_texts) which has 2933 bird classes. Each class has 10 descriptions.

Step 4: text_num = test_texts[0].shape[0] (For each bird, 10 vectors corresponding to the 10 descriptions will be present).

Step 5: for every i in testset_size *text_num

    Generate output image by passing through the trained model and store

in the form of numpy arrays (.npy output file)

Step 6: Calculate inception score to evaluate visual reality

---

4 Implementation Details

In the Text encoder part, a char CNN RNN model is implemented. The Char CNN RNN model is prevalent in the Text-to-Image task, and is used to process image descriptions to obtain embeddings that contain visual-relevant features. In order to achieve competitive performance, robustness to mistakes, and scalability to huge vocabulary, the

CNN-RNN model is expanded to train a visual semantic embedding "from scratch" at the character level. Visually discriminative text representations of previously undiscovered categories can be extracted using a character level model. The result is the creation of text embeddings.

Given a batch of text embeddings ϕt with dimension 1024, we concatenate and normalize it as latent codes with a batch of random noise vectors with dimension 100 before the transitional mapping subnetwork M of the Style GAN. The output from the mapping network is given to the generator module and the GAN training takes place. The Bridge GAN model is trained on the local machine using the NVIDIA Quadro P5000 GPU.

4.1 Dataset

The dataset most frequently used for fine-grained visual categorization tasks is Caltech-UCSD Birds-200-2011 (CUB-200-2011). 11,788 photos, 5,994 for training and 5,794 for testing, of 200 bird subcategories are included. Each image contains extensive annotations, including 312 binary characteristics, 1 bounding box, 15 part positions, and 1 sub category title.

4.2 Hyperparameters

The following are the hyperparameters that are used to fine tune the training process for GAN and RNN model as shown in Tables 1 and 2.

Table 1. Hyperparameters for GAN

Hyperparameter	Value
Number of mapping layers	8
Number of activations in the mapping layers	512
Learning rate multiplier for the mapping layers	0.01
Activation function	Leaky RELU
Learning rate - Generator and Discriminator	0.001
Optimizer	Adam
Generator optimizer values (beta1, beta2, epsilon)	0.0, 0.99, 1e-8
Discriminator optimizer values (beta1, beta2, epsilon)	0.0, 0.99, 1e-8
Activation function for Generator and Discriminator	Leaky RELU

Table 2. Hyperparameters for RNN models

Parameter	Model 1	Model 2
RNN dimension	256	512
Max pool layer	True	False
Model type	fixed_rnn	fixed_gru
RNN steps	8	18
Activation function	Relu	Sigmoid and tanH

4.3 Evaluation Metrics

Root mean square deviation (RMSE) - RMSE is employed to quantify the discrepancies between samples predicted by the system and the values actually observed. The formula is represented below in Eq. 1.

$$RMSE = \sqrt{\sum_{t=1}^{T} (\hat{y}_t - y_t)^2} \tag{1}$$

Peak signal to noise ratio (PSNR) - The fidelity of a signal's representation depends on the ratio between the maximal power and the noise. PSNR is typically stated as a logarithmic number using the decibel scale. The formula is represented below in Eq. 2.

$$PSNR = 10.log_{10}\left(\frac{MAX_I^2}{MSE}\right) = 20.log_{10}(MAX_I) - 10.log_{10}(MSE) \tag{2}$$

where MAX_I is the maximum possible pixel value, MSE is the mean square error.

Structural Similarity Index Measure (SSIM) - The formula for SSIM that incorporates luminance masking and contrast masking terms is represented below in Eq. 3.

$$SSIM(x, y) = \frac{(2\mu_x\mu_y + c_1)(2\sigma_{xy} + c_2)}{(\mu_x^2 + \mu_y^2 + c_1)(\sigma_x^2 + \sigma_y^2 + c_2)} \tag{3}$$

Feature Similarity Index Matrix (FSIM) - Index of Feature Similarity process maps the features and compares the two photos' likenesses. Phase Congruency (PC) and Gradient Magnitude (GM) are two criteria that must be explained in detail in order to characterise FSIM. The formula is represented below in Eq. 4.

$$FSIM = \frac{\sum_{x\varepsilon\Omega} S_L(x).PC_m(x)}{\sum_{x\varepsilon\Omega} PC_m(x)} \tag{4}$$

5 Results and Discussion

Text descriptions are fed and the model is trained to obtain the text embeddings. For getting the text embeddings for the descriptions, the one-hot encoded form of the text is given to that trained char CNN RNN model. For each class taken, the mean of the generated text embeddings is taken and finally one embedding per class is considered. The embedding value is obtained from the char CNN model. With the obtained text embeddings from the model and the image features in the T7 format, the average precision score is calculated and the average of all classes is calculated for getting the average top-1 accuracy. The average precision score which is the average of the matching scores between the image features and text features for each of the bird classes considered for Model 1 is 0.5520. The average precision score which is the average of the matching scores between the image features and text features for each of the bird classes considered for Model 2 is 0.4545. The images in the dataset are of varied dimensions. To ensure every image is of the same dimension, resizing is done and the images obtained are of the dimension 256×256.

TensorFlow (TF) records are created from the downsized images and text embeddings generated from the char CNN-RNN model. When a series of these records serializes to binary, the result is a TF Record. Comparatively speaking to all other data formats, the binary format requires less capacity for storing. The number of fully connected layers in the transitional mapping subnetwork is set to 8 from the various values tried in the implementation. Each completely connected layer has a 512-dimensional architecture, and the activation functions used is Leaky ReLUs. After the transitional mapping subnetwork, we can obtain a batch of 512-dimensional interpretable representation.

A Style GAN is used in the GAN section. Style GAN offered some modifications to the progressive GAN architecture's generator section. The discriminator architecture, however, resembles baseline progressive GAN quite a bit. The proposed model consists of different blocks where each block includes 3 layers. These layers converts the input from the dimension of $m \times m$ into $2 m \times 2 m$ with the help of 2 convolution and 1 upscale layer. The resolutions of the output photos gradually increase during the model training. The generator G first creates graphics with an 8×8 resolution and eventually reaches 256×256 resolution. The basic learning rate is 1×10^{-3} and increases gradually to 2×103 with increasing resolution, while the Adam optimizer approach is included in the proposed system to minimize the loss between the actual and predicted.

In the GAN part, a Style GAN is implemented. Style GAN uses the baseline progressive GAN architecture and proposed some changes in the generator part of it. However, the discriminator architecture is quite similar to baseline progressive GAN. The proposed model consists of different blocks where each block includes 3 layers. These layers converts the input from the dimension of $m \times m$ into $2 m \times 2 m$ with the help of 2 convolution and 1 upscale layer. The generator G produces images with 8×8 dimension during the start and moves to 256×256 dimension. The Adam optimizer approach is included in the proposed system to minimize the loss between the actual and predicted. The learning rate of the proposed system is 0.001 for GAN and 0.01 for mapping layers. The proposed framework is capable of producing images with a resolution of 256×256. The test data is tested with the trained GAN model to obtain the associated images.

Input: *A bird with a light brown tint, a white head, and an orange beak.*

(a). Dataset image
for the same class

(b). Generated image

(c). Generated
image for different class

Fig. 2. Generated images of different class

Figure 2(b) is the generated image for the same class considering as Image 1 and Fig. 2(c) is the generated image for a different class considering as Image 2 as shown in Fig. 2. The RMSE score is less for the generated image of the same class and it is comparatively higher for the generated image of different class as the generator has produced an image for the same class description with less deviation as shown in Table 3. PSNR approximation of reconstruction quality is higher for the generated image from the same class compared to generated image from a different class. Structural similarity index is higher for the same class image when compared to other due to more similarities in structural information for the generated image from the same class. Feature based similarity index is higher for the same class when compared to other due to more similar features in the generated image from the same class to that of the reference image. The different metrics along with their corresponding scores are shown in Fig. 3.

Table 3. Performance Analysis

Metrics	FSIM	SSIM	RMSE	PSNR
Image 1	0.3084	0.9051	0.0181	34.809
Image 2	0.2854	0.7593	0.0271	31.322

5.1 Comparative Analysis

The proposed Bridge-GAN model is tested for the Inceptions core for the CUB dataset with 4 different GAN model. From the Table 4, it is inferred that Bridge GAN model has outperformed the other models. The comparison of the different models in shown in Table 4.

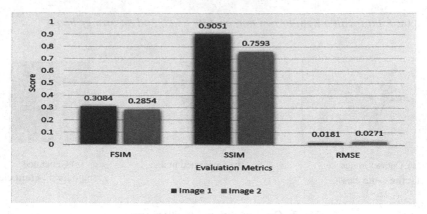

Fig. 3. Evaluation Metrics Graph

Table 4. Comparative analysis of Inception score

Models	Inception score
GAN-INT-CLS	2.88 ± 0.04
GAWWN	3.62 ± 0.07
Stack GAN++	4.04 ± 0.05
DGattGAN	4.45 ± 0.05
Dualattn-GAN	4.59 ± 0.07
Bridge-GAN (Proposed System)	4.75 ± 0.06

The first model is a GAN-INT-CLS model that has achieved a inception score of 2.88. The Bridge GAN model that uses a transitional space, has achieved a score of 4.75 which is nearly a double-manifold increase from the baseline model. The GAWWN model has achieved an inception score of 3.62 which is 1.13 units lesser than the proposed model. Even though, the Stack GAN++ which uses 2-stage Generative adversarial network architecture achieved an inception score of 4.04, it is still lesser than Bridge GAN's score by 0.71 units. The DGattGAN and the Dualattn-GAN models have achieved almost a similar score with a difference of 0.14 units. The Table 5 shows the generated images by the proposed system for sample text descriptions.

Table 5. Generated images for certain text descriptions

S.No	Description	Generated Image
1.	The long, flat beak and broad wings of this bird make it easily recognisable.	
2.	The bill is blunt-tipped and black, the head is light brown with a tiny white marking between the eye and the beak, and the wings are long, slender, and brown with white markings on the secondaries.	
3.	A bird with a light brown tint, a white head, and an orange beak.	
4.	This enormous white bird's eye is brown, and its bill is long and curved.	
5.	This bird has a long, grainy neck and a slender, pastel orange/blue beak that droops at the tip.	

6 Conclusion

The suggested Bridge GAN model produces synthetic images from text descriptions automatically with a high level of visual realism and consistency in the content. The proposed systems incorporates Bridge GAN and char CNN – RNN model to generate the image in high content consistency. By expanding the CNN-RNN model at the character level, fine grained visually meaningful text embeddings are employed to train the network, producing competitive performance, robustness to mistakes, and scalability to vast vocabulary. The best quantitative outcomes from studies on the CUB-200-2011 birds dataset thus serve to confirm the efficacy of the proposed Bridge-GAN. The dataset for CUB-200-2011 birds was used to train the suggested model. Other generic datasets, such as MS-COCO datasets, and others can be included in this. By using the suggested Bridge-GAN technique, it is also expected to produce images with improved resolution and visual realism. Moreover, real-time image synthesis from text descriptions has not yet been accomplished. It is also possible to create a user-friendly interface that takes the shape of a website to collect the user's text input and show them the results in real time.

References

1. Frolov, S., Hinz, T., Raue, F., Hees, J., Dengel, A.: Adversarial text-to-image synthesis: a review. Neural Netw. **144**, 187–209 (2021)
2. Dong, Y., Zhang, Y., Ma, L., Wang, Z., Luo, J.: Unsupervised text-to-image synthesis. Pattern Recognit. **110**, 107573 (2021). https://doi.org/10.1016/j.patcog.2020.107573
3. Bankar, S.A., Ket, S.: An analysis of text-to-image synthesis. In: Proceedings of the International Conference on Smart Data Intelligence (ICSMDI 2021) (2021)
4. Tan, Y.X., Lee, C.P., Neo, M., Lim, K.M.: Text-to-image synthesis with self-supervised learning. Pattern Recognit. Lett. **157**, 119–126 (2022)
5. Hossain, M.Z., Sohel, F., Shiratuddin, M.F., Laga, H., Bennamoun, M.: Text to image synthesis for improved image captioning. IEEE Access **9**, 64918–64928 (2021)
6. Zhang, Z., Xie, Y., Yang, L.: Photographic text-to-image synthesis with a hierarchically-nested adversarial network. In: Proceedings of the IEEE Conference on Computer Vision and Pattern Recognition, pp. 6199–6208 (2018)
7. Sun, J., Zhou, Y., Zhang, B.: ResFPA-GAN: text-to-image synthesis with generative adversarial network based on residual block feature pyramid attention. In: 2019 IEEE International Conference on Advanced Robotics and its Social Impacts (ARSO), pp. 317–322. IEEE (2019)
8. Reed, S.E., Akata, Z., Mohan, S., Tenka, S., Schiele, B., Lee, H.: Learning what and where to draw. Adv. Neural Inf. Process. Syst. **29**, 217–225 (2018)
9. Mansimov, E., Parisotto, E., Ba, J.L., Salakhutdinov, R.: Generating images from captions with attention. arXiv preprint arXiv:1511.02793 (2015)
10. Odena, A., Olah, C., Shlens, J.: Conditional image synthesis with auxiliary classifier GANs. In: International Conference on Machine Learning, pp. 2642–2651. PMLR (2017)
11. Zhang, H., et al.: StackGAN++: realistic image synthesis with stacked generative adversarial networks. IEEE Trans. Pattern Anal. Mach. Intell. **41**(8), 1947–1962 (2018)
12. Peng, Y., Qi, J.: Reinforced cross-media correlation learning by context-aware bidirectional translation. IEEE Trans. Circuits Syst. Video Technol. **30**(6), 1718–1731 (2019)
13. Gregor, K., Danihelka, I., Graves, A., Rezende, D., Wierstra, D.: DRAW: a recurrent neural network for image generation. In: International Conference on Machine Learning, pp. 1462–1471. PMLR (2015)
14. Dash, A., Gamboa, J.C.B., Ahmed, S., Liwicki, M., Afzal, M.Z.: TAC-GAN-text conditioned auxiliary classifier generative adversarial network. arXiv preprint arXiv:1703.06412 (2017)
15. Gajendran, S., Manjula, D., Sugumaran, V.: Character level and word level embedding with bidirectional LSTM–dynamic recurrent neural network for biomedical named entity recognition from literature. J. Biomed. Inform. **112**, 103609 (2020). https://doi.org/10.1016/j.jbi.2020.103609

Evaluation of Transformer-Based Models for Punctuation and Capitalization Restoration in Spanish and Portuguese

Ronghao Pan[iD], José Antonio García-Díaz[✉][iD], and Rafael Valencia-García[iD]

Departamento de Informática y Sistemas, Facultad de Informática,
Universidad de Murcia, 30100 Murcia, Espinardo, Spain
{ronghao.pan,joseantonio.garcia8,valencia}@um.es

Abstract. Punctuation restoration plays a key role as a post-processing task in various text generation methods, such as Automatic Speech Recognition (ASR), and Machine Translation (MT). Despite its importance, the results of ASR systems and other generation models used in these tasks often produce texts that lack punctuation, which is difficult for human readers and might limit the performance of many downstream text processing tasks for web analytics, such as sentiment analysis, sarcasm detection or hate-speech identification including stereotypes, sexism, and misogyny. Thus, there are many techniques for restoring text punctuation, but most solutions like Condition Random Field (CRF) and pre-trained models such as the BERT, have been widely applied. In addition, they focus only on English and on restoring punctuation, without considering the restoration of capitalization. Recently, there has been a growing interest in an alternative method of addressing the problem of punctuation restoration, which is to transform it into a sequence labeling task. In this sense, we propose a capitalization and punctuation restoration system based on Transformers models and a sequence labeling approach for Spanish and Portuguese. Both models obtained good results: a macro-averaged F1-score of 59.90% and overall performance of 93.87% for Spanish and macro-averaged F1-score of 76.94% and 93.66% overall performance for Portuguese. In addition, they are also able to restore capitalization, identifying proper names, names of countries and organizations.

Keywords: Punctuation restoration · Capitalization restoration · Natural Language Processing · Spanish · Portuguese

1 Introduction

Advances in the field of Artificial Intelligence (AI) and Deep Learning (DL) have driven the development of increasingly accurate and efficient Automatic Speech Recognition (ASR) systems, models of Speech-To-Text and Machine Translation, leading to the development of a wide range of applications in various domains,

E. Métais et al. (Eds.): NLDB 2023, LNCS 13913, pp. 243–256, 2023.
https://doi.org/10.1007/978-3-031-35320-8_17

including voice assistants, customer care or healthcare among others. However, ASR system and the generation models employed in those tasks often generate as output a stream of words without punctuation, which significantly reduces their readability and overall comprehensibility, especially in cases where there is ambiguity in the interpretation [13]. In addition, the most advanced Natural Language Processing (NLP) models are trained mostly with punctuated text, such as the BERT model, which has been trained with Toronto Book Corpus and Wikipedia. Therefore, an unpunctuated output set generated would reduce its usefulness in these models for specific tasks, such as hate speech detection, business intelligence, fake news and deceptive language, or detection of harmful content, as it would seriously degrade the performance of the linguistic models. For example, in [4] there is a performance difference of more than 10% when the models are trained with newspaper texts and tested with unpunctuated transcripts for the Named Entity Recognition (NER) task. Therefore, punctuation and capitalization restoration is one of the most important post-processing tasks of text generation methods.

Lexical features have become a popular choice for training models in the task of punctuation restoration, as they can be trained on a variety of text sources that contain punctuation, including Wikipedia, articles, news articles, publicly accessible newspapers, and other large-scale texts. The widespread availability of such texts further contributes to the appeal of lexical features in this task. As for machine learning models, the Conditional Random Field (CRF) has been widely used [22]. Lately, deep learning models such as recurrent or convolutional (LSTM or CNN) neural networks and transformers have also been used [18,19, 23]. Recent developments in pre-trained models based on Transformers such as BERT, RoBERTa, and XLM-RoBERTa, have been explored and are very useful for the problem of punctuation restoration.

In this work, we present various sequence tagging models for punctuation and capitalization restoration for Spanish and Portuguese. These models are composed of a transformer architecture based on fine-tuning a pre-trained language model in order to use the prior knowledge for the identification of capital letters and punctuation marks. Currently, for Spanish and Portuguese, there are different monolingual and multilingual models based on BERT or RoBERTa, with different performances. Thus, this work also analyses the behavior of different current pre-trained models for the task of automatic restoration of punctuation and capital letter.

In addressing the challenge of automatic restoration of punctuation and capitalization for Spanish and Portuguese, we make the following contributions: (1) we evaluated the OpusParaCrawl dataset [3]; (2) we examine the feasibility of fine-tuning different pre-trained monolingual and multilingual models for this task; and (3) we demonstrate that our proposal can outperform the performance of previous approaches.

This paper is structured as follows: Sect. 2 presents an overview of the state of the art of punctuation and capitalization restoration system. In Sect. 3, materials and methods are presented and described in detail. Section 4 presents the performed experiment and the results obtained by different pre-trained language models, and an error analysis is conducted. Finally, in Sect. 5 the conclusions and future work are discussed.

2   Related Work

Nowadays, automatic punctuation and capitalization restoration tasks have been extensively studied in many systems and are constantly evolving. These approaches can be broadly divided into three categories according to the features applied [21]: those using prosody features derived from acoustic information, those using lexical features, and the combination of the previous two features-based methods. Lately, for the task of punctuation of restoration, lexical features have been widely used because the model can be trained using any punctuation and because of the availability of large-scale texts [1].

In recent years, the problem of punctuation retrieval has been addressed with different approaches, from the use of deep learning algorithms, such as [18], which proposed a neural network model based on LSTM to restore English punctuation marks to the use of architectures based on Transformer model [23]. Recent advances in transformer-based pre-trained models have proven to be successful in many NLP tasks, so new transformer-based approaches based on BERT-type architectures have emerged [9], which have been shown to achieve values of up to 83.9% on the F1-score in the well-known and reference IWSLT 2012 dataset [11].

Regarding punctuation retrieval in Spanish and Portuguese, new models have recently emerged, such as [23], which is a punctuation restoration system in Spanish customer support transcripts using transfer learning, and a BERT-based automatic punctuation and capitalization system for Spanish and Basque [12]. Both models have used a medium training corpus, so the performance of certain punctuation is quite low, as in [12], which has obtained an f1 score of 11.9% for the closed exclamation mark. The difference between our model from existing punctuation restoration models is that we have used a larger training corpus, which allows us to increase the performance of certain lesser-used punctuation marks, such as exclamation and colons. In addition, our sequence labeling model can jointly identify punctuation marks and capital letters. Concerning punctuation restoration in Portuguese, in [14] the authors performed an experimental analysis comparing a bidirectional LSTM model with CRF and BERT to predict punctuation in Brazilian Portuguese. The BERT-based model [14] is a similar approach to ours for punctuation restoration, but it only predicts three punctuation marks (comma, period, and question mark) and does not identify capital letters, and only BERT-based models have been tested.

The system presented in this paper addresses 5 different punctuation marks for Spanish and Portuguese, which are described in Sect. 3. Both models are composed of a transformer architecture but, unlike prior works that solely studied one architecture (BERT), we experiment with different pre-trained models based on BERT, and RoBERTa, thus analyzing the monolingual and multilingual models used.

3   Materials and Methods

In this work, we create a punctuation and capitalization restoration system using the OpusParaCrawl [3] dataset. Our method can be summarized as follows (see Fig. 1): first, the Spanish and Portuguese datasets are cleaned, and each sentence is divided into a set of tokens. Second, the Splitter module divides the corpus into training, evaluation, and testing according to the task. Finally, the fine-tuning approach of pre-trained monolingual and multilingual models is evaluated for punctuation and capitalization restoration tasks.

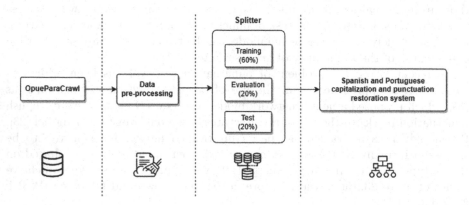

Fig. 1. Overall architecture of the system.

3.1   Dataset

We used OpusParaCrawl [3] dataset for Spanish and Portuguese capitalization and punctuation restoration, which consists of parallel corpora from Web Crawls collected in the ParaCrawl project. These datasets contain 42 languages, and 43 bitexts with a total number of 3.13G sentence fragments by crawling hundreds of thousands of websites, using open-source tools. Usually, parallel corpora are essential for building high-quality machine translation systems and have found uses in many other natural language applications, such as paraphrases learning [2]. The reason for using this database is its size and the number of exclamatory and interrogative sentences it contains, which is larger than other existing corpora. Besides, the texts of this dataset are already divided into sentences and have all punctuation marks for each language. Specifically, we have used the "es-ca" partition of OpusParaCrawl for the restoration of Spanish punctuation and capitalization, and it contains a total of 17.2M sentences and 774.58M words written in Spanish. For Portuguese, we used the "pt-en" partition, which contains 84.9M sentences and 2.74G words written in Portuguese.

3.2 Data Pre-processing

To solve the task of recovering punctuation and capitalization, we perform a common pre-processing step, in which we (1) remove all non-target punctuation marks; (2) divide the texts into words; and (3) label the words with their corresponding tags.

Instead of covering all possible punctuation marks in Spanish and Portuguese, we only include 5 types of target punctuation that are commonly used and are important to improve the readability of the transcription: period (.), comma (,), question (?), exclamation (!), and colon (:). For capitalization restoration, the same approach has been used as for punctuation, so that for each punctuation mark two labels have been added to identify whether the word is upper or lower case. For example, for the comma, we have two labels: ,u indicates that the token is of uppercase type and has the comma, and ,l denotes that the token is of lowercase type. However, in Spanish interrogative and exclamation sentences there is always a mark indicating the beginning of the sentence (¿ and ¡), so in the Spanish punctuation restoration model, 6 more classification labels are added with respect to Portuguese: ¿l (lower case with an open question mark), ¿u (upper case with an open question mark), ¡l (lower case with an open exclamation mark), ¡u (upper case with an open exclamation mark), ¿?l (indicates that the sequence consists of a single token and is of interrogative type), and ¡!u (indicates that the sequence consists of a single token and is of exclamatory type). Finally, for the Spanish punctuation and capitalization restoration model, there are a total of 18 classes to be predicted by the model, and for Portuguese 12 classes.

3.3 Splitter Module

The Splitter module is responsible for extracting the training, evaluation, and testing dataset with a 60–20–20 ratio. As discussed in Sect. 3.1, the dataset is very large, so we have used only 2,153,297 sentences (48,598,391 words) for Spanish and 2,974,059 sentences (48,598,391 words) for Portuguese. Table 1 details the dataset used for Spanish and Portuguese, showing the distribution of each label.

3.4 Punctuation and Capitalization Restoration System

The problem of punctuation and capitalization restoration has been approached as a sequence labeling task, which consists of a sequence of token classifications, in which the model predicts the punctuation marks that each word in the input text may have. In Fig. 2, the system architecture is shown. Briefly, it can be described as follows. First, we take the training and evaluation dataset to train a pre-trained model. Second, we extract the tokens from the dataset using the tokenizer of the pre-trained model. This ensures that the words in the dataset are split in the same tokens as the pre-trained model. Third, the fine-tuning process is carried out, which consists of adjusting or adapting the model for a specific task, taking advantage of the modern Large Language Models (LLMs) prior knowledge. Finally, a token classification layer is added to classify each token in the input sentence into the correct category. As can be seen in Fig. 2, the input sentence "qué estás haciendo" does not have any punctuation, and the model predicts that the word "qué" is uppercase type with open question mark, the word "estás" is lowercase type, and the word "haciendo" is lowercase and has a question mark after it to produce the output sentence "¿Qué estás haciendo?".

Different monolingual and multilingual models for the task of punctuation and capitalization restoration in Spanish and Portuguese have been evaluated. The Spanish models are: (1) BETO [6], (2) ALBETO [7], (3) DistilBETO [7], (4) MarIA [10], and (5) BERTIN [16]. The Portuguese model are: (1) BERTimbau Base [17], and (2) BR_BERTo[1]. We also evaluate XLM-RoBERTa as a multilingual transformer [8]. The main feature of transformer networks is their self-attention mechanism, whereby each word in the input can learn what relation it has with the others [20]. All models are based on different transformers-based

Table 1. Distribution of the datasets.

	Spanish			Portuguese		
Symbol	Train	Eval	Test	Train	Eval	Test
l	24,766,487	6,188,709	7,735,761	22,357,554	5,583,964	6,983,933
u	3,227,725	805,128	1,008,684	5,270,270	1,318,219	1,647,823
?u	4,069	1,025	1,312	21,604	5,485	6,948
?l	26,267	6,536	8,188	37,581	9,464	11,736
!u	2,795	693	863	10,317	2,587	3,168
!l	16,385	4,087	5,047	31,965	7,929	10,003
,u	402,341	100,313	125,855	537,272	133,382	166,797
,l	1,327,308	331,192	414,603	1,284,072	321,069	400,403
.u	198,155	49,693	62,001	283,580	70,426	88,629
.l	948,916	237,060	296,425	980,717	245,831	306,616
:u	40,150	10,094	12,424	129,261	32,133	40,237
:l	110,445	27,523	34,133	165,170	41,216	51,030
¿u	23,675	5,971	7,422	–	–	–
¿l	5,049	1,225	1,582	–	–	–
¡u	5,724	1,445	1,791	–	–	–
¡l	3,022	818	991	–	–	–
¿?u	356	82	91	–	–	–
¡!u	494	111	150	–	–	–
Total	31,109,363	7,771,705	9,717,323	31,109,363	7,771,705	9,717,323

---

[1] https://huggingface.co/rdenadai/BR_BERTo.

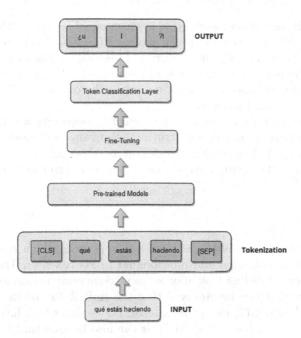

Fig. 2. Overall architecture of capitalization and punctuation restoration system.

models, such as BERT, RoBERTa or XLM-RoBERTa, and all of them need the input data to be preprocessed by the tokenization process, which consists of decomposing a larger entity into smaller components called *tokens*. For tokenization, we use the same tokenizer used in the pre-trained model. The models used in this study use the tokenization of sub-words with the WordPiece algorithm as BERT or the Byte-Pair Encoding (BPE) algorithm in the RoBERTa and XLM-RoBERTa-based models, so there are words that split into several tokens as in the case of BERT frequent tokens are grouped into one token and less frequent tokens are split into frequent tokens [5]. Therefore, it is necessary to adjust the sub-word labels and treat special tokens so that they are ignored during training. For this purpose, we have applied the following techniques proposed in [15]:

- Assign -100 labels to special tokens such as [CLS], [SEP], $< s >$ and $< /s >$ so that they are ignored during training.
- Assign all sub-words the same label as the first sub-word to solve the sub-word tokenization problem.

4   Results and Analysis

To compare the performance of the models, we rely on the weighted and macro-averaged F1-score as reference metrics. Both metrics consider precision and recall, but they differ in how they weight the contributions of each class. The macro-average F1-score is calculated by taking the average of the F1 score for each class. This means that each class is given equal weight in the calculation and gives information about the performance of the model with respect to each class independently. The weighted-average F1-score, on the other hand, takes into account the number of instances in each class, giving more weight to the classes with more instances. Thus, it measures the overall performance of the model in an unbalanced dataset.

To perform an error analysis and check where models give wrong predictions, a normalized confusion matrix with truth labels of the best model for each language has been used. A normalized confusion matrix consists of a table showing the distribution of the predictions of a model compared to the truth label of the data.

4.1 Spanish

Table 2 shows the results obtained with our approach, which consists of fine-tuning different monolingual and multilingual LLMs based on Transformers to perform a sequence labeling task in order to retrieve punctuation and capitalization of a sentence. It can be observed that the RoBERTa architecture achieves better results than BERT, except for the BETO model, which has achieved the best macro-averaged F1-score (59.90%). It can also be seen that the lightweight version of BETO and distilled BETO (ALBETO and DistilBETO) are the worst performers, with 57.46% and 57.90% in the macro-averaged F1-score. The two best scores are achieved by BETO (59.90%) and XLM-RoBERTa (59.60%), outperforming two of the RoBERTa-based models trained on a large Spanish corpus, such as MarIA (58.84% in M-F1) and BERTIN (58.33% in M-F1). When comparing the results obtained with the monolingual and multilingual models, there is a slight advantage for the models trained only in Spanish, as in the case of BETO and XLM-RoBERTa. Therefore, it is preferable to obtain specific pretrained models for the target language rather than to use multilingual variants. Comparing our Spanish punctuation and capitalization restoration system (see Table 3) with one of the existing ones like [12], our model improves the overall performance of their system. However, these results should be taken with caution, as we are comparing different test splits.

The error analysis is conducted with the BETO model. Figure 3 shows its confusion matrix. It can be observed that BETO does not make many relevant wrong classifications, i.e., it does not confuse punctuation symbols that separate a sentence (such as a comma, and colon) with those indicating the end of a sentence. BETO mislabeled the labels contained in the exclamation. The ratio of wrong classification of the labels indicating the end of an exclamatory sentence (!u and !l) is skewed for labels that denote the end of a sentence (.u and .l) with 59.16% and 36.62%. This is because both punctuation marks are placed at the end of the sentence and the only difference is that exclamations are used to show emphasis or an emotional exclamation. Therefore, across texts it is difficult to identify the emotions of a sentence. On the other hand, labels indicating the beginning of an exclamatory sentence (¡u and ¡l) are often confused with those denoting the absence of punctuation marks (u and l) with 79.90% and 72.94%.

Table 2. Results of different LLMs for Spanish punctuation and capitalization restoration system. We report the weighted averaged precision, recall and F1-score(W-P, W-R, W-F1), and macro averaged F1-score (M-F1).

Model	W-P	W-R	W-F1	M-F1
BETO	**93.834**	93.930	**93.873**	**59.902**
ALBETO	93.756	93.902	93.809	57.457
DistilBETO	93.680	93.810	93.729	57.897
MarIA	93.685	93.791	93.732	58.843
BERTIN	93.589	93.691	93.634	58.333
XLM-R	93.883	**94.001**	93.927	59.660

Table 3. Classification report of the BETO fine-tuned for Spanish punctuation and capitalization restoration.

Symbol	Precision	Recall	F1-score	Symbol	Precision	Recall	F1-score
!l	44.673	22.485	29.906	!u	38.664	20.693	26.958
,l	77.283	74.257	75.740	,u	77.219	75.968	76.588
.l	87.383	89.740	88.546	.u	83.910	82.688	83.295
:l	66.490	60.658	63.440	:u	64.131	55.231	59.349
?l	78.102	72.646	75.275	?u	76.876	70.368	73.478
l	96.939	97.430	97.184	u	89.868	89.199	89.532
¡!u	19.731	17.886	18.763	¡l	36.240	11.377	17.318
¡u	46.696	14.888	22.577	¿?u	48.039	47.573	47.805
¿l	60.305	51.675	55.657	¿u	77.653	76.014	76.825

Overall	Precision	Recall	F1-score
Macro avg	65.009	57.265	59.902
Weighted avg	93.834	93.930	93.873

This is because the dataset contains many exclamation marks that do not have the open exclamation marks in an exclamatory sentence, so the proportion of open and close exclamation marks are different, as shown in Table 1. One solution proposed in future work to solve this problem is to add some heuristic conditions in the post-processing to mitigate this type of error. In addition, the ratio of wrong classification of labels indicating exclamatory pronouns (¡!u) is skewed for .l and u, being the percentage of wrong classification of 26.83% and 24.39%, respectively.

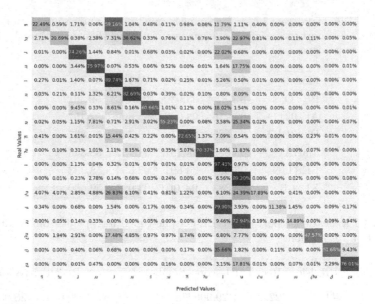

Fig. 3. Confusion matrix of BETO for Spanish punctuation and capitalization restoration system.

4.2 Portuguese

As for the Portuguese, two monolingual models (BERTimbau and BR_BERTo) and multilingual (XLM-RoBERTa) are evaluated (see Table 4). The BR_BERTo model has obtained the most limited result (74.84% in macro-averaged F1-score), as it has been pre-trained with a smaller Portuguese corpora size compared to two other models. The two best scores are achieved by XLM-RoBERTa (76.94%) and BERTimbau (76.93%), with a difference of about 0.01% in the macro F1-score. In this case, the multilingual model is slightly better than the model pre-trained with the target language. Comparing the performance of our best Portuguese punctuation and capitalization restoration system with one of the existing models called *bert-restore-punctuation-ptbr*[2], which consists of a BERTimbau fine-tuned for punctuation and capitalization restoration in the WikiLingua corpus. The difference between our system and theirs is that ours only predicts the 5 most relevant punctuation marks (see Sect. 3.4) for audio transcription reliability and theirs predicts a total of 8 punctuation marks (! ? . , - : ; '). However, through the table of results shown on the Huggingface page, it can be observed that their training set is unbalanced, so they have obtained bad results in classifying words with semicolons, apostrophes, hyphen, exclamation, and interrogation with upper case words. In contrast, our corpus is larger and more balanced, so we have achieved improved prediction for most punctuation marks, as shown in Table 5.

---

[2] https://huggingface.co/dominguesm/bert-restore-punctuation-ptbr.

Table 4. Results of different LLMs for Portuguese punctuation and capitalization restoration system. We report the weighted averaged precision, recall and F1-score(W-P, W-R, W-F1), and macro averaged F1-score (M-F1).

Model	W-P	W-R	W-F1	M-F1
BERTimbau	93.461	93.540	93.489	76.938
BR_BERTo	93.462	93.579	93.496	74.840
XLM-R	**93.637**	**93.730**	**93.663**	**76.944**

Table 5. Classification report of the XLM-RoBERTa fine-tuned for Portuguese punctuation and capitalization restoration.

Symbol	Precision	Recall	F1-score	Symbol	Precision	Recall	F1-score
!l	61.082	22.363	32.740	!u	67.722	37.911	48.610
,l	81.189	78.316	79.726	,u	82.364	79.850	81.087
.l	87.215	89.521	88.353	.u	87.059	82.964	84.962
:l	79.770	71.399	75.353	:u	82.149	73.897	77.805
?l	78.523	73.913	76.148	?u	91.289	88.597	89.923
l	96.153	97.218	96.682	u	92.611	91.281	91.941

Overall	Precision	Recall	F1-score
Macro avg	82.260	73.936	76.944
Weighted avg	93.637	93.730	93.663

Fig. 4. Confusion matrix of XLM-RoBERTa for Portuguese punctuation and capitalization restoration system.

To perform the error analysis, we used the XLM-RoBERTa model and a normalized confusion matrix (see Fig. 4). XLM-RoBERTa does not make many relevant classification errors and frequently confuses exclamation marks with the period, with a percentage of 58.33% and 23.18%. In addition, the misclassification ratio of :u and :l is skewed for labels identifying the absence of punctuation marks (u and l), with 16.75% and 14.91%.

5   Conclusions and Further Work

This paper presents models of capitalization and punctuation restoration for Spanish and Portuguese, based on a transfer learning approach through fine-tuning different pre-trained models to jointly restore punctuation and capitalization. The system has been trained for 5 types of punctuation and 2 types of capitalization. In addition, the models can identify certain proper names for the capitalization restoration task. Both models have been evaluated with the Opus-ParaCrawl dataset. The best performance is obtained by BETO for Spanish and XLM-RoBERTa for Portuguese, with a macro-averaged F1-score of 59.90% and overall performance of 93.87% for the Spanish, and a macro-averaged F1-score of 76.94% and 93.66% overall performance for the Portuguese.

As future work, it is proposed to establish a set of simple heuristics in the post-processing of the Spanish punctuation restoration model to mitigate the error caused by unmatched predictions for paired punctuation marks, such as interrogative and exclamation marks. It also proposed to compare our model with other existing models using the same test set to see the improvement of our model with respect to the others. And the last proposal is to develop a model that takes into account the relationships of the previous sentence with the following sentence to increase the accuracy of the models and resolve the errors discussed in Sect. 4.

Acknowledgments. This work is part of the research projects AIInFunds (PDC2021-121112-I00) and LT-SWM (TED2021-131167B-I00) funded by MCIN/AEI/10.13039/501100011033 and by the European Union NextGenerationEU/PRTR. This work is also part of the research project LaTe4PSP (PID2019-107652RB-I00/AEI/ 10.13039/501100011033) funded by MCIN/AEI/10.13039/501100011033. In addition, José Antonio García-Díaz is supported by Banco Santander and the University of Murcia through the Doctorado Industrial programme.

References

1. Alam, T., Khan, A., Alam, F.: Punctuation restoration using transformer models for high-and low-resource languages. In: Proceedings of the Sixth Workshop on Noisy User-Generated Text (W-NUT 2020), pp. 132–142. Association for Computational Linguistics, Online (2020). https://doi.org/10.18653/v1/2020.wnut-1.18

2. Bannard, C., Callison-Burch, C.: Paraphrasing with bilingual parallel corpora. In: Proceedings of the 43rd Annual Meeting of the Association for Computational Linguistics (ACL 2005), pp. 597–604. Association for Computational Linguistics, Ann Arbor, Michigan (2005). https://doi.org/10.3115/1219840.1219914

3. Bañón, M., et al.: ParaCrawl: web-scale acquisition of parallel corpora. In: Proceedings of the 58th Annual Meeting of the Association for Computational Linguistics, pp. 4555–4567. Association for Computational Linguistics, Online (2020). https://doi.org/10.18653/v1/2020.acl-main.417

4. Basili, R., Bosco, C., Delmonte, R., Moschitti, A., Simi, M. (eds.): Harmonization and Development of Resources and Tools for Italian Natural Language Processing within the PARLI Project. SCI, vol. 589. Springer, Cham (2015). https://doi.org/10.1007/978-3-319-14206-7

5. Bostrom, K., Durrett, G.: Byte pair encoding is suboptimal for language model pretraining. CoRR abs/2004.03720 (2020). https://arxiv.org/abs/2004.03720

6. Cañete, J., Chaperon, G., Fuentes, R., Ho, J.H., Kang, H., Pérez, J.: Spanish pre-trained BERT model and evaluation data. PML4DC ICLR **2020**(2020), 1–10 (2020)

7. Cañete, J., Donoso, S., Bravo-Marquez, F., Carvallo, A., Araujo, V.: ALBETO and DistilBETO: lightweight Spanish language models. In: Proceedings of the Thirteenth Language Resources and Evaluation Conference, pp. 4291–4298. Marseille, France (2022)

8. Conneau, A., et al.: Unsupervised cross-lingual representation learning at scale. In: Proceedings of the 58th Annual Meeting of the Association for Computational Linguistics, pp. 8440–8451. Association for Computational Linguistics, Online (2020). https://doi.org/10.18653/v1/2020.acl-main.747

9. Courtland, M., Faulkner, A., McElvain, G.: Efficient automatic punctuation restoration using bidirectional transformers with robust inference. In: Proceedings of the 17th International Conference on Spoken Language Translation, pp. 272–279. Association for Computational Linguistics, Online (2020). https://doi.org/10.18653/v1/2020.iwslt-1.33

10. Fandiño, A.G., et al.: Maria: Spanish language models. Procesamiento del Lenguaje Natural 68 (2022). https://doi.org/10.26342/2022-68-3

11. Federico, M., Cettolo, M., Bentivogli, L., Paul, M., Stüker, S.: Overview of the IWSLT 2012 evaluation campaign. In: Proceedings of the 9th International Workshop on Spoken Language Translation: Evaluation Campaign, pp. 12–33. Hong Kong, Table of contents (2012). https://aclanthology.org/2012.iwslt-evaluation.1

12. González-Docasal, A., García-Pablos, A., Arzelus, H., Álvarez, A.: AutoPunct: a BERT-based automatic punctuation and capitalisation system for Spanish and basque. Procesamiento del Lenguaje Natural **67**, 59–68 (2021). http://journal.sepln.org/sepln/ojs/ojs/index.php/pln/article/view/6377

13. Jones, D., et al.: Measuring the readability of automatic speech-to-text transcripts. In: 8th European Conference on Speech Communication and Technology, EUROSPEECH 2003 - INTERSPEECH 2003, Geneva, Switzerland, 1–4 September 2003. ISCA (2003). https://doi.org/10.21437/Eurospeech

14. Lima, T.B.D., et al.: Sequence labeling algorithms for punctuation restoration in Brazilian Portuguese texts. In: Xavier-Junior, J.C., Rios, R.A. (eds.) Intelligent Systems (BRACIS 2022). LNCS, vol. 13654, pp. 616–630. Springer, Cham (2022). https://doi.org/10.1007/978-3-031-21689-3_43

15. Pan, R., García-Díaz, J.A., Vicente, P.J.V., Valencia-García, R.: Evaluation of transformer-based models for punctuation and capitalization restoration in Catalan

and Galician. Proces. del Leng. Natural **70**, 27–38 (2023). http://journal.sepln.org/sepln/ojs/ojs/index.php/pln/article/view/6476

16. De la Rosa, J.G., Ponferrada, E., Romero, M., Villegas, P., González de Prado Salas, P., Grandury, M.: Bertin: efficient pre-training of a Spanish language model using perplexity sampling. Procesamiento del Lenguaje Natural **68**, 13–23 (2022). http://journal.sepln.org/sepln/ojs/ojs/index.php/pln/article/view/6403

17. Souza, F., Nogueira, R., Lotufo, R.: BERTimbau: pretrained BERT models for Brazilian Portuguese. In: 9th Brazilian Conference on Intelligent Systems, BRACIS, Rio Grande do Sul, Brazil, 20–23 October (2020). (To appear)

18. Tilk, O., Alumäe, T.: LSTM for punctuation restoration in speech transcripts. In: Sixteenth Annual Conference of the International Speech Communication Association (2015). https://doi.org/10.21437/Interspeech

19. Tündik, M.A., Szaszák, G.: Joint word- and character-level embedding CNN-RNN models for punctuation restoration. In: 2018 9th IEEE International Conference on Cognitive Infocommunications (CogInfoCom), pp. 000135–000140 (2018). https://doi.org/10.1109/CogInfoCom.2018.8639876

20. Yi, J., Tao, J.: Self-attention based model for punctuation prediction using word and speech embeddings. In: 2019 IEEE International Conference on Acoustics, Speech and Signal Processing (ICASSP 2019), pp. 7270–7274 (2019). https://doi.org/10.1109/ICASSP.2019.8682260

21. Yi, J., Tao, J., Bai, Y., Tian, Z., Fan, C.: Adversarial transfer learning for punctuation restoration (2020). https://doi.org/10.48550/ARXIV.2004.00248

22. Zhang, D., Wu, S., Yang, N., Li, M.: Punctuation prediction with transition-based parsing. In: Proceedings of the 51st Annual Meeting of the Association for Computational Linguistics, vol. 1, pp. 752–760. Association for Computational Linguistics, Sofia, Bulgaria (2013). https://aclanthology.org/P13-1074

23. Zhu, X., Gardiner, S., Rossouw, D., Roldán, T., Corston-Oliver, S.: Punctuation restoration in Spanish customer support transcripts using transfer learning. In: Proceedings of the Third Workshop on Deep Learning for Low-Resource Natural Language Processing, pp. 80–89. Association for Computational Linguistics, Hybrid (2022). https://doi.org/10.18653/v1/2022.deeplo-1.9

Sentence-to-Label Generation Framework for Multi-task Learning of Japanese Sentence Classification and Named Entity Recognition

Chengguang Gan[1]([⊠]) [iD], Qinghao Zhang[2], and Tatsunori Mori[1] [iD]

[1] Yokohama National University, Yokohama, Japan
gan-chengguan-pw@ynu.jp, tmori@ynu.ac.jp
[2] Department of Information Convergence Engineering, Pusan National University, Busan, South Korea
zhangqinghao@pusan.ac.kr

Abstract. Information extraction (IE) is a crucial subfield within natural language processing. In this study, we introduce a Sentence Classification and Named Entity Recognition Multi-task (SCNM) approach that combines Sentence Classification (SC) and Named Entity Recognition (NER). We develop a Sentence-to-Label Generation (SLG) framework for SCNM and construct a Wikipedia dataset containing both SC and NER. Using a format converter, we unify input formats and employ a generative model to generate SC-labels, NER-labels, and associated text segments. We propose a Constraint Mechanism (CM) to improve generated format accuracy. Our results show SC accuracy increased by 1.13 points and NER by 1.06 points in SCNM compared to standalone tasks, with CM raising format accuracy from 63.61 to 100. The findings indicate mutual reinforcement effects between SC and NER, and integration enhances both tasks' performance.

Keywords: Sentence classification · Named entity recognition · Prompt · Japanese · Information extraction · Transformer

1 Introduction

In the realm of information extraction, numerous specialized tasks exist, such as named entity recognition [7,11,15], relation extraction [10], event extraction [3], sentence classification [19], sentiment analysis [9,13], and more. With the advent of the Transformer architecture, pre-training and fine-tuning paradigms have gained widespread adoption. Typically, models undergo unsupervised pre-training on a large-scale, general corpus, such as Wikipedia text, in order to acquire foundational knowledge. These pre-trained models are then fine-tuned for specific downstream tasks. However, due to the considerable variation in data features and requirements across tasks, adapting a single dataset and model to multiple tasks simultaneously is challenging. Consequently, researchers often create dedicated datasets for distinct IE tasks and employ these for fine-tuning

E. Métais et al. (Eds.): NLDB 2023, LNCS 13913, pp. 257–270, 2023.
https://doi.org/10.1007/978-3-031-35320-8_18

Fig. 1. The illustration depicts the interrelationship between the labels of Named Entity Recognition (NER) and Sentence Classification (SC) within a single sentence.

pre-trained models. Moreover, IE methods have evolved from sequence labeling tasks utilizing Long Short-Term Memory (LSTM) [4] to seq to seq generative IE methods [8]. The emergence of generative approaches indicates the feasibility of addressing multiple tasks with a single model by unifying input and output formats. In the present study, illustrated by Fig. 1, the SC and NER tasks are fed as inputs to their respective fine-tuned models. Then models generate corresponding labels/spans for each task, respectively.

While generic pre-training knowledge can be beneficial for various downstream tasks, the possibility of mutual reinforcement effects between tasks remains an open question. To explore this, we hypothesize that mutual reinforcement effects exists between different tasks. To test this hypothesis, we focus on Named Entity Recognition (NER) and Sentence Classification (SC) as the most representative tasks in IE, as illustrated in Fig. 1. In the SC task, a model generates sentence classification labels given an input sentence. In the NER task, a model identifies entity spans in the input sentence and generates corresponding labels and spans. Many task scenarios require simultaneous sentence classification and entity extraction, but no existing dataset satisfies both requirements. Furthermore, SC and NER tasks exhibit correlations in the labels they extract. For instance, a sentence mentioning "Shinzo Abe" likely pertains to Social, and a Social sentence is more likely to contain names of Social figures and countries. Consequently, we investigate whether leveraging the interrelationship between SC and NER tasks can improve model performance. In this context, we propose a novel framework for handling both Japanese SC and NER tasks. The primary contributions of this work include:

1. Integrating SC and NER tasks into a new Sentence Classification and Named Entity Recognition Multi-task (SCNM) task and constructing an SCNM dataset by annotating SC labels on the existing Wikipedia Japanese NER dataset.
2. Proposing a Sentence-to-Label Generation Framework (SLG) for addressing the SCNM task, comprising format converter construction, incremental training, and the development of a format Constraint Mechanism (CM). The format converter enables the SLG to handle the SCNM task, as well as SC or NER tasks separately, highlighting its generalizability.
3. Demonstrating through ablation experiments that SC and NER tasks are mutual reinforcement effects. The performance of a model trained by combining both tasks surpasses that of a model fine-tuned on a single task, supporting the notion that $1 + 1 > 2$. This finding offers insights for future scenarios requiring SCNM.

The remainder of this paper is structured as follows: Some related work and prior studies are presented in Sect. 2. In Sect. 3, we describe the task setup and the construction of the SCNM dataset used in our study. Section 4 presents the Sentence-to-Label Generation Framework, which encompasses the format converter 4.1, Incremental Learning 4.2, and Constraint Mechanism 4.3. Lastly, Sect. 5 discusses the results of our SLG framework experiments, as well as various ablation studies to evaluate the effectiveness of the proposed approach.

2 Related Work

In this section, we provide a comprehensive overview of previous studies on generative IE methodologies. Furthermore, we delineate the similarities and distinctions between these prior works and our current research, thereby highlighting the novel contributions of our study.

Word-Level. In [18], the authors propose a novel Seq2Seq framework that addresses flat, nested, and discontinuous NER subtasks through entity span sequence generation. Similarly, [1] used a self-describing mechanism for few-shot NER, which leverages mention describing and entity generation. GenIE [5] uses the transformer model to extract unstructured text relationally through global structural constraint. And LightNER [2] is addresses class transfer by constructing a unified learnable verbalizer of entity categories and tackles domain transfer with a pluggable guidance module. InstructionNER [16] and UIE [8] have also developed frameworks for word-level IE tasks.

Sentence-Level. In terms of using sentences label to improve the NER effect. Joint learning framework used BiLSTM model and attention, CRF layer to improve the effectiveness of NER through sentence labeling [6]. MGADE that uses a dual-attention mechanism to concurrently address two Adverse Drug Event (ADE) tasks: ADE entity recognition at the word level (fine-grained) and ADE assertive sentence classification (coarse-grained). The model takes advantage of the interdependencies between these two levels of granularity to improve the performance of both tasks [17].

In conclusion, this study employed a generative model for Sentence-to-Label conversion, distinguishing itself from previous studies by pioneering the utilization of mutual reinforcement effects between SC and NER tasks. This novel approach effectively enhanced the accuracy of both tasks. Additionally, we introduced the SLG framework, which enables the model to adeptly manage both SC and NER tasks simultaneously.

3 Task Setup and Dataset Constructed

Before delving into the SLG, let us first describe the structure of the SCNM task. SCNM involves the classification of both sentence-level and word-level information within a single sentence. As illustration of Fig. 2, given an input sentence (i.e., In 2020, Shinzo Abe resigned as Prime Minister of Japan), the model is

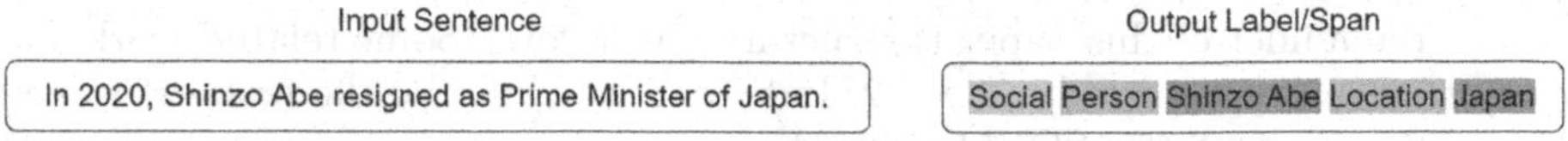

Input Sentence

Output Label/Span

In 2020, Shinzo Abe resigned as Prime Minister of Japan.

Social Person Shinzo Abe Location Japan

Fig. 2. The illustration of Sentence Classification and Named Entity Recognition Multi-task (SCNM) task.

expected to generate a classification label (i.e., Social) for the sentence, along with named entity labels (i.e., Preson, Location) and the corresponding word spans (i.e., Shinzo Abe, Japan) present in the sentence. Moreover, when selecting and constructing the dataset, it is crucial to encompass a wide range of content, and the classification labels should be generic rather than specific to a narrow domain. Considering these factors, we chose the Japanese Wikipedia-based NER dataset [12] for our SCNM dataset foundation. It consists of 5,343 sentences (4,859 with named entities, 484 without) and includes 8 categories (13,185 total named entities): person, company, political org., other org., location, public facility, product, and event. This diverse and broad dataset is ideal for the SCNM task.

Following the selection of the NER dataset, we annotated sentence classification labels based on the original dataset. We partitioned the Wikipedia sentences into five primary categories: social, literature and art, academic, technical, and natural. All 5,343 sentences were categorized into these five groups, ultimately resulting in the construction of the SCNM dataset. Figure 2 illustrates a specific instance of the input and output by the SCNM task.

3.1 Evaluation

Upon constructing the SCNM dataset, the primary challenge we encounter is devising a comprehensive set of evaluation metrics for this new dataset. We categorize the SCNM evaluation metrics into two distinct classes: label evaluation and format evaluation.

Text Evaluation. As illustrated in Fig. 3, we present several instances of both generated and actual text, labeled numerically (1–5) for further analysis. Given that the combined task of SC and NER precludes the computation of traditional metrics (e.g., precision recall f1-score) in the conventional manner, generative IE deviates from the traditional sequence tagging model. Specifically, in the generative IE approach, a token does not correspond to a label. Furthermore, the number of generated named entities and word spans is variable (e.g., 3), as is the number of generated text, which may also contain extraneous text (e.g., 4).

Consequently, we employ accuracy as the evaluation metric, when generate text 1 is all equal to actual text 5, it counts as a correct text 1. Although this evaluation criterion may seem somewhat stringent, it is well-suited for SCNM tasks. We denote generated text as G and actual text as A. The $|A \cap G|$ is represented by $C_{\text{generated text}}$ (the total number of matches text between G and

Fig. 3. The illustration of text and format evaluation. 1 and 0 represents a correctly or incorrectly generated text, and the total number of all correctly generated text in the test set adds up to C.

A), while the total number of actual text (i.e., total number of samples in the test set) is denoted by $T_{\text{actual text}}$.

$$\text{SCNM Accuracy} = \frac{C_{\text{generated text}}}{T_{\text{actual text}}} \qquad (1)$$

In addition, we also computed accuracy for SC and NER in the SCNM task separately. Specifically, the SC-label and all remaining NER-label/span in generated text and actual text were split. Then the accuracy is calculated separately.

$$\text{SC Accuracy} = \frac{C_{\text{SC}}}{T_{\text{SC}}} \qquad \text{NER Accuracy} = \frac{C_{\text{NER}}}{T_{\text{NER}}} \qquad (2)$$

Format Evaluation. In generative IE, a key metric is the ability to produce outputs in the right format. Due to the uncontrollable nature of generative models, there's a high chance of generating duplicate words or incoherent sentences. Incorrect output formats likely lead to wrong label classification (e.g., 4). Thus, we augment label evaluation with format generation accuracy assessment.

This additional evaluation aims to gauge a model's proficiency in controlling the generated format. If the first generated text becomes SC-label and the subsequent generated ones are NER-label and span, it is counted as a format correct number (regardless of whether the generated SC-label and NER-label are correct or not, they are counted as format correct). As illustrated in Fig. 3 (e.g., 1 2 3). The total number of generated text with correct format is C_{format}, and the total number of actual text is T_{format}. The Format Accuracy is defined as:

$$\text{Format Accuracy} = \frac{C_{\text{format}}}{T_{\text{format}}} \qquad (3)$$

4 Sentence-to-Label Generation Framework

In the preceding section, the SCNM task setting and dataset construction were presented. This section offers a thorough overview of the Sentence-to-Label (SL)

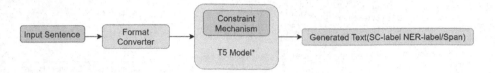

Fig. 4. The illustration of overview for Sentence-to-Label Generate (SLG) Framework. The T5 model* is the vanilla T5 model with incremental learned using Shinra NER corpus.

framework, followed by a detailed explanation of each component of the SLG in three separate subsections.

An overview of the SLG framework is depicted in Fig. 4. Initially, the Shinra NER corpus[1] is reformatted using a format converter. Subsequently, the transformed corpus serves as a basis for incremental learning in the model. The SCNM dataset, converted by the format converter, is then fine-tuned for the model. Prior to the model's Decoder generating prediction results, a Constraint Mechanism (CM) is incorporated to enhance the model's format generation capabilities. Lastly, the SC-label, NER-label, and corresponding word span are sequentially outputted.

4.1 Format Converter

In this subsection, we explore multiple converter formats and evaluate performance in later experiment sections. The most effective format is chosen for our converter.

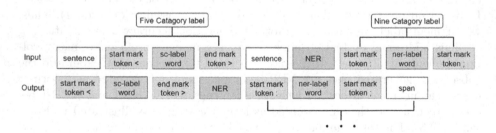

Fig. 5. The illustration of format converter.

As show in Fig. 5, the optimal format is determined from the experimental outcomes. For the input sequence of the model, the original sentence is positioned at the beginning, succeeded by five SC-label words. The start and end tokens, "<" and ">", respectively, enclose all SC-labels. Subsequently, the original sentence is repeated immediately after the above end mark token">". To signal the model's

---

[1] http://shinra-project.info/shinra2020jp/data_download/.

initiation of NER-label generation and corresponding word span, a prompt word "NER" is appended after the sentence.

Due to the presence of negative sentences in the SCNM dataset that lack named entities, an additional "None" label is introduced for negative cases, augmenting the original eight NER-labels. Consequently, a total of nine NER-labeled words follow the prompt word. To indicate the commencement and termination of the NER-label word, the start and end tokens, ":", and ";", are employed, respectively. The distinct mark tokens for SC and NER labels demonstrate superior performance in the experiments, as compared to identical mark tokens.

Regarding the output format of the model, the overall and input token order is maintained consistently. However, it is crucial to note that only one of the predicted SC-label words is utilized, rather than all five words present in the input. Following the starting word "NER", the NER-label word and corresponding word span derived from the sentence are provided. Utilizing the format converter, the model demonstrates versatility in managing diverse tasks, such as SC, NER, and SCNM. These tasks can be effectively addressed either individually or concurrently. And through format converter, the model learns the correct format to generate a uniform format. A specific example of the input and output sequence is show in Fig. 6.

Input	In 2020, Shinzo Abe resigned as Prime Minister of Japan. <Social><Literature and Art><Academic><Technical><Natural> In 2020, Shinzo Abe resigned as Prime Minister of Japan. NER:Person;:Company;:Political Organization;:Other Organization; :Location;:Public Facility;:Product;:Event;:None;
Output	<Social>NER:Person;Shinzo Abe:Location;Japan

Fig. 6. A specific example of an input converted using the format converter, and the corresponding generated output.

4.2 Incremental Learning

In this subsection, we elucidate the process of applying incremental learning (IL) to the vanilla T5 model[2] using the Shinra NER corpus, as well as the underlying rationale. The T5 model is primarily pre-trained for sequence-to-sequence (seq2seq) tasks in text processing [14]. However, it lacks specific pre-training for word-level attributes, such as named entities. Our objective is to implement IL in a seq2seq format, tailored for named entities, without causing the model to lose its pre-trained knowledge.

---

[2] https://huggingface.co/sonoisa/t5-base-japanese.

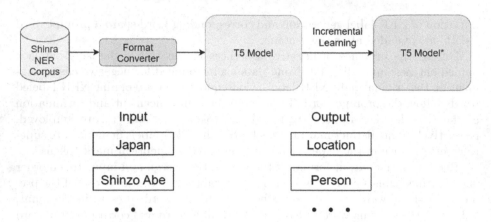

Fig. 7. The illustration of incremental learning. And IL specific format converter for Shira NER corpus.

We selected the Shinra2020-JP corpus as the data source for IL. The Shinra project, an extended named entity recognition (NER) endeavor, is constructed based on the Japanese Wikipedia. Consequently, the corpus encompasses a wide array of named entities derived from Wikipedia. In other words, this corpus contains various named entities of wikipedia. The categories of named entities are: facility, event, organization, location, airport name, city, company, Compound, person. It is a relatively comprehensive and extensive NER corpus. The dataset is used for incremental learning of the T5 model after a simple format transformation (e.g., input:Japan, output:Location). The total number of samples is 14117 and there are no duplicate samples. As illustrated in the Fig. 7, the T5 model employed within the SLG framework is ultimately acquired.

4.3 Constraint Mechanism

To enhance the accuracy of the model's output format, we introduce an efficient and straightforward Constraint Mechanism (CM). Let X_1 denote the initial token predicted by the Decoder, with the total predicted sequence comprising n tokens. The predicted sequence can be represented as $(X_1, X_2, \ldots, X_n)$. The prediction probability for the second token X_2 can be formulated as the subsequent equation:

$$P(X_2|X_1) = Decoder_2(X_1, Encoder(Inputs)) \qquad (4)$$

Here, $Encoder(Inputs)$ denotes the vector resulting from the computation of the input by the next layer of Encoder. $Decoder_2$ denotes the result of the computation of the vector output by encoder and the first token vector output by Decoder of the first layer is passed to the second layer Deocder.

In Fig. 8, a specific example is presented. The output text refers to the desired output sequence that should be generated accurately. Notably, the first token of every output text within the SCNM dataset remains constant, represented

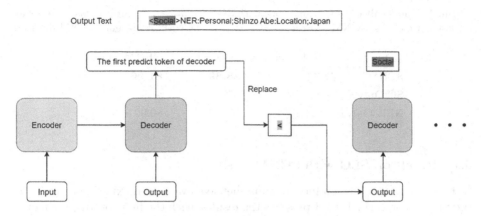

Fig. 8. The processes of Constraint Mechanism (CM).

by the "$<$" symbol. Consequently, the initial token of each predicted sequence is compelled to be replaced with the "$<$" token. In other words, this substitution corresponds to the numerical value of the "$<$" symbol in the T5 model's vocabulary.

Adopting this approach ensures that the first predicted token in each newly generated output text is accurate, which in turn enhances the precision of subsequent token predictions. The ultimate experimental outcomes corroborate that the CM technique effectively augments the model's capacity to generate accurate formats, thereby improving the overall correctness of SCNM tasks.

5 Experiments

In this chapter, we present a comprehensive series of experiments conducted on our proposed SLG framework and its application to SCNM tasks. Our aim is to demonstrate the effectiveness of the SLG framework and the synergistic effect of integrating the SC and NER tasks.

Given that the Japanese T5 model is only available in base size, we employ the T5-base as the underlying model weight for the SLG framework. To ensure robustness, we conduct each experiment three times, and the final result is obtained by averaging the outcomes. The proportion used for dividing the data into the training set and the test set is 9:1. We adopt a randomized approach to data set partitioning, using the parameter "Random Seed=None" to guarantee distinct training and testing sets for each iteration. For an in-depth discussion of the evaluation metrics utilized, please refer to Sect. 3.1.

Table 1. The result of SLG framework with SCNM dataset. Accuracy was used for all evaluation metrics. SCNM represents SCNM task. SCNM* represents SCNM dataset.

Dataset	SCNM Accuracy	SC Accuracy	NER Accuracy
SCNM*	**72.41**	**88.89**	**81.96**
SC Only	–	87.76	–
NER Only	–	–	80.90

5.1   Result on SLG with SCNM Task

In this subsection, we conduct a comprehensive evaluation experiment utilizing the SLG framework. Table 1 presents the results, with the first row displaying the metrics SCNM, SC, and NER, which correspond to the overall accuracy of the SCNM dataset, the accuracy of the SC dataset individually, and the accuracy of the NER dataset individually.

Three distinct datasets are outlined in the first column. "SCNM*" represents the full SCNM dataset, encompassing both SC and NER tasks. "SC Only" and "NER Only" signify the evaluation of the SC and NER datasets independently. To achieve this, we employ a format converter to separate the SC and NER components within the SCNM dataset, resulting in two distinct datasets (i.e., SC dataset and NER dataset). All three datasets are assessed using the SLG framework.

The evaluation reveals that the SCNM task attains a notable score of 72.41, even under rigorous evaluation metrics. Furthermore, by integrating the SC and NER tasks, the accuracy of NER improves by 1.06 compared to evaluating the NER task individually. Similarly, the SC task accuracy increased by 1.13 compared to evaluating it separately. The experimental outcomes highlight the exceptional performance of the SLG framework in handling the SCNM task, as well as the mutual reinforcement effects observed between the SC and NER tasks.

5.2   Compare the Effect of Different Formats on Results

In order to investigate the impact of various formats on the outcomes, we compared four distinct formats. Table 2 displays these formats, where the first row represents the input text and the second row signifies the output text. Given that the number of NER-label span pairs generated in each sentence is indefinite, we use *x to denote the count of generated NER-label span pairs. Moreover, since there are five SC-labels in the input text, we represent this with *5. The corresponding NER-labels total nine, denoted by *9, which includes eight labels from the original dataset and one additional "None" label.

In the experimental setup, we aimed to minimize the influence of external factors on the results. Therefore, only the original T5-base model was employed in the format comparison experiment, with the random seed and other hyper-parameters held constant.

Table 2 reveals that the accuracy of the simplest format is considerably low on the SCNM dataset, particularly when the input consists solely of sentences. In this case, the accuracy is 0, with all results being incorrect. This is due to the model's inability to generate the desired format accurately. As a result, even if the SC or NER labels are generated correctly, they are still considered errors based on the strict evaluation criteria. The second format introduced a simple prompt word, "sentence NER", which slightly improved accuracy to 0.19; however, the accuracy remained substantially low.

In the third and fourth formats, we incorporated all the SC-labels (five label words) and NER-labels (nine label words) into the input text. Upon adding sufficient prompt words to the input text, the accuracy of the third format increased to 0.37 and 0.56 respectively. Lastly, we modified the start and end mark tokens of the SC-label to "<" and ">", respectively, to facilitate the model's differentiation between SC-label and NER-label. Consequently, the accuracy significantly improved to 29.40, surpassing the results of all previous formats. This format comparison experiment highlights the critical role of prompt design in obtaining accurate outcomes.

Table 2. The result of compared different format with SCNM tasks. And without IL and CM. The first line is input text, and second line is output text.

Different Format	Accuracy
{sentence} :SC-label;(:NER-label;span)*x	0
sentence:{sentence} label:SC-label;NER(:NER-label;span)*x	0.19
{sentence}category(:SC-label;)*5{sentence}NER(:NER-label)*9 category:SC-label;NER(:NER-label;span)*x	0.37
{sentence}(:SC-label;)*5{sentence}NER(:NER-label)*9 :SC-label;NER(:NER-label;span)*x	0.56
{sentence}(<SC-label>)*5{sentence}NER(:NER-label)*9 :SC-label;NER(<NER-label>span)*x	**29.40**

5.3   Ablation Study

To assess the impact of SL and CM on the outcomes within the SLG framework, we carried out a series of ablation experiments. Table 3 illustrates that, upon removing Incremental Learning, the Named Entity Recognition NER accuracy within the SCNM dataset experienced a substantial decline of 15.98. Concurrently, the SC in the SCNM dataset also saw a reduction of 3.18. These findings highlight that incremental training not only enhances NER in the SCNM dataset but also exerts a positive influence on SC. This observation aligns with our initial hypothesis that SC and NER tasks exhibit a mutual reinforcement effects.

Conversely, when CM was eliminated from the SLG framework, the format accuracy of the model plummeted to 63.61. Consequently, the SCNM, SC, and NER metrics also witnessed significant decreases, falling to 46.38, 55.99, and 52.62, respectively. These experimental outcomes underscore the efficacy of our proposed CM approach. By effectively managing the initial token generated by the model, we can guide the subsequent tokens towards accurate generation, thereby improving the model's overall performance.

Table 3. The result of IL or CM with ablation experiment.

Method	SCNM Accuracy	SC Accuracy	NER Accuracy	Format Accuracy
SLG	**72.41**	**88.89**	**81.96**	**100**
w/o IL	56.18	85.71	65.98	99.50
w/o CM	46.38	55.99	52.62	63.61

6   Conclusion and Future Work

In this study, we integrate Sentence Classification (SC) and Named Entity Recognition (NER) tasks, leveraging their shared knowledge to enhance accuracy. We propose the SCNM task and construct a comprehensive dataset from Wikipedia. Our experiments demonstrate mutual reinforcement effects between SC and NER, and introduce the versatile Sentence-to-Label Generate (SLG) framework for handling both tasks concurrently or individually through a Format Converter.

Future work includes exploring alternative language models, assessing the SLG framework on other SC and NER datasets, and creating domain-specific SCNM datasets to evaluate the framework's adaptability and effectiveness.

Acknowledgements. This research was partially supported by JSPS KAKENHI Grant Numbers JP23H00491 and JP22K00502.

References

1. Chen, J., Liu, Q., Lin, H., Han, X., Sun, L.: Few-shot named entity recognition with self-describing networks. In: Proceedings of the 60th Annual Meeting of the Association for Computational Linguistics, Dublin, Ireland (Volume 1: Long Papers), pp. 5711–5722. Association for Computational Linguistics (2022). https://doi.org/10.18653/v1/2022.acl-long.392. https://aclanthology.org/2022.acl-long.392
2. Chen, X., et al.: LightNER: a lightweight tuning paradigm for low-resource NER via pluggable prompting. In: Proceedings of the 29th International Conference on Computational Linguistics, Gyeongju, Republic of Korea, pp. 2374–2387. International Committee on Computational Linguistics (2022). https://aclanthology.org/2022.coling-1.209

3. Etzioni, O., Banko, M., Soderland, S., Weld, D.S.: Open information extraction from the web. Commun. ACM **51**(12), 68–74 (2008)
4. Huang, Z., Xu, W., Yu, K.: Bidirectional LSTM-CRF models for sequence tagging. arXiv preprint arXiv:1508.01991 (2015)
5. Josifoski, M., De Cao, N., Peyrard, M., Petroni, F., West, R.: GenIE: generative information extraction. In: Proceedings of the 2022 Conference of the North American Chapter of the Association for Computational Linguistics: Human Language Technologies, Seattle, USA, pp. 4626–4643. Association for Computational Linguistics (2022). https://doi.org/10.18653/v1/2022.naacl-main.342. https://aclanthology.org/2022.naacl-main.342
6. Kruengkrai, C., Nguyen, T.H., Aljunied, S.M., Bing, L.: Improving low-resource named entity recognition using joint sentence and token labeling. In: Proceedings of the 58th Annual Meeting of the Association for Computational Linguistics, pp. 5898–5905. Association for Computational Linguistics, Online (2020). https://doi.org/10.18653/v1/2020.acl-main.523. https://aclanthology.org/2020.acl-main.523
7. Lample, G., Ballesteros, M., Subramanian, S., Kawakami, K., Dyer, C.: Neural architectures for named entity recognition. In: Proceedings of the 2016 Conference of the North American Chapter of the Association for Computational Linguistics: Human Language Technologies, San Diego, California, pp. 260–270. Association for Computational Linguistics (2016). https://doi.org/10.18653/v1/N16-1030. https://aclanthology.org/N16-1030
8. Lu, Y., et al.: Unified structure generation for universal information extraction. In: Proceedings of the 60th Annual Meeting of the Association for Computational Linguistics, Dublin, Ireland (Volume 1: Long Papers), pp. 5755–5772. Association for Computational Linguistics (2022). https://doi.org/10.18653/v1/2022.acl-long.395. https://aclanthology.org/2022.acl-long.395
9. Medhat, W., Hassan, A., Korashy, H.: Sentiment analysis algorithms and applications: a survey. Ain Shams Eng. J. **5**(4), 1093–1113 (2014)
10. Mintz, M., Bills, S., Snow, R., Jurafsky, D.: Distant supervision for relation extraction without labeled data. In: Proceedings of the Joint Conference of the 47th Annual Meeting of the ACL and the 4th International Joint Conference on Natural Language Processing of the AFNLP, Suntec, Singapore, pp. 1003–1011. Association for Computational Linguistics (2009). https://aclanthology.org/P00-1113
11. Nadeau, D., Sekine, S.: A survey of named entity recognition and classification. Lingvisticae Investigationes **30**(1), 3–26 (2007)
12. Omi, T.: Construction of a Japanese named entity recognition dataset using Wikipedia. In: 27th Annual Conference of the Association for Natural Language Processing (2021)
13. Pang, B., Lee, L., Vaithyanathan, S.: Thumbs up? Sentiment classification using machine learning techniques. In: Proceedings of the 2002 Conference on Empirical Methods in Natural Language Processing (EMNLP 2002), pp. 79–86. Association for Computational Linguistics (2002). https://doi.org/10.3115/1118693.1118704. https://aclanthology.org/W02-1011
14. Raffel, C., et al.: Exploring the limits of transfer learning with a unified text-to-text transformer. J. Mach. Learn. Res. **21**(1), 5485–5551 (2020)
15. Ritter, A., Clark, S., Etzioni, O., et al.: Named entity recognition in tweets: an experimental study. In: Proceedings of the 2011 Conference on Empirical Methods in Natural Language Processing, pp. 1524–1534 (2011)
16. Wang, L., et al.: InstructionNER: a multi-task instruction-based generative framework for few-shot NER. arXiv preprint arXiv:2203.03903 (2022)

17. Wunnava, S., Qin, X., Kakar, T., Kong, X., Rundensteiner, E.: A dual-attention network for joint named entity recognition and sentence classification of adverse drug events. In: Findings of the Association for Computational Linguistics: EMNLP 2020, pp. 3414–3423. Association for Computational Linguistics, Online (2020). https://doi.org/10.18653/v1/2020.findings-emnlp.306. https://aclanthology.org/2020.findings-emnlp.306

18. Yan, H., Gui, T., Dai, J., Guo, Q., Zhang, Z., Qiu, X.: A unified generative framework for various NER subtasks. In: Proceedings of the 59th Annual Meeting of the Association for Computational Linguistics and the 11th International Joint Conference on Natural Language Processing (Volume 1: Long Papers), pp. 5808–5822. Association for Computational Linguistics, Online (2021). https://doi.org/10.18653/v1/2021.acl-long.451. https://aclanthology.org/2021.acl-long.451

19. Zhang, Y., Wallace, B.: A sensitivity analysis of (and practitioners' guide to) convolutional neural networks for sentence classification. arXiv preprint arXiv:1510.03820 (2015)

Could KeyWord Masking Strategy Improve Language Model?

Mariya Borovikova[1,3]([⊠]) [iD], Arnaud Ferré[1] [iD], Robert Bossy[1] [iD],
Mathieu Roche[2,3] [iD], and Claire Nédellec[1] [iD]

[1] MaIAGE, Université Paris-Saclay, INRAE, Domaine de Vilvert,
78352 Jouy-en-Josas, France
`mariya.borovikova@universite-paris-saclay.fr`
[2] CIRAD, 34398 Montpellier, France
[3] TETIS, Univ. Montpellier, AgroParisTech, CIRAD, CNRS, INRAE,
34090 Montpellier, France

Abstract. This paper presents an enhanced approach for adapting a
Language Model (LM) to a specific domain, with a focus on Named
Entity Recognition (NER) and Named Entity Linking (NEL) tasks. Traditional NER/NEL methods require a large amounts of labeled data,
which is time and resource intensive to produce. Unsupervised and semi-
supervised approaches overcome this limitation but suffer from a lower
quality. Our approach, called KeyWord Masking (KWM), fine-tunes a
Language Model (LM) for the Masked Language Modeling (MLM) task
in a special way. Our experiments demonstrate that KWM outperforms
traditional methods in restoring domain-specific entities. This work is
a preliminary step towards developing a more sophisticated NER/NEL
system for domain-specific data.

Keywords: Language Model · Named Entity Recognition and
Linking · domain adaptation

1 Introduction

Named Entity Recognition (NER) and Named Entity Linking (NEL), also known
as Named Entity Disambiguation and Named Entity Normalisation, are important tasks of Natural Language Processing that aim to detect named entities
from unstructured text, categorize them (NER) and then link to a knowledge
base (NEL) (see Fig. 1). Traditional approaches to the task [6,29,34] require
a huge amount of manually labeled data which is resource consuming to produce. Unsupervised [16] and semi-supervised [27] approaches exceed the limit
of traditional approaches, but the quality of the results obtained from domain-
specific texts tends to diminish [41]. Labelled data scarcity is a major obstacle in
achieving high-quality NER and NEL in the biological and biomedical domains.
However, lists of relevant terms (lexicons) are usually available. Our work is an
original contribution that aims to improve a few-shot technique by fine-tuning a

E. Métais et al. (Eds.): NLDB 2023, LNCS 13913, pp. 271–284, 2023.
https://doi.org/10.1007/978-3-031-35320-8_19

272   M. Borovikova et al.

BERT-based model [10] for the Masked LM (MLM) task on biomedical and epidemiological data. The Masked LM (MLM) task, as introduced in [10], involves predicting or restoring missing tokens in a text given its context. To accomplish this goal, a LM takes a text as input and replaces a random subset of its tokens by a special mask token ([MASK]). The model's performance is then evaluated using accuracy and perplexity metrics. Usually, while adapting an LM to more specific data, the model is fine-tuned on a smaller amount of the relevant texts in the same way. However, the masking procedure can vary depending on a particular purpose of the system. Traditional approaches, such as random masking, may not adequately account for the specific characteristics of these texts. This motivates our proposed approach, which focuses on leveraging semantic information to guide the masking process. Specifically, we pre-fine-tune a BERT-based model to mask only the domain-relevant tokens taken from the lexicons, guided by the assumption that this approach will better account for the linguistic nuances present in these texts. More precisely, we conduct our experiments in the biology and biomedical domains, leveraging publicly available datasets containing biomedical and human disease epidemiology news texts, as well as an in-house dataset focused specifically on plant disease epidemiology. This paper presents a preliminary step towards a more advanced NER/NEL system that could be applied to any domain-specific data. Our work is a part of the BEYOND project [1]. The primary objective of the BEYOND project is to improve epidemiological surveillance strategies. This involves the development of novel risk indicators for plant diseases and the proposal of new surveillance plans to achieve this goal. The rest of the paper is organized as follows: In Sect. 2, we provide a detailed review of related work. In Sect. 3, we describe our proposed method. In Sect. 4, we present our experimental setup and results. Finally, we conclude the paper and discuss future work in Sect. 5.

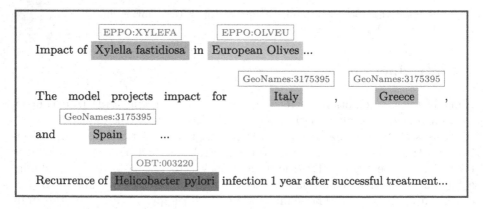

Fig. 1. This figure provides an example of NER/NEL tasks where short passages are labeled with different entity types (i.e., pests in red, plants in green, microorganisms in emerald, and locations in blue) along with their unique identifiers and the specific resource in the format of Database:id. (Color figure online)

2   Related Work

The state-of-the-art NER/NEL models rely on supervised Machine Learning algorithms such as DeepType [29], C-Norm [11], GAN-BERT [18]. Besides, a fine-tuned BERT-based LM with various architectural modifications are mostly used to resolve both NER [33,39] and NEL [5,40] tasks.

Traditional unsupervised approaches rely on lexicon-based rules to identify entities within text, often using pre-existing dictionaries or knowledge bases. For example, the system presented in [28] uses syntactic and semantic rules applied to every word in the text, while an approach proposed in [38] involves searching for noun phrases in the text that differ from terms in a given Database by only a few symbols. Modern unsupervised approaches imply the usage of clustering strategies, such as kNN [35]. The state-of-the-art unsupervised NER method, Cyclener [16], trains two functions: one that generates Named entities (NE) from the input text, and another that generates text from a set of NE. The two functions are trained iteratively in a cycle, where the output of one function is used as the input to the other. One of the notable strengths of Cyclener is that it does not require annotated texts, but instead relies on a random set of annotations with the same NE distribution as the texts being analyzed.

Recent research on few-shot named entity recognition (NER) has primarily focused on two approaches: transfer learning and meta-learning. In transfer learning, models pre-trained on large datasets for the same or similar tasks are fine-tuned on smaller, target datasets [8,13,17,22,23].

On the other hand, proponents of the meta-learning approach train a model on domain-specific data for various tasks and then adapt it to perform the NER/NEL task with only a few examples [12,20,21,24]. One of the leading meta-learning approaches is proposed in [21], where a generative model rewrites all mentions, and their dense representations are compared with those of the entities in the database in terms of cosine distance. However, we were particularly interested in a transfer learning approach for domain-specific data proposed in [13]. The authors pre-train word embeddings on a large corpus of domain-specific texts, and then fine-tune them on a small labeled NER dataset. What makes this approach interesting is that it relies solely on raw texts written on the same topic during the pre-training stage and significantly improves the NER model's performance.

In addition to these approaches, some researchers have explored using MLM as a preliminary step of training a model for a NER task. For instance, in [26], the authors aim to enhance question-answering systems in the biomedical domain by fine-tuning the LM by masking some of the entities recognized by the SciSpacy system [25]. This approach is similar to the one we propose, but it requires a pre-trained NER system.

Our approach to improve the NER/NEL model relies on the intuition of [13] and [26], which is that by masking relevant domain-specific words during MLM pre-training, the model can learn to better represent domain-specific knowledge and improve the performance for other tasks on the same domain. These works were of particular interest to us due to their success in improving algorithm performance without requiring annotated data, but using raw texts from a specific domain instead. However, [26] requires an existing NER system, and both [13] and [26] rely on training and fine-tuning the system on the same corpus, which may lead to unpredictable behavior when applied to new data. To address these limitations, we propose using a KeyWord Masking strategy for a MLM task that we introduce in the Sect. 3.1.

3   Methodology

Building on the insights from [26], we propose that masking some mentions of the relevant entity types can substantially enhance the NER/NEL algorithm performance. Specifically, we compile a comprehensive list of those mentions, based on the entity type semantics, before the fine-tuning. In this section, we describe in detail the KeyWord Masking strategy and the datasets involved. An overview of our approach is shown in Fig. 2.

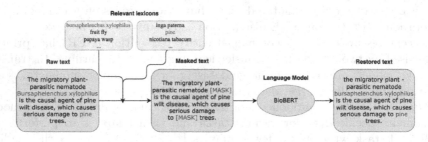

Fig. 2. Overview of the KeyWord Masking approach. Relevant entity type mentions are masked in the raw text, based on a comprehensive list compiled from entity type semantics. The Language Model then restores these masked terms.

3.1   Masking Strategy

The MLM task consists in restoring randomly masked tokens in the input text based on the context provided by the surrounding tokens. Traditional approaches mask randomly chosen tokens (conventionally 15% [36]). Since the final objective of our system is to identify particular entities, we will prioritize masking these mentions. More precisely, we have a lexicon for each entity type which varies for different datasets (see Table 1 and Sect. 3.2). These lists were compiled by gathering relevant terms from domain-specific databases. Then, the list items are masked in the training corpus (see Algorithm 1). If the ratio of the masked tokens is below 15%, other tokens are randomly masked while ensuring that if a token is a part of a word, the entire word is masked. The complete process of fine-tuning the model is described in Algorithm 1.

Algorithm 1. KeyWord Masking

Input: raw texts corpus *Corpus*, relevant lexicons *Lexicons* and Language Model M

1:   *min.loss* ← +∞
2:   *patience* ← 5
3: **while** *patience* > 0 **do**
4:     **for each** *lexicon* ∈ *Lexicons* **do**
5:       **for each** *text* ∈ *Corpus* **do**
6:         **for each** *term* ∈ *lexicon* **do** REPLACE(*text, term, mask*)
7:         **end for**
8:         **while** $\frac{length(mask)}{length(text)} < 0.15$ **do**
9:             REPLACE.RANDOM.ELEMENT(*text, mask*)
10:         **end while**
11:       **end for**
12:       FINE-TUNE(M)
13:       **if** $LOSS(M) < min.loss$ **then**
14:         *min.loss* ← +∞
15:         *patience* ← 5
16:       **else**
17:         *patience* ← *patience* − 1
18:       **end if**
19:     **end for**
20: **end while**

3.2 Domain-Specific Terms Lists

Domain-specific lexicons were created for each dataset separately. For the Plant Health domain, we consulted two sources: a list of pests treated by PESV and a list of pests studied in the BEYOND project. The PESV's list was selected because the Platform monitors plants health at the international level and includes the most dangerous and frequently encountered pests worldwide. The BEYOND project's pests complements the PESV's list with additional pathogens that represent diverse dissemination means. We collected all pests and vulnerable plants names in the EPPO (European and Mediterranean Plant Protection Organization) database [4] and the NCBI taxonomy [32]. The list of plants was compiled using the Encyclopedia of Life resource. By leveraging these sources, the resulting list of pests, pathogens and plants is representative of the types of entities relevant to the specific domain of plant health management.

For Microbiology, we have used a subset of the NCBI taxonomy that contains scientific names of microorganisms.

For geographical entities, we relied on a list of countries and cities from the GeoNames database [2]. The GeoNames database is a comprehensive geographical database for named geographic locations worldwide. Each record in the database contains information, e.g. the name of the location, its coordinates, population size.

Table 1. Masked entities by datasets

Dataset subject matter	Entity type	Number	Examples
Plant Health	Plant	151	*vitis vinifera subsp. vinifera, red rice, tree*
	Pest	96	*l@f. odoratissimum tr4, leafhopper, triozida*
Microbiology (Bacterias and their habitats)	Microorganism	6758474	*Chainia INMI 1349, JRF 142, P.insecticola*
	Habitat	4522	*Ornithodoros moubata, donkey, wild tree*
	Phenotype	574	*oval-shaped, endophytic, osmophile*
Locations (Geographical data in News)	Location (Countries, Cities)	2132976	*Tianxia, Munich, Australian*

3.3   Evaluation Method

After fine-tuning our model, the annotated entities of the evaluation dataset are masked. More specifically, we have two evaluation strategies. We mask (1) all the domain-specific entities, i.e. *Pests* and *Plants* for a Plant Health dataset, or (2) random words ($\approx$15%). Then, we use the base (non-fine tuned) model, the model fine-tuned in a usual way and the model fine-tuned in a way described in Sect. 3.1 to restore the masked entities. Further, we measure the performance of models for the MLM task by calculating the standard metrics of accuracy and perplexity. Accuracy is the ratio of the number of correct predictions to the number of all the predictions made by a model. Perplexity is calculated as follows:

$$Perplexity(M) = \exp(CrossEntropyLoss(M))$$
$$= \exp(-\sum_{t \in v} L(t|context) * \log_2 P(t|context)),$$

where M is a language model, t is a token from the vocabulary v of the language model, $L(t|context)$ is the true probability of occurrence of token t in the given context, and $P(t|context)$ is the probability of the occurrence of token t predicted by the model M in the given context. It is used to quantify the dissimilarity between the predicted and actual probability distributions of the text.

The relationship between perplexity and accuracy is not always straightforward. While accuracy assesses how well the model predicts each token, perplexity measures the overall quality of the model's predictions by considering the probability of the entire generated text. Therefore, these two metrics are complementary in evaluating the performance of MLM models, providing a more nuanced assessment of the model's quality.

3.4   Training Data

We would like to evaluate the effectiveness of our approach across different types of domain-specific data. To achieve this, we have chosen three distinct semantic groups of entities types we intend to mask: Plant Health, Microbiology, and Locations. The first two domains are highly specialized and differ significantly from one another, while the third includes entities types that are more likely to appear in general news articles.

Plant Health. In the Plant Health domain, we focus on adapting a LM to *Plant* and *Pest* species. For this purpose, we used an extended version of the corpus we received from the Plateforme d'Épidémiosurveillance en Santé Végétale (PESV) [3], which includes scientific reports and news about plants diseases, their vectors and corresponding pathogens. Additionally, we collected texts that describe plants and/or pests (encyclopedic articles, other scientific reports, etc.) or texts similar to those which will be further processed by the real-time NER+NEL system (news, official reports, etc.). Namely, our efforts were focused on gathering texts from relevant websites where the license explicitly permitted the utilization of the data (e.g., UK Plant Health Information Portal, Missouri Botanical Garden Website, https://www.hortweek.com/news). As a result, we obtained 1311 texts with an average length ranging from 10000 to 20000 characters.

Microbiology. In the Microbiology domain, we fine-tune a LM with a focus on *Microorganisms*, *Habitats* and *Phenotypes*. We accomplish the fine-tuning on the Bacteria Biotope 2019 corpus [7]. The corpus is a dataset of scientific publications related to bacteria and their habitats, and it is annotated for NER/NEL and Relation extraction tasks. We use raw texts from a training set of the corpus to fine-tune a LM specifically for this domain.

General-Domain News. In the General-domain news domain, we focus on *Location* entities and use raw texts from the English conll2003 corpus [31], which is a subset of the Reuters news stories.

4   Experiments

4.1   Evaluation Data

To evaluate the performance of our approach, we created or sourced from a publicly available NER/NEL dataset a separate test set for each training set based on its theme. Named entity statistics are provided in Table 2.

Plant Health. To the best of our knowledge, there is currently no publicly available dataset for NER/NEL in the Plant Health domain. Therefore, we have constructed a very small one that we introduce here. "Plant Health Risks Identification from textual data" is a new open-source test dataset for the evaluation of NER/NEL in the Plant Health domain. It is a small dataset of 23 representative manually annotated texts that contain relevant and representative information on Plant Health Monitoring. Specifically, these texts are official reports or news articles and describe the occurrence of a pest on a particular plant in a specific geographical zone. During the text selection process, we consulted with experts in the Plant Health domain from the EPPO (European and Mediterranean Plant Protection Organization) and requested a list of the currently monitoring pests. We then collected texts that cover all the pests from the list, with each pest occurring multiple times under different names to ensure comprehensive coverage. We made sure that there is no document overlap between the training and test sets. During the manual annotation process, we labeled the mentions of four entity types (see Table 2). Only two of them, *Pest* and *Plant*, are used for the method described in this article. To normalize the entities, we assigned EPPO [4] and NCBI [32] labels for *Plant* and *Pest* entities respectively. The other two annotated entities types, *Date* and *Location*, will be used in subsequent work for NER/NEL system evaluation. We used *GeoNames* [2] labels for *Location* entities, while temporal entities were normalized with the TIMEX3 [9] format. The dataset with its full annotation guide and a more detailed description are publicly available through open access and can be found at the following link[1].

Microbiology. To evaluate the performance of our approach in restoring entities related to microbiology, we use the Bacteria Biotope 2019 corpus [7] development set which contains 100 documents.

Geographical Data. In order to measure the quality of our method in reconstructing geographical entities, we use the GeoVirus corpus [14]. The dataset consists of 229 news articles that describe events related to epidemics and/or global disease outbreaks.

Table 2. Test corpora statistics

Dataset	Plant Health					Bacteria Biotope (dev)				GeoVirus
Entity type	Plant	Pest	Date	Location	All	Microorganism	Habitat	Phenotype	All	Location
Total entities	86	188	93	131	400	402	610	161	1073	1981
Unique entities	24	43	61	71	199	137	130	44	311	569

4.2 Experimental Protocol

All the data and results processing were conducted using Python Programming language 3.8 [30]. The main libraries used for this project are: PyTorch [15] and transformers [37].

In our experiments, we have fine-tuned BERT [10] and BioBERT [19] models. We selected BERT because it is a widely used model across various domains, and BioBERT, as it is the current State-of-the-art model in the biomedical domain,

---

[1] https://entrepot.recherche.data.gouv.fr/dataset.xhtml?persistentId=doi%3A10.
57745%2FHVPITE.

which includes Microbiology and Plant Health. Both models were chosen for their ease of use and relatively light computational requirements.

For both models training is done with an Adam optimizer and a learning rate $5e-5$ for 40 epochs.

4.3 Results

Tables 3 and 4, along with Figs. 3 and 4 present the results based on accuracy and perplexity indicators, respectively. The evaluation of BERT and BioBERT models was performed on different datasets with and without fine-tuning, using standard masking and a KeyWord Masking approach (KWM). The *Dataset* column indicates the evaluation dataset. The *Masked tokens* column describes whether random or domain-specific tokens were masked during the evaluation process. When masking specific entities, all the entities mentioned in Tables 3 and 4 were masked in the texts. The *Model* column contains the name of the pre-trained model, and the columns *without fine-tuning*, *standard masking*, and *KWM* contain the corresponding accuracy or perplexity indicators. The best results for each dataset and model are shown in bold. To ensure the reliability of our results, we trained our models 10 times and present the mean and standard deviation values.

Our experiments reveal a clear distinction between the two masking strategies. Models fine-tuned with the KWM strategy outperform those fine-tuned using the standard approach for restoring domain-specific entities. Conversely, for random word masking, models fine-tuned using the standard approach perform better than those fine-tuned with KWM. Moreover, we observe that BioBERT outperforms BERT on the biomedical (Bacteria Biotope (BB)) and epidemiological (Plant Health) texts, whereas BERT performs better on general domain texts (GeoVirus).

Another observation concerns the perplexity. A lower perplexity value indicates that the model is more confident in predicting the next token. Our results show that the perplexity is consistently lower on the test set when using the standard fine-tuning approach. This implies that the model fine-tuned with the standard approach has a higher level of confidence in predicting a masked token. This finding underscores the importance of fine-tuning methodology in achieving optimal performance in the MLM task.

4.4 Discussion

Based on our findings, the strategy of masking the keywords is advantageous for restoring domain-specific mentions. Therefore, we assume that models fine-tuned in this way captures better the semantics of the masked words lexical group and that it will improve the quality while being used for the NER/NEL task where the entities belong to the same lexical group. However, this masking approach seems to worsen the overall understanding of the language and seems to have no advantage unless it is specifically targeted towards a related lexical group of masked tokens.

Table 3. Accuracy comparison of BERT and BioBERT models fine-tuned by different masking techniques. The values in bold are the best for each task and model.

Dataset	Masked tokens	Model	without fine-tuning	standard masking	KWM
Plant Health	*Plants* and *Pests* entities	BERT	0.02	0.09 ± 0.02	**0.21 ± 0.02**
		BioBERT	0.04	0.14 ± 0.02	**0.56 ± 0.03**
	Random	BERT	0.37	**0.52 ± 0.02**	0.3 ± 0.02
		BioBERT	0.41	**0.56 ± 0.02**	0.46 ± 0.02
BB	*Microorganisms*, *Habitats* and *Phenotypes* entities	BERT	0.02	0.02 ± 0.01	**0.06 ± 0.01**
		BioBERT	0.03	0.03 ± 0.01	**0.08 ± 0.03**
	Random	BERT	0.37	**0.38 ± 0.01**	0.12 ± 0.00
		BioBERT	**0.46**	0.43 ± 0.01	0.15 ± 0.00
GeoVirus	*Locations* entities	BERT	0.08	0.14 ± 0.03	**0.21 ± 0.1**
	Random	BERT	0.30	**0.41 ± 0.03**	0.08 ± 0.00

Table 4. Perplexity of BERT and BioBERT models fine-tuned by different masking techniques. The values in bold are the best for each task.

Dataset	Masked tokens	Model	without fine-tuning	standard masking	KWM
Plant Health	*Plants* and *Pests* entities	BERT	12253.5	**2.7 ± 0.2**	5.1 ± 2.1
		BioBERT	968.5	2.2 ± 0.2	**1.3 ± 0.3**
	Random	BERT	11350.6	**1.9 ± 0.2**	2.7 ± 1.1
		BioBERT	1014.3	**1.7 ± 0.2**	2.2 ± 0.1
BB	*Microorganisms*, *Habitats* and *Phenotypes* entities	BERT	26170240	**6.2 ± 3.2**	6.7 ± 1.4
		BioBERT	313426	6.3 ± 2.1	**5.9 ± 2.3**
	Random	BERT	2605567.2	**1.9 ± 0.5**	3.4 ± 0.4
		BioBERT	61243.3	**1.7 ± 0.9**	3.1 ± 1.9
GeoVirus	*Locations* entities	BERT	2432350	**4.8 ± 3.6**	15 ± 2.7
	Random	BERT	2875939	**7.3 ± 5.2**	20 ± 6.1

This is reasonable, as the standard fine-tuning approach involves training the language model on the entire text data with randomly chosen tokens to mask, while the KWM strategy trains the model to focus on implicit information that is helpful in predicting specific entities. We believe our method can enhance the performance of MLMs in NER/NEL tasks, but it may reduce its ability to capture the overall structure and patterns of the input data, making it less suitable for general text processing. Further research is needed to determine whether KWM fine-tuned LMs will perform well for NER/NEL tasks, and we plan to conduct additional testing in future work.

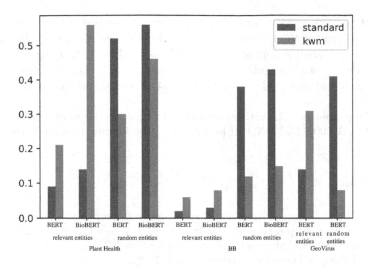

Fig. 3. Accuracy comparison.

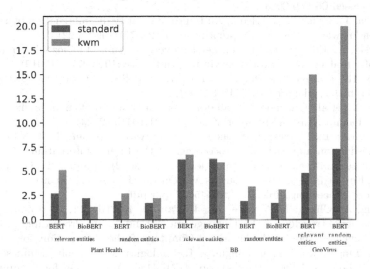

Fig. 4. Perplexity comparison.

5 Conclusion

In this work, we aimed to improve the LM understanding of domain-specific entities in the fields of biomedicine and epidemiology for it further usage. The results of our experiments show that our approach outperforms the traditional methods on restoring domain-specific entities. Our code is available on https:// github.com/project178/KeyWord-Masking-strategy.

This work is a preliminary step towards developing an effective NER/NEL system for domain-specific data. Future research will focus on exploring the impact of various lexicons and corpora (diversity, coverage, etc.) on the performance of our method. We will also explore combining our approach with unsupervised or semi-supervised NER/NEL algorithms. These experiments will provide a deeper understanding of the factors that influence the effectiveness of our approach and will guide the development of a more advanced system.

Acknowledgements. The authors would like to express their sincere gratitude to the ANR-20-PCPA-0002, BEYOND [1] for providing the funding that made this research possible.

References

1. BEYOND: Building epidemiological surveillance & prophylaxis with observations near & distant. https://www6.inrae.fr/beyond/. Accessed 06 Feb 2023
2. GeoNames. https://gd.eppo.int/. Accessed 06 Feb 2023
3. PESV. https://gd.eppo.int/. Accessed 06 Feb 2023
4. EPPO (2023). EPPO Global Database (available online). https://plateforme-esv.fr. Accessed 06 Feb 2023
5. Ayoola, T., Fisher, J., Pierleoni, A.: Improving entity disambiguation by reasoning over a knowledge base. arXiv preprint arXiv:2207.04106 (2022)
6. Baevski, A., Edunov, S., Liu, Y., Zettlemoyer, L., Auli, M.: Cloze-driven pretraining of self-attention networks. arXiv preprint arXiv:1903.07785 (2019)
7. Bossy, R., Deléger, L., Chaix, E., Ba, M., Nédellec, C.: Bacteria Biotope 2019 (2022). https://doi.org/10.57745/PCQFC2
8. Chen, X., et al.: One model for all domains: collaborative domain-prefix tuning for cross-domain NER. arXiv preprint arXiv:2301.10410 (2023)
9. Derczynski, L., Llorens, H., Saquete, E.: Massively increasing TIMEX3 resources: a transduction approach. In: Proceedings of the Eighth International Conference on Language Resources and Evaluation (LREC 2012), Istanbul, Turkey, pp. 3754–3761. European Language Resources Association (ELRA) (2012). http://www.lrec-conf.org/proceedings/lrec2012/pdf/451_Paper.pdf
10. Devlin, J., Chang, M.W., Lee, K., Toutanova, K.: BERT: pre-training of deep bidirectional transformers for language understanding. In: Proceedings of the 2019 Conference of the North American Chapter of the Association for Computational Linguistics: Human Language Technologies, Minneapolis, Minnesota (Volume 1: Long and Short Papers), pp. 4171–4186. Association for Computational Linguistics (2019). https://doi.org/10.18653/v1/N19-1423. https://aclanthology.org/N19-1423
11. Ferré, A., Deléger, L., Bossy, R., Zweigenbaum, P., Nédellec, C.: C-norm: a neural approach to few-shot entity normalization. BMC Bioinform. **21**(23), 1–19 (2020)
12. Fritzler, A., Logacheva, V., Kretov, M.: Few-shot classification in named entity recognition task. In: Proceedings of the 34th ACM/SIGAPP Symposium on Applied Computing, pp. 993–1000 (2019)
13. Gligic, L., Kormilitzin, A., Goldberg, P., Nevado-Holgado, A.: Named entity recognition in electronic health records using transfer learning bootstrapped neural networks. Neural Netw. **121**, 132–139 (2020)
14. Gritta, M., Pilehvar, M.T., Collier, N.: Which Melbourne? Augmenting geocoding with maps. In: Proceedings of the 56th Annual Meeting of the Association for Computational Linguistics (Volume 1: Long Papers), pp. 1285–1296 (2018)

15. Imambi, S., Prakash, K.B., Kanagachidambaresan, G.: PyTorch. In: Programming with TensorFlow: Solution for Edge Computing Applications, pp. 87–104 (2021)
16. Iovine, A., Fang, A., Fetahu, B., Rokhlenko, O., Malmasi, S.: CycleNER: an unsupervised training approach for named entity recognition. In: Proceedings of the ACM Web Conference 2022, pp. 2916–2924 (2022)
17. Jia, C., Liang, X., Zhang, Y.: Cross-domain NER using cross-domain language modeling. In: Proceedings of the 57th Annual Meeting of the Association for Computational Linguistics, pp. 2464–2474 (2019)
18. Jiang, S., Cormier, S., Angarita, R., Rousseaux, F.: Improving text mining in plant health domain with GAN and/or pre-trained language model. Front. Artif. Intell. **6** (2023)
19. Lee, J., et al.: BioBERT: a pre-trained biomedical language representation model for biomedical text mining. Bioinformatics **36**(4), 1234–1240 (2020)
20. Li, J., Chiu, B., Feng, S., Wang, H.: Few-shot named entity recognition via meta-learning. IEEE Trans. Knowl. Data Eng. **34**(9), 4245–4256 (2022). https://doi.org/10.1109/TKDE.2020.3038670
21. Li, X., et al.: Effective few-shot named entity linking by meta-learning. In: 2022 IEEE 38th International Conference on Data Engineering (ICDE), pp. 178–191. IEEE (2022)
22. Liu, Z., Jiang, F., Hu, Y., Shi, C., Fung, P.: NER-BERT: a pre-trained model for low-resource entity tagging. arXiv preprint arXiv:2112.00405 (2021)
23. Liu, Z., et al.: CrossNER: evaluating cross-domain named entity recognition. In: Proceedings of the AAAI Conference on Artificial Intelligence, vol. 35, pp. 13452–13460 (2021)
24. Ming, H., Yang, J., Jiang, L., Pan, Y., An, N.: Few-shot nested named entity recognition. arXiv e-prints, pp. arXiv-2212 (2022)
25. Neumann, M., King, D., Beltagy, I., Ammar, W.: ScispaCy: fast and robust models for biomedical natural language processing. In: BioNLP 2019, p. 319 (2019)
26. Pergola, G., Kochkina, E., Gui, L., Liakata, M., He, Y.: Boosting low-resource biomedical QA via entity-aware masking strategies. In: Proceedings of the 16th Conference of the European Chapter of the Association for Computational Linguistics: Main Volume, pp. 1977–1985 (2021)
27. Peters, M.E., Ammar, W., Bhagavatula, C., Power, R.: Semi-supervised sequence tagging with bidirectional language models. arXiv preprint arXiv:1705.00108 (2017)
28. Popovski, G., Kochev, S., Korousic-Seljak, B., Eftimov, T.: Foodie: a rule-based named-entity recognition method for food information extraction. ICPRAM **12**, 915 (2019)
29. Raiman, J., Raiman, O.: Deeptype: multilingual entity linking by neural type system evolution. In: Proceedings of the AAAI Conference on Artificial Intelligence, vol. 32 (2018)
30. van Rossum, G.: Python programming language. **3**(8), 15 (2022). https://www.python.org/downloads/release/python-3815/. Accessed 06 Feb 2023
31. Sang, E.F., De Meulder, F.: Introduction to the CoNLL-2003 shared task: language-independent named entity recognition. arXiv preprint cs/0306050 (2003)
32. Schoch, C., et al.: NCBI taxonomy: a comprehensive update on curation, resources and tools. Database **2020** (2020). https://doi.org/10.1093/database/baaa062. https://www.ncbi.nlm.nih.gov/taxonomy. Accessed 06 Feb 2023
33. Ushio, A., Camacho-Collados, J.: T-NER: an all-round python library for transformer-based named entity recognition. arXiv preprint arXiv:2209.12616 (2022)

34. Wang, C., Sun, X., Yu, H., Zhang, W.: Entity disambiguation leveraging multi-perspective attention. IEEE Access **7**, 113963–113974 (2019)
35. Wang, S., et al.: k NN-NER: named entity recognition with nearest neighbor search. arXiv preprint arXiv:2203.17103 (2022)
36. Wettig, A., Gao, T., Zhong, Z., Chen, D.: Should you mask 15% in masked language modeling? arXiv preprint arXiv:2202.08005 (2022)
37. Wolf, T., et al.: Transformers: state-of-the-art natural language processing. In: Proceedings of the 2020 Conference on Empirical Methods in Natural Language Processing: System Demonstrations, pp. 38–45. Association for Computational Linguistics, Online (2020). https://www.aclweb.org/anthology/2020.emnlp-demos.6
38. Xu, J., Gan, L., Cheng, M., Wu, Q.: Unsupervised medical entity recognition and linking in Chinese online medical text. J. Healthcare Eng. **2018** (2018)
39. Yamada, I., Asai, A., Shindo, H., Takeda, H., Matsumoto, Y.: LUKE: deep contextualized entity representations with entity-aware self-attention. In: Proceedings of the 2020 Conference on Empirical Methods in Natural Language Processing (EMNLP), pp. 6442–6454. Association for Computational Linguistics, Online (2020). https://doi.org/10.18653/v1/2020.emnlp-main.523. https://aclanthology.org/2020.emnlp-main.523
40. Yamada, I., Washio, K., Shindo, H., Matsumoto, Y.: Global entity disambiguation with BERT. In: Proceedings of the 2022 Conference of the North American Chapter of the Association for Computational Linguistics: Human Language Technologies, pp. 3264–3271 (2022)
41. Zhang, S., Elhadad, N.: Unsupervised biomedical named entity recognition: experiments with clinical and biological texts. J. Biomed. Inform. **46**(6), 1088–1098 (2013)

Regularization, Semi-supervision, and Supervision for a Plausible Attention-Based Explanation

Duc Hau Nguyen[1] (ID), Cyrielle Mallart[3] (ID), Guillaume Gravier[1(✉)] (ID), and Pascale Sébillot[2] (ID)

[1] Univ Rennes, CNRS, Inria - IRISA, Rennes, France
{duc-hau.nguyen,guig}@irisa.fr
[2] Univ Rennes, CNRS, Inria, INSA Rennes - IRISA, Rennes, France
pascale.sebillot@irisa.fr
[3] University of Rennes 2, Rennes, France
cyrielle.mallart@univ-rennes2.fr

Abstract. Attention mechanism is contributing to the majority of recent advances in machine learning for natural language processing. Additionally, it results in an attention map that shows the proportional influence of each input in its decision. Empirical studies postulate that attention maps can be provided as an explanation for model output. However, it is still questionable to ask whether this explanation helps regular people to understand and accept the model output (the plausibility of the explanation). Recent studies show that attention weights in RNN encoders are hardly plausible because they spread on input tokens. We thus propose three additional constraints to the learning objective function to improve the plausibility of the attention map: regularization to increase the attention weight sparsity, semi-supervision to supervise the map by a heuristic and supervision by human annotation. Results show that all techniques can improve the attention map plausibility at some level. We also observe that specific instructions for human annotation might have a negative effect on classification performance. Beyond the attention map, results on text classification tasks also show that the contextualization layer plays a crucial role in finding the right space for finding plausible tokens, no matter how constraints bring the gain.

Keywords: Attention mechanism · Explainability · Plausibilty · Regularization · Semi-supervision · Supervision

1 Introduction

Attention mechanisms [15] play a crucial role in recent success across many natural language processing (NLP) tasks and are present in most recent neural models. As a layer in a complex neural network, the attention mechanism

Work partially funded by grant ANR-19-CE38-0011-03 from the French national research agency (ANR).

attributes a weight to each input token and encodes each into a context vector through a weighted sum of the input vectors. When this context vector is used for prediction, the weight vector, also called *attention map* [11], can be considered as an explanation by showing the degree of influence of each input token to the prediction.

Despite the potential of attention maps as a form of explanation, there are concerns [11] about their validity on two properties that are not guaranteed: faithfulness and plausibility. Faithfulness, a widely discussed problem [3,19], focuses on whether the weight associated with a token reflects its influence on the prediction. Plausibility refers to the extent to which the attention map can resemble human reasoning [19,31].

While plausibility is an interesting feature that allows to present an easily comprehensible way to individuals with limited knowledge of neural models without additional computational costs, the contributions in this direction remain limited and rare. Given that multiple studies have suggested that raw attention weights lack plausibility (see, e.g., [20]), the issue of forcing their plausibility is an obvious one that calls for further exploration. As it is proven possible to incorporate constraints on attention while maintaining satisfactory performance [12,25,31], we propose three approaches for enforcing plausibility constraints on attention maps, namely, sparsity regularization, semi-supervised learning, and supervised learning.

The main contributions in this paper are: (1) we can to some extent force the model plausibility (as demonstrated by supervision) at no accuracy cost, (2) both regularization and semi-supervision can optimize the plausibility but the latter offers a solution without compromising performance and (3) the deep contextualization is harmful to attention plausibility. The last result provides insight into why this hardly transfers to transformers.

2   Related Works

The attention mechanism is widely used as a possible feature to explain the model decision [23,28]. However, the local explanation is facing an issue that the attention map can be manipulated while keeping the same prediction [12,29,31]. While this feature is considered as a weak faithful explanation [1,27], this enables the selection of a plausible map.

Among the few studies on attention supervision, [18] showed that supervision can harm classification performance in sentiment classification tasks. Regularization was considered to circumvent the issue of a rather flat distribution of attention weights as reported by [13]. [19] suggested an additional constraint in the learning objective to force this representation to be sparse.

To overcome the lack of human references in many datasets, many contributions offer task-specific solutions, such as [22] guiding attention based on topic-related vocabulary and [14] using a WordNet-based heuristic for evidence inference, while [20] provides an effective heuristic map that is closer to human annotation but only for natural language inference (NLI). While the authors of existing techniques have not fully explored their effects and limitations in different tasks, this study aims to provide a comprehensive view of how different techniques improve attention plausibility.

Hard attention, also referred to as rationalized learning in the literature [5], is an alternative form of the attention mechanism that comprises two components: a generator function that masks irrelevant input tokens, and a predictor that is trained to make predictions on the remaining inputs. While hard-attention is advantageous with respect to soft-attention in robustness and faithfulness aspects, it introduced a trade-off between sparsity and accuracy because the full context is inaccessible [24].

Other post-zhoc explanation techniques can provide faithful explanations (such as gradient-based methods or feature suppression), however with two main drawbacks: (i) incurring additional computational costs during each inference and (ii) offering benefits only to the model developer, without the flexibility to impose constraints for plausible explanations [2] while its explanation cannot be guaranteed to be plausible for end-users [3,21].

To the best of our knowledge, no existing study has brought a broad and comprehensive overview of how different techniques improve attention plausibility. Although regularization techniques are independent of human annotation and heuristics can overcome the lack of human annotation, it is still unclear how they improve plausibility compared to supervision. Furthermore, the authors of the existing techniques suggest improvement without questioning their implications and limitations in different tasks, especially in soft-attention models. This study focuses on addressing these fundamental issues and does not include a comparative analysis of hard-attention techniques and post-hoc explanation methods but they are promising for future works.

3   Tasks and Datasets

To ensure the generalization of our findings across different tasks, we investigate three different datasets from the ERASER benchmark [6] and [30] designed for plausibility studies.

The e-SNLI corpus [4], a reference dataset in NLI, consists of pairs of sentences, a premise and a hypothesis with a label stating whether the hypothesis entails, contradicts, or is unrelated to the premise. The annotators also answered the question *Why is a pair of sentences in a relation of entailment, neutrality, or contradiction?* by highlighting the relevant words in both the premise and hypothesis and providing a short explanatory text. The corpus consists of 549,367 sentence pairs for training and 9,842 pairs for the validation and test sets respectively. Note that the SNLI corpus is known to have artifacts [10], where some lexical fields appear mostly in one class. Also, the annotation instruction in e-SNLI leads to some particularities, such as not highlighting the common words between premise and hypothesis, thus making the annotation not convincing in some cases.

The HateXPlain dataset [17] was conceived by gathering posts from social networks that were labeled for the detection of hate speech. Each post belongs

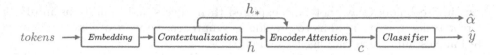

Fig. 1. Generic architecture of a RNN-based attention model for classification.

to either one of three labels: offensive, hateful, and normal speech. Annotators were also instructed to highlight the relevant part of the post to justify their choice of a label. Overall, the corpus consists of 15,383 posts for training, 1,922 for validation, and 1,924 for testing.

The Yelp-Hat dataset [26] was obtained by gathering reviews on restaurants from a website and by asking reviewers to highlight parts of the text to justify their choice. The corpus consists of 3,482 reviews for training and validation[1]. Yelp-Hat was split randomly into 2,436 sentences for training and 1,046 for validation.

4   Attention Mechanism on RNN Encoders

Being one of the most studied in NLP yet the most controversial in the explainability debate [3], we employ the attention model with RNN encoders. Preliminary experiments on BERT-like self-attention models have shown little hope in finding a single layer or head to provide plausible explanations.

The model, illustrated in Fig. 1, consists of an embedding layer and a bi-LSTM layer, which produce contextualized token representations h_i, for $i \in [1, L]$ in a sentence of length L, as well as a sentence embedding h_*, which is the concatenation of the forward and backward last state. The attention encoder assigns weights $\hat{\alpha}_i$ to each h_i and computes a context vector c through a weighted sum. Finally, a multilayer perceptron classifier is applied to c for prediction. We also consider attention weights on each input token in the loss function. To simplify notation, we use the notation $h = [h_1, ..., h_L]^\intercal = [h_i]_{i=1}^{L}$ to denote the sequence of bi-LSTM outputs and $\hat{\alpha} = [\hat{\alpha}_i]_{i=1}^{L}$ to denote the attention weights. In this paper, we distinguish the model attention map $\hat{\alpha}$ from α which refers to the human annotation binary map.

The attention layer is adapted differently for various tasks. We begin by describing the attention layer formally as a function that takes query q, key k, and value v as input and generates c and $\hat{\alpha}$ as output according to [15]:

$$c, \hat{\alpha} = \text{Attention}(q, k, v). \tag{1}$$

In text classification, the attention layer queries the text embedding ($q = h_*$) and use the token contextualized vectors as both key and value ($k = v = h$). The prediction is made on c. In NLI, we use text embeddings of the premise or

---

[1] 15 "incoherent" samples were excluded, such as incompatible annotation maps and number of tokens in reviews.

hypothesis as query ($q = \bar{h}_*$) and keys/values are bi-LSTM representations from the opposite sentence ($k = v = h$). As a result, we obtain two context vectors, c_p for the premise and c_h for the hypothesis, which are concatenated $[c_p \oplus c_h]$ for prediction.

5   Constraints on the Objective Function

We propose to control the behavior of the attention layer to improve its plausibility by extending the loss function to include a term on the attention

$$\mathcal{L}(y, \hat{y}, \hat{\alpha}) = \mathcal{L}_c(y, \hat{y}) + \lambda \, \mathcal{L}_a(\hat{\alpha}) \tag{2}$$

where we combine the classification loss $\mathcal{L}_c$ (cross-entropy loss) with a constraint on attention map $\mathcal{L}_a(\hat{\alpha})$ weighted by $\lambda \in [0, 1]$. We detail hereunder the different forms for $\mathcal{L}_a$ in three approaches.

5.1   Sparsity Regularization

The sparsity constraint can be expressed in many different ways, which have different but marginal effects on convergence speed, or on the resulting explanation [13,19]. Shannon entropy offers a straightforward yet effective method to measure sparsity, where high entropy values indicate uniform weight distributions and low values indicate sparse ones. We incorporate Shannon entropy as a loss function, defined as

$$\mathcal{L}_a(\hat{\alpha}) = - \sum_{i=1}^{L} \hat{\alpha}_i \log_L(\hat{\alpha}_i). \tag{3}$$

5.2   Supervision from Reference Annotation

A difficulty in supervising attention layers with a reference annotation is that attention weights and reference annotations are conceptually of different nature. The former are weights such that $\sum \hat{\alpha}_i = 1$ while the latter are binary indicators of whether a token is useful for a plausible explanation or not. Contrary to [22], supervision directly on the attention map $\hat{\alpha}_i$ did not work out in practice in the models and tasks that we consider. Thus, we propose instead to supervise on $\hat{\beta}_i = \text{sigmoid}(\hat{a}_i)$ (similar to logistic attention [16]), where $\hat{a}_i$ are the attention weights taken before the softmax that is applied within the Attention() function of Eq. 1. Due to the sparsity in the human annotation α, the traditional loss function would put too much emphasis on non-annotated tokens so we rather use the Jaccard loss function from [7] to avoid this bias, i.e.,

$$\mathcal{L}_a(\hat{\beta}, \alpha) = \frac{\hat{\beta}^T \alpha}{\sum_{i}^{L} \hat{\beta}_i + \sum_{i}^{L} \alpha_i - \hat{\beta}^T \alpha}. \tag{4}$$

Note that $\hat{\beta}$ is only used in the loss function, c is still computed based on softmax attention map $\hat{\alpha}$.

5.3   Semi-supervision from Heuristics

Supervising with the reference human annotation aims at demonstrating whether supervision can be used to improve plausibility or not in an ideal scenario. This is however not realistic as human annotations are seldom available for this task and are costly to obtain. We thus investigate semi-supervision with annotations generated by simple heuristic rules. Indeed, [20] show that a simple heuristic attention map exploiting part-of-speech (POS) tags offers decent plausibility in the NLI task. The heuristic builds on the observation that verbs, nouns and adjectives (save for those in a small shortlist, such as auxiliary verbs) account for a fair amount of the tokens deemed as informative by human annotators[2]. In the e-SNLI dataset, 73.42% of the tokens in the human annotation fall in this category. To a slightly lesser extent, this is also observed on the HateXPlain and Yelp-Hat datasets used of text classification with more than 53% of the annotated tokens in this category.

We construct the heuristic map $\tilde{\alpha} = [\tilde{\alpha}_i]_{i=1}^{L}$ such that $\tilde{\alpha}_i = 0$ for tokens that are not nouns, verbs, adjectives, or stop-words, and reweight the remaining tokens based on the task. For classification tasks, the weight is the frequency of the token in the reference annotation. For NLI task, the weight is the sum of cosine similarities between the token and all tokens in the other sentence, applied equally to premise and hypothesis. Finally in all tasks, the heuristic map $\tilde{\alpha}$ is renormalized on a per-sentence basis, which transformed it into a probability vector. The Kullback-Leibler divergence

$$\mathcal{L}_a(\hat{\alpha}, \tilde{\alpha}) = \tilde{\alpha} \times [log(\tilde{\alpha}) - log(\hat{\alpha})] \tag{5}$$

is used to measure the loss between two probability vectors, $\tilde{\alpha}$ and $\hat{\alpha}$:

Our proposed heuristic for text classification has a limit as it indirectly relies on human annotations to weight each token, but one could make use of semantic lexicons such as SentiWordNet or VerbNet to craft heuristic weights for noun, verb, and adjective tokens.

6   Implementation and Training Parameters

To ensure consistency, the text data are pre-processed by tokenizing, lemmatizing, and lowercasing using the *spaCy* library. A unique vocabulary was generated for each dataset using the training set. All models reported in this study were initialized with the same GloVE embeddings (glove.42B.300d) and utilized ReLu activation functions with a softmax at the output of the classifier. The training settings were kept at their default configurations, including a learning rate of $lr = 1e-3$ and a stabilizer of $\epsilon = 1e-8$, as per community standards. To account for model variability, all runs were repeated three times.

Regarding evaluation, assessing the plausibility of attention maps faces three challenges: (1) the attention weights are continuous, (2) the magnitude of its

---

[2] POS tags were detected with spaCy using the *en_core_web_sm* pipeline, which claims an accuracy of 97.2% in POS tagging.

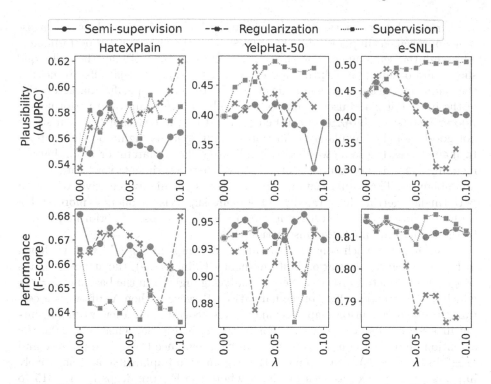

Fig. 2. Plausibility (AUPRC, top) and performance (F-score, bottom) on HateXPlain, YelpHat-50, and e-SNLI.

values depends on the sentence length and (3) only a few tokens are highlighted (class imbalance). To address these challenges, we apply a min-max scaler on the attention map and use the Area Under Recall/Precision curve (AURPC) as proposed in ERASER [6] to measure how close it is to human annotation. Additionally, we report Recall and Specificity by applying a threshold of 0.5 (the value is chosen following the ERASER benchmark [6]) for further insights.

Code to reproduce all experiments is available via github[3].

7   Experimental Results

Firstly, the study investigates whether enhancing the plausibility of attention map is feasible without compromising classification performance. To answer this question, we evaluate three methods, namely, semi-supervision (solid line with round marker), regularization (dashed line with X marker), and supervision (dotted line with square marker) based on plausibility (AUPRC) and task performance (F-score) as reported in Fig. 2. The figure showcases the evolution of the two metrics across three datasets under λ values ranging from $[0, 0.1]$ in a single bi-LSTM contextualization layer setting.

---

[3] https://github.com/Kihansi95/Linkmedia_AttentionPlausibilityByConstraint.

Across all three datasets, supervision and regularization show a consistent improvement in plausibility while preserving the classification performance. Although the semi-supervision shows little effect in HateXPlain, the technique shows improvement in YelpHat and e-SNLI. This suggests that effectiveness of the semi-supervision strategy in general depends on the specific characteristics of the input data, and users cannot always rely on it for improved performance. Poorer results on HateXplain can be explained by the fact that the heuristic is not good enough as explanation in HateXPlain depends highly on the context: In many cases, the same words could indicate either a hateful or a non-hateful meaning. This is not the case of YelpHat where sentiment words are rather unambiguous. The regularization approach turns out highly sensitive to λ, with performance getting hurt rapidly, while semi-supervision offers a more stable solution. Notice that supervision in e-SNLI leads to a loss of performance, due to the artifact in annotation instruction [10].

The impact of each constraint on attention maps in the NLI task is shown in Fig. 3. When regularization is strengthened (λ increases), the attention maps progressively delete words that were initially highlighted in the baseline ($\lambda = 0$), which is the intended effect of regularization. However, when λ surpasses a certain threshold, attention maps become too concentrated on a few words, resulting in less plausible explanations. For instance, in Fig. 3a, when $\lambda = 0.06$, the attention maps focus on only one word in each sentence ("with" in premise and "rug" in hypothesis), which renders the explanation implausible and negatively impacts performance (as seen in Fig. 2, where the F-score drops from 0.815 to around 0.793).

In the case of supervision, attention maps gradually delete words from the baseline model, resulting in more plausible explanations that match the words highlighted by annotators. The constraint, however, does not ensure complete alignment with human annotations as shown in Fig. 3b, where the attention map of $\lambda = 0.1$ does not select the words "two" and "on" to explain in hypothesis. In fact, with 10% of the loss devoted to making attention maps closer to human annotations, words selected by human annotation may not all be necessary for prediction. As can be seem from Fig. 2, the attention maps cannot be constrained to be more similar to human annotations beyond $\lambda = 0.06$.

In semi-supervision, attention maps tend to retain the focus on words obtained from heuristic maps and do not impact performance. For instance, in the hypothesis attention map when $\lambda = 0.04$ (Fig. 3c), the constraint deletes the words "two", "are", "on" and enforces attention values on "children" to match the heuristic map.

To confirm these observations, we report in Fig. 4 recall and specificity of attention maps as a function of λ: while regularization encourages the selection of true positives (increase in recall), it tends to ignore some plausible words as indicated by the drop in specificity (we have more false negatives), as shown in e-SNLI and HateXPlain. This leads to a more conservative model that prefers to drop some words than highlight words that are not plausible. With supervision,

	Premise	Hypothesis	Label
GROUNDTRUTH	Two children re laying on a rug with some wooden bricks laid out in a square between them .	Two children are on a rug .	entailment
Baseline	Two children re laying on a rug with some wooden bricks laid out in a square between them .	Two children are on a rug .	entailment
λ=0.01	Two children re laying on a rug with some wooden bricks laid out in a square between them .	Two children are on a rug .	entailment
λ=0.02	Two children re laying on a rug with some wooden bricks laid out in a square between them .	Two children are on a rug .	entailment
λ=0.06	Two children re laying on a rug with some wooden bricks laid out in a square between them .	Two children are on a rug .	entailment

(a) regularization of attention

	Premise	Hypothesis	Label
GROUNDTRUTH	Two children re laying on a rug with some wooden bricks laid out in a square between them .	Two children are on a rug .	entailment
Baseline	Two children re laying on a rug with some wooden bricks laid out in a square between them .	Two children are on a rug .	entailment
λ=0.03	Two children re laying on a rug with some wooden bricks laid out in a square between them .	Two children are on a rug .	entailment
λ=0.05	Two children re laying on a rug with some wooden bricks laid out in a square between them .	Two children are on a rug .	entailment
λ=0.1	Two children re laying on a rug with some wooden bricks laid out in a square between them .	Two children are on a rug .	entailment

(b) supervision of attention

	Premise	Hypothesis	Label
GROUNDTRUTH	Two children re laying on a rug with some wooden bricks laid out in a square between them .	Two children are on a rug .	entailment
HEURISTIC	Two children re laying on a rug with some wooden bricks laid out in a square between them .	Two children are on a rug .	entailment
Baseline	Two children re laying on a rug with some wooden bricks laid out in a square between them .	Two children are on a rug .	entailment
λ=0.01	Two children re laying on a rug with some wooden bricks laid out in a square between them .	Two children are on a rug .	entailment
λ=0.03	Two children re laying on a rug with some wooden bricks laid out in a square between them .	Two children are on a rug .	entailment
λ=0.04	Two children re laying on a rug with some wooden bricks laid out in a square between them .	Two children are on a rug .	entailment

(c) semi-supervision of attention

Fig. 3. Examples of attention maps on one of the e-SNLI entailment pair.

the model does the opposite and highlights more correct words by taking the risk of selecting more non-plausible words, thus increasing the false positive rate.

We further study the impact of the LSTM-based contextualization on plausibility. By stacking multiple layers of contextualization, a more semantically meaningful (or deeper) representation of each token can be obtained but also results in a uniform attention map across the entire sentence [8,9]. As regulariza-

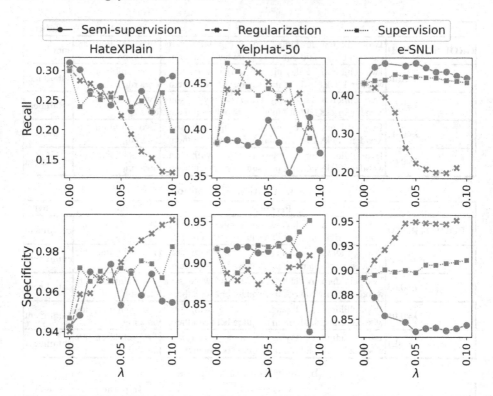

Fig. 4. Recall (top) and specificity (bottom) of attention map against annotation.

tion and semi-supervision can remove words from the attention map and make it sparse, we explore their potential to overcome the limitation of flat attention distribution in deeply contextualized models. Figure 5a reports results on the three tasks with one layer (in red (bullets)), three layers (green (crosses)), and five layers (blue (squares)) of bi-LSTMs contextualization, considering the three attention regularization strategies. Note that the scale of λ is different in each dataset. The effect of regularization depends on the task. In easy tasks (YelpHat), regularization does not yield improvement in plausibility. Surprisingly, the semi-supervision can actually improve in the case of the YelpHat corpus, overreaching supervision. In fact, the model's plausibility converges to the AURPC of the heuristic map (0.6546 in YelpHat-50 and 0.5224 for HateXPlain). Although semi-supervision can offer a stable solution in classification tasks, its utility in complex tasks such as NLI and HateXPlain requires careful design. Finally, deeper contextualization with several bi-LSTM layers makes it harder to obtain a plausible attention map, no matter the technique. This suggests that the contextualization by selectively keeping important features for classification suppressed other information that allow the attention layer to distinguish input tokens between them.

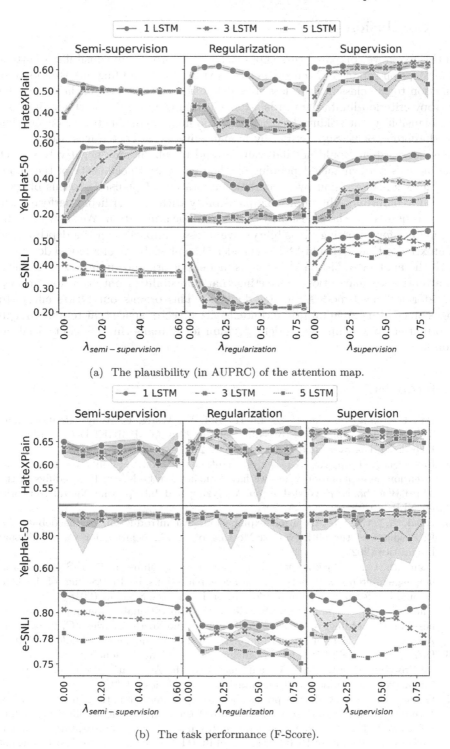

(a) The plausibility (in AUPRC) of the attention map.

(b) The task performance (F-Score).

Fig. 5. Plausibility and performance in 3 datasets, for 3 techniques, for 3 settings.

8   Conclusion

In this work, we compared three approaches to improve the plausibility of attention maps on top of RNN encoders at no extra cost, by adding an attention loss function to the classification loss. Regularization of the attention layer with an entropy criterion limits the words attended to in the model, marginally improving plausibility but risking the deletion of too many plausible tokens or focusing on the wrong ones. Supervision by human annotation encourages attention to focus on words it would not naturally attend to, but it may negatively impact the model's performance depending on the quality and peculiarity of the annotation. Semi-supervision by a heuristic annotation of plausible tokens offers a valuable compromise by improving plausibility without sacrificing performance, but it is limited by the plausibility of the heuristic annotation. We show that the techniques for enforcing plausibility have a lesser impact than the depth of the contextualization with a bi-LSTM encoder. The plausibility of a model decreases with the number of bi-LSTM layers as model performance improves, regardless of attention regularization, suggesting that plausibility from attention in deep transformer-based models remains doubtful. This orients our future efforts to focus on creating an appropriate contextualized vector space that retains enough information to explain the model's decision for humans through contextualization layers.

References

1. Bai, B., Liang, J., Zhang, G., Li, H., Bai, K., Wang, F.: Why attentions may not be interpretable? In: Proceedings of the 27th ACM SIGKDD Conference on Knowledge Discovery and Data Mining (2021)
2. Bastings, J., Filippova, K.: The elephant in the interpretability room: why use attention as explanation when we have saliency methods? In: Proceedings of the Third BlackboxNLP Workshop on Analyzing and Interpreting Neural Networks for NLP (2020)
3. Bibal, A., et al.: Is Attention explanation? An introduction to the debate. In: Proceedings of the 60th Annual Meeting of the Association for Computational Linguistics (2022)
4. Camburu, O.M., Rocktäschel, T., Lukasiewicz, T., Blunsom, P.: E-SNLI: natural language inference with natural language explanations. In: Proceedings of the 32nd Annual Conference on Neural Information Processing Systems (2018)
5. Chen, H., He, J., Narasimhan, K., Chen, D.: Can rationalization improve robustness? In: Proceedings of the 2022 Conference of the North American Chapter of the Association for Computational Linguistics: Human Language Technologies (2022)
6. DeYoung, J., et al.: ERASER: a benchmark to evaluate rationalized NLP models. In: Proceedings of the 58th Annual Meeting of the Association for Computational Linguistics. Association for Computational Linguistics (2020)
7. Duque-Arias, D., et al.: On power Jaccard losses for semantic segmentation. In: 16th International Conference on Computer Vision Theory and Applications (2021)
8. Ethayarajh, K.: How contextual are contextualized word representations? Comparing the geometry of BERT, ELMo, and GPT-2 embeddings. In: Proceedings of

the 2019 Conference on Empirical Methods in Natural Language Processing and the 9th International Joint Conference on Natural Language Processing (2019)

9. Fosse, L., Nguyen, D.H., Sébillot, P., Gravier, G.: Une étude statistique des plongements dans les modèles transformers pour le français. In: 29th Conference Traitement Automatique des Langues Naturelles (2022)

10. Gururangan, S., Swayamdipta, S., Levy, O., Schwartz, R., Bowman, S., Smith, N.A.: Annotation artifacts in natural language inference data. In: Proceedings of the 2018 Conference of the North American Chapter of the Association for Computational Linguistics (2018)

11. Jacovi, A., Goldberg, Y.: Towards faithfully interpretable NLP systems: how should we define and evaluate faithfulness? In: Proceedings of the 58th Annual Meeting of the Association for Computational Linguistics (2020)

12. Jain, S., Wallace, B.C.: Attention is not explanation. In: Proceedings of the 2019 Conference of the North American Chapter of the Association for Computational Linguistics. Minneapolis, Minnesota (2019)

13. Jia, W., Dai, D., Xiao, X., Wu, H.: ARNOR: attention regularization based noise reduction for distant supervision relation classification. In: Proceedings of the 57th Annual Meeting of the Association for Computational Linguistics (2019)

14. Lehman, E., DeYoung, J., Barzilay, R., Wallace, B.C.: Inferring which medical treatments work from reports of clinical trials. In: Proceedings of the 2019 Conference of the North American Chapter of the Association for Computational Linguistics (2019)

15. Luong, T., Pham, H., Manning, C.D.: Effective approaches to attention-based neural machine translation. In: Proceedings of the Conference on Empirical Methods in Natural Language Processing (2015)

16. Martins, A., Astudillo, R.: From softmax to sparsemax: A sparse model of attention and multi-label classification. In: Proceedings of the 33rd International Conference on Machine Learning (2016)

17. Mathew, B., Saha, P., Yimam, S.M., Biemann, C., Goyal, P., Mukherjee, A.: HateXplain: a benchmark dataset for explainable hate speech detection. In: Proceedings of the AAAI Conference on Artificial Intelligence (2021)

18. McGuire, E.S., Tomuro, N.: Sentiment analysis with cognitive attention supervision. In: Proceedings of the Canadian Conference on Artificial Intelligence (2021)

19. Mohankumar, A.K., Nema, P., Narasimhan, S., Khapra, M.M., Srinivasan, B.V., Ravindran, B.: Towards transparent and explainable attention models. In: Proceedings of the 58th Annual Meeting of the Association for Computational Linguistics (2020)

20. Nguyen, D.H., Gravier, G., Sébillot, P.: A Study of the plausibility of attention between RNN encoders in natural language inference. In: 20th IEEE International Conference on Machine Learning and Applications (2021)

21. Nguyen, D.H., Gravier, G., Sébillot, P.: Filtrage et régularisation pour améliorer la plausibilité des poids d'attention dans la tâche d'inférence en langue naturelle. In: Traitement Automatique Des Langues Naturelles (2022)

22. Nguyen, M., Nguyen, T.H.: Who is killed by police: introducing supervised attention for hierarchical LSTMs. In: Proceedings of the 27th International Conference on Computational Linguistics (2018)

23. Ousidhoum, N., Zhao, X., Fang, T., Song, Y., Yeung, D.Y.: Probing toxic content in large pre-trained language models. In: Proceedings of the 59th Annual Meeting of the Association for Computational Linguistics and the 11th International Joint Conference on Natural Language Processing (2021)

24. Paranjape, B., Joshi, M., Thickstun, J., Hajishirzi, H., Zettlemoyer, L.: An information bottleneck approach for controlling conciseness in rationale extraction. In: Proceedings of the 2020 Conference on Empirical Methods in Natural Language Processing (2020)
25. Pruthi, D., Gupta, M., Dhingra, B., Neubig, G., Lipton, Z.C.: Learning to deceive with attention-based explanations. In: Proceedings of the 58th Annual Meeting of the Association for Computational Linguistics (2020)
26. Sen, C., Hartvigsen, T., Yin, B., Kong, X., Rundensteiner, E.: Human attention maps for text classification: do humans and neural networks focus on the same words? In: Proceedings of the 58th Annual Meeting of the Association for Computational Linguistics (2020)
27. Serrano, S., Smith, N.A.: Is attention interpretable? In: Proceedings of the 57th Annual Meeting of the Association for Computational Linguistics (2019)
28. Sun, X., Lu, W.: Understanding attention for text classification. In: Proceedings of the 58th Annual Meeting of the Association for Computational Linguistics (2020)
29. Vashishth, S., Upadhyay, S., Tomar, G.S., Faruqui, M.: Attention interpretability across NLP tasks. CoRR (2019)
30. Wiegreffe, S., Marasović, A.: Teach me to explain: a review of datasets for explainable natural language processing. In: Proceedings of the Neural Information Processing Systems Track on Datasets and Benchmark, vol. 1 (2021)
31. Wiegreffe, S., Pinter, Y.: Attention is not not explanation. In: Proceedings of the 2019 Conference on Empirical Methods in Natural Language Processing and the 9th International Joint Conference on Natural Language Processing (2019)

Node-Weighted Centrality Ranking for Unsupervised Long Document Summarization

Tuba Gokhan$^{(\boxtimes)}$, Phillip Smith , and Mark Lee

University of Birmingham, Edgbaston, Birmingham B15 2TT, UK
txg857@alumni.bham.ac.uk, p.smith.7@cs.bham.ac.uk, m.g.lee@bham.ac.uk

Abstract. Supervised methods have demonstrated superior performance to unsupervised methods in text summarization. However, supervised methods heavily rely on human-generated summaries, which can be costly and difficult to obtain in large quantities. They also face challenges in summarizing long documents due to input length restrictions. Graph-based methods are frequently employed in unsupervised text summarization owing to their capacity to examine interrelationships between. However, these methods usually depend on unique node weights, resulting in limited mapping capabilities and weak performance on long documents. To address these difficulties, this study proposes an unsupervised method that employs a graph model with augmented node weights with a novel centrality ranking algorithm. Comprehensive experiments on standard datasets demonstrate the effectiveness of the proposed method, which outperforms both unsupervised and supervised techniques when evaluated using the ROUGE metric.

Keywords: SentenceBERT · Ranking · Sentence Centrality · Unsupervised · Latent Semantic Analysis · Sentence Feature Scoring

1 Introduction

The purpose of single-document summarization is to condense a text while retaining the most significant information that was presented in the original document [24]. Supervised neural network-based methods are successful in short document summarization, but they require large-scale, domain-specific training datasets [38] and have input length limitations [36]. Unsupervised extractive summarization methods can overcome these limitations as they do not require domain-specific training datasets and have fewer length limitations. To address these issues associated with long document summarization, unsupervised methods are being investigated in this paper. Unsupervised graph-based methods have become a widely used approach in text summarization, as they enable the exploration of complex interrelationships between textual components by creating graph representations, allowing for a comprehensive understanding of the

E. Métais et al. (Eds.): NLDB 2023, LNCS 13913, pp. 299–312, 2023.
https://doi.org/10.1007/978-3-031-35320-8_21

underlying content structure. In unsupervised graph-based methods for summarization, sentences are represented as nodes, and weighted edges indicate the degree of similarity between them. Centrality measures are commonly used for graph analysis, but in many cases, node weights are ignored due to the difficulty in identifying the mapping between node characteristics and values [33]. However, fully-weighted graphs that consider node weights can provide a more accurate analysis [33]. Centrality-based text summarization models rely on sentence similarity, but additional factors beyond similarity need to be considered to accurately determine sentence importance. A more comprehensive evaluation of the relationship between sentences and documents can improve centrality measures. In this paper, we argue that node-weighted graphs can enhance these measures.

Based on these findings, we propose a novel **No**de-**W**eighted Centrality **Ran**king (**NoWRANK**) approach for unsupervised graph-based long document extractive summarization. In our approach, we create an undirected fully weighted graph model for each document. First, to define augmented node weights (i.e., sentences) we use two well-known summarization methods on our two different models: Latent Semantic Analysis [9] and Sentence Feature Scoring [35]. Secondly, we employ Sentence-BERT [27] to better capture sentence meaning and compute sentence similarity and define the weight of edges. Finally, we apply our novel Node-Weighted Centrality Ranking method to the node-weighted graphs. NoWRANK is developed based on eigenvector centrality [28] by including node-weights. We evaluate our approach to the summarization of long scientific datasets from PubMed and arXiv [7]. Our experimental results demonstrate that our method outperforms earlier state-of-the-art unsupervised graph-based summarization algorithms and surpasses strong unsupervised baselines. In addition, our straightforward, unsupervised method also shows performance equivalent to that of state-of-the-art supervised neural models trained in large documents.

2   Related Work

Extractive summarization using graphs, where nodes represent text units and links show semantic similarity, has been used since the late 1990s [29]. The nodes are sentences or paragraphs of a document, and two nodes are linked if the respective text units shared a common vocabulary. In advanced techniques for unsupervised summarization, graph-based ranking algorithms are used to evaluate the importance of a sentence for inclusion in the summary. A document is shown as a graph whose nodes correspond to sentences and whose edges are weighted according to their similarity. The centrality of a node (i.e., sentence) can be determined by computing nodes degree or utilizing a ranking algorithm like PAGERANK [5].

TEXTRANK [21] is a popular method for extractive graph-based single-document summarization. It uses PAGERANK and a Markov chain model to calculate the importance of each node. PAGERANK gives relative scores to each node in the graph based on a basic cursive principle, which says that links to nodes with a high score add more to the score of the node in question. This is different from degree centrality, which only looks at local connections. While TEXTRANK calculates similarity by evaluating the co-occurrence of words with another well-known PAGERANK-based algorithm, LEXRANK [10] integrates TF-IDF values into the edge weights. PACSUM [38] present a graph method in which deep learning models are used to calculate sentence similarities, and similar to other studies, the PAGERANK algorithm is used to calculate sentence centrality and assumes that the relative location of two nodes influences the contribution of those nodes to their respective centrality. HIPORANK [8] enhances PACSUM by integrating hierarchical and positional information into the directed centrality algorithm. By incorporating a sentence-document weight, FAR [15] pays greater attention to a variety of factors. Hence the score for sentence centrality is increased by the weight.

3   Methodology

In this section, we present our methodology for long document extractive summarization by introducing a ranking algorithm and the calculation of node and edge weights for the proposed graph model.

3.1   Calculation of Node Weights

The proposed node-weighted graph model has been designed to enable easy integration with various approaches. The key aspect is to define the characteristic attributes of sentences in the document, which are distinct from similarity and can be measured through node weights. These characteristics can be evaluated in several ways. Our system applies a novel perspective by assigning node weights to two statistical text summarization methods, and evaluating their effectiveness.

Latent Semantic Analysis. The concept of employing Latent Semantic Analysis (LSA) for text summarization has been published by Gong & Liu [12]. Inspired by Latent Semantic Indexing, they used singular value decomposition to summarize generic text. Since then, various LSA-based summarizing techniques have been developed [2,6,13,14,25,34].

This study analyses a corpus using the LSA algorithm to identify node weights. The corpus is first parsed into individual sentences, and a term-document matrix is created that represents the frequency of each word in each sentence. Singular value decomposition (SVD) is then applied to the matrix to identify the most important relationships between words and sentences, and the dimensionality of the matrix is reduced to facilitate this identification.

Each sentence in the corpus is subsequently scored based on its similarity to the essential concepts or topics identified using the LSA algorithm. Sentences with the highest similarity to these concepts are regarded as the most important and are allocated higher scores. The sentences in the corpus are then ranked according to their scores, with the highest-scoring sentences being considered the most important. The values obtained from this process are then used to assign node weights. Figure 1(a) illustrates the node weights for a sample document.

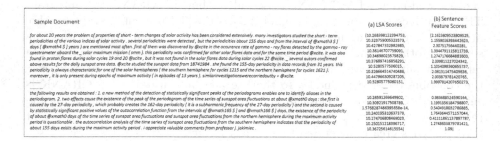

Fig. 1. A sample document fragments from arXiv dataset. (a) Node weight values based on LSA (b) Node weight values based on sentence feature scoring

Sentence Features Scoring. Sentence feature scoring is a commonly used method for summarization. While only the statistically obtained values are used in the summary in the early approaches, these features are included in the language models in the recent period [1,11,19,20,32].

In this study, we focus on four features selected for sentence scoring in text summarization - Sentence length, Sentence position, Proper nouns, and Numerical tokens - for capturing the salient information in a sentence and providing a good indication of its importance or relevance in the context of the corpus. Sentence length is a commonly used feature in text summarization, as it can indicate a sentence's complexity and level of detail. Longer sentences typically contain more information [32]. Sentence position is also crucial as sentences that appear at the beginning or end of a paragraph or section may be more significant or provide important contextual information [32]. Proper nouns and numerical tokens can also provide valuable information for summarization [35]. Proper nouns, such as names of people or places, can often indicate important entities or topics in the text. At the same time, numerical tokens can signify vital statistics or numerical data that may be key to understanding the content. This study combines these features, and the resultant values are assigned to serve as relevant node weights. Figure 1(b) shows the node weights for a sample document.

3.2   Calculation of Edge Weights

Our approach to text summarization is based on a graph-based model, in which the sentences of a document are represented as nodes, and edges capture the relationships between them. To measure the similarity between the sentences, we utilized various methods that can be integrated into our graph model. Specifically, we employed Sentence-BERT, a variant of the widely used BERT model that is pre-trained on sentence-level tasks. We can encode each sentence's semantic meaning using this method into a dense vector representation.

To determine the edge weights in our graph, we calculated the cosine similarity between each pair of sentence vectors. Cosine similarity is a commonly used metric in natural language processing that measures the similarity between two vectors and ranges from 0 (no similarity) to 1 (identical). Using an undirected graph, we assigned these values as the edge weights to construct the graph, allowing us to identify the most critical sentences in the document based on their relationships.

3.3   Ranking via NoWRANK

Eigenvector centrality [4], one of the most prevalent centrality metrics, offers advantages over other measures of centrality since it can evaluate a node's impact on a graph. Eigenvector centrality, which forms the basis of the PAGERANK [5] algorithm, is an extension of degree centrality. In degree centrality, the degree of a node is solely the total number of linked nodes, but eigenvector centrality takes into account both the total number of neighbouring nodes and the significance of the adjacent node. According to eigenvector centrality, not all connections are equal.

For a given weighted graph $G = (V, E)$ of nodes in V are connected by edges in E. Each edge e_{ij} connects nodes v_i and v_j with w_{ij}, where v_i and $v_j \in V$ and $e_{ij} \in E$. Every weighted graph has an associated adjacency matrix defined as:

$$A_{i,j} = \begin{cases} w_{ij} & \text{if node i is linked to node j} \\ 0 & \text{otherwise} \end{cases} \tag{1}$$

where A_{ij} is a symmetric NxN matrix, where N is the total number of nodes.

In this study, we introduce an innovative ranking approach for text summarization that enhances the efficacy of eigenvector centrality while overcoming its shortcomings. Eigenvector centrality is a potent method for determining the relative significance of nodes in a graph. However, it does not fully capture the intricacies of text summarization, where each node represents a sentence. Our approach tackles this issue by integrating the calculation of node weights, resulting in a more comprehensive solution for text summarization. Specifically, we integrate the node weights into the generation of the adjacency matrix in our method.

Given a document D, it contains a set of sentences $(s_1, s_2, ..., s_n)$. Graph-based algorithms treats D as a graph $G = (V; E)$ and $A = (a_{i,j})$ is the adjacency matrix. New formula for adjacency matrix calculation can be defined as:

$$a_{[i,j]} = e_{[si,sj]} + (v_{si} + v_{sj}) * k \tag{2}$$

where A_{ij} is a symmetric NxN matrix, N is the total number of nodes, k is constant value for normalization.

The relative Node-Weighted Centrality, score of vertex v can be defined as:

$$v_i = \frac{1}{\lambda} \sum_{j=1}^{N} A_{i,j} v_j \tag{3}$$

In the last step, we apply Eq. 2 and generate an adjacency matrix. The k value was set to 0.01. Next, we rank the sentences using Eq. 3 and determine the six most important sentences for long documents, and the three most important sentences for short documents that should be included in the summary.

4   Experimental Setup

In this section we assess the performance of NoWRANK on the document summarization. We first introduce the datasets that we used, then give our preprocessing and implementation details.

4.1   Summarization Datasets

For the purpose of validating the effectiveness of the proposed method on documents, we conduct experiments on four widely-used datasets gathered from numerous contexts.

CNN/DailyMail (CNN/DM) [31] and New York Times (NYT) [30] are the standard single-document datasets with manually-written summaries. According to Zheng and Lapata [38], some summaries are extremely short and formulaic for evaluating extractive summarization systems. We eliminate documents with summaries under 50 words to address this issue.

PubMed and arXiv [7] are two large-scale datasets of long and structured scientific articles that uses the abstract section as the ground-truth summary and the long body section as the document.

4.2   Implementation Details

The NLTK library [3] is employed in our experiments to utilize the nltk.tokenize and nltk.tag packages. The first step in constructing the graph is to determine the node weights. Our study employs two distinct graph models for this purpose. In the first model, we utilize the Latent Semantic Analysis (LSA) method described in Sect. 3.1 to define node weights. We have extended the LsaSummarizer method in the Sumy[1] library and have computed scores for each sentence, which are then assigned as node weights. In the second graph model, we have adopted the methodology proposed in [32] to calculate the node weights for each sentence based on its sentence position, length, proper noun, and numerical token values. The scores for each sentence are the summation of these values.

---

[1] https://pypi.org/project/sumy/.

We have calculated the edge weights, which indicate the similarity between sentences. We used the publicly available Sentence-BERT model *roberta-base-nli-stsb-mean-tokens*[2] to initialize our sentence embeddings for each dataset. This model transforms sentences into 768-dimensional dense vector representations. We have computed sentence similarities by measuring the Cosine Distance between the sentence embedding vectors.

5 Results and Analysis

5.1 Automated Evaluation

We use the ROUGE metric [16] for evaluation. ROUGE-1 and ROUGE-2 measure the unigram and bigram matches, ROUGE-L measures the longest common subsequence matches, between the candidate and the gold summary. The py-rouge package[3] is used to calculate these ROUGE scores. In Table 1, we compare our approach with previous unsupervised and supervised methods for long document extractive summarization.

Table 1. Test set results on the arXiv and PubMed datasets using ROUGE F1. Results are taken from [8,15] Underlined values indicate the highest values in supervised methods, and bold values indicate the highest values in unsupervised methods.

Category	Method	arXiv			PubMed		
		R-1	R-2	R-L	R-1	R-2	R-L
Upper Bound	ORACLE	53.88	23.05	34.90	55.05	27.48	38.66
Baselines	LEAD	33.66	8.94	22.19	35.63	12.28	25.17
	LEXRANK [10]	33.85	10.73	28.99	39.19	13.89	34.59
Supervised	SummaRuNNer [22]	42.81	16.52	28.23	43.89	18.78	30.36
	GlobalLocalCont [36]	43.62	17.36	29.14	44.85	19.70	31.43
	Sent-PTR [26]	42.32	15.63	38.06	43.30	17.92	39.47
Unsupervised	PACSUM [38]	39.33	12.19	34.18	39.79	14.00	36.09
	FAR [15]	40.92	**13.75**	35.56	41.98	15.66	37.58
	HIPORANK [8]	39.34	12.56	34.89	43.58	**17.00**	39.31
Current Work	NoWRANK$_{LSA}$	**43.05**	12.98	**39.27**	44.05	15.53	**41.92**
	NoWRANK$_{Sentence\_Feature}$	42.33	12.73	**40.54**	44.27	15.72	**43.51**

Upper bound and baseline techniques are included in the first block of both tables. ORACLE [22] can be seen as the upper bound of extractive models in which the baseline greedily extracts the sentences. ORACLE optimizes the ROUGE-L score in accordance with the gold summary. LEAD and LEXRANK [10] are strong unsupervised baselines. LEAD extracts the document's first k

---

[2] https://huggingface.co/sentence-transformers/roberta-base-nli-stsb-mean-tokens.
[3] https://pypi.org/project/py-rouge/.

Table 2. Test set results on the CNN/DM and NYT datasets using ROUGE F1. Results are taken from [8,15] Underlined values indicate the highest values in supervised methods, and bold values indicate the highest values in unsupervised methods.

Category	Method	CNN/DM			NYT		
		R-1	R-2	R-L	R-1	R-2	R-L
Upper Bound	ORACLE	52.59	17.62	36.67	61.63	41.54	58.11
Baselines	LEAD-3	40.49	17.66	36.75	35.50	17.20	32.00
	LEXRANK [10]	34.68	12.82	31.12	30.75	10.49	26.58
Supervised	EXTRACTION [37]	40.70	18.00	36.80	44.30	25.50	37.10
	REFRESH [23]	41.30	18.40	35.70	41.30	22.00	37.80
	BertExt [18]	43.25	20.24	39.63	–	–	–
Unsupervised	PACSUM [38]	40.70	17.80	36.90	41.40	21.70	37.50
	FAR [15]	40.83	17.85	36.91	41.61	**21.88**	37.59
	Liu et al. [17]	**41.60**	**18.50**	37.80	42.20	21.80	**38.20**
Current Work	NoWRANK$_{LSA}$	39.45	14.02	**39.13**	44.03	20.32	36.41
	NoWRANK$_{Sentence\_Feature}$	39.94	14.42	**39.58**	45.19	21.60	37.75

sentences to provide a summary. LEXRANK is the one of earliest approach to including graph structure in the summarization method. In the second block of each table, there are supervised neural extractive summarization methods.

We compare our method with SummaRuNNer [22], GlobalLocalCont [36], Sent-PTR [26] in Table 1, EXTRACTION [37], REFRESH [23], BertExt [17] in Table 2. Graph-Based unsupervised extractive summarization methods are presented in the third blocks of each table (See Sect. 2).

In the last blocks, we present an evaluation of NoWRANK. Our experimental results indicate that NoWRANK outperforms all other unsupervised graph-based methods by a substantial margin in terms of ROUGE-1,2,L F1 scores on both the arXiv and PubMed datasets (See Table 1). Additionally, our method achieves higher Rouge-L scores than the supervised methods in both datasets. However, our evaluation on short documents, Table 2, reveals that our methods are unable to achieve a level of performance that would have made a significant difference. This is because the node weight scores increase as the document length increases. Consequently, more weighted nodes lead to a higher sensitivity of the ranking algorithm, which ultimately improves the quality of the summarization. Our primary objectives are to highlight the significance of node weights in graph-based approaches and to develop an unsupervised model that is specific to the domain and applicable to long documents. In addition to meeting our objectives, our results demonstrate successful summarization of long documents in comparison to other state-of-the-art methods.

5.2   Sentence Position Distribution

We compare the position distribution of extracted sentences for PACSUM, HIPORANK, and ORACLE in order to further evaluate the performance of

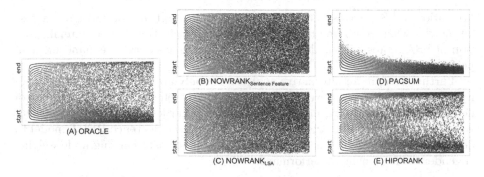

Fig. 2. The sentence position distribution of extracted sentences by different models on the PubMed validation set. On the x-axis, documents are ordered by article length, from shortest to longest.

NoWRANK on the PubMed validation dataset. The position distribution of extracted sentences is visualized in Fig. 2.

ORACLE is the upper bound for extractive summarization models. The ORACLE's summaries are generated by greedily selecting a subset of sentences in a document. As shown in Fig. 2, the ORACLE-selected sentences are distributed uniformly throughout all positions. The distribution of both NoWRANK generated summarization systems closely matches that of ORACLE. While PAC-SUM and ORACLE display a similar distribution in short documents, PACSUM focuses at the beginning of long documents. The similarity in distributions of sentence positions between our models and the ORACLE may explain how our model outperforms PACSUM. NoWRANK and HIPORANK have roughly similar distributions. Both models are quite comparable to ORACLE. The main difference is that as the document size enlarges, HIPORANK focuses on the beginning and ending parts of the document, while NoWRANK shows a homogeneous distribution regardless of size.

5.3 Ablation Study

Table 3. Ablation Study on PubMed and NYT test sets using ROUGE F1.

	PubMed			NYT		
	R-1	R-2	R-L	R-1	R-2	R-L
NoWRANK$_{Sentence\_Feature}$	44.27	15.72	43.51	45.19	21.60	37.75
NoWRANK$_{LSA}$	44.05	15.53	41.92	44.03	20.32	36.41
LSA	33.23	9.00	31.89	32.57	11.07	25.66
Eigenvector Centrality	43.99	15.54	41.90	42.84	19.02	35.02

Table 3 demonstrates an analysis of the contributions of our model's components on standard and long document datasets. The outcomes reveal that the exclusive utilization of LSA across both datasets leads to suboptimal performance across all metrics when compared to our proposed approach. However, the amalgamation of LSA scores with node weights results in a considerable enhancement in performance.

Furthermore, in an alternative analysis, we only applied eigenvector centrality, without taking node weights into account. In effect, with the removal of node weights, our ranking methodology can be regarded as equivalent to eigenvector centrality. In this experiment, we employed the Sentence-BERT model to determine edge weights. The findings demonstrate that discarding node weights engenders a decrement in performance.

5.4 Discussion

The present study is devoted to the extractive summarization of long documents, with the goal of achieving high-performance outcomes. However, it is worth noting that the same level of performance is not necessarily attainable in the case of short documents. This is due to the fact that node weights are assigned larger values in longer documents, thereby enhancing the sensitivity of the ranking algorithm and the quality of the summarization. Nonetheless, the method developed herein exhibits limitations in relation to light-weighted node ranking. To overcome this, more specialized techniques for ranking and scoring node weights will be explored in forthcoming research endeavors.

Moreover, when comparing our method with ORACLE, it becomes apparent that our sentence selection displays a relatively homogeneous distribution. This is partly attributable to our system's lack of section information, which constitutes a critical component of scientific documents. While section information has the potential to enhance the quality of summarization in scientific publications, the majority of corpora do not contain such data. To address this limitation, we intend to incorporate a section selection stage in future work, with the aim of accommodating diverse corpora.

6   Conclusion

This paper presents an unsupervised graph-based model for extractive summarization of long documents, with a focus on the importance of nodes in graph-based summarization. Specifically, we introduce a novel node-weighted graph model and a centrality ranking algorithm. To gauge the effectiveness of the ranking algorithm, we utilize two distinct node-weighted graph models. The proposed approach is systematically evaluated using lengthy documents sourced from PubMed and arXiv. The evaluation results demonstrate that our efficient unsupervised method surpasses the performance of prior unsupervised graph-based summarization models by significant margins, while achieving comparable performance to state-of-the-art supervised models.

In conclusion, there are still many opportunities for future research in this area that could build upon the findings of this study and contribute to a deeper understanding of text summarization. Moving forward, we aim to investigate the scalability of the proposed approach to larger datasets or longer documents, which could limit its practical application. Moreover, we intend to explore the feasibility of applying our approach to multi-document summarization and enhancing the representation of node-weights in the context of multi-documents.

Acknowledgments. The first author would like to acknowledge the Ministry of National Education of Turkey for the financial support of her research activity.

References

1. Abuobieda, A., Salim, N., Albaham, A.T., Osman, A.H., Kumar, Y.J.: Text summarization features selection method using pseudo genetic-based model. In: 2012 International Conference on Information Retrieval & Knowledge Management, pp. 193–197. IEEE (2012)
2. Babar, S., Thorat, S.: Improving text summarization using fuzzy logic & latent semantic analysis. Int. J. Innov. Res. Adv. Eng. (IJIRAE) **1**(4), 170-177 (2014)
3. Bird, S., Loper, E.: NLTK: the natural language toolkit. In: Proceedings of the ACL Interactive Poster and Demonstration Sessions, pp. 214–217. Association for Computational Linguistics, Barcelona, Spain, July 2004. https://aclanthology.org/P04-3031
4. Bonacich, P.: Factoring and weighting approaches to status scores and clique identification. J. Math. Sociol. **2**(1), 113–120 (1972). https://doi.org/10.1080/0022250X.1972.9989806
5. Brin, S., Page, L.: The anatomy of a large-scale hypertextual Web search engine. Comput. Netw. ISDN Syst. **30**(1), 107–117 (1998). https://doi.org/10.1016/S0169-7552(98)00110-X, https://www.sciencedirect.com/science/article/pii/S016975529800110X
6. Cagliero, L., Garza, P., Baralis, E.: Elsa: a multilingual document summarization algorithm based on frequent itemsets and latent semantic analysis. ACM Trans. Inf. Syst. (TOIS) **37**(2), 1–33 (2019)
7. Cohan, A., et al.: A discourse-aware attention model for abstractive summarization of long documents. In: Proceedings of the 2018 Conference of the North American Chapter of the Association for Computational Linguistics: Human Language Technologies, vol. 2 (Short Papers), pp. 615–621. Association for Computational Linguistics, New Orleans, Louisiana, June 2018. https://doi.org/10.18653/v1/N18-2097, https://aclanthology.org/N18-2097
8. Dong, Y., Mircea, A., Cheung, J.C.K.: Discourse-aware unsupervised summarization for long scientific documents. In: Proceedings of the 16th Conference of the European Chapter of the Association for Computational Linguistics: Main Volume, pp. 1089–1102. Association for Computational Linguistics, Online, April 2021. https://doi.org/10.18653/v1/2021.eacl-main.93, https://aclanthology.org/2021.eacl-main.93
9. Dumais, S.T., et al.: Latent semantic analysis. Annu. Rev. Inf. Sci. Technol. **38**(1), 188–230 (2004)

10. Erkan, G., Radev, D.R.: LexRank: graph-based lexical centrality as salience in text summarization. J. Artif. Intell. Res. **22**, 457–479 (2004). https://doi.org/10.1613/jair.1523

11. Fattah, M.A.: A hybrid machine learning model for multi-document summarization. Appl. Intell. **40**(4), 592–600 (2013). https://doi.org/10.1007/s10489-013-0490-0

12. Gong, Y., Liu, X.: Generic text summarization using relevance measure and latent semantic analysis. In: Proceedings of the 24th Annual International ACM SIGIR Conference on Research and Development in Information Retrieval, pp. 19–25 (2001)

13. Gupta, H., Patel, M.: Method of text summarization using LSA and sentence based topic modelling with Bert. In: 2021 International Conference on Artificial Intelligence and Smart Systems (ICAIS), pp. 511–517. IEEE (2021)

14. John, A., Premjith, P., Wilscy, M.: Extractive multi-document summarization using population-based multicriteria optimization. Expert Syst. Appl. **86**, 385–397 (2017)

15. Liang, X., Wu, S., Li, M., Li, Z.: Improving unsupervised extractive summarization with facet-aware modeling. In: Findings of the Association for Computational Linguistics: ACL-IJCNLP 2021, pp. 1685–1697. Association for Computational Linguistics, Stroudsburg, PA, USA (2021). https://doi.org/10.18653/v1/2021.findings-acl.147

16. Lin, C.Y.: ROUGE: a package for automatic evaluation of summaries. In: Text Summarization Branches Out, pp. 74–81. Association for Computational Linguistics, Barcelona, Spain, July 2004. https://aclanthology.org/W04-1013

17. Liu, J., Hughes, D.J.D., Yang, Y.: Unsupervised extractive text summarization with distance-augmented sentence graphs. In: Proceedings of the 44th International ACM SIGIR Conference on Research and Development in Information Retrieval, pp. 2313–2317. ACM, New York, NY, USA, July 2021. https://doi.org/10.1145/3404835.3463111

18. Liu, Y., Lapata, M.: Text summarization with pretrained encoders. In: Proceedings of the 2019 Conference on Empirical Methods in Natural Language Processing and the 9th International Joint Conference on Natural Language Processing (EMNLP-IJCNLP), pp. 3730–3740. Association for Computational Linguistics, Hong Kong, China, November 2019. https://doi.org/10.18653/v1/D19-1387, https://aclanthology.org/D19-1387

19. Luhn, H.P.: The automatic creation of literature abstracts. IBM J. Res. Dev. **2**(2), 159–165 (1958). https://doi.org/10.1147/rd.22.0159

20. Mendoza, M., Bonilla, S., Noguera, C., Cobos, C., León, E.: Extractive single-document summarization based on genetic operators and guided local search. Expert Syst. Appl. **41**(9), 4158–4169 (2014)

21. Mihalcea, R., Tarau, P.: TextRank: bringing order into text. In: Proceedings of the 2004 Conference on Empirical Methods in Natural Language Processing, pp. 404–411. Association for Computational Linguistics, Barcelona, Spain, July 2004. https://aclanthology.org/W04-3252

22. Nallapati, R., Zhai, F., Zhou, B.: Summarunner: a recurrent neural network based sequence model for extractive summarization of documents. In: Thirty-first AAAI Conference on Artificial Intelligence (2017)

23. Narayan, S., Cohen, S.B., Lapata, M.: Ranking sentences for extractive summarization with reinforcement learning. In: Proceedings of the 2018 Conference of the North American Chapter of the Association for Computational Linguistics: Human Language Technologies, vol. 1 (Long Papers), pp. 1747–1759. Association for Computational Linguistics, New Orleans, Louisiana, June 2018. https://doi.org/10.18653/v1/N18-1158, https://aclanthology.org/N18-1158

24. Nenkova, A., McKeown, K., et al.: Automatic summarization. Found. Trends® Inf. Retr. **5**(2–3), 103–233 (2011)

25. Ozsoy, M., Cicekli, I., Alpaslan, F.: Text summarization of Turkish texts using latent semantic analysis. In: Proceedings of the 23rd international conference on computational linguistics (Coling 2010), pp. 869–876 (2010)

26. Pilault, J., Li, R., Subramanian, S., Pal, C.: On extractive and abstractive neural document summarization with transformer language models. In: Proceedings of the 2020 Conference on Empirical Methods in Natural Language Processing (EMNLP), pp. 9308–9319. Association for Computational Linguistics, Online, November 2020. https://doi.org/10.18653/v1/2020.emnlp-main.748, https://aclanthology.org/2020.emnlp-main.748

27. Reimers, N., Gurevych, I.: Sentence-BERT: sentence embeddings using Siamese BERT-networks. In: Proceedings of the 2019 Conference on Empirical Methods in Natural Language Processing and the 9th International Joint Conference on Natural Language Processing (EMNLP-IJCNLP), pp. 3982–3992. Association for Computational Linguistics, Hong Kong, China, November 2019. https://doi.org/10.18653/v1/D19-1410, https://aclanthology.org/D19-1410

28. Ruhnau, B.: Eigenvector-centrality - a node-centrality? Soc. Netw. **22**(4), 357–365 (2000). https://doi.org/10.1016/S0378-8733(00)00031-9, https://www.sciencedirect.com/science/article/pii/S0378873300000319

29. Salton, G., Allan, J., Buckley, C., Singhal, A.: Automatic analysis, theme generation, and summarization of machine-readable texts. Science **264**(5164), 1421–1426 (1994)

30. Sandhaus, E.: The New York Times Annotated Corpus LDC2008T19. Linguistic Data Consortium, Philadelphia (2008). https://catalog.ldc.upenn.edu/LDC2008T19

31. See, A., Liu, P.J., Manning, C.D.: Get to the point: summarization with pointer-generator networks. In: Proceedings of the 55th Annual Meeting of the Association for Computational Linguistics (Volume 1: Long Papers), pp. 1073–1083. Association for Computational Linguistics, Vancouver, Canada, July 2017. https://doi.org/10.18653/v1/P17-1099, https://www.aclweb.org/anthology/P17-1099

32. Shirwandkar, N.S., Kulkarni, S.: Extractive text summarization using deep learning. In: 2018 Fourth International Conference on Computing Communication Control and Automation (ICCUBEA), pp. 1–5 (2018). https://doi.org/10.1109/ICCUBEA.2018.8697465

33. Singh, A., Singh, R.R., Iyengar, S.R.S.: Node-weighted centrality: a new way of centrality hybridization. Comput. Soc. Netw. **7**(1), 1–33 (2020). https://doi.org/10.1186/s40649-020-00081-w

34. Steinberger, J., Jezek, K.: Using latent semantic analysis in text summarization and summary evaluation. Proc. ISIM **4**, 93–100 (2004)

35. Suanmali, L., Binwahlan, M.S., Salim, N.: Sentence features fusion for text summarization using fuzzy logic. In: 2009 Ninth International Conference on Hybrid Intelligent Systems, vol. 1, pp. 142–146 (2009). https://doi.org/10.1109/HIS.2009.
36

36. Xiao, W., Carenini, G.: Extractive summarization of long documents by combining global and local context. In: Proceedings of the 2019 Conference on Empirical Methods in Natural Language Processing and the 9th International Joint Conference on Natural Language Processing (EMNLP-IJCNLP), pp. 3011–3021. Association for Computational Linguistics, Hong Kong, China, November 2019. https://doi.org/10.18653/v1/D19-1298, https://aclanthology.org/D19-1298

37. Xu, J., Durrett, G.: Neural extractive text summarization with syntactic compression. In: Proceedings of the 2019 Conference on Empirical Methods in Natural Language Processing and the 9th International Joint Conference on Natural Language Processing (EMNLP-IJCNLP), pp. 3292–3303. Association for Computational Linguistics, Hong Kong, China, November 2019. https://doi.org/10.18653/v1/D19-1324, https://aclanthology.org/D19-1324

38. Zheng, H., Lapata, M.: Sentence centrality revisited for unsupervised summarization. In: Proceedings of the 57th Annual Meeting of the Association for Computational Linguistics, pp. 6236–6247. Association for Computational Linguistics, Stroudsburg, PA, USA (2019). https://doi.org/10.18653/v1/P19-1628

Characterization of the City of the Future from a Science Fiction Corpus

Sami Guembour[1,2](✉) (iD), Chuanming Dong[1,3] (iD), and Catherine Dominguès[1,4] (iD)

[1] LASTIG, Univ Gustave Eiffel, ENSG, IGN, Paris, France
{sami.guembour,chuanming.dong,catherine.domingues}@ign.fr
[2] Université Paris Cité, Paris, France
[3] ADEME, Agence de l'Environnement et de la Maîtrise de l'Energie, Paris, France
[4] I-SITE FUTURE, Paris, France

Abstract. The article focuses on the characterization of the city of the future in a science fiction novel corpus, using natural language processing techniques and methods. It aims to analyze the images of the city through its elements (places, urban objects, etc.) and the functions associated with them. A terminological resource enables to identify the specific elements of the city.

Clustering algorithms and dimension reduction techniques are used iteratively to identify the elements of the city of the future, and their main functions based on the science fiction novels. The results show that, the city of the future, as the current one, is mainly concerned with mobility and dwelling.

Keywords: future urban · city · science fiction · corpus · clustering · dimension reduction · NLP

1 Introduction

The city concentrates a large number of current issues in connection with the lifestyles it promotes and climate change, and these issues are also relevant for questioning the city of the future. In this context, the PARVIS project[1] aimed to study images of the future city, in order to identify futuristic urban imaginations, particularly in the field of climate change. It was deployed through different research fields: literature, natural language processing, geography, architecture, music and sound creation, literary creation. Different modes of expression were explored and combined. The project also implemented a research-creation process which enabled the production of literary, sound, video and theatrical works.

This paper[2] is part of that project. It focuses on the analysis of the literary corpus defined within the framework of the project, using natural language pro-

---

[1] PARVIS is for **Paroles de villes** [Words from cities]; (https://parvis.hypotheses.org/).

[2] Additional information related to this article can be accessed at the following address: https://github.com/SamiGuembour/Characterization-of-the-city-of-the-future-from-Sci-Fi-corpus.

E. Métais et al. (Eds.): NLDB 2023, LNCS 13913, pp. 313–325, 2023.
https://doi.org/10.1007/978-3-031-35320-8_22

cessing tools and methods. It aims to characterize the city from the urban objects and elements it contains, and the urban and social functions of these objects and elements. The scale of urban objects is varied and the relation between objects and city can be direct: the city contains streets and buildings, or through several whole/part relations: a window is a part of a building which is a part of the city, the city therefore contains a window. In this article, in order to facilitate the reference of these urban objects and elements, they will be referred by OOC (as an abbreviation for *Object Of the City*).

Section 2 describes the construction of the corpus concerning the city in science fiction (sci-fi) imaginaries (named SciFiCityCorpus). The method for identifying OOCs and the urban and social functions associated with them in SciFiCityCorpus is described in Sect. 3. Finally, Sect. 4 presents some perspectives.

2   Construction of SciFiCityCorpus

Many sources of information are relevant to anticipate and imagine the city of the future. Within the framework of PARVIS, a corpus of novels has been compiled. The hypothesis is that, although authors and languages may differ one another, works are received, put into circulation, valued in a coordinated way by a community of sci-fi readers. The works thus make connections and exclusions, defining relevant traits and admitting continuities [1].

As these works are published, a sci-fi specific intertext has been made. Intertext is "the set of texts that the reader or writer can connect to the one in front of him or her, the set of texts that he or she can find in memory when reading a specific passage"[3] [10]. The genre of science fiction presents properties of serial literatures and is characterized by a "reading effect formulated by a community of readers, who identify, at one moment and one context, affinities between works, fictions, authors, themes, and who establish from then series between the latter and a labeling (a genre name) that constructs in turn, by recursive effect, a generic concept" (see footnote 3) [2]. The works thus make connections and exclusions, defining relevant traits and admitting continuities [1] that include recurrent concepts (for example: ansible, teleportation, cloning), technical objects (spacecraft, laser gun), places (Middle-earth in *The Lord of the Rings* by J. R. R. TOLKIEN, Aurora in ASIMOV's work), characters (androids, clones), tropes (intergalactic journey, duplicate of a living person, effective telepathy), etc. Thus it makes it possible to explain the presence of certain elements as well as their transformations, their deformations, their modifications.

Sci-fi is thus a cumulative genre where certain elements of the narratives can be shared by the authors of the genre [3]. This property legitimizes the approach of the article. The proposal consists in identifying the common characteristics of the city of the future in the sci-fi novel corpus.

PARVIS Corpus. The corpus of the PARVIS project aims to describe the city of the future in sci-fi literature and taking into account the imaginaries

---

[3] Translation by the authors.

related to climate disruption. It is characterized by these thematics: city and climate change. The cultural area of production of the PARVIS novels is North Western and in particular Franco-British-American. The corpus is the product of a research crossing the corpus of critical literature on climate fiction, various climate fiction lists produced by readers and consumers on cataloging media and the databases of the National Library of France[4]. The kept novels are those that make reference, from the diegetic, thematic and aesthetic points of view, to the two themes on which PARVIS focuses: the climatic issue and the urban issue. The corpus collection ends in 2020, to avoid adding works whose creation and production context was marked by the lockdown due to the COVID-19 pandemic. The starting point is 1961, the date of publication of *The Wind from Nowhere*, the novel by J.G. BALLARD, that inaugurates and illustrates the sub-genre of climate fiction (cli-fi), within the sci-fi genre. In the cli-fi novels, the Earth has been subjected to theogenic, xenogenic, geological, anthropogenic disturbances that the scientific and technical progress could not stop. These disturbances have caused floods, droughts, mega-fires, heat waves, ice ages, tornadoes or hurricanes, and have led to the setting up of violent, liberticidal or totalitarian dystopias.

All novels in the corpus[5] are in French, translated or written natively in this language. Table 1 describes the textometric characteristics of PARVIS corpus(see footnote 1).

SciFiCityLexicon. TOPALOV, urban planner and researcher, proposed in [4] a lexicon of the city. The lexicon gathers 533 words, mostly nouns, that designate OOCs divided into four themes: *Agglomération* [Urban area], *Circulation* [Mobility], *Division* [Division] and *Habitation* [Dwelling], a word can be associated with several themes, such as *ville* [city] which appears both in *Agglomération* and *Division*. However, not all the lexicon words are present in PARVIS corpus, only 183 words appear; we name SciFiCityLexicon the subset of the lexicon of the city that contains these 183 words.

SciFiCityCorpus. PARVIS corpus gathers sci-fi novels which address two issues: the city and/or climate change. However, the city is not an important element in all the novels. The researchers who collected and selected the novels in the corpus also annotated them with keywords, including *city*. However, this annotation is subjective and differs from one annotator to another. Therefore, a more objective and quantifiable criterion was sought. A terminology resource was therefore used to extract from PARVIS corpus the novels in which the city is an important background. The selection rule is as follows: a novel in PARVIS corpus is considered to describe the city of the future if it contains numerous and varied SciFiCityLexicon words.

However, some words in the SciFiCityLexicon are polysemous and their meanings in the novels are not all related to the city; for example, the word *cité* can have the lemma *cité* [city] which belongs to SciFiCityLexicon but also

---

[4] https://www.bnf.fr/fr.

[5] For a well-argued description, see the description made by Nadège Pérelle, (https://parvis.hypotheses.org/3400) from which the previous comments were extracted.

be the past participle of the verb *citer* [quote] which does not belong to the vocabulary of the city. Therefore, in a first step, all the occurrences of polysemous terms were disambiguated[6] in the PARVIS novel set.

The initial hypothesis assumes the cumulative construction of a set of notions shared by sci-fi novels, particularly in the description of the future city. Consequently, a novel that would contain many occurrences of the SciFiCityLexicon words through the massive use of a single word (or a small number of words) would not validate the selection criterion. Indeed, it would correspond to an a priori singular use, and thus not shared in the sci-fi intertext, of the corresponding concept(s).

Consequently, the selection of the SciFiCityCorpus novels is the result of a clustering (unsupervised learning) of the PARVIS corpus novels based on the SciFiCityLexicon word frequencies (disambiguated and lemmatized). The algorithm used for the clustering is Spherical K-means (which is, according to [6], the best suited for directional data) with 2 classes: novels that describe the city vs novels that do not. The results of the algorithm showed that 18 of the novels(see footnote 2) describe the city and form SciFiCityCorpus, and the other 113 are discarded. Finally, this method of clustering to identify the novels which describe the city was favored to the method of the topic modeling, because the emitted hypothesis consisted in considering that in these novels of science fiction, the city is not the main subject, but a frame in which the characters and the plot fit.

The SciFiCityCorpus numerical characteristics (see footnote 2) are reported in the Table 1. The 20 most frequent OOCs after disambiguation (see footnote 6) as shown in Fig. 1, are (in descending order of frequency): *porte* [door], *ville* [city], *lieu* [place], *maison* [house], *route* [road], *chemin* [path], *chambre* [room], *rue* [street], *passage* [passing], *zone* [area], *voie* [way], *cité* [town], *siège* [headquarter], *cercle* [ring], *camp* [camp], *place* [square], *tour* [tower], *pont* [bridge], *village* [village], *région* [region]. The OOCs are often places of zonal implantation: *marché* [market] or *place* [square], but not only; they can also refer to places of linear implantation: *chemin* [path] or architectural elements: *porte* [door]. They potentially carry diegetic elements of the future city in SciFiCityCorpus.

3   The OOCs and Their Functions Mentioned in SciFiCityCorpus

As the novels that describe the city have been identified through the SciFiCityLexicon words, we can assume that not all the lexicon words have the same weight in the clustering, and thus that not all the OOCs used in the novels

---

[6] The disambiguation of polysemous terms relies on CamemBERT [5]. It is based on classification of the context vectors of sentences containing an ambiguous word. Among the 20 most frequent OOCs in the corpus, 14 are polysemous. A classifier was created for each of the 14 ambiguous words and trained with sentences extracted from the corpus. The accuracies of the trained classifiers were all above 90%. The description of the disambiguation task is not part of this article.

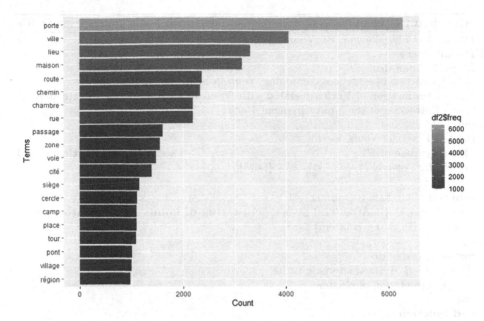

Fig. 1. The 20 most frequent OOCs in PARVIS corpus

Table 1. Textometric characteristics of PARVIS and SciFiCityCorpus corpuses

Indicators	PARVIS corpus	SciFiCityCorpus
#novels	131	18
#words	29 038 420	2 268 884
#sentences	1 056 287	153 131

have an equivalent importance in the description of the city of the future. The task now is to identify the OOCs that decide whether a novel belongs in the "sci-fi novel set in a city" class. This objective was translated into a co-clustering [7] (simultaneous unsupervised row and column clustering) of the novels and the SciFiCityLexicon words they contain (i.e., an array of (18 × 183)). Two clusters are built on the frequencies of the words (disambiguated and lemmatized) in the novels. The Fig. 2 shows a first cluster with 102 words having very low frequencies in the SciFiCityCorpus novels, and a second cluster that contains a set of 81 words with higher frequencies, which become discriminating.

The next step is to identify the functions associated with these OOCs. In linguistic terms, these are designated by nouns, and the functions by verbs such as *voyager* [travel]. The method developed aims to identify the verbs expressing actions and associated with the most frequently evoked OOCs; it is based on an iterative clustering (function CLUSTERING used twice), described in Algorithm 1.

Algorithm 1. Identification of verbs associated with nouns designating OOCs

Data: *SciFiCityCorpus*, 81 *Noun*
Result: *Verb*
foreach *Noun* **do**
  | - Extraction of sentences containing *Noun* in SciFiCityCorpus ;
  | - Identification of *Verb* associated with *Noun* ;   ▷ see: § **Syntactic parser**
  | - Extraction of the 5 most frequent *Verb* ;
end
result *R*1 : 81x5 (*Noun, Verb*) ;
 Interpretation of *R*1 ;   ▷ see: § **Interpretation of R1**
 result *R*2 : matrix (**Noun, *Verb* - {faire}) ;

function CLUSTERING(*matrix*) :
- n * *cluster* ← HCA(*matrix*) ; ▷ see: §**clustering of nouns by associated verbs**
- visualize (PCA(n * *cluster*)) ;
- $R' ← ∅$;
foreach *cluster* **do**
  | - $R' ← R' +$ {characteristic verbs} ;
  | - Interpretation of *cluster*
end
end function
Clustering (*R*2)   ▷ see: § **Noun clustering - first iteration**
result *R*3 : *R*2 - *R'*
Clustering (*R*3)   ▷ see: § **Noun clustering - second iteration**

Syntactic Parser: A synctactic dependency parser was used to identify the verbs linked to the OOCs. The parser is *DependencyParser*[7] which is compatible with Python and demonstrated efficiency in extracting actions related to pollution events [8].

The parser was applied to all sentences containing one of the 81 discriminating nouns . It takes as input a sentence, tokenizes it, and returns several features for each sentence token: the lemma, the label according to its part of speech (noun, verb, determiner, etc.), and the head (i.e. the word on which it depends syntactically).

The extraction of functions is performed by taking the lemmas of tokens having both the label "verb", and a discriminating OOC noun as head (i.e. the lemmas of verbs which have a syntactic dependence with a discriminating OOC noun). For example, for the sentence: *La porte s'ouvre mais l'homme refuse de sortir.* [The door opens but the man refuses to come out.], *porte* is a discriminating OOC noun, the parser indicates that *s'ouvre* has the label *verb* (lemma: *s'ouvrir*) and has *porte* as head; the conclusion is that *s'ouvrir* is a function associated with *porte*.

Interpretation of R1: R1 contains the nouns (OOCs) and the 5 most frequent verbs associated with each. The examination of these verbs shows that *faire*

---

[7] https://spacy.io/api/dependencyparser.

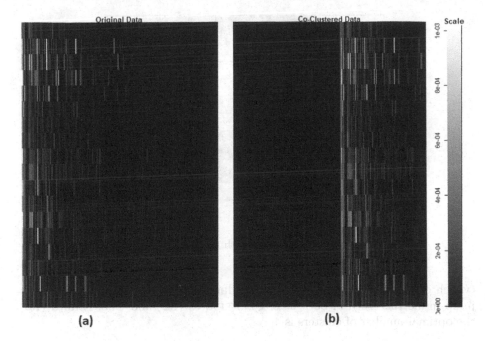

Fig. 2. (a): Original data matrix with novels on rows and SciFiCityLexicon words on columns, (b): checkerboard pattern in novels by SciFiCityLexicon word matrix obtained after performing co-clustering. The word frequency is represented by a scale on the right (higher frequency in white, and lower frequency in black). The blue line separates on the right the discriminating words (i.e. having a high enough frequency for the occurrences are visible and draw a clear bar) and on the left the others (i.e. non-discriminating because of low or null frequencies which draw invisible points). (Color figure online)

[do] is associated with a majority of nouns. Linguistically, this presence can be explained by its role as a support verb In these constructions, *faire* does not provide information on the action associated with the noun naming the OOC; so, *faire* has been removed from the verbs associated with the nouns. The resulting data structure is a matrix of 81 rows (the 81 discriminant OOC) and 5 columns (containing the 4 (if *faire* was part of the list) or 5 verbs most frequently associated with the noun).

This matrix was analyzed to classify the OOCs according to their functions. The verb *faire* was removed from the top 5 functions table (matrix) because of its predominant use (as a support verb).

Clustering of Nouns by Associated Verbs: The CLUSTERING() function applies to the matrix of verbs associated with nouns. The objective is to classify the nouns designating the OOCs according to the associated verbs (their functions). The clustering (unsupervised learning) is done using an Hierarchical Classification Algorithm (HCA) [9], using the package *Factominer* [11]. In the definition of HCA, the number of clusters is chosen using the elbow method

Verbs	Cluster 1	Cluster 2	Cluster 3	Cluster 4
avoir	-2.31	-4.97	0.896	6.35
abandonner	-1.11	-2.39	-1.53	4.85
quitter	0.781	-2.71	0.743	1.72
parcourir	2.9	-1.42	-0.904	0.243
traverser	6.51	-3.73	-1.04	0.233
envahir	2.9	-0.221	-0.904	-1.07
monter	-0.658	2.17	-0.904	-1.07
franchir	2.9	0.543	-1.3	-1.54
atteindre	4.02	-1.31	0.201	-1.71
trouver	-1.07	-4	8.33	-2.44

Fig. 3. Verb contributions for each cluster obtained by HCA

(which consists of taking the number of clusters corresponding to the greatest jump in inertias [13]); in both uses: CLUSTERING (R2) and CLUSTERING (R3), the optimal number of clusters is 4.

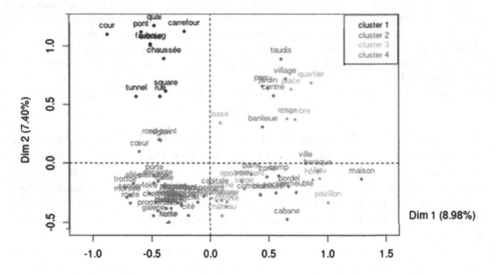

Fig. 4. Clusters of OOCs obtained by HCA (PCA visualization)

Noun Clustering - First Iteration: The R2 clustering enables a first organization of OOCs based on their associated verbs/functions. Figure 3 shows the verbs that characterize each cluster. In order to interpret the clusters obtained and to understand the relationships between the verbs that characterize each cluster, the clustering results were visualized in Fig. 4 through a Principal Component Analysis (PCA) [12]. It should be noted that the low sum of inertias of the first two axes does not affect the results obtained, since PCA was only used to visualize the clusters of OOCs.

Cluster 1 is characterized by the verbs *traverser* [traverse] (most important positive contribution), then *atteindre* [reach], *franchir* [cross], *parcourir* [travel], *envahir* [invade] which describe movement. They are associated with public places that are the origin, destination or steps of this movement, for example *tunnel*, *rue* [street], *pont* [bridge]. Their influence is limited by a border (named by nouns also included in this cluster): bord de *l'autoroute* [edge of the "highway"], bord du *faubourg* [edge of the "suburb"]. In cluster 3, *trouver* [find] concentrates almost all the positive inertia. The corresponding places: *forteresse* [fortress], *colonie* [colony], *château* [castle], *appartement* [apartment], *hôtel* [hotel] can be considered as a refuge. An interpretation could be that these refuge elements are the result of a (positive) search described in the novels. The cluster 4 is characterized positively (important contributions) by the verbs *avoir* [have] and *abandonner* [abandon] (where *abandonner* can be seen as a synonym for a negative form of *avoir*), and negatively by *trouver* [find]. The corresponding OOCs are thus evoked by their links of possession (or abandonment) with the protagonists of the novels; they do not have to be found, they are directly possessed or abandoned. They are public places (*ville* [city], *village*, *banlieue* [suburb], *parc* [park]) that are not owned but for which the verb *avoir* constructs a whole/-part relationship with other OOCs such as *banlieue* and *parc* which are part of *ville*. Other nouns name private places, which can be owned or abandoned: *maison* [house], *cabane* [cabin], *baraque* [shack], *ferme* [farm]. The cluster 2, weakly characterized by *monter* [mount] and groups OOCs that are not possessed, abandoned, found or reached (the verbs that characterize the other clusters) or/and are characterized by their height.

Verbs	Cluster 1	Cluster 2	Cluster 3	Cluster 4
suivre	-0,98	-1,11	-4,31	8,94
reprendre	-0,837	-0,949	-0,97	3,4
longer	1,03	0,784	-2,96	2,74
devoir	4,3	-0,534	-2,07	-0,471
regagner	-0,675	2,33	-0,782	-0,675
construire	6,23	0,332	-3,68	-0,837
dresser	7,64	-0,949	-3,68	-0,837
quitter	-1,11	8,94	-4,88	-1.11

Fig. 5. Verb contributions for each cluster obtained from HCA - 2nd iteration -

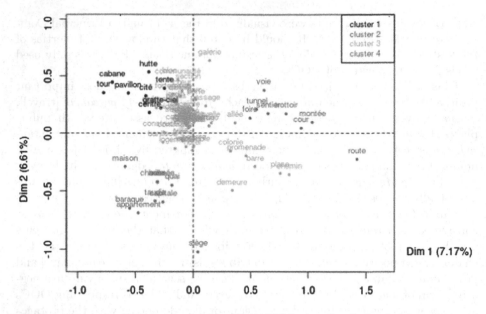

Fig. 6. Clusters of OOCs obtained by HCA (PCA visualization) - 2nd iteration -

Noun Clustering - Second Iteration: The first iteration of clustering enabled to identify and interpret the most characteristic functions (i.e. whose inertia is high, positive or negative) of the OOCs. The second iteration (function CLUS-TERING on the R3 matrix) aims to identify the second level functions, less frequent, but still recognizable once the most frequent functions have been eliminated. Figure 5 illustrates the verbs that characterize each cluster, and Fig. 6 shows the dispersion of OOCs from this second iteration of clustering. The cluster 4 is characterized (positive and significant contributions) by the verbs *suivre* [follow], *reprendre* [get back] and *longer* [go along]; this connotation of linear hold is confirmed by the nature of the cluster's (public) places: *voie* [way], *tunnel* [tunnel], *sentier* [trail], *route* [road], *trottoir* [sidewalk]. The verbs *quitter* [leave] and *regagner* [get back] are associated with cluster 2 they add a non-permanent temporal dimension to the stay actions performed in the places of the cluster, which can only be regained if they have been left. These places *maison* [house], *appartement* [apartment], *quai* [dock], *capitale* [capital], *taudis* [slum], *baraque* [hut], *siège* [seat] constitute the origins and destinations of movements. The grouping of OOCs in cluster 1 is guided by the verbs *construire* [build] and *dresser* [erect]. The OOCs in the cluster fall under the architectural theme; they are thus erected and built but also characterized by their lifespan: temporary and connoted to poverty as *hutte* [hut], *cabane* [cabin], *tente* [tent], or durable, monumental (in height) and symbols of wealth: *gratte-ciel* [skyscraper], *tour* [tower]. The last cluster (3) brings together OOCs that are not characterized in the corpus by their length, their border, their modes of access or intermittent stay.

A third iteration of noun clustering was performed by eliminating verbs that contributed in the clusters of the second iteration. The results of this clustering showed that in each cluster, all the verbs that characterize it have similar contributions that are not significantly high, indicating that no function is significantly associated with a cluster of OOCs. Consequently, this third iteration of clustering was not meaningful in the search for new functions of OOCs in the city of the future. As a result, it was decided to stop at only two iterations.

4 Conclusions and Prospects

This work provides a qualitative and quantitative representation of what human imagination thinks the city of the future should or would look like. A holistic end-to-end process has been described for identifying the features of the city of the future from the questions imagined and analysed by science fiction writers. As in any creative device, science fiction writers project their questions and interests into their literary works. These questions are therefore based on their direct human experience, on the social and political environment of their time and on their personal concerns and sensitivities.

The literary genre of science fiction is characterised by its fictional, poetic and cognitive codes. SUVIN defines sci-fi as *the literature of cognitive estrangement* [14]. Its generic specificity is based on the notion of *novum* [15] which consists in the use of an object, a phenomenon, etc. which is foreign to the experience and the encyclopaedic knowledge acquired by or accessible to the reader. And the invented word is considered as a trigger of estrangement[8] [16]. Consequently, places in the city would be imagined by the authors as novum and would be named by invented words. Invented words were identified using Unitex [18] software in the following way: words unknown to the general language dictionaries provided by the tool are considered invented. Only words whose initial is not capitalized were taken into account since the OOCs searched are generic (those whose initial is capitalized were considered a priori as proper names). Their frequency has been computed. The frequency of the most frequent unknown word (*fourmite* in *Exodes* by J.-M. Ligny) has been compared with the discrimant OOC whose frequency is the lower. Its frequency is lower, which means that even if *fourmite* designated a place (in fact, it designates an animal), it could not have been considered as discriminating.

The SciFiCityLexicon words are divided into four themes (p. 3). In Sect. 3, the results of the co-clustering show that 81 OOCs are discriminating. 57 of them belong to the themes of *Circulation* [Mobility] and *Habitation* [Dwelling], i.e. more than 70%. This allows us to conclude that when the city is evoked in SciFiCityCorpus, it is done so through the vocabulary, and thus the themes of mobility (*rue* [street], *pont* [bridge], *chemin* [path]) and dwelling (*maison* [house], *tente* [tent], *chambre* [bedroom]).

In both levels of clustering, mobility and dwelling are the most evoked city themes in the novels through a vocabulary that can be interpreted as the quest

---

[8] Other estrangement clues are analysed in [17].

for a place of refuge (fortress, castle, colony, etc.) where the quest may be eventful (to cross, reach, travel, invade, etc.) and renewed (to leave, get back).

These preoccupations differ little from those of the current citizens except that, for the latter, the refuge is more often an apartment. A notable difference lies in a type of settlement: the colony, which is frequently mentioned in SciFiCityCorpus. The term may refer to the theme shared by many works of sci-fi where it is about leaving the Earth to implant a human colony on another planet. In the contexte of cli-fi narratives, it can also refer to the type of settlement of people forced to leave their homes which have become uninhabitable. The habitat is evoked in a contrasting way; *huts*, *tents*, *cabins* evoke lack of security and poverty of people fleeing the city; they co-occurrence and contrast with non-precarious housing as *towers* and *skyscrapers* which connote wealth and technical prowess.

One of the limitations of this work is the exclusion of predicative nouns[9] which can express functions too. Taking them into account could modify the most frequent functions associated with OOC.

The analysis did not show the appearance, nor the reuse in the whole corpus, of new places or new functions that would be mandatory to describe the city of the future. A study with the same tools and methods but limited to a corpus characterized by its narrative unity, *Tetralogy Of Transformation*[10] by J.G. BALLARD, is in progress and will enable to validate this working method, in a complementary way to this work.

Acknowledgements. This work was supported by I-SITE FUTURE (http://www.future-isite.fr/accueil/?L=0) within the PARVIS project framework (2019–2022, https://parvis.hypotheses.org/a-propos).

The authors would like to thank the reviewers who helped improve the quality of this paper.

References

1. Broderick, D.: Reading by Starlight: Postmodern Science Fiction, First edition in 1995 ed. Routledge, Abingdon (2005)
2. Letourneux, M.: Fictions à la chaîne - Littératures sérielles et culture médiatique, Média Diffusion, Paris, France (2017)
3. Sadoul, J.: Histoire de la science-fiction moderne 1911–1984. Robert Laffont, Paris, France (1984)
4. Topalov, C., de Lille, L.C., Depaule, J.-C., Marin, B.: L'aventure des mots de la ville. Robert Laffont, Paris, France (2010)
5. Martin, L., et al.: Camembert: a tasty french language model, arXiv preprint arXiv:1911.03894 (2019)
6. M. Ait-Saada, F. Role, M. Nadif, Classification non supervisée de documents à partir des modèles transformeurs, Revue des Nouvelles Technologies de l'Information Extraction et Gestion des Connaissances, RNTI-E-38, pp. 331–338 (2022)

---

[9] A predicative noun associated with a support verb has the same meaning as the predicate as in *to have a travel* and *to travel*.

[10] *The Wind from Nowhere* (1961), *The Drowned World* (1962), *The Burning World* (1964) and *The Crystal World* (1966).

7. Bhatia, P., Iovleff, S., Govaert, G.: Blockcluster: an R package for model based co-clustering. J. Stat. Softw. **76** (2014). https://doi.org/10.18637/jss.v076.i09

8. Dong, C., Gambette, P., Dominguès, C.: Extracting event-related information from a corpus regarding soil industrial pollution. In: KDIR 2021, volume 1 of 13th International Conference on Knowledge Discovery and Information Retrieval, SciTePress, Setúbal, Portugal, 2021, pp. 217–224 (2021). https://hal.archives-ouvertes.fr/hal-03366097. https://doi.org/10.5220/0010656700003064

9. Gao, X., Wu, S.: Hierarchical clustering algorithm for binary data based on cosine similarity. In: 2018 8th International Conference on Logistics, Informatics and Service Sciences (LISS), 2018, pp. 1–6 (2018). https://doi.org/10.1109/LISS.2018.8593222

10. Riffaterre, M.: L' intertexte inconnu. In: Littérature, JSTOR, 1981, pp. 4–7 (1981)

11. Lê, S., Josse, J., Husson, F., et al.: Factominer: an R package for multivariate analysis. J. Stat. Softw. **25**, 1–18 (2008)

12. Abdi, H., Williams, L.J.: Principal component analysis. WIREs Comput. Stat. **2**, 433–459 (2010). https://wires.onlinelibrary.wiley.com/doi/abs/10.1002/wics.101

13. Zambelli, A.: A data-driven approach to estimating the number of clusters in hierarchical clustering, F1000Research, no. 5 (2016). https://doi.org/10.12688/f1000research.10103.1

14. Suvin, D.: On the poetics of the science fiction genre, JSTOR (1972)

15. Suvin, D.: Pour une poétique de la science-fiction: études en théorie et en histoire d'un genre littéraire, Presses de l'Université du Québec (1977)

16. Langlet, I.: La science-fiction: lecture et poétique d'un genre littéraire, Armand Colin (2006)

17. Huz, A.: Démêlés avec le novum: démontages et remontages de la notion dans une perspective culturelle intermédiatique, ReS Futurae. Revue d'études sur la science-fiction (2020)

18. Paumier, S., et al.: UNITEX 3.3 User Manual (2021). https://hal.archives-ouvertes.fr/hal-03589580

On the Rule-Based Extraction
of Statistics Reported in Scientific Papers

Tobias Kalmbach$^{(\boxtimes)}$, Marcel Hoffmann$^{(\boxtimes)}$ iD, Nicolas Lell$^{(\boxtimes)}$ iD,
and Ansgar Scherp$^{(\boxtimes)}$ iD

Universität Ulm, Ulm, Germany
{tobias.kalmbach,marcel.hoffman,nicolas.lell,ansgar.scherp}@uni-ulm.de

Abstract. The identification and extraction of statistics in scientific papers as nested entities is an indispensable feature for analyzing scientific papers at a large scale. STEREO is a tool for extracting statistics from scientific papers using a set of regular expressions. Key feature of the tool is that it supports statistics reported in American Psychology Association (APA) style, as well as non-APA style such as only a reported p-value. The original STEREO rule set has been extensively trained in the life sciences domain using preprints of the CORD-19 dataset. We analyze this rule set with its hundreds of regular expressions using a regular expression inclusion algorithm. We transfer the condensed rule set to papers in the domain of Human-Computer-Interaction (HCI). Our experiments show that only 13 new R^+ rules and 77 new R^- rules are needed to conduct this transfer. A higher percentage of APA-conform statistics were found in the HCI domain (26%) compared to the life sciences domain (only 1.8%). We compare the statistics extraction from PDFs vs. LaTeX source files, finding the latter more reliable.

An extended version with detailed examples is provided on arXiv [11] and the source code is here: https://github.com/Tobi2K/statistics-extraction.

Keywords: statistics extraction · nested entities · regular expressions

1 Introduction

An abundance of scientific papers are published daily. The large and rapidly growing number of papers is too extensive to scan manually. In particular, assessing the published results in terms of insights generated by the statistical analyses such as significance tests is very challenging. A quick overview of the statistics in a paper can also be useful for the authors to find statistical errors in their studies, i.e., to verify and check them. Moreover, extracting sentences containing statistics together with metadata (authors, title, etc.) can enable researchers to get an impression of an article without the need to read it. Tools like *statcheck* [16] provide very accurate extraction of statistics reported in accordance with the commonly used writing style guide of the American Psychology Association

© The Author(s), under exclusive license to Springer Nature Switzerland AG 2023
E. Métais et al. (Eds.): NLDB 2023, LNCS 13913, pp. 326–338, 2023.
https://doi.org/10.1007/978-3-031-35320-8_23

(APA) [2]. However, previous research found less than one percent of APA-conform statistics in a sample of $113,000$ statistics extracted from pre-prints in the life sciences [7]. In this work, we extend STEREO (STat ExtRaction Experimental cOnditions) [7], an automatic statistics extraction pipeline for statistics presented in APA as well as non-APA notation.

STEREO learns regular expressions (rules) to decide whether a sentence contains statistics (R^+ rules) or not (R^- rules) using active wrapper learning. The R^+ rules are used to extract the statistic's type and values. During the application of STEREO on the life sciences dataset CORD-19 [20] containing preprints of papers about the corona virus and related viruses, a total of 85 R^+ rules for statistics detection (with 52 sub-rules for value extraction) and $1,425$ R^- rules were learned. Inspecting these rules shows that rules, which were added later in the learning process, generalize better and previously added rules become obsolete.

Reducing the number of rules can help to identify common patterns of non-APA statistics, e.g., incomplete reporting, and derive recommendations to improve statistics reporting. Subsequently, general rule patterns that indicate a sentence does not contain a statistic can serve as guidance for future active wrapper approaches. One can make use of these general rule patterns to avoid creating excess rules. Following this reasoning, we apply a DFA-based (Deterministic Finite Automaton) algorithm introduced by Chen and Xu [5] to minimize the existing set of regular expressions.

We transfer STEREO to a new scientific domain, namely Human-Computer-Interaction (HCI), to investigate the generalization of the STEREO rules and potentially find new rules for statistics extraction. This includes finding uncovered statistic types and other non-APA conform reporting of statistics. We further extend the STEREO rules from text to also support statistic extraction from LaTeX files. In summary, this work makes the following contributions:

- We analyze the extraction rules from STEREO and achieve a rule set reduction of 34%, which results in 31% less runtime needed to apply the reduced rule set compared to the full rule set.
- We extend the rule set by repeating the active wrapper learning from STEREO on the HCI domain, adding 13 new R^+ rules and 77 R^- rules.
- Using the new rule set, we identify that 26% of all statistics extracted from HCI preprints are in APA style, while in the life sciences domain we found only 1.8% of statistics to be conform to APA.
- We compare the extraction from LaTeX versus PDF files. The extraction precision is high in both cases. However, we miss 20% of the statistics in PDF due to transformation errors from PDF to text.

Below we discuss related work on statistics extraction and regular expression inclusion. Section 3 presents the experimental apparatus. The results are reported in Sect. 4 and discussed in Sect. 5, before we conclude.

2 Related Work

Statistics Extraction. Statistic extraction poses several challenges like different writing styles or usage of number separators and might even require to parse formulaic expressions [9]. Teja et al. [12] presented a regular expression-based approach to extract statistics from scientific papers. They use a single regular expression to match the p-value per statistical test. For example, a regular expression to match a t-test is `t(df)=float, p (<, >, =) float`. A similar approach is pursued by *statcheck* [16], an R package that allows to extract and verify the consistency of statistics reported following APA guidelines. If all information required by APA is provided, e.g., the p-value and degrees of freedom, statcheck can check if the reported statistics is plausible. Recomputing the statistics is not possible since this would require access to the raw data. Schmidt [19] disputed the effectiveness of *statcheck*. They criticize the testing conducted in the *statcheck* authors' follow-up paper [15]. Schmidt [19] argues that *statcheck* simply does not detect many reported statistics due to the strong assumption that they must be reported following APA. This questions the overall performance of *statcheck*, even though it is widely used [8,17,18].

The approaches by both Nuijten et al. [16] and Teja et al. [12] are limited to only match APA-style statistics. Böschen [3] presented a text-mining approach on XML documents. They differentiate between computable results, where the p-value is given and can be recalculated; checkable results, where the p-value is not given but can be calculated; and uncomputable results, where the p-value cannot be calculated due to some information missing. The extraction algorithm by Böschen [3] works as follows: Sentences are only selected if they contain at least one letter, followed by an operator ($<, >, =, \leq, \geq$), which in turn is followed by a number. Surrounding text is removed using regular expressions. Individual heuristics are applied to extract the recognized test statistics, the operator, degrees of freedom, and p-value to cope with varying reporting styles. As the requirements are not as strict as *statcheck*'s, Böschen [3] generally finds more statistics. STEREO [7] uses active wrapper learning to learn regular expressions (rules) that determine whether or not a sentence contains statistics. The rules are divided into R^+ rules that match statistics and R^- rules that denote that a sentence does not include statistics. R^+ rules have additional sub-rules, which are used to capture specific parts of the statistic (e.g., the p-value) after the statistic type has been identified by the main R^+ rule. During the active wrapper learning, every sentence that does not contain a number is ignored. For any remaining sentences not matched by any rules, the user is prompted to create a new rule to cover the new case. STEREO achieved a precision close to 100% for APA-conform statistics and 95% for non-APA statistics on the CORD-19 dataset.

Rule Set Inclusion Algorithms. Regarding regular expression inclusion, i.e., minimal rule set computation, many algorithms are limited to determining inclusion using one-unambiguous regular expressions. One-unambiguous regular expressions [4] are a subset of regular expressions that can match every word (in their respective language) in a unique way without looking ahead. For example, $(a_1|b_1)^*(a_2|\epsilon)$ (numbered for clarity) is not one-unambiguous, as the word baa can be formed as $b_1a_1a_1$ or $b_1a_1a_2$. However, $(a|b)^*$ describes the same language but is one-unambiguous. Chen and Xu [5] presented two algorithms for regular expression inclusion. The first is an automata-based algorithm that converts the given one-unambiguous regular expressions into Deterministic Finite Automatons (DFAs) and subsequently checks the created DFAs for inclusion. The second algorithm is a derivative-based algorithm. Derivatives of regular expressions are sub-expressions, which are valid regular expressions themselves. The idea is that if an expression A is included in an expression B, all derivatives of A are also derivatives of B. The algorithm generates all derivatives of both expressions. If all derivatives of one expression are included in the other, the first expression is included in the second. Nipkow and Traytel [14] presented a framework to determine if two given regular expressions are equivalent. Equivalence is a stricter requirement than the inclusion of Chen and Xu [5]. The framework dynamically creates an automata from one regular expression and uses "computations on regular expression-like objects" [14, p. 2] as a substitute for the traditional transition table. Hovland [10] presented an approach that uses an inference system instead of automata to inductively determine a binary relationship between one-unambiguous regular expressions. The algorithm guarantees polynomial runtime, which can be slower than the quadratic runtime of Chen and Xu [5].

3   Experimental Apparatus

Datasets. We have two types of datasets: The original rule set from STEREO and the scientific papers in life sciences and the new HCI domain.

STEREO's rule set for the life sciences was created using the COVID-19 Open Research Dataset (CORD-19). We apply minimal rule set analysis on this dataset. The dataset consists of $1,510$ manually created rules, divided into 85 R^+ and $1,425$ R^- rules. Each rule has an incremental ID (determined at the time of creation) and its corresponding regular expression. Implicitly, a higher rule ID means that the rule has been added later in the process of applying the active wrapper. We assume that it is unlikely that the 85 R^+ rules can be optimized greatly, as these rules are designed to match specific information present in the reporting of a statistics. This makes it unlikely that one R^+ rule is included in another. However, the $1,425$ R^- rules can be optimized to improve runtime performance as well as maintainability by revealing common patterns used to identify sentences as non-statistic.

The pre-print papers in life sciences and HCI: The COVID-19 Open Research Dataset [20] is the original dataset used in STEREO that can be used to evaluate the minimal rule set. This dataset contains 110,427 papers provided in JSON-format on COVID-19, SARS-CoV-2, and all corona viruses in general. In STEREO, the date of access is given as 21st September 2020. The CORD-19 dataset version 52^1, which we use for comparison, is a close match. Note, that our version of the dataset is slightly newer and contains a few more papers than the version used in STEREO. Thus, we rerun the experiments of the original paper for a fair analysis of the rule set.

The arXiv Dataset [6] has over 1.7 million STEM papers.[2] It includes metadata like author, category, etc. We filter for HCI, which studies the use of technology, focusing on the interface between people and computers [13]. HCI is a strong domain for publishing studies and the corresponding statistics. There are $9,730$ papers tagged with the "cs.HC" (HCI tag on arxiv.org) category. We only use papers with HCI as primary tag. For a fair comparison of the statistics extraction on PDF and LaTeX, we only use papers that are provided in both formats. With these restrictions, $4,023$ papers remain.

Preprocessing. For the rule set inclusion, we transform the regular expressions provided by STEREO from the original Python format into a formal representation that is required for the inclusion algorithm of Chen and Xu [5]. For the transfer of STEREO's rules from the life sciences to HCI, we parse the content to plain text while removing all `table`, `figure`, `lstlisting`, and `tikzpicture` environments. As in STEREO, line breaks are removed and the plain text is split into sentences using the regular expression `\.\s?[A-Z]`. Every sentence that does not contain a digit is removed. The corresponding PDF files are converted to raw text using *pdftotext*[3]. Then the same processing (line breaks, split sentences, keep numbers) is applied. This results in $9,393,662$ sentences for the CORD-19 dataset and $222,544$ sentences for the HCI domain.

Procedure. We compute the minimal set of R^+ and R^- rules on the STEREO rule set for life sciences using the M_{E_1}-directed version of the algorithm from Chen and Xu [5]. Although the runtime of this algorithm is quadratic in length of the expressions, it is sufficient as our regular expressions are usually short (<100 characters) resulting in a good trade-off between runtime and effort to implement it. We do a pairwise comparison of the rules in the set. A rule that is already covered by some other rule is removed.

We randomly sample two times 200 papers (about 5% of all papers) from the $4,023$ papers in the HCI dataset, one sample contains LaTeX the other PDF files. On these samples, we repeat the active wrapper induction from STEREO to learn new rules for the extraction of statistics from HCI papers. Specifically, we split the input into sentences and STEREO checks for every digit in the sentence if it is covered by an existing rule. In case of any uncovered digit, the active learning approach of STEREO prompts a user interface and asks an expert to add a new R^+ or R^- rule, based on whether the sentence contains statistic or not. Each new rule is assigned an incremental ID. This step produces our new rules that are added to the STEREO rule set. As we use new input formats,

---

[1] (publication: 2020-09-21, accessed: 2022-07-11) https://www.kaggle.com/datasets/ allen-institute-for-ai/CORD-19-research-challenge/versions/52.

[2] https://www.kaggle.com/datasets/Cornell-University/arxiv (2022-07-11).

[3] https://pypi.org/project/pdftotext/.

i.e., LaTeX versus PDF, this results in new, format-specific rules. The goal is to further improve the robustness and completeness of the extraction.

Finally, we evaluate the precision for every statistic type following the evaluation procedure of STEREO [7]. We extract all sentences from all papers in the respective corpus that are matched by R^+ rules. We then sample 200 sentences for every statistic type, or use all extracted sentences if there were fewer than 200 extractions, to manually check if the statistic types are matched and extracted correctly. We also measure the difference in APA versus non-APA reporting. Furthermore, we extract 200 sentences matched by R^- rules from random documents, which we did not use for rule learning. This is to test whether R^- rules do not reject statistics, i.e., we have false negatives. Lastly, we extract 200 sentences that were neither matched by any R^+ nor R^- rule to check for unrecognized statistics or data format transformation errors, i.e., errors that were introduced when transforming a paper from the input format (e.g., PDF) to plain text [7].

Measures. For the rule set inclusion, we measure runtime and number of included rules per rule. Furthermore, we check that the reduced and the original rule set cover the same sentences. Finally, we compare the time required to match 200 sentences with the original rule set versus the reduced R^- rule set.

For the experiments on comparing statistics extraction in HCI versus life sciences and from LaTeX versus PDF files, we use precision of the extraction. We calculate it on 200 rules per statistic type or the maximum amount when there are less than 200 extractions.

4   Results

Rule Set Inclusion. After running the rule inclusion algorithm for the R^- rules, 483 unique rules out of the total 1,426 rules were included by others. This is a reduction of 33.8%. 1,253 rules included no other rules, 83 included one, and 28 included two rules. However, the analysis also revealed that 13 rules included more than 20 rules, and 4 had more than 100 rules included. These rules can be seen in Table 1. Naturally, some rules were included more than once. Figure 1a shows how often rules were included in other rules. The rule `figure \d{1,2}` was the most included one with 14 inclusions, and `table \d+` was the second-most included rule with 13 inclusions.

We show the included rules sorted by rule ID (grouped in hundreds) in Fig. 1b. The ID of each rule reflects when it was created in the active wrapper process, i.e., rules with lower IDs were created earlier than rules with higher IDs. We observe that many rules that were included by others had a rule ID between 400 and 700. Furthermore, approximately 47% of included rules had an ID below 500 and 88% had an ID below 1,000. In general, lower ID rules are included in higher ID rules.

We also ran the inclusion algorithm on the R^+ rules to double check whether optimization is possible. We observe that one rule was removed. This inclusion

332   T. Kalmbach et al.

Table 1. R^- rules sorted in descending order by the number of included rules and having more than 50 inclusions.

Regular Expression	# included rules
`[a-zA-Z]{3,}\s?\d+[\.\,\s\dabcdef]*`	173
`[a-zA-Z]{2,}\s?\d+(\.\d)?`	173
`[a-zA-Z]{3,}\s?\d+[\.\,\s\d]*`	171
`[a-zA-Z]{3,};?\s?\d+`	130
`[a-zA-Z"]+\s?\d{1,3}$`	83
`[a-zA-Z]{3,20}\s\d+(\,\d+)*(\.\d+)?`	72
`[a-zA-Z]{3,20}\d+`	71
`[a-zA-Z]{3,}\s-?\d+(\.\d+)?`	62
`\d+(\,\d+)*(\.\d+)?\s[a-zA-Z]{3,10}`	51

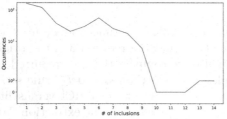

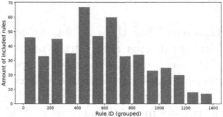

(a) Number of times a rule was included by other rules.

(b) Amount of rules included in other rules, sorted by ID, grouped by hundreds.

Fig. 1. Left: 166 rules were included once, one rule was included 14 times. Right: Amount of inclusions based on rule ID. The Rule ID reflects the order in which a rule was created in STEREO's [7] wrapper induction (see Sect. 3).

was an exact duplicate that most likely was added by mistake. Thus, the R^+ rules do not need further consideration for rule set minimization.

Transfer of the Rules to the HCI Domain. Using the LaTeX files, we added 13 new R^+ rules and 77 R^- rules. Furthermore, we manually changed 6 previously added R^- rules to be more general. For example changing `m^2` to `m^[2|3]` to capture both square and cubic meters. The R^+ rules added two new statistics types, the Z-Test and ANOVA without an r-value. The statistics covered by our rules are those frequently used in HCI literature [13]. In the original implementation of STEREO, all ANOVA tests that did not contain a r-value were seen as non-APA. However, we found that APA guidelines do allow ANOVA to be reported without an r-value [1]. Therefore, when referencing the percentage of APA-conform statistics in a corpus, we mention both including and excluding ANOVA tests without an r-value. For both the Z-Test and ANOVA without an r-value, only APA conform extraction rules were added.

Table 2. Number (*num*) of extracted statistics and precision (P) over min(200, *num*) for APA and non-APA conform reporting on HCI papers. Separately considering the extraction from PDF and LaTeX files.

| | APA conform | | | | non-APA conform | | | |
| | PDF | | LaTeX | | PDF | | LaTeX | |
Statistic Type	*num*	P	*num*	P	*num*	P	*num*	P
Student's *t*-test	440	100%	634	100%	38	97.4%	69	100%
Pearson Correlation	48	100%	65	100%	76	96%	94	96.8%
Spearman Correlation	2	100%	1	100%	59	90.7%	64	89%
ANOVA	0	N/A	0	N/A	2	100%	0	N/A
ANOVA without *r*-value	1,059	100%	1,097	100%	0	N/A	0	N/A
Mann-Whitney-U	0	N/A	0	N/A	270	92%	425	94%
Wilcoxon Signed-Rank	0	N/A	0	N/A	0	N/A	0	N/A
Chi-Square	53	100%	85	100%	14	100%	718	100%
Z-Test	66	100%	195	100%	0	N/A	0	N/A
Total supported statistics	1,668		2,077		459		1,370	

For the PDF files, nine R^- rules and no R^+ rule had to be added. These new R^- rules where added because the PDF to text conversion includes page numbers and citations, which are not contained in the LaTeX files of the HCI dataset and the JSON files of the CORD-19 dataset.

In total, transferring STEREO from the life sciences to the HCI domain required adding 99 rules, including 13 R^+ rules to cover Z-Tests and ANOVA without *r*-value.

Precision of Statistics Extraction for the HCI Dataset. Our R^+ rules extract the same statistic types used in STEREO [7] (Pearson's Correlation, Spearman Correlation, Student's *t*-test, ANOVA, Mann-Whitney-U Test, Wilcoxon Signed-Rank Test, and Chi-Square Test). These statistic types were chosen as they were commonly found in scientific papers. We added two new types of statistics found often in HCI papers, the Z-Test and ANOVA without an *r*-value.

In the 4,023 HCI papers, the R^+ rules matched 6,321 sentences from the PDF files and 7,669 sentences from the LaTeX files. Normalizing this to the total amount of sentences in both file types, these numbers correspond to about 3% of the sentences. Table 2 shows all reported statistics categorized by type and whether the statistics matched APA style or not. For every statistic type, more statistics were extracted from LaTeX files than from PDF files. The only exception is the Spearman Correlation in the case of APA conform and LaTeX. We denote 'Other Statistics' as all statistic types which are extracted by STEREO but are not assigned a specific APA or non-APA type. It includes a range of statistics not yet captured by the rule set, e.g., interquartile range or Kolmogorov-Smirnov tests. We do not list 'Other Statistics' in the result tables. Using PDF files, about 26% of the extracted statistics were APA conform (9% when treating ANOVA without *r*-value as non-APA). With LaTeX files, 27% of extracted statistics were APA conform (13% when considering ANOVA without r-value as non-APA).

On PDF files, the precision for APA statistics was 100% and ranged from 90% to 100% for non-APA statistics (see Table 2). 'Other Statistics' had a precision of 54.5% with 4,194 extracted statistics. Similarly, using the LaTeX files, we achieved 100% precision for APA conform statistics and precision ranging from 89% to 100%, otherwise. 'Other Statistics' had an increased precision of 60.5% but only 4,184 extracted statistics. Adding the 'Other Statistics', we extracted 1,668 APA conform and 4,653 non-APA conform statistics on PDF files. On the LaTeX files, we extracted 2,077 APA conform and 5,554 non-APA conform statistics in total.

Precision of the Statistics Extraction for the CORD-19 Dataset. The number of statistics extractions and their precision on the CORD-19 dataset are presented in Table 3. As expected, we achieve similar results as the original STEREO paper. Please note that, as mentioned earlier, STEREO used a slightly older version of the dataset than the one available to us. The most statistic was extracted for 'Other Statistics' with 114,242 and a precision of 98.5%. In total, 2,189 APA conform and 120,516 non-APA conform statistics were extracted. For the supported statistic types, non-APA conform Pearson Correlations were extracted the most, by a large margin. Of the extracted statistics, 1.8% were APA conform (0.8% when treating ANOVA without r-value as non-APA). As for the HCI dataset, the APA-conform extractions achieved a precision of 100%. For non-APA conform statistics, the precision ranged from 94.5% to 100%.

Table 3. Number (num) of extracted statistics for APA and non-APA conform reporting on CORD-19 papers. Precision (P) is calculated on 200 samples per type or all samples if there are less.

	APA conform		non-APA conform	
Statistic Type	num	P	num	P
Student's t-test	662	100%	210	97%
Pearson Correlation	113	100%	5,034	98.5%
Spearman Correlation	1	100%	551	100%
ANOVA	0	N/A	2	100%
ANOVA without r-value	1,239	100%	0	N/A
Mann-Whitney-U	2	100%	419	94.5%
Wilcoxon Signed-Rank	0	N/A	0	N/A
Chi-Square	69	100%	58	100%
Z-Test	103	100%	0	N/A
Total supported statistics	2,189		6,274	

R^- *Rule Evaluation.* We evaluate the R^- rules on 200 randomly selected sentences from the HCI dataset as well as the CORD-19 dataset. We aim to test if any reported statistic was falsely matched by R^- rules, i. e., results in a false negative. Our investigation shows that for both datasets, all 200 sentences were correctly identified as non-statistics. We measure the runtime using the HCI dataset and compare the reduced rule set with the full rule set. The full rule set takes 122.4 s (averaged over 5 runs), while the reduced rule set takes 84.5 s (averaged over 5 runs). This is a performance gain of about 31% for the reduced rule set.

We extract 200 sentences that contain a number but were not matched by any R^- or R^+ rules. We assess whether these uncaptured sentences report a statistic or not, or whether they contain a transformation error regardless of the content (see Table 4). 92% of uncaptured sentences did not contain any statistics. The most missed statistics (8.5%) were in CORD-19, whereas using the PDF files in the HCI domain missed the fewest (2.5%). Using the CORD-19 dataset resulted in the most transformation errors, while using LaTeX did not have transformation errors.

Table 4. Evaluation of sentences not covered by R^- or R^+ rules. Evaluated on a sample of 200 sentences taken from the respective datasets.

Dataset	Statistic missed	No statistic contained	Transformation error
CORD-19 + JSON	17 (9%)	174 (87%)	9 (5%)
HCI + LaTeX	14 (7%)	186 (93%)	0 (0%)
HCI + PDF	5 (3%)	192 (96%)	3 (2%)

5 Discussion

Statistics Extraction from the Datasets. Using the HCI dataset, about 26% of the extracted statistics were APA conform. This is a large difference to the 1.8% of APA conform statistics in the CORD-19 dataset. Nonetheless, this means that the remaining 74% for HCI and 98.2% for CORD-19 of reported statistics are non-APA conform. This makes understanding the scientific progress and relying on studies very difficult for researchers, as discussed in the introduction. Since all APA-conform statistics follow a very strict and well-defined pattern, they achieve a precision of 100%. However, non-APA Mann-Whitney-U test rules need refinement, as in all scenarios, some Wilcoxon Signed-Rank tests were falsely identified as Mann-Whitney-U tests.

Generally, we could extract more statistics from LaTeX files than using PDF files in the HCI dataset. Note that the dataset contains only preprints that are available in both formats. This means we loose statistics in the process of converting PDF to text and learning rules to find those statistics in the text. However, it is encouraging that regardless of the file format, the precision of the extracted statistics is generally high for both PDF and LaTeX.

In LATEX files and in the CORD-19 dataset, page numbers, as well as citations, were automatically removed or never generated. However, converted PDF files contained citations, which in turn included pages of an article in a journal or ACM identifiers. These had a high diversity of representation, which makes defining new R^- rules to capture them very difficult. Some examples of these variations can be seen in the following:

- `Human Factors in Computing Systems. dl.acm.org, 2853-2859.`
- `ACM, New York, NY, USA, 285-296.`
- `Computer Graphics 19, 12 (2013), 2713-2722.`
- `Virtual Environ. 7(3), 225- 240 (1998).`
- `Thousand Oaks, CA, 508-510 (2007) [49]`

In the end, we added the rule `\),\s\d{1,4}[--]\d{2,4}[.)]` to capture most cases. Tables could not be removed from the PDF input, leading to some extra rules. However, most numbers were already matched by the previously added R^- and R^+ rules.

We performed a detailed analysis on the large deviation of the precision (Table 2) for'Other Statistics', which are statistics we extract but do not determine the type of, compared to explicitly captured statistic types, i.e., those that are supported by specific and typed R^+ rules. We identified a rule in STEREO that is `\([P|p] \s? <?=? \s? \d (\.\d+)?\)`. This rule also captures the string `(P1)`, which is not a statistic and produced false positive. Thus, we change the rule to `\([P|p] \s? [<=]+ \s? \d (\.\d+)?\)`. We re-run the evaluation and retrieve 2,337 'Other Statistics'. Now the precision goes up to 97.5% for the PDF files. For the LATEX files, 'Other Statistics' extractions are reduced to 2,254, with a precision increase to 98.5%.

Inspecting the Reduced Set of R^- Rules. We applied the rule set inclusion algorithm from Chen and Xu [5] to reduce the rule set of STEREO. The goal is to improve STEREO's runtime, which we observe to be by about one third. A detailed inspection on the rule inclusion in Fig. 1b shows that later added rules are more likely to include one or more other rules. Note, "later" refers to the point in time a rule was added during the active wrapper learning process, i.e., a higher rule ID was assigned to it (see Sect. 3). We assume that later rules were added with more background knowledge of the STEREO tool and thus they tend to be more general. The most included rule is `figure \d{1,2}`. Later rules like `(...| fig | figure | Table |...)\s*\d+(\s*[\.\,]\s*\d+)*` (shortened) include the first rule and do not only match a figure, but also tables and equations.

The structure of rules with many inclusions is mostly similar. Every rule, which included more than 100 other rules, leveraged numbers being preceded or followed by a word. Fore example, `[a-zA-Z]{3,}` covers rules of the same structure designed for special physical units like `\d[mM]` matching meter information.

6 Conclusion

We analyzed STEREO, which extracts statistics from papers using a set of regular expressions. We apply a rule set inclusion algorithm that removed a third of the rules. We extend the rule set to the HCI domain. We repeated the active wrapper learning from STEREO on a sample of 200 papers, i. e., 222,544 sentences. We only had to add 13 R^+ and 77 R^- rules to cover this new domain. This is a small fraction of newly required rules compared to the 1,510 original rules in STEREO. We apply the extended statistics extraction rule set to the whole HCI dataset. We find that only 26% of extracted statistics were APA conform in the HCI domain, compared to only 1.8% for the CORD-19 dataset.

We compare the use of PDF versus LaTeX files in the HCI domain. The overall extraction precision is high independent of the format. For PDF converted to text, we observe a few transformation errors, which do not occur with LaTeX.

In future studies, one could further analyze Wilcoxon Signed-Rank tests that were often falsely captured as Mann-Whitney-U tests. While Wilcoxon Signed-Rank and Mann-Whitney-U have similar reporting styles, exploiting more surrounding context might better separate these two types.

Acknowledgements. This work is co-funded under the 2LIKE project by the German Federal Ministry of Education and Research (BMBF) and the Ministry of Science, Research and the Arts Baden-Württemberg within the funding line Artificial Intelligence in Higher Education.

References

1. APA: Publication manual of the American Psychological Association 2020: the official guide to APA style. American Psychological Association, 7 edn. (2020)
2. Bentley, M., Peerenboom, C., Hodge, F., Passano, E.B., Warren, H., Washburn, M.: Instructions in regard to preparation of manuscript. Psyc. Bulletin (1929)
3. Böschen, I.: Evaluation of JATSdecoder as an automated text extraction tool for statistical results in scientific reports. Scientific Reports (2021)
4. Brüggemann-Klein, A., Wood, D.: One-unambiguous regular languages. Inf. Comput. **679**, 95–106 (1998)
5. Chen, H., Xu, Z.: Inclusion algorithms for one-unambiguous regular expressions and their applications. Sci. Comput. Program. **193**, 102436 ff (2020)
6. Clement, C.B., Bierbaum, M., O'Keeffe, K.P., Alemi, A.A.: On the use of ArXiv as a dataset (2019). https://arxiv.org/abs/1905.00075
7. Epp, S., Hoffmann, M., Lell, N., Mohr, M., Scherp, A.: STEREO: a pipeline for extracting experiment statistics, conditions, and topics from scientific papers. In: iiWAS. ACM (2021)
8. Freedman, L.P., Venugopalan, G., Wisman, R.: Reproducibility 2020: progress and priorities. F1000Research (2017)
9. Göpfert, J., Kuckertz, P., Weinand, J., Kotzur, L., Stolten, D.: Measurement extraction with natural language processing: a review. In: EMNLP. ACL, December 2022
10. Hovland, D.: The inclusion problem for regular expressions. J. Comput. Syst. Sci. **78**(6), 1795–1813 (2012)

11. Kalmbach, T., Hoffmann, M., Lell, N., Scherp, A.: Reducing a set of regular expressions and analyzing differences of domain-specific statistic reporting. CoRR abs/2211.13632 (2022). https://arxiv.org/pdf/2211.13632v2.pdf
12. Lanka, S.S.T., Rajtmajer, S.M., Wu, J., Giles, C.L.: Extraction and evaluation of statistical information from social and behavioral science papers. In: Companion of The Web Conference 2021. ACM/IW3C2 (2021)
13. Lazar, J., Feng, J., Hochheiser, H.: Research Methods in Human-Computer Interaction. Morgan Kaufmann, Burlington (2017)
14. Nipkow, T., Traytel, D.: Unified decision procedures for regular expression equivalence. In: Klein, G., Gamboa, R. (eds.) ITP 2014. LNCS, vol. 8558, pp. 450–466. Springer, Cham (2014). https://doi.org/10.1007/978-3-319-08970-6_29
15. Nuijten, M.B., van Assen, M.A.L.M., Hartgerink, C.H.J., Epskamp, S., Wicherts, J.M.: The validity of the tool statcheck in discovering statistical reporting inconsistencies (2017). psyarxiv.com/tcxaj
16. Nuijten, M.B., Hartgerink, C.H., Van Assen, M.A., Epskamp, S., Wicherts, J.M.: The prevalence of statistical reporting errors in psychology (1985–2013). Behavior research methods (2016)
17. PsychOpen: Psychopen uses statcheck tool for quality check. PsychOpen (2017)
18. Sakaluk, J.K., Graham, C.A.: Promoting transparent reporting of conflicts of interests and statistical analyses at the journal of sex research. J. Sex Res. **55**(1), 1–6 (2018)
19. Schmidt, T.: Statcheck does not work: all the numbers. reply to Nuijten et al. (2017) (2017). psyarxiv.com/hr6qy
20. Wang, L.L., Lo, K., Chandrasekhar, Y., Reas, R., Yang, J., et al.: CORD-19: the COVID-19 Open Research Dataset. CoRR abs/2004.10706 (2020)

GRAM: Grammar-Based Refined-Label Representing Mechanism in the Hierarchical Semantic Parsing Task

Dinh-Truong Do[✉], Minh-Phuong Nguyen, and Le-Minh Nguyen

Japan Advanced Institute of Science and Technology, Ishikawa, Japan
{truongdo,phuongnm,nguyenml}@jaist.ac.jp

Abstract. In this study, we proposed an efficient method to improve the performance of the hierarchical semantic parsing task by strengthening the meaning representation of the label candidate set via inductive grammar. In particular, grammar was first synthesized from the logical representations of training annotated data. Then, the model utilizes it as additional structured information for all expression label predictions. The grammar was also used to prevent unpromising directions in the semantic parsing process dynamically. The experimental results on the three well-known semantic parsing datasets, TOP, TOPv2 (low-resource settings), and ATIS, showed that our proposed method work effectiveness, which achieved new state-of-the-art (SOTA) results on TOP and TOPv2 datasets, and competitive results on the ATIS dataset.

Keywords: Hierarchical semantic parsing · Grammar · Task-Oriented Dialog

1 Introduction

Task-oriented dialog (TOD) systems are computer systems that assist users in achieving specific objectives [15,23], which have widespread applications in both modern business and daily life [24]. At the core of these systems, semantic parsers play an important role in mapping natural language utterances into machine-understandable representations. By utilizing these representations, TOD systems can understand the user's intentions and generate suitable responses accordingly. Therefore, developing effective semantic parsers is a crucial aspect of building TOD systems.

Given a query, a semantic parser is responsible for identifying the user *intents* (e.g., "get event information") and determining the entities that are relevant to those intents, called *slots* (e.g., "the organizer"). Traditional semantic parsing methods, such as intent detection and slot-filling, consider only a single intention for each user utterance [4, 16]. However, the use of hierarchical representation [9] has introduced a new challenge known as hierarchical semantic parsing (HSP), where the model must identify multiple-level intentions and nested slots based on the query. This representation demonstrated the importance of nested sub-logic composition in a TOD system [1]. While this representation is flexible enough to capture the meaning of complex utterances, it also raises challenges to semantic parsing models to accurately identify the appropriate label and

© The Author(s), under exclusive license to Springer Nature Switzerland AG 2023
E. Métais et al. (Eds.): NLDB 2023, LNCS 13913, pp. 339–351, 2023.
https://doi.org/10.1007/978-3-031-35320-8_24

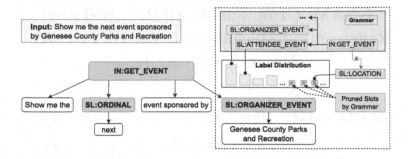

Fig. 1. Our mechanism (GRAM) uses grammar in hierarchical semantic parsing.

corresponding span hierarchically. In this work, we focus on the problem of similar label confusion in HSP, which is common for slots like SL:ORGANIZER_EVENT and SL:ATTENDEE_EVENT, which have close meanings.

Recently, based on the success of the pre-trained language model (LM) (e.g., BERT), the HSP task achieved impressive results [15,25]. However, these works do not pay attention to the meaning of labels in the parsing process. Intuition from the other tasks [6,14], we hypothesize that refined representing vectors of possible labels based on grammar can help the model reduce confusion in recognizing similar labels. For example, in Fig. 1, considering the current parsing step of intent IN:GET_EVENT, the candidates are its children nodes generated by a grammar synthesized from training data: SL:ORGANIZER_EVENT, SL:ATTENDEE_EVENT, etc. In our proposed model (GRAM), these possible labels are encoded by an embedding layer and used to compute the following label predictions. This allowed our model to focus on the important information (candidate set) and make better predictions by preventing unpromising decoding directions (e.g., SL:LOCATION in Fig. 1). Our method effectively injects structured information on grammar into the model, thus enhancing the performance of semantic parsers. Besides, this method is generalized enough to apply to another kind of semantic logical representation, such as λ-calculus [7] or other structure parsing systems. Indeed, our contributions to this paper are as follows:

- We propose a novel method for exacting and using grammar as additional structured information in the hierarchical semantic parsing task to improve label representation and prevent the unpromising predicting directions.
- An experimental experiment shows that our method achieves SOTA results on the TOP dataset [9] and the TOPv2 dataset [5] (low-resource settings), and promising results on the ATIS dataset [10].

The remainder of this paper is organized into five sections. Section 2 provides an overview of related works. In Sect. 3, we provide a detailed description of our proposed method, GRAM. Sections 4 and 5 present our experiments and results analysis. Finally, in Sect. 6, we conclude this paper.

2   Related Work

Hierarchical Semantic Parsing. TOP [9] and TOPv2 [5] datasets were created to evaluate methods for the hierarchical semantic parsing task and several approaches have been introduced to tackle the challenges of these datasets. To deal with complex queries, Rongali et al. [19] developed a unified architecture based on sequence-to-sequence (S2S) models and a pointer generator network. Aghajanyan et al. [1] converted the hierarchical representation to a new form, called decoupled representation, to deal with the problem of discontinuities in English and then used S2S models based on the pointer generator architecture to predict this. Einolghozati et al. [8] proposed a shift-reduce based on Recurrent Neural Network (RNN) Grammars with improvements of incorporating contextualized embeddings, ensembling, and pairwise re-ranking via a language model. Zhu et al. [25] developed a non-autoregressive parser based on an insertion transformer to speed up the inference time. Finally, the RINE model [15] led the SOTA results by splitting the parsing process into multiple steps, where the input of the current step is the output of the previous step. However, the SOTA model ignores the schema constraint information of hierarchical representation. This motivates us to synthesize grammar from the hierarchical representation of annotated data and use it for the prediction process.

Grammar-Constrained Neural Network Models. Incorporating grammar constraints with deep neural networks has received considerable attention from researchers. Yin et al. [22] introduced a neural code generation approach that generates an abstract syntax tree by following a series of actions dictated by a grammar model, which encodes the syntax of the programming language as prior knowledge. Xiao et al. [21] proposed an RNN-based approach for semantic parsing that takes into account grammar constraints of logical form. Specifically, this model used a constrained loss to optimize the model's parameters. More recently, Baranowski et al. [2] extracted a context-free grammar from the target logical form of the semantic parsing task. These grammar constraints were then enforced with an LR parser [12] to maintain syntactically valid sequences throughout decoding. In comparison, besides using grammar to maintain valid label predictions as in prior research, we also leverage grammar as additional structured information for performing label predictions. To the best of our knowledge, we are the first to integrate grammar constraints with label embedding [14] to tackle the problem of similar label confusion in the hierarchical semantic parsing task.

3   Method

3.1   Overview

Figure 2 illustrates an overview of our method, GRAM. Firstly, from the annotated training data, we synthesize a grammar based on the parent-child relations in the hierarchical representation. This results in an inductive grammar with the root represented by a special label ROOT. Secondly, we train our GRAM model, which uses the recursive insertion-based method [15] enhanced by label embedding [14] and grammar constraints to tackle the problem of hierarchical semantic parsing. The parsing process consists of multiple sub-node prediction steps. At each parsing step, a pre-trained LM [13] serves as an encoder to obtain hidden states of the input. Two classifiers are then employed to predict the start and end positions of the span. For label prediction, the label embedding method is used to assist the model in learning the latent features of label categories, which serves as additional information to reduce confusion between labels. To this end, we apply a grammar-based masking strategy to the label embedding to focus the model on relevant labels (candidate set) rather than all label types, thus reducing the model resources required to distinguish unpromising label types. The masked label embedding is then utilized to create the final representation of the label type, which is used to predict the label.

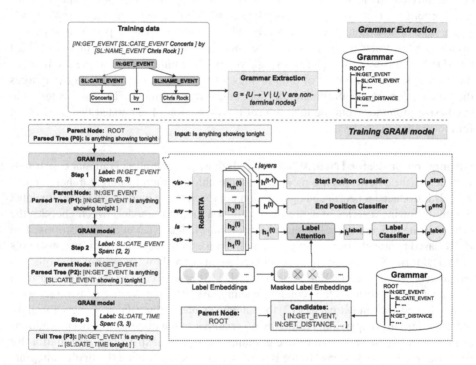

Fig. 2. Overview of our method

3.2   Recursive Insertion-Based Method

Before introducing our model, we describe the recursive insertion-based method [15]. In this method, the parsing process can be formally represented as an incremental chain of sub-parsed trees, $P = [P_0, P_1, P_2, ..., P_n]$ where n is the total number of parsing steps required to obtain the full-parsed tree (e.g., $n = 3$ in the example of Fig. 2). P_0 represents the original input utterance. At the ith step, the model takes the output of the previous parsed tree P_{i-1} as input and predicts the node label with its corresponding span. This label is inserted into the previous parsed tree based on the position of the predicted span to form the current parsed tree P_i. The process recursively runs until a special end-of-prediction signal (EOP) is encountered.

3.3 Grammar Constraints

Our observation revealed that the relationship between parent nodes and child nodes in the hierarchical representation typically follows some constraints. For example, the intent IN:GET_LOCATIONS is associated with slots containing location information, such as SL:LOCATION or SL:POINT_ON_MAP. These relationships are useful during the hierarchical parsing process as they can prevent the model from making unpromising label predictions. Therefore, we introduce a grammar-based mechanism and aggregate it with our recursive insertion-based model to improve the label prediction performance. In particular, from the annotated training data, we extract grammar $\mathcal{G} = \{U \to V | \ U, V$ are non-terminal nodes$\}$ (e.g., IN:GET_LOCATION $\to$ SL:LOCATION). Aggregating the extracted grammar into the recursive insertion-based model means that at each step of parsing process, the model only needs to consider a pool of candidates for predicting label type instead of all label categories (e.g., $\mathcal{G}$(IN:GET_EVENT) is candidate set of parent node IN:GET_EVENT).

3.4 Modeling

Training. At the ith step of the parsing process, the inputs are the linearized representation containing m tokens of the parsed tree, $P_i = [x_1, x_2, ..., x_m]$, and the parent node U. Given these inputs, the model needs to predict a node label in the label set $L = [l_1, l_2, ..., l_{|L|}]$ and its corresponding span (i, j) with $i, j \in [0, m]$.

Firstly, we use the label embedding method [14] to represent the set of label categories L. This method transforms label categories from the label space to the embedding space, which captures the semantic meaning of label categories.

$$e_i = E^l(l_i) \tag{1}$$

where E^l indicates the label embedding lookup table and e_i denotes the vector representation of label type in the embedding space. At the start, the parameters in the lookup table are randomly initialized, which will be updated during the training process.

Then, using a pre-trained LM [13] as an encoder, the input sequence P_i is encoded to obtain its hidden states. Following Mansimov et al. [15], we use the hidden states of the two last transformer layers to compute the probabilities of start and end positions.

$$p_k^{start} = \text{softmax}(W_s h_{x_k}^{(t)} + b_s) \tag{2}$$

$$p_k^{end} = \text{softmax}(W_e h_{x_k}^{(t-1)} + b_e) \tag{3}$$

where W_* and b_* are the learnable parameters, t is the index of the last transformer layer in the pre-trained LM, and x_k is the kth token in the input sequence.

For label prediction, given the hidden state of [CLS] token in the last transformer layer and the label embedding $e = [e_1, e_2, ..., e_{|L|}]$, a multi-head attention layer [20] is applied to obtain the attention vector h^{attn}. For computing this attention vector, we use the sentence embedding $h^{(t)}_{[CLS]}$ as the query, and the label embedding as the key and value. Especially, an attention mask generated by grammar is used to cause only the promising label predictions to be attended. Let set C as the candidate set generated from the extracted grammar G and the parent node U. We define a masking matrix M to inject grammar information to the model with values set 0 for all labels in C and 1 for otherwise. To this end, the promising label meaning vector contributes to the node label prediction via the dependencies between the sentence context vector and candidate label set. Following that, the attention vector h^{attn} is concatenated with the hidden state of $[CLS]$ token $h^{(t)}_{[CLS]}$ to create the hidden state of label type h^{nodeLb}. This hidden state is then put into a linear layer to get the probabilities of label type p^{nodeLb}.

$$M_i = \begin{cases} 0 & \text{if} \quad l_i \in C \\ 1 & \text{otherwise} \end{cases} \tag{4}$$

$$h^{attn} = \text{MHA}(h^{(t)}_{[CLS]}, e, e, M) \tag{5}$$

$$h^{nodeLb} = \text{concat}(h^{attn}, h^{(t)}_{[CLS]}) \tag{6}$$

$$p^{nodeLb} = \text{softmax}(W_{lb}h^{nodeLb} + b_{lb}) \tag{7}$$

Since h^{attn} is the result of the attention mechanism of $h^{(t)}_{[CLS]}$ with only a pool of label candidates through the masking mechanism. That guides the model to focus only on the valid candidate set C, therefore reducing the resource needed to distinguish other labels which are not in C. In addition, h^{attn} is concated with $h^{(t)}_{[CLS]}$ to form the final hidden state h^{nodeLb}, which means that h^{nodeLb} not only contains the latent knowledge of label categories but also carry the semantic information from the language model. Finally, the cross-entropy (CE) losses are computed based on the gold label and the resulting probabilities of label and span.

$$Loss_{nodeLb} = \text{CE}(g^{nodeLb}, p^{nodeLb}) \tag{8}$$

$$Loss_{start} = \sum_k \text{CE}(g^{start}_k, p^{start}_k) \tag{9}$$

$$Loss_{end} = \sum_k \text{CE}(g^{end}_k, p^{end}_k) \tag{10}$$

$$Loss_{final} = Loss_{nodeLb} + Loss_{start} + Loss_{end} \tag{11}$$

Inference In the inference phase, we also use the grammar to correct the parsing process to prune the unpromising decoding directions. However, the challenge in this phase is the lack of information about the parent node to generate a candidate set. To meet this challenge, a simple strategy is applied where we first predict the span of the label and then use this information to figure out what the parent node should be. For example, considering the third step 3rd with given input P_2 in Fig. 2, there is no information about the parent node of the current label should be IN:GET_EVENT or SL:CATE_EVENT.

Therefore, we perform the span prediction first and get the span *"tonight"*. Based on the position of this span in the given parsed tree P_2, the parent node of the current label should be IN:GET_EVENT. Once obtaining the parent node, we use it with the extracted grammar to generate a set of candidates C. Based on this candidate set, we prune the decoding directions of the labels not in the set. To accomplish this, we set the probabilities of all labels $c \notin C$ to zero.

4 Experiment

4.1 Dataset and Evaluation Metric

In this study, we evaluated our method by using three well-known English semantic parsing datasets including TOP [9], TOPv2 [5], and ATIS [10]. Similar to prior works [1, 15, 19], our primary evaluation metric was the exact match (EM). The EM score was calculated based on the number of predicted trees that exactly matched the gold trees.

TOP. The dataset contains utterances in two domains: *navigation* and *event*. There are 25 intents and 36 slots in the dataset. The mean depth of the trees is 2.54, and the mean length of the utterances is 8.93 tokens. Following the previous works [8, 15, 19, 25], we eliminated all the utterances containing the UNSUPPORTED intent which resulted in 28,414 training, 4,032 valid, and 8,241 test utterances.

TOPv2. The dataset is designed to focus on low-resource settings. In this study, we used the low-resource version of the *reminder* and *weather* domains. Whereas the weather domain only has 7 intents and 11 slots, the reminder domain has 19 intents and 32 slots. The low-resource versions are created by using a *sample per intent and slot* (SPIS) threshold from the original training data. Specifically, when an intent or a slot occurs with less than a defined number of SPIS, all parsed trees containing this intent/slot will be chosen as low-resource samples. In this research, we used the low-resource settings at 500 SPIS and 25 SPIS. At 500 SPIS, the reminder domain has 4788 training and 1871 validation utterances, while the weather domain contains 2372 training and 1202 validation utterances. At 25 SPIS, the reminder domain has 493 training and 337 validation utterances, while the weather domain contains 176 training and 147 validation utterances. There are, respectively, 5767 and 5682 test utterances in the reminder and weather domains in both SPIS settings.

ATIS. The dataset is a collection of utterances taken from users who were booking flights. There are 21 intents and 120 slots in the ATIS dataset. In this study, we used the same data division as Nguyen et al. [17]. The training, validation, and test sets contain 4478, 500, and 893 utterances, respectively. However, the ATIS dataset used the BIO format for representing data samples instead of hierarchical representation [9]. Therefore, we built a hierarchical representation version of the ATIS dataset to evaluate our method. It's worth noting that we did not change any labels or spans in the dataset, we only converted the format from BIO to hierarchical representation so that our results can be directly compared to previous works on the ATIS dataset.

4.2   Experimental Setting

Baseline. We reproduced the RINE model [15] as a strong baseline. For the hyperparameters, we used the same values as those specified in the original paper.

GRAM[1]**.** We used RoBERTa-large and RoBERTa-base pre-trained language models [13] as our backbone encoders. For the TOP dataset, we set the number of warmup steps to 1000, using Adam optimizer [11] with a peak learning rate at 1e-05. The training process takes a mini-batch of size 32, with a max length of 512 tokens. Since the label embedding lookup table (Sect. 3.4) is randomly initialized at the beginning of the training process. This randomness can cause the model's performance to be inconsistent. To address this, we froze the RoBERTa encoder for the first $\{0, 1, 3, \mathbf{5}, 7\}$[2] epochs and trained only the label embedding layer on these epochs. For the TOPv2 dataset, we used the same settings as the TOP dataset, except for a batch size of 16 at 500 SPIS and a batch size of 8 and 10 epochs for freezing RoBERTa encoders at 25 SPIS. For the ATIS dataset, we used the same settings as the TOPv2 dataset at 25 SPIS.

4.3   Main Results

Table 1. Performance comparison on the TOP and TOPv2 test sets.

Method	Pre-trained	TOP	TOPv2			
			Weather		Reminder	
			25 SPIS	500 SPIS	25 SPIS	500 SPIS
RNNG ensem. + SVMRank [8]	ELMo	87.25	–	–	–	–
S2S-Ptr [19]	RoBERTa	86.67	–	–	–	–
Decoupled S2S-Ptr [1]	RoBERTa	87.10	–	–	–	–
Seq2seq-Ptr [5]	BART	–	71.60	84.90	55.70	71.90
Insertion Transformer + S2S [25]	RoBERTa	86.74	–	–	–	–
RINE^{base} [15]	RoBERTa	87.14	74.53	87.80	68.71	80.30
RINE^{large} [15]	RoBERTa	87.57	77.03	87.50	71.10	81.31
GRAM^{base} (ours)	RoBERTa	87.19	75.95	**88.40**	69.74	81.39
GRAM^{large} (ours)	RoBERTa	**87.85**	**78.83**	88.06	**71.44**	**82.19**

Table 1 shows the results on the TOP and TOPv2 test sets of our method and other previous works. In the TOP dataset, our models outperformed all other methods. Particularly, it achieved a higher score than the autoregressive S2S model with pointer network [19] by 1.18 EM and the current SOTA method RINE [15] by 0.28 EM scores. These results demonstrate the value of incorporating grammar in our model when performing the TOP dataset. In the TOPv2 dataset, our models outperformed other methods in all SPIS settings of both the reminder and weather domains. Specifically, at 25 SPIS settings, our method outperformed the baseline by 1.80 EM and 0.34 EM, and at 500 SPIS settings,

---

[1] Our source code and the converted version of the ATIS dataset are publicly available at https://github.com/truongdo619/GRAM.

[2] The values resulting in the best performance are **bold**.

Table 2. Performance comparison for ATIS test set.

Method	EM
BERT-Joint [3]	88.20
JointBERT [4]	88.20
Stack-propagation [18]	88.60
JointBERT-CAE + CRF [17]	88.40
JointBERT-CAE [17]	**88.70**
RINE^{large} (ours)	88.06
GRAM^{large} (ours)	88.69

Table 3. Results of ablation study on validation set of TOP dataset. Denotations ✓ and ✗ indicate whether corresponding component was used or not, respectively. Δ denotes difference in EM scores between the full-setting model with other models.

Method	Settings		EM	Δ
	Grammar-based Label Embedding	Pruning Label by Grammar		
GRAM	✓	✓	87.90	
	✓	✗	87.82	–0.08
	✓*	✗	87.66	–0.24
	✗	✓	87.74	–0.16
Baseline	✗	✗	87.57	–0.33

* Without freezing RoBERTa to training label embedding first (Sect. 4.2).

our method outperformed the baseline by 0.90 EM and 0.88 EM in the weather and reminder domains, respectively. These results show that even under the conditions of minimal annotated training data, our technique still achieves significant improvements. In addition, the RoBERTa-base [13] version of our method performed better than the RoBERTa-base version of RINE in all settings. This proves the solid improvement of our grammar integration mechanism on the different pre-trained models.

Table 2 shows the results of the ATIS test set of our method and other prior works. Our method outperformed the baseline and achieved competitive results when compared with the current best method JointBERT-CAE [17]. These results proved the solid improvement of our integration mechanism, in which our method is generalized enough to apply to other semantic parsing datasets other than TOP and its variants.

5 Analysis

5.1 Statistical Analysis of Label Confusion

In the parsing process, an intent typically comes up with similar slots that are easily confused. Therefore, we conducted a statistical analysis to inspect the ability of our model to distinguish the slots within an intent (Fig. 3). For analysis, we select the intent IN:GET_EVENT, which has the most errors in the TOP test set. We then compared the F1 score improvement for all slots within this intent using our GRAM model and the baseline model, as shown in Fig. 3b. We found that the advancement of our model is shown in both high and low occurrence slots. For example, we observed an improvement of 0.022 F1 score for the SL:ORGANIZER_EVENT slot, which was mainly due to the reduction in confusion with the SL:ATTENDEE_EVENT slot (Fig. 3a). Although our model improves on almost slots, it still remains confusing in special slot SL:ATTRIBUTE_EVENT. We argue that because this slot has more general meaning compared with other specific slots. These results proved the effectiveness of incorporating latent label knowledge through grammar-based label embedding to reduce confusion between analogous labels.

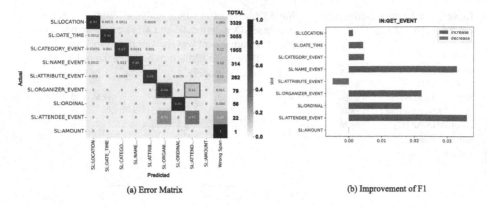

(a) Error Matrix   (b) Improvement of F1

Fig. 3. Error matrix of baseline and distribution of slot F1 improvement between GRAM compared with baseline in the TOP test set, sorted by occurrence.

5.2 Ablation Study

To evaluate the impact of using grammar-based label embedding to diminish label confusion in the training phase and grammar to prevent unpromising label predictions in the inference phase, we compared our full-setting model with each combination of component settings and the baseline (Table 3). We found that using grammar to prevent the unpromising label predictions in the inference phase led to improve performance on the TOP dataset (0.17 EM score higher than with the baseline model). Besides that, using grammar-based label embedding to diminish the label confusion in the training phase further improved performance on the TOP dataset (0.25 EM score higher than with the baseline model). In addition, we found the advancement of freezing the RoBERTa encoder for some first epochs to train only the label embedding layer on these epochs (0.16 EM score higher than without freezing). We attribute this to helping the weights of the label embedding layer be more stable, it provides a good starting point for the fine-tuning process.

5.3 Case Study

Table 4 shows the difference in our model output compared to the baseline model on the TOP dataset. In the first example, the baseline model is confused between two labels, SL:ORGANIZER_EVENT and SL:NAME_EVENT, which both convey event information. In contrast, our model which incorporates grammar-based label embedding to reduce confusion about similar labels accurately predicted the output. In the second example, our model predicted the slot SL:POINT_ON_MAP after the intent IN:GET_LOCATION, whereas the baseline predicted the slot SL:NAME_EVENT. This difference occurred because the extracted grammar does not contain the constraint (IN:GET_LOCATION → SL:NAME_EVENT). This emphasizes the importance of using grammar to prevent unpromising label predictions in our method. The last example is the most difficult because it contains a tree with a depth of 5, which indicates that the tree structure is highly complex. Both models were unable to provide accurate

Table 4. Comparison of outputs of baseline (RINE) and our model (GRAM) on the validation set of TOP.

Type	Ouput
Input	Show me the next event sponsored by Genesee County Parks and Recreation
Ground-Truth	[IN:GET_EVENT Show me the [SL:ORDINAL next] event sponsored by [SL:ORGANIZER_EVENT Genesee County Parks and Recreation]]
Baseline	[IN:GET_EVENT Show me the [SL:ORDINAL next] event sponsored by [SL:NAME_EVENT Genesee County Parks and Recreation]] ✗
GRAM	[IN:GET_EVENT Show me the [SL:ORDINAL next] event sponsored by [SL:ORGANIZER_EVENT Genesee County Parks and Recreation]] ✓
Input	Where is the nearest Tom Thumb
Ground-Truth	[IN:GET_LOCATION Where is the [SL:LOC_MOD nearest] [SL:POINT_ON_MAP Tom Thumb]]
Baseline	[IN:GET_LOCATION Where is the [SL:LOC_MOD nearest] [SL:NAME_EVENT Tom Thumb]] ✗
GRAM	[IN:GET_LOCATION Where is the [SL:LOC_MOD nearest] [SL:POINT_ON_MAP Tom Thumb]] ✓
Input	traffic near me right now
Ground-Truth	[IN:GET_INFO_TRAFFIC What 's the traffic like [SL:LOCATION [IN:GET_LOCATION [SL:LOCATION _MODIFIER [IN:GET_LOCATION [SL:SEARCH_RADIUS around] [SL:LOCATION Sturgis]]]]]]
Baseline	[IN:GET_INFO_TRAFFIC What 's the traffic like [SL:LOCATION [IN:GET_LOCATION [SL:SEARCH _RADIUS around] [SL:LOCATION Sturgis]]]] ✗
GRAM	[IN:GET_INFO_TRAFFIC What 's the traffic like [SL:LOCATION [IN:GET_LOCATION [SL:SEARCH _RADIUS around] [SL:LOCATION Sturgis]]]] ✗

predictions, indicating that developing techniques to handle such complex queries is an interesting topic for future work.

6   Conclusion

In conclusion, this research has proposed an effective method for improving the hierarchical semantic parsing task by strengthening the meaning representation of the label candidate set via grammar constraints. Our approach synthesized grammar from logical representations of training annotated data, and utilized it as additional structured information for all expression label predictions. Additionally, we also leveraged the grammar to dynamically prevent unpromising directions in the semantic parsing process. The effectiveness of our method was demonstrated by experimental results on three semantic parsing datasets, TOP, TOPv2, and ATIS.

Acknowledgments. This work is supported by AOARD grant FA23862214039.

References

1. Aghajanyan, A., et al.: Conversational semantic parsing. In: Proceedings of the 2020 Conference on Empirical Methods in Natural Language Processing (EMNLP), pp. 5026–5035. Association for Computational Linguistics, Online, November 2020. https://aclanthology. org/2020.emnlp-main.408

2. Baranowski, A., Hochgeschwender, N.: Grammar-constrained neural semantic parsing with LR parsers. In: Findings of the Association for Computational Linguistics: ACL-IJCNLP 2021, pp. 1275–1279. Association for Computational Linguistics, Online, August 2021. https://aclanthology.org/2021.findings-acl.108

3. Castellucci, G., Bellomaria, V., Favalli, A., Romagnoli, R.: Multi-lingual intent detection and slot filling in a joint bert-based model. arXiv preprint arXiv:1907.02884 (2019). https://arxiv.org/abs/1907.02884

4. Chen, Q., Zhuo, Z., Wang, W.: Bert for joint intent classification and slot filling. arXiv preprint arXiv:1902.10909 (2019). https://arxiv.org/abs/1902.10909

5. Chen, X., Ghoshal, A., Mehdad, Y., Zettlemoyer, L., Gupta, S.: Low-resource domain adaptation for compositional task-oriented semantic parsing. In: Proceedings of the 2020 Conference on Empirical Methods in Natural Language Processing (EMNLP), pp. 5090–5100. Association for Computational Linguistics, Online, November 2020. https://aclanthology.org/2020.emnlp-main.413

6. Cui, L., Zhang, Y.: Hierarchically-refined label attention network for sequence labeling. In: Proceedings of the 2019 Conference on Empirical Methods in Natural Language Processing and the 9th International Joint Conference on Natural Language Processing (EMNLP-IJCNLP), pp. 4115–4128. Association for Computational Linguistics, Hong Kong, China, November 2019. https://aclanthology.org/D19-1422

7. Dong, L., Lapata, M.: Language to logical form with neural attention. In: Proceedings of the 54th Annual Meeting of the Association for Computational Linguistics (Volume 1: Long Papers), pp. 33–43. Association for Computational Linguistics, Berlin, Germany, August 2016. https://aclanthology.org/P16-1004

8. Einolghozati, A., et al.: Improving semantic parsing for task oriented dialog. arXiv preprint arXiv:1902.06000 (2019). https://doi.org/10.48550/ARXIV.1902.06000

9. Gupta, S., Shah, R., Mohit, M., Kumar, A., Lewis, M.: Semantic parsing for task oriented dialog using hierarchical representations. In: Proceedings of the 2018 Conference on Empirical Methods in Natural Language Processing, pp. 2787–2792. Association for Computational Linguistics, Brussels, Belgium (Oct-Nov 2018). https://aclanthology.org/D18-1300

10. Hemphill, C.T., Godfrey, J.J., Doddington, G.R.: The ATIS spoken language systems pilot corpus. In: Speech and Natural Language: Proceedings of a Workshop Held at Hidden Valley, Pennsylvania, 24–27 June 1990. https://aclanthology.org/H90-1021

11. Kingma, D.P., Ba, J.: Adam: a method for stochastic optimization. arXiv preprint arXiv:1412.6980 (2014). https://doi.org/10.48550/ARXIV.1412.6980

12. Knuth, D.E.: On the translation of languages from left to right. Inf. Control 8(6), 607–639 (1965). https://www.sciencedirect.com/science/article/pii/S0019995865904262

13. Liu, Y., et al.: Roberta: A robustly optimized bert pretraining approach. arXiv preprint arXiv:1907.11692 (2019). https://doi.org/10.48550/arXiv.1907.11692

14. Liu, Y., Zhao, J., Hu, J., Li, R., Jin, Q.: DialogueEIN: emotion interaction network for dialogue affective analysis. In: Proceedings of the 29th International Conference on Computational Linguistics, pp. 684–693. International Committee on Computational Linguistics, Gyeongju, Republic of Korea, October 2022. https://aclanthology.org/2022.coling-1.57

15. Mansimov, E., Zhang, Y.: Semantic parsing in task-oriented dialog with recursive insertion-based encoder. In: Proceedings of the AAAI Conference on Artificial Intelligence, vol. 36, pp. 11067–11075 (2022). https://doi.org/10.1609/aaai.v36i10.21355

16. Mesnil, G., He, X., Deng, L., Bengio, Y.: Investigation of recurrent-neural-network architectures and learning methods for spoken language understanding. In: Proceedings of the Interspeech 2013, pp. 3771–3775 (2013). https://doi.org/10.21437/Interspeech.2013-596

17. Phuong, N.M., Le, T., Minh, N.L.: CAE: mechanism to diminish the class imbalanced in SLU slot filling task. In: Bădică, C., Treur, J., Benslimane, D., Hnatkowska, B., Krótkiewicz, M.

(eds.) Advances in Computational Collective Intelligence. ICCCI 2022. CCIS, vol. 1653, pp. 150–163. Springer, Cham (2022). https://doi.org/10.1007/978-3-031-16210-7_12

18. Qin, L., Che, W., Li, Y., Wen, H., Liu, T.: A stack-propagation framework with token-level intent detection for spoken language understanding. In: Proceedings of the 2019 Conference on Empirical Methods in Natural Language Processing and the 9th International Joint Conference on Natural Language Processing (EMNLP-IJCNLP), pp. 2078–2087. Association for Computational Linguistics, Hong Kong, China, November 2019. https://aclanthology.org/D19-1214

19. Rongali, S., Soldaini, L., Monti, E., Hamza, W.: Don't parse, generate! a sequence to sequence architecture for task-oriented semantic parsing. In: Proceedings of The Web Conference 2020, pp. 2962–2968 (2020). https://doi.org/10.1145/3366423.3380064

20. Vaswani, A., et al.: Attention is all you need, p. 30 (2017)

21. Xiao, C., Dymetman, M., Gardent, C.: Sequence-based structured prediction for semantic parsing. In: Proceedings of the 54th Annual Meeting of the Association for Computational Linguistics (Volume 1: Long Papers), pp. 1341–1350. Association for Computational Linguistics, Berlin, Germany, August 2016. https://aclanthology.org/P16-1127

22. Yin, P., Neubig, G.: A syntactic neural model for general-purpose code generation. In: Proceedings of the 55th Annual Meeting of the Association for Computational Linguistics (Volume 1: Long Papers), pp. 440–450. Association for Computational Linguistics, Vancouver, Canada, July 2017. https://aclanthology.org/P17-1041

23. Zhang, Z., Huang, M., Zhao, Z., Ji, F., Chen, H., Zhu, X.: Memory-augmented dialogue management for task-oriented dialogue systems. ACM Trans. Inf. Syst. (TOIS) 37(3), 1–30 (2019). https://dl.acm.org/doi/abs/10.1145/3317612

24. Zhang, Z., Takanobu, R., Zhu, Q., Huang, M., Zhu, X.: Recent advances and challenges in task-oriented dialog systems. Sci. China Technol. Sci. 63(10), 2011–2027 (2020). https://doi.org/10.1007/s11432-016-0037-0

25. Zhu, Q., Khan, H., Soltan, S., Rawls, S., Hamza, W.: Don't parse, insert: multilingual semantic parsing with insertion based decoding. In: Proceedings of the 24th Conference on Computational Natural Language Learning, pp. 496–506. Association for Computational Linguistics, Online, November 2020. https://doi.org/10.18653/v1/2020.conll-1.40

Expanding Domain-Specific Knowledge Graphs with Unknown Facts

Miao Hu$^{(\boxtimes)}$, Zhiwei Lin, and Adele Marshall

School of Mathematics and Physics, Queen's University Belfast, Belfast, UK
{mhu05,z.lin,a.h.marshall}@qub.ac.uk

Abstract. Many knowledge graphs have been created to support intelligent applications, such as search engines and recommendation systems. Some domain-specific knowledge graphs contain similar contents in nature (e.g., the FreeBase contains information about actors and movies which are the core of the IMDB). Adding relevant facts or triples from one knowledge graph into another domain-specific knowledge graph is key to expanding the coverage of the knowledge graph. The facts from one knowledge graph may contain unknown entities or relations that do not occur in the existing knowledge graphs, but it doesn't mean that these facts are not relevant and hence can not be added to an existing domain-specific knowledge graph. However, adding irrelevant facts will violate the inherent nature of the existing knowledge graph. In other words, the facts that conform to the subject matter of the existing domain-specific knowledge graph only can be added. Therefore, it is vital to filter out irrelevant facts in order to avoid such violations. This paper presents an embedding method called UFD to compute the relevance of the unknown facts to an existing domain-specific knowledge graph so that the relevant new facts from another knowledge graph can be added to the existing domain-specific knowledge graph. A new dataset, called UFD-303K, is created for evaluating unknown fact detection. The experiments show that our embedding method is very effective at distinguishing and adding relevant unknown facts to the existing knowledge graph. The code and datasets of this paper can be obtained from GitHub (https://github.com/MiaoHu-Pro/UFD).

Keywords: Domain-specific knowledge graph · Knowledge graph expanding · Unknown facts detection · BERT pre-trained model

1 Introduction

Knowledge graphs are widely used in many information systems such as search engines and recommender systems. A *knowledge graph* (KG) $G = \{(h, r, t) | h, t \in E, r \in R\}$ is a set of triples where E is a set of entities, R is a set of relations between the entities. A triple (h, r, t) denotes that the head entity h has a relation of r with a tail entity t. For example, as shown in Fig. 1, ('Tom Cruise', '/film/producer/film', 'Mission:Impossible') is a triple where the head entity is 'Tom Cruise', the relation is '/film/producer/film', and the tail entity is 'Mission:Impossible'.

The *Domain-specific Knowledge Graph* (Ds-KG) is described as "Domain Knowledge Graph is an explicit conceptualisation to a high-level subject-matter domain and

E. Métais et al. (Eds.): NLDB 2023, LNCS 13913, pp. 352–364, 2023.
https://doi.org/10.1007/978-3-031-35320-8_25

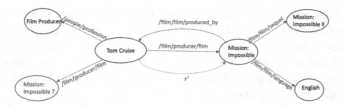

Fig. 1. An example of a sub-graph from FreeBase, where the nodes are entities, and the directed edges represent relationships between the entities. There are 2 relations, '/film/film/produced_by' and '/film/producer/film', between 'Tom Cruise' and 'Mission:Impossible'. And a new relation r' is introduced from out-of-KG. Then, an unknown fact, ('Tom Cruise', r', 'Mission:Impossible'), is emerging. By analogy, a new entity, 'Mission:impossible 7', is introduced, which constructs an unknown fact ('Tom Cruise', '/film/producer/film', 'Mission:Impossible 7'). Before adding them to the existing knowledge graph, it is necessary to judge whether these unknown facts constructed by new entities or new relations are relevant to the current knowledge graph.

its specific subdomains are represented in terms of semantically interrelated entities and relations." in [1]. In other words, Ds-KG is a knowledge representation for a specific domain application. Large-scale domain-specific knowledge graphs (such as FreeBase[1] and IMDB[2]) have played key roles in supporting intelligent question-answering, recommendation systems, and search engines [7]. Some of them may contain similar contents to some extent, for example, the FreeBase knowledge graph also contains facts[3] about movies, TV series, which overlaps with the content in the IMDB knowledge graph. Some of the facts in FreeBase conform to the subject matter of the IMDB, and these facts can be introduced into IMDB from FreeBase, which is a crucial way to enrich the IMDB.

Adding relevant facts from one knowledge graph U into another knowledge graph G is instrumental as this will help to enrich the content in the knowledge graph G and consequently improve the intelligent systems that use the knowledge graph G. Adding facts from one knowledge graph U into another existing domain specific knowledge graph G is not easy, as not all the facts in U are relevant to the subject matter of the contents in G. Adding irrelevant facts may violate the inherent nature of the existing knowledge graph. In other words, we hope to introduce new facts that conform to the subject matters of the existing domain-specific knowledge graph [1]. For example, the triple of ('Geoffrey Hinton', 'recipient of', '2018 ACM A.M. Turing Award') about a computer scientist is certainly irrelevant to the IMDB knowledge graph as the IMDB knowledge graph contains triples about movies, TV programs and actors. Such facts should not be added to the IMDB knowledge graph to avoid violation. The facts from U may contain entities or relations that are not in G. Such facts constructed by new entities or relations are denoted as unknown/new facts for graph G in this paper[4].

---

[1] www.freebase.com.

[2] IMDB is the world's most popular and authoritative source for movie, TV and celebrity content (https://www.imdb.com/).

[3] 'facts' and 'triples' are used interchangeably without confusion in this paper.

[4] 'unknown facts' and 'new facts' are used interchangeably in this paper.

Making sure as many relevant facts from U as possible are added to an existing knowledge graph G is key to enriching G but also preventing violating the inherent subject matter of the knowledge graph. This paper proposes to address this issue by learning embeddings to detect if an unknown fact is relevant to the subject matter of an existing knowledge graph so that only those relevant facts are added to an existing domain-specific knowledge graph.

For a fact $(h', r', t') \in U$, this paper focus on the following cases for this fact to be added to an existing knowledge graph $G = (E, R)$:

1. $r' \in R$, $h' \notin E$, or $t' \notin E$: at least one of the head or tail entities is unknown to the existing knowledge graph G;
2. $r' \notin R$: the relation is unknown to the existing knowledge graph G. This should also include the case where $r' \notin R$, $h' \notin E$, and $t' \notin E$.

For example, in Fig. 1, there are 2 relations between 'Tom Cruise' and 'Mission:Impossible'. There may be a new relation r' between the two entities, and the r' does not exist in R. On the other hand, the title of the new film 'Mission:Impossible 7', the latest movie starring 'Tom Cruise', that will be released in 2023, is a new entity, and it is now not in the entity set E. Therefore, it is necessary to detect whether the unknown facts constructed by new entities or new relations, such as ('Tom Cruise', '/film/producer/film' ,'Mission:Impossible 7'), are relevant or not to the subject of knowledge graph G before adding them into G.

Manually adding unknown facts into the existing knowledge graph is time-consuming and makes it difficult to validate if the unknown facts should belong to the knowledge graph. This paper seeks to show how to expand an existing domain-specific knowledge graph by adding relevant facts obtained from other knowledge graphs. The contributions of this work are as follows:

1. A novel knowledge graph expansion strategy is proposed, using unknown facts from other knowledge graphs;
2. A new embedding method via the composition of word information is introduced to embed a given fact and to judge if it should be added to the existing knowledge graph;
3. A new large dataset, UFD-303K, is created for this task. The experiments with UFD-303K show that our embedding method is effective for determining whether unknown facts are relevant and whether they should be added to the existing knowledge graph.

2   Related Work

Many KGs have been built but they are still incomplete [13, 19] due to missing entities or relations. Therefore, adding new entities or relations had been instrumental to improving the completeness of the existing graphs. This section presents key notation and related work about improving knowledge graph completeness.

2.1 Knowledge Graph Completion

There has been work about *knowledge graph completion* for 'closed' knowledge graphs using link prediction. The *translation-based models*, proposed in TransE [2], interpret each relation as a translating operation from a head entity to a tail entity for a triple $(h, r, t) \in G$, i.e., $\mathbf{h} + \mathbf{r} \approx \mathbf{t}$, where $\mathbf{h}, \mathbf{r}, \mathbf{t} \in \mathbb{R}^n$ are used to denote the embeddings for h, r, t, respectively. The learning objective is to minimise the loss of the score function $f_{\mathbf{r}}(\mathbf{h}, \mathbf{t}) = \|\mathbf{h} + \mathbf{r} - \mathbf{t}\|$ for all the triples in G. The TransH [21] projects h and t to the relationship-specific hyperplane to allow entities to play different roles in different relationships. The RotatE [15] treats the relation r as a rotating operation from h to t. The RESCAL [11] represents each relation as a full rank matrix and defines the score function as $f_{\mathbf{r}}(\mathbf{h}, \mathbf{t}) = \mathbf{h}^\top \mathbf{M_r} \mathbf{t}$. As full rank matrices are prone to over-fitting, recent work turns to make additional assumptions on $\mathbf{M_r}$. For example, DistMult [24] assumes $\mathbf{M_r}$ to be a diagonal matrix, which also utilizes the multi-linear dot product as the scoring function. To better model asymmetric and inverse relations, DistMult was extended by introducing complex-valued embeddings, followed by the proposal of ComplEx [17].

The above models are referred to as shallow models as they cannot capture the potential connection between entities and relationships well. *CNN-based* approaches have been proposed to capture the expressive features, such as, ConvE [4] and ConvKB [10]. ConvE and ConvKB take advantage of CNNs, which improves the expressive power by increasing the interactions between entities and relations.

However, the above models ignore the neighbourhood information in the process of embedding. The *Graph Convolutional Network-based methods* (GCNs) were proposed to address this issue, such as R-GCN [12], which is the first to show that the GCNs can be applied to model relational data. To explicitly and sufficiently model the Semantic Evidence into knowledge embedding, a new method SE-GNN [8] was proposed, where the three-level Semantic Evidence (entity level, relation level and triple-level) are modelled explicitly by the corresponding neighbour pattern and merged sufficiently by the multi-layer aggregation, which contributes to obtaining more extrapolative knowledge representation.

2.2 Knowledge Graph Completion with Unknown Entities

The above methods only focus on a closed knowledge graph, which enriches the knowledge graph by complementing the relationships between entities. However, with the growing volume of data on the Internet, new entities are constantly emerging over time. The entities obtained from the out-of-knowledge graph (called out-of-KG for short in this paper) have been used to enrich the existing knowledge graph [13, 14, 20, 22].

Zhang [20] first proposed a novel method of jointly embedding entities and words into the same continuous vector space, resulting in the prediction of facts containing entities that comes from the out-of-KG. In order to enhance the entities' semantic information, the entity description was used to help with knowledge graph embedding. For example, DKRL [22] employed two encoder methods, continuous Bag-of-words and convolutional neural network (CNN), to embed entity description and then to train models based TransE framework. The ConMask [14] used the CNN attention mechanism to mark which words in the entity description are related to the relation, and then generating target entity embedding. Shah et al. [13] proposed an open-word knowledge graph completion framework, OWE, based on any pre-trained embedding model, such as TransE. This framework aims to establish a mapping between entity descriptions and their pre-trained embeddings.

The above embedding methods use new entities from the out-of-KG to enrich the existing knowledge graph via word embeddings. However, they are not able to tell whether the new facts constructed with unknown entities are relevant to the existing knowledge graph and hence the new facts may violate the inherent coherence of the existing knowledge graph.

The entity alignment approach [9,23] aims to expand an existing knowledge graph by linking or aligning two entities from two different knowledge graphs that describe the same real-world object. For example, let G_1 and G_2 be two knowledge graphs to be aligned. If an entity e_1 in G_1 corresponds to another entity e_2 in G_2, we call (e_1, e_2) an alignment pair. The task of entity alignment is to find all alignment pairs across two knowledge graphs. Related work also includes extracting facts from texts to enrich an existing knowledge graph [6,25]. However, most of the existing work relies on the pre-defined relations, which are used to guide the extraction of facts from texts.

2.3 Remarks

This paper proposes to expand a domain-specific knowledge graph G by adding unknown facts from another knowledge graph U, where either the entities or the relations from U may be unknown to G. This is significantly different from and more challenging than the above mentioned work. As the unknown facts may contain new entities or relations which did not exist in G, we need to make sure that only the facts that are relevant to the subject matter of G from U can be added into G to avoid potential violation of the inherent subject matter of G.

3   Unknown Fact Detection

This section introduces a novel approach by learning word embeddings for the entities and relations, in order to detect if the unknown facts from U are relevant to the existing knowledge graph so that as many relevant facts from U as possible are added into G.

3.1   Constructing Description for Facts

We use a sub-graph (shown in Fig. 2) from the created UFD-303K dataset as an example. For each entity, a brief description (known as Mention in this paper) was obtained from WiKidata[5]. Each Mention (usually in a phrase or a sentence) provides a brief explanation for its associated entity. For example, the entity 'Titanic' has a Mention with '1997 American romantic disaster film directed by James Cameron'.

A triple (h, r, t) in a knowledge graph is used to denote a fact, i.e., the head entity h has a relation of r with the tail entity t. For example, as shown in Fig. 2, a triple $\tau =$

---

[5] https://www.wikidata.org/wiki/Wikidata:Main_Page.

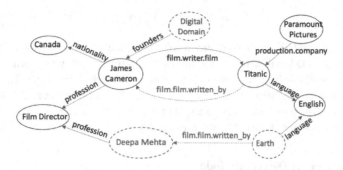

Fig. 2. A sub-graph of the UFD-303K dataset, the new dataset proposed by this work and the more details will be given in Sect. 4.1. The data use the format of (entity name, mention). For example, the format for entity 'James Cameron' is ('James Cameron', 'Canadian film director') and the format for entity 'Titanic' is ('Titanic', '1997 American romantic disaster film directed by James Cameron'). The new entities and new relations are introduced marked as red. (Color figure online)

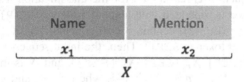

Fig. 3. The structure for representing entity or relation X.

('James Cameron', 'film.writer.film', 'Titanic') can be described as $D(\tau)$ = (James Cameron has a relation of film.writer.film with Titanic.). In order to enhance the semantic information for the triple, the external explanation information, such as the Mention, can be used to construct a meaningful description for the triple.

In this work, an entity or relation representation consists of 2 components (Name, Mention), as shown in Fig. 3. Here, the Name will refer to either the actual entity or relation and the Mention is usually a phrase or a sentence to interpret an entity. In order to increase the interaction between entities and the relation, we use the sentence template $\{r,$ which is between h and $t.\}$ to create a corresponding Mention for a relation within the facts. Let X be an entity or a relation, and X contains 2 components as shown in Fig. 3,

$$X = (x_1, x_2),\qquad(1)$$

where x_1 is a list of words for Name and x_2 is a list of words for Mention as shown in Fig. 3. For example, given an entity, 'Titanic', x_1 refers to itself, and x_2 denotes its Mention, '1997 American romantic disaster film directed by James Cameron'. Then, the entity 'Titanic' can be described as $X_{Titanic}$ = (Titanic, 1997 American romantic disaster film directed by James Cameron.). As a result, given a triple $\tau = (h, r, t)$, its new description can be represented as:

$$D(\tau) = (X_h; X_r; X_t), \tag{2}$$

where X_h, X_r, and X_t represent the word sequence of h, r, and t, which is initialized by Eq. (1). Finally, for τ = ('James Cameron', 'film.writer.film', 'Titanic'), it will be described by the new description constructed by Eq. (2), i.e., $D(\tau)$ = (James Cameron, Canadian film director; film.writer.film, which is between James Cameron and Titanic; Titanic, 1997 American romantic disaster film directed by James Cameron.).

3.2 Unknown Fact Detection Model

BERT [5] is a pre-trained language model based on a multilayer bidirectional Transformer encoder [18]. In this work, we fine-tune the pre-trained BERT for Unknown Fact Detection, known as UFD. The triple description will be concatenated together into a single sequence as input. The first token of every sequence is always a special classification token ([CLS]). The final hidden state corresponding to this token is used as the aggregated sequence representation for the classification task. Each component of the triple description is separated with a special token ([SEP]). For example, the triple description $D(\tau)$ (Eq. (2)) contain 3 components, X_h, X_r, and X_t, which are separated with a special token ([SEP]). Then, the input sequence will be represented as S = ([CLS] X_h [SEP] X_r [SEP] X_t [SEP]), and N is the number of tokens in the sequence, $N = |S| = m + n + k + 4$, where m, n, and k denote the number of tokens in X_h, X_r, and X_t, respectively. The pre-trained WordPice embeddings was used to initialize input tokens [5]. The final hidden vector of the special [CLS] token as $C_\tau \in \mathbb{R}^H$, where H is the hidden state size in pre-trained BERT. The only new parameters introduced during fine-tuning are classification layer weights $W \in \mathbb{R}^{K \times H}$, where K is the number of labels. Then, we compute a standard classification loss with C_τ and W (Eq. (3)).

3.3 Training

Finally, we train the model by optimizing a cross entropy loss:

$$L = \sum_{\tau \in G \cup G^-} (y_\tau \log(p_\tau) + (1 - y_\tau) \log(1 - p_\tau)), \tag{3}$$

where

$$p_\tau = \text{softmax}(C_\tau W^T), \tag{4}$$

$p_\tau \in \mathbb{R}^2$, which is two probability values $p_\tau = [p_{\tau_1}, p_{\tau_2}]$, indicating relevant probability and irrelevant probability, respectively. If the former p_{τ_1} is greater than the latter p_{τ_2}, the triplet is considered as related to the existing knowledge graph, and this triple can be introduced into the graph. $y_\tau \in \{0, 1\}$ indicates a negative or positive label, and G^- is the set of negative triples (fake triples) that are constructed by positive triples, and these all 'negative' triples are irrelevant to the existing knowledge G. This set is obtained using $G^- = G_1^- \cup G_2^- \cup G_3^- \cup G_4^- \cup G_5^-$ by considering 5 different cases as shown below to replace the entities or relations, for $\forall (h, r, t) \in G$:

$$G_1^- = \{(\overline{h_i}, r, t)|1 \leq i \leq m\},$$
$$G_2^- = \{(h, r, \overline{t_i})|1 \leq i \leq m\},$$
$$G_3^- = \{(\overline{h_i}, r, \overline{t_i})|1 \leq i \leq m\},$$
$$G_4^- = \{(h, \overline{r_i}, t)|1 \leq i \leq n\},$$
$$G_5^- = \{(\overline{h_i}, \overline{r_i}, \overline{t_i})|1 \leq i \leq n\},$$

where $\overline{h_i} \neq h$, and $\overline{t_i} \neq t$ are random samples from E, and $\overline{r_i} \neq r$ are random samples from R. In our experiments, we set $m = 1$ and $n = 2$.

4 Experiments

In this section, we evaluate our method for the unknown fact detection task. If a new fact is detected as relevant to the existing knowledge, it can be added to the knowledge graph. Otherwise, it should not be added. As such, this unknown fact detection is a binary classification task which is based on a score (Eq. 4) to tell whether a given fact (h, r, t) conforms to the subject matter of the existing domain-specific knowledge graph.

4.1 Datasets

Table 1. Statistics of the datasets. E_k, E_t, and E_u are the sets of entities, and R_k, R_t, R_u are the set of relations, where $E_k \subset E_t$, $R_k \subset R_t$, $E_t \cap E_u = \emptyset$, and $R_t \cap R_u = \emptyset$. The dataset contains 97309 ($E_t \cup E_u$) entities and 4762 ($R_t \cup R_u$) relations to construct Train and Test (303569 triples in total). In testing set, E indicates the entity or the relation occurs in the training set while O means they do not occur in the training set.

			#Triples	#Entities		#Relations	
				In-KG	Out-of-KG	In-KG	Out-of-KG
UFD-303K	#Train	E - E - E	243998	49391 (E_t)	0	1734 (R_t)	0
	#Test	E - O - E	3234	16516 (E_k)	47918 (E_u)	1282 (R_k)	3028 (R_u)
		E - $\overleftarrow{O}$ - E	8289				
		O - E - O	11829				
		O - E - E	10026				
		E - E - O	7261				
		O - O - O	8145				
		O - $\overleftarrow{O}$ - O	10787				

In this work, we create a new dataset called UFD-303K from FreeBase. Table 1 is a summary of the entities and relations in UFD-303K. This dataset is split into 2 parts,

#Train (training set) and #Test (test set), to represent two knowledge graphs and #Train ∩ #Test = ∅. We assume that #Train is an existing domain-specific knowledge graph, and we introduce facts that conform to the subject matter of #Train from another knowledge graph #Test.

As shown in Table 1, the set of known entities is denoted as E_t and $|E_t| = 49391$. The set of known relations is denoted as R_t and $|R_t| = 1734$. Both E_t and R_t are used to build the training set using the facts from FreeBase. R_t does not have any two relations that are inverse relationship to each other. The set of 47918 new entities E_u has no common entities with E_t, and the set of 3028 relations R_u has no common relations with R_t.

For the dataset, the #Test (test set) includes 7 kinds of type triples: E-$\overleftarrow{O}$-E, E-O-E, O-E-O, O-E-E, E-E-O, O-$\overleftarrow{O}$-O, O-O-O, where E indicates the entity or the relation that occurs in the training set, while O means they do not occur in the training set. The $\overleftarrow{O}$ indicates that the new relations have reverse relations in training data. For example, as shown in Fig. 2, ('Earth', 'film.film.written_by', 'Deepa Mehta') is an unknown fact, belonging to the O-$\overleftarrow{O}$-O type, where all elements, 'Earth' $\in E_u$, 'film.film.written_by' $\in R_u$, and 'Deepa Mehta' $\in E_u$, are unknown. The relation 'film.film.written_by' in R_u is an inverse relationship of 'film.writer.film' in R_t.

4.2 Hyper-parameter Settings

We choose the pre-trained BERT-Base model with 12 layers, 12 self-attention heads and $H = 768$ [5]. Following the original BERT, we set the following hyper-parameters in our model to fine-tune: The batch size is 32; The learning rate is set among {5e−5, 3e−5, 0.001}; The N is set among {100, 200, 300, 400}; The number of epochs is set among {2, 5, 10}. Unknown fact detection is a binary classification task and therefore $K = 2$ in this work.

4.3 Unknown Fact Detection Results

In this section, we evaluate the performance of our method on a new dataset, UFD-303K, using accuracy, recall, precision, and F_1. However, the UFD-303K only provides positive triples. A testing set with negative triples are created for the 7 cases as Table 1 shows the number of positive triples. For each positive triple in the testing set, two negative triples are created by replacing head or tail entity with two randomly selected entities from $E_t \cup E_u$. The details are shown in Table 2.

The training set denotes an existing domain knowledge graph and is used to train a model, and the test set simulates the unknown facts obtained from other knowledge graphs. We use the trained model to detect whether these unknown facts are relevant to the subject matter of existing knowledge graph (the training set). Table 3 shows the results of facts detection on 7 test cases. From the results, we observe that the predicted performance of the E-$\overleftarrow{O}$-E case is better than the E-O-E, especially on Recall. Also, we observe that the O-$\overleftarrow{O}$-O obtained detection results are better than O-O-O because the relations of the O-$\overleftarrow{O}$-O cases have inverse relationships in the training set. As noted by [16], if the test set contains the inverse relations of the training set, the inverse relations

Table 2. A testing set with negative triples are created for the 7 cases as Table 1 shows the number of positive triples. For each positive triple in the testing set, two negative triples are created by replacing head or tail entity with two randomly selected entities from $E_t \cup E_u$.

7 cases	$r' \notin R$, and $h', t' \in E$		$r' \in R$, and h' or $t' \notin E$			$r' \notin R$, and $h', t' \notin E$	
	E - $\overleftarrow{O}$ - E	E - O - E	O - E - O	O - E - E	E - E - O	O - $\overleftarrow{O}$ - O	O - O - O
#Test (positive)	8289	3234	11829	10026	7261	10787	8145
#Test (negative)	16578	6468	23658	20052	14522	21574	16290

Table 3. Experimental results on unknown fact detection for 7 test cases using true positive (TP), true negative (TN), false positive (FP) and false negative (FN). They are used to calculate accuracy, recall, precision and F_1 score

7 cases	$r' \notin R$, and $h', t' \in E$		$r' \in R$, and h' or $t' \notin E$			$r' \notin R$, and $h', t' \notin E$	
	E - $\overleftarrow{O}$ - E	E - O - E	O - E - O	O - E - E	E - E - O	O - $\overleftarrow{O}$ - O	O - O - O
TN	16410	6420	23456	19779	14354	21409	16154
FP	168	48	202	273	168	165	136
FN	840	589	1750	918	630	1942	2328
TP	7449	2645	10079	9108	6631	8845	5817
$Accuracy$	0.9594	0.9343	0.9449	0.9604	0.9633	0.9348	0.8991
$Recall$	0.8986	0.8178	0.8520	0.9084	0.9132	0.8199	0.7141
$Precision$	0.9779	0.9821	0.9803	0.9708	0.9752	0.9816	0.9771
F_1	0.9366	0.8925	0.9117	0.9386	0.9432	0.8935	0.8252

can help to obtain a good predicting result. This is because the inverse relations may have some common knowledge with the training data. For the result of unknown facts consisting of the new entity (O-E-O, O-E-E, and E-E-O cases), we obtained comparable performance on O-E-E and E-E-O cases, and higher than O-E-O case.

Table 4. Unknown fact detection on WN18RR and YAGO3-10 test set. TNR (True Negative Rate) indicates the ratio of true negative and total negative, i.e., $TNR = TN/(TN + FP)$

	WN18RR (test set)	YAGO3-10 (test set)
#Test	3134	5000
TN	2571	4269
FP	563	731
TNR	0.8203	0.8538

We also need to make sure that our model does not classify the irrelevant triples as relevant to the existing knowledge graph. We use WN18RR[6] [10], and YAGO3-10[7] [4]

---

[6] WN18RR is a sub-set of a lexical database of English.
[7] YAGO3-10 is a sub-set of large semantic knowledge base, derived from Wikipedia, WordNet, and other data sources.

as irrelevant triples since they are different KGs from the UFD-303K. We would expect as high TN and TNR as possible as we do not want to add those irrelevant triples from WN18RR and YAGO3-10 into UFD-303K.

The training set of UFD-303K is used to train the model. After the training process, the test set of WN18RR and YAGO3-10 are detected by the trained model. The WN18RR and YAGO3-10 is O-O-O case according to the division in Table 1, where both entities and relations are unknown to UFD-303K. The experimental results are shown in Table 4, from which we observe that TNR is 82.03 % for WN18RR and 85.38 % for YAGO3-10. From Table 3 and 4, our method can detect the relevant triples (shows in Table 3) from U but also is effective to filter out the irrelevant triples (shows in Table 4) .

5   Conclusion and Future Work

In this paper, we propose a novel strategy to expand an existing domain-specific knowledge graph with relevant unknown facts that may come from other knowledge graphs; A new embedding method, UFD, is introduced to learn embeddings for entities and relations to judge unknown triples. This method is validated using a new dataset (UFD-303K), and the experiments show that our embedding method effectively distinguishes the relevance of unknown facts to an existing domain-specific knowledge graph.

Our future work will include canonicalisation for entities and relations [3] to reduce information redundancy, caused by adding new facts into the existing knowledge graph. For example, if the entity 'James Cameron' occurs in an existing domain-specific knowledge graph, adding a new triple with the entity 'James Francis Cameron' into this existing knowledge graph may potentially duplicate the information when 'James Francis Cameron' and 'James Cameron' in fact refer to the same person.

References

1. Abu-Salih, B.: Domain-specific knowledge graphs: a survey. J. Netw. Comput. Appl. **185**, 103076 (2021)
2. Bordes, A., Usunier, N., Garcia-Duran, A., Weston, J., Yakhnenko, O.: Translating embeddings for modeling multi-relational data. In: Neural Information Processing Systems (NIPS), pp. 1–9 (2013)
3. Dash, S., Rossiello, G., Mihindukulasooriya, N., Bagchi, S., Gliozzo, A.: Open knowledge graphs canonicalization using variational autoencoders. In: Proceedings of the 2021 Conference on Empirical Methods in Natural Language Processing, EMNLP 2021, pp. 10379–10394 (2021)
4. Dettmers, T., Minervini, P., Stenetorp, P., Riedel, S.: Convolutional 2d knowledge graph embeddings. In: Proceedings of the Thirty-Second AAAI Conference on Artificial Intelligence, pp. 1811–1818 (2018)
5. Devlin, J., Chang, M., Lee, K., Toutanova, K.: BERT: pre-training of deep bidirectional transformers for language understanding. In: Proceedings of the 2019 Conference of the North American Chapter of the Association for Computational Linguistics: Human Language Technologies, pp. 4171–4186 (2019)

6. Hwang, E., Lee, J., Yang, T., Patel, D., Zhang, D., McCallum, A.: Event-event relation extraction using probabilistic box embedding. In: Muresan, S., Nakov, P., Villavicencio, A. (eds.) Proceedings of the 60th Annual Meeting of the Association for Computational Linguistics (Volume 2: Short Papers), pp. 235–244. ACL 2022, Dublin, Ireland, 22–27 May 22–27 2022. Association for Computational Linguistics (2022)

7. Ji, S., Pan, S., Cambria, E., Marttinen, P., Philip, S.Y.: A survey on knowledge graphs: representation, acquisition, and applications. IEEE Trans. Neural Netw. Learn. Syst. **33**, 1–21 (2021)

8. Li, R., et al.: How does knowledge graph embedding extrapolate to unseen data: a semantic evidence view. In: Thirty-Sixth AAAI Conference on Artificial Intelligence, pp. 5781–5791. AAAI, (2022)

9. Mao, X., et al.: An effective and efficient entity alignment decoding algorithm via third-order tensor isomorphism. In: Proceedings of the 60th Annual Meeting of the Association for Computational Linguistics (Volume 1: Long Papers), pp. 5888–5898. ACL 2022, Dublin, Ireland, 22–27 May 22–27 2022 (2022)

10. Nguyen, D.Q., Nguyen, T.D., Nguyen, D.Q., Phung, D.Q.: A novel embedding model for knowledge base completion based on convolutional neural network. In: Proceedings of the 2018 Conference of the North American Chapter of the Association for Computational Linguistics: Human Language Technologies, Volume 2 (Short Papers), pp. 327–333 (2018)

11. Nickel, M., Tresp, V., Kriegel, H.: A three-way model for collective learning on multi-relational data. In: Proceedings of the 28th International Conference on Machine Learning, pp. 809–816. ICML 2011, Bellevue, 28 June 28–July 2 2011 (2011)

12. Schlichtkrull, M., Kipf, T.N., Bloem, P., van den Berg, R., Titov, I., Welling, M.: Modeling relational data with graph convolutional networks. In: Gangemi, A., et al. (eds.) ESWC 2018. LNCS, vol. 10843, pp. 593–607. Springer, Cham (2018). https://doi.org/10.1007/978-3-319-93417-4_38

13. Shah, H., Villmow, J., Ulges, A., Schwanecke, U., Shafait, F.: An open-world extension to knowledge graph completion models. In: Proceedings of the AAAI Conference on Artificial Intelligence, vol. 33, pp. 3044–3051 (2019)

14. Shi, B., Weninger, T.: Open-world knowledge graph completion. In: Proceedings of the Thirty-Second AAAI Conference on Artificial Intelligence, (AAAI-18), New Orleans, Louisiana, USA, 2–7 February 2018, pp. 1957–1964 (2018)

15. Sun, Z., Deng, Z., Nie, J., Tang, J.: Rotate: Knowledge graph embedding by relational rotation in complex space. In: 7th International Conference on Learning Representations, ICLR, pp. 1–18 (2019)

16. Toutanova, K., Chen, D.: Observed versus latent features for knowledge base and text inference. In: Proceedings of the 3rd Workshop on Continuous Vector Space Models and their Compositionality, pp. 57–66 (2015)

17. Trouillon, T., Welbl, J., Riedel, S., Gaussier, É., Bouchard, G.: Complex embeddings for simple link prediction. In: International Conference on Machine Learning, pp. 2071–2080 (2016)

18. Vaswani, A., et al.: Attention is all you need. In: Advances in Neural Information Processing Systems 30: Annual Conference on Neural Information Processing Systems, pp. 5998–6008 (2017)

19. Wang, B., Shen, T., Long, G., Zhou, T., Wang, Y., Chang, Y.: Structure-augmented text representation learning for efficient knowledge graph completion. In: WWW 2021: The Web Conference 2021, Virtual Event / Ljubljana, Slovenia, 19–23 April 19–23 2021, pp. 1737–1748 (2021)

20. Wang, Z., Zhang, J., Feng, J., Chen, Z.: Knowledge graph and text jointly embedding. In: Proceedings of the 2014 Conference on Empirical Methods in Natural Language Processing, pp. 1591–1601 (2014)

21. Wang, Z., Zhang, J., Feng, J., Chen, Z.: Knowledge graph embedding by translating on hyperplanes. In: Proceedings of the Twenty-Eighth AAAI Conference on Artificial Intelligence, 27–31 July 27–31 2014, Québec City, Québec, Canada, pp. 1112–1119 (2014)

22. Xie, R., Liu, Z., Jia, J., Luan, H., Sun, M.: Representation learning of knowledge graphs with entity descriptions. In: Proceedings of the Thirtieth AAAI Conference on Artificial Intelligence, 12–17 February 12–17 2016, Phoenix, pp. 2659–2665 (2016)

23. Yan, Y., Liu, L., Ban, Y., Jing, B., Tong, H.: Dynamic knowledge graph alignment. In: Proceedings of the AAAI Conference on Artificial Intelligence, vol. 35, pp. 4564–4572 (2021)

24. Yang, B., Yih, W., He, X., Gao, J., Deng, L.: Embedding entities and relations for learning and inference in knowledge bases. In: 3rd International Conference on Learning Representations, pp. 1–12. ICLR 2015, San Diego, 7–9 May 7–9 2015, Conference Track Proceedings (2015)

25. Zhu, H., Lin, Y., Liu, Z., Fu, J., Chua, T., Sun, M.: Graph neural networks with generated parameters for relation extraction. In: Proceedings of the 57th Conference of the Association for Computational Linguistics, ACL 2019, Florence, Italy, 28 July–2 August 2019, Volume 1: Long Papers, pp. 1331–1339 (2019)

Knowledge Graph Representation Learning via Generated Descriptions

Miao Hu$^{(\boxtimes)}$ (iD), Zhiwei Lin, and Adele Marshall (iD)

School of Mathematics and Physics, Queen's University Belfast, Belfast, UK
{mhu05,z.lin,a.h.marshall}@qub.ac.uk

Abstract. Knowledge graph representation learning (KGRL) aims to project the entities and relations into a continuous low-dimensional knowledge graph space to be used for knowledge graph completion and detecting new triples. Using textual descriptions for entity representation learning has been a key topic. However, the current work has two major constraints: (1) some entities do not have any associated descriptions; (2) the associated descriptions are usually phrases, and they do not contain enough information. This paper presents a novel KGRL method for learning effective embeddings by generating meaningful descriptive sentences from entities' connections. The experiments using four public datasets and a new proposed dataset show that the **N**ew **D**escription-Embodied **K**nowledge **G**raph **E**mbedding (NDKGE for short) approach introduced in this paper outperforms most of the existing work in the task of link prediction. The code and datasets of this paper can be obtained from GitHub (https://github.com/MiaoHu-Pro/NDKGE.)

Keywords: Knowledge graph embedding · Entity description · Constructing new descriptions · Link prediction

1 Introduction

A *knowledge graph* $G = \{(h,r,t)|h,t \in E, r \in R\}$ [4,10] contains a set of nodes E for entities and a set of edges R for the relations between the entities. A *triple* (h,r,t) in a knowledge graph, $(h,r,t) \in G$, where $h,t \in E$ and a $r \subset R$. Triple (h,r,t) is usually used to denote a fact where a head entity h has a relation of r with a tail entity t. For example, as shown in Fig. 1, ('Tom Cruise', '/film/producer/film', 'Mission: Impossible') is a triple where the head entity is 'Tom Cruise', the relation is 'film/producer/film', and the tail entity is 'Mission: Impossible'. Large scale knowledge graphs, such as FreeBase, have played key roles in supporting intelligent question answering, recommendation systems, and searches engines. However, most of them were built collaboratively by humans, where emerging relationships and entities may not be included. This is so-called *incompleteness* and *sparseness* of knowledge graph [10]. Thus, it is important to enrich knowledge graphs automatically to reduce those issues.

Knowledge graph representation learning (KGRL), also known as *knowledge graph embedding* (KGE), aims to automatically enrich knowledge graphs by representing entities and their relations into a continuous low-dimensional vector space so that the missing entities and relations can be inferred using those embeddings [4]. Two key tasks,

E. Métais et al. (Eds.): NLDB 2023, LNCS 13913, pp. 365–378, 2023.
https://doi.org/10.1007/978-3-031-35320-8_26

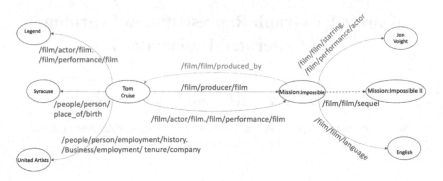

Fig. 1. An example of a sub-graph from the FB15K [4] dataset, where the nodes are entities, and the directed edges represent relationships between the entities. The head entity 'Tom Cruise' has two relations pointing at the tail entity 'Mission:Impossible' while the entity 'Mission:Impossible' is the head entity to the tail entity of 'Tom Cruise' with a relation of '/film/film/produced_by'. Most entities in the FB15K dataset contain a mention to explain the entity. For example, the entity 'Tom Cruise' has a mention of 'American actor and film producer' and the entity 'Mission:Impossible' has a mention of '1996 film directed by Brian De Palma'.

link prediction and triple classification, have been proposed by [4] to consolidate a knowledge graph G, where both tasks are about making sure if a triple (h, r, t) exists in the knowledge graph, i.e., $(h, r, t) \in G$.

The early work, such as *translation-based models* [1,4,5,7,23], treats a triple (h, r, t) as a translation operation from head entity h to tail entity t via a relation r. Recently, researchers realised the importance of using textual information for learning effective embeddings [2,9,22]. These approaches use the associated descriptions for entities, or they extract relevant entity description information from external sources to help learning knowledge graph embedding. Although these methods have improved the performance in the link prediction task by using external information for the entities, they have the following key constraints:

1. the associated descriptions, also called *mention* are usually a phrase, which does not have enough meaningful information without enough context. For example, the mention for 'Tom Cruise' is 'American actor and film producer' as show in Fig. 1. This does not provide enough detail to explain who 'Tom Cruise' is as it does not have any information regarding what films he had been involved in.
2. the associated description is not always available. For example, in the FB15K dataset, some entities do not have the associated descriptions;
3. the associated description obtained from external sources may not be accurate and may introduce noise into the training data.

To address these problems, this paper proposes a novel description-based KGE approach, known as New Description-Embodied Knowledge Graph Embedding (NDKGE for short), by creating a new description from their neighbours for each entity. The difference from all previous methods is: we use entities' neighbours to construct a sentence-level description and then learn meaningful embeddings from the text. This NDKGE approach does not rely on external sources and it is believed that the generated description will help the algorithm to learn more meaningful and effective knowledge graph embeddings. The contributions of this paper include:

1. Sentence-level semantic description for entities generated by aggregating neighbour-hood information;
2. A new data structure including an ID, name, mention, and a generated description introduced to represent an entity and a relation;
3. Experiments conducted to show that the sentence-level description is very useful for learning effective embeddings.

2 Related Work

This section presents key notation and related work in knowledge graph representation learning. For a triple $(h, r, t) \in G$, $\mathbf{h}, \mathbf{r}, \mathbf{t} \in \mathbb{R}^n$ is used to denote their embeddings, respectively.

TransE [4] interprets each relation as a translating operation from a head entity to a tail entity, i.e., $\mathbf{h} + \mathbf{r} \approx \mathbf{t}$. The learning objective is to minimise the loss of the score function

$$f_{\mathbf{r}}(\mathbf{h}, \mathbf{t}) = \|\mathbf{h} + \mathbf{r} - \mathbf{t}\| \tag{1}$$

for all the triples in G, where we take to be the L_1-norm. Studies have shown that the TransE performs well for 1-to-1 relations, but its performance drops significantly for 1-to-N, N-to-1, and N-to-N relations [28]. TransH [28] tries to solve the issues in the TransE by projecting h and t to the relationship-specific hyperplane, in order to allow entities to play different roles in different relationships. The PTransE [14] believes that multi-step relation paths contain rich inference patterns between entities. It considers relation paths as translations between entities. The TransE-EMM [17] introduced a neighbourhood mixture model for knowledge base completion by combining neighbour-based vector representations for entities. Compared with the TransE-EMM, our method relies on the generated entity descriptions to conduct embedding rather than computing entity representations directly based on neighbourhood entities and relations. The RotatE [23] treats the relation r as a rotating operation from h to t. The HAKE [35] models semantic hierarchies map entities into the polar coordinate system. It is inspired by the fact that concentric circles in the polar coordinate system can naturally reflect hierarchy. The BoxE [1] encodes relations as axis-aligned hyper-rectangles (or boxes) and entities as points in the d-dimensional euclidian space. The PairRE [7] uses two vectors for relation representation. These vectors project the corresponding head and tail entities to Euclidean space, where the distance between the projected vectors is minimized. The DualE [5] uses dual quaternion to unify translation and rotation in one model, where the new model can solve symmetry, antisymmetry, inversion, composition and multiple relations problems.

RESCAL [18] represents each relation as a full rank matrix and defines the score function as $f_{\mathbf{r}}(\mathbf{h}, \mathbf{t}) = \mathbf{h}^\top \mathbf{M_r} \mathbf{t}$. As full rank matrices are prone to over-fitting, recent work turns to make additional assumptions on $\mathbf{M_r}$. For example, DistMult [33] assumes

M_r to be a diagonal matrix, which also utilizes the multi-linear dot product as the scoring function. However, for general knowledge graphs, these simplified models are often less expressive and powerful. To better model asymmetric and inverse relations, DistMult was extended by introducing complex-valued embeddings, followed by the proposal of ComplEx [26]. The SimplE [11] uses the same diagonal constraint as Dist-Mult. It models each fact in two forms (a direct and an inverse form). To represent such forms, It embeds each entity e in separate head and tail vectors e_h and e_t, and each relation r in individual direct and inverse vectors V_r and V_{-r}, which is fully expressive and can successfully model asymmetric relations. KGE-CL [32] proposed a simple yet efficient contrastive learning framework, which can capture the semantic similarity of the related entities and entity-relation couples in different triples, thus improving the expressiveness of embeddings.

The CNN-based approaches, such as ConvE [8] and ConvKB [16], improve the expressive power by increasing the interactions between entities and relations. CapsE [27] employs a capsule network to model the entries in the triple at the same dimension.

The Graph Convolutional Network-based methods (GCNs) were proposed to do embedding, such as R-GCN [20], which is the first to show that the GCNs can be applied to model relational data. This method aims to conduct the central node embedding by aggregating its neighbourhood information [12]. To explicitly and sufficiently model the Semantic Evidence into knowledge embedding, a new method SE-GNN [13] was proposed, where the three-level Semantic Evidence (entity level, relation level and triple-level) are modelled explicitly by the corresponding neighbour pattern and merged sufficiently by the multi-layer aggregation, which contributes to obtaining more extrapolative knowledge representation.

Text-based models take advantage of entity descriptions to help knowledge graph embedding. The majority of knowledge graphs include a brief entity description, called mention, for entities. Each mention, usually in a phrase, briefly explains its associated entity. Jointly (desp) [36] utilized an alternative alignment model that is not dependent on Wikipedia anchors and is based on text descriptions of entities. DKRL [30] employed two encoder methods, continuous Bag-of-words (CBOW) and convolutional neural network (CNN), to embed entity description and then to train models based on TransE. Jointly (LSTM) [31] used three encoder methods for joint knowledge graph embedding with structural and entity description and set the gating mechanism to integrate representations of structure and text into a unified architecture. ConMask [22] used the CNN attention mechanism to mark which words in the entity description are related to the relations and then generate target entity embedding. An et al. [2] proposed an accurate text-enhanced KG representation framework (AATE_E), which can utilize accurate textual information extracted from additional text to enhance the knowledge representations. Shah et al. [21] proposed an open-word detection framework, OWE, based on any pre-trained embedding model, such as TransE [4]. This framework aims to establish a mapping between entity descriptions and their pre-trained embeddings. Hu et al. [9] proposed to model the whole auxiliary text corpus with a graph and present an end-to-end text-graph enhanced KG embedding.

The above textual-based methods must satisfy a precondition, which is the entity descriptions, or available relevant texts. In other words, if the entity descriptions or related text are missing or can not be obtained, these methods will be unable to perform knowledge graph embedding. This paper proposes a model, NDKGE, which is a textual-based model. NDKGE aims to solve the problem of unavailable descriptions and creates a high-quality description for entities.

3 Constructing New Entity Description for Knowledge Graph Embedding

This section presents a novel method to create descriptions for entities by aggregating the entity's neighbours' information in order to learn effective representations for entities and their relations.

3.1 Word-Level and Sentence-Level Semantics

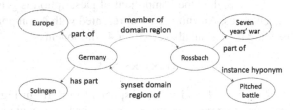

Fig. 2. A sub-graph of the WN18 dataset. The data use the format of (ID, entity name, mention). For example, the format for entity 'Germany' is (08766988, 'Germany', 'a republic in central Europe') and the format for entity 'Rossbach' is (01292928, 'Rossbach', 'a battle in the Seven Years' War (1757)').

The existing textual-based methods, such as SSP [29], AATE_E [2], and Teger-TransE [9] use the pre-defined descriptions which are associated with the entities in a knowledge graph. For example, in the WN18 dataset, the format for entity 'Germany' is (08766988, 'Germany', 'a republic in central Europe') as shown in Fig. 2, where 'a republic in central Europe' is the *mention* that is associated to 'Germany' and 08766988 is its unique ID.

However, not every entity has its associated description and the associated mention can be too brief to provide enough detail about the entity. With brief mentions or without any associated mentions, the performance could be compromised. As such, this paper aims to represent entities using more informative descriptions generated from their neighbours.

In this work, a new entity representation consists of four components (ID, Name, Mention, and Description), as shown in Fig. 3, where ID, Name, and Mention can be obtained from those existing knowledge graphs. Here, the Name will refer to either the actual entity or relation and the Mention is usually a phrase to interpret an entity (when the Name refers to an entity).

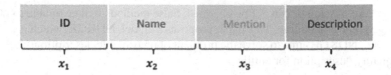

Fig. 3. The structure for representing entity or relation x. An entity may contain all four components but a relation will only contains (ID, Name), where name is the relation name.

The component of Description for each entity x is obtained by generating a set of sentences $D(x)$, where $D(x) = \{x$ has a relation of r with $y : \forall (x, r, y) \in G\}$, from which k sentences are randomly picked ($k \leq |D(x)|$) and concatenated to construct a Description for entity x. For example, according to Fig. 2, if entity x is 'Germany', then $D(x)=\{$'Germany has a relation of part of with Europe.', 'Germany has a relation of member of domain region with Europe.', 'Germany has a relation of has part with Solingen.'$\}$, which has three sentences. If $k = 3$, then the component of Description is generated by concatenating the three sentences. An entity x is represented with 4 components as shown in Fig. 3. The embedding for x shall also consider 4 components

$$\mathbf{x} = \{\mathbf{x}_1, \mathbf{x}_2, \mathbf{x}_3, \mathbf{x}_4\}, \tag{2}$$

where $\mathbf{x}_i \in \mathbb{R}^n$ for $1 \leq i \leq 4$, and $\mathbf{x}_1$ corresponds to the ID in Fig. 3. For $\mathbf{x}_2$, $\mathbf{x}_3$ and $\mathbf{x}_4$, as their corresponding components x_2, x_3, x_4 in Fig. 3 contain tokens/words, word embeddings are used to initiate $\mathbf{x}_2$, $\mathbf{x}_3$ and $\mathbf{x}_4$. Let $W \subseteq \mathbb{R}^n$ be the set of word embeddings and suppose x_i ($2 \leq i \leq 4$) contains n tokens $(x_{i_1}, \ldots, x_{i_n})$, then

$$\mathbf{x}_i = \frac{1}{n} \sum_{j=1}^{n} \mathbf{x}_{i_j} \tag{3}$$

where $\mathbf{x}_{i_j} \in W$ is the embedding for token x_{i_j}.

Algorithm 1 shows a function to calculate the embeddings $(\mathbf{h}, \mathbf{r}, \mathbf{t})$ for a triple $(h, r, t) \in G$, where the representation of entities ($\mathbf{h}$ or $\mathbf{t}$) and relations ($\mathbf{r}$) will be calculated according to different settings such as '*mention*' and '*description*'. For example, $\mathbf{h}$ =representation(h,'*description*') and $\mathbf{t}$ =representation(t,'*description*') will use the contextual information in the Description that are generated as shown in Fig. 3. As a relation does not have a Mention and no Description is generated, $\mathbf{r}$ is obtained using $\mathbf{r}$ =representation(r,'*name*'). The entities h or t, and relations r denote $\mathbf{x}$ represented by the Eq. (2). After $(\mathbf{h}, \mathbf{r}, \mathbf{t})$ is obtained, the TransE score function Eq. (1) is used for optimizing $(\mathbf{h}, \mathbf{r}, \mathbf{t})$.

3.2 Training

Our model uses the vectors constructed above as input. The embedding of the entities and relations is obtained after the model training is completed. We use the max-margin criterion [4] for training, and define the following loss function to optimize the model:

Algorithm 1: Generating initial embedding vectors for entities or relations x

---

Data: A knowledge graph G; A set of word embeddings W
Input: Entity or relation x (represented with Eq. (2)), method y for combining
embedding vectors
Result: Embedding vector $\mathbf{v}_x$ for input x
Function representation(x, y):

    Initialize $\mathbf{x}_1$ by a random vector or pre-trained embeddings [16];
    Calculate $\mathbf{x}_2$ using Eq. (3) ;
    if $y = $ *'name'* **then**
        | $\mathbf{x}_2 = \mathbf{x}_2$;
    end
    if $y = $ *'mention'* **then**
        | $\mathbf{x}_2 = \mathbf{x}_2 + \mathbf{x}_3$;
    end
    else if $y = $ *'description'* **then**
        | $\mathbf{x}_2 = \mathbf{x}_2 + \mathbf{x}_3 + \mathbf{x}_4$;
    end
    return $\mathbf{v}_x = \mathbf{x}_1 \oplus \mathbf{x}_2$ (The $\oplus$ denotes that two vectors are concatenated.);

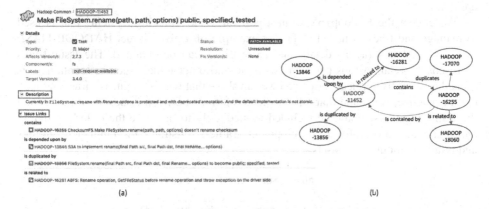

(a)   (b)

Fig. 4. A summary of the issues in Issue Tracker System. For the given issue, HADOOP-11452, has several attributes, such as Type, Status, and Priority, as shown in (a). On the other hand, the description (known as Mention in this work) and Issue Links were provided. And these Issue Links can be represented to a graph as shown in (b). In this paper, the links between issues are known as relations, and the issues are known as entities.

$$L = \sum_{(h,r,t)\in G} \sum_{(h',r,t')\in G'} \max(\gamma + f_{\mathbf{r}}(\mathbf{h},\mathbf{t}) \tag{4}$$
$$- f_{\mathbf{r}}(\mathbf{h}',\mathbf{t}'), 0)$$

where (h', r, t') is the negative triple, and γ is a hyper-parameter representing the max-margin between positive triples scores and negative triples scores. G' is the negative triple set generated by positive triples G with head or tail randomly replaced by another entity. Most importantly, the head and tail can not be replaced at the same time [4].

$$G' = \{(h', r, t) \,|h' \in E\} \cup \{(h, r, t') \,|t' \in E\} \qquad (5)$$

In the training process, our model needs to learn the parameter set $\theta = \{\mathbf{E}, \mathbf{R}\}$ where $\mathbf{E} = \{\mathbf{h}, \mathbf{t}|\forall(h, r, t) \in G\}$, $\mathbf{R} = \{\mathbf{r}|\forall r \in R\}$ stand for the embeddings for entities and relations.

4   Experiments

4.1   Datasets

In this paper, four commonly used datasets, FB15K [4], WN18 [29], FB15K237 [8], WN18RR [8], and a new dataset Hadoop16K proposed by this work are used to evaluate NDKGE model on link prediction task. FB15K and WN18 are extracted from the FreeBase[1] and WordNet[2] respectively. FB15K237 and WN18RR were considered as challenging datasets, which is a subset of FB15K and WN18 where inverse relations are removed.

We collect the Hadoop16K from a popular Issue Tracking System[3] that is used to manage and track issues [15]. For an example of a given issue, HADOOP-11452, as shown in Fig. 4 (a), its details and Issue Links can be obtained. The Issue Links represent the relationships between this issue and other issues, such as 'contains', 'is related to', and 'is duplicated by', and we can show that with a graph, as shown in Fig. 4 (b). In practice, we found that a lot of links/relations between issues are missing, and these missing links should be included immediately to facilitate the orderly progress and maintenance of software development. Table 1 illustrates the number of entities and relations about the datasets.

Table 1. Summary of datasets.

Dataset	#Rel	#Ent	#Train	#Valid	#Test
FB15K	1345	14951	483142	50000	59071
WN18	18	40943	141442	5000	5000
FB15K237	237	14541	272115	17535	20466
WN18RR	11	40943	86835	3034	3134
Hadoop16K	31	12249	15791	1974	1974

4.2   Parameter Settings

The experiments use different margin γ from $\{0.5, 1, 3, 5\}$ and the learning rate λ is set among $\{0.01, 0.05, 0.5, 1\}$. Also, we set the dimension of ID embedding $\mathbf{x}_1$ in

---

[1] www.freebase.com.
[2] https://wordnet.princeton.edu/.
[3] https://issues.apache.org/.

Algorithm 1 among $\{20, 50, 100, 200\}$, and the dimension of textual embedding x_2 among $\{50, 100, 200, 300\}$. The number k of neighbours for generating descriptions is $|D(x)|$. The measure of dissimilarity is L_1 distance. At the same time, the experiment conducts a setting *description* for using Name, Mention and generated sentence-level Description.

4.3 Link Prediction

Link prediction aims to complete a triple (h, r, t) with h or t missing. For example, to predict t given an in-complete triple $(h, r, ?)$ or predict h given $(?, r, t)$. We use two evaluation metrics in accordance with [4]: (1) the mean rank of correct entities; (2) the proportion of valid entities in the top 10 for the entity. In addition, we use the evaluation settings "Filter" [4,28]. Tables 2, 3 show the results of entity prediction.

As illustrated in Table 2, compared with *translation-based models* such as RotatE [23], PairRE [7], and DualE [5] that only encode entity/relation ID, our method can achieve high performances by using not only entity/relation ID but also textual information (entity name, mention and description). This indicates that related textual information is very helpful for effective knowledge graph embeddings. Also, we observe that our method is better than other text-based method, such as ConMask [22], and Teger-TransE [9], this indicates that the newly constructed entity description is reasonable and better than the original text. For WN18 dataset, our method achieves the best performance in Mean Rank (MR) and Hits@10 compared with all baselines. It even also surpasses the latest method such as PairRE [7] and DualE [5] in Hits@10.

Table 3 shows that our model NDKGE significantly outperforms the state-of-the-art models on the WN18RR. Our NDKGE with the `description` setting can obtain 0.699 for Hits@10, which is 10% higher than the state-of-the-art RESCAL-CL [32] to obtain 0.597. Also, our method achieved comparable performance to the benchmark models on the FB15K237, less than the latest method such as DualE [5], and ComplEx-CL [32]. The main reason could be that the FB15K237 is significantly density: 1) The multi-relationships between entities are common: for example, multi-relational facts (that is, N-to-N relations type) account for more than 70% in the test set [25]; 2) According to statistics of FB15K237, the average number of neighbours for entities is 18.8, and the maximum number of neighbours for entities is 1325, which is denser than WN18RR. The latter has the average number of neighbours at 2.1 and the maximum number of neighbours at 462. As a result, our NDKGE achieves higher performance on WN18RR than FB15K237.

On Hadoop16K, our method achieves the best performance in MR and Hits@10 compared with other state-of-the-art benchmarks. Compared with FB15K237, the Hadoop16K has a sparse structure. For example, the statistics of the test set found that the proportions of N-1, 1-N and N-N relation types were 11.5%, 10.8% and 0%, respectively. At the same time, counting the number of neighbours of entities, we found the maximum number of neighbours of its entities is 84, and the average number of neighbours is 1.2, much smaller than 1325 and 18.8 in FB15K237.

From all the results on the five datasets we report above, we find that connecting newly created sentence descriptions can obtain good experimental results, which

Table 2. Results of link prediction on FB15K and WN18.

Datasets	FB15K		WN18	
Metric	Mean Rank	Hits@10	Mean Rank	Hits@10
TransE [4]	119	0.661	280	0.899
TransH [28]	87	0.644	303	0.867
Jointly(desp) [36]	39	0.773	-	-
DKRL(CNN) [30]	91	0.674	-	-
Jointly(A-LSTM) [31]	73	0.755	123	0.909
SSP(Joint) [29]	82	0.790	156	0.932
AATE_E [2]	76	0.761	123	0.941
ConMask [22]	98	0.620	-	-
RotatE [23]	40	0.884	309	0.959
RPJE [19]	40	**0.903**	-	0.951
Teger-TransE [9]	72	0.763	168	0.947
PairRE [7]	<u>37</u>	<u>0.896</u>	-	-
DualE [5]	**21**	<u>0.896</u>	156	<u>0.962</u>
NDKGE	45	0.842	**13**	**0.976**

Table 3. Results of link prediction on FB15K237 and WN18RR.

Datasets	WN18RR		FB15K237		Hadoop16K	
Metric	Mean Rank	Hits@10	Mean Rank	Hits@10	Mean Rank	Hits@10
TransE [4]	3526	0.477	234	0.480	401	0.738
TransH [28]	6356	0.350	334	0.395	559	0.823
DistMult [33]	7000	0.504	512	0.446	530	0.586
ComplEx [26]	7882	0.530	546	0.450	555	0.793
R-GCN [20]	6700	0.207	600	0.300	-	-
ConvE [8]	4464	0.531	245	0.497	-	-
ConvKB [16]	3433	0.524	309	0.421	<u>282</u>	0.855
QuatE [34]	3472	0.564	176	0.495	-	-
RotatE [23]	3340	0.571	177	0.533	385	0.859
TuckER [3]	-	0.526	-	0.544	-	-
HAKE [35]	-	0.582	-	0.545	-	-
GC-OTE [24]	-	0.583	-	0.550	-	-
ATTH [6]	-	0.573	-	0.540	-	-
BoxE [1]	3117	0.523	163	0.538	481	0.851
PairRE [7]	-	-	160	0.544	379	0.850
DualE [5]	2270	0.492	**91**	<u>0.559</u>	1144	0.854
SE-GNN [13]	3211	0.572	<u>157</u>	0.549	-	-
RESCAL-CL [32]	-	<u>0.597</u>	-	0.554	-	0.812
ComplEx-CL [32]	-	0.595	-	**0.564**	-	<u>0.882</u>
NDKGE	**166**	**0.699**	187	0.547	**219**	**0.900**

Table 4. Ablation study for WN18, FB15K, WN18RR, and FB15K237.

Datasets	WN18		FB15K		WN18RR		FB15K237	
Metric	MR	Hits@10	MR	Hits@10	MR	Hits@10	MR	Hits@10
NDKGE(*name*)	158	0.848	330	0.558	1530	0.486	273	0.449
NDKGE(*mention*)	40	0.948	76	0.725	307	0.621	263	0.516
NDKGE(*description*)	13	0.976	45	0.842	166	0.699	187	0.547

Table 5. Ablation study for Hadoop16K.

Datasets	Hadoop16K	
Metric	MR	Hits@1
NDKGE(*name*)	289	0.744
NDKGE(*mention*)	275	0.766
NDKGE(*description*)	219	0.778

means that the sentence-level description can provide the model with richer semantic information and help to learn more effective knowledge embeddings for application tasks.

4.4 Ablation Study

Algorithm 1 shows a function to calculate the embeddings $(\mathbf{h}, \mathbf{r}, \mathbf{t})$ for a triple $(h, r, t) \in G$, where we conduct ablation study on five datasets using three different settings: *name*, *mention*, and *description*. Table 4 shows the result of ablation study on WN18, FB15K, WN18RR and FB15K237. For WN18, The MR is reduced from 158 to 13 and Hits@10 rises from 0.848 to 0.976 when using the *name* and *description* settings, respectively. For FB15K, in Hits@10, using the *description* setting to obtain 0.842 is 28.4% higher than using *name* setting to obtain 0.558, and 11.7% higher than using *mention* setting to obtain 0.725. The MR is reduced from 1530 to 166, Hits@10 increases from 0.486 to 0.699 in WN18RR and Hits@10 achieves 0.699 using *description* setting and 21.3% higher than using *name* setting to obtain 0.486, and 7.8% higher than using the *mention* setting to obtain 62.1. For FB15K237, Hits@10 increases from 0.449 to 0.547 by using *name* and *description* settings, respectively.

Table 5 shows the ablation study result on Hadoop16K. Statistics show that about 45% of entities have only one link, so getting higher Hits@1 makes more sense in industrial practice. We report the results of MR and Hits@1 under the three settings, *name*, *mention*, and *description*. With the addition of the newly created description, MR decreases from 289 to 219, and Hits@1 rises from 0.744 to 0.778. The ablation study on five datasets shows that the link prediction performance increases with newly created sentence-level descriptions, which means adding new descriptions to help knowledge graph embedding is meaningful in practice.

5   Conclusion and Future Work

This paper introduces the NDKGE approach, which uses neighbour information to create a description for an entity. The method helps to address the issue in the existing text-based methods where some entities may not have their associated mentions or the related text description can not be obtained from external sources. We conduct the link prediction task on five datasets, FB15K, FB15K237, WN18, WN18RR, and Hadoop16K. The experimental results show that the knowledge graph embeddings with the generated descriptions can outperform the existing work when each entity has fewer relations with other entities, such as in the WN18RR and Hadoop16K. This paper only focused on using the score function from TransE, which already shows promising results. We will consider the other score functions in our future work. Future work will also focus on extending the generated description for detecting unknown entities that are introduced from out-of-the KG.

References

1. Abboud, R., Ceylan, İ.İ., Lukasiewicz, T., Salvatori, T.: Boxe: A box embedding model for knowledge base completion. In: Advances in Neural Information Processing Systems 33: Annual Conference on Neural Information Processing Systems, pp. 9649–9661 (2020)
2. An, B., Chen, B., Han, X., Sun, L.: Accurate text-enhanced knowledge graph representation learning. In: Proceedings of the 2018 Conference of the North American Chapter of the Association for Computational Linguistics: Human Language Technologies, New Orleans, Louisiana, USA, vol. 1 (Long Papers), pp. 745–755 (2018)
3. Balazevic, I., Allen, C., Hospedales, T.M.: Tucker: tensor factorization for knowledge graph completion. In: Proceedings of the 2019 Conference on Empirical Methods in Natural Language Processing, Hong Kong, China, pp. 5184–5193 (2019)
4. Bordes, A., Usunier, N., Garcia-Duran, A., Weston, J., Yakhnenko, O.: Translating embeddings for modeling multi-relational data. In: Neural Information Processing Systems (NIPS), pp. 1–9 (2013)
5. Cao, Z., Xu, Q., Yang, Z., Cao, X., Huang, Q.: Dual quaternion knowledge graph embeddings. In: Thirty-Fifth AAAI Conference on Artificial Intelligence, Virtual Event, pp. 6894–6902 (2021)
6. Chami, I., Wolf, A., Juan, D., Sala, F., Ravi, S., Ré, C.: Low-dimensional hyperbolic knowledge graph embeddings. In: Proceedings of the 58th Annual Meeting of the Association for Computational Linguistics, Online, pp. 6901–6914 (2020)
7. Chao, L., He, J., Wang, T., Chu, W.: Pairre: knowledge graph embeddings via paired relation vectors. In: Proceedings of the 59th Annual Meeting of the Association for Computational Linguistics and the 11th International Joint Conference on Natural Language Processing, (vol. 1: Long Papers), Virtual Event, pp. 4360–4369 (2021)
8. Dettmers, T., Minervini, P., Stenetorp, P., Riedel, S.: Convolutional 2d knowledge graph embeddings. In: Proceedings of the Thirty-Second AAAI Conference on Artificial Intelligence, pp. 1811–1818 (2018)
9. Hu, L., et al.: Text-graph enhanced knowledge graph representation learning. Front. Artif. Intell. **4**, 118–127 (2021)
10. Ji, S., Pan, S., Cambria, E., Marttinen, P., Philip, S.Y.: A survey on knowledge graphs: representation, acquisition, and applications. IEEE Trans. Neural Netw. Learn. Syst. **33**, 1–21 (2021)

11. Kazemi, S.M., Poole, D.: Simple embedding for link prediction in knowledge graphs. In: Advances in Neural Information Processing Systems 31: Annual Conference on Neural Information Processing Systems, Montréal, Canada, pp. 4289–4300 (2018)
12. Kipf, T.N., Welling, M.: Semi-supervised classification with graph convolutional networks. In: 5th International Conference on Learning Representations, Toulon, France, Conference Track Proceedings, pp. 1–14 (2017)
13. Li, R., et al.: How does knowledge graph embedding extrapolate to unseen data: a semantic evidence view. In: Thirty-Sixth AAAI Conference on Artificial Intelligence, AAAI, pp. 5781–5791 (2022)
14. Lin, Y., Liu, Z., Luan, H., Sun, M., Rao, S., Liu, S.: Modeling relation paths for representation learning of knowledge bases. In: Proceedings of the 2015 Conference on Empirical Methods in Natural Language Processing, Lisbon, Portugal, pp. 705–714 (2015)
15. Montgomery, L., Lüders, C.M., Maalej, W.: An alternative issue tracking dataset of public jira repositories. In: IEEE/ACM 19th International Conference on Mining Software Repositories, Pittsburgh, PA, USA, pp. 73–77 (2022)
16. Nguyen, D.Q., Nguyen, T.D., Nguyen, D.Q., Phung, D.Q.: A novel embedding model for knowledge base completion based on convolutional neural network. In: Proceedings of the 2018 Conference of the North American Chapter of the Association for Computational Linguistics: Human Language Technologies, vol. 2 (Short Papers), pp. 327–333 (2018)
17. Nguyen, D.Q., Sirts, K., Qu, L., Johnson, M.: Neighborhood mixture model for knowledge base completion. In: Proceedings of the 20th SIGNLL Conference on Computational Natural Language Learning, Berlin, Germany, pp. 40–50 (2016)
18. Nickel, M., Tresp, V., Kriegel, H.: A three-way model for collective learning on multi-relational data. In: Proceedings of the 28th International Conference on Machine Learning, Bellevue, Washington, USA, pp. 809–816 (2011)
19. Niu, G., et al.: Rule-guided compositional representation learning on knowledge graphs. In: Proceedings of the AAAI Conference on Artificial Intelligence, vol. 34, pp. 2950–2958 (2020)
20. Schlichtkrull, M., Kipf, T.N., Bloem, P., Van Den Berg, R., Titov, I., Welling, M.: Modeling relational data with graph convolutional networks. In: European semantic web conference, pp. 593–607 (2018)
21. Shah, H., Villmow, J., Ulges, A., Schwanecke, U., Shafait, F.: An open-world extension to knowledge graph completion models. In: Proceedings of the AAAI Conference on Artificial Intelligence, vol. 33, pp. 3044–3051 (2019)
22. Shi, B., Weninger, T.: Open-world knowledge graph completion. In: Proceedings of the Thirty-Second AAAI Conference on Artificial Intelligence, New Orleans, Louisiana, USA, pp. 1957–1964 (2018)
23. Sun, Z., Deng, Z., Nie, J., Tang, J.: Rotate: knowledge graph embedding by relational rotation in complex space. In: 7th International Conference on Learning Representations, New Orleans, LA, USA, pp. 1–18 (2019)
24. Tang, Y., Huang, J., Wang, G., He, X., Zhou, B.: Orthogonal relation transforms with graph context modeling for knowledge graph embedding. In: Proceedings of the 58th Annual Meeting of the Association for Computational Linguistics, Online, pp. 2713–2722 (2020)
25. Toutanova, K., Chen, D.: Observed versus latent features for knowledge base and text inference. In: Proceedings of the 3rd Workshop on Continuous Vector Space Models and their Compositionality, pp. 57–66 (2015)
26. Trouillon, T., Welbl, J., Riedel, S., Gaussier, É., Bouchard, G.: Complex embeddings for simple link prediction. In: International Conference on Machine Learning, pp. 2071–2080 (2016)

27. Vu, T., Nguyen, T.D., Nguyen, D.Q., Phung, D., et al.: A capsule network-based embedding model for knowledge graph completion and search personalization. In: Proceedings of the 2019 Conference of the North American Chapter of the Association for Computational Linguistics: Human Language Technologies, vol. 1 (Long and Short Papers), pp. 2180–2189 (2019)

28. Wang, Z., Zhang, J., Feng, J., Chen, Z.: Knowledge graph embedding by translating on hyperplanes. In: Proceedings of the Twenty-Eighth AAAI Conference on Artificial Intelligence, Québec City, Québec, Canada, pp. 1112–1119 (2014)

29. Xiao, H., Huang, M., Meng, L., Zhu, X.: SSP: semantic space projection for knowledge graph embedding with text descriptions. In: Proceedings of the Thirty-First AAAI Conference on Artificial Intelligence, San Francisco, California, USA, pp. 3104–3110 (2017)

30. Xie, R., Liu, Z., Jia, J., Luan, H., Sun, M.: Representation learning of knowledge graphs with entity descriptions. In: Proceedings of the Thirtieth AAAI Conference on Artificial Intelligence, Phoenix, Arizona, USA, pp. 2659–2665 (2016)

31. Xu, J., Qiu, X., Chen, K., Huang, X.: Knowledge graph representation with jointly structural and textual encoding. In: Proceedings of the Twenty-Sixth International Joint Conference on Artificial Intelligence, Melbourne, Australia, pp. 1318–1324 (2017)

32. Xu, W., Luo, Z., Liu, W., Bian, J., Yin, J., Liu, T.: KGE-CL: contrastive learning of knowledge graph embeddings, pp. 1–14 (2022)

33. Yang, B., Yih, W., He, X., Gao, J., Deng, L.: Embedding entities and relations for learning and inference in knowledge bases. In: 3rd International Conference on Learning Representations, San Diego, CA, USA, Conference Track Proceedings, pp. 1–12 (2015)

34. Zhang, S., Tay, Y., Yao, L., Liu, Q.: Quaternion knowledge graph embeddings. In: Advances in Neural Information Processing Systems 32: Annual Conference on Neural Information Processing Systems, Vancouver, BC, Canada, pp. 2731–2741 (2019)

35. Zhang, Z., Cai, J., Zhang, Y., Wang, J.: Learning hierarchy-aware knowledge graph embeddings for link prediction. In: The Thirty-Fourth AAAI Conference on Artificial Intelligence, pp. 3065–3072 (2020)

36. Zhong, H., Zhang, J., Wang, Z., Wan, H., Chen, Z.: Aligning knowledge and text embeddings by entity descriptions. In: Proceedings of the 2015 Conference on Empirical Methods in Natural Language Processing, pp. 267–272 (2015)

LonXplain: Lonesomeness as a Consequence of Mental Disturbance in Reddit Posts

Muskan Garg[1,4], Chandni Saxena[2], Debabrata Samanta[3(✉)],
and Bonnie J. Dorr[4]

[1] Mayo Clinic, Rochester, MN, USA
garg.muskan@mayo.edu
[2] The Chinese University of Hong Kong, Ma Liu Shui, Hong Kong, SAR
chandnisaxena@cse.cuhk.edu.hk
[3] Rochester Institute of Technology, Pristina, Kosovo
debabrata.samanta369@gmail.com
[4] University of Florida, Gainesville, FL, USA
bonniejdorr@ufl.edu

Abstract. Social media is a potential source of information that infers latent mental states through Natural Language Processing (NLP). While narrating real-life experiences, social media users convey their feeling of loneliness or isolated lifestyle, impacting their mental well-being. Existing literature on psychological theories points to *loneliness* as the major consequence of *interpersonal risk factors*, propounding the need to investigate loneliness as a major aspect of mental disturbance. We formulate *lonesomeness detection* in social media posts as an **explainable** binary classification problem, discovering the users at-risk, suggesting the need of resilience for early control. To the best of our knowledge, there is no existing explainable dataset, i.e., one with human-readable, annotated text spans, to facilitate further research and development in loneliness detection causing mental disturbance [9]. In this work, three experts: a senior clinical psychologist, a rehabilitation counselor, and a social NLP researcher define annotation schemes and perplexity guidelines to mark the presence or absence of lonesomeness, along with the marking of text-spans in original posts as *explanation*, in 3, 521 Reddit posts. We expect the public release of our dataset, LONXPLAIN, and traditional classifiers as baselines via GitHub (https://github.com/drmuskangarg/lonesomeness_dataset).

Keywords: dataset · interpersonal risk factor · loneliness · mental health · Reddit post

1 Introduction

According to the *World Health Organization*,[1] one in three older people feel lonely. Loneliness has a serious impact on older people's physical and mental

---

[1] https://www.who.int/teams/social-determinants-of-health/demographic-change-and-healthy-ageing/social-isolation-and-loneliness.

E. Métais et al. (Eds.): NLDB 2023, LNCS 13913, pp. 379–390, 2023.
https://doi.org/10.1007/978-3-031-35320-8_27

health, quality of life, and their longevity. According to the *Loneliness and the Workplace: 2020 U.S. Report*, three in five Americans (61%) report the feeling of loneliness, compared to more than half (54%) in 2018 [16]. Older adults are at high risk for morbidity and mortality due to prolonged isolation, especially during the COVID-19 [8] era. To this end, researchers demonstrate loneliness as a major concern for increased risk of depression, anxiety, and stress thereby affecting cognitive functioning, sleep quality, and overall well-being [7]. We define *lonesomeness* as an unpleasant emotional response to perceived isolation through mind and character, especially in terms of concerns for social lifestyle. The anonymous nature of Reddit social media platform provides an opportunity for its users to express their thoughts, concerns, and experiences with ease. We leverage Reddit to formulate a new annotation scheme and perplexity guidelines for constructing an explainable annotated dataset for Lonesomeness. We start with an example of how this information is reported in social media texts.

Example: Within the last month, I have lost my best friend and my grandmother, to whom I was very close with (both passed away). This time last year, I was involved in an incident where I was assaulted (we were not dating at the time), and it is bringing up some bad memories for me. I am continuously mentioning about moving cities on my own. I am all by myself now and have no one to speak to!

In this example, a person is upset about losing all loved ones and coping with the memories of manipulative situations in their life. Red colored words depict explanations for lonesomeness and blue colored words represent the triggering circumstances.

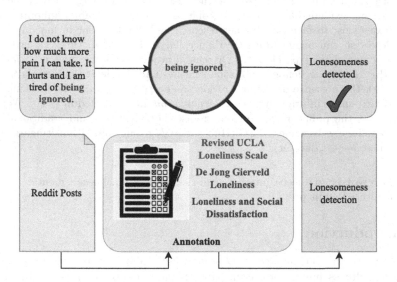

Fig. 1. Overview of classifying lonesomeness in Reddit Posts.

Sociologists Weiss *et al.* in 1975 [22] introduce a *theory of loneliness* suggesting the need for six social needs to prevent loneliness in stressful situations: (i) attachment, (ii) social integration, (iii) nurturing, (iv) reassurance of worth, (v) sense of reliable alliance and (vi) guidance. Furthermore, Baumeister *et al.* [5] explains various indices of social isolation associated with suicide as living alone, and low social support across the lifespan. In recent investigations of attachment style, Nottage *et al.* [18] argue that loneliness mediates a positive association between attachment style and depressive symptoms. Loneliness results in disrupted work-life balance, emotional exhaustion, insomnia and depression [6]. With this background, the annotation guidelines are developed through the collaborative efforts of three experts (a clinical psychologist, a rehabilitation counselor and a social NLP researcher) for early detection of lonesomeness, which if left untreated, may cause chronic disease such as self harm or suicide risk.

We examine potential indicators of mental disturbance in Reddit posts, aiming to discover users at risk through explainable lonesomeness annotations, as shown in Fig. 1. We first introduce the Reddit dataset for lonesomeness detection in social media posts reflecting mental disturbance. Our data annotation scheme is designed to facilitate the discovery of users with (potential) underlying tendencies toward self harm, including suicide, through loneliness detection. We construct this scheme using three clinical questionnaires: (i) UCLA Loneliness Scale [21], (ii) De Jong Gierveld Loneliness Scale [19], and (iii) Loneliness and Social Dissatisfaction scale [3].

Table 1. Historical evolution of language resources for determining lonesomeness in texts. There is no existing publicly available or explainable dataset for identifying loneliness as an interpersonal risk factor for mental disturbance.

Dataset	Media	Size	Xplain	Avail.
Kivran *et al.* 2014 [13]	Twitter	4454	No	No
Badal *et al.* 2021 [4]	Interviews	97 adults	No	No
Mohney *et al.* 2019 [14]	Twitter	22477	No	No
Ours	Reddit	3522	Yes	Yes

The quantitative literature on loneliness and mental health has limited, openly available language resources due to the sensitive nature of the data. Examples are shown in Table 1. We aim to fill this gap by introducing a new dataset for lonesomeness classification with human-generated explanations and to make it publicly available on Github. Our **contributions** are summarized as follows:

- We define an experts-driven annotation scheme for Lonesomeness detection.
- We deploy the annotation scheme to construct and release LONXPLAIN, a new dataset containing 3521 instances for early detection of textitlonesomeness that thwarts belongingness and potentially leads to self harm.

– We deploy existing classifiers and investigate explainability through Local Interpretable Model-Agnostic Explanations (LIME), suggesting an initial step toward more responsible AI models.

2   Corpus Construction

We collect Reddit posts through The Python Reddit API Wrapper (PRAW) API, from 02 December 2021 to 06 January 2022 maintaining a consistent flow of 100 posts per day. The subreddits extracted for this dataset are those most widely used in the discussion forum for depression (r/depression) and suicide risk (r/SuicideWatch). We manually filter out irrelevant posts with empty strings and/or posts containing only URLs.

We further clean and preprocess the dataset and filter out the data samples (posts) longer than 300 words, to simplify the complexity of a given task. The length of a single sample in the original dataset varies from 1 to more than 4000 words, highlighting the need for bounding the length, thus inducing comparatively consistent data points for developing AI models. We define the experts-driven annotation scheme, train and employ three student annotators for data annotation and compute inter-annotator agreement to ensure the coherence and reliability of the annotations. We emphasize FAIR principles [23] while constructing and releasing LONXPLAIN.

2.1   Annotation Scheme

Dunn introduces six dimensions of wellness (spiritual, social, intellectual, vocations, emotional, and physical), affecting users' mental well-being. A key consequence of mental disturbance is a tendency toward the negative end of the scale for these dimensions, e.g., loneliness derives from negative values associated with the spiritual, social, and emotional dimensions. Further intensification may lead to thwarted belongingness [2], suicidal tendencies, and self harm.

Bringing together the two disiplines of Natural Language Processing (NLP) and clinical psychology, we adopt an annotation approach that leverages both the application of NLP to Reddit posts and clinicial questionnaires on loneliness detection, as two concrete baselines. The annotations are based on two research questions: (i) "RQ1: *Does the text contain indicators of lonesomeness which alarms suicidal risk or self harm in a person?,*" and (ii) "RQ2: *What should be the extent to which annotators are supposed to read in-between-the-lines for marking the text-spans indicating the presence or absence of lonesomeness.*"

Our experts access three clinical questionnaires used by mental health practitioner, to define lonesomeness annotation guidelines. The UCLA Loneliness Scale [21] that measures loneliness was adapted to distinguish among three dimensions of loneliness: *social loneliness* (the absence of a social network), *emotional loneliness* (the absence of a close and intimate relationship), and *existential loneliness* (the feeling of being disconnected from the larger world). The De Jong Gierveld Loneliness Scale [19] is a 6-item self-report questionnaire over

5-point Likert scale (ranging from 0 (not at all) to 4 (completely)) that assesses two dimensions of loneliness: *emotional loneliness* and *social loneliness*.

From Loneliness and Social Dissatisfaction scale [3] we use 10 out of 20 items, reflecting loneliness on a 5-point Likert scale, ranging from 1 (strongly disagree) to 5 (strongly agree). The experts annotate 40 data points using fine-grained guidelines seperately at 3 different places to avoid any influence. Furthermore, we find the possibility of dilemmas due to the psychology-driven subjective and complex nature of the task.

2.2 Perplexity Guidelines

We propose perplexity guidelines to simplify the task and facilitate future annotations. We observe following:

1. **Lonesomeness in the Past**: A person with a history of loneliness may still be at risk of self harm or suicide. For instance,'*I was so upset being lonely before Christmas and today I am celebrating New Year with friends'*. We define rules to capture indicators of prior lonesomeness such as attending a celebration to fill the void associated with this negative emotion. With both negative and positive clauses in the example above, the NLP expert would deem this neutral, yet our clinical psychologist discerns the presence of lonesomeness, with both clauses contributing to its likelihood. This post is thus marked as presenting lonesomeness, an indicator that the author is potentially at risk.

2. **Ambiguity with *Social Lonesomeness***: Major societal events such as breakups, marriage, best friend related issues may be mentioned in different contexts, suggesting different perceptions. We formulate two annotation rules: (i) Any feeling of void/missing/regrets/or even mentioning such events with negative words is marked as the presence of lonesomeness. Example: *'But I just miss her SO. much. It's like she set the bar so high that all I can do is just stare at it.'*, (ii) Mentions of fights/ quarrels/ general stories are marked with absence of lonesomeness. Example: *'My husband and I just had a huge argument and he stormed out. I should be crying or stopping him or something. But I decided to take a handful of benzos instead.'*.

2.3 Annotation Task

We employ three postgraduate students, trained by experts on manual annotations. Professional training and guidelines are supported by perplexity guidelines. After three successive trial sessions to annotate 40 samples in each round, we ensure their **coherence** and understanding of the task for further annotations.

Each data sample is annotated by three annotators in three different places to confirm the **authenticity** of the task. We restrict the annotations to 100 per day, to maintain the **quality** of the task and **consistency**. We further validate three annotated files using Fliess' Kappa inter-observer agreement study to ensure **reliability** of the dataset, where kappa is calculated at 71.83%, and carry out agreement studies for lonesomeness detection. We obtain final annotations based on a *majority voting mechanism* and experts' opinions, resulting in LONXPLAIN dataset. Furthermore, the explanations are annotated by a group of 3 experts to ensure the nature of LONXPLAIN as *psychology-grounded* and *NLP-driven*. We deploy FAIR principle [23] by releasing LONXPLAIN data in a public repository of Github, making it **findable** and **accessible**. The comma separated format contains <text, label, explanations> in English language, ensuring the **interoperability** and **re-usability**. We illustrate the samples of LONXPLAIN in Table 2, with blue and red color indicating the presence of *cause* [10] and *consequence* [11], respectively. This task of early consequence detection, may prevent chronic disease such as depression and self-harm tendencies in the near future.

Table 2. An annotated dataset example illustrates causes (blue colored text-span) and lonesomeness as a consequence (red colored text-span) of mental disturbance in Reddit posts. Not all posts contain information about cause and/or consequences.

Text	Label	Exp.
Just a sense of impending doom, this year is going to be shit. I'm starting to think things never actually do get better. All of my friends are out partying right now ← (Consequence) and I'm at home getting lectured by my family← (Cause) on my negative attitude. Anyway, happy new year I guess	Present	my friends are out partying
All of us on here are probably feeling alone and lonely← (Consequence) and depressed and like everyone else out there is having an awesome time← (Cause) except us, so why don't we have our own "party"? (In a way). Let's get to know each other! What is something really funny to you guys? It can be a joke/a meme/a video/a story of yours/whatever. Let's help each other feel less alone	Present	feeling alone and lonely
There is literally no point in life. We live and we die. And life has been hell to me← (Cause) so far so why should I even bother finishing. I am almost at the point where I am about to say **** it and quit	Absent	-

3   Data Analyses

Corpus construction is accompanied by fine-grained analyses for: (i) statistical information about the dataset and (ii) overlapping terms and syntactic similarity based on word cloud and keyword extraction. In this section, we further discuss the linguistic challenges with supporting psychological theories for LONXPLAIN.

3.1   Statistical Information

LONXPLAIN contains 3,521 data points among which 54.71% are labeled as positive sample, depicting the presence of lonesomeness in a given text. We observe the statistics for number of words and sentences in both the `Text` and `Explanation` (see Table 3). The average number of Text words is 4 and the maximum number of words reported as explainable in text spans is 19, highlighting the need for identifying focused words for classification.

Table 3. The statistics of LONXPLAIN for determining the presence or absence of lonesomeness in a given Reddit post.

Column	Feature	Lonesomeness	
		Absent	Present
Labels	Number of Posts	1595	1927
Text	Average number of Words	≈97	≈135
	Maximum number of Words	300	300
	Total number of Words	153459	258992
	Average number of Sentences	≈7	≈ 9
	Maximum number of Sentences	42	32
	Total number of Sentences	9618	16302
Explanation	Average number of Words	-	≈4
	Maximum number of Words	-	19
	Total number of Words	-	6647

3.2 Overlapping Information

We investigate words that represent class 0: absence of lonesomeness and class 1: presence of lonesomeness in a given text. Words such as `life`, `im`, `feel`, and `people` indicate a very large syntactic overlap between these classes (see Fig. 2). However, a seemingly neutral (or even positive) word like `friend` indicates a discussion about interpersonal relations, which be an indicator of a negative mental state. We further obtain word clouds for explainable text-spans indicating label 1 in LONXPLAIN. We find that words such as `lonely`, `alone`, `friend`, `someone`, `talk` may be indicators of the presence of lonesomeness.

For keyword extraction, we use KeyBERT, a pre-trained model that finds the sub-phrases in a data sample reflecting the semantics of the original text. BERT extracts *document embeddings* as a document-level representation and *word embeddings* for N-gram words/phrases [12]. Consider a top-20 word list for each of label 0 ($K0$) and label 1 ($K1$):

$K0$: *sleepiness, depresses, tiredness, relapses, fatigue, suffer, insomnia, suffers, stressed, sleepless, selfobsessed, stress, numbness, cry, diagnosis, sleepy, moodiness, depressants, stressors, fatigued.*

Fig. 2. The wordcloud for label 0: absence of lonesomeness (left), label 1: presence of lonesomeness (center), and Word cloud evolved from explainable text-spans (right)

$K1$: *dumped, hopelessness, introvert, breakup, hopeless, loneliness, heart-broken, dejected, introverted, psychopath, breakdown, graduation, break-downs, overcome, depressant, solace, counseling, befriend, sociopaths, abandonment.*

Although some important terms are missed by KeyBERT, e.g., `homelessness` and `isolated`, most of the terms in $K1$ indicate lonesomeness. Thus, KeyBERT plays a pivotal role in LonXplain, as an example of a context-aware AI classifier that lends itself to explainable output, and (more generally) responsible AI.

4   Experiments and Evaluation

We formulate the problem of lonesomeness detection as a binary class classification problem, define the performance evaluation metrics, and discuss the existing classifiers. Following this, we present the experimental setup and implement the existing classifiers for setting up baselines on LONXPLAIN. The explainable AI method, LIME [17], is used to find text-spans responsible for decision making, highlighting the scope of improvement.

Problem Formulation. We define the task of identifying Lonesomeness L and its explanation E in a given document D. The ground-truth contains a tuple $< D(text), L(bool), E(text) >$ for every data point in a comma separated format. A corpus of D documents where $D = \{d_1, d_2, ..., d_n\}$ for n documents where n = 3,522 in LONXPLAIN. We develop a binary classification model for every document D_i to classify it as L_i.

4.1   Experimental Setup

Evaluation Metrics. We evaluate the performance of our experiments in terms of precision, recall and f-score. Accuracy is a simple and intuitive measure of overall performance that is easy to interpret. However, accuracy alone may not be a good measure of performance for imbalanced datasets, where one class (e.g., user's lonely posts) is not equal to the other (e.g., user's non-lonely posts). In such cases, a model that always predicts the majority class can achieve high accuracy, but will not be useful for detecting the minority class. In this work, our task is to identify lonesomeness and not to identify a user's non-lonely posts. Thus, we consider Accuracy as an important metrics for evaluation.

Baselines. We compare results with linear classifiers using word embedding Word2Vec [15]. We further use GloVe [20] to obtain word embeddings and deploy them on two Recurrent Neural Networks (RNN): Long Short Term Memory (LSTM) and Gated Recurrent Unit (GRU) for performance evaluation.

1. **LSTM:** Long Short-Term Memory networks (LSTM) take a sequence of data as an input and make predictions at individual time steps of the sequential data. We apply a LSTM model for classifying texts that indicate lonesomeness versus those that do not.
2. **GRU:** Gated Recurrent Units (GRU) use connections between the sequence of nodes to resolve the *vanishing gradient problem*. Since the textual sequences in the LONXPLAIN present a mixed context, GRU's non-sequential nature offers improvement over LSTM.

We additionally built out versions of each approach above with bidirectional RNNs (BiLSTM, BiGRU, respectively), where the input sequence is processed in both forward and backward directions. This enrichment enables the above technologies to capture the past and future context of the input sequence— yielding a significant advantage over the standard RNN formalism.

Hyperparameters. We used grid-search optimization to derive the optimal parameters for each method. For consistency, we used the same experimental settings for all models with 10-fold cross-validation, reporting the average score. Varying length posts are padded and trained for 150 epochs with early stopping, and patience of 20 epochs. Thus, we set hyperparameters for our experiments with transformer-based models as $H = 256$, $O =$ Adam, learning rate $= 1 \times 10^{-3}$, and batch size 128.

4.2   Experimental Results

Table 4 reports precision, recall and f-score for all classifiers, resulting in non-reliable Accuracy for real-time use. Word2vec achieved the lowest Accuracy of 0.64. We postulate this low performance because word2vec is unable to capture contextual information. GloVe + GRU, a state-of-the-art deep learning model, achieved the highest performance among all recurrent neural network models, counterparts with an F1-score and Accuracy of 0.77 and 0.78, respectively.

We further examine the explanations for Recurrent neural network models through Local Interpretable Model-Agnostic Explanations (LIME). LIME provide a human-understandable explanation of how the model arrived at its

Table 4. Main results: Comparison of SOTA baselines. Score of each metric is averaged over 10-folds.

Model	Absent			Present			Accuracy
	P	R	F	P	R	F	
Word2Vec + RF	0.61	0.55	0.58	0.66	0.72	0.69	0.64
GloVe + LSTM	0.60	0.82	0.70	0.81	0.58	0.68	0.69
GloVe+BiLSTM	0.80	0.59	0.68	0.74	0.89	0.81	0.76
GloVe + GRU	0.72	0.80	0.75	0.83	0.76	0.79	0.77
Glove + BiGRU	0.70	0.84	0.76	0.85	0.73	0.79	0.78

Table 5. Performance evaluation of explanations obtained through LIME

Model	ROUGE-1 P	ROUGE-2 R	ROUGE-1 F
LSTM	0.50	0.12	0.18
BiLSTM	0.58	0.15	0.22
GRU	0.53	0.14	0.21
BiGRU	0.55	0.14	0.21

prediction of lonesomneness in a given text. We further use ROUGE-1 scores to validate the explanations obtained through LIME, over all positive samples in test data with explainable text-spans in ground-truth of LonXplain (see Table 5). We observe that all explanations are comparable and achieve high precision as compared to recall. In the near future, we plan to formulate better explainable approaches by incorporating clinical questionnaires in language models. Consider the following text T1:

> T1: What bothers me is the soul crushing loneliness, i haven't had a girlfriend in years and I haven't been physically touched in what seems like forever. I spend all day in a shitty little side room by myself writing and hardly see hide nor hair of another person besides my dad most of the time. I'm pretty done with it all to be honest, I don't really see any reason to continue living like this.

BiGRU decides label 1 for T1 with 0.96 prediction probability, highlighting the text-spans: (i) focused by BiGRU for making decision (blue + red colored text), (ii) marked as explanations in the ground truth of LonXplain (red colored text), and (iii) missed text-spans by BiGRU (brown colored text).

5   Conclusion and Future Work

We present LonXplain, a new dataset for identifying lonesomeness through human-annotated extractive explanations from Reddit posts, consisting of 3,522 English Reddit posts labeled across binary labels. In future work, we plan to enhance the dataset with more samples and develop new models tailored explicitly to lonesomeness detection.

The implications of our work are the potential to improve public health surveillance and to support other health applications that would benefit from the detection of lonesomeness. Automatic detection of lonesomeness in the posts at early stage of mental health issues has the potential for preventing prospective chronic diseases. We define annotation guidelines based on three clinical questionnaires. If accommodated as external knowledge from a lexical resource, the outcome of our study has the potential to improve existing classifiers. We keep this idea as an open research direction.

Ethical Considerations and Broader Impact. We emphasize that the sensitive nature of our work necessitates that we use publicly available Reddit posts in a purely observational manner. This research intends to improve public health surveillance and other health applications that automatically identify lonesomeness on Reddit. To adhere to privacy constraints, we do not disclose any personal information such as demographics, location, and personal details of social media user while making LONXPLAIN publicly available [24]. The annotations scheme is carried out under the observation of a senior clinical psychologist, a rehabilitation counselor, and a social NLP expert. This research is purely observational and we do not claim any solution for clinical diagnosis at this stage [1]. Reddit posts might subject to biased demographics such as race, location and gender of a user. Therefore, we do not claim *diversity* in our dataset. Our dataset is susceptible to the prejudices and biases of our student annotators. There will be no ethical issues or legal impact with our dataset and is subject to IRB approval.

Acknowledgement. We would like to sincerely thank the postgraduate student annotators, Ritika Bhardwaj, Astha Jain, and Amrit Chadha, for their dedicated work in the annotation process. We are grateful to Veena Krishnan, a senior clinical psychologist, and Ruchi Joshi, a rehabilitation counselor, for their unwavering support during the project. Furthermore, we would like to express our heartfelt appreciation to Prof. Sunghwan Sohn for consistently guiding and supporting us.

References

1. Gaur, M., et al.: Iseeq: Information seeking question generation using dynamic meta-information retrieval and knowledge graphs (2022)
2. Ghosh, S., et al.: Am i no good? towards detecting perceived burdensomeness and thwarted belongingness from suicide notes. In: IJCAI (2022)
3. Asher, S., Wheeler, V.: Children's loneliness and social dissatisfaction scale. Child Dev. **55**(4), 1456–1464 (1984)
4. Badal, V.D., et al.: Do words matter? detecting social isolation and loneliness in older adults using natural language processing. Front. Psychiatry **12**, 1932 (2021)
5. Baumeister, R.F., Leary, M.R.: The need to belong: Desire for interpersonal attachments as a fundamental human motivation. Interpers. Dev. 57–89 (2017)
6. Becker, W.J., Belkin, L.Y., Tuskey, S.E., Conroy, S.A.: Surviving remotely: how job control and loneliness during a forced shift to remote work impacted employee work behaviors and well-being. Hum. Resour. Manage. **61**, 449–464 (2022)

7. Cacioppo, J.T., Hughes, M.E., Waite, L.J., Hawkley, L.C., Thisted, R.A.: Loneliness as a specific risk factor for depressive symptoms: cross-sectional and longitudinal analyses. Psychol. Aging **21**(1), 140 (2006)

8. Donovan, N.J., Blazer, D.: Social isolation and loneliness in older adults: review and commentary of a national academies report. Am. J. Geriatr. Psychiatry **28**(12), 1233–1244 (2020)

9. Garg, M.: Mental health analysis in social media posts: a survey. Arch. Comput. Methods Eng. **30**, 1–24 (2023)

10. Garg, M., et al.: CAMS: an annotated corpus for causal analysis of mental health issues in social media posts. In: Language Resources Evaluation Conference (LREC) (2022)

11. Ghosh, S., Maurya, D.K., Ekbal, A., Bhattacharyya, P.: EM-PERSONA: emotion-assisted deep neural framework for personality subtyping from suicide notes. In: Proceedings of the 29th International Conference on Computational Linguistics, pp. 1098–1105 (2022)

12. Grootendorst, M.: Keybert: Minimal keyword extraction with bert. Zenodo (2020)

13. Kivran-Swaine, F., Ting, J., Brubaker, J., Teodoro, R., Naaman, M.: Understanding loneliness in social awareness streams: expressions and responses. In: Proceedings of the International AAAI Conference on Web and Social Media, vol. 8, pp. 256–265 (2014)

14. Mahoney, J., et al.: Feeling alone among 317 million others: disclosures of loneliness on twitter. Comput. Hum. Behav. **98**, 20–30 (2019)

15. Mikolov, T., Sutskever, I., Chen, K., Corrado, G.S., Dean, J.: Distributed representations of words and phrases and their compositionality. In: Burges, C.J.C., Bottou, L., Welling, M., Ghahramani, Z., Weinberger, K.Q. (eds.) Advances in Neural Information Processing Systems, vol. 26, pp. 3111–3119. Curran Associates, Inc. (2013). http://papers.nips.cc/paper/5021-distributed-representations-of-words-and-phrases-and-their-compositionality.pdf

16. Nemecek, D.: Loneliness and the workplace: 2020 us report. Cigna, January (2020)

17. Nguyen, D.: Comparing automatic and human evaluation of local explanations for text classification. In: Proceedings of the 2018 Conference of the North American Chapter of the Association for Computational Linguistics: Human Language Technologies, vol. 1 (Long Papers), pp. 1069–1078 (2018)

18. Nottage, M.K., et al.: Loneliness mediates the association between insecure attachment and mental health among university students. Personality Individ. Differ. **185**, 111233 (2022)

19. Penning, M.J., Liu, G., Chou, P.H.B.: Measuring loneliness among middle-aged and older adults: the UCLA and de Jong Gierveld loneliness scales. Soc. Indic. Res. **118**, 1147–1166 (2014)

20. Pennington, J., Socher, R., Manning, C.: Glove: global vectors for word representation. In: Proceedings of the 2014 Conference on Empirical Methods in Natural Language Processing (EMNLP), pp. 1532–1543 (2014)

21. Russell, D., Peplau, L.A., Cutrona, C.E.: The revised UCLA loneliness scale: concurrent and discriminant validity evidence. J. Pers. Soc. Psychol. **39**(3), 472 (1980)

22. Weiss, R.: Loneliness: The Experience of Emotional and Social Isolation. MIT press, Cambridge (1975)

23. Wilkinson, M.D., et al.: The fair guiding principles for scientific data management and stewardship. Sci. Data **3**(1), 1–9 (2016)

24. Zirikly, A., Dredze, M.: Explaining models of mental health via clinically grounded auxiliary tasks. In: CLPsych (2022)

A Comparative Study of Evaluation Metrics for Long-Document Financial Narrative Summarization with Transformers

Nadhem Zmandar(✉)📷, Mahmoud El-Haj📷, and Paul Rayson📷

UCREL NLP Group, School of Computing and Communications, Lancaster University,
Lancaster, UK
{n.zmandar,m.el-haj,p.rayson}@lancaster.ac.uk

Abstract. There are more than 2,000 listed companies on the UK's London Stock Exchange, divided into 11 sectors who are required to communicate their financial results at least twice in a single financial year. UK annual reports are very lengthy documents with around 80 pages on average. In this study, we aim to benchmark a variety of summarisation methods on a set of different pre-trained transformers with different extraction techniques. In addition, we considered multiple evaluation metrics in order to investigate their differing behaviour and applicability on a dataset from the Financial Narrative Summarisation (FNS 2020) shared task, which is composed of annual reports published by firms listed on the London Stock Exchange and their corresponding summaries. We hypothesise that some evaluation metrics do not reflect true summarisation ability and propose a novel BRUGEscore metric, as the harmonic mean of ROUGE-2 and BERTscore. Finally, we perform a statistical significance test on our results to verify whether they are statistically robust, alongside an adversarial analysis task with three different corruption methods.

Keywords: Long Document sumamrization · Evaluation Metrics · Benchmarking

1 Introduction

With the proliferation of firms worldwide, the amount of financial disclosures and financial texts (or narratives) in various languages and formats has risen dramatically. Consequently, the study of natural language processing (NLP) methods that automatically summarize content has become a rapidly growing research area [22] [8].

In fact, financial reporting and communication requirements have expanded significantly in recent years, particularly following the 2008 financial crisis. Financial communications and investor relations management are becoming increasingly critical to the financial markets and fund management industry. Regulated financial markets mandate that all listed companies regularly communicate their financial activities to stakeholders by publishing financial reports and other financial narratives.

Financial narratives are employed by firms to communicate with their stakeholders, including investors, shareholders, customers, employees, financial analysts, regulators,

ⓒ The Author(s), under exclusive license to Springer Nature Switzerland AG 2023
E. Métais et al. (Eds.): NLDB 2023, LNCS 13913, pp. 391–403, 2023.
https://doi.org/10.1007/978-3-031-35320-8_28

lenders, rating agencies, and suppliers. Through financial communications, stakeholders can assess how well the company is creating value.

The aim of this study is to create and evaluate summarization benchmarks for UK financial narratives, investigate the effect of long document methods, and examine their interactions with various metrics, including ROUGE, in order to assess their suitability for this domain. Additionally, we will introduce a statistical testing method for system-generated financial summaries and the novel BRUGEscore.

2   Background

Summarizing text is a complex task, and standard evaluation metrics such as accuracy, recall, and precision are not suitable for text summarization. In recent years, several metrics have been introduced that are specifically designed for evaluating the quality of machine-generated summaries. In this study, we used the following metrics:

- **ROUGE**: Recall-Oriented Understudy for Gisting Evaluation is a metric used to evaluate the quality of machine-generated summaries by comparing them with a set of human-produced reference summaries. ROUGE measures the number of overlapping textual units, such as n-grams or word sequences, between the generated summary and the reference summaries.
- **BERTScore**: BERTScore is an embedding-based evaluation metric that aligns generated and reference summaries on a token level. Token alignments are computed to maximize the cosine similarity between contextualized token embeddings from the BERT transformer.
- **BARTScore**: BARTScore is an unsupervised evaluation metric used for generative tasks such as machine translation, text summarization, and text generation. It offers a number of variants, depending on the language model used, that can be flexibly applied to evaluate generated text from different perspectives such as informativeness, fluency, or factuality.
- **METEOR**: METEOR computes an alignment between candidate and reference sentences by mapping unigrams in the generated summary to 0 or 1 unigrams in the reference, based on stemming, synonyms, and paraphrastic matches.
- **Bleurt**: Bleurt is a transfer learning-based metric for natural language generation that compares a candidate summary with a reference summary to determine how well the candidate summary conveys the meaning of the reference summary.
- **BRUGEscore**: BRUGEscore is our novel proposed metric, calculated as the harmonic mean of ROUGE-2 and BERTscore. It combines elements of word overlap and embedding cosine similarity into a single score.

Table 1 provides a summary of the features of these metrics, including whether they are embedding-based or n-gram-based.

2.1   Related Work

Text summarization has shown promising applications in the financial domain [7]. Prior works in this field have explored a range of approaches. The Summariser system [15] employed sentence linkage heuristics, while a query-based company-tailored

Table 1. Summary of the features of the evaluation metrics used in this study

Metric	Embeddings	Language Model	n-gram
ROUGE	No	N.A	n-gram
BERTScore	Yes	Roberta Large	1-gram
BARTScore	Yes	Bart Large	1-gram
METEOR	No	N.A	1-gram
Bleurt	Yes	BERT-lg	Sequence
BRUGEscore	Yes	N.A	2-gram

summarization system was proposed in [9]. Recently, statistical features with heuristic approaches were used to summarise financial textual disclosures [3]. The Financial Narrative Summarisation (FNS) task of the Multiling 2019 workshop involved generating structured summaries from financial narrative disclosures. The FNS 2020 task [6] resulted in the first large scale experimental results and state-of-the-art summarisation methods applied to financial data, focusing on annual reports produced by UK firms listed on the London Stock Exchange (LSE). The participating systems used a variety of techniques, ranging from rule-based extraction methods to traditional machine learning methods and high-performing deep learning models.

Prior works on UK annual report summarization include [16], who used a transformer-based encoder-decoder extractive summarisation approach based on the T5 pre-trained model. Abhishek Singh [20] proposed a Pointer Network and T5-based summarization approach to extract relevant narrative sentences in a particular order to have a logical flow in the summary. Lei Li [13] used Determinantal Point Processes to build a Statistical learning Extractive Financial Narrative auto Summarizer. Jaime Baldeon Suarez, [1] combined financial word embeddings and knowledge-based features for financial text summarisation, and Moreno La Quatra [11] developed an end-to-end training framework for financial report summarisation in English.

In comparison to prior works, we explore the impact of different transformer model architectures, the task and data used to pre-train transformer models, as well as correlations between automated metrics within the task of summarising UK annual reports. Our work is distinct as UK annual reports are long, unstructured in plain text, technically written, and subjective. Our study aims to address the challenging components of Financial Narrative Summarisation, and this effort is further promoted by the 2021 Financial Narrative Summarisation task (FNS 2021) in the FNP 2021 workshop.

To address the memory efficiency issue of transformers, we cannot simply pass the entire input annual report and gold standard to the model and fine-tune it. Instead, we need to determine which parts of the report to pass to the transformer. Through dataset analysis, we found that the gold standards are typically extracted from the first third of the report, where the chairman or CEO message and financial highlights are usually located. Therefore, we will pass the first k tokens to the model, where k depends on the model architecture, pre-training, and memory efficiency. Then, the model will be trained to predict the first n tokens of the system summary. On the test dataset of 500 UK annual reports, the model will predict the first n tokens, and we will continue the extraction of the remaining k tokens by determining which part of the report matches the predicted n tokens. This approach transforms the summarization problem into a task of predicting the start of the summary, allowing us to adapt sequence-to-sequence transformer models to summarize long documents where the reference summary is a continuous extracted part of the original text. We refer to this technique as the block-based summarization approach. This technique surpasses the memory efficiency issue of some transformers and is motivated by the fact that reference summaries are extracted from the financial annual report as a block. To our knowledge, this is the best approach for adapting encoder-decoder transformer models to summarize long documents.

We describe several techniques for summarization in this paper, including transformer-based [16], reinforcement learning-based [23], unsupervised learning using LSA, BERT extractive [14], and SBERT extractive summarisation [19]. We also compare the results of these techniques to four toplines and baseline summarizes, as we show later in the papers, and finally, we use Lead-1000 (the first 1000 words) as a strong baseline summarizer [17].

The block-based summarization approach is described as a method of adapting sequence-to-sequence transformer models to summarize long documents where the reference summary is a continuous extracted part of the original text [16]. RL-based summarization is also discussed as a suitable approach for maximizing a predefined metric [23]. Finally, we briefly explain LSA [10], BERT extractive [14], and SBERT extractive [19] as unsupervised techniques that can be used to identify important sentences in a document.

3   Dataset

The dataset used for this study is composed of UK annual reports in English from the financial summarisation shared task (FNS 2021) [22]. It contains 3,863 annual reports for firms listed on the London Stock Exchange (LSE) covering the period between 2002 and 2017, with an average length of 52,000 tokens. The dataset also includes 9,873 gold standard summaries. The dataset is randomly split into training (75%), testing, and validation (25%). Table 2 shows the dataset details.

Table 2. FNS 2021 Shared Task Dataset

Data Type	Train	Validate	Test
Report full text	3,000	363	500
Gold summaries	9,873	1,250	1,673

The dataset used for training presents several gold standard summaries for each annual report (between one and five) [22]. We wanted to use multiple references to make the process more objective since we did not have a human-generated reference summary as a good gold standard. The gold standards used in this study were Financial Highlights, Letter to the Shareholders, Financial Statements, and Auditor's Report.

4 Experimental Work

In our experiments, we used various transformer models used in the study, including the T5 transformer [18], LongFormer Encoder-Decoder [2], as well as BART, Pegasus, and BERT [4,12,21].

In our study, we investigated whether using multiple gold standard summaries would improve the performance of summarization models. To fine-tune the models, we first considered the issue of gold summary standards. We trained T5, Pegasus, and BART using two different strategies. The first strategy involved using all available gold standards, which meant creating multiple pairs for each report. The second strategy was to choose only one gold summary that maximized the ROUGE metric [23], which was the aim of the FNS task. Our preliminary study found that training on a multi-referenced dataset did not significantly improve the ROUGE result and was computationally expensive. Therefore, we chose to train our models using only one reference summary per annual report. We set our reward function as ROUGE-2 and selected the gold standard summary that maximized the ROUGE-2 score with the annual report. This enables our system sumamrisers to maximize the Rouge metric with all the reference summaries.

For hyperparameter search, a comprehensive grid search is a common approach. However, due to the significant computational power and time required, we opted for a simpler strategy. We selected hyperparameters that maximize the input length and target length for our models, as detailed in Table 3. In this study, we used metrics that support multiple references to evaluate the performance of our models. To compute the score between the system summary and all the gold standards, we used the Rouge.2.0 java jar[1] file for ROUGE evaluation. We removed English stop-words but did not use an English stemmer. For other metrics, we used the implementation from the original authors or the implementation of the Hugging Face team on the datasets library. Table 4 provides a summary of the results. We compared the best version of each transformer model with different baselines and toplines, as well as our new BRUGEscore. F1 scores were reported for each metric, including four variants of the rouge score (R1, R2, R-L, R-SU4), BERT and BART scores, Meteor and Bleurt scores. To compute the embedded representation, we used the Roberta-large-mnli and Bart-large-mnli language models for BERTScore and BARTScore, respectively.

Table 3. Description of hyperparameters during training on the FNS dataset

Transformer	model_name	max_input	max_target	batch_size	train_epochs
T5	t5-small	4096	512	4	5
LED base	allenai/led-base-16384	8000	1000	4	5
LED large	allenai/led-large-16384	4096	512	4	5
Pegasus	google/pegasus-large	1024	256	4	5
BART	facebook/bart-base	1024	128	4	5

---

[1] https://github.com/kavgan/ROUGE-2.0.

The results suggest that model-based metrics give good results on the financial dataset, and that Bleurt is not a suitable metric to evaluate system performance. T5 is the best text-to-text model for the dataset, performing well alongside Longformer Encoder-Decoder. LED base is memory-efficient and performs very well on the dataset, while LED Large did not perform as well due to limited GPU memory. The BRUGEscore shows a harmonic mean between the Rouge2 score and BERT score, giving an equilibrium between sentence semantics and exact 2-gram matching. Lead-1000 is a strong benchmark in this task, indicating the superiority of transformer-based summarisation over deep learning and reinforcement learning methods.

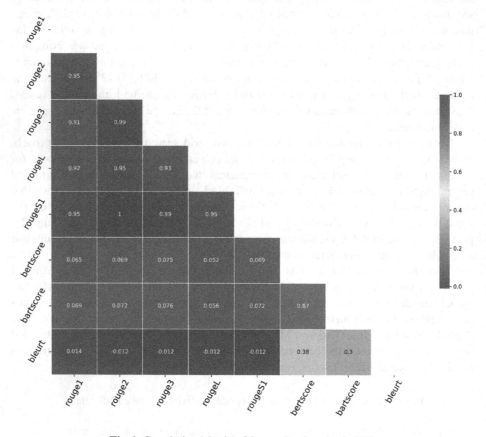

Fig. 1. Correlation Matrix of Scores Produced using T5

Figure 1 shows the correlation matrix of different evaluation metrics' scores using summaries produced by the T5 transformer models which was pre-trained on the FNS test dataset[2]. The correlation plot shows that the different variants of the ROUGE metric are highly correlated, motivating the use of only one ROUGE variant in the evalu-

---

[2] We only display the T5 matrix as it aligns with our conclusion, and the matrices of the other transformers exhibit similar patterns.

ation process. Additionally, BERTScore and BARTScore are highly correlated, while BERTscore, BARTscore, and Bleurt are not correlated with the different variants of ROUGE.

Table 4. F-measure scores for Rouge-1, Rouge-2, Rouge-L, SU4, BERTScore, BARTScore, Bleurt, and Meteor, ranked based on Rouge-2 F1 measure. The abbreviations used are BE for BERT score (roberta-large-mnli), BA for BART score (bart-large-mnli), and BR for BRUGEscore.

System/Metric	R-1/F	R-2/F	R-L/F	R-SU4/ F	BE/F	BA/F	bleurt	meteor	BR
T5-Small-96	0.496	0.374	0.487	0.417	0.910	0.830	-0.836972	0.184	0.530
LED-base-128	0.492	0.370	0.484	0.413	0.899	0.816	-0.849750	0.182	0.524
Pegasus	0.476	0.350	0.467	0.394	0.847	0.759	-0.925372	0.174	0.495
BART	0.453	0.317	0.440	0.365	0.852	0.774	-0.928474	0.176	0.462
Lead-1000	0.443	0.307	0.431	0.356	0.774	0.694	-1.039358	0.162	0.440
RNN-LSTM-RL	0.459	0.270	0.431	0.268	0.761	0.647	-1.027724	0.175	0.399
MUSE-topline	0.433	0.234	0.419	0.253	0.756	0.655	-1.045138	0.163	0.357
LSA	0.321	0.140	0.287	0.187	0.782	0.651	-0.945594	0.160	0.237
SBERT-extractive	0.322	0.139	0.276	0.187	0.781	0.647	-0.973918	0.159	0.236
BERT-extractive	0.312	0.134	0.263	0.182	0.771	0.632	-0.987254	0.121	0.228
LexRank	0.264	0.120	0.253	0.140	0.732	0.580	-1.051438	0.088	0.206
POLY-BASELINE	0.274	0.105	0.212	0.135	0.723	0.565	-1.060618	0.109	0.183
TextRank	0.172	0.070	0.242	0.079	0.727	0.576	-1.074088	0.088	0.128

5 Statistical Significance

To compare the performance of two algorithms or models, we need to prove that the evaluation metric, denoted by 'e', is greater for one system than the other. However, this is not sufficient as we also need to check the statistical significance of the difference in performance between the two algorithms. The common practice in NLP is to claim superiority of one algorithm over another only if the difference in results is statistically significant. To do that, we use significance levels and p-values to determine whether the test results are statistically significant, to avoid false discoveries. We follow the guidelines from the Hitchhiker's Guide to Testing Statistical Significance in NLP" [5]. We model our problem as a "no difference" (null hypothesis H0) or "difference" (H1) and choose the bootstrap test to verify the significance of our results. We apply our test to the difference between the series of results generated by each system, report the p-values of ROUGE-2, ROUGE-L, BERTscore, and Bleurt score as shown in Tables 6 to 9 in Appendix A. We present the p-values of ROUGE-2, ROUGE-L, BERTscore, and Bleurt score in the tables obtained through the Bootstrap method. These p-values, when compared to the significance level (0,1), indicate the significance of the performance difference between the two systems. Cells that are not coloured red indicate a statistically insignificant difference, allowing us to claim with 90% confidence that system one system outperforms the other using a specific metric.

6   Adversarial Analysis

To assess the robustness of the metrics, we also conducted an adversarial analysis on the predicted summaries. Adversarial attacks are text perturbations designed to test the effectiveness of the metrics. Our experiments involved corrupting a set of summaries generated by the T5 small model, which was the best-performing model on the test dataset. We tested the ability of the metrics to resist different sources of noise using **a) BERT mask-filling, b) word-dropping, and c) word permutation** methods. BERT mask-filling and word-dropping are derived from the method used to pre-train BLEURT, while word permutation tests the metrics' sensitivity to syntax by swapping the ordering of two adjacent tokens in the summary. We chose four values of chunks to avoid creating a bias in the distribution of corrupted tokens: 4, 6, 8, and 10. By uniformly distributing the corruption across the text, we can evaluate how well the metrics reflect the difference between the corrupted and uncorrupted text. We anticipate that higher-quality summaries will be more robust to noise. Word-dropping simulates some of the common issues that can arise with extractive summarization. BERT mask-filling is a denoising encoding task that is challenging for BERT score since it assumes that the predicted word by a BERT model is better in this context than the original word in the system summary. Word permutation will penalize the n-gram based metrics but will favour model-based metrics like BERT score and BART score.

To compare the original and corrupted summaries, we use a strict comparison where the original summary must be strictly better than the corrupted one. Table 5 shows the results for the three adversarial tasks with a chunk length of 10. The accuracy value represents the percentage of non-corrupted summaries that received better scores than their corrupted counterparts. An accuracy of 0.00 indicates that the corrupted and non-corrupted summaries received the same scores, as with ROUGE-1 during the word permutation corruption test. This is because ROUGE-1 is insensitive to syntax.

BERTScore and BARTScore achieved an accuracy score of 60% across the three different tasks. These results suggest that **ROUGE** is better suited for extractive summarization while model-based metrics are more suitable for abstractive summarization. ROUGE evaluates summaries on a word-by-word basis, whereas model-based metrics consider the context as a whole. The results also show that ROUGE-2 performed best on the word permutation and BERT mask-filling tasks, while ROUGE-3 performed best on the word dropping task. When the corruption is applied to a single token in a sentence, it disrupts the n-gram sequence, which impacts ROUGE-n when n is greater than 1. Bleurt returned poor results, confirming that it is more suitable for comparing different models than evaluating a single model.

Table 5. Mean accuracy by metric on the three corruption tasks. We apply three types of corruptions on the system generated summaries. We create a corruption every 10 chunks. Each metric is used to score the original and the corrupted versions of these summaries. This task should give the uncorrupted version a higher score to make sure that the metric is sensitive to corrupted summaries. The results reported shows the accuracy by metric on this task. All standard deviations were small (less than 0.2%). The experiments were performed on the FNS dataset using the best performing system which is the small version of T5 transformer

Metric	Word dropping_10 (%)	Word Permutation_10 (%)	Bert Mask filling_10(%)
ROUGE-1	0.826	0.000	0.982
ROUGE-2	0.958	1	0.99
ROUGE-3	0.968	0.998	0.992
ROUGE-S1	0.958	1	0.99
ROUGE-S2	0.946	0.996	0.992
ROUGE-L	0.922	0.978	0.99
ROUGE-SU4	0.88	0.994	0.992
BERTScore	0.608	0.63	0.668
BARTScore	0.636	0.6	0.656
BLEURT	0.556	0.632	0.574

7   Conclusion and Future Work

This paper tackled the task of automatic financial extractive summarisation of UK annual reports using various transformer models and unsupervised baselines. We proposed a set of model-based evaluation metrics, including a new metric called BRUGEscore, which outperformed ROUGE metric variants. We analyzed the results and performed adversarial analysis on the system-generated summaries to verify the robustness of the metrics. In the future, we plan to perform a human evaluation task on our dataset, measure the correlation with existing evaluation metrics, and work on improving the quality of the reference summaries. All PyTorch models are hosted on a private huggingface repository and will be released once the paper is accepted.

8   Limitations

The lack of gold standards, specifically human-generated summaries by domain experts, is the biggest technical challenge facing the financial text summarisation research community. We currently use extracted sections from annual reports as gold summaries. Furthermore, the results are limited to this English dataset, and the performance of evaluation metrics on other languages cannot be guaranteed, especially for language model-based models that are pretrained on English. Financial datasets are also large and scalable, requiring significant computational capacities. Finally, the jargon used in financial disclosures is different from 'general' language, and there is an urgent need to pre-train financial-specific language models for use in such studies.

Appendix A

Table 6. The p-values of the BERT score results using the Bootstrap test are presented in each column, where column i includes the p-values of system i and the p-values of the remaining n-i systems.

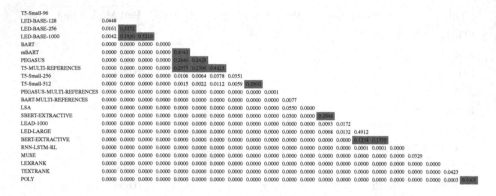

Table 7. The p-values of the Bleurt score results using the Bootstrap test are presented in each column, where column i includes the p-values of system i and the p-values of the remaining n-i systems.

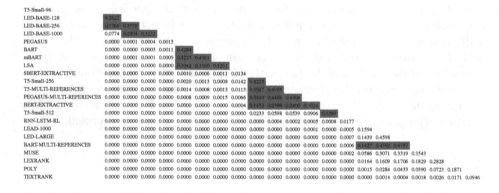

Table 8. The p-values of the Rouge-2 score results using the Bootstrap test are presented in each column, where column i includes the p-values of system i and the p-values of the remaining n-i systems.

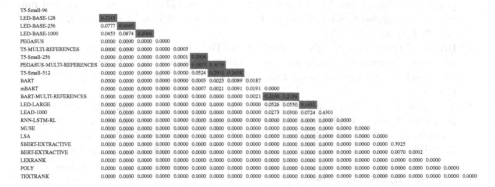

Table 9. The p-values of the Rouge-L score results using the Bootstrap test are presented in each column, where column i includes the p-values of system i and the p-values of the remaining n-i systems.

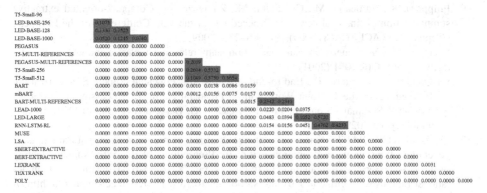

References

1. Baldeon Suarez, J., Martínez, P., Martínez, J.L.: Combining financial word embeddings and knowledge-based features for financial text summarization UC3M-MC System at FNS-2020. In: Proceedings of the 1st Joint Workshop on Financial Narrative Processing and MultiLing Financial Summarisation, pp. 112–117. COLING, Barcelona, Spain (Online) (2020). https://aclanthology.org/2020.fnp-1.19
2. Beltagy, I., Peters, M.E., Cohan, A.: Longformer: the long-document transformer. arXiv:2004.05150 [cs] (2020). http://arxiv.org/abs/2004.05150
3. Cardinaels, E., Hollander, S., White, B.J.: Automatic summarization of earnings releases: attributes and effects on investors' judgments. Rev. Acc. Stud. **24**(3), 860–890 (2019)

4. Devlin, J., Chang, M.W., Lee, K., Toutanova, K.: BERT: pre-training of deep bidirectional transformers for language understanding. In: Proceedings of the 2019 Conference of the North American Chapter of the Association for Computational Linguistics: Human Language Technologies, vol. 1 (Long and Short Papers), pp. 4171–4186. Association for Computational Linguistics, Minneapolis (2019). https://doi.org/10.18653/v1/N19-1423, https://aclanthology.org/N19-1423

5. Dror, R., Baumer, G., Shlomov, S., Reichart, R.: The hitchhiker's guide to testing statistical significance in natural language processing. In: Proceedings of the 56th Annual Meeting of the Association for Computational Linguistics (vol. 1: Long Papers). vol. 1, p. 1383–1392 (2018)

6. El-Haj, M., Litvak, M., Pittaras, N., Giannakopoulos, G., et al.: The financial narrative summarisation shared task (FNS 2020). In: Proceedings of the 1st Joint Workshop on Financial Narrative Processing and MultiLing Financial Summarisation, pp. 1–12 (2020)

7. El-Haj, M., Rayson, P., Walker, M., Young, S., Simaki, V.: In search of meaning: lessons, resources and next steps for computational analysis of financial discourse. J. Bus. Finan. Acc. **46**(3–4), 265–306 (2019)

8. El-Haj, M., et al.: The financial narrative summarisation shared task (FNS 2022). In: Proceedings of the 4th Financial Narrative Processing Workshop @LREC2022, pp. 43–52. European Language Resources Association, Marseille (2022). https://aclanthology.org/2022.fnp-1.6

9. Filippova, K., Surdeanu, M., Ciaramita, M., Zaragoza, H.: Company-oriented extractive summarization of financial news. In: Proceedings of the 12th Conference of the European Chapter of the ACL (EACL 2009), pp. 246–254 (2009)

10. Gong, Y., Liu, X.: Generic text summarization using relevance measure and latent semantic analysis. In: SIGIR 2001 (2001)

11. La Quatra, M., Cagliero, L.: End-to-end Training For Financial Report Summarization. In: Proceedings of the 1st Joint Workshop on Financial Narrative Processing and MultiLing Financial Summarisation, pp. 118–123. COLING, Barcelona (Online) (2020). https://aclanthology.org/2020.fnp-1.20

12. Lewis, M., et al.: BART: Denoising sequence-to-sequence pre-training for natural language generation, translation, and comprehension. In: Proceedings of the 58th Annual Meeting of the Association for Computational Linguistics, pp. 7871–7880. Association for Computational Linguistics, Online (2020). https://doi.org/10.18653/v1/2020.acl-main.703, https://aclanthology.org/2020.acl-main.703

13. Li, L., Jiang, Y., Liu, Y.: Extractive financial narrative summarisation based on DPPs. In: Proceedings of the 1st Joint Workshop on Financial Narrative Processing and MultiLing Financial Summarisation, pp. 100–104. COLING, Barcelona (Online) (2020). https://aclanthology.org/2020.fnp-1.17

14. Miller, D.: Leveraging Bert for extractive text summarization on lectures (2019)

15. de Oliveira, P.C.F., Ahmad, K., Gillam, L.: A financial news summarization system based on lexical cohesion. In: Proceedings of the International Conference on Terminology and Knowledge Engineering, Nancy, France (2002)

16. Orzhenovskii, M.: T5-LONG-EXTRACT at FNS-2021 shared task. In: Proceedings of the 3rd Financial Narrative Processing Workshop, pp. 67–69. Association for Computational Linguistics, Lancaster, United Kingdom (2021). https://aclanthology.org/2021.fnp-1.12

17. Radev, D.R., Jing, H., Styś, M., Tam, D.: Centroid-based summarization of multiple documents. Inf. Process. Manage. **40**(6), 919–938 (2004)

18. Raffel, C., et al.: Exploring the limits of transfer learning with a unified text-to-text transformer. arXiv:1910.10683 [cs, stat] (Jul 2020). http://arxiv.org/abs/1910.10683

19. Reimers, N., Gurevych, I.: Sentence-BERT: Sentence embeddings using Siamese BERT-networks. In: Proceedings of the 2019 Conference on Empirical Methods in Natural Language Processing and the 9th International Joint Conference on Natural Language Processing (EMNLP-IJCNLP), pp. 3982–3992. Association for Computational Linguistics, Hong Kong, China (2019). https://doi.org/10.18653/v1/D19-1410, https://aclanthology.org/D19-1410

20. Singh, A.: PoinT-5: pointer network and t-5 based financial narrative summarisation. In: Proceedings of the 1st Joint Workshop on Financial Narrative Processing and MultiLing Financial Summarisation. pp. 105–111. COLING, Barcelona, Spain (Online) (2020), https://aclanthology.org/2020.fnp-1.18

21. Zhang, J., Zhao, Y., Saleh, M., Liu, P.J.: PEGASUS: pre-training with extracted gap-sentences for abstractive summarization. arXiv:1912.08777 [cs] (2020). http://arxiv.org/abs/1912.08777

22. Zmandar, N., El-Haj, M., Rayson, P., Abura'Ed, A., Litvak, M., Giannakopoulos, G., Pittaras, N.: The financial narrative summarisation shared task FNS 2021. In: Proceedings of the 3rd Financial Narrative Processing Workshop, pp. 120–125. Association for Computational Linguistics, Lancaster, United Kingdom (2021). https://aclanthology.org/2021.fnp-1.22

23. Zmandar, N., Singh, A., El-Haj, M., Rayson, P.: Joint abstractive and extractive method for long financial document summarization. In: Proceedings of the 3rd Financial Narrative Processing Workshop, pp. 99–105. Association for Computational Linguistics, Lancaster, United Kingdom (2021). https://aclanthology.org/2021.fnp-1.19

Effective Information Retrieval, Question Answering and Abstractive Summarization on Large-Scale Biomedical Document Corpora

Naveen Shenoy[1], Pratham Nayak[1], Sarthak Jain[1],
S. Sowmya Kamath[1(✉)], and Vijayan Sugumaran[2]

[1] Department of Information Technology, National Institute of Technology
Karnataka, Surathkal 575025, India
sowmyakamath@nitk.edu.in
[2] Department of Decision and Information Sciences, Oakland University, Rochester,
MI 48309, USA

Abstract. During the COVID-19 pandemic, a concentrated effort was made to collate published literature on SARS-Cov-2 and other coronaviruses for the benefit of the medical community. One such initiative is the COVID-19 Open Research Dataset which contains over 400,000 published research articles. To expedite access to relevant information sources for health workers and researchers, it is vital to design effective information retrieval and information extraction systems. In this article, an IR approach leveraging transformer-based models to enable question-answering and abstractive summarization is presented. Various keyword-based and neural-network-based models are experimented with and incorporated to reduce the search space and determine relevant sentences from the vast corpus for ranked retrieval. For abstractive summarization, candidate sentences are determined using a combination of various standard scoring metrics. Finally, the summary and the user query are utilized for supporting question answering. The proposed model is evaluated based on standard metrics on the standard CovidQA dataset for both natural language and keyword queries. The proposed approach achieved promising performance for both query classes, while outperforming various unsupervised baselines.

Keywords: Information retrieval · PageRank · Question-answering · Abstractive Summarization · Transformer models

1 Introduction

Since its emergence in late 2019, the Novel Coronavirus Disease (COVID-19) has escalated into a worldwide pandemic in a very short span of time. In spite of stringent protocols adopted by most countries to contain its spread, the mutating nature of the virus posed serious challenges. Researchers have long studied

E. Métais et al. (Eds.): NLDB 2023, LNCS 13913, pp. 404–415, 2023.
https://doi.org/10.1007/978-3-031-35320-8_29

the Coronaviridae family of viruses, and a huge volume of scientific literature exists already. During the pandemic, a major escalation in research efforts on all aspects of this field to understand the causes, impact, genetics, and also ways for mitigating the impact was seen. For effective utilization of these worldwide efforts and research outcomes, ensuring access to factual and authentic sources of information on important topics related to COVID-19 for the use of medical practitioners, researchers, and other personnel received much importance. This led to concerted efforts and initiatives for creating large-scale centralized repositories of literature, like the COVID-19 Open Research Dataset (CORD-19) [22] consisting of more than 1,000,000 documents with over 400,000 full-text research articles about SARS-CoV-2, COVID-19 and other related topics.

Challenges related to enabling effective information retrieval and relevant knowledge extraction from such large-scale unstructured data repositories is, however, a major challenge. The users typically range from information seekers who need natural language keyword-based querying to researchers who may require support for highly intuitive knowledge discovery techniques for further development of therapeutics and vaccines. Furthermore, finding relevant information in all such cases is more critical due to the numerous false information and rumors that people tend to disseminate fast due to ignorance. Therefore, an efficient and effective system to find the most relevant scientific literature to support intelligent retrieval applications is a critical requirement.

Large-scale information retrieval (IR) systems are designed to facilitate effective matching between given query terms and the most relevant documents from vast document corpora. However, clinical and biomedical text is quite different in structure and distribution of words in comparison to standard text. This makes information retrieval over clinical/scientific articles a difficult task which cannot be addressed using generalized IR techniques. Word embeddings are common for representing documents and hence obtaining vector representations for documents which can be compared with vector representations for the queries for similarity. Word embeddings trained specifically for representing biomedical texts, such as BioBERT, SciBERT and ClinicalBERT, are extensively being used. However, since COVID-19 is a very recent disease, most clinical-based embeddings are not trained on its data. Due to COVID-19 literature having its own style of representation and distribution of text, direct use of BioBERT or SciBERT embeddings may not be optimal.

Several tools and search engines dedicated to information retrieval on COVID-19 articles trained exclusively on the CORD-19 dataset have been developed. Some notable efforts include AWS CORD-19 Search [3] and Neural Covidex [24]. These search engines have been developed specifically to address the tasks of keyword-based search, question answering (QA), and FAQ matching. Techniques based on NLP, keyword search, and knowledge graphs were used extensively in the development of these engines. However, these efforts overlook certain aspects, such as common citation similarity of specific sections in an article, like paper abstracts and titles. Also, most efforts focus on individual end-user tasks like IR and QA and overlook the need for different styles of information seeking.

Often, the relevant document list returned to the user in response to a keyword search may be long, and it requires manual effort to effectively peruse these documents. Hence, supporting intuitive summarization may also add value to the user's information-seeking experience.

In this article, an integrated framework for information retrieval, question answering, and abstractive summarization is proposed for supporting intuitive information-seeking processes in large document corpora like CORD-19. User queries can range from general information regarding COVID-19 to information regarding precautions, vaccines, and therapeutics. The framework automatically generates summaries by analyzing the information value from the sentences retrieved from relevant documents. Also, the proposed framework also enables question answering, which takes the generated summary as context and the user questions as input to provide answers to user questions. The CORD-19 dataset was used for the experimental evaluation of the proposed framework.

The remainder of the paper is organized as follows. In Sect. 2, a discussion on relevant recent work in the domain of interest is presented. The proposed methodology and related processes for supporting summarization and question-answering are discussed in detail in Sect. 3. In Sect. 4, the experimental validation of the proposed framework and the observed results are presented, followed by conclusions and future research directions in Sect. 5.

2   Related Work

The challenges related to the design of IR systems for large corpora have been extensively studied and researched over the past few decades. Several works have utilized classical IR models, topic modeling [4,11], transformer-based models, while others have adapted these for specialized tasks [1,21] and domains like healthcare, finance, law etc. Our study focuses on existing works addressing the challenges of IR in large-scale scientific literature corpora.

For creating the CORD-19 dataset, the most promising contributions were carefully analyzed by a team of doctors and other medical experts, and a formal literature review was undertaken. The resultant data is of a semi-structured nature consisting of questions and answers as values. The CovidQA dataset [19] is a question-answering dataset built over the CORD data, consisting of natural language questions, their keyword versions, the possible answers from the documents of the dataset, along with the document ids. Since CovidQA contains a small number of question-and-answer pairs, it cannot be used for training neural network-based models. The dataset can be used in fine-tuning tasks for testing or evaluation purposes. The Stanford Question-Answering Dataset (SQuAD) [17] and the Microsoft MAchine Reading COmprehension Dataset (MS-MARCO) [14] were used to fine-tune BERT, BioBERT and T5 [16] models for Question-Answering. T5 fine-tuned on the MS-MARCO dataset outperformed other models. Various other question-answering datasets in the biomedical domain have been proposed, BioASQ [20] being one of them. One issue with the provided questions is that they differ from the tasks in the TREC-COVID challenge.

Das et al. [7] proposed an IR system built of graph community detection over similarity networks built using paper abstracts and text. Initially, BioSentVec [6] was used to create the initial graph between the documents and the common citation information between the two papers. Further, ego-splitting was applied to the graph to generate local clusters. BioBERT [12] embeddings were then used to map the query to certain documents and select those clusters reducing the search space. Finally, only sentences from the reduced set were used for information retrieval and question answering. A major drawback of this work is the lack of evaluation of the proposed question-answering and information retrieval system. Apart from this, no ablation study has been performed to suggest which modules of the model contribute to the approach's effectiveness. Esteva et al. [9] performed information retrieval with support for question answering on the CORD-19 dataset using deep neural models. They used a combination of Siamese BERT model along with keyword-based models, which included BM25 and TF-IDF. However, a major drawback of this work is that it does not incorporate techniques for relevance feedback.

Tang et al. [19] performed extensive experiments and presented the results of various baseline models evaluated on the CovidQA dataset. They reported that BM25 outperformed unsupervised approaches such as the BERT-based models, including vanilla BERT [8], BioBERT [12], and SciBERT [2]. It has also been reported that BERT-based models, both unsupervised and fine-tuned versions, performed poorly when compared to the best match-based IR models for keyword-based queries. This is because BERT is trained to understand the meaning behind the text, which is often absent in keyword queries. Bhatia et al. [3] developed a COVID-19 IR system (ACS) with question answering, passage ranking and document ranking. ACS used knowledge graphs to model the entities such as citations, authors, their institutions, scholarly articles etc. Topic modeling was also performed to group documents into overlapping topics, such as virology, epidemiology, etc., to help group or cluster the documents. However, ACS performs information retrieval by finding the relevant passage and hence does not support summarization. Zhang et al. [24] proposed an IR system to find relevant documents for a given query, where each paragraph across the corpus is ranked using BM25 and each document is ranked the same as the best-ranked paragraph from the document. The shortlisted documents are then filtered for relevancy using monoT5 model that is trained to return true/false depending on whether the given query/document pair is relevant or not. The final output only consists of a ranked list of relevant documents and tasks such as question-answering or summarization are not attempted.

3   Proposed Methodology

The proposed workflow and its constituent processes are depicted in Fig. 1. For the experimental evaluation of the proposed integrated framework, the COVID-19 Open Research Dataset (CORD-19) was employed. It provides more than 400,000 full-text research articles, and on average, each document contains hundreds of sentences. Firstly, the documents available in the CORD-19 dataset are preprocessed, split into sentences using heuristic algorithms, and then cleaned using standard preprocessing pipelines. The Okapi BM25 model [18] is used to generate scores for each of the sentences. Also, BioSentVec is used to convert documents into embeddings, which are then compared with the query embeddings and scored using cosine similarity. A combination of both these scores is used to shortlist candidate sentences. These sentences are used to construct a graph based on the cosine similarity of BioSentVec embeddings. Next, the PageRank algorithm is applied to the generated graph to score all the sentences.

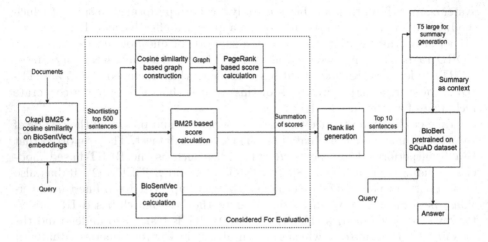

Fig. 1. Proposed workflow

Next, a combination of all three scores obtained from Okapi BM25, BioSentVec, and PageRank is used to generate the final rank list. This combined score considers both word-level scores of the Okapi model as well as semantic-level scores of the BioSentVec model making the two approaches complementary to each other. The top sentences are used to generate a summary using the T5 model, after which the summary and query are used to find the exact answer using a BioBERT model trained on the SQuAD dataset. For the evaluation of the model, the CovidQA dataset is employed. This can be used to benchmark the IR model via sentence retrieval evaluation using the provided answer relevance details as per standard metrics.

Search Space Reduction. As the CORD-19 dataset consists of more than 400,000 scientific articles, each with hundreds of sentences, information retrieval over search a large search space is a computationally expensive task. It is thus necessary to reduce the search space and select the sentences which are to be used to perform summarization and question-answering. To reduce the search space from the set of all sentences from the CORD-19 corpus, we use the Okapi BM25 model scores computed for each document along with the scores generated using BioSentVec [6] embeddings.

Okapi BM25 is a probabilistic retrieval framework based on the bag of words retrieval that ranks documents based on the query terms in them. Here, the order of the words or the proximity of the words in the document is not considered. If Q is a query containing n terms and D is a document, then the similarity between the query and the document is given by Eq. (1) where K and b are constants, $f(q_i, D)$ is the frequency of the ith query term in the document D, $|D|$ is the length of the document, $avgdoclen$ is the average document length across the corpus. The term $IDF(q_i)$ is the inverse document frequency of the ith query term computed as per Eq. (2), where, N is the total number of documents in the corpus and $n(q_i)$ is the number of documents containing the term q_i.

$$Sim(Q, D) = \sum_{i=1}^{n} \frac{(k_1 + 1)f(q_i, D)}{k_1(1 - b + b\frac{|D|}{avgdoclen}) + f(q_i, D)} IDF(q_i) \tag{1}$$

$$IDF(q_i) = \ln(\frac{N - n(q_i) + 0.5}{n(q_i) + 0.5} + 1) \tag{2}$$

BioSentVec [6] is a deep learning-based model trained on a corpus of over 30,000,000 clinical and bio-medical research articles from PubMed [5], and MIMIC-III [10] databases, which are publicly available. BioSentVec was trained using a Continuous Bag of Words (CBOW) based sent2vec model. Experiments based on differing n-gram models and window sizes led to the attainment of 700-dimensional vectors when trained using a bigram sent2vec model with a window size of 30. Hence, the BioSentVec embedding for a sentence turns out to be a 700-dimensional vector. BioSentVec was trained on two tasks, clinical sentence similarity, and biomedical multi-label text classification. For sentence similarity, BioSentVec was evaluated on two datasets, BIOSSES and MedSTS, using both supervised and unsupervised approaches. Supervised approaches were mainly multi-layer deep learning models with BioSentVec embeddings as the input.

In our work, the BioSentVec score between a query and a sentence is the cosine similarity between the BioSentVec embeddings of the query and the sentence. We consider the final score for a sentence as the arithmetic sum of the BM25 score and the cosine similarity of the BioSentVec embeddings of the sentence and the query, both normalized to give equal weightage to the BM25 and BioSentVec models. A total of 500 sentences are shortlisted in this phase.

Ranking Optimization. In this stage, further shortlisting of the sentences is performed. The shortlisted sentences and the semantic relation between them are modeled in the form of a graph. Ideally, two sentences which are semantically similar to each other should have an edge between them. At the same time, it should be ensured that semantically related sentences which are unrelated to the query should not contain an edge between them. As a solution, a graph between the sentences is created where an edge between two sentences exists if and only if the cosine similarity between the BioSentVec embeddings of the two sentences, as well as the cosine similarity of the embeddings of each sentence with that of the query, are above a specific threshold. This threshold is determined empirically based on experimentation and thus set to 0.1. The chosen threshold value should be such that neither the graph should be too dense nor too sparse. A sparse graph can lead to a biased selection of the nodes or sentences, while a dense graph may result in noise for the PageRank algorithm in further steps.

The PageRank algorithm [23] is employed for traversal of the constructed graph for finding the most relevant sentences for summarization. PageRank (PR) is an iterative algorithm that computes the rank of each node in a given directed graph. PR gives scores to each of the nodes or sentences based on how influential they are. The rank of each node is computed using Eq. (3), where $PR(p_i)$ is the page rank of p_i, d is the damping factor, N is the total number of nodes in the graph, $M(p_i)$ is the set of all nodes with an outgoing edge to p_i and $L(p_i)$ is the out-degree of p_i.

$$PR(p_i) = \frac{1-d}{N} + \sum_{p_j \in M(p_i)} \frac{PR(p_j)}{L(p_j)} \tag{3}$$

Since the graph construction process is slow, the number of sentences on which the PageRank algorithm can be executed is limited. To shortlist the final set of sentences from the corpus, the PageRank score, BM25 score and BioSentVec score are considered for each shortlisted sentence. After normalizing all scores, the arithmetic sum of the PageRank score, BM25 score and BioSentVec scores are used to rank each sentence. The top 10 sentences are finally selected from the generated rank list for undertaking the task of summary generation.

Summarization. In the proposed framework, the T5-large model is used for abstractive text summarization. T5 (Text-to-Text transfer transformer) [16] is a transformer-based model trained on masked language modeling. It can perform various tasks such as text classification, question answering, machine translation, and abstractive summarization. T5-large is used to summarize the top 10 sentences from the previous stage in an abstractive manner, to provide a summary. Abstractive summarization produces novel sentences that are not present in the input. In order to obtain a short and concise summary from the retrieved text, only 10 sentences from the previous step are input to the T5-large summarizer.

Question Answering. For question answering, a BioBERT model pre-trained on the SQuAD [17] dataset is used. SQuAD contains for each training example a query, a context text to answer the query and the exact answer. The SQuAD BioBERT model takes the input query along with a limited-sized context as the input. Since no context is provided during information retrieval in our case apart from the query itself, we leverage the summary generated from the top 10 sentences from the T5-large model as context for our question-answering task using BioBERT. The output answer provided by the BioBERT model is generally concise, which is, in turn, supported by the concise context provided to it.

4   Experimental Evaluation and Results

For experimental validation of the proposed approach, the Covid-19 Open Research Dataset (CORD-19) is used. Each of the 400,000+ research articles in the dataset is made available with all its constituent sections, such as abstract, body, reference entries, etc. For evaluation, we use CovidQA [19], a question-answering dataset created using the CORD dataset. It comprises questions in the form of natural language & keyword queries, along with the exact answer and the document in which it occurs. A query may have multiple answers from different documents from the CORD corpus. In our work, the version of CORD from April 10, i.e. Round 1 of the TREC-COVID challenge, was used. The dataset contains 130 question-answer pairs and 27 unique topics (or questions). The answers to the queries form a set of 85 documents from CORD. On average, each question contains 1.6 answers. The exact answer may be present in several sentences of the given document. The answer can be from the abstract, body text or even the reference entries.

For obtaining sentences from the text, a heuristic algorithm covers the cases of text containing abbreviations, hyphens, colons, etc. For further preprocessing, all the sentences are converted to lowercase, and additional whitespaces are removed. For the BM25 modeling, additional preprocessing is done. This includes removing normalization, lemmatization, and stop word removal. Along with standard English stopwords, around 26 paper-specific stopwords like Elsevier, fig, copyright, table, org, et, etc., are also considered as stopwords.

Baselines. The baseline models for evaluation can be categorized into two categories. The first type consists of models which consider keywords for ranking documents. The second type is neural-based, i.e., BERT. For the keyword-based model, we use Okapi BM25 [18], a probabilistic IR model based on the bag of words strategy that ranks documents based on the query terms appearing in them. For neural network-based models, we consider vanilla BERT [8] as well as SciBERT [2], and BioBERT [12]. SciBERT is trained on scientific texts such as SciERC [13], which contain computer science abstracts. BioBERT, on the other hand, is trained on bio-medical datasets such as MIMIC-III [10] and PubMed [5]. The Bio-BERT model fine-tuned on the Stanford Question Answering Dataset (SQuAD) for the question-answering task using techniques defined by [15].

Evaluation Metrics. The CovidQA dataset is used to evaluate the proposed model on the question-answering task. Given a query and a document containing the answer to the query, the system ranks all the sentences. To be deemed correct, the chosen sentence must contain the answer as a substring. To evaluate the generated rank list, three evaluation metrics are used. These include precision, recall and mean reciprocal rank (MRR). Since there is a large imbalance in the number of questions per topic and per document, micro-averaging is used to compute the final precision, recall and MRR scores.

- *Precision@1 (P@1)*: For a single query, P@1 shows whether the top sentence in the generated rank list contains the answer or not.
- *Recall@3 (R@3)*: For a single query, R@3 is the total number of relevant sentences in the top 3 of the rank list divided by the total number of sentences containing the answer.
- *Mean Reciprocal Rank (MRR)*: RR for a query is the inverse of the rank of the first sentence containing the answer in the generated rank list. The MRR score is the mean of the individual RR values across all queries.

4.1   Results and Discussion

Several experiments were undertaken to assess the performance of the proposed approach against the baseline models of BM25, BERT, SciBERT, BioBERT and BioBERT trained on SQuAD proposed by Tang et al. [19]. Table 1 shows the comparison of the proposed approach with the baseline models for natural language and keyword queries. The proposed model outperformed all baselines in terms of the P@1 score. For R@3 and MRR, the proposed model outperforms all baselines except the SQuAD fine-tuned BioBERT model.

Table 1. Performance on Natural Language (NL) Queries and Keyword Queries of CovidQA

Model	NL Queries			Keyword Queries		
	P@1	R@3	MRR	P@1	R@3	MRR
Random [19]	0.012	0.034	-	0.012	0.034	-
BM25 [19]	0.150	0.216	0.243	0.150	0.216	0.243
BERT [19]	0.081	0.117	0.159	0.073	0.164	0.187
SciBERT [19]	0.040	0.056	0.099	0.024	0.064	0.094
BioBERT [19]	0.097	0.142	0.170	0.129	0.145	0.185
BioBERT (SQuAD fine-tuned) [19]	0.161	**0.403**	**0.336**	0.056	0.093	0.135
BM25 + BioSentVec + PageRank (*proposed*)	**0.177**	0.244	0.268	**0.162**	**0.236**	**0.258**

The lower performance on R@3 and MRR implies that the proposed model performs well in ranking a relevant sentence at the top ranked position but not so well in ranking relevant sentences in the first three positions. Surprisingly, BM25 performed second best in terms of R@3 and MRR, even outperforming the BERT counterparts. The best performance amongst the baseline models was achieved by the BioBERT question-answering model. The comparison of the proposed approach with the baseline models for keyword queries provided in the CovidQA dataset are also shown here. It can be observed that, in this case, the proposed model outperformed all baseline models for all metrics. The low

---

Table 2. Summaries and answers generated by T5 and BioBERT (SQuAD) for some sample queries

Query	Summary	Answer
common symptoms of covid 19	the most common symptoms of covid-19 are fever, cough and tiredness. the most common symptoms of covid-19 are fever, dry cough, and malaise/fatigue. covid screening for that visitor depends on resource availability and symptoms.	fever, cough and tiredness
how to mitigate covid transmission?	social measures for mitigating covid transmission, including social distancing and sheltering in place, have not been examined. risk of transmission during rugby matches is very low but efforts should be made to further mitigate disease transmission within environment.	travel bans and sheltering in place

performance of BERT-based models could be because the keyword query lacks natural language semantics which they heavily rely on.

The summaries and answers generated by T5 and BioBERT (SQuAD) for some sample queries are shown in Table 2. It can be observed that the generated summaries are concise and contain relevant information with respect to the query. For a sample query *"how to mitigate covid transmission"*, the summary contains 2 sentences from the 10 sentences that are shortlisted after Pagerank, BM25, and BioSentVec. Further, question answering using this summary as context provides a to-the-point answer, i.e. *"travel bans and sheltering in place"*.

4.2 Ablation Studies

Table 3 shows the results of the ablation study performed for natural language and keyword queries of the CovidQA dataset by considering a combination of different subsets of scoring algorithms. Based on the observations, the final model performs optimally, as a major performance boost is provided by BM25, followed by BioSentVec, and then PageRank. The performance drop is maximum without BM25 and minimum without PageRank. The results of the ablation study performed for keyword queries of the CovidQA dataset by considering a combination of different subsets of scoring algorithms (shown in Table 3), also revealed similar observations and performance variations for the various combinations are exactly similar to that of the natural language queries.

Table 3. Ablation study on CovidQA - Natural Language (NL) queries *vs.* Keyword queries

Model	NL Queries			Keyword Queries		
	P@1	R@3	MRR	P@1	R@3	MRR
BioSentVec + PageRank	0.138	0.216	0.247	0.138	0.208	0.248
BM25 + PageRank	0.154	0.215	0.248	0.146	0.215	0.244
BM25 + BioSentVec	0.169	**0.244**	0.264	0.154	**0.236**	0.254
BM25 + BioSentVec + PageRank (*proposed*)	**0.177**	**0.244**	**0.268**	**0.162**	**0.236**	**0.258**

5   Conclusion and Future Work

In this paper, an integrated information retrieval framework built on the BM25 IR model, BioSentVec model, and PageRank algorithm for enabling automated abstractive summarization and question answering was presented. The proposed model was experimentally validated on the large-scale scientific document corpus called CORD-19 and the CovidQA dataset. Search space reduction techniques were incorporated to reduce the computational complexity of searching in large document collections. During the experimental evaluation, the proposed approach outperformed the standard BM25 and BERT-based models (both unsupervised and fine-tuned on the SQuAD dataset). The summarization and question-answering functionalities provided meaningful and reasonable answers. Ablation studies were performed, which showed that the enhanced performance was greatly influenced by the BM25 model, followed by the BioSentVec model, and then the PageRank algorithm. Further, it was observed that the performance of the proposed model was consistent for both natural language-based and keyword-based queries, which is not the case for BERT-based models. As part of future work, we plan to integrate a relevant feedback loop to make the process of COVID-19 information retrieval faster and more efficient.

References

1. Bachina, S., Balumuri, S., Kamath, S.: Ensemble ALBERT and RoBERTa for span prediction in question answering. In: Proceedings of 59th Annual Meeting of the Association for Computational Linguistics and 11th International Joint Conference on Natural Language Processing (ACL-IJCNLP 2021), pp. 63–68 (2021)
2. Beltagy, I., Lo, K., Cohan, A.: Scibert: A pretrained language model for scientific text. arXiv preprint arXiv:1903.10676 (2019)
3. Bhatia, P., et al.: AWS CORD-19 search: a neural search engine for COVID-19 literature. In: Shaban-Nejad, A., Michalowski, M., Bianco, S. (eds.) W3PHAI 2021. SCI, vol. 1013, pp. 131–145. Springer, Cham (2021). https://doi.org/10.1007/978-3-030-93080-6_11
4. Bhopale, A.P., Shevgoor, S.K.: Temporal topic modeling of scholarly publications for future trend forecasting. In: Reddy, P.K., Sureka, A., Chakravarthy, S., Bhalla, S. (eds.) BDA 2017. LNCS, vol. 10721, pp. 144–163. Springer, Cham (2017). https://doi.org/10.1007/978-3-319-72413-3_10
5. Canese, K., Weis, S.: Pubmed: the bibliographic database. The NCBI handbook, vol. 2(1) (2013)
6. Chen, Q., Peng, Y., Lu, Z.: Biosentvec: creating sentence embeddings for biomedical texts. In: 2019 IEEE International Conference on Healthcare Informatics, pp. 1–5. IEEE (2019)
7. Das, D., et al.: Information retrieval and extraction on COVID-19 clinical articles using graph community detection and bio-Bert embeddings. In: Proceedings of the 1st Workshop on NLP for COVID-19 at ACL 2020 (2020)
8. Devlin, J., Chang, M.W., Lee, K., Toutanova, K.: BERT: Pre-training of deep bidirectional transformers for language understanding. arXiv:1810.04805 (2018)

9. Esteva, A., et al.: COVID-19 information retrieval with deep-learning based semantic search, question answering, and abstractive summarization. NPJ Digital Med. **4**(1), 1–9 (2021)
10. Johnson, A.E., et al.: Mimic-iii, a freely accessible critical care database. Sci. Data **3**(1), 160035 (2016)
11. Krishnan, G.S., Sowmya Kamath, S., Sugumaran, V.: Predicting vaccine hesitancy and vaccine sentiment using topic modeling and evolutionary optimization. In: Métais, E., Meziane, F., Horacek, H., Kapetanios, E. (eds.) NLDB 2021. LNCS, vol. 12801, pp. 255–263. Springer, Cham (2021). https://doi.org/10.1007/978-3-030-80599-9_23
12. Lee, J., et al.: BioBERT: a pre-trained biomedical language representation model for biomedical text mining. Bioinformatics **36**(4), 1234–1240 (2020)
13. Luan, Y., He, L., Ostendorf, M., Hajishirzi, H.: Multi-task identification of entities, relations, and coreference for scientific knowledge graph construction. arXiv preprint arXiv:1808.09602 (2018)
14. Nguyen, T., et al.: MS MARCO: a human generated machine reading comprehension dataset. In: CoCo@ NIPs (2016)
15. Nogueira, R., Jiang, Z., Lin, J.: Document ranking with a pretrained sequence-to-sequence model. arXiv preprint arXiv:2003.06713 (2020)
16. Raffel, C., et al.: Exploring the limits of transfer learning with a unified text-to-text transformer. J. Mach. Learn. Res. **21**(140), 1–67 (2020)
17. Rajpurkar, P., Zhang, J., Lopyrev, K., Liang, P.: Squad: 100,000+ questions for machine comprehension of text. arXiv preprint arXiv:1606.05250 (2016)
18. Robertson, S.E., Walker, S., Beaulieu, M., Gatford, M., Payne, A.: Okapi at TREC-4. Nist Special Publication Sp pp. 73–96 (1996)
19. Tang, R., et al.: Rapidly bootstrapping a question answering dataset for COVID-19. arXiv preprint arXiv:2004.11339 (2020)
20. Tsatsaronis, G., et al.: An overview of the BIOASQ large-scale biomedical semantic indexing and question answering competition. BMC Bioinform. **16**(1), 1–28 (2015)
21. Upadhya, B.A., Udupa, S.: Deep neural network models for question classification in community question-answering forums. In: 2019 10th International Conference on Computing, Communication and Networking Technologies. IEEE (2019)
22. Wang, L.L., Lo, K., Chandrasekhar, Y., Reas, R., Yang, J., et al.: Cord-19: The covid-19 open research dataset (2020)
23. Xing, W., Ghorbani, A.: Weighted pagerank algorithm. In: Proceedings. Second Annual Conference on Communication Networks and Services Research, 2004, pp. 305–314. IEEE (2004)
24. Zhang, E., Gupta, N., Tang, R., Han, X., Pradeep, R., et al.: Covidex: neural ranking models and keyword search infrastructure for the COVID-19 open research dataset (2020). https://doi.org/10.48550/ARXIV.2007.07846

Abstractive Summarization Based Question-Answer System For Structural Information

Menaka Pushpa Arthur[1]([✉]), Thakor Jayraj Rameshchandra[2],
and Manjula Dhanabalachandran[2]

[1] Associate Professor, School of Computer Science and Engineering, Vellore Institute
of Technology, Chennai Campus, Chennai 600 127, Tamil Nadu, India
menakapushpa.a@vit.ac.in
[2] School of Computer Science and Engineering, Vellore Institute of Technology,
Chennai Campus, Chennai 600 127, Tamil Nadu, India

Abstract. Query-based answer summarization is the process by which
the answer from structured information like books is extracted in a concise fashion based on the given query, with minimal loss of information.
Whether an abstractive or extractive answer summarization technique
gets executed automatically depends on the information that is being
extracted with respect to the question raised. The lexical relationship
between sentence-to-sentence and query-to-sentence reduces the conflict
between answer summary and user query and also improves the quality of the answer summary. For the fastest content retrieval from the
structured information, book, our system finds the semantic and syntactic similarity between the subtitles of each chapter and the query. This
work uses techniques of the Natural Language Processing paradigm along
with some of the advanced Deep Learning techniques such as attention
mechanism and Transfer Learning. The implementation results demonstrate the accuracy and efficiency of the extracted answer summary for
the respective query, without compromising the quality of content.

Keywords: NLP · Deep Learning · QA System · Abstractive
summary · Extractive summary · semantic and syntactic similarity

1 Introduction

The Question-Answering (QA) system has been one such field that has gained
the attention of people in the last decade. The automated QA system has now
become an integral part of today's world. Research scholars and engineers are
now focusing on the development of such expert systems for broader domains
such as industrial automation, the Government sector, the corporate sector as
well as in pedagogical domain. The development of an automated QA expert
system requires knowledge of Information Retrieval and Natural Language Processing. Humans are more interested in getting concise and easily readable short
answers rather than going through long texts from different hyperlinks and wast-
ing their valuable time. Therefore, in order to provide a more accurate and point-
to-point answer, automated text summarization plays an important role. With

E. Métais et al. (Eds.): NLDB 2023, LNCS 13913, pp. 416–427, 2023.
https://doi.org/10.1007/978-3-031-35320-8_30

the development and advancements in the text summarization domain, we can get an overview of long articles within minutes by getting a compressed summary that covers the highlights of the article.

One such domain where the application of an automated QA system and text summarization plays an important role is, getting a concise answer when prompted with a question from the book. In general, there are two techniques of text summarization: Extractive and Abstractive. Extractive summarization is a technique that generates a summary by extracting important sentences from the given text as input thereby maintaining the same syntax. Whereas abstractive summarization is an approach where the semantic structure is the same but the syntactic structure is modified. It generates and adds words that are semantically the same and thereby producing a human-like summary. With this motive of using the abstractive summarization technique, we came up with the idea of developing an abstractive question-answering system for structured information such as books. Given an abstractive question as input by the user, the system will generate a more human-like and concise answer by scanning through the entire book and picking up relevant portions which can be fed into the system for abstractive text summarization. The main objectives of our proposed systems are;

- Query-based answer extractive or abstractive Summarization technique. Accuracy and efficiency of the resultant answer are ensured by Natural Language Processing techniques
- Optimized Search and Summarization Algorithms and frameworks like metadata for quick response systems for larger books

The rest of this paper is organized as follows. Section 2 describes related work in answer extractive and abstractive summarization. Our proposed method is introduced in Sect. 3. In Sect. 4 experimental results are presented and discussed. In Sect. 5, we have given conclusions and our future works.

2 Literature Review

A number of different techniques have been implemented now for developing a robust and effective QA system. Domain-specific research for QA systems is also going on and taking place in different fields. An expert QA system called AnswerBus developed by Zhiping Zheng [1] accepts a question in the form of query in five different languages and retrieves the answer in the English language. Brian L. Cairns et al. developed a QA system called MiPACQ [2] for health professionals in the medical domain. The system developed by Darshan Kapashi and Pararth Shah [3] which answers questions of reading comprehension in the form of a single word or a sentence. They used LSTM model for supervised training and weakly supervised training. More research work on QA systems using neural networks and memory networks like LSTM has been carried out by different authors [4–8] and institutions.

Alessandro Moschitti in his work [9] uses Rocchio and SVM text classifiers for extracting statistical features like TF-IDF from a collection of documents 'd'.

This TF-IDF feature is then used in the categorization of question and passage ranking along with the filtering of answers. A statistical language modeling approach [10,11] was carried out by different researchers. The focus of their work is to treat QA as a problem of classification. They use a probabilistic model which helps them to identify the probability distribution over a set of words given in the form of a sequence. Many pattern-matching approaches [12,13] to extract the answer patterns based on the question as well as to create a knowledge base have been implemented. With the availability of pre-trained models, tasks to find an answer based on a given query have become easier and simpler than ever. One such implementation using a pre-trained model called BERT is used by A. Lamurias and F. Couto [14]. Q. Cao et al. in their work [15] use pre-trained transformers: BERT and XLNet to improve the performance of QA by reducing the time to answer the given question. More similar kinds of works using transformers have been carried out in [16–18].

2.1 Text Summarization

There are a number of techniques for text summarization [19] detail-based, number of input documents-based, query-based, language-based, etc. In general, for text summarization, there are two main approaches: extractive and abstractive. Extractive summarization technique generates the synopsis by collecting a set of important sentences and phrases. These sentences are usually collected based on statistical features. On the other hand, abstractive summarization tries to focus on the semantics of the given information to summarize. It tries to generate a more human-like summary by linking the key concepts with self-generated words. A. Khan et al. in their work [20] use graph-based algorithm to generate the summary of movie reviews. For calculating semantic similarity they use an undirected weighted graph in which the graph nodes consist of sentences that are to be considered for similarity and the edges between nodes denote the weight in the form of semantic similarity. A Template-based method implemented by T. Oya et al. in their work [21] generates an abstractive summary for meeting conversations among different people. They generate a template from a human-written summary by making a word graph.

An ontology-based summarization has also been carried out [22] for Arabic text. In this work, a focus on domain-specific knowledge is given. They use Arabic WordNet as a corpus to enhance the knowledge base and use a decision tree algorithm to generate a summary after pre-processing steps are done using NLP and relationship extraction. I. Moawad and M. Aref in their work [23] on abstractive text summarization use a graph reduction approach. R Paulus, C Xiong and R Socher in their work [24] describe a reinforcement learning-based model with an attention mechanism. Y Keneshloo, N Ramakrishnan and CK Reddy in their work [25] use transfer learning to achieve a state-of-art model. They analyze how existing models failed to provide good generalization and therefore use the Pointer-Generator model by fine-tuning. More works on abstractive summarization using transfer learning can be found in [26–28].

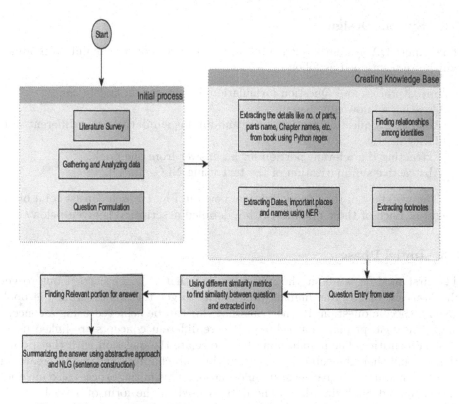

Fig. 1. Block diagram of Abstractive Summarization-based QA System

3 Question-Answer System

3.1 Methodology

The idea of the project is to present a concise human-like answer for a given question using Natural Language Processing (NLP) and Deep learning (DL) techniques from structural information like books. The system tries to present the answer in the form of an abstractive summary as the answer portions will be extracted from the entire book and therefore will be inconsistent and unorganized. The data given to the expert system should be organized in some way such that the system can infer patterns from it. The data is provided in the form of a book and it is used to create a knowledge base (KB). From this knowledge base, the relevant data is extracted based on the patterns to find the similarity with the given user-defined question. Using the different similarity metrics, a similarity measure is calculated to find the similarity between different data extracted from KB and the question. After this, a relevant portion of the answer is extracted from the book and fed into the deep learning model to generate an abstractive summary.

3.2 System Design

The expert QA system implemented in this project consists mainly 5 modules which are mentioned as follows:

- Initial process and Question formulation for evaluation and testing.
- Creating a knowledge base.
- Accepting a question from the user and finding similarity using different similarity metrics.
- Extracting the relevant portion for an answer from the book.
- Abstractive summarization of the text using NLG and DL.

The workflow of the five modules is shown in Fig. 1 which consists of a block diagram. Each of these modules with a detailed description is given below.

3.3 Initial Phase

The first module is about the initial process that is to be carried out to get the overview of how the human mind works to get the answer from the book given a specific question. It turns out that this can be achieved using a concept map. The concept map is a technique where different concepts are linked using the main entities. The human mind tries to relate the question with the specific chapter and then the sub-chapter. From this sub-chapters, it tries to create an abstract summary to give accurate information. This initial process also includes gathering and analyzing data. The data is used in the form of a book and is taken from the Project Gutenberg website. Project Gutenberg is a website that contains a collection of ebooks from all over the world. The name of the book used is "India Under British Rule" in the text format with UTF-8 encoding. Figure 2 shows the sample structure of the book which is to be used as data.

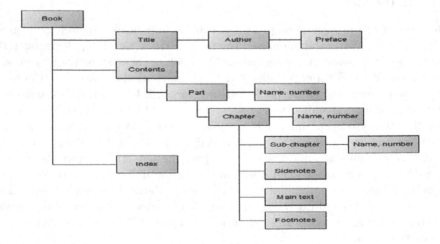

Fig. 2. Structure of the Structural Information i.e., Book

3.4 Knowledge Base Creation

Second module consists of creating a knowledge base. The main aim of creating a KB is to store structured information by the content from the book. The structured information contains the number of parts in the book, number of chapters, number of sub-chapters, dates, period of the event, footnotes (here sidenotes), etc. It also consists of visualization of how words in the sentence are related to each other along with named entity recognition (NER). In this process of creating KB and visualizing the data is mainly done using Python regex and NLP libraries. Figure 3 shows the sample dependency relation in a sentence. The sentence is "The 22-year-old recently won ATP Challenger tournament." This section deals with how the knowledge base is created for the given data.

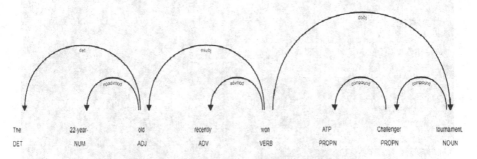

Fig. 3. Sample Dependency Graph of the Sentence

```
All the keys of the dictionary:

dict_keys(['Title', 'Author', 'Contents', 'Parts', 'Part-I', 'Part-II', 'Chapter 1', 'Chapter 2',

Key and value of part 1 contents
dict_keys(['Name', 'Chapters', 'Chapter Name', 'Chapter Periods', 'PageNo'])

dict_values(['EAST INDIA COMPANY', [1, 2, 3, 4, 5, 6], ['FIRST PERIOD: FACTORIES, FORTRESSES, TOW

Part-I Chapter names:
FIRST PERIOD: FACTORIES, FORTRESSES, TOWNS.
SECOND PERIOD: BENGAL PROVINCES.
THIRD PERIOD: IMPERIAL GOVERNMENT.
FOURTH PERIOD: RISE TO ASIATIC POWER.
SEPOY REVOLT: BENGAL, DELHI, PUNJAB.
SEPOY REVOLT: NORTH WEST, CAWNPORE, LUCKNOW.

Key and value of part 2 contents
dict_keys(['Name', 'Chapters', 'Chapter Name', 'Chapter Period', 'PageNo'])

dict_values(['BRITISH CROWN', [1], ['CONSTITUTIONAL GOVERNMENT.'], ['1858-1886.'], '275-302'])

Part-II Chapter names:
CONSTITUTIONAL GOVERNMENT.
```

Fig. 4. Structure of System Generated Knowledge Base (KB)

The knowledge base is a type of data container that contains all the required information in a structured way. This structured information is further used to filter the content that is to be sent for the summarization process. The data to be given in the system is in the form of a book. Different sections of the book details like title, author name, content, main text, remove footnotes, etc. Using appropriate customized functions, the required information is extracted and stored in a dictionary which acts as our KB. The sample structure of KB created is shown in Fig. 4.

```
2. Describe the Hands of Black Town
Sub Chap: 3
[Sidenote: Right and Left Hands.]

3. Discuss the difficulties faced in Black town of Madras.
Sub Chap: 4
[Sidenote: Hindu town under British rule.]
[Sidenote: Protection of Hindus.]
[Sidenote: Question of taxation.]

4. Discuss the slavery practiced under Mohammedan rule and by portuguese.
Sub Chap: 6
[Sidenote: Slavery under Hindu rule.]
[Sidenote: Mohammedan slavery.]
[Sidenote: Mogul restrictions.]
[Sidenote: Portuguese slave trade.]
[Sidenote: Kidnapping from Bengal.]
```

Fig. 5. Sample questions with ground truth

3.5   Finding Similarity Score

In this module, user input is accepted and it is used to find the similarity between different chapter names and sidenotes. Here four different similarity metrics are used to find the similarity and compare in order to check which metric gives the best result. These four metrics are Cosine similarity, Wu Palmer similarity, Path similarity, and Leacock Chodorow similarity. These similarity metrics are used in a similarity algorithm that has been designed to check the syntactic and semantic similarity. Once a question is accepted by the user, the system tries to get the relevant portion of the text from the book. As there are references of one topic in different chapters of the book, it is very difficult to get the exact portion. Therefore, using similarity measure, semantic and syntactic similarity is found between the question and chapters, and question and sub-chapters. Four different similarity metrics are used to find similarity. After using finding similarity score using these metrics, they are compared with the ground truth shown in Fig. 5, and the best-performing similarity metric is used. Top 'k' scores are used to get better results. The chapter corresponding to this similarity scores are used and further again score is calculated between the question and sub-chapter of that chapter. These similarity metrics are very much based on synset, hypernym, and hyponym concepts.

A synset is a group of words that are synonyms of each other. These words are considered the same semantically but they differ in terms of their part of speech (noun, verb, adjective, etc.). For example, the synonyms of bird and wood are shown with different part of speech. In order to get synsets, wordnet is used. Wordnet is a large corpora just like English dictionary but it is in a more organized and structured way. Hypernyms are words with a very abstract meaning. An example can be, the animal is a hypernym of tiger or lion. On the other hand, hyponyms are words with a very specific meaning than a general term applicable to them. For example, toothpaste is a hyponym for toiletries.

3.6 Abstractive Summary Extraction

Here, a relevant portion of the answer that is to be summarized is extracted. As the answer has to be extracted from the entire book, there will be a relation and reference of concepts between chapters. Due to this, it is not feasible to select the result with the best similarity score. And so, the highest similarity score is associated with the chapter names selected and used to further filter the content. Once the Chapter is selected, similarity with sub-chapters is calculated and then a few top-scoring sub-chapters are selected to further filter the content using sidenotes. Sidenotes prove to be most useful to get the final content.

Once the final content is obtained, it is used for the abstractive summarization process. First, the data is pre-processed as per the requirement and then sent for training. Data in the form of a sequence will be fed into the system. In order to process the text and convert it into a text-to-text format a transformer-based architecture is used. For obtaining better results, the transfer learning concept is used in which the pre-trained model is used to fine-tune the model based on our dataset. The pre-trained models are generally trained on large datasets like CNN/daily mail. In the general abstract architecture used for the transfer learning-based transformer approach, the encoder-decoder model is used with a feed-forward neural network and attention layers stacked up in each of them. The transformer is made up of multiple encoders and decoders. Each encoder consists of a multi-head attention layer and feed-forward neural network layers. Each decoder consists of masked attention layers, attention layers, and feed-forward neural network layers. The inputs are passed in the form of word embeddings to the encoder. The output from the last encoder from the stack of encoders is passed onto the decoder in the stack of decoders. The decoder also consists of an additional attention layer which helps it to focus on specific part of sentences. Here the given question is "Explain how British won against Portuguese". All four similarity metrics are shown for comparison with ground truth. That score is shown in Fig. 6. The similarity with chapter names, sub-chapter names of the highest scoring chapter, and the sidenotes of that highest scoring chapter. Using this similarity metric the relevant portion is extracted and passed on for abstractive text summarization.

Explain how did British won against portuguese.

Chapter Sidenotes	Cosine similarity	Path similarity	LCH similarity	WuPalmer similarity
Rise of British rule	0.191	0.594	0.482	0.646
NORTHERN INDIA: the Great Mogul	0.15	0.079	0.492	0.186
SOUTHERN INDIA: Mohammedan Sultans and Hindu Rajas	0.331	0.083	0.505	0.153
Portuguese fortresses	0.234	0.514	0.31	0.575
British traders at Surat	0.281	0.748	0.31	0.775
British defeat the Portuguese	0.36	0.781	0.409	0.808
British factory at Surat, 1612	0.15	0.748	0.295	0.775
Factory life	0.157	0.081	0.513	0.168
Foreign guests	0.173	0.155	0.325	0.238
British and Moguls	0.315	0.748	0.325	0.775
Trade on the eastern coast	0.081	0.17	0.518	0.313
British territory and fortress at Madras, 1639	0.141	0.798	0.427	0.825
Fort St. George and Black Town	0.274	0.076	0.496	0.182
Despotic rule	0.0	0.155	0.34	0.25
Portuguese and Dutch neighbours	0.348	0.581	0.298	0.642
Dutch trade in India	0.189	0.166	0.397	0.283
Right and Left Hands	0.216	0.164	0.5	0.263
Mohammedan invasion	0.184	0.079	0.518	0.156
Troubles with Dutch and French, 1670	0.186	0.093	0.548	0.226
Increase of population	0.212	0.11	0.609	0.321
Fort St. George, 1670-86	0.13	0.065	0.473	0.139
Hindu town under British rule	0.366	0.517	0.478	0.562

Fig. 6. Similarity Score between Question and Chapter names

4   Results Discussion

To calculate the accuracy ROUGE metric was used. It operates by comparing an autonomously produced summary or translation to a list of reference summaries (usually human-authored). Three type of ROUGE measures are used namely ROUGE - 1, ROUGE - 2, and ROUGE - L. ROUGE - 1 and ROUGE - 2 uses unigram and bigram concept to check the overlap of words from the generated summary to reference summary. ROUGE-L uses LCS to determine the longest-matched sequence of words. LCS has the advantage of not requiring consecutive matches but rather in-sequence matches that reflect sentence-level word order. Each measure consists of precision, recall and F-1 score. A ROUGE - 1 score having 0.33 precision and 0.34 recall shows that there is only approximately 33% overlapping of words as compared to the original. The performance of the proposed system is analyzed and given in Fig. 7.

{'rouge-1': {'f': 0.3338497404541722, 'p': 0.33031250325666299, 'r': 0.3480848883384189}, 'rouge-2': {'f': 0.13071194761908414, 'p': 0.1297652024065983, 'r': 0.13426891144918662}, 'rouge-l': {'f': 0.3092670883281174, 'p': 0.36147439771089407, 'r': 0.2880819280478676}}

Fig. 7. Performance metrics of the Generated Answer Summary

5 Conclusion

Till now no such systems have been created which can answer a given question from the book. In this work, an attempt to make an Abstractive Summarization-based Question Answer system for structural information shows that an expert system can be made for answering a given question from the book. The book here represents a structured piece of information that is used to create a Knowledge Base for the system. As the contents in the book are interrelated with references to one another in different chapters, it becomes necessary to present the answer in a concise form and present a more human-like summarized answer. This work shows that Natural Language Generation and Transfer Learning approaches can be used for the abstractive text summarization process. Though the outputs obtained are not perfect as compared to the human summary, they are still acceptable. A more dynamic generalized system can be created such that it can answer any question from any given book. Currently, in this work, the results obtained are book specific. But approaches like transfer learning can be used to build a generalized system and predict the correct answers. Also, more precise and accurate data such as human-generated summaries from the book would also have helped in a better way to train the model and evaluate the summaries.

References

1. Zheng, Z.: AnswerBus question answering system. In: Human Language Technology Conference (HLT 2002), vol. 27 (2002)
2. Cairns, B.L., et al.: The MiPACQ clinical question answering system. AMIA Ann. Symp. Proc. AMIA Symp. **2011**, 171–180 (2011)
3. Kapashi, D., Shah, P.: Answering reading comprehension using memory networks. Report for Stanford University Course cs224d (2015)
4. Sukhbaatar, S., Szlam, A., Weston, J., Fergus, R.: End-to-end memory networks. arXiv preprint arXiv:1503.08895 (2015)
5. Andreas, J., Rohrbach, M., Darrell, T., Klein, D.: Learning to compose neural networks for question answering. arXiv preprint arXiv:1601.01705 (2016)
6. Budiharto, W., Andreas, V., Gunawan, A.A.S.: Deep learning-based question answering system for intelligent humanoid robot. J. Big Data **7**(1), 1–10 (2020)
7. Wang, D., Nyberg, E.: A long short-term memory model for answer sentence selection in question answering. In: Proceedings of the 53rd Annual Meeting of the Association for Computational Linguistics and the 7th International Joint Conference on Natural Language Processing (Volume 2: Short Papers), pp. 707–712 (2015)
8. Wang, L., Zhang, Yu., Liu, T.: A deep learning approach for question answering over knowledge base. In: Lin, C.-Y., Xue, N., Zhao, D., Huang, X., Feng, Y. (eds.) ICCPOL/NLPCC -2016. LNCS (LNAI), vol. 10102, pp. 885–892. Springer, Cham (2016). https://doi.org/10.1007/978-3-319-50496-4_82
9. Moschitti, A.: Answer filtering via text categorization in question answering systems. In: Proceedings of the 15th IEEE International Conference on Tools with Artificial Intelligence, pp. 241–248. IEEE (2003)

10. Whittaker, E., Furui, S., Klakow, D.: A statistical classification approach to question answering using web data. In: 2005 International Conference on Cyberworlds (CW'05), pp. 8-pp. IEEE (2005)

11. Heie, M.H., Whittaker, E.W., Furui, S.: Question answering using statistical language modelling. Comput. Speech Lang. **26**(3), 193–209 (2012)

12. Er, N.P., Cicekli, I.: A factoid question answering system using answer pattern matching. In: Proceedings of the Sixth International Joint Conference on Natural Language Processing, pp. 854–858 (2013)

13. Schlaefer, N., Gieselmann, P., Schaaf, T., Waibel, A.: A pattern learning approach to question answering within the ephyra framework. In: Sojka, P., Kopeček, I., Pala, K. (eds.) TSD 2006. LNCS (LNAI), vol. 4188, pp. 687–694. Springer, Heidelberg (2006). https://doi.org/10.1007/11846406_86

14. Lukovnikov, D., Fischer, A., Lehmann, J.: Pretrained transformers for simple question answering over knowledge graphs. In: Ghidini, C., et al. (eds.) ISWC 2019. LNCS, vol. 11778, pp. 470–486. Springer, Cham (2019). https://doi.org/10.1007/978-3-030-30793-6_27

15. Cao, Q., Trivedi, H., Balasubramanian, A., Balasubramanian, N.: Deformer: Decomposing pre-trained transformers for faster question answering. arXiv preprint arXiv:2005.00697 (2020)

16. Schmidt, L., Weeds, J., Higgins, J.: Data mining in clinical trial text: Transformers for classification and question answering tasks. arXiv preprint arXiv:2001.11268 (2020)

17. Resta, M., Arioli, D., Fagnani, A., Attardi, G.: Transformer models for question answering at BioASQ 2019. In: Cellier, P., Driessens, K. (eds.) ECML PKDD 2019. CCIS, vol. 1168, pp. 711–726. Springer, Cham (2020). https://doi.org/10.1007/978-3-030-43887-6_63

18. Siblini, W., Challal, M., Pasqual, C.: Delaying Interaction Layers in Transformer-based Encoders for Efficient Open Domain Question Answering. arXiv preprint arXiv:2010.08422 (2020)

19. Munot, N., Govilkar, S.S.: Comparative study of text summarization methods. Int. J. Comput. Appl. **102**(12), 1–5 (2014)

20. Khan, A., et al.: Movie review summarization using supervised learning and graph-based ranking algorithm. Comput. Intell. Neurosci. **2020** (2020)

21. Oya, T., Mehdad, Y., Carenini, G., Ng, R.: A template-based abstractive meeting summarization: Leveraging summary and source text relationships. In: Proceedings of the 8th International Natural Language Generation Conference (INLG), pp. 45–53 (2014)

22. Imam, I., Nounou, N., Hamouda, A., Khalek, H.A.A.: An ontology-based summarization system for Arabic documents (OSSAD). Int. J. Comput. Appl. **74**(17), 38–43 (2013)

23. Moawad, I. F., Aref, M.: Semantic graph reduction approach for abstractive text summarization. In: 2012 Seventh International Conference on Computer Engineering & Systems (ICCES), pp. 132–138. IEEE (2012)

24. Paulus, R., Xiong, C., Socher, R.: A deep reinforced model for abstractive summarization. arXiv preprint arXiv:1705.04304 (2017)

25. Keneshloo, Y., Ramakrishnan, N., Reddy, C.K.: Deep transfer reinforcement learning for text summarization. In: Proceedings of the 2019 SIAM International Conference on Data Mining, pp. 675–683. Society for Industrial and Applied Mathematics (2019)

26. Laskar, M.T.R., Hoque, E., Huang, J.: Query focused abstractive summarization via incorporating query relevance and transfer learning with transformer models. In: Goutte, C., Zhu, X. (eds.) Canadian AI 2020. LNCS (LNAI), vol. 12109, pp. 342–348. Springer, Cham (2020). https://doi.org/10.1007/978-3-030-47358-7_35
27. Sarkhel, R., Keymanesh, M., Nandi, A., Parthasarathy, S.: Transfer Learning for Abstractive Summarization at Controllable Budgets. arXiv preprint arXiv:2002.07845 (2020)
28. Raffel, C., et al.: Exploring the limits of transfer learning with a unified text-to-text transformer. arXiv preprint arXiv:1910.10683 (2019)

Adversarial Capsule Networks for Romanian Satire Detection and Sentiment Analysis

Sebastian-Vasile Echim[1], Răzvan-Alexandru Smădu[1], Andrei-Marius Avram[1], Dumitru-Clementin Cercel[1(✉)], and Florin Pop[1,2]

[1] Faculty of Automatic Control and Computers, University Politehnica of Bucharest, Bucharest, Romania
sebastian.echim@stud.aero.upb.ro,
{razvan.smadu,andrei_marius.avram}@stud.acs.upb.ro,
{dumitru.cercel,florin.pop}@upb.ro
[2] National Institute for Research and Development in Informatics - ICI Bucharest, Bucharest, Romania

Abstract. Satire detection and sentiment analysis are intensively explored natural language processing (NLP) tasks that study the identification of the satirical tone from texts and extracting sentiments in relationship with their targets. In languages with fewer research resources, an alternative is to produce artificial examples based on character-level adversarial processes to overcome dataset size limitations. Such samples are proven to act as a regularization method, thus improving the robustness of models. In this work, we improve the well-known NLP models (i.e., Convolutional Neural Networks, Long Short-Term Memory (LSTM), Bidirectional LSTM, Gated Recurrent Units (GRUs), and Bidirectional GRUs) with adversarial training and capsule networks. The fine-tuned models are used for satire detection and sentiment analysis tasks in the Romanian language. The proposed framework outperforms the existing methods for the two tasks, achieving up to 99.08% accuracy, thus confirming the improvements added by the capsule layers and the adversarial training in NLP approaches.

Keywords: Natural Language Processing · Satire Detection · Sentiment Analysis · Capsule Networks · Adversarial Training

1 Introduction

Satirical news is a type of entertainment that employ satire to criticize and ridicule, in a humorous way, the key figures from society, socio-political points, or notable events [27,38]. Although it does not aim to misinform, it mimics the style of regular news. Therefore, it has a sizeable deceptive potential, driven by the current increase in social media consumption and the higher rates of distrust in official news streams [20].

Furthermore, sentiment analysis is regarded as a successful task in determining the opinions and feelings of people, especially in online shops where customer feedback analysis can lead to better customer service [37]. Limited resources in languages such as Romanian make it challenging to develop large-scale machine learning systems since the largest datasets present up to tens of thousands of examples [27]. Therefore, various

E. Métais et al. (Eds.): NLDB 2023, LNCS 13913, pp. 428–442, 2023.
https://doi.org/10.1007/978-3-031-35320-8_31

techniques should be proposed and investigated to address these challenges on such datasets.

Adversarial training is an effective defense strategy to increase the robustness and generalization of the models intrinsically. Introduced by Szegedy et al. [33] and analyzed by Goodfellow et al. [8], adversarial examples are augmented data points generated by applying a small perturbation to the input samples. It was initially employed in computer vision, where input images were altered with a small perturbation [8,18,36]. More recently, adversarial training gained popularity in NLP. The text input is a discrete signal; therefore, the perturbation is applied to the word embeddings in a continuous space [22]. The application of adversarial training in our experiments is motivated by the potential to improve the robustness and generalization of models with limited training resources.

This paper aims to introduce robust high-performing networks employing adversarial training and capsule layers [28] for satire detection in a Romanian corpus of news articles [27] and sentiment analysis for a Romanian dataset [34]. Our experiments include training models suitable for NLP tasks as follows: Convolutional Neural Networks (CNNs) [12], Gated Recurrent Units (GRUs) [3], Bidirectional GRUs (BiGRUs), CNN-BiGRU, Long Short-Term Memory (LSTM) [10], Bidirectional LSTM (BiLSTM), and CNN-BiLSTM. Starting from Zhao et al. [41], we compare the networks against their adversarial capsule flavors. Next, the best-performing network is subjected to an in-depth analysis concerning the impact on the performance of the capsule model and the training with adversarial examples. Thus, we test the effect of capsule hyperparameters varying the number of primary and condensed capsules [41]. Also, we assess the performance of our model employing Romanian GPT-2 (RoGPT-2) [24] for data augmentation up to 10,000 text continuation examples. Finally, we discuss several misclassified test inputs for the sentiment analysis task.

The main contributions in this work are as follows: (i) we thoroughly experiment with various configurations to assess the performances of the investigated approaches, namely adversarial augmentations and capsule layers; (ii) we show that the best-performing model uses BiGRU with capsule networks, while the most improvements were seen when incorporating RoGPT-2-based augmentations; (iii) we investigate the effects of analyzed components through t-SNE plots [17] and ablation studies; and (iv) we achieve state-of-the-art results on the two Romanian datasets.

2 Related Work

2.1 Capsule Networks in NLP

Firstly presented by Sabour et al. [28], the capsule neural networks are machine learning systems that model hierarchical relationships regarding object properties (such as pose, size, or texture) in an attempt to resemble the biological structure of neurons. Among other limitations, capsule networks are addressing the max pooling problem of the CNNs, which allows for translation invariance, making them vulnerable to adversarial attacks [15]. While it has been demonstrated that capsule networks are successful in image classification [28], there is also a general preference for exploring their potential in NLP tasks, especially in text classification. Several works [11,42] took the lead in this topic, showing that using different approaches, such as static and dynamic routing, the capsule models provided competitive results on popular benchmarks.

Several studies were performed in topic classification and sentiment analysis using capsule networks. Srivastava et al. [30] addressed the identification of aggression and other activities, such as hate speech and trolling, using a model based on the dynamic routing algorithm [42] involving LSTM as a feature extractor, two capsule layers (namely, a primary capsule layer and a convolutional capsule layer), and finally, the focal loss [16] to handle the class imbalance. The resulting model outperformed several robust baseline algorithms in terms of accuracy; however, a more complex data preprocessing was expected to improve the results further.

For the sentiment analysis task, Zhang et al. [40] proposed CapsuleDAR, a capsule model successfully combined with the domain adaptation technique via correlation alignment [32] and semantic rules. The model architecture consisted of a base and a rule network. The base network employed a capsule network for sentiment prediction, consisting of several layers: embedding, convolutional, capsule, and classification. The rule network involved a rule capsule layer before the classification layer. Extensive experiments were conducted on review datasets from four product domains, which showed that the model achieved state-of-the-art results. Additionally, their ablation study showed that the accuracy decreased sharply when the capsule layers were removed.

Su et al. [31] tackled limitations of Bidirectional Encoder Representations from Transformers (BERT) [4] and XLNet [39], such as local context awareness constraints, by incorporating capsule networks. Their model considered an XLNet layer with 12 Transformer-XL blocks on top of which the capsule layer extracted space- and hierarchy-related features from the text sequence. Experiments illustrated that capsule layers provided improved results compared with XLNet, BERT, and other classical feature-based approaches.

Moreover, Saha et al. [29] introduced a speech act classifier for microblog text posts based on capsule layers on top of BERT. The model took advantage of the joint optimization features of the BERT embeddings and the capsule layers to learn cumulative features related to speech acts. The proposed model outperformed the baseline models and showed the ability to understand subtle differences among tweets.

2.2 Romanian NLP Tasks

In recent years, several datasets have emerged aiming to improve the performance of the learning algorithms on Romanian NLP tasks. Apart from the two datasets used in this work, researchers have also introduced the Romanian Named Entity Corpus (RONEC) [6] for named entity recognition[1], the Moldavian and Romanian Dialectal Corpus (MOROCO) [2] for dialect and topic classification, the Legal Named Entity Recognition corpus (LegalNERo) [26] for legal named entity recognition, and the Romanian Semantic Textual Similarity dataset (RoSTS)[2] for finding the semantic similarity between two sentences.

Lately, the language model space for Romanian was also improved with the introduction of Romanian BERT (BERT-ro) [5], RoGPT-2, ALR-BERT [23], and

---

[1] A new version of RONEC is available at https://github.com/dumitrescustefan/ronec.

[2] https://github.com/dumitrescustefan/RO-STS.

DistilMulti-BERT [1]. In addition, all the results for these systems have been centralized in the Romanian Language Leaderboard (LiRo) [7], a leaderboard similar to the General Language Understanding Evaluation (GLUE) benchmark [35] that tracks over ten Romanian NLP tasks.

3 Datasets

In this work, we rely on two of the most recent Romanian language text datasets: a corpus of news articles, henceforth called SaRoCo [27], and one composed of positive and negative reviews crawled from a Romanian website, henceforth called LaRoSeDa [34].

3.1 Satirical News

SaRoCo is one of the most comprehensive public corpora for satirical news detection, eclipsed only by an English corpus [38] with 185,029 news articles and a German one [20] with 329,862 news articles. SaRoCo includes 55,608 samples, of which 27,628 are satirical and 27,980 are non-satirical (or regular). Each sample consists of a title, a body, and a label. On average, an entire news article has 515.24 tokens for the body and 24.97 tokens for the title. The average number of sentences and words per sentence are 17 and 305, respectively. The labeling process is automated, as the news source only publishes satirical or regular content.

3.2 Product Reviews

LaRoSeDa is one of the largest corpora for sentiment analysis in the Romanian language. It was created based on the observation that the freely available Romanian language datasets were significantly reduced in size. This dataset totals 15,000 online store product reviews, either positive or negative, for which the ratings were also collected for labeling purposes. Thus, assuming that the ratings might reflect the polarity of the text, each review rated with one or two stars was considered negative. In contrast, the four or five-star labels were considered positive. The labeling process resulted in 7,500 positive reviews (235,474 words) and 7,500 negative reviews (304,813 words). The average number of sentences and words per review is 4 and 36, respectively.

4 Methodology

The generic adversarial capsule network we employ is presented in Fig. 1. It consists of a sub-module that can represent any widely-used NLP model, followed by capsule layers. Concretely, we use primary capsules and capsule flattening layers to facilitate the projection into condensed capsules passed as input for a routing mechanism to obtain the class probabilities. To increase robustness, we feed regular and adversarial samples into the model. In what follows, we detail the employed components.

Word Embeddings. Each word is associated with a fixed-length numerical vector, allowing us to express semantic and syntactic relations, such as context, synonymy, and antonymy. Depending on the model, the embedding representation has various sizes.

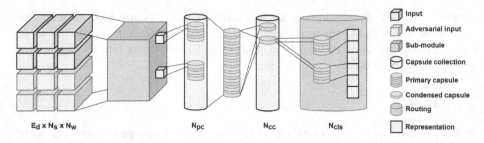

Fig. 1. Our generic adversarial capsule architecture, where E_d denotes the embedding size, N_s is the number of sentences, N_w is the number of words per sentence, N_{pc} is the number of primary capsules, N_{cc} is the number of condensed capsules, and N_{cls} is the number of classes to which the routing algorithm will converge.

To use a continuous representation of the input data, we employ two different types of embeddings: BERT- and non-BERT-based. On the RoBERT model [19], we rely on embeddings delivered by the model with a dimension $E_d = 768$, whereas, for the non-BERT models, we abide by Onose et al. [25] in terms of distributed word representations and choose Contemporary Romanian Language (CoRoLa) [21] with an embedding dimension $E_d = 300$, Nordic Language Processing Laboratory (NLPL) [14], having the size $E_d = 100$, and Common Crawl (CC) [9] with $E_d = 300$.

Adversarial Examples. To increase the robustness of our networks, we create adversarial examples by replacing characters in words. Using the letters of the Romanian alphabet, we randomly substitute one character per word, depending on the sentence size: one replacement for less than five words per sentence, two replacements for 5 to 20 words per sentence, and three replacements for more than 20 words per sentence.

Primary Capsule Layer. This layer transforms the feature maps obtained by passing the input through the sub-module into groups of neurons to represent each element in the current layer, enabling the ability to preserve more information. By using 1×1 filters, we determine the capsule $\boldsymbol{p}_i$ from the projection p_{ij} of the feature maps [41]:

$$\boldsymbol{p}_i = squash(p_{i1} \oplus p_{i2} \oplus \cdots \oplus p_{id}) \in \mathbb{R}^d \tag{1}$$

where d is the primary capsule dimension, $\oplus$ is the concatenation operator, and $squash(\cdot)$ adds non-linearity in the model:

$$squash(\boldsymbol{x}) = \frac{\|\boldsymbol{x}\|^2}{1 + \|\boldsymbol{x}\|^2} \frac{\boldsymbol{x}}{\|\boldsymbol{x}\|} \tag{2}$$

Compression Layer. Because it requires extensive computational resources in the routing process (i.e., the fully connected part of the capsule framework), we need to reduce the number of primary capsules. We follow the approach proposed by Zhao et al. [41], which uses capsule compression to determine the input of the routing layer $\boldsymbol{u}_j$. Each condensed capsule $\hat{\boldsymbol{u}}_j$ represents a weighted sum over all the primary capsules:

$$\hat{\boldsymbol{u}}_j = \sum_i b_i \boldsymbol{p}_i \in \mathbb{R}^d \tag{3}$$

Routing Layer. It conveys the transition layer between the condensed capsules to the representation layer. It is denoted by a routing method to overcome the loss of information determined by a usual pooling method. In our capsule framework, we choose Dynamic Routing with three iterations [28].

Representation Layer. In the binary classification tasks, the last slice of our generic architecture is represented by the probability of a text input being satirical or regular for SaRoCo and positive or negative sentiment for LaRoSeDa.

5 Experimental Setup

5.1 Model Parameters

Firstly, we use CoRoLa, CC featuring 300-dimensional, and NLPL with 100-dimensional state space vectors for reconstruction at the embeddings level. We choose n-gram kernels with three sizes (i.e., 3, 4, and 5) and 300 filters each for the CNN submodule. Also, for the Capsule layers, we use $N_{pc} = 8$ primary capsules and $N_{cc} = 128$ condensed capsules, which we fully connect through Dynamic Routing and obtain N_t lists with N_{cls} elements. For each element in the list, the argument of the maximum value represents the predicted label, where "1" is a satirical text or a positive review, whereas "0" is a non-satirical text or a negative review. Secondly, for the GRU and LSTM sub-modules, we employ one layer and a hidden state dimension of 300 for both unidirectional and bidirectional versions. Finally, for the RoBERT model, we choose the base version of the Transformer with vector dimensions of 768, followed by a fully connected layer with the size of 64, tanh activation function, and a fully connected layer with N_{cls} output neurons.

5.2 Training Parameters

The number of texts chosen from SaRoCo is $N_t = 30,000$ (15,000 satirical and 15,000 non-satirical) with a maximum $N_s = 5$ sentences per document and $N_w - 60$ words per sentence. For LaRoSeDa, we use 6,810 positive and 6,810 negative reviews for training, with $N_s = 3$ sentences per document and $N_w = 60$ words per sentence. The optimizer is Adam [13], and the loss function is binary cross-entropy. We set the learning rate to $5e - 5$ with linear decay and train for 20 epochs. The batch size is 32, and the train/validation/test split is 70%/20%/10%.

6 Results

This section presents the performance analysis of our models from quantitative and qualitative perspectives, as well as a comparison with previous works for the chosen datasets.

Initial Results. Table 1 shows our results on the SaRoCo and LaRoSeDa datasets. The experiments with varying embeddings other than RoBERT (i.e., CC, CoRoLa, and NLPL) show that NLPL determines better performance overall. This was unexpected because CoRoLa covers over one billion Romanian tokens, while CC and NLPL contain considerably fewer tokens. For the SaRoCo dataset, the best model on the CC embeddings uses the BiGRU sub-module, achieving a 95.80% test accuracy. For the CoRoLa corpus, the GRU and BiGRU sub-modules perform equally, resulting in a 95.77% test accuracy. Also, the best NLPL embedding model considers the BiGRU sub-module, scoring a 96.15% test accuracy. On the LaRoSeDa dataset, we find the best model obtaining a 96.06% test accuracy based on GRU with NLPL embeddings. Moreover, training on the RoBERT embeddings brings the highest performance when combined with the BiGRU sub-module, achieving a test accuracy of 98.32% on SaRoCo and 98.60% on LaRoSeDa.

The score differences between our results on the two datasets are less than 0.5%. Therefore, a performance difference is expected due to the more considerable proportion of data for SaRoCo. Thus, there is no concrete insight into whether the satire detection task is more complex than the sentiment analysis one, especially in the binary classification setup. Still, since the training set size for LaRoSeDa is considerably smaller than that of the SaRoCo one, the slight performance difference shows polarization support on sentiment analysis.

We further assess the feature representation quality for each sub-module using the two-dimensional t-SNE visualizations upon the best-performing training results. Figure 2 shows different clustering representations in most cases. For the SaRoCo dataset, the best delimitation is observed on the BiGRU sub-module, which is validated by the best performance achieved for the NLPL embeddings as shown in Table 1. A similar effect applies to the BiGRU sub-module trained and evaluated on LaRoSeDa. Considering these results, the next set of experiments is performed based on the higher performance achieved with and without BERT embeddings, namely, the BiGRU sub-module with RoBERT and NLPL embeddings, respectively.

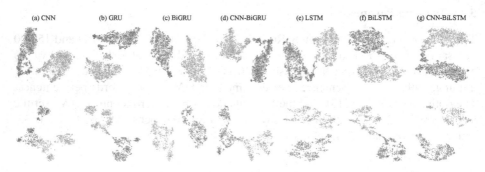

Fig. 2. t-SNE plots for each sub-module from the best-performing adversarial capsule network. The first row depicts the evaluation on SaRoCo, where blue indicates negative sentiment and orange represents positive one. The second row is for LaRoSeDa, where blue is for the non-satirical text, and orange is for the satirical one. The higher density on SaRoCo is because of a larger test dataset.

Table 1. Accuracy (Acc) of the generic adversarial capsule network with different word embeddings and sub-modules.

Embeddings	Sub-module	SaRoCo		LaRoSeDa	
		Valid. Acc(%)	Test Acc(%)	Valid. Acc(%)	Test Acc(%)
CC (300)	CNN	95.57	95.34	**95.52**	95.19
	GRU	95.92	95.70	95.29	95.33
	BiGRU	**96.02**	**95.80**	95.19	**95.53**
	CNN-BiGRU	95.90	95.60	95.16	94.39
	LSTM	95.70	95.54	95.09	94.53
	BiLSTM	95.67	95.47	95.19	94.46
	CNN-BiLSTM	95.57	95.00	95.09	95.06
CoRoLa (300)	CNN	95.49	95.60	95.19	95.26
	GRU	95.97	**95.77**	95.39	95.59
	BiGRU	**95.99**	**95.77**	95.46	**95.60**
	CNN-BiGRU	95.82	95.67	95.42	95.19
	LSTM	95.85	95.70	95.39	94.86
	BiLSTM	95.90	95.70	**95.56**	95.26
	CNN-BiLSTM	95.65	95.50	95.52	94.73
NLPL (100)	CNN	95.79	95.80	95.29	95.86
	GRU	96.04	95.80	**95.92**	**96.06**
	BiGRU	**96.10**	**96.15**	95.79	95.83
	CNN-BiGRU	95.60	95.80	95.32	95.19
	LSTM	95.74	95.64	95.52	95.79
	BiLSTM	95.44	95.70	95.29	94.99
	CNN-BiLSTM	95.45	95.57	95.22	95.39
RoBERT (768)	CNN	98.17	98.09	98.50	98.56
	GRU	98.07	98.17	98.39	98.49
	BiGRU	**98.27**	**98.32**	**98.54**	**98.60**
	CNN-BiGRU	98.07	98.24	98.42	98.45
	LSTM	98.07	98.24	98.36	98.39
	BiLSTM	98.10	98.17	98.46	98.49
	CNN-BiLSTM	98.04	98.24	98.46	98.52
BERT-ro [27]		82.41	73.00	-	-
Char-CNN [27]		73.42	69.66	-	-
HISK+BOWE-BERT+SOMs [34]		-	-	-	90.90

Comparison to Existing Methods. The results of Rogoz et al. [27] on the SaRoCo dataset show a more than 25% gain for our models compared to the BERT-ro approach, while our models outperform the character-level CNN by more than 29%. Human performance is a notable figure in deciding whether a selection of 200 news articles extracted from the dataset is satirical. Rogoz et al. [27] explored the idea, involving

Table 2. Accuracy for various capsule hyperparameters.

Dataset	N_{pc}			N_{cc}		
	2	8	32	32	128	256
SaRoCo	96.07	96.13	**96.17**	95.95	**96.02**	96.00
LaRoSeDa	95.23	**95.52**	95.50	95.01	**95.46**	95.12

ten human annotators and indicated that the human performance is at 87.35% accuracy. Our approach surpasses this result by more than 11%. In addition, the results shown by Tache et al. [34] on the LaRoSeDa dataset prove the competitive performance of our proposed approach. Thus, our results are 7–8% higher than their best model, HISK+BOWE-BERT+SOMs, which comprises histogram intersection string kernels, bag-of-words with BERT embeddings, and self-organizing maps.

Capsule Hyperparameter Variation. Fig. 1 depicts the hyperparameters of the capsule layers of our generic network, represented by N_{pc} (i.e., the number of primary capsules) and N_{cc} (i.e., the number of condensed capsules). We test the impact of these hyperparameters on the BiGRU sub-module with NLPL embeddings. We present the average for three runs per experiment. The chosen values for the hyperparameters are $N_{pc} = \{2, 8, 32\}$ and $N_{cc} = \{32, 128, 256\}$ (see Table 2).

During experiments, we observed that large values for N_{pc} considerably impact the training time. This is mainly due to the operations over high-dimensional matrices in the $squash(\cdot)$ function from the iterative Dynamic Routing algorithm (see Eq. 2). Results from Table 2 support the intuition that a larger N_{pc} would bring better results. The model trained on SaRoCo with $N_{pc} = 32$ achieves the highest accuracy of 96.17%; nevertheless, the difference between choosing 8 and 32 is minimal. For SaRoCo and LaRoSeDa, the best overall performance is achieved in a setting with $N_{cc} = 128$, attaining accuracy scores of 96.02% and 95.46%, respectively. Based on both sets of results, we note that, for better performance, a hyperparameter search should be extended to the capsule hyperparameters.

Ablation Study. Motivated by the noteworthy closeness in performance between the BiGRU-based models with NLPL and RoBERT embeddings, respectively, we perform an ablation study, slicing the generic model into four categories: baselines (i.e., NLPL-BiGRU and RoBERT-BiGRU), adversarial (Adv), Capsule, and Adv+Capsule. The best results on the test datasets are brought by the most complex models in terms of training and architecture, with a 96.02% test accuracy for SaRoCo and a 95.82% test accuracy for LaRoSeDa using the NLPL embeddings, as well as a 98.30% test accuracy for SaRoCo and a 98.61% test accuracy for LaRoSeDa using the RoBERT embeddings (see Table 3).

Regarding model complexity, we determine that except for the adversarial training on a baseline BiGRU model, the performance improves when capsule layers are added on top of it, irrespective of including the perturbed data in training. The increase in performance on the SaRoCo dataset with our model is by 0.45% for the NLPL embeddings and by 0.10% for the RoBERT embeddings. We observe a decrease of 2.73% when the most undersized model (i.e., NLPL-BiGRU) is compared with the most complex one (i.e., RoBERT-BiGRU+Adv+Capsule). For the LaRoSeDa dataset, we gain 1.18%

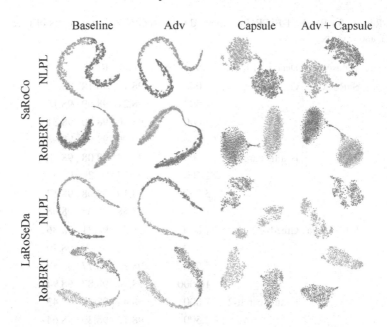

Fig. 3. t-SNE plots on embedding space for each model from the ablation study.

Table 3. Ablation study.

Model	SaRoCo		LaRoSeDa	
	Valid. Acc(%)	Test Acc(%)	Valid. Acc(%)	Test Acc(%)
NLPL-BiGRU	94.80	95.57	92.73	94.64
+Adv	95.17	95.50	93.17	95.30
+Capsule	95.57	95.67	93.61	95.67
+Adv+Capsule	**95.90**	**96.02**	**95.61**	**95.82**
RoBERT-BiGRU	98.23	98.20	98.68	98.16
+Adv	**98.47**	98.00	**98.83**	97.94
+Capsule	98.33	98.27	98.68	98.46
+Adv+Capsule	98.45	**98.30**	98.75	**98.61**

using the NLPL embeddings and 0.45% with the RoBERT embeddings, respectively. Also, the test accuracy difference between the most complex and the most undersized models is 3.97%, determining that the network conveys more value for the sentiment analysis task.

The two-dimensional t-SNE embeddings depicted in Fig. 3 show the contrast between the capsule- and non-capsule-based models. The embeddings obtained with the BiGRU alone feature a specific chained distribution, with clusters defined by halving the sequence. The RoBERT embeddings convey a similar partition. In contrast, the capsule networks will mostly feature well-separated embedding clusters. No significant embedding change occurs when adversarial training is included.

Table 4. Results for RoBERT-BiGRU augmented with RoGPT-2 data in terms of precision (P), recall (R), and accuracy (Acc).

Dataset	Decoder Method	No. of Aug.	P(%)	R(%)	Acc(%)
SaRoCo	Greedy	1,000	98.15	98.18	98.16
		2,500	98.21	98.09	98.15
		5,000	98.36	98.20	98.31
		10,000	99.06	99.08	**99.08**
	Beam-search-2	1,000	98.24	98.08	98.23
		2,500	98.37	98.29	98.34
		5,000	98.19	98.08	98.17
		10,000	98.58	98.65	**98.68**
LaRoSeDa	Greedy	1,000	98.39	98.31	98.36
		2,500	98.82	98.52	98.70
		5,000	98.85	98.77	98.87
		10,000	98.94	98.87	**98.94**
	Beam-search-2	1,000	98.44	98.40	98.43
		2,500	98.72	98.49	98.64
		5,000	98.90	98.80	**98.87**
		10,000	98.82	98.70	98.77

Data Augmentation. Next, we incorporate the RoGPT-2 text continuation examples on a set of samples using two strategies for the decoder (i.e., greedy and beam-search-2). We perform experiments with the RoBERT-BiGRU model and show that the generative effort increases the overall performance for both tasks (see Table 4). In most cases, the RoBERT embeddings bring increased performance on the LaRoSeDa dataset as a consequence of the polarized effect of the product reviews, being strongly positive or negative. This polarization impact also applies to the models trained on augmented data. Data augmentation using the greedy decoder method achieves the best performance on SaRoCo, with a 99.08% test accuracy, employing 10,000 expanded texts, compared with the best accuracy of 98.68% obtained with beam-search-2. Furthermore, on LaRoSeDa, we determine similar performance on the greedy search algorithm with the best accuracy of 98.94% for 10,000 augmented texts. However, for the second dataset, more generated data will not necessarily determine the best performance as in the beam-search-2 scenario, using 10,000 augmented texts slightly underperforms in contrast with 5,000 examples.

Discussions. RoBERT-BiGRU, augmented with RoGPT-2 samples, correctly classifies 1,344 out of 1,362 examples from the LaRoSeDa test dataset. Due to spatial constraints, Table 5 depicts only the shortest eight misclassified texts out of 18, for which ground truth, predicted, and human annotated labels are shown. Two human annotators concluded from these examples that three indecisions and five classifications contradict the expected ones. The uncertain results and the negative misclassifications are expected to have been 3-out-of-5 stars ratings, which were assumed negative when the dataset was

Table 5. Examples from LaRoSeDa predicted with RoBERT-BiGRU. Ground truth (GT), Predicted (Pred) and Human labels are shown. P stands for Positive, N for Negative, and I for Indecisive.

Romanian text	English translation	GT	Pred	Human
o boxa ok din punct de vedere calitate pret daca este cumparata de unde trebuie. aici nu apare nici numele complet al boxei iar descrierea este saraca, plus pretul cu mult peste cat o gasesti in alte magazine	a good speaker in terms of quality and price if it is bought from the right place. the speaker's full name does not appear here and the description is poor, plus the price is much higher than what you can find in other stores	P	N	I
bun doar pentru incarcare (nu face conexiune, nu incarca rapid modelul nexus x). nu pare sa fie universal. nu realizeaza conexiune. voi mai incerca cu diverse cabluri micro usb si revin daca reusesc sa conectez telefonul la calculator	good only for charging (doesn't connect, doesn't fast charge the nexus x model). it doesn't seem to be universal. it doesn't connect. I will try with various micro usb cables and return if I can connect the phone to the computer	P	N	N
imi place. o bratara feminina care isi face bine treaba. se sincronizeaza foarte bine cu android - samsung. bateria are autonomie zile cu functia pulse ox activata, fara aceasta functie scrie ca ar avea zile, dar nu am incercat	I like it. a feminine bracelet that does its job well. it synchronizes very well with android - samsung. the battery has an autonomy of days with the pulse ox function activated, without this function, it says it would have days, but I have not tried it	N	P	P
aproape multumit. am cumparat acest produs in urma cu o luna si pana acum doua zile am fost foarte multumit de el. bateria asigura o autonomie de - zile, finisajele sunt ok	almost satisfied. I bought this product a month ago and until two days ago I was very satisfied with it. the battery ensures the autonomy of - days, the finishes are ok	N	P	P
bun. folie calitativ buna dar nepotrivita pentru ecrane curbate. raman - milimetri dezlipiti pe margine. personal as recomanda folie de plastic pentru ecrane curbate dupa experienta asta	good. good quality foil but not suitable for curved screens. it remains - millimetres unglued on the edge. I would personally recommend a plastic film for curved screens after this experience	N	P	I
multumita! este foarte buna sunet clar! doar ca are probleme la conectarea cu bluetooth, il gaseste greu sau face nazuri km a conectare trebuie sa caut de multi ori bluetooth-ul. in rest e ok	pleased! it is a very good clear sound! it's just that it has problems connecting with bluetooth, it finds it hard or it's difficult to connect, I have to look for bluetooth many times. the rest is ok	N	P	P
recomand. claritate, sunet bun si un microfon super, fara fire, doar o cutiuta miniona de incarcare! pretul este mult sub cel de la apple. multumit de produs	I recommend it. clarity, good sound and a great microphone, no wires, just a tiny charging box! the price is much lower than that of apple. happy about the product	N	P	P
decent. il folosesc cu un samsung si nici pe departe nu are incarcare fast charge. daca nu te grabesti si ai rabdare sa astepti, merge	decent. I use it with a Samsung, which doesn't even have a fast charge. It will work if you are not in a hurry and have the patience to wait	N	P	I

created. Furthermore, we observe strongly positive texts such as "I like it. A feminine bracelet that does its job well", "I was very satisfied with it", "happy about the product", "I recommend it", and "pleased! it is a very good clear sound!" have negative ground truth in the dataset. However, these are positive examples for the model and human annotators. Thus, we determine noise in the LaRoSeDa dataset, which is expected for datasets gathered from online sources, as the origin of the noise can be introduced by the page user or by automated data extractors.

7 Conclusions

Satire detection and sentiment analysis are important NLP tasks for which literature provides an ample palette of models and applications. Despite the more polarization expected on the product review task in contrast with the increased passivity of satirical texts, our models properly encapsulate the meaning represented by relevant features. In the syntactic and semantic context of our tasks, there is a slight difference in performance for the CC, CoRoLa, and NLPL embeddings, whereas fine-tuning the pre-trained RoBERT model brings up to 3% performance improvement. We showed in many experiments that our parameterized capsule framework can be adapted to specific problems. Moreover, we can improve the capsule network by employing data augmentation using generative models such as RoGPT-2, achieving a maximum gain of 0.6%. Based on our results, the potential of such an architecture is of increased significance, thus enabling further work in this direction.

Acknowledgements. The research has been funded by the University Politehnica of Bucharest through the PubArt program.

References

1. Avram, A.M., et al.: Distilling the knowledge of Romanian BERTs using multiple teachers. In: Proceedings of the Thirteenth Language Resources and Evaluation Conference, pp. 374–384 (2022)
2. Butnaru, A., Ionescu, R.T.: MOROCO: the Moldavian and Romanian dialectal corpus. In: Proceedings of the 57th Annual Meeting of the Association for Computational Linguistics, pp. 688–698 (2019)
3. Cho, K., van Merrienboer, B., Bahdanau, D., Bengio, Y.: On the properties of neural machine translation: encoder-decoder approaches, pp. 103–111 (2014). https://doi.org/10.3115/v1/W14-4012
4. Devlin, J., Chang, M.W., Lee, K., Toutanova, K.: BERT: Pre-training of deep bidirectional transformers for language understanding. arXiv preprint arXiv:1810.04805 (2018)
5. Dumitrescu, S., Avram, A.M., Pyysalo, S.: The birth of Romanian BERT. In: Findings of the Association for Computational Linguistics: EMNLP 2020, pp. 4324–4328 (2020)
6. Dumitrescu, Ş.D., Avram, A.M.: Introducing RONEC-the Romanian named entity corpus. In: Proceedings of the 12th Language Resources and Evaluation Conference, pp. 4436–4443 (2020)
7. Dumitrescu, S.D., et al.: LiRo: Benchmark and leaderboard for Romanian language tasks. In: Thirty-fifth Conference on Neural Information Processing Systems Datasets and Benchmarks Track (Round 1) (2021)
8. Goodfellow, I.J., Shlens, J., Szegedy, C.: Explaining and harnessing adversarial examples. arXiv preprint arXiv:1412.6572 (2014)
9. Graves, A., Schmidhuber, J.: Framewise phoneme classification with bidirectional LSTM networks. In: Proceedings. 2005 IEEE International Joint Conference on Neural Networks, vol. 4, pp. 2047–2052 (2005). https://doi.org/10.1109/IJCNN.2005.1556215

10. Hochreiter, S., Schmidhuber, J.: Long short-term memory. Neural Comput. **9**(8), 1735–1780 (1997)
11. Kim, J., Jang, S., Park, E., Choi, S.: Text classification using capsules. Neurocomputing **376**, 214–221 (2020)
12. Kim, Y.: Convolutional neural networks for sentence classification. In: Proceedings of the 2014 Conference on Empirical Methods in Natural Language Processing (EMNLP), pp. 1746–1751 (2014). https://doi.org/10.3115/v1/d14-1181
13. Kingma, D.P., Ba, J.: Adam: a method for stochastic optimization. arXiv preprint arXiv:1412.6980 (2014)
14. Kutuzov, A., Barnes, J., Velldal, E., Øvrelid, L., Oepen, S.: Large-scale contextualised language modelling for Norwegian. arXiv preprint arXiv:2104.06546 (2021)
15. Kwabena Patrick, M., Felix Adekoya, A., Abra Mighty, A., Edward, B.Y.: Capsule networks - a survey. J. King Saud Univ. Comput. Inf. Sci. **34**(1), 1295–1310 (2022)
16. Lin, T.Y., Goyal, P., Girshick, R., He, K., Dollár, P.: Focal loss for dense object detection. In: Proceedings of the IEEE International Conference on Computer Vision, pp. 2980–2988 (2017)
17. Van der Maaten, L., Hinton, G.: Visualizing data using t-SNE. J. Mach. Learn. Res. **9**(11), 1–27 (2008)
18. Madry, A., Makelov, A., Schmidt, L., Tsipras, D., Vladu, A.: Towards deep learning models resistant to adversarial attacks. In: 6th International Conference on Learning Representations, ICLR 2018, Vancouver, BC, Canada, 30 April – 3 May 2018, Conference Track Proceedings. OpenReview.net (2018). https://openreview.net/forum?id=rJzIBfZAb
19. Masala, M., Ruseti, S., Dascalu, M.: Robert-a Romanian BERT model. In: Proceedings of the 28th International Conference on Computational Linguistics, pp. 6626–6637 (2020)
20. McHardy, R., Adel, H., Klinger, R.: Adversarial training for satire detection: controlling for confounding variables. In: Proceedings of the 2019 Conference of the North American Chapter of the Association for Computational Linguistics: Human Language Technologies, Volume 1 (Long and Short Papers), pp. 660–665. Association for Computational Linguistics, Minneapolis, Minnesota (2019). https://doi.org/10.18653/v1/N19-1069
21. Mititelu, V.B., Tufiş, D., Irimia, E.: The reference corpus of the contemporary Romanian language (CoRoLa). In: Proceedings of the Eleventh International Conference on Language Resources and Evaluation (LREC 2018) (2018)
22. Miyato, T., Dai, A.M., Goodfellow, I.J.: Adversarial training methods for semi-supervised text classification. In: 5th International Conference on Learning Representations, ICLR 2017, Toulon, France, 24–26 April 2017, Conference Track Proceedings. OpenReview.net (2017)
23. Nicolae, D.C., Yadav, R.K., Tufiş, D.: A lite Romanian BERT: ALR-BERT. Computers **11**(4), 57 (2022)
24. Niculescu, M.A., Ruseti, S., Dascalu, M.: Rogpt2: Romanian gpt2 for text generation. In: 2021 IEEE 33rd International Conference on Tools with Artificial Intelligence (ICTAI), pp. 1154–1161. IEEE (2021)
25. Onose, C., Cercel, D.C., Trausan-Matu, S.: SC-UPB at the VarDial 2019 evaluation campaign: Moldavian vs. Romanian cross-dialect topic identification. In: Proceedings of the Sixth Workshop on NLP for Similar Languages, Varieties and Dialects, pp. 172–177. Association for Computational Linguistics, Ann Arbor, Michigan (2019). https://doi.org/10.18653/v1/W19-1418
26. Păiş, V., Mitrofan, M., Gasan, C.L., Coneschi, V., Ianov, A.: Named entity recognition in the Romanian legal domain. In: Proceedings of the Natural Legal Language Processing Workshop 2021, pp. 9–18 (2021)
27. Rogoz, A.C., Gaman, M., Ionescu, R.T.: SaRoCo: detecting satire in a novel Romanian corpus of news articles. In: Proceedings of the 16th Conference of the European Chapter of the

Association for Computational Linguistics: Main Volume. Association for Computational Linguistics, Online (2021). https://arxiv.org/pdf/2105.06456.pdf

28. Sabour, S., Frosst, N., Hinton, G.E.: Dynamic routing between capsules. In: Advances in Neural Information Processing Systems, vol. 30 (2017)

29. Saha, T., Ramesh Jayashree, S., Saha, S., Bhattacharyya, P.: Bert-caps: a transformer-based capsule network for tweet act classification. IEEE Trans. Comput. Soc. Syst. **7**(5), 1168–1179 (2020). https://doi.org/10.1109/TCSS.2020.3014128

30. Srivastava, S., Khurana, P., Tewari, V.: Identifying aggression and toxicity in comments using capsule network. In: Proceedings of the First Workshop on Trolling, Aggression and Cyberbullying (TRAC-2018), pp. 98–105. Association for Computational Linguistics, Santa Fe, New Mexico, USA (2018). https://aclanthology.org/W18-4412

31. Su, J., Yu, S., Luo, D.: Enhancing aspect-based sentiment analysis with capsule network. IEEE Access **8**, 100551–100561 (2020). https://doi.org/10.1109/ACCESS.2020.2997675

32. Sun, B., Feng, J., Saenko, K.: Correlation alignment for unsupervised domain adaptation. In: Csurka, G. (ed.) Domain Adaptation in Computer Vision Applications. ACVPR, pp. 153–171. Springer, Cham (2017). https://doi.org/10.1007/978-3-319-58347-1_8

33. Szegedy, C., et al.: Intriguing properties of neural networks. In: Bengio, Y., LeCun, Y. (eds.) 2nd International Conference on Learning Representations, ICLR 2014, Banff, AB, Canada, 14–16 April 2014, Conference Track Proceedings (2014). http://arxiv.org/abs/1312.6199

34. Tache, A., Gaman, M., Ionescu, R.T.: Clustering word embeddings with self-organizing maps. application on LaRoSeDa - a large Romanian sentiment data set. In: Proceedings of the 16th Conference of the European Chapter of the Association for Computational Linguistics: Main Volume, pp. 949–956. Association for Computational Linguistics, Online (2021). https://www.aclweb.org/anthology/2021.eacl-main.81

35. Wang, A., Singh, A., Michael, J., Hill, F., Levy, O., Bowman, S.: Glue: a multi-task benchmark and analysis platform for natural language understanding. In: Proceedings of the 2018 EMNLP Workshop BlackboxNLP: Analyzing and Interpreting Neural Networks for NLP, pp. 353–355 (2018)

36. Xiao, C., Li, B., Zhu, J.Y., He, W., Liu, M., Song, D.: Generating adversarial examples with adversarial networks. In: 27th International Joint Conference on Artificial Intelligence, IJCAI 2018, pp. 3905–3911. International Joint Conferences on Artificial Intelligence (2018)

37. Xu, G., Meng, Y., Qiu, X., Yu, Z., Wu, X.: Sentiment analysis of comment texts based on BiLSTM. IEEE Access **7**, 51522–51532 (2019). https://doi.org/10.1109/ACCESS.2019.2909919

38. Yang, F., Mukherjee, A., Dragut, E.: Satirical news detection and analysis using attention mechanism and linguistic features. In: Proceedings of the 2017 Conference on Empirical Methods in Natural Language Processing, pp. 1979–1989. Association for Computational Linguistics, Copenhagen, Denmark (2017). https://doi.org/10.18653/v1/D17-1211

39. Yang, Z., Dai, Z., Yang, Y., Carbonell, J., Salakhutdinov, R.R., Le, Q.V.: XLNET: Generalized autoregressive pretraining for language understanding. In: Advances in Neural Information Processing Systems, vol. 32 (2019)

40. Zhang, B., Xu, X., Yang, M., Chen, X., Ye, Y.: Cross-domain sentiment classification by capsule network with semantic rules. IEEE Access **6**, 58284–58294 (2018). https://doi.org/10.1109/ACCESS.2018.2874623

41. Zhao, W., Peng, H., Eger, S., Cambria, E., Yang, M.: Towards scalable and reliable capsule networks for challenging NLP applications. In: Proceedings of the 57th Annual Meeting of the Association for Computational Linguistics, pp. 1549–1559. Association for Computational Linguistics, Florence, Italy (2019). https://doi.org/10.18653/v1/P19-1150

42. Zhao, W., Ye, J., Yang, M., Lei, Z., Zhang, S., Zhao, Z.: Investigating capsule networks with dynamic routing for text classification. In: Proceedings of the 2018 Conference on Empirical Methods in Natural Language Processing, pp. 3110–3119 (2018)

Short papers

Short papers

A Few-Shot Approach to Resume Information Extraction via Prompts

Chengguang Gan$^{(\boxtimes)}$ (ID) and Tatsunori Mori (ID)

Yokohama National University, Yokohama, Japan
`gan-chengguan-pw@ynu.jp, tmori@ynu.ac.jp`

Abstract. Prompt learning's near fine-tune performance on text classification tasks has attracted the NLP community. This paper applies it to resume information extraction, improving existing methods for this task. We created manual templates and verbalizers tailored to resume texts and compared the performance of Masked Language Model (MLM) and Seq2Seq PLMs. Also, we enhanced the verbalizer design for Knowledgeable Prompt-tuning, contributing to prompt template design across NLP tasks. We present the Manual Knowledgeable Verbalizer (MKV), a rule for constructing verbalizers for specific applications. Our tests show that MKV rules yield more effective, robust templates and verbalizers than existing methods. Our MKV approach resolved sample imbalance, surpassing current automatic prompt methods. This study underscores the value of tailored prompt learning for resume extraction, stressing the importance of custom-designed templates and verbalizers.

Keywords: resume · prompt · few-shot learning · template · verbalizer · information extraction · text classification

1 Introduction

With the introduction of the Transformer architecture [19], large-scale language models pre-trained on unsupervised tasks have consistently achieved state-of-the-art results on a wide range of NLP tasks. The most prominent of these models include the Encoder-based BERT [1], a task-based MLM pre-trained model primarily used for classification tasks, and its modified version, RoBERTa [11]. Another example is the T5 model [13], which uses the Seq2Seq MLM pre-training method. The pre-training and fine-tuning paradigm was widely applied to various NLP downstream tasks until 2020, when a novel pre-training and prompt paradigm was proposed.

The first prompt-based approach for text classification tasks, which utilizes models to answer cloze questions and predict labels, was proposed for sentiment classification [16]. This approach was shown to achieve higher accuracy than the traditional fine-tuning paradigm, even with limited training data. The underlying principle of prompt learning involves using manually designed templates to wrap sentences, which are then masked to provide the target label relation

E. Métais et al. (Eds.): NLDB 2023, LNCS 13913, pp. 445–455, 2023.
https://doi.org/10.1007/978-3-031-35320-8_32

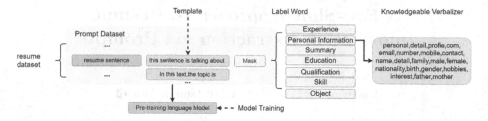

Fig. 1. Illustration of the process of prompt learning for the resume information extraction task.

words. This masked text is then input into the model, which predicts the corresponding label relation words. The development of manual prompt templates led to the exploration of automatic prompt generation methods. These methods are broadly categorized into two groups: discrete prompts and continuous prompts [9].

As previously noted, prompt methods have demonstrated exceptional performance across various benchmark datasets. However, their efficacy in unique practical scenarios, such as information extraction from resumes, remains a question. This application is of great significance to businesses, given the daily influx of resumes. Though deep learning has facilitated automated resume screening, the resource demand for annotating resume texts for Pretrained Language Model (PLM) fine-tuning can be prohibitive. Prompt methods, requiring only a few labeled resume texts, present an economical solution, particularly for small businesses or niche industries. In this study, we leverage a seven-category sentence classification of English resume data [3]. This approach transforms the resume extraction task into a sentence classification task, aligns with the current research focus in prompt learning, and offers practical value, especially for organizations with limited resources. Moreover, the recurring specific words in resumes are ideal for constructing a Knowledgeable Verbalizer (KV), a technique known for its state-of-the-art (SOTA) results [6]. Thus, we focus on information extraction from resumes in this study.

As depicted in Fig. 1, the sentence to be classified, denoted as X, is inputted into the wrap class. Following this, an indicative template sentence is appended. Subsequently, a mask token is integrated into the prompted sentence, representing the label relation word to be forecasted, such as "{X} this sentence is about {mask}". Consequently, a sentence classification problem is reframed as a fill-in-the-blanks (mask token) task. The Masked Language Model (MLM) explicitly addresses this issue. As a result, prompting enables the downstream task to align more closely with the pre-training task, facilitating rapid model adaptation for small datasets. The Knowledgeable Verbalizer (KV) extends a single label relation word to cover multiple associated terms. Initially, the output probability of each relevant word for the mask token is calculated. These probabilities are then consolidated, and the class with the highest probability of associated words is selected as the sentence's predicted outcome, i.e., the mask token word. In conclusion, KV with a manually designed template has achieved superior scores across numerous datasets compared to other prompt methods' baseline scores. Therefore, our initial hypothesis in this study was that the amalgamation of manually designed templates and KV is the most effective among current mainstream prompt methods. We conducted subsequent comparison experiments to validate this hypothesis. To assess the impact of different templates on the results, we devised several alternative templates for comparison experiments. The results suggest that the efficacy of prompt-learning is significantly impacted by template design. A baseline KV was created for resume text classification using the original Knowledgeable Prompt-learning method [6] and compared with the KV designed based on our refined rules. We term the KV constructed following our proposed rule as Manual Knowledgeable Verbalizer (MKV). On the 25-shot and 50-shot tasks, performance increased significantly from 54.96% to 63.65% and 59.72% to 76.53% respectively. These findings indicate our proposed MKV is more suited for the resume extraction task. We conducted comparative experiments on two models using 25/50/10-shot tasks and two distinct training techniques to compare the encoder structure of BERT and the Seq2Seq structure of the T5 model in the context of prompt-learning. In summary, our primary contributions include:

1. Development of a comprehensive set of prompt-learning techniques for the few-shot resume information extraction task.

2. Proposal of KV construction rules, based on the original Knowledgeable Prompt-tuning (KPT), that are more compatible with resume text. This provides insights for subsequent researchers to develop KVs for practical application scenarios.

3. Comparison of manual template construction with automatic template generation for the prompt method. We have demonstrated that, in the current state of prompt-learning for resume text, a method employing manually crafted prompts surpasses one using automatically generated prompts.

2 Related Work

The research related to this paper is divided into two main groups. Prompt templates and constructs of prompt verbalizer.

Prompt Template. Since PET(Pattern-Exploiting Training) [16] was proposed, a surge of prompt research has been started. A PET follow-up study mentioned that smaller size models, such as BERT-base, are also capable of few-shot learning [17]. There are also some other studies of discrete prompts [4,14,18]. The idea behind a discrete prompt is that the words in the template are real. The reason for this is because in coordinate space, the words are in a discrete state. Another hand, as all token-level prompts have been automatically generated, some research has gone a step further by replacing the token-level prompt template in the token representation with continuous vectors directly and training these prompts instead of the fine-tune model(A.K.A Continuous Prompt) [5,7,8,10,12]. Using continuous vectors, we can find the best set of vectors to replace the discrete prompt template.

Prompt Verbalizer. The automatic construction method of verbalizer in few-shot learning is explored [15]. There are also corresponding verbalizers for some of the prompt methods mentioned in the previous paragraph, such as manual, soft and automatic verbalizers. Finally, the KV in this study also has better performance than other verbalizers [6].

3   Task Setup

In this work, we select the resume information sentence classification dataset as the experimental object. Hence, this study also considers the task setting from a practical application scenario. Suppose an IT company needs to fine-tune its company resume information extraction model. First, a training dataset consisting of several hundred resumes needs to be constructed. This results in the need to annotate tens of thousands of sentences. This is a non-negligible cost for a small company. Also, some small start-up companies may not have hundreds of resumes to create a training dataset. Thus, it is essential to minimize the investment of company human resource in producing training datasets for company.

In summary, we set the task to be in the case of annotating only one or two resumes. The resume dataset was extracted from 15,000 original resumes and 1000 of them were used as tagged objects [3][1]. In addition, the total number of sentence samples in this dataset is 78786, and the total number of annotated resumes is 1000. So it is calculated that each resume contains about 79 sentences on average.

4   Prompt Design

In this section, we firstly designed a series of prompt templates for resumes. Secondly, we presented a different KV construction method from the original KPT depending on the textual characteristics of the resume (Fig. 1).

4.1   Manual Template

For the manually designed templates, we divided into two design thoughts. One is the generic template that is commonly used in prior studies (e.g., "{input sentence} In this sentence, the topic is {mask}."). Another type of template is designed for resume documents (e.g., "{input sentence} this sentence belongs in the {mask} section of the resume."). Based on this, we designed a series of templates specifically for the resume text. By inserting words like "resume" and "curriculum vitae" into the templates, which are strongly related to the classification text. It is anticipated that the performance of the few-shot learning of resume text would improve with the specific design of templates and MKV.

---

[1] https://www.kaggle.com/datasets/oo7kartik/resume-text-batch.

4.2 Knowledgeable Verbalizer

In this study, KV from the KPT paper is utilized [6]. In their study, KV is constructed by introducing external knowledge. As an example, consider the class label "experience". By using related word search sites, the words that appear frequently in conjunction with "experience" are tallied, and the top 100 words with the highest frequency are selected to constitute KV[2]. There are seven word sets for class labels to construct the KV.

As shown in Fig. 2, the text of the "personal information" in the original manuscript of a resume was selected to illustrate the MKV construction rules of our proposal. In summary, we present two rules for selecting the label relation word. 1. Words that frequently appear in sentence of the target class with resume text. 2. This word does not often occur in other classes. Thus, the words marked with gray background in the figure can be selected according to the two rules mentioned above. Two of them, "languages" and "address", are marked with a black background. The word "languages" often appears in "skill" classes for programming languages. The "address" is a word that appears not only in personal information as a home address. It also appears in "experience" classes for company addresses. So the above two words will not be selected in the label relation word set of personal information.

Fig. 2. Example of label-related word selection for the *personal information* class in resume when constructing Knowledgeable Verbalizer(Although the data comes from open source websites, mosaic is given to the part involving privacy.).

5 Experiments Setup

This study aims to investigate the impact of various factors on the outcomes of limited opportunity resume learning, as well as to assess the efficacy of our proposed MKV construction rules for Prompt Learning of resume material. We performed multiple comparative tests between the prompt's template and verbalizer, evaluated the performance of several prompting methods against MKV, and examined the effectiveness of two structurally distinct PLM models in few-shot resume learning. These experiments utilized a specially created resume dataset.

For efficient iteration of different experiments, we used Openprompt[3], an Open-Source Framework for Prompt-learning [2]. We used the F1-micro as the

---

[2] https://relatedwords.org/.
[3] https://github.com/thunlp/OpenPrompt.

evaluation metric for all experiments. Given that few-shot learning typically allows only a limited number of training samples per class, we employed a random seed to extract the training set from our unbalanced dataset of resumes. This approach maintained the original sample distribution, thereby preserving the inherent imbalance of the resume samples. Distinct random seeds were used for the 25/50/100-shot experiments.

Initially, we conducted two comparison experiments to determine the most efficient template and Knowledge Verbalizer (KV). One experiment compared different manual templates, while the other compared the performance of our proposed MKV construction method with the original KV construction method. After establishing the performance of Manual Template (MT) and Manual Knowledge Verbalizer (MKV), they were compared with three other types of templates and verbalizers.

The methods we considered include: 1) The Automatic method, where the model generates discrete prompt template words automatically, 2) Soft prompt method, where by optimizing the vectors of the embedding layer, soft prompts are utilized, 3) P-tuning method, where token-level templates are replaced with dense vectors, which are trained to predict the masked words, and 4) Prefix prompt approach, where task-specific continuous sequence prefixes are trained instead of the entire transformer model.

Finally, to investigate the fine-tuning and prompt-tuning performance of RoBERTa$_{large}$ and T5$_{large}$, we conducted an additional experiment. The scores from the first three experiments were obtained after 4 training epochs, while the PLM comparison experiment used scores adjusted to the best epoch based on test set scores. To evaluate the performance of KV and MKV in the context of sample imbalance, we created and analyzed the confusion matrix of the 50-shot test dataset for both methods.

Table 1. The result of 0-shot was compared with different Template. Use the manual template(MT) and Manual knowledgeable verbalizer(MKV).

Method	Template	F1-score
MT+MKV	{input sentence} In this sentence, the topic is {mask}	33.45
	{input sentence} this sentence is talking about {mask}	55.77
	{input sentence}this sentence belongs in the {mask} section of the resume	61.32
	{input sentence}this sentence belongs in the {mask} section of the curriculum vitae	**62.09**

6 Results and Analysis

6.1 Comparison Between Different Manual Templates

Table 1 showcases experimental results from comparing four distinct templates. To eliminate confounding variables such as training samples, we adopted a 0-shot training strategy, directly predicting the test set using the original parameters of PLMs. This amplifies the impact of each template's efficacy. The top two are universal prompt templates suitable for any classification task. Contrarily, we developed two templates specifically for the resume dataset; incorporating "resume" into the templates notably enhanced the outcomes.

Another noteworthy observation is the 0.77 point score increment following the substitution of "resume" with "curriculum vitae". We hypothesize this arises from the polysemous nature of "resume" (e.g., n.summary, v.recover), creating ambiguity when used within the template sentence. Replacing "resume" with the unambiguous term "curriculum vitae" consequently improved the score.

Table 2. The results of 25/50/100-shot was compared with different Knowledgeable Verbalizer construction method.

Total Label Set Size(KV method)	25-shot	50-shot	100-shot
700(KV-baseline)	54.96	59.72	66.46
63(Ours MKV)	**63.65**	**76.53**	**76.72**

6.2 Compare Different Verbalizers

Subsequently, we compare the performance of the original KV construction method and our proposed method. As shown in Table 2, the total label set size means the sum of the extended words of the seven categories. To start with, for baseline, we follow the method in the original paper to obtain a set of related words to each sentence class by retrieving webpages with the class label as a query [6]. Later, we constructed a total of 63 MKVs according to the rule proposed in Sect. 4.2. For the KV comparison test in this section, we used the fourth manual template in Table 1 ({text} this sentence belongs in the {mask} section of the curriculum vitae.). MKV is 8.69/16.81/10.26 point higher than the origin KV on 25/50/100-shot. This result also demonstrates the effectiveness of our improved MKV.

6.3 Comparison of Different Prompt Methods

Since the OpenPrompt framework divides the process of prompt-tuning into two main parts: Template and Verbalizer (See in Fig. 1), these two parts can be used in combination at will. Hence, we have selected four representative Templates

Table 3. Compare the results of different prompt methods at 25/50/100-shot. MT, MV is the abbreviation of Manual Template and Verbalizer. ST, SV is the abbreviation of Soft Template and Verbalizer. PT, PFT is the abbreviation of P-tuning Template and Prefix-tuning Template. AutoV is the abbreviation of AutomaticVerbalizer. MKV is the abbreviation of Manual Knowledgeable Verbalizer.

Prompt Method	F1-score			
Template	Verbalizer	25-shot	50-shot	100-shot
MT	MKV	63.65	**76.53**	**76.72**
	MV	51.95	70.18	72.89
	SV	51.49	55.37	64.29
	AutoV	14.72	14.48	13.93
ST	MKV	**63.92**	70.42	73.91
	MV	39.93	57.91	65.42
	SV	33.69	53.60	60.29
	AutoV	14.72	14.48	13.93
PT	MKV	62.82	68.19	72.33
	MV	42.11	55.97	65.65
	SV	16.43	50.42	64.04
	AutoV	14.48	14.28	15.12
PFT	MKV	60.88	67.29	73.60
	MV	40.36	55.62	62.73
	SV	39.13	53.56	57.62
	AutoV	14.85	14.65	13.96

and four Verbalizer methods and compared their few-shot learning effectiveness with each other. As shown in Table 3, In the 50/100-shot experiments, the combination of MT+MKV achieved the best results. Especially in the 50-shot experiment, the combination of MT+MKV scored 6.11 point higher than the second place ST+MKV. However, in the 25-shot experiment, the ST+MKV combination was slightly higher than the MT+MKV combination. Overall, the MT+MKV method that we propose outperforms the other four template and verbalizer combinations. This further validates the effectiveness and robustness of our MKV constructed for the resume classification dataset.

6.4   Results on T5 and RoBERTa Model

In our final experiment, we compared the performance of the RoBERTa model, trained using Masked Language Model (MLM) within an Encoder structure, and the T5 model, implemented with an Encoder-Decoder structure, on a resume classification task. Unlike previous model comparison experiments where training was conducted for a fixed four epochs, we adjusted the training duration to the optimal number of epochs based on the test dataset score. This approach

Table 4. Compare the few-shot (25/50/100-shot) learning results of RoBERTa$_{large}$ and T5$_{large}$ models under different methods.

Model	Method	Examples	F1-score
RoBERTa$_{large}$(baseline)	Fine-tune	25	58.70
		50	66.10
		100	73.78
T5a$_{large}$(baseline)	Fine-tune	25	47.33
		50	58.97
		100	70.46
RoBERTa$_{large}$	MT+MKV	25	57.48
		50	71.50
		100	71.85
T5$_{large}$	MT+MKV	25	**63.65**
		50	**76.53**
		100	**78.01**

better demonstrates the peak performance of both models using the two methods, thereby facilitating a more accurate comparison for determining the more suitable model for the few-shot learning task on the resume dataset.

As illustrated in Table 4, the T5 model, when trained using the fine-tuning approach, underperforms the RoBERTa model in the 25/50/100-shot outcomes. However, the 25/50/100-shot results outperform the RoBERTa model when the T5 model is trained using the MT+MKV prompt-learning method. Notably, the corresponding improvements are 6.17, 5.03, and 6.16 points respectively.

Additionally, the RoBERTa model, when provided with a larger number of training samples, exhibits a performance gain of 1.93 points at the 100-shot level, with the fine-tune method compared to the prompt-learning method. Interestingly, the score difference between the 50-shot and 100-shot instances using the MT+MKV method with the RoBERTa model is minimal, despite doubling the sample size. This suggests limited efficiency in the use of larger samples within this context. This observation aligns with the findings of [7], which propose that the performance of prompt-tuning improves with an increase in the number of parameters within the model.

6.5   Analysis of the Confusion Matrix

The "experience" category in a resume dataset features the largest sample size at 41,114, while "qualification" has the smallest at 974, leading to a notable imbalance. This imbalance challenges the use of few-shot learning models. Our proposed MKV method's effectiveness in addressing this imbalance is demonstrated through a confusion matrix comparison in Fig. 3.

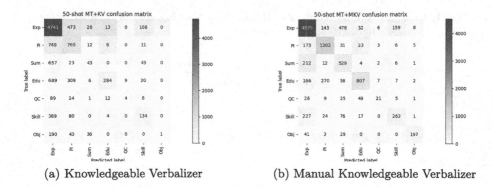

(a) Knowledgeable Verbalizer   (b) Manual Knowledgeable Verbalizer

Fig. 3. Confuse Matrix of MT+KV and MT+MKV in 50-shot on T5$_{large}$ model.

To begin with, an analysis of the confusion matrix for the labels "summary", "qualification", "education", "skill", and "object" using the original KV method, as depicted in Fig. 3(a), reveals a substantial misclassification rate. These labels are associated with a smaller proportion of samples, many of which are erroneously classified into the categories of "experience" and "personal information", which represent a larger proportion of the sample. Furthermore, the distribution observed in the confusion matrix of the KV method corroborates the trend suggested in Fig. 3(a): the fewer the number of samples in a class, the lower the number of correct classifications.

Conversely, the application of our proposed MKV method shows a considerable improvement in addressing classification errors associated with sample imbalance, as shown in Fig. 3(b). This lends credence to the effectiveness of the MKV approach, crafted according to our rule, in maintaining high performance even in the presence of highly unbalanced samples.

7   Conclusion

In this study, we use the prompt technique on the resume dataset for few-shot learning. We created templates informed by resume sentence structures and assessed their utility. Additionally, we refined the construction of a knowledgeable verbalizer, relying on Knowledgeable Prompt Tuning (KPT). For this, we devised construction rules for the MKV, tailored to the textual features of resumes. Experimental evaluations demonstrate our MKV's effectiveness and robustness. While the final outcomes were satisfactory, they also elucidated the constraints inherent in the utilized prompt methodology. It is anticipated that future endeavors will develop a more universal prompt approach, capable of addressing a variety of industries and accommodating diverse resume formats.

Acknowledgements. This research was partially supported by JSPS KAKENHI Grant Numbers JP23H00491 and JP22K00502.

References

1. Devlin, J., Chang, M.W., Lee, K., Toutanova, K.: BERT: pre-training of deep bidirectional transformers for language understanding. In: Proceedings of the NAACL (2019)
2. Ding, N., et al.: OpenPrompt: an open-source framework for prompt-learning. In: Proceedings of the ACL (2022)
3. Gan, C., Mori, T.: Construction of English resume corpus and test with pre-trained language models. arXiv preprint arXiv:2208.03219 (2022)
4. Gao, T., Fisch, A., Chen, D.: Making pre-trained language models better few-shot learners. In: Proceedings of the ACL-IJCNLP (Aug 2021)
5. Hambardzumyan, K., Khachatrian, H., May, J.: WARP: word-level adversarial reprogramming. In: Proceedings of the ACL-IJCNLP (2021)
6. Hu, S., et al.: Knowledgeable prompt-tuning: incorporating knowledge into prompt verbalizer for text classification. In: Proceedings of the ACL (2022)
7. Lester, B., Al-Rfou, R., Constant, N.: The power of scale for parameter-efficient prompt tuning. In: Proceedings of the EMNLP (2021)
8. Li, X.L., Liang, P.: Prefix-tuning: optimizing continuous prompts for generation. In: Proceedings of the ACL-IJCNLP (2021)
9. Liu, P., Yuan, W., Fu, J., Jiang, Z., Hayashi, H., Neubig, G.: Pre-train, prompt, and predict: a systematic survey of prompting methods in natural language processing. ACM Comput. Surv. 55(9), 1–35 (2023)
10. Liu, X., et al.: P-tuning: Prompt tuning can be comparable to fine-tuning across scales and tasks. In: Proceedings of the ACL (2022)
11. Liu, Y., et al.: Roberta: a robustly optimized BERT pretraining approach. arXiv preprint arXiv:1907.11692 (2019)
12. Qin, G., Eisner, J.: Learning how to ask: querying LMs with mixtures of soft prompts. In: Proceedings of the NAACL (2021)
13. Raffel, C., et al.: Exploring the limits of transfer learning with a unified text-to-text transformer. J. Mach. Learn. Res. 21(1), 5485–5551 (2020)
14. Reynolds, L., McDonell, K.: Prompt programming for large language models: beyond the few-shot paradigm. In: Extended Abstracts of the 2021 CHI Conference on Human Factors in Computing Systems, pp. 1–7 (2021)
15. Schick, T., Schmid, H., Schütze, H.: Automatically identifying words that can serve as labels for few-shot text classification. In: Proceedings of the ICCL (2020)
16. Schick, T., Schütze, H.: Exploiting cloze-questions for few-shot text classification and natural language inference. In: Proceedings of the EACL (2021)
17. Schick, T., Schütze, H.: It's not just size that matters: small language models are also few-shot learners. In: Proceedings of the NAACL (2021)
18. Tam, D., R. Menon, R., Bansal, M., Srivastava, S., Raffel, C.: Improving and simplifying pattern exploiting training. In: Proceedings of the EMNLP (2021)
19. Vaswani, A., et al.: Attention is all you need. In: Advances in Neural Information Processing Systems, vol. 30 (2017)

Decoding Strategies for Code Conciseness and Efficiency in Transformer-Generated Programs

Brendan Kondracki[✉][iD]

Columbia University, New York, NY 10027, USA
bk2793@columbia.edu

Abstract. In recent years, tremendous strides have been made in the area of program synthesis due to the leveraging of highly parameterized transformer models. Such models have demonstrated near human levels of performance on tasks such as bug detection, computer language translation, and competitive programming. Unfortunately, little research has been done in the exploration of decoding methodologies for such models, despite the semantic and structural differences between human and programming languages. In this paper, we propose extensions to commonly used decoding strategies, which incorporate additional constraints on non-concise and inefficient program generations. Our approaches have shown comparable performance on program generation tasks while producing programs requiring fewer lines of code and a reduced number of looping operations on average compared to traditional methods of decoding.

Keywords: Program Synthesis · CodeT5 · Transformers · Decoding

1 Introduction

Historically, the creation of computer programs has required the use of experienced computer scientists in order to take high level objectives and convert them into well defined program instructions. More recently, however, a great deal of research has been done in the automation of such programming tasks through the use of highly-parameterized transformer models. Although these models have shown promising results on program generation and understanding tasks, very little research has been done on decoding methodologies tailored to programming language. For example, popular program synthesis models such as Codex [1] and AlphaCode [2] utilize standard decoding methods such as nucleus [3] and top-k sampling [4]. In addition, few experimental results have been found analyzing the structural and semantic changes in generated programs when decoded using different strategies.

In this paper, we introduce modified beam search decoding strategies which include re-ranking terms aimed at reducing the number of lines of code generated, as well as reducing the computational cost of programs from looping

© The Author(s), under exclusive license to Springer Nature Switzerland AG 2023
E. Métais et al. (Eds.): NLDB 2023, LNCS 13913, pp. 456–466, 2023.
https://doi.org/10.1007/978-3-031-35320-8_33

operations. In addition, we also integrate our re-ranking approaches into more advanced decoding techniques such as NeuroLogic A* [9]. We finally analyze the effects that such decoding strategies have on program properties such as compile/runtime errors, lines of code/looping operations generated, test case performance, and structural/semantic overlap with human generated programs.

2 Related Work

Numerous approaches have been taken recently to leverage pretrained transformer models for the task of program synthesis. Such approaches include encoder-decoder models such as CodeT5 [5], where a T5 model trained on both natural and programming language was fine-tuned on a number of downstream tasks such a code defect and clone detection. A critical element in the pretraining of CodeT5 was the utilization of a masked identifier prediction (MIP) objective, in which code identifiers such as function and variable names were masked with a unique sentinel token and predicted in an auto-regressive manner. Despite the flexibility in the model's ability to accomodate multiple programming related tasks, its performance on program synthesis specifically was not heavily evaluated.

Another model which focused on such performance was AlphaCode [2], where an encoder-decoder transformer was fine-tuned on a large competitive program dataset consisting of problem/solution pairs from a number of popular competition sites. This model proved to be highly effective, achieving a performance on unseen competition problems ranked in the top 54.3% of human respondents.

In addition to encoder-decoder models, decoder-only models have also shown successes in program synthesis. OpenAI's Codex model [1] was created by fine-tuning GPT language models on publicly available GitHub code. These models showed promising results on benchmarks such as the APPS dataset [6], where functional correctness of generated programs was consistently higher than that of non-modified GPT models.

Regardless of the structure a language model might take on, the choice of decoding strategy must always be made prior to generating outputs. Naive approaches such a greedy decoding have proven to be sub-optimal in practice due to its inability to produce diverse generations, as well as its difficulty capturing the highest probability generation. Sampling techniques have been a commonly used alternative to this greedy approach due to the introduction of randomness/diversity in token selection. Top-k sampling [4] is one method which samples from the top-k highest probability tokens at each step in the model's generation. A common issue with top-k, however, is the difficulty in determining an optimal k value without prior knowledge of the probability distribution at each time-step. Nucleus sampling [3] is a slightly different approach, where instead of defining the number of tokens to sample from, a probability value p is defined, whereby the first n tokens which attribute a total mass of p are sampled.

Although generation diverseness is a desirable trait in many natural language tasks, different properties such as program efficiency and code conciseness are often held in higher importance in the domain of programming language. One decoding approach which aims to maximize the overall probability of a generation is beam search, whereby a set of N highest-probability sequences are maintained at each step in the decoding. As such, we feel that this decoding strategy can yield promising results if explored further in this domain.

A more recent expansion to the beam search method of decoding is Neuro-Logic A*, which builds upon the constrained generation technique, NeuroLogic [10], with the use of an additional look ahead heuristic for estimating the future value of a generation. Since no work thus far has evaluated program synthesis models with this more advanced decoding strategy, we decided to incorporate it into our experiments as well.

There is a rectangle in a coordinate plane. The coordinates of the four vertices are (0,0), (W,0), (W,H), and (0,H). You are given a point (x,y) which is within the rectangle or on its border. We will draw a straight line passing through (x,y) to cut the rectangle into two parts. Find the maximum possible area of the part whose area is not larger than that of the other. Additionally, determine if there are multiple ways to cut the rectangle and achieve that maximum.

——Constraints——
- $1 \leq W, H \leq 10^9$
- $0 \leq x \leq W$
- $0 \leq y \leq H$
- All values in input are integers.
——Input——
Input is given from Standard Input in the following format: W H x y
——Output——
Print the maximum possible area of the part whose area is not larger than that of the other, followed by 1 if there are multiple ways to cut the rectangle and achieve that maximum, and 0 otherwise. The area printed will be judged correct when its absolute or relative error is at most 10^{-9}.
——Sample Input——
2 3 1 2
——Sample Output——
3.000000 0
The line x=1 gives the optimal cut, and no other line does

Fig. 1. Example problem statement from APPS dataset

3   Data

Although the end goal of our decoding methods is to produce more concise and efficient code, we must ensure that doing so does not come at a significant cost of correctness. To evaluate this, we will utilize the APPS dataset [6], which provides a set of natural language coding prompts, as well as test cases for ensuring that generated programming solutions correctly solve the problem (Fig. 1). The data is split into training and testing sets, where each set consists of 5,000 problems with their corresponding test cases. In total, the dataset also contains 232,421 ground truth solutions across all training and testing problems.

In order to format our examples to be used for model training/evaluation, we follow the same structure as proposed by Hendrycks et al., 2021. Namely, for each problem statement, we create a model input of the form:

"\nQUESTION:\n" + q_str + "\n" + $starter\_code\_str$ + "\n" + "\nUse Call-Based Format\n\nANSWER:\n"

where q_str is the original problem text, and $starter\_code\_str$ is any starter code provided (such as function definitions) or the empty string otherwise. The "Use Call-Based Format" text is used to specify that problem inputs should be expected based on an explicit function call. In the event where inputs are passed in through standard input, we instead use the string "Use Standard Input Format".

Since we plan to evaluate our decoding approaches on a custom fine-tuned CodeT5 model, we exclude any problems whose total input tokens size exceeds 512 (the maximum allowed for T5 models). For each problem statement in our training set, we create an (input, output) example across all available ground truth solutions. This yielded 86,338 training examples in total.

4   Methods

As mentioned in Sect. 2, we plan to expand upon the beam search decoding method to analyze how the introduction of program specific re-ranking terms affect model generations. The traditional beam search algorithm builds upon the greedy next-best token decoding strategy by considering a set of N highest-probability sequences at each step. Since the sequence probabilities are computed through a summation of the log conditional probabilities for each token, a standard beam search is naturally biased towards shorter sequences. In practice, an additional length normalization term is multiplied to remove this bias when ranking the possible sequences. The below equation represents the sequence scores generated through a length-normalized beam search:

$$\frac{1}{T} \cdot \sum_{t=1}^{T} log P(y_t | y_{t-1}, ..., y_1, x) \tag{1}$$

where T is the sequence length, x is the original model input, and y_t is the output token at time step t.

We will first expand this scoring approach by adding an additional penalty to the length normalization term for any newline characters generated in the sequence in order to prioritize outputs containing fewer lines of code. In addition, we will multiply this value by a new hyper-parameter, λ, in order to experiment with varying degrees of penalization. This will yield a new beam search equation of the form:

$$\frac{1 + (\lambda N_T)}{T} \cdot \sum_{t=1}^{T} log P(y_t | y_{t-1}, ..., y_1, x) \tag{2}$$

An additional expansion to the beam search methodology we will incorporate is a penalization term for the number of looping operations included in a generation. Similarly to our previous approach, we will include a new hyper-parameter, γ, which will control the extent of penalization over the number of *for* and *while* loops in a model generation.

Our final implementation will include the use of NeuroLogic A* decoding. In the constrained generation setting, this approach can take in a set of lexical constraints in CNF form and reward candidate generations based on their ability to satisfy such constraints. Since our program synthesis setting does not require any forms of lexical constraints, we will utilize the unconstrained implementation of NeuroLogic A*. This approach incorporates an additional heuristic term to the sequence scoring function of beam search to evaluate the future value of generations in the current beam. This heuristic calculates the log-likelihood of each candidate sequence up to a certain look-ahead length, and takes the form:

$$h(y \leq t + l) = \alpha log p(y_{t+1:t+l} | y \leq t, x) \tag{3}$$

where α is a hyper-parameter which controls how much influence the heuristic has over the final generation scores, and l represents the total number of look-ahead steps. Our experiments include analysis over the traditional unconstrained NeuroLogic A* implementation, as well as implementations incorporating our newline and looping penalization terms into NeuroLogic A*'s beam search scoring function.

The first model we chose to analyze the effects of our decoding methods on was CodeT5. Since the default model was not trained on the APPS dataset, we decided to fine-tune the 220 million parameter CodeT5-base model using our currated training examples. Due to computation and time constraints, we trained our CodeT5 model over 3 epochs using AdamW optimization with an initial learning rate of 1×10^{-4}. In addition, we utilized a batch size of 8, with 32 gradient accumulation steps, yielding an effective global batch size of 256. In addition to analyzing the performance of CodeT5, we also evaluated results on a 1.5 billion parameter GPT-2 model trained on the APPS dataset already, provided by Hendrycks et al., 2021. Due to time and system constraints, all NeuroLogic A* experiments were conducted solely with the GPT-2 model.

5   Experiments

Due to the computational bottleneck of evaluating numerous solution generations across multiple tests cases, we decided to limit our analysis to 400 interview level problems from the APPS test data split. We conducted our experiments

Table 1. Evaluation results across CodeT5 and GPT-2 models. %*pass@k* represents the average percentage of test cases passed across best out-of-k solutions for each problem.

Model	Decoding Method	%pass@1	%pass@2	%pass@4
CodeT5	Beam Search, $\lambda = 0$	0.418	0.489	0.897
	Beam Search, $\lambda = 0.25$	0.518	0.711	1.041
	Beam Search, $\lambda = 0.75$	0.518	0.711	1.041
	Beam Search, $\gamma = 1$	0.422	0.493	0.863
	Beam Search, $\gamma = 2$	0.426	0.552	0.923
	Nucleus, p = 0.95	0.693	0.911	1.471
GPT-2	Beam Search, $\lambda = 0$	0.796	0.952	1.178
	Beam Search, $\lambda = 0.25$	0.796	0.952	1.178
	Beam Search, $\lambda = 0.75$	0.796	0.952	1.178
	Beam Search, $\gamma = 1$	0.804	0.948	1.178
	Beam Search, $\gamma = 2$	0.804	0.948	1.178
	Nucleus, p = 0.95	0.585	0.889	1.797
	NeuroLogic A*, $\lambda = 0$	0.796	0.952	1.178
	NeuroLogic A*, $\lambda = 0.25$	0.745	0.948	1.193
	NeuroLogic A*, $\lambda = 0.75$	0.745	0.948	1.193
	NeuroLogic A*, $\gamma = 1$	0.826	0.967	1.163
	NeuroLogic A*, $\gamma = 2$	0.826	0.967	1.163

over 3 variations of our proposed beam search algorithm, with λ values of 0, 0.25, and 0.75 (where $\lambda = 0$ represents the standard length-normalized beam search algorithm), as well as 2 additional loop-penalized variations with γ values of 1 and 2. These λ and γ values were also utilized in our NeuroLogic A* decoding experiments as well. For both beam search and NeuroLogic A* experiments, we utilized a beam size of 4. After observing the results obtained by Lu et al. 2021a, we decided to use a look-ahead length of 5 for our NeuroLogic A* heuristic, as values past this point observed a deterioration in performance. In order to determine the proper value of the α parameter for the A* approach, we conducted an ablation over a small subset of 75 problems with values of 0.1, 0.25, 0.5, and 0.75. We found there to be no difference in terms of the percentage of test cases passed for all 4 values. However, we found marginally fewer runtime and compile errors with α values between 0.25–0.75. As a result, we decided to utilize a value of $\alpha = 0.5$ for all NeuroLogic A* experiments. In addition, we also compared these results against the nucleus sampling strategy with $p = 0.95$. The first metric we analyzed was the %*pass@k*, which represents the percentage of tests cases passed across the best performing solutions out-of-k generations per problem. In addition, we also compared the average number of lines generated and average number of looping operations for the best performing solutions across the various decoding strategies. Finally, since functional correctness can often times inaccurately capture the semantic and structural equivalence between program excerpts, we decided to evaluate each generated program against the set of provided human generated solutions from the APPS test data using the CodeBLEU metric [7]. This metric takes the following form:

$$CodeBLEU = \alpha \cdot BLEU + \beta \cdot BLEU_{weight} + \gamma \cdot Match_{ast} + \theta \cdot Match_{df} \quad (4)$$

where $BLEU_{weight}$ represents a weighted BLEU [8] score where programming language specific keywords such as "if" and "return" are given higher weights compared to the remaining text, $Match_{ast}$ represents the syntactic match between candidate and reference subtrees generated with the tree-sitter parser[1], and $Match_{df}$ represents the semantic data flow match between candidate and reference solutions. We followed the guidelines provided by the CodeBLEU authors in terms of the optimal hyper-parameter values, and utilized $\alpha = \beta = 0.1, \gamma = \theta = 0.4$.

Table 2. Evaluation results across CodeT5 and GPT-2 models. *lines@k* represents the average number of lines generated for the best performing solutions out-of-k for each problem. *loops@k* represents the average number of loops generated for the best performing solutions out-of-k for each problem.

Model	Decoding Method	lines/loops@1	lines/loops@2	lines/loops@4
CodeT5	Beam Search, $\lambda = 0$	13.132/1.175	13.132/1.175	13.137/1.175
	Beam Search, $\lambda = 0.25$	6.352/0.557	6.352/0.557	6.372/0.56
	Beam Search, $\lambda = 0.75$	6.295/0.547	6.295/0.547	6.315/0.55
	Beam Search, $\gamma = 1$	95.73/0.597	95.73/0.597	95.742/0.597
	Beam Search, $\gamma = 2$	88.647/0.57	88.647/0.57	88.66/0.57
	Nucleus, p = 0.95	12.345/1.27	12.355/1.262	12.372/1.255
GPT-2	Beam Search, $\lambda = 0$	14.0/1.417	14.07/1.422	14.147/1.425
	Beam Search, $\lambda = 0.25$	14.0/1.417	14.07/1.422	14.147/1.425
	Beam Search, $\lambda = 0.75$	14.0/1.417	14.07/1.422	14.147/1.425
	Beam Search, $\gamma = 1$	13.985/1.365	14.032/1.367	14.12/1.372
	Beam Search, $\gamma = 2$	13.985/1.365	14.032/1.367	14.12/1.372
	Nucleus, p = 0.95	17.99/1.89	18.06/1.885	18.135/1.885
	NeuroLogic A*, $\lambda = 0$	14.0/1.417	14.07/1.422	14.147/1.425
	NeuroLogic A*, $\lambda = 0.25$	13.682/1.4	13.802/1.402	13.917/1.407
	NeuroLogic A*, $\lambda = 0.75$	13.682/1.4	13.802/1.402	13.917/1.407
	NeuroLogic A*, $\gamma = 1$	13.902/1.34	13.982/1.342	14.032/1.345
	NeuroLogic A*, $\gamma = 2$	13.902/1.34	13.982/1.342	14.032/1.345

---

[1] https://github.com/tree-sitter/tree-sitter.

6   Results

Looking at Table 1, we can see that our line-penalized beam search methods perform better at all %pass@k checkpoints using our CodeT5 model, and identical performance when utilizing the GPT-2 model. In both cases, we also see a sharp difference in performance between the nucleus sampling approach and all beam search variations when evaluating up to 4 solutions. Comparing the line-penalized NeuroLogic A* methods with traditional beam search decoding, we see that NeuroLogic A* outperforms beam search when evaluating up to 4 solutions.

Looking at Table 2, we can see a comparison between the average number of lines of code generated for the best performing solutions out-of-k. We see in the CodeT5 case, there is a noticeable difference in the number of lines generated on average between the line-penalized beam search methods and the standard beam search/nucleus sampling methods. We see that in all %pass@k evaluations, the CodeT5 model is able to achieve better test case performance than standard beam search, while producing fewer than half the number of lines of code on average. In addition, when looking at the loop-penalized decoding approaches, we see better performance at the %pass@1 and %pass@2 checkpoints compared to standard beam search across both models.

Table 3. Average CodeBLEU score for all model/decoding strategies evaluated with APPS test data

Model	Decoding Method	CodeBLEU
CodeT5	Beam Search, $\lambda = 0$	0.237
	Beam Search, $\lambda = 0.25$	0.234
	Beam Search, $\lambda = 0.75$	0.234
	Beam Search, $\gamma = 1$	0.235
	Beam Search, $\gamma = 2$	0.235
	Nucleus, p = 0.95	0.288
GPT-2	Beam Search, $\lambda=0$	0.290
	Beam Search, $\lambda = 0.25$	0.290
	Beam Search, $\lambda = 0.75$	0.290
	Beam Search, $\gamma = 1$	0.288
	Beam Search, $\gamma = 2$	0.288
	Nucleus, p = 0.95	0.319
	NeuroLogic A*, $\lambda = 0$	0.290
	NeuroLogic A*, $\lambda = 0.25$	0.289
	NeuroLogic A*, $\lambda = 0.75$	0.289
	NeuroLogic A*, $\gamma = 1$	0.289
	NeuroLogic A*, $\gamma = 2$	0.289

Fig. 2. Example code generation from GPT-2 model. The left is code generated from standard beam search decoding, the right is from the newline-penalized NeuroLogic A* with $\lambda = 0.75$

Table 4. Comparison of the average percentage of runtime and compile errors across all generated solutions from each model/decoding strategy.

Model	Decoding Method	Runtime Error %	Compile Error %
CodeT5	Beam Search, $\lambda = 0$	91.945	0.558
	Beam Search, $\lambda = 0.25$	90.912	0.342
	Beam Search, $\lambda = 0.75$	90.952	0.327
	Beam Search, $\gamma = 1$	91.637	0.787
	Beam Search, $\gamma = 2$	91.045	0.778
	Nucleus, p $= 0.95$	84.765	1.306
GPT-2	Beam Search, $\lambda=0$	83.957	0.083
	Beam Search, $\lambda = 0.25$	83.957	0.083
	Beam Search, $\lambda = 0.75$	83.957	0.083
	Beam Search, $\gamma = 1$	83.947	0.085
	Beam Search, $\gamma = 2$	83.947	0.086
	Nucleus, p $= 0.95$	85.995	0.290
	NeuroLogic A*, $\lambda = 0$	83.857	0.083
	NeuroLogic A*, $\lambda = 0.25$	84.018	0.086
	NeuroLogic A*, $\lambda = 0.75$	84.018	0.086
	NeuroLogic A*, $\gamma = 1$	82.844	0.078
	NeuroLogic A*, $\gamma = 2$	82.844	0.078

Table 3 gives a breakdown of the average CodeBLEU score obtained for each decoding approach, where the average was taken amongst the highest scoring generation for each problem in the test set. The scores were obtained utilizing all provided human written sample solutions for each problem as references. As expected, the GPT-2 model scores higher across the board compared to each equivalent decoding approach from the CodeT5 model. In addition, we see that within each model's respective group, the generated solutions from nucleus sampling score the highest. This suggests that the diversity due to randomness assumptions often used to justify such a sampling technique for natural language generation may prove to be equally justifiable in the context of programming language.

Figure 2 shows two example GPT-2 model generations for a particular problem. The left is a generation using standard beam search which passes 0 test cases, while the right is generated using the newline penalized NeuroLogic A* strategy with $\lambda = 0.75$, which passes 5 test cases. As we can see from the highlighted portions of the code, the standard beam search generation includes unnecessary and redundant code with the creation of a "_starting_point" function, which in turn simply calls the main function of the program. The NeuroLogic A* generation instead calls the main function directly, choosing to bypass the creation of unnecessary functions such as this.

7   Error Analysis

In Table 4, we observe the percentage of runtime and compile errors in all code generations outputted by each of our models/decoding methods. As we can see, across all models and methods, the vast majority of programs generated result in an error at runtime, while very few solutions contain errors prior to runtime. Intuitively, this shows that although our models have great difficulty generating a functionally correct program, they have very little trouble generating code which is structurally/syntactically sound.

Comparing results across each decoding method, we see that nucleus sampling when applied to our CodeT5 and GPT-2 models has a noticeably higher percentage of compile errors compared to the beam search based approaches. This occurrence is not surprising due to the randomness inherent in nucleus sampling. Such randomness can lead to sub-optimal token choices during sequence generations, leading to possible syntax errors.

An interesting pattern found in the loop-penalized beam search experiments for the CodeT5 model is a drastic increase in the number of newlines generated compared to other approaches. Examining the generated solutions, we find that a large number of programs are appended with continuous newline tokens, only to be stopped due to maximum length constraints. This could be due to the model's inability to find high probability solutions when penalties are assigned to looping operators, however further research would need to be conducted to analyze this further.

8   Conclusion

We introduced variants to both traditional (beam search) and advanced (NeuroLogic A*) decoding strategies which attempt to optimize the conciseness and efficiency of model generated programs. Our results have shown that incorporating additional penalization terms for program elements such as newlines and looping operators can yield new sequence variations which perform on par or better than their non-penalized counterparts. Our experiments have also given new insights into the strengths and weaknesses of sampling and non-sampling based decoding algorithms with regards to properties such as programming errors and semantic/syntactic overlap with human generated programs. One of the most apparent conclusions drawn from our experiments is the value in including randomness from techniques such as nucleus sampling, not only to produce more human-like generations, but generations which are functionally correct as well.

Future work can greatly expand upon the results gathered here by evaluating a larger degree of data outside the small test set utilized in this paper. In addition, it would be interesting to see how the different decoding approaches illustrated here would affect the performance of state of the art models such as Codex and AlphaCode.

The code repository for the implementation of this research can be found at: github.com/brendankon/NLP_Gen_Sum_Project.

References

1. Chen, M., et al.: Evaluating large language models trained on code. arXiv:2107.03374 (2021)
2. Li, Y., et al.: Competition-level code generation with AlphaCode. arXiv:2203.07814 (2022)
3. Holtzman, A., Buys, J., Du, L., Forbes, M., Choi, Y.: The curious case of neural text degeneration. arXiv:1904.09751 (2020)
4. Fan, A., Lewis, M., Dauphin, Y.: Hierarchical neural story generation. arXiv:1805.04833 (2018)
5. Wang, Y., Wang, W., Joty, S., Hoi, S.C.H.: Code T5: identifier-aware unified pre-trained encoder-decoder models for code understanding and generation. arXiv preprint arXiv:2109.00859 (2021)
6. Hendrycks, D., et al.: Measuring coding challenge competence with apps. arXiv preprint arXiv:2105.09938 (2021)
7. Ren, S., et al.: CodeBLEU: a method for automatic evaluation of code synthesis. arXiv:2009.10297 (2020)
8. Papineni, K., Roukos, S., Ward, T., Zhu, W.: Bleu: a method for automatic evaluation of machine translation. In: ACL (2002)
9. Lu, X., et al.: NeuroLogic A*esque decoding: constrained text generation with lookahead heuristics. arXiv:2112.08726 (2021)
10. Lu, X., West, P., Zellers, R., Le Bras, R., Bhagavatula, C., Choi, Y.: NeuroLogic decoding: (un)supervised neural text generation with predicate logic constraints. arXiv:2010.12884 (2021)

SP-BERT: A Language Model for Political Text in Scandinavian Languages

Tu My Doan[✉][iD], Benjamin Kille[iD], and Jon Atle Gulla[iD]

Norwegian University of Science and Technology, Trondheim, Norway
{tu.m.doan,benjamin.u.kille,jon.atle.gulla}@ntnu.no

Abstract. Language models are at the core of modern Natural Language Processing. We present a new BERT-style language model dedicated to political texts in Scandinavian languages. Concretely, we introduce SP-BERT, a model trained with parliamentary speeches in Norwegian, Swedish, Danish, and Icelandic. To show its utility, we evaluate its ability to predict the speakers' party affiliation and explore language shifts of politicians transitioning between Cabinet and Opposition.

Keywords: SP-BERT · Scandinavian LM · Political Text Mining

1 Introduction

Political texts are pervasive. They are available in many forms from political manifestos, over political speeches, and debates, to news articles. They constitute an important resource for social and political study. Analysing political texts raises challenges when dealing with large amounts of data. The complexity of political languages and their nuances make the task even more challenging, especially for those lacking political background. Political domain is also known to be complex, and hard to analyze. This holds also for Norwegian politics. The use of language, both written and spoken, plays a crucial role in shaping political discourse and decision-making.

Large Language Models (LLMs) are proven to be powerful tools in the field of Natural Language Processing (NLP). Pre-trained LLMs capture the language's complexity and represent texts. However, LM resources are rare for Norwegian politics. To fill in the gap, we introduce SP-BERT—a pre-trained BERT LM for Scandinavian Politics in four languages: Norwegian, Swedish, Danish and Icelandic. As a use case, we use SP-BERT to identify the shifts in Norwegian politics by learning text representation. We also analyse the changes in word choices by politicians when they switch positions (Opposition vs. Cabinet). We aim to gain a deeper understanding of the current state of Norwegian politics through linguistic strategies used by politicians and political parties. Furthermore, language models' ability to efficiently process vast amounts of data enables faster analysis for political domain than traditional methods. We define two research questions:

© The Author(s), under exclusive license to Springer Nature Switzerland AG 2023
E. Métais et al. (Eds.): NLDB 2023, LNCS 13913, pp. 467–477, 2023.
https://doi.org/10.1007/978-3-031-35320-8_34

- Does the LM trained exclusively on political text outperform the multilingual BERT and/or language-specific BERT model on the task of classifying Norwegian and Swedish political text? (RQ_1)
- Does being in government/opposition change how politicians express their views in Norwegian politics? In which way? (RQ_2).

The rest of the paper is structured as follow: Sect. 2 conveys related work for LM in Politics, and political analysis. Details about SP-BERT model are described in Sect. 3. Section 4 discusses shifts in Norwegian political speeches. Section 5 concludes the paper with suggestions for future research.

2   Related Work

This section presents related work concerning language models for politics and analyzing political texts.

2.1   Language Models for Politics

Since its introduction, BERT [4] has been used for various tasks in NLP. Especially for English, BERT achieves state-of-the-art results. Working with languages other than English represents a challenge. Researchers either rely on multilingual models, such as mBERT [4], or gather data and pre-train a model dedicated to their target language. Training is both costly and time-consuming. In Northern Europe, we find NB-BERT [11] and NorBERT [12] for Norwegian, and models for Swedish [17], Danish [9], Finish [23], and Icelandic [20]. To capture as much of the language as possible, researchers tend to include as much text as possible. This leads to generic models. In contrast, for English we observe more specialized models. Liu et al. [15] trained a language model for political texts that focuses on ideology and stance detection. Hu et al. [8] presented ConfliBERT dedicated to deal with texts concerning political conflict and violence. To the best of our knowledge, there is not yet a model that deals with politics for smaller-scale language such as the language family in Northern Europe.

2.2   Political Analysis

Political Science relies on analysing texts. Abercrombie and Batista-Navarro [1] study the semantic changes in UK Parliamentary Debates. Chen et al. [3] focus on analysing the political bias and unfairness of news articles at different levels in the US. Maronikolakis et al. [18] analyse the political parody in social media for US, UK, and the rest of the world. Walter et al. [24] analyse the ideological bias for German parliamentary proceedings. Magnusson et al. [16] analyse the Swedish parliamentary debates.

The numerous examples of text analyses for Political Science demonstrates the need for tools to process more texts. Hence, we build a large pre-trained language model specifically for political texts to support political research. Shared culture and language in Northern Europe let us assume that the model will provide a benefit to all political scientists in that region.

3   SP-BERT Language Model

We introduce SP-BERT, a pre-trained language model for political text in Norway, Sweden, Denmark, and Iceland. The section describes the data sources, pre-processing, the training procedure, and an evaluation set up.

3.1   Corpora

We focus on data sources for Norwegian, Swedish, Danish, and Icelandic that relate to politics. Parliamentary speeches fulfil that requirement.

Norwegian Datasets: We obtain parliamentary speeches from three sources:

- The Talk of Norway (ToN) [13]: a rich annotated dataset containing 250 373 speeches from the Norwegian Parliament in the period from 1998 to 2016.
- Norwegian Parliamentary Speech Corpus (NPSC) [21]: a speech dataset with recordings from Norwegian Parliamentary meetings from 2017 to 2018. The dataset has 64 531 sentences from about 9722 speeches.
- Due to low number of speeches in Norwegian Parliamentary, we decided to crawl more data from the Norwegian Parliamentary website using their API[1]. We have collected data from 01 Jan 2019 up to end of February 2023. As a result, we obtained 3158 additional speeches.

Swedish Dataset: Data come from the ParlSpeech(V2) dataset [19]—a full-text corpora of 6.3M parliamentary speeches from nine European countries. Data were collected from 2 October 1990 to 21 December 2018. The corpus contains 355 059 speeches. In addition, we obtained more recent data from the Swedish Parliament website[2].

Danish Dataset: The Danish parliamentary speeches also come from the same source as the Swedish [19]. This corpus contains 455 076 Danish speeches from 7 October 1997 to 20 December 2018.

Icelandic Dataset: We use data coming from the IGC-Parl corpus [22]. There are 388 650 speeches in the time span from 1911 to 2020.

3.2   Data Pre-processing

We pre-processed the texts collected from all sources. Typically, speeches start off with a short reference to the parliament's president. We employed a set of regular expression to remove those. Further, we eliminated redundant white spaces and removed markup. We removed speeches with less than 60 tokens as these were frequently questions or answers and not speeches. As a result, we obtained a data set of about 1.44 million speeches. They split into 16 % Norwegian, 32 % Danish, 25 % Swedish, and 27 % Icelandic. We took part of the data to form two evaluation sets (see Table 1), and kept the rest for training.

---

[1] https://data.stortinget.no/om-datatjenesten/bruksvilkar/.
[2] https://data.riksdagen.se/data/anforanden/.

Table 1. Evaluation datasets summary. The numerical values represent the labels we use in fine-tuning classifiers. For Task 1, we labelled data based on political leaning of the party. In Task 2, data was labelled based on political party.

Task 1: Political Leaning Classification				
Label (Political Leaning)	# items	Label (Political Leaning)		# items
0: Left	1300	0: Left		18 802
1: Right	1471	1: Right		18 308
Sum	2771	Sum		37 110
Task 2: Party Affiliation Classification				
Label (Party Name)	# items	Label (Party Name)		# items
0: Right	539	0: Moderate Rally		6418
1: Left	256	1: Sweden's Social Democratic Labor		11 897
2: Labor	604	2: The Christian Democrats		2981
3: Center	334	3: Left		3296
4: Progress	473	4: Green		3504
5: Christian People's	203	5: Liberals		2053
6: Socialist Left	362	6: Center		2601
		7: Sweden Democrats		4360
Sum	2771	Sum		37 110

3.3   Experimental Setup

Pre-training Setup. To train SP-BERT[3], we follow the approach by original BERT paper [4]. Since removing Next Sentence Prediction (NSP) loss helps improve the performance in downstream tasks [14], we only keep the Masked Language Model (MLM) training objective. The architecture of mBERT model [4] is similar to the original BERT. It has 12 layers, 12 attention heads, and 768 hidden dimensions. As we want to build a pre-trained LM for multi-languages, mBERT serves as a good starting point[4]. This model has already been trained on more than 100 languages including Norwegian (Bokmål and Nynorsk), Swedish, Danish, and Icelandic. We first train the model for 1M steps on batch size 128, sequence length 256, learning rate 1×10^{-4}, with Adam optimizer [10] on NVIDIA A100 80 GB GPUs. Later, we change the sequence length to 512, batch size 64 and continue the training for another 0.5M steps to learn better context.

Fine-Tuning Setup. To find the best hyper-parameters for each task, we experiment with batch size of 64, learning rate $\in \{5e-5, 4e-5, 3e-5\}$, sequence length of 512 for max 10 epochs. To evaluate the performance, we use *Accuracy* and F_1 score. Besides doing full fine-tuning the classifier, we also explore using class weight[5] when dealing with imbalanced dataset following the work done in [5].

---

[3] https://huggingface.co/tumd/sp-bert.
[4] https://huggingface.co/bert-base-multilingual-cased.
[5] https://scikit-learn.org/stable/modules/generated/sklearn.utils.class_weight.
  compute_class_weight.html.

3.4   Evaluation

We are interested in the performance for politics-specific tasks. Consequently, we define two evaluation tasks to assess the model's performance. There is no public data set for this purpose which is why we created two datasets. One of them is in Norwegian while the other is in Swedish. We fine-tune a classifier for political text. Table 1 shows the distribution of speeches.

- **Task 1 (Binary Classification)** The task concerns classifying the speech's political leaning. We matched the parties to either left or right following discussions with experts.
- **Task 2 (Multi-label Classification)** We define a multi-class problem in predicting the speaker's party affiliation. We omit parties that have very few items in each language (see Table 1).

3.5   Results and Discussions

Table 2 shows results on both binary and multi-label task. The left column shows the model. We consider three models for each language. First, the multilingual BERT model serves as a baseline. Second, we use a language-specific BERT model. Third, we present our proposed model. Besides, we illustrate a fine-tuned version of each model which puts more weights on the minority classes. For the binary classification, we present the accuracy for each model. SP-BERT achieves the best accuracy for Norwegian. The Swedish BERT model performs slightly better for Swedish.

Concerning the multi-class problem, we show the accuracy, macro F_1 score, as well as the accuracy for the best and worst class. For Norwegian, we observe a similar picture. SP-BERT performs best. The Swedish BERT model performs somewhat better for Swedish. Looking at the column with the worst class-specific score, we notice that the weighting improves the performance. Either the score for the class improves or a different class becomes the worst performing.

In our analysis, we follow the work in [6] who define a method to compare two binary classifiers. Suppose, we compare two binary classifiers A and B. Both supply a set of predictions for L given texts $\{\hat{y}_A\}_{\alpha=1}^L$ and $\{\hat{y}_B\}_{\alpha=1}^L$. We distinguish three cases: $\hat{y}_A = \hat{y}_B$ indicating that both classifiers agree; $\hat{y}_A = y, \hat{y}_B \neq y$ indicating that classifier A predicts correctly whereas B fails; $\hat{y}_A \neq y, \hat{y}_B = y$ indicating that classifier A fails whereas B predicts correctly. Goutte and Gaussier [6] show that having counted the number of instances for the three cases, we can approximate the distributions with a Dirichlet:

$$\Pr(\pi|Z, \alpha) \sim \text{Dirichlet}(N_1 + \alpha_1, N_2 + \alpha_2, N_3 + \alpha_3), \tag{1}$$

where π refers to the probability of each case, Z refers to the counts (N_1, N_2, N_3), and α captures the prior information. In our evaluation, we consider $\alpha = \frac{1}{2}$. We employ Markov Chain Monte Carlo (MCMC) with NUTS [7] and four chains to generate 100 000 samples from the posterior distributions in each comparison.

Table 2. Results of the sequence classification for Task 1 and 2. We report the Accuracy for both tasks, and the best and worst class performance with F_{1macro} for Task 2. The values are highlighted with gradient colors with incremental intensity from low to high. Best values in the group have more intense color.

Model	Task 1	Task 2			
	Acc	Acc	(best)	(worst)	F_{1macro}
Norwegian					
bert-base-multilingual-cased [a]	0.627	0.360	0.515 (3)	0.208 (5)	0.358
nb-bert-base [b]	0.643	0.450	0.603 (3)	0.250 (5)	0.449
sp-bert-base (ours)	0.636	0.465	0.620 (4)	0.268 (2)	0.457
weight-bert-base-multilingual-cased	0.571	0.409	0.598 (4)	0.308 (6)	0.410
weight-nb-bert-base	0.602	0.418	0.542 (5)	0.283 (2)	0.426
weight-sp-bert-base (ours)	0.638	0.470	0.641 (4)	0.286 (1)	0.465
Swedish					
bert-base-multilingual-cased [a]	0.822	0.651	0.825 (1)	0.440 (5)	0.593
bert-base-swedish-cased [c]	0.877	0.692	0.856 (1)	0.370 (6)	0.625
sp-bert-base (ours)	0.871	0.681	0.858 (1)	0.399 (6)	0.626
weight-bert-base-multilingual-cased	0.855	0.603	0.716 (1)	0.400 (6)	0.554
weight-bert-base-swedish-cased	0.882	0.664	0.728 (1)	0.516 (2)	0.630
weight-sp-bert-base (ours)	0.878	0.663	0.757 (3)	0.465 (6)	0.619

[a] https://github.com/google-research/bert
[b] https://github.com/NBAiLab/notram
[c] https://huggingface.co/KB/bert-base-swedish-cased

Figure 1 shows the posterior distributions for two comparisons (more comparisons omitted due to space limitations). Each plot presents two densities. The densities express the probability that one language model performs better than the other.

4   Identifying Shifts in Norwegian Politics

We investigate the shifts in the position of politicians and parties.

4.1   Politicians' Position Shifts with SP-BERT Representations

First, we take the ToN data[6] and check whether Principal Component Analysis (PCA) projects speeches into discernible sub-spaces. Concretely, we take speeches of politicians about the same topic if they gave them both as member

---

[6] Due to space limitation, we omit the detailed pre-processing steps.

of the government and opposition. Subsequently, we apply PCA to their embeddings obtained with SP-BERT model. Specifically, we fine-tuned SP-BERT on classifying party position (Opposition/Cabinet) to help model learn about the party position differences, thus, improve visualization of obtained embeddings.

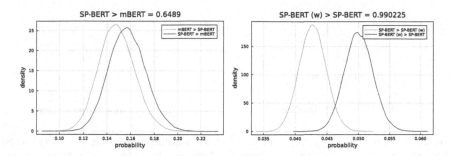

Fig. 1. Exemplary comparison of SP-BERT versus mBERT (Norwegian), and weighted SP-BERT versus SP-BERT (Swedish).

To capture the changes in political position, we filter a list of politicians with fairly balanced number of their given speeches for specific topics per party. First, we visualize the embeddings with PCA and then use k-means clustering to verify whether the text representations and the clusters are aligned.

We analyze seven political parties and a number of politicians. We learn that not all cases, there are significant shifts in the way politicians speak when they change their political position. Fortunately, some cases show distinctions quite well. We only show here some plots that we think are interesting (see Fig. 2). The PCA projects all speeches onto two dimensions. Both plots show a noticeable grouping between speeches of Cabinet or Opposition. The k-means clustering confirms the insight from PCA with few exceptions.

4.2 Parties' Position Shifts in Word Choices with POS Tagging

To understand politicians' word choices better when they change political roles, we utilize a part-of-speech (POS) tagger. We lemmatize nouns, verbs, and adjectives with SpaCy[7]. We focus on words of more than four characters to remove less expressive terms. We compute the frequencies with which politicians use these words and distinguish between cabinet and opposition. We obtain two values between 0.0 and 1.0 for each term. We plot these values onto a two-dimensional scatter plot labelled with the term. With a log-scale, we avoid cluttering. The diagonal line expresses that both usages are equal. In other words, the politicians use the term as often in cabinet speeches as in opposition speeches. On the other hand, terms that are far from the line are either used predominantly

---

[7] https://spacy.io.

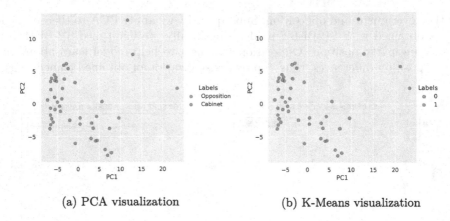

(a) PCA visualization   (b) K-Means visualization

Fig. 2. Visualization of speeches given by Anders Anundsen (Progress Party) about Ministries. In (a), we notice two clusters produces by the PCA. In (b), K-Means confirms with clustering with a few mis-classified speeches at the intersection of both clusters.

in cabinet (lower) or opposition (upper). Figure 3 shows two examples of politicians' word choices when changing roles. Figure 3a illustrates the usage of nouns by members of the Center Party. The colour shows the output of a sentiment lexicon [2]. The plot shows the 30 most frequently used nouns. We omit the plots for the remaining parties and verbs, and adjectives due to space limitations. We observe that terms related to infrastructure are more commonly used in cabinet speeches. Terms related to health-care such as Hospital (sykehus) appear more often in opposition speeches.

We also compare the usage of nouns related to health for all parties. Figure 3b uses the same display but shows all parties for a selection of health-related terms. Parties are colour-coded. The terms are in Norwegian. Due to space restrictions, we omit the plots for other topics such as transport, or education. We can clearly see that some parties cover health-care more when they are in government whereas others cover it in opposition. For instance, the Labour Party (Arbeiderpartiet, AP) covers health topics predominantly in government. Conversely, the Center party (Senterpartiet, S) talks more about it in opposition.

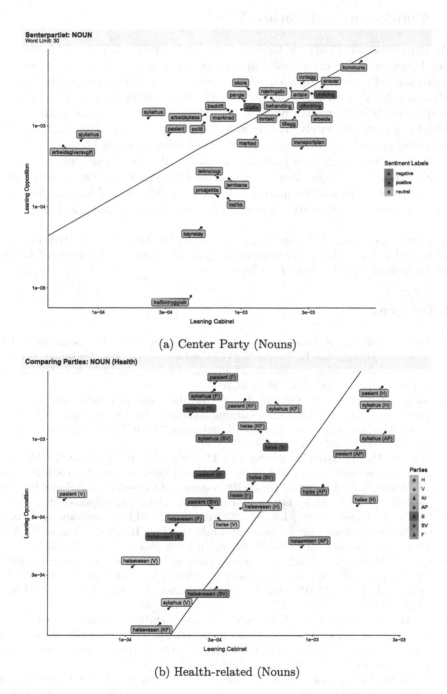

(a) Center Party (Nouns)

(b) Health-related (Nouns)

Fig. 3. Plots depicting the word usage by Norwegian parliamentarians in cabinet and opposition.

5   Conclusion and Future Work

We introduced SP-BERT, a language model for political texts in Scandinavian languages. The model will support political and social research in that researchers will be able to adequately represent texts and process them more automatically. Our investigation finds clear differences in the use of nouns concerning health in Norwegian politics. Results show that the model helps classifying texts more accurately. This is just one exemplary case that highlights the use of automated text processing for political sciences using language models. Language-specific model can perform similarly well or better in some instances.

We will add language models pre-trained for politics that can generate and transform texts. We want to apply SP-BERT to additional problems in the scope of politics, such as automatic viewpoints identification and sentiment analysis.

Acknowledgements. This work is done as part of the Trondheim Analytica project and funded under Digital Transformation program at Norwegian University of Science and Technology (NTNU), 7034 Trondheim, Norway.

References

1. Abercrombie, G., Batista-Navarro, R.: Semantic change in the language of UK parliamentary debates. In: Proceedings of the 1st International Workshop on Computational Approaches to Historical Language Change, pp. 210–215. ACL (2019). https://doi.org/10.18653/v1/W19-4726
2. Barnes, J., Touileb, S., Øvrelid, L., Velldal, E.: Lexicon information in neural sentiment analysis: a multi-task learning approach. In: Proceedings of the 22nd Nordic Conference on Computational Linguistics, Turku, Finland (2019). https://www.aclweb.org/anthology/W19-6119/
3. Chen, W.F., Al Khatib, K., Wachsmuth, H., Stein, B.: Analyzing political bias and unfairness in news articles at different levels of granularity. In: Proceedings of the 4th Workshop on Natural Language Processing and Computational Social Science, pp. 149–154. ACL (2020). https://doi.org/10.18653/v1/2020.nlpcss-1.16
4. Devlin, J., Chang, M.W., Lee, K., Toutanova, K.: BERT: pre-training of deep bidirectional transformers for language understanding. In: Proceedings of NAACL 2019, pp. 4171–4186. ACL (2019). https://doi.org/10.18653/v1/N19-1423
5. Doan, T.M., Kille, B., Gulla, J.A.: Using language models for classifying the party affiliation of political texts. In: Rosso, P., Basile, V., Martínez, R., Métais, E., Meziane, F. (eds.) NLDB 2022. LNCS, vol. 13286, pp. 382–393. Springer, Cham (2022). https://doi.org/10.1007/978-3-031-08473-7_35
6. Goutte, C., Gaussier, E.: A probabilistic interpretation of precision, recall and F-score, with implication for evaluation. In: Losada, D.E., Fernández-Luna, J.M. (eds.) ECIR 2005. LNCS, vol. 3408, pp. 345–359. Springer, Heidelberg (2005). https://doi.org/10.1007/978-3-540-31865-1_25
7. Hoffman, M.D., Gelman, A., et al.: The no-U-turn sampler: adaptively setting path lengths in Hamiltonian Monte Carlo. J. Mach. Learn. Res. **15**(1), 1593–1623 (2014)
8. Hu, Y., et al.: ConfliBERT: a pre-trained language model for political conflict and violence. In: Proceedings of NAACL 2022, pp. 5469–5482. ACL (2022). https://doi.org/10.18653/v1/2022.naacl-main.400

9. Hvingelby, R., Pauli, A.B., Barrett, M., Rosted, C., Lidegaard, L.M., Søgaard, A.: DaNE: a named entity resource for Danish. In: Proceedings of the 12th Language Resources and Evaluation Conference, pp. 4597–4604 (2020)

10. Kingma, D.P., Ba, J.: Adam: a method for stochastic optimization. arXiv preprint arXiv:1412.6980 (2014)

11. Kummervold, P.E., De la Rosa, J., Wetjen, F., Brygfjeld, S.A.: Operationalizing a national digital library: the case for a Norwegian transformer model. In: Proceedings of NoDaLiDa 2021, pp. 20–29 (2021)

12. Kutuzov, A., Barnes, J., Velldal, E., Øvrelid, L., Oepen, S.: Large-scale contextualised language modelling for Norwegian. In: Proceedings of NoDaLiDa 2021, pp. 30–40. Linköping University Electronic Press, Sweden, Reykjavik, Iceland (2021)

13. Lapponi, E., Søyland, M.G., Velldal, E., Oepen, S.: The talk of Norway: a richly annotated corpus of the Norwegian parliament, 1998–2016. Lang. Resour. Eval. **52**(3), 873–893 (2018). https://doi.org/10.1007/s10579-018-9411-5

14. Liu, Y., et al.: RoBERTa: a robustly optimized BERT pretraining approach. arXiv preprint arXiv:1907.11692 (2019)

15. Liu, Y., Zhang, X.F., Wegsman, D., Beauchamp, N., Wang, L.: POLITICS: pretraining with same-story article comparison for ideology prediction and stance detection. In: Findings of the Association for Computational Linguistics: NAACL 2022, pp. 1354–1374. ACL (2022). https://doi.org/10.18653/v1/2022.findings-naacl.101

16. Magnusson, M., Öhrvall, R., Barrling, K., Mimno, D.: Voices from the far right: a text analysis of Swedish parliamentary debates (2018)

17. Malmsten, M., Börjeson, L., Haffenden, C.: Playing with words at the national library of Sweden - making a Swedish BERT. CoRR abs/2007.01658 (2020)

18. Maronikolakis, A., Sánchez Villegas, D., Preotiuc-Pietro, D., Aletras, N.: Analyzing political parody in social media. In: Proceedings of the 58th Annual Meeting of the Association for Computational Linguistics, pp. 4373–4384. ACL (2020). https://doi.org/10.18653/v1/2020.acl-main.403

19. Rauh, C., Schwalbach, J.: The ParlSpeech V2 data set: full-text corpora of 6.3 million parliamentary speeches in the key legislative chambers of nine representative democracies (2020). https://doi.org/10.7910/DVN/L4OAKN

20. Snæbjarnarson, V., et al.: A warm start and a clean crawled corpus — a recipe for good language models. In: Proceedings of the 13rd Language Resources and Evaluation Conference, pp. 4356–4366. European Language Resources Association, Marseille (2022)

21. Solberg, P.E., Ortiz, P.: The Norwegian parliamentary speech corpus. arXiv preprint arXiv:2201.10881 (2022)

22. Steingrímsson, S., Barkarson, S., Örnólfsson, G.T.: IGC-Parl: icelandic corpus of parliamentary proceedings. In: Proceedings of the Second ParlaCLARIN Workshop, pp. 11–17. European Language Resources Association (2020). ISBN 979-10-95546-47-4

23. Virtanen, A., et al.: Multilingual is not enough: BERT for Finnish. arXiv preprint arXiv:1912.07076 (2019)

24. Walter, T., Kirschner, C., Eger, S., Glavaš, G., Lauscher, A., Ponzetto, S.P.: Diachronic analysis of German parliamentary proceedings: ideological shifts through the lens of political biases. In: 2021 ACM/IEEE Joint Conference on Digital Libraries (JCDL), pp. 51–60 (2021). https://doi.org/10.1109/JCDL52503.2021.00017

Improving Context-Awareness on Multi-Turn Dialogue Modeling with Extractive Summarization Techniques

Yujie Xing$^{(\boxtimes)}$ and Jon Atle Gulla

Norwegian University of Science and Technology, Trondheim, Norway
{yujie.xing,jon.atle.gulla}@ntnu.no

Abstract. The study of context-awareness in multi-turn generation-based dialogue modeling is an important but relatively underexplored topic. Prior research has employed hierarchical structures to enhance the context-awareness of dialogue models. This paper aims to address this issue by utilizing two extractive summarization techniques, namely the PMI topic model and the ORACLE algorithm, to filter out unimportant utterances within a given context. Our proposed approach is assessed on both non-hierarchical and hierarchical models using the *distracting test*, which evaluates the level of attention given to each utterance. Our proposed methods gain significant improvement over the baselines in the distracting test.

Keywords: Multi-Turn Response Generation · Conversational Agent · Summarization

1 Introduction

Although generation-based dialogue models have achieved much progress in recent years, multi-turn dialogue models are still facing challenges. Recent works deal with multi-turn using modified attention mechanisms and hierarchical structures. One focus of dealing with multi-turn is the ability of context-awareness on a dialogue model, which requires a model to pay more attention to important utterances while less attention to unimportant ones. An example of important/unimportant utterances is given by Table 1.

ⓒ The Author(s), under exclusive license to Springer Nature Switzerland AG 2023
E. Métais et al. (Eds.): NLDB 2023, LNCS 13913, pp. 478–488, 2023.
https://doi.org/10.1007/978-3-031-35320-8_35

Table 1. An example of important utterances and unimportant utterances under the same context in the Ubuntu chatlog dataset [9]. Unimportant utterances are marked in red.

User	Utterances
Taru	Haha sucker.
Kuja	?
Taru	Anyways, you made the changes right?
Kuja	Yes.
Taru	Then from the terminal type: sudo apt-get update
Kuja	I did

In Table 1, the first two utterances ("Haha sucker." and "?") are unimportant utterances that are irrelevant to the main topic of the context. A multi-turn dialogue model with good ability on context awareness should identify and ignore these unimportant utterances and focus only on the important ones. Thus, we propose that one way to improve the context awareness of a model is to **filter out** the unimportant utterances, which is a task similar to summarization: given a reference and a source, an extractive summarization algorithm extracts all utterances related to the reference and eliminate all others in the source. In the case of dialogue models, we do not have a reference for the context; nevertheless, the last utterance in the context, i.e., the *query*, plays a crucial role in generating the response. In most cases, responses aim to provide answers to the *query* while utilizing other utterances in the context as the source for answering. We denote all utterances in a context except for the last one as *source*. This paper investigates improving context awareness for multi-turn dialogue models by filtering out unimportant utterances from the *source* using extractive summarization techniques with the *query* as the reference.

There are a few works that combine summarization with dialogue models. One of the techniques used in these works is the topic model, where a keyword is predicted from the *query* and the entire corpus to help a model generate detailed responses. In our paper, we also use a PMI topic model to extract keywords from the context, while instead of using the keywords to support the generation task, we pass the keywords directly to the dialogue model. Additionally, we explore the ORACLE algorithm, a widely-used algorithm for generating gold labels for extractive summarization, to filter out utterances unrelated to *query* before passing them to the dialogue model.

For evaluation, we use an evaluation method tailored for multi-turn dialogue models. Since most multi-turn dialogue models have attention mechanisms and they rely on the mechanism to assign different extents of focus to each utterance in the context, we use the **distracting test** to measure if a model pays more attention to the important utterances and less to the unimportant ones. The test simply adds distracting utterances to each dialogue and compares the attention scores on these distracting (unimportant) utterances with the original (important) utterances in the *source*, thus measures the ability of context awareness for a dialogue model.

This paper is organized as follows. In Sect. 2, we introduce related works. In Sect. 3 and Sect. 4, we introduce the model to be examined, the summarization techniques to be integrated, and the evaluation metrics. In Sect. 5, we describe our experiment settings, and we report the results in Sect. 6.

2   Related Work

Previous works try to improve context-awareness on dialogue modeling through the hierarchical structure. [13,14] first introduce the hierarchical structure to dialogue models. [17] evaluate different methods of integrating context utterances in hierarchical structures, and [21] further evaluate the effectiveness of static and dynamic attention mechanism. In our paper, we examine our context-summarization module with both different methods of integrating context utterances and two kinds of attention mechanisms.

A similar direction of combining summarization and multi-turn dialogue modeling is the integration of topic models, though current works in this direction are all on single-turn dialogues. [6] uses a classifier to select the keyword for a given query from a pre-generated keyword list. [10,20] use PMI to choose a keyword for given query from a big corpus. Similarly, [2,18] uses a topic model to predict the keyword out from vocabulary words. In our paper, we also examine if a topic model can improve the context-awareness of dialogue models.

As mentioned in [19], a typical way to construct labeled data for extractive summarization is to set ROUGE. Most works including [5] construct gold label sequences by greedily optimizing ROUGE-1, which is the algorithm ORACLE. Further, although in this paper we stick to extractive summarization due to lack of suitable conversational datasets for abstractive summarization, we expect the very soon coming of this kind of dataset from [3].

3   Models to be Examined

We use an LSTM Seq2Seq model with attention [1,4,16] as the base model, since it is a common model for conversational systems [7,12].

The basic task of conversational agents is to predict the next word given all the past and current words of the context and response, and to make the generated response as similar to the original response as possible. Formally, the task can be described as follows. Probability of response Y given context X is predicted as:

$$P(Y|X) = \prod_{t=1}^{n} p(y_t|y_1, \ldots, y_{t-1}, X), \tag{1}$$

where $X = x_1, \ldots, x_m$ and $Y = y_1, \ldots, y_n$ are a context-response pair.

3.1   LSTM Seq2Seq Model with Attention

We simplify an LSTM structure with attention mechanism as $LSTM^*$ since it is well introduced in previous work [7]. We calculate the hidden vector h_t at step t as:

$$h_t = LSTM^*(h_{t-1}, c_t, E(z_t)), \qquad (2)$$

where $h_{t-1} \in \mathbb{R}^{dim}$ is the hidden vector at step $t - 1$, dim is the dimension of hidden vectors, and $E(z_t)$ is the word embedding for token $z_t \in \{x_1, ..., x_m, y_1, ..., y_{n-1}\}$. The context vector c_t is inputted only to the decoder at step t.

3.2   Attention Mechanism and Utterance Integration

We examine both hierarchical and non-hierarchical structures. For hierarchical structures, following [21], we examine two attention mechanisms, namely static and dynamic attention mechanisms. Following [17], we examine hierarchical models with or without utterance integration LSTM units.

For the non-hierarchical structured model, there are no utterance vectors. Hidden vectors of all words in the encoder are concatenated and used in the attention mechanism. Denoting the concatenated vector as $\mathcal{H}$ ($\mathcal{H} = [h_1, h_2, ..., h_m]$), we calculate the context vector c_t for each decoder step as

$$c_t = \mathcal{H} \cdot (softmax(\mathcal{H}^\top \cdot h_{t-1})) . \qquad (3)$$

For the hierarchically structured models, we denote the last utterance of the context as the *query*, and the other utterances as the *source*. At each step where an utterance ends, we collect the hidden vector of its last word as the hidden vector of the utterance, thus compared to the non-hierarchical structured model, we have much fewer hidden vectors from the encoder. Denoting the hidden vector of kth utterance as H_k, the hidden vector of the *query* as H_q, and the concatenated vector of the *source* and the *query* as $\mathcal{H}_c$ ($\mathcal{H}_c = [H_1, H_2, ..., H_q]$), we calculate the context vector c_t for static attention mechanism as

$$c_t = \mathcal{H}_c \cdot (softmax(\mathcal{H}_c^\top \cdot H_q)) \qquad (4)$$

where it is easy to see that static attention does not change during steps in the decoder. And we calculate c_t for dynamic attention mechanism as

$$c_t = \mathcal{H}_c \cdot (softmax(\mathcal{H}_c^\top \cdot h_{t-1})) . \qquad (5)$$

In the decoder, c_t is input to the next step t, and each token's hidden vector h_{t-1} is combined with c_t to predict the next token.

Finally, with the utterance integration LSTM unit, the hidden vector to be put into the first step of the decoder is different from the regular h_m; instead, the vector is calculated by integrating $H_1, H_2, ... H_q$ through a separate LSTM unit.

4 Proposed Methods

4.1 PMI-Context

The method PMI-context uses a Pointwise Mutual Information (PMI) to select the k most relevant words in a *source* given a *query*. Given a word x_c in a *source*, the total PMI of x_c given a *query* $= x_{q1}, ..., x_{ql}$ is calculated following [20]:

$$\mathrm{PMI}(x_{q1}, ..., x_{ql}, x_c) \approx \sum_i^l \mathrm{PMI}(x_{qi}, x_c) . \tag{6}$$

The selected k keywords $x_{c1}, ..., x_{ck}$ and the *query* are combined through the static attention mechanism described in Eq. (4) to calculate the context vector c_t. Note that here a *query* does not attend to itself, but only to the selected keywords. The context vector c_t, the selected k keywords, and the *query* are then inputted into the LSTM unit as described in the following adapted version of Eq. (2):

$$h_t = LSTM^*(h_{t-1}, c_t, E(z_t')) , \tag{7}$$

where $z_t' \in \{x_{c1}, ..., x_{ck}, x_{q1}, ..., x_{ql}, y_1, ..., y_{n-1}\}$.

4.2 ORACLE-Context

The method ORACLE-context is based on an extractive summarization algorithm named the ORACLE algorithm. It uses the ORACLE algorithm to extract relevant utterances from the *source* by greedily optimizing ROUGE-1 using the *query* as the summarization reference. The extracted k most relevant utterances are then inputted into the LSTM unit as described in the following adapted version of Eq. (2):

$$h_t = LSTM^*(h_{t-1}, c_t, E(z_t'')) , \tag{8}$$

where $z_t'' \in \{x_{c1}^1, x_{c2}^1, ..., x_{c1}^k, x_{c2}^k, ..., x_{q1}, ..., x_{ql}, y_1, ..., y_{n-1}\}$, and $X_i = x_{c1}^i, x_{c2}^i, ...$ ($i \in \{1, ..., k\}$) denotes for each of the extracted k most relevant utterances.

This method intends to filter out irrelevant utterances from the *source* given the *query* and delete the utterances from the inputs to the dialogue model, which helps the model to pay attention correctly to the important utterances.

4.3 Evaluation

Since perplexity is considered not a good measure of how good a conversation is [8], besides perplexity, we examine whether the model pays attention to the correct utterance through a simple **distracting test**.

In the distracting test, for each dialogue, we insert several distracting utterances into the dialogue. The distracting utterance can be anything that does not belong to the original dialogue. Then we compare the attention scores of the distracting utterances with the attention scores of the original utterances. A well-performing model should pay less attention to the distracting utterances but more attention to the original utterances. For an utterance H_k in the context, the score is calculated as

$$\begin{cases} \frac{\exp(H_k^\top \cdot H_q)}{\sum_k \exp(H_k^\top \cdot H_q)} & \text{Static attention} \\ \mathbf{mean}_t \left(\frac{\exp(H_k^\top \cdot h_t)}{\sum_k \exp(H_k^\top \cdot h_t)} \right) & \text{Dynamic attention} \end{cases} \tag{9}$$

To avoid bias, we weigh the attention score with the utterance amount, or the total word amount of *source* plus *query* divided by the word amount of the utterance to be examined. That gives us 100% for any utterance that is paid average attention among *source* plus *query*, i.e. $\frac{1}{k}$ attention for a total of k utterances in *source* plus *query*.

5 Experiment Setup

5.1 Dataset

We use the Ubuntu chatlogs dataset [9], which contains dialogues about solving technical problems of Ubuntu, as the training and testing corpus. We have about $0.48M$ dialogues for training, $20K$ dialogues for validation, and $10K$ dialogues for testing. These are the original settings of the Ubuntu chatlogs dataset. We removed all single-turn dialogues, since single-turns do not have contexts that we need to study on. The last utterance in the context is treated as *query*, and the other utterances are treated as *source*.

For the distracting test, we set the amount of distracting utterances for each dialogue as 2. We have 3 distracting test datasets: 1) dataset distracted with utterances containing frequent words, which are "why should I help you" and "I have my right"; 2) dataset distracted with utterances containing rare words, which are "would you have lunch?" and "I should have lunch"; 3) dataset distracted with utterances randomly picked from the training set.

5.2 Training

Our methods are built on a basic LSTM Seq2Seq model. We used Pytorch [11] for implementation. The LSTM model has 4 layers and the dimension is 512. The training procedure was with a batch size of 256, a learning rate of 1.0, and a gradient clip threshold of 5. The vocabulary size is 25000 and the dropout rate is 0.2.

5.3 Models to Be Examined

For the method PMI-context, we examine the maximum keyword amounts of both 10-word level and 30-word level. For the method ORACLE-context, we examine the maximum extracted utterance amounts of both 5-utterance level and 10-utterance level. Also, we examine ORACLE-context on 5 model variants, namely static attention with utterance integration LSTM unit, static attention without utterance integration LSTM unit, dynamic attention with utterance integration LSTM unit, and dynamic attention without utterance integration LSTM unit. Among these variants, one is non-hierarchical structured, and the other four are hierarchical structured.

6   Results

We show the perplexity and attention scores of the models to be examined. For comparison, we also show scores of non-hierarchical model trained on either the whole context (*source* and *query*) or only *query*. The results are shown in Table 2.

For the distracting test, besides the attention scores of the distracting utterances, we also show the average attention scores of the *source*. A lower score indicates that more attention is paid to the *query* instead of the *source*. In addition, we calculate the ratio between the attention scores of the distracting utterances and those of the original utterances in the *source*, to show how much attention is paid to the distracting utterances compared to the *source*. A lower ratio indicates that the model is less distracted by the distracting utterances.

Table 2 shows that the non-hierarchical model with the ORACLE-context method of 10-utterance level has the best perplexity and the lowest attention scores' ratio for the frequent and rare distracting datasets, which indicates that this model is the least distracted from frequent and rare distracting utterances. Among the four kinds of hierarchical models, the variant of static attention mechanism with utterance integration LSTM unit (Static+UttLSTM) gets the best performance on the random distracting dataset, and most of the other variants manage to exceed the non-hierarchical model on the random distracting dataset, from which we can infer that the hierarchical models are less distracted from random distracting utterances. PMI-context method of the 30-word level also gains a good perplexity, but since perplexity is not a good method for evaluating responses' quality, more evaluation is needed.

It is easy to notice that while the perplexity scores of the ORACLE-context models show marginal improvement over the baselines, they outperform the baselines in the distracting test, which is a better evaluation metric for the ability of context-awareness. To assess the efficacy of the ORACLE algorithm, we further investigated the filtered-out and extracted utterances. Results show that approximately 79%, 84%, and 82% of the distracting utterances were filtered out in each of the three distracting datasets, respectively. In contrast, the algorithm extracted a considerable portion of the first and second utterances closest to the *query*, which are typically regarded as important utterances in a *source*, and these make up 30% and 43% of the total extracted utterances, respectively. This means that the ORACLE algorithm does filter out unimportant utterances to some extent.

It is surprising to see that the models have the worst performance for the distracting dataset with rare utterances. It is obvious for humans to identify

Table 2. Perplexity (Perp), attention score of distracting utterances (Distract, %), attention score of average original utterances in the *source* (Avg., %), and their ratio (ratio). The best attention scores of distracting utterances and the best ratios are bolded.

(a) Results on the random distract testset

Method	Model	Original		Distract: random		
		Perp	Avg.	Perp	Distract (ratio)	Avg.
\	Non-hier (*query* only)	49.5	100	\		
	Non-hier	49.8	94.7	49.8	94.4 (0.99)	95.4
PMI	PMI-10	49.5	\	49.5	\	
	PMI-30	47.8	\	47.8	\	
ORACLE-5	Non-hier	48.1	86.2	48.7	82.4 (0.94)	87.2
	static	49.0	68.0	49.3	56.8 (0.81)	70.0
	static+UttLSTM	51.3	52.8	51.6	**41.2 (0.76)**	54.1
	dynamic	49.7	86.8	50.2	81.4 (0.93)	88.0
	dynamic+UttLSTM	50.7	93.8	51.2	91.3 (0.97)	94.4
ORACLE-10	Non-hier	**47.1**	86.5	**47.7**	82.5 (0.94)	87.4
	static	49.5	60.7	49.9	**47.1 (0.75)**	62.4
	static+UttLSTM	47.7	54.1	48.0	43.5 (0.79)	55.3
	dynamic	49.9	85.5	50.3	80.0 (0.92)	86.7
	dynamic+UttLSTM	49.6	95.0	49.9	93.4 (0.98)	95.3

(b) Results on the frequent and rare distracting dataset

Method	Model	Distract: frequent			Distract: rare		
		Perp	Distract (ratio)	Avg.	Perp	Distract (ratio)	Avg.
\	Non-hier (*query* only)	\			\		
	Non-hier	49.7	94.3 (0.98)	95.8	49.8	94.4 (0.99)	95.5
PMI	PMI-10	49.5	\		49.5	\	
	PMI-30	47.8	\		47.8	\	
ORACLE-5	Non-hier	48.3	74.8 (0.86)	86.9	48.4	78.1 (0.90)	86.3
	static	49.1	65.1 (0.95)	68.7	49.2	63.0 (0.91)	69.3
	static+UttLSTM	51.4	46.9 (0.88)	53.4	51.4	**48.3 (0.90)**	53.5
	dynamic	49.9	79.3 (0.90)	88.3	50.0	83.0 (0.95)	87.5
	dynamic+UttLSTM	50.8	89.3 (0.95)	94.6	50.9	94.3 (1.01)	93.0
ORACLE-10	Non-hier	**47.3**	69.9 (0.80)	87.3	**47.3**	**74.3 (0.86)**	86.8
	static	49.7	51.0 (0.83)	61.7	49.7	55.3 (0.90)	61.5
	static+UttLSTM	47.7	**46.8 (0.86)**	54.7	47.9	51.1 (0.95)	54.1
	dynamic	50.1	79.3 (0.92)	86.4	50.1	87.9 (1.03)	85.0
	dynamic+UttLSTM	49.7	91.1 (0.95)	95.9	49.8	94.6 (1.00)	94.3

"Would you have lunch?" and "I should have lunch" as distracting utterances, while although the ORACLE algorithm only keeps 16% of these distracting utterances, the model still cannot learn to pay less attention to them.

7   Conclusions

We have integrated extractive summarization techniques with multi-turn dialogue models to improve their ability of context-awareness. The techniques that we have examined are PMI topic model and ORACLE algorithm; we have integrated them with both non-hierarchical and hierarchical dialogue models. For evaluation, we have employed the distracting test to evaluate the context-awareness of each model. With extractive summarization techniques integrated, we find significant improvements in distracting tests for the multi-turn conversational agents. For future works, more summarization techniques can be considered, and more evaluation metrics can be used.

Acknowledgement. This paper is funded by the collaborative project of DNB ASA and Norwegian University of Science and Technology (NTNU). We have also received assistance on computing resources from the IDUN cluster of NTNU [15]. We would like to thank Pinar Øzturk for her helpful comments.

References

1. Bahdanau, D., Cho, K., Bengio, Y.: Neural machine translation by jointly learning to align and translate. In: 3rd International Conference on Learning Representations, ICLR 2015, San Diego, CA, USA, 7–9 May 2015, Conference Track Proceedings (2015). http://arxiv.org/abs/1409.0473
2. Baheti, A., Ritter, A., Li, J., Dolan, B.: Generating more interesting responses in neural conversation models with distributional constraints. In: Proceedings of the 2018 Conference on Empirical Methods in Natural Language Processing, pp. 3970–3980. Association for Computational Linguistics (2018). http://aclweb.org/anthology/D18-1431
3. Gliwa, B., Mochol, I., Biesek, M., Wawer, A.: SAMSum corpus: a human-annotated dialogue dataset for abstractive summarization. In: Proceedings of the 2nd Workshop on New Frontiers in Summarization, pp. 70–79. Association for Computational Linguistics, Hong Kong, China (2019). https://doi.org/10.18653/v1/D19-5409, https://www.aclweb.org/anthology/D19-5409
4. Hochreiter, S., Schmidhuber, J.: Long short-term memory. Neural Comput. **9**(8), 1735–1780 (1997). https://doi.org/10.1162/neco.1997.9.8.1735
5. Kedzie, C., McKeown, K.R., III, H.D.: Content selection in deep learning models of summarization. In: Riloff, E., Chiang, D., Hockenmaier, J., Tsujii, J. (eds.) Proceedings of the 2018 Conference on Empirical Methods in Natural Language Processing, Brussels, Belgium, 31 October - 4 November 2018, pp. 1818–1828. Association for Computational Linguistics (2018). https://doi.org/10.18653/v1/d18-1208
6. Li, J., Sun, X.: A syntactically constrained bidirectional-asynchronous approach for emotional conversation generation. In: Proceedings of the 2018 Conference on Empirical Methods in Natural Language Processing, pp. 678–683. Association for Computational Linguistics, Brussels, Belgium (2018). http://www.aclweb.org/anthology/D18-1071
7. Li, J., Galley, M., Brockett, C., Spithourakis, G., Gao, J., Dolan, B.: A persona-based neural conversation model. In: Proceedings of the 54th Annual Meeting of

the Association for Computational Linguistics (Volume 1: Long Papers), pp. 994–1003. Association for Computational Linguistics (2016). https://doi.org/10.18653/v1/P16-1094, http://aclweb.org/anthology/P16-1094

8. Liu, C.W., Lowe, R., Serban, I., Noseworthy, M., Charlin, L., Pineau, J.: How not to evaluate your dialogue system: an empirical study of unsupervised evaluation metrics for dialogue response generation. In: Proceedings of the 2016 Conference on Empirical Methods in Natural Language Processing, pp. 2122–2132. Association for Computational Linguistics (2016). https://doi.org/10.18653/v1/D16-1230, http://aclweb.org/anthology/D16-1230

9. Lowe, R., Pow, N., Serban, I., Pineau, J.: The ubuntu dialogue corpus: a large dataset for research in unstructured multi-turn dialogue systems. In: Proceedings of the 16th Annual Meeting of the Special Interest Group on Discourse and Dialogue, pp. 285–294. Association for Computational Linguistics (2015). https://doi.org/10.18653/v1/W15-4640, http://aclweb.org/anthology/W15-4640

10. Mou, L., Song, Y., Yan, R., Li, G., Zhang, L., Jin, Z.: Sequence to backward and forward sequences: a content-introducing approach to generative short-text conversation. In: Proceedings of COLING 2016, the 26th International Conference on Computational Linguistics: Technical Papers, pp. 3349–3358. The COLING 2016 Organizing Committee (2016). http://aclweb.org/anthology/C16-1316

11. Paszke, A., et al.: Automatic differentiation in PyTorch. In: NIPS-W (2017)

12. See, A., Roller, S., Kiela, D., Weston, J.: What makes a good conversation? How controllable attributes affect human judgments. arXiv:1902.08654 [cs] (2019). http://arxiv.org/abs/1902.08654

13. Serban, I.V., Sordoni, A., Bengio, Y., Courville, A., Pineau, J.: Building end-to-end dialogue systems using generative hierarchical neural network models. In: 13th AAAI Conference on Artificial Intelligence (2016). https://www.aaai.org/ocs/index.php/AAAI/AAAI16/paper/view/11957

14. Serban, I.V., et al.: A hierarchical latent variable encoder-decoder model for generating dialogues. In: 31st AAAI Conference on Artificial Intelligence (2017). https://www.aaai.org/ocs/index.php/AAAI/AAAI17/paper/view/14567

15. Själander, M., Jahre, M., Tufte, G., Reissmann, N.: EPIC: an energy-efficient, high-performance GPGPU computing research infrastructure (2019)

16. Sutskever, I., Vinyals, O., Le, Q.V.: Sequence to sequence learning with neural networks. In: Ghahramani, Z., Welling, M., Cortes, C., Lawrence, N.D., Weinberger, K.Q. (eds.) Advances in Neural Information Processing Systems 27, pp. 3104–3112. Curran Associates, Inc. (2014). http://papers.nips.cc/paper/5346-sequence-to-sequence-learning-with-neural-networks.pdf

17. Tian, Z., Yan, R., Mou, L., Song, Y., Feng, Y., Zhao, D.: How to make context more useful? An empirical study on context-aware neural conversational models. In: Proceedings of the 55th Annual Meeting of the Association for Computational Linguistics (Volume 2: Short Papers), pp. 231–236. Association for Computational Linguistics (2017). https://doi.org/10.18653/v1/P17-2036, http://aclweb.org/anthology/P17-2036

18. Xing, C., et al.: Topic aware neural response generation. In: 31st AAAI Conference on Artificial Intelligence (2017). https://www.aaai.org/ocs/index.php/AAAI/AAAI17/paper/view/14563

19. Yao, J., Wan, X., Xiao, J.: Recent advances in document summarization. Knowl. Inf. Syst. **53**(2), 297–336 (2017). https://doi.org/10.1007/s10115-017-1042-4

20. Yao, L., Zhang, Y., Feng, Y., Zhao, D., Yan, R.: Towards implicit content-introducing for generative short-text conversation systems. In: Proceedings of the

2017 Conference on Empirical Methods in Natural Language Processing, pp. 2190–2199. Association for Computational Linguistics (2017). https://doi.org/10.18653/v1/D17-1233, http://aclweb.org/anthology/D17-1233

21. Zhang, W., Cui, Y., Wang, Y., Zhu, Q., Li, L., Zhou, L., Liu, T.: Context-sensitive generation of open-domain conversational responses. In: Proceedings of the 27th International Conference on Computational Linguistics, pp. 2437–2447. Association for Computational Linguistics (2018). http://aclweb.org/anthology/C18-1206

Document Knowledge Transfer for Aspect-Based Sentiment Classification Using a Left-Center-Right Separated Neural Network with Rotatory Attention

Emily Fields, Gonem Lau, Robbert Rog, Alexander Sternfeld,
and Flavius Frasincar(✉) ⓘ

Erasmus University of Rotterdam, Burgemeester Oudlaan 50, 3062 Rotterdam, PA,
The Netherlands
{505456ef,500202gl,492751rr,492825as}@student.eur.nl,
frasincar@ese.eur.nl

Abstract. Hybrid Aspect-Based Sentiment Classification (ABSC) methods make use of domain-specific, costly ontologies to make up for the lack of available aspect-level data. This paper proposes two forms of transfer learning to exploit the plenteous amount of available document data for sentiment classification. Specifically, two forms of document knowledge transfer, pretraining (PRET) and multi-task learning (MULT), are considered in various combinations to extend the state-of-the-art LCR-Rot-hop++ model. For both the SemEval 2015 and 2016 datasets, we find an improvement over the LCR-Rot-hop++ neural model. Overall, the pure MULT model performs well across both datasets. Additionally, there is an optimal amount of document knowledge that can be injected, after which the performance deteriorates due to the extra focus on the auxiliary task. We observe that with transfer learning and L1 and L2 loss regularisation, the LCR-Rot-hop++ model is able to outperform the HAABSA++ hybrid model on the (larger) SemEval 2016 dataset. Thus, we conclude that transfer learning is a feasible and computationally cheap substitute for the ontology step of hybrid ABSC models.

Keywords: LCR-Rot-hop++ · Transfer Learning · Pretraining · Multi-Task Learning

1 Introduction

In the pre-Web era, it was often difficult for companies to gauge the opinions of their large customer bases. While the increasing popularity of the Web provided a virtually inexhaustible source of data, machine learning methods had to be developed for extracting insights from this information. One particularly interesting insight is to extract a sentiment from a segment of text, for example a review. This is what drove the development of Sentiment Analysis in the field of Natural Language Processing (NLP) [9].

© The Author(s), under exclusive license to Springer Nature Switzerland AG 2023
E. Métais et al. (Eds.): NLDB 2023, LNCS 13913, pp. 489–499, 2023.
https://doi.org/10.1007/978-3-031-35320-8_36

This paper specifically considers Aspect-Based Sentiment Analysis (ABSA). ABSA consists of two steps: Aspect Detection (AD) and Aspect-Based Sentiment Classification (ABSC). AD is the task of finding an aspect, such as price, quality, or service of an entity, within a text or review. This paper will focus on ABSC exclusively, which involves determining the sentiment of a given aspect within a given sentence [1,14]. It is common practice to divide sentiment into three classes: positive, neutral, and negative.

Traditionally, dictionary-based approaches such as that in [7] have been used, but with the rise of deep learning and the ever-increasing computational power of modern machines, a range of new techniques for ABSC have become available. Of the basic "deep" models, the Bidirectional Long Short-Term Memory Network (BiLSTM) at first appeared to be the most promising, as illustrated in [5]. Over the years, however, more sophisticated BiLSTM methods have been developed. One of these is the Left-Center-Right Separated BiLSTM with Rotatory Attention (LCR-Rot) [20], which utilises separately trained BiLSTM networks for the context to the left of the aspect, the aspect itself, and the context to the right of the aspect, and has been found to outperform previously proposed LSTM-variations [20]. Even more recently, the LCR-Rot model has been extended with respect to both the attention mechanism and the word embeddings. Namely, the LCR-Rot-hop model presented in [19] iteratively applies the attention mechanism, while the LCR-Rot-hop++ model proposed in [18] builds on this to include hierarchical attention and deep contextual word embeddings.

Over the past years, a collection of techniques called Transfer Learning (TL) has surged in popularity as a method to improve the performance of machine learning methods [10]. More formally, TL involves training a model on auxiliary tasks to improve the performance of the main task. This is particularly interesting when there is few data available for our task at hand. One such method is MULTi-task learning (MULT), where a model is trained on two tasks simultaneously, as applied in the widely used language model called Bidirectional Encoder Representation from Transformers (BERT) [4]. An alternative method is PRE-Training (PRET), which involves first learning an auxiliary task after which the model is trained for the main task. The latter step is called Fine-Tuning (FT), meaning a TL model is trained once more on just the main task.

A lack of training data in the same domain as the test data is a persistent issue in machine learning [10]. In ABSC, this is reflected by the limited availability of aspect-level data. As there is more annotated sentiment data available at a document level, i.e., review texts with star ratings, this information can be exploited using TL techniques. [6], for example, showed an improvement in the performance of ABSC in BiLSTMs when PRET and MULT are utilised. We consider four approaches for document knowledge transfer in the state-of-the-art LCR-Rot-hop++ neural model, inspired by [6]. The first approach is PRET+FT, in which the model is first pretrained on the document knowledge and then fine-tuned. The second is MULT, where the sentiment of a document and of an aspect are determined simultaneously. While the method proposed in [6] does not include a regularisation term, we extend the approach by including a regularisation term in the loss function as in [19]. The third method is a combination of both PRET and MULT, called PRET+MULT, in which the model is first pretrained at a document level on part of the data, before MULT is applied to the rest of the data. Last, in the fourth and fifth approaches, we develop new methods that incorporate FT into the TL approach, in two models called MULT+FT and PRET+MULT+FT.

The present work extends the existing literature by implementing document knowledge transfer on the state-of-the-art LCR-Rot-hop++ neural model, with the aim to further improve its accuracy. Moreover, different L1 and L2 regularisation terms are combined to improve upon the previous works. The Python source code of our models can be found at https://github.com/Gogonemnem/LCR-Rot-hop-plus-plus-TL.

The paper continues as follows. First, the related works and their results are discussed in more detail in Sect. 2, after which the data is illustrated in Sect. 3. Subsequently, the methodology is presented in Sect. 4. Thereafter, the results are compared with those obtained in the previous literature in Sect. 5. Last, conclusions with the main findings and suggestions for future research are presented in Sect. 6.

2 Related Work

The performance of the LCR-Rot-hop++ model depends on the scale of the available training data, as limited training data can lead to a lower accuracy. Ideally, one would use aspect-level data, as the model is used for sentiment analysis at the aspect level. However, the availability of annotated aspect-level data is limited [6,10]. To illustrate, both [18,19] use the standard SemEval 2015 [12] and SemEval 2016 [11] datasets, which are relatively small. Due to the limited availability of aspect-level data, the LCR-Rot-hop++ model may not reach its full potential. To overcome this issue, one can consider coarser data, such as document-level or sentence-level data. There is an abundance of this type of data, for instance Yelp reviews [16].

Document knowledge transfer can be motivated from three perspectives: human learning, pedagogy, and machine learning [13]. From the point of view of human learning, it is clear that we frequently use knowledge acquired from learning related tasks when learning a new task. Equally, from a pedagogical perspective, we often learn the foundations first, before using this knowledge to learn more complex skills. Last, document knowledge transfer improves generalisation by introducing an inductive bias, which creates a preference for hypotheses that explain more than one task [2]. In this paper, we investigate which method for document knowledge transfer performs best, specifically, we consider combinations of PRETraining (PRET), MULTi-task learning (MULT), and Fine-Tuning (FT).

PRET. Pretraining is the act of training a model on a task semantically related to your target task, prior to training for your target task [6,13]. This technique has shown great success in language models such as BERT in [4]. BERT was trained to perform two tasks which helped the model understand language, after which it can be fine-tuned for a wider variety of language tasks. As shown in [6], pretraining a BiLSTM on document-level data improved the results obtained on an aspect level.

MULT. In contrast to PRET, when using MULT the model is trained for the target task and the semantically related task simultaneously [13]. The purpose of this is to improve generalisation, which might lead to more effective knowledge transfer. For example, [15] demonstrated that multi-task learning is able to produce good word embeddings.

FT. In PRET and MULT, one uses the semantically-related task to improve performance on the target task. With FT, one only trains on the target task. Therefore, it is necessary in combination with PRET, but optional with MULT. To illustrate, the BERT language model is first trained using a MULT approach on general language tasks, after which it can be trained for specific tasks using an FT approach [4].

3 Data

The datasets used for ABSC are the SemEval 2015 [12] and SemEval 2016 [11] datasets. Specifically, our analysis focuses on restaurant reviews. Each review consists of one or more sentences, and each sentence contains the sentiment on one or more aspects. The sentiment can either be positive, neutral, or negative. In our research we focus on explicit aspects, which means that the aspect is present in the sentence. Figure 1 shows an example sentence from the SemEval 2016 dataset in the XML markup language. This example shows that, in a review, multiple aspects can be present and the sentiment towards different aspects may differ. Table 1 gives the descriptive statistics of the SemEval 2015 and the SemEval 2016 data sets. One can notice that there are relatively few neutral reviews. Furthermore, in most data the positive class is the majority class, except for the test data of the SemEval 2015 [12] dataset. The 2015 dataset is a subset of the 2016 dataset, and is noticeably smaller.

We use a document-level dataset from Yelp2014 [17] for pretraining, as it matches the domain of our aspect-level data: restaurants. However, these reviews are classified on a 5-point scale. Therefore, the reviews will be labeled in the following way: reviews with ratings > 3, $= 3$, and < 3 are labeled as positive, neutral, and negative, respectively. Similar to [6], a balanced sample of 30,000 is extracted from the dataset to obtain our pretraining corpus. As Table 1 shows, there is a significant lack of neutral examples in the aspect-level data. Therefore, the balancing of the pretraining corpus allows the model to see an ample amount of documents for each category. To make our data suitable for multi-task learning, each aspect-level data point is paired with a random document from our

```
<sentence id="Z#3:0">
    <text>Excellent food, although the interior could use some help.</
        text>
    <Opinions>
        <Opinion target="food" category="FOOD#QUALITY" polarity="positive"
            from="10" to="14"/>
        <Opinion target="interior" category="AMBIENCE#GENERAL" polarity="
            negative" from="29" to="37"/>
    </Opinions>
</sentence>
```

Fig. 1. A sentence from the SemEval 2016 dataset.

sample. As there are many more documents available than aspects, we upsample our aspect-level data with a factor of three. This value was chosen based on intuition, as too little upsampling will not allow us to exploit many documents, whereas too much upsampling will likely lead the model to overfit due to the duplicates in the aspect data.

Table 1. Descriptive statistics of the SemEval 2015 and SemEval 2016 datasets, split into training and test data.

Dataset	Positive		Neutral		Negative		Total
	Freq	%	Freq	%	Freq	%	Freq
SemEval-2015 training data	963	75.3	36	2.8	280	21.9	1279
SemEval-2015 test data	354	34.7	38	6.3	208	59.0	600
SemEval-2016 training data	1321	70.1	73	3.9	490	26.0	1884
SemEval-2016 test data	487	74.4	32	4.9	136	20.8	655

4 Methodology

This section discusses the methodology used to obtain the results. First, the two methods for document knowledge transfer (PRET and MULT) are elaborated upon, along with the various combinations in which they are applied. Then, the experimental setup for obtaining the results is given.

4.1 Knowledge Transfer

This paper considers several different approaches for document knowledge transfer. Each approach consists of one or more of the following building blocks: PRET, MULT, and FT. In this section, each building block is described separately. Furthermore, Fig. 2 displays which compositions of PRET, MULT, and FT are used in this work. In the notation of each building block, we consider two tasks τ_1 and τ_2. Let τ_2 be our task of interest, namely ABSC. In contrast, τ_1 is sentiment classification at a document level, which is semantically related to our main task. Therefore, teaching our model to execute τ_1 will enlighten it with knowledge that can be used for better executing τ_2.

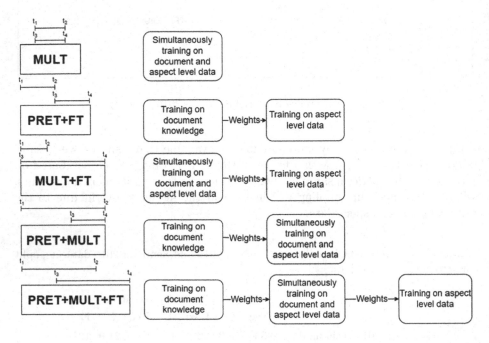

Fig. 2. An overview of the different document knowledge transfer approaches. The target task is executed in the time interval $[t_3, t_4]$, whereas the semantically related task is executed in the time interval $[t_1, t_2]$

PRET. In the pretraining stage only τ_1 is executed, which trains the model for sentiment analysis at a document level. Specifically, the documents are put through the left, center, and right BiLSTM, after which the final hidden layers of all words are pooled (averaged). The pooled hidden layers of the three BiLSTMs are concatenated and fed into a classification layer. The aim of this stage is to pretrain the BiLSTMs, as it is expected that the BiLSTM weights obtained in the PRET stage transfer the information from the document-level sentiment classification to improve the accuracy at the aspect level.

MULT. During the multi-task stage, tasks τ_1 and τ_2 are executed simultaneously. In this approach, the three BiLSTMs are trained simultaneously on the document-level data and on their corresponding part of the aspect-level data (left, target, or right). Each aspect-level data point is paired to a document-level data point. Thus, the embedding layer and the three BiLSTMs in the LCR-Rothop++ model are shared for τ_1 and τ_2. The document-level data is processed the same as in the PRET stage. For the aspect-level data, the outputs from the BiLSTMs are directed to the corresponding attention mechanism, which finally leads to probabilities regarding the aspect-based sentiment.

The parameters are set by minimising the loss function below.

$$L = J + \lambda U + \omega \|\Theta\|_1 + \Omega \|\Theta\|^2 \tag{1}$$

In this loss function, J is the mean loss per training batch corresponding to our primary task τ_2. Likewise, U is the mean loss per training batch corresponding to our secondary task τ_1. The loss U is weighted with a parameter $\lambda \in (0,1)$, which can be interpreted as the importance of τ_1 for performing τ_2. Last, ω and Ω denote the weights of the L1 and L2 regularisation terms, respectively. The L1 regularisation considers the absolute value of the coefficients, whereas the L2 regularisation considers the squared value of the coefficients.

FT. The fine-tuning stage can be used as the final stage for training a model. In the FT stage, only τ_2 is executed. In this context, this means that only ABSC is performed. The goal of this stage is to tweak the model, such that it performs best for the target task. Whereas previous stages have taught the model more general knowledge, the FT stage aims at preparing the model solely for the target task.

4.2 Experimental Setup

To verify the added value of the TL approaches, we test all combinations as presented in the previous section and compare their performance to the benchmark model without document knowledge transfer. The following section describes in more detail how we find the best models for each combination.

Hyperparameter Tuning. Hyperband is used to find the optimal hyperparameters [8]. As hypertuning all models over all stages is computationally infeasible, a heuristic is used for setting the hyperparameters. Namely, for each dataset, the optimal hyperparameters for the MULT model and the FT model are computed. These hyperparameters are generalised over all building blocks of the model. Models which use hyperparameters from the tuned FT model are referred to as FT-based models. Models which use hyperparameters from the tuned MULT model are referred to as MULT-based models. Thus, each approach in Fig. 2 is executed using both the FT hyperparameters and the MULT hyperparameters. For the FT-based PRET+MULT+FT model, λ has not been optimised in the hypertuning. Hence, the λ from MULT tuning is generalised to this model as well. Note that we do not run an FT-based model for MULT nor PRET+MULT, nor a MULT-based model for PRET+FT, as these parameter and TL approach combinations are likely to be suboptimal. We use 80% of the training data to optimize the loss function and the remaining 20% as validation to select the best hyperparameters.

Model Training. Early stopping is applied to determine the number of training epochs with different levels of patience for the stages. This means that when the performance on the validation set has not increased during the patience epochs, the epochs after the current best epoch, training is stopped and the optimal model weights are restored. For the PRET stage, the performance measure is the validation loss (categorical cross-entropy). The PRET corpus is large compared to the aspect level data, so for computational efficiency a relatively low patience of 3 is chosen here. Similarly, for the MULT stage, we use early stopping with respect to the combined validation loss described in [6]. We allow a higher patience of 10 as the per epoch time is considerably lower, making it more affordable. Last, for the FT stage, early stopping is done with respect to the validation accuracy, as this is our measure of interest. Again, a patience of 10 is used. The loss functions in all stages, including the benchmark LCR-Rot-hop++, are regularised to prevent overfitting. Both L1 and L2 regularisation are used, the weights of which are optimised by the aforementioned hyperband for both FT-based and MULT-based models.

Model Evaluation. We evaluate the various approaches using the out-of-sample accuracy measure. This measure allows us to see, after training, how often a model correctly predicts the sentiment of an aspect. We note that this measure weights the performance for each sentiment class according to how many observations there are for each sentiment, meaning it does not heavily penalise poor performance in a small sentiment class. As we observe in our data that there are very few neutral observations compared to positive and negative observations, we acknowledge that poor model performance when predicting a neutral sentiment might not be strongly reflected in the accuracy.

5   Results

Table 2 shows the results of the benchmark LCR-Rot-hop++ model with different hyperparameters and different combinations of document knowledge transfer approaches, for the data of SemEval 2015 and SemEval 2016. All losses, including that of the benchmark LCR-Rot-hop++ model without document knowledge transfer, are regularised using the L1 and L2 regularisation terms, allowing for a fair comparison. We find that several TL models outperform the benchmark LCR-Rot-hop++ model, for both datasets, suggesting there is added value in incorporating document knowledge transfer in the base model.

For the SemEval 2015 dataset, all models with TL outperform the benchmark model. The largest improvement in accuracy, 6.50% points, is observed for the MULT model. For the SemEval 2016 dataset, on the other hand, several models with TL do not outperform the benchmark, namely FT-based MULT+FT and PRET+MULT+FT, and MULT-based PRET+MULT and PRET+MULT+FT. Still, the remaining models do outperform the benchmark, with the biggest improvements observed for the PRET+FT and MULT models, which exceed the accuracy of the benchmark model by 1.83 and 1.76% points, respectively.

Table 2. Results of LCR-Rot-hop++ with various forms of document knowledge transfer, alongside the benchmark model without document knowledge transfer, for the SemEval 2015 and SemEval 2016 datasets.

Settings	Accuracy	
	SemEval 2015	SemEval 2016
Benchmark model		
LCR-Rot-hop++	74.00%	86.87%
FT-based models		
MULT+FT	77.00%	85.95%
PRET+FT	78.00%	88.70%
PRET+MULT+FT	79.67%	86.56%
MULT-based models		
MULT	80.50%	88.63%
MULT+FT	74.50%	87.18%
PRET+MULT	76.67%	85.04%
PRET+MULT+FT	77.67%	86.87%

Note. The FT-based models are constructed using the optimal hyperparameters from a model with only the FT stage, as is the LCR-Rot-hop++ benchmark model. The MULT-based models use the optimal hyperparameters for a pure MULT model.

The differences in performance for this dataset are smaller, likely because it is larger and more balanced. Given that TL aims to handle limited data availability and data imbalance by supplying the model with additional examples of a similar task, it is indeed to be expected that these approaches have greater impact in the 2015 dataset.

Based on the accuracy measures, we conclude that the analysed TL models can boost the accuracy of the existing LCR-Rot-hop++ model. Overall, the MULT model performs best, as it leads to the greatest improvements in accuracy across the two datasets. In comparison to the existing state-of-the-art HAABSA++ model, we observe that our MULT model outperforms HAABSA++ for the SemEval 2016 dataset, by 1.63% points, but performs slightly worse for the 2015 dataset, by 1.2% points.

One plausible reason for MULT outperforming PRET approaches is catastrophic forgetting [3]. Knowledge learned in the PRET stage might be forgotten when the model is retrained on the main task. In MULT, the main and auxiliary tasks are learned simultaneously, making the document knowledge more recent and prevalent. As shown in [3], multi-task learning provides a solution to catastrophic forgetting.

6   Conclusion

ABSC models are constrained due to the limited availability of aspect-level training data. In this paper, we aim to overcome this limitation by using document-level training data to train the state-of-the-art LCR-Rot-hop++ model. The results show that the most successful transfer learning approach is multi-task learning, particularly when faced with a small and imbalanced dataset such as SemEval 2015. Likely, multi-task learning outperforms the pretraining approach due to catastrophic forgetting; document knowledge acquired in pretraining is partly forgotten when the model is retrained on aspects. Multi-task learning solves this problem by fitting on the main and auxiliary task simultaneously, preventing this type of forgetting [3].

Our best approach, the MULT model, yields a 6.5% points increase relative to the state-of-the-art LCR-Rot-hop++ model with L1 and L2 regularisation for the SemEval 2015 dataset, as well as a 1.76% point increase for the SemEval 2016 dataset. Furthermore, this model outperforms the HAABSA++ model for the SemEval 2016 dataset. Therefore, we conclude that the inclusion of L1 and L2 regularisation terms along with the MULT method of document knowledge transfer can under certain circumstances effectively compensate for the exclusion of an ontology reasoning. Hence, this updated model can serve as a computationally cheaper alternative to existing hybrid models, without any significant loss in performance.

A suggestion for future research is to investigate different deep learning architectures for incorporating document knowledge transfer. One example of a different architecture is adding a shared BiLSTM layer below the LCR-Rot-hop++ model, instead of sharing the left, middle, and right BiLSTM. Furthermore, future research can investigate models that exploit sentence- or paragraph-level knowledge, besides document-level knowledge.

References

1. Brauwers, G., Frasincar, F.: A survey on aspect-based sentiment classification. ACM Comput. Surveys **55**(4), 65:1–65:37 (2023)
2. Caruana, R.: Multitask Learning: a Knowledge-Based Source of Inductive Bias. In: 10th International Conference on Machine Learning (ICML 1993), pp. 41–48. Morgan Kaufmann (1993)
3. Chen, S., Hou, Y., Cui, Y., Che, W., Liu, T., Yu, X.: Recall and learn: fine-tuning deep pretrained language models with less forgetting. In: Proceedings of the 2020 Conference on Empirical Methods in Natural Language Processing (EMNLP 2020). ACL (2020)
4. Devlin, J., Chang, M.W., Lee, K., Toutanova, K.: BERT: pre-training of deep bidirectional transformers for language understanding. In: 17th Conference of the North American Chapter of the Association for Computational Linguistics: Human Language Technologies (NAACL-HLT 2019), pp. 4171–4186. ACL (2019)
5. Graves, A., Schmidhuber, J.: Framewise phoneme classification with bidirectional LSTM and other neural network architecture. Neural Netw. **18**(5–6), 602–610 (2005)

6. He, R., Lee, W.S., Ng, H.T., Dahlmeier, D.: Exploiting document knowledge for aspect-level sentiment classification. In: 56th Annual Meeting of the Association for Computational Linguistics (ACL 2018), pp. 579–585. ACL (2018)
7. Hu, M., Liu, B.: Mining and summarizing customer reviews. In: 10th ACM SIGKDD International Conference on Knowledge Discovery and Data Mining (KDD 2004), pp. 168–177. ACM (2004)
8. Li, L., Jamieson, K., DeSalvo, G., Rostamizadeh, A., Talwalkar, A.: Hyperband: a novel bandit-based approach to hyperparameter optimization. J. Mach. Learn. Res. 18(1), 6765–6816 (2018)
9. Liu, B.: Sentiment Analysis: Mining Opinions, Sentiments, and Emotions 2nd (edn.) Cambridge University Press (2020)
10. Pan, S.J., Yang, Q.: A survey on transfer learning. IEEE Trans. Knowl. Data Eng. 22(10), 1345–1359 (2010)
11. Pontiki, M., et al.: SemEval-2016 Task 5: aspect based sentiment analysis. In: 10th International Workshop on Semantic Evaluation (SemEval 2016), pp. 19–30. ACL (2016)
12. Pontiki, M., Galanis, D., Papageorgiou, H., Manandhar, S., Androutsopoulos, I.: SemEval-2015 Task 12: aspect based sentiment analysis. In: 9th International Workshop on Semantic Evaluation (SemEval 2015), pp. 486–495. ACL (2015)
13. Ruder, S.: Neural transfer learning for natural language processing. Ph.D. thesis, National University of Ireland, Galway (2019)
14. Schouten, K., Frasincar, F.: Survey on aspect-level sentiment analysis. IEEE Trans. Knowl. Data Eng. 28(3), 813–830 (2016)
15. Subramanian, S., Trischler, A., Bengio, Y., Pal, C.J.: Learning general purpose distributed sentence representations via large scale multi-task learning. In: 6th International Conference on Learning Representation (ICLR 2018). OpenReview.net (2018)
16. Tang, D., Qin, B., Liu, T.: Learning semantic representations of users and products for document level sentiment classification. In: 53rd Meeting of the Association for Computational Linguistics (ACL 2015), pp. 1014–1023. ACL (2015)
17. Tang, D., Qin, B., Liu, T.: Aspect level sentiment classification with deep memory network. In: 2016 Conference on Empirical Methods in Natural Language Processing (EMNLP 2016), pp. 214–222. ACL (2016)
18. Truşcă, M.M., Wassenberg, D., Frasincar, F., Dekker, R.: A hybrid approach for aspect-based sentiment analysis using deep contextual word embeddings and hierarchical attention. In: Bielikova, M., Mikkonen, T., Pautasso, C. (eds.) ICWE 2020. LNCS, vol. 12128, pp. 365–380. Springer, Cham (2020). https://doi.org/10.1007/978-3-030-50578-3_25
19. Wallaart, O., Frasincar, F.: A hybrid approach for aspect-based sentiment analysis using a lexicalized domain ontology and attentional neural models. In: Hitzler, P., et al. (eds.) ESWC 2019. LNCS, vol. 11503, pp. 363–378. Springer, Cham (2019). https://doi.org/10.1007/978-3-030-21348-0_24
20. Zheng, S., Xia, R.: Left-center-right separated neural network for aspect-based sentiment analysis with rotatory attention. arXiv preprint arXiv:1802.00892 (2018)

Argument and Counter-Argument Generation: A Critical Survey

Xiaoou Wang$^{(\boxtimes)}$, Elena Cabrio, and Serena Villata

Université Côte d'Azur, CNRS, Inria, I3S, Sophia Antipolis, France
{xiaoou.wang,elena.cabrio,serena.villata}@univ-cotedazur.fr

Abstract. Argument Generation (AG) is becoming an increasingly active research topic in Natural Language Processing (NLP), and a large variety of terms has been used to highlight different aspects and methods of AG such as argument construction, argument retrieval, argument synthesis and argument summarization, producing a vast literature. This article aims to draw a comprehensive picture of the literature concerning argument generation and counter-argument generation (CAG). Despite the increasing interest on this topic, no attempt has been made yet to critically review the diverse and rich literature in AG and CAG. By confronting works from the relevant subareas of NLP, we provide a holistic vision that is essential for future works aiming to produce understandable, convincing and ethically sound arguments and counter-arguments.

Keywords: Argument generation · Counter-argument generation · Argument retrieval · Argument mining

1 Introduction

Argument Mining (AM) is a research area which aims at identifying and classifying argumentative structures from text. The increasing interest in the literature for this area, due to its applications in tacking substantial societal challenges as propaganda detection, fact-checking and *explainable Artificial Intelligence*, resulted in the publication of several surveys [13,30]. The research area of AM has now been expanded to the generation of natural language arguments. To this date, *Argument Generation (AG)* is still considered as a hard task and no standard methods exist. To the best of our knowledge, no survey has been published on this subject. A recent paper by Lauscher *et al.* [29] discussed the role of knowledge in the general context of argumentation including AM, argument assessment, argument reasoning and AG, without focusing on the state of the art of this latter domain as well as the main trends and challenges faced by most researchers. However, researches in AG are clearly on the rise and a huge variety of methods have been explored. Also, multiple research directions have been sketched, from the perspective of generating argumentative components (e.g., claim, premise and enthymeme) as well as the employment of rhetorical strategies [45] and users' beliefs [1] to guide the argument generation. Applications

E. Métais et al. (Eds.): NLDB 2023, LNCS 13913, pp. 500–510, 2023.
https://doi.org/10.1007/978-3-031-35320-8_37

of AG are diverse and numerous, of which the most relevant are *writing assistance* [48], *legal decision making* [6], *collective decision making* [12] and *Counter Narrative Generation* [43] to fight online hate speech.

In this paper, we aim to lay out a comprehensive picture of the studies on AG and *Counter-argument Generation (CAG)*, where counter-arguments are in essence arguments against other arguments. Due to the large variety of topics and research communities covered by AG and CAG, studies published in these two fields often fail to cite each other. It is important to underline that AG is a complex task including multiple subtasks and it is essential to have a holistic view of the ongoing works in all the relevant subareas in order to design reliable end-to-end argumentative systems. With the idea of federating relevant communities in mind, we propose the current survey with the following contributions:

1. We draw a historical view of the development of studies in AG and CAG, providing a detailed outline of the main results and trends in various subareas of AG and CAG, along with a summary of the main datasets for these tasks.
2. We discuss the main issues and some open challenges in AG and CAG.
3. We point out 4 most promising research directions in AG and CAG.

2 Data to Text Argument Generation

Studies on argument generation started around the 1990s in the spirit of recommender systems. Considerable research has been devoted to developing computational models for automatically generating and presenting *evaluative arguments*. The general idea of these studies was to design computer systems serving as advisors to support humans in similar communicative settings. These studies were mainly concerned with producing short texts from structured data such as knowledge graphs representing domain knowledge as well as users. We call this family of approaches *Data to Text Generation*.

The general principles of data to text generation were formalized by Carenini [14] and applied to their *Generator of Evaluative Arguments* recommending houses to a client. The generation process first involves a deep generation phase which is agnostic of the target language since it consists mainly in the selection of knowledge chunks based on the comparison of a *User Model* and a *Domain Model* (e.g., the profile of a buyer and the profile of a house), and the selection of the argumentative strategy. The second phase, *content realization*, involves the actual text generation requiring specific grammatical knowledge of the target language such as verbal inflections and logical connectors.

Data to text generation is cumbersome since it involves a lot of manual work to build the knowledge bases and the actual knowledge acquisition process has to be restarted whenever a new domain is being tackled. Around the beginning of the 2010s, a shift took place in argument generation: first, the design of debating systems started to draw the attention of researchers (a prominent event was the Project Debater[1] of IBM, started in 2012); secondly, inspired by techniques

---

[1] https://www.research.ibm.com/artificial-intelligence/project-debater/.

in *Natural Language Generation (NLG)*, researchers adopt a *Text to Text Generation* approach, which can either be further divided into several subtasks or generate full arguments in an end-to-end fashion.

3 Text to Text Argument Generation

This section provides a complete outline of the main trends in AG and CAG using the text to text approach, summarized in Table 1.

3.1 Generation of Argument Components

A claim forms the basis of an argument, being the assertion that the argument aims to establish. Therefore, claim construction may be viewed as a first step in argument generation. It should be noted that *Claim Generation (CG)* is different from *Claim Retrieval* which consists in employing argument mining to identify existing claims in a corpus. To retrieve arguments, Levy et al. [32] have developed the task of *Context-dependent Claim Detection* whose objective is to identify supporting and attacking claims related to a topic from a Wikipedia corpus. The tasks of *Evidence Retrieval* [38] and *Claim Stance Classification* [7] are also related topics for the AG task. The goal here is to retrieve pro and con arguments for a given query. In the following sections, however, we will focus mainly on claim generation.

In its simplest form, *Claim Generation* takes a debate topic as input and the output is a concise assertion with a clear stance on this topic. To automatically generate new claims, Bilu and Slonim [10] used traditional linguistic features for predicting the suitability of candidate claims. Concretely, the authors drew insights from the fact that a predicate on a certain topic can be used to other topics under certain constraints. For instance, the predicate "is a violation of free speech" can be applied both to "banning violent video games" and "Internet censorship". Their framework employs two stages: first, given a topic, word2vec embeddings are used to select top k similar predicates from a Predicate Lexicon; second, the top-k predicates are combined with new topics and a logistic regression classifier is used to predict if the new claim is valid or not, using features such as n-grams. Gretz *et al.* [21] expanded this framework by leveraging GPT-2 to generate claims on topics and showed the potential of large language models in this task. Furthermore, Alshomary *et al.* [1] studied how to encode specific beliefs into generated claims.

Contrastive Claim Generation (CAG) is motivated by the observation that negation has an important function in argumentation. Bilu *et al.* [9] proposed a rule-based system to augment a set of claims by automatically suggesting a meaningful negation, which means that an opposite claim must be grammatically correct, semantically clear and logically valid. The authors concluded from this study that explicit negation is not always possible. To better tackle this issue, Hidey and McKeown [24] used a sequence to sequence model to encode the original claim with an attention mechanism. They used a sequence of words and a sequence of edits as encoder representations and found that the latter is more effective. Another line of research, initiated by Chen *et al.* [16], is related to CAG. The authors proposed to use autoencoders for the task of *Bias Flipping* (i.e., switch the left or right bias of an article). An encoder conditioned on the source bias is used to encode the input text, while a decoder conditioned on the target bias decodes the encoder representation into a new text.

Bar-Haim *et al.* [7] introduced the task of *Premise Target Identification (PTI)* which identifies the target in a premise. Based on this task, Alshomary *et al.* [5] initiated the task of *Conclusion Target Inference (CTI)*, inspired by the observation that conclusions are not often explicitly formulated. They used a BIO sequence labeling to detect the boundary of the target of premises, then a ranking model [47] to select the premise target that is the most representative of the conclusion target. The authors also explored the use of a triplet neural network to select the most similar conclusion target to a premise target from a knowledge base containing all the conclusion targets. A hybrid approach, however, yielded the best results.

The last subtask of AG is called *Enthymeme Reconstruction (ER)*, where an enthymeme is an implicit premise that clarifies how a conclusion is inferred from the given premises. Boltužić and Šnajder [11] studied how to identify such enthymemes given the other components. Similarly, Habernal *et al.* [23] present the task of identifying the correct enthymeme from two options. More recently, a large dataset [15] studying abductive reasoning in narrative text was created to enable the use of neural models in this line of research.

3.2   Generation of Full Arguments

Rule-Based Argument Generation. Sato *et al.* [40] presented the first end-to-end rule-based retrieval system to generate argument scripts in the first round of a debate. A user first selects a motion and a stance which agrees or disagrees with the motion. A *Motion Analysis component* then extracts the target of the motion and its stance. The *Value Selection component* selects the 5 most relevant talking points. Then the *Sentence Retrieval Component* retrieves sentences relevant to each value from the corpus, and finally, the *Sentence Rephrasing component* arranges the retrieved sentences to build the final argument.

Summarization-Based Approach. Due to the complexity to maintain the components in systems like [40], some studies proposed to use a neural summarization approach. Instead of producing single-sided arguments, summarization-based approaches also generate arguments representing both stances, which is particularly useful for controversial topics. From the perspective of argument generation, Alshomary *et al.* [2] argued that the objective of argument summarization is to extract snippets containing the main claim and the supporting reason of an argument. This task is called *Argument Snippet Generation (ASG)*. The authors addressed two goals of ASG: representativeness based on how much the core information of an argument is kept, and argumentativeness. They modified the LexRank algorithm [19] to account for the representativeness and improved argumentativeness of sentences by using lexicons of discourse and claim markers. One limitation of this approach is redundancy: since the summarization is based on top-ranked arguments retrieved by an argument search engine, there is no guarantee that the snippets represent different aspects. To tackle this redundancy issue, Alshomary et al. [3] adapted an approach from comparative summarization which was designed to answer questions like "What is different between the coverage in NYTimes and BBC?". The authors defined an argument snippet as contrastive if it highlights the uniqueness of an input argument compared to other arguments returned by an argument search engine. They extended the graph-based approach of [2], which ranks sentences based on their centrality and argumentativeness, by encoding an extra term to account for the sentence's similarity to other arguments. Their results showed a clear improvement, with a tradeoff between representativeness and contrastiveness.

Other Research Directions in AG. One of the emerging research areas in full argument generation is *Audience-oriented Argument Generation*. Alshomary et al. [1] implemented audience-based features in AG to enhance the persuasiveness of the generated arguments. They trained a BERT-based classifier to identify morals such as care, fairness and loyalty in arguments and used the Project Debater's API to generate arguments based on morals on 6 topics. In *Rhetoric-based Argument Generation*, Wachsmuth et al. [45] created a benchmark dataset with manually synthesized arguments that follow rhetorical strategies, containing 260 argumentative texts on 10 topic-stance pairs. Based on this dataset, El baff et al. [18] proposed a computational model to generate arguments according to a specific rhetorical strategy (Logos vs. Pathos) by imitating the process of selecting, arranging, and phrasing *Argumentative Discourse Units* (ADUs). Concretely, their approach viewed AG as a Language Modeling Task by considering ADUs as words and arguments as sentences. They first identified different ADU types using clustering then learned to select unit types matching the given strategy. The selected units are then arranged according to their argumentative roles (Thesis, Con, Pro). Finally, the argument is phrased by predicting the best set of semantically related ADUs for the arranged structure using supervised regression. Finally, the dialogue aspect of AG is getting more and more attention from researchers. Graph-based [36], rule-based [20] and retrieval-based neural generative systems [31] have all been explored, with more or less success and very different metrics for evaluation.

Counter-Argument Generation. Besides Sato et al. [40]'s value-based AG system, Wachsmuth et al. [46] designed another rule-based system to retrieve a counter-argument by identifying opposing conclusions to a given claim in the debate pool *idebate.org*. Concretely, their system detects similar conclusions with dissimilar premises and considers such arguments as counter-arguments. However, neural CAG is by far the most investigated approach because of the inherent overhead of maintaining rule-based systems. Hua and Wang [26] tackled this task in two steps: evidence retrieval and text generation. The authors first retrieved relevant Wikipedia articles using sentences in the original argument and then re-ranked the articles' paragraphs using TF-IDF similarity to the argument. The top-ranked sentences, concatenated with the input argument, were encoded and fed to the decoder producing first some keyphrases, then the counterarguments per se by attending to the keyphrases at the same time. Hua *et al.* [25]'s model further improves the previous method by extracting (instead of generating) keyphrases from the input statement. Also, it ranks evidence passages by their keyphrase overlap with the input statement and also their sentiment toward the input statement to encourage counter-evidence. More recently, Alshomary *et al.* [4] proposed to attack an argument by challenging the validity of one of its premises on the CMV dataset [28]. Concretely, the task is divided into two subtasks: Weak-Premise Ranking using the learn-to-rank framework [35] and Premise Attack Generation. For the generation part, they used OpenAI's GPT [37] as a pretrained language model and a joint-learning approach combining next-token prediction and counter-argument classification (given two concatenated segments, decide whether the second is a counter-argument to the first). Their approach did not outperform the baseline of [27], however, a manual evaluation in terms of content richness, correctness and grammaticality showed that their approach yielded better results.

Table 1. Datasets in AG and CAG classified by subareas.

Task	Datasets	Source	Size
CG	[22]	Crowd annotation	30k arguments, 71 topics
	[38]	Wikipedia articles	2.3k claims, 58 topics
Belief-based CG	[1]	debate.org	51k claims, 27k topics
CCG	[24]	Reddit	1,083,520 pairs of contrastive claims
Bias Flipping	[16]	Biased headlines from allsides.com	6458 claim-like headlines
CG or PTI	[7]	Wikipedia articles	2,394 claims, 55 topics
CTI	[47]	idebate.org	2,259 arguments, 676 topics
ER	[23]	Comments section of the New York Times	2k arguments with two enthymemes of which one is correct
	[8]	Extended from a collection of five sentence stories	7,2k argument-hypothesis pairs
ASG	[2]	args.me	83 arguments along with two-sentence snippets
AG and CAG	[45]	Written by experts based on pools of ADUs representing pros and cons	130 logos-oriented and 130 pathos-oriented arguments, 10 topics
	[26]	Change My View (CMV) channel of Reddit	26,525 arguments, 305,475 counter-arguments
	[4]	CMV	111.9k triples of argument, weak premise and counter-argument

4   Challenges and Open Research Directions

Despite the rich literature produced in AG and CAG, these two fields are still rapidly evolving and many challenges remain to be addressed. In this section, we highlight some of the most important challenges faced in AG and CAG.

Evaluation. Most automatic evaluation metrics used in CG and CAG are some commonly adopted metrics in machine translation and summarization such as BLEU, ROUGE and METEOR. Although automatic metrics are necessary for large-scale evaluation, the above-mentioned metrics are not specifically designed for argumentation and do not capture the essential qualities of an argument such as *cogency* (when an argument contains acceptable premises that are relevant to the argument's conclusion and that are sufficient to draw the conclusion), and *reasonableness* (when an argument contributes to the resolution of the given issue in a sufficient way that is acceptable to the target audience) [44]. In [25,26], despite some encouraging results using BLEU and ROUGE, for both studies, human evaluation shows that the quality of fully-generated counter-arguments is yet lower than that of a simple concatenation of evidence passages in terms of topical relevance and counterness. In fact, the simple criteria of understandability of an argument is far from being reached. In [16], out of 200 generated headlines, only 73 were understandable. The rule-based system of Sato *et al.* [40] has the same drawback (50 out of 86 sentences are judged as non-understandable). In addition, Chen *et al.* [16] found that for a successful flipping (CAG), the overlapping of generated and ground-truth headlines is very low, making overlap-based metrics unreliable. As for manual evaluation, a huge variety of author-dependent metrics is defined in the literature, making the cross-study comparability difficult. Studies concerning automatic argument quality evaluation [34,41] are arising and should be integrated to AG and CAG.

Argumentation Strategies Other Than Rhetoric. Argumentation strategies such as hypothetical reasoning, reasoning by cases, premise-to-goal arguments such as inference to the best explanation [33] have been the focus of the earliest studies in AG [49]. Current studies are mainly focused on the computational aspects and concentrate less on these aspects, which are however important to produce convincing arguments according to different audiences, in the same vein of the modeling of users' beliefs in AG and CAG systems.

Other Challenges. Although the main goal of argumentation is to convince instead of proving the truthfulness of a thesis, the truthfulness issue must be considered to fight against online disinformation. In the case of retrieval-based systems, the reliability of the retrieved claims and evidences must be checked. Recent studies have started investigating the automatic evaluation of fairness in argument retrieval [17], the automated fact-checking of claims [39] and the automatic detection of insufficiently supported arguments [42]. These dimensions are particularly relevant to prevent the spread of disinformation, especially in view of the increasing use of large language models such as GPT which, trained on datasets such as CMV [28], is prone to inject bias and unreliable information in the generated texts. Last but not least, when the argument is not sufficiently elaborated, clarification questions should be triggered to request additional information to have a meaningful dialogue with the end user. This line of research has already been introduced in question answering, but a deeper investigation is required in AG and CAG.

Notes on Ethical Issues. As for many other NLP methods, AG has the potential of being misused, as it allows to automatically generate a variety of potentially false assertions regarding a topic of interest. Also, as discussed above, current methods in AG and CAG inherit the biases and truthfulness issues of the underlying language models. While ethical issues must be considered when AG systems are deployed at a large scale, two points are worth noting: *i)* the main objective of AG and CAG is to generate coherent and understandable (counter-)arguments based on a given input, which still remains the biggest challenge to be resolved; *ii)* AG and CAG systems allow for arguments to be generated on both stances towards a topic, thus if one side on a topic is misrepresented, it would be easily uncovered and this can contribute to the discovery of the inherent bias pertaining to large generative language models.

5 Conclusions

Studies on AG and CAG are clearly on the rise, with multiple subareas and research directions. In this work, we draw a comprehensive outline of the subareas of AG and CAG as well as the biggest challenges in these two research fields. Our comparative examination of the existing literature highlights four promising lines of future research: *i)* the integration of users' beliefs and preferences in AG, which is reminiscent of early studies on AG in recommender systems where the user's profile play a role; *ii)* the development of intelligent argument dialogue systems, since arguments must be exchanged in a continuous fashion to reach a consensus; *iii)* the design of novel evaluation metrics concerning the quality of automatically generated arguments, and *iv)* the integration of fact-checking into AG to produce consistent, verified and sound arguments. All these challenges call for more innovative and reliable methods which would eventually allow for applications of AG and CAG in a even larger diversity of scenarios.

Acknowledgements. This work has been partially supported by the ANR project ATTENTION (ANR21-CE23-0037) and the French government through the 3IA Côte d'Azur Investments in the Future project managed by the National Research Agency (ANR) with the reference number ANR-19-P3IA-0002.

References

1. Alshomary, M., Chen, W.F., Gurcke, T., Wachsmuth, H.: Belief-based generation of argumentative claims. In: Proceedings of the 16th Conference of the European Chapter of the Association for Computational Linguistics: Main Volume (2021)

2. Alshomary, M., Düsterhus, N., Wachsmuth, H.: Extractive snippet generation for arguments. In: Proceedings of the 43rd International ACM SIGIR Conference on Research and Development in Information Retrieval, pp. 1969–1972. ACM, Virtual Event China (2020)

3. Alshomary, M., Rieskamp, J., Wachsmuth, H.: Generating contrastive snippets for argument search. In: Toni, F., Polberg, S., Booth, R., Caminada, M., Kido, H. (eds.) Frontiers in Artificial Intelligence and Applications. IOS Press (2022)

4. Alshomary, M., Syed, S., Dhar, A., Potthast, M., Wachsmuth, H.: Counter-argument generation by attacking weak premises. In: Findings of the Association for Computational Linguistics: ACL-IJCNLP 2021, pp. 1816–1827. Association for Computational Linguistics (2021)

5. Alshomary, M., Syed, S., Potthast, M., Wachsmuth, H.: Target inference in argument conclusion generation. In: Proceedings of the 58th Annual Meeting of the Association for Computational Linguistics, pp. 4334–4345. Association for Computational Linguistics (2020)

6. Ashley, K.D., Walker, V.R.: Toward constructing evidence-based legal arguments using legal decision documents and machine learning. In: Proceedings of the Fourteenth International Conference on Artificial Intelligence and Law, pp. 176–180 (2013)

7. Bar-Haim, R., Bhattacharya, I., Dinuzzo, F., Saha, A., Slonim, N.: Stance classification of context-dependent claims. In: Proceedings of the 15th Conference of the European Chapter of the Association for Computational Linguistics: Volume 1, Long Papers, pp. 251–261 (2017)

8. Bhagavatula, C., et al.: Abductive commonsense reasoning. arXiv preprint arXiv:1908.05739 (2019)

9. Bilu, Y., Hershcovich, D., Slonim, N.: Automatic claim negation: why, how and when. In: Proceedings of the 2nd Workshop on Argumentation Mining, pp. 84–93. Association for Computational Linguistics, Denver (2015)

10. Bilu, Y., Slonim, N.: Claim synthesis via predicate recycling. In: Proceedings of the 54th Annual Meeting of the Association for Computational Linguistics (Volume 2: Short Papers), pp. 525–530 (2016)

11. Boltužić, F., Šnajder, J.: Fill the gap! Analyzing implicit premises between claims from online debates. In: Proceedings of the Third Workshop on Argument Mining (ArgMining2016), pp. 124–133 (2016)

12. Bose, T., Reina, A., Marshall, J.A.: Collective decision-making. Curr. Opin. Behav. Sci. 16, 30–34 (2017)

13. Cabrio, E., Villata, S.: Five years of argument mining: a data-driven analysis. In: Proceedings of the Twenty-Seventh International Joint Conference on Artificial Intelligence, pp. 5427–5433. International Joint Conferences on Artificial Intelligence Organization, Stockholm (2018)

14. Carenini, G.: GEA: a complete, modular system for generating evaluative arguments. In: Alexandrov, V.N., Dongarra, J.J., Juliano, B.A., Renner, R.S., Tan, C.J.K. (eds.) ICCS 2001. LNCS, vol. 2073, pp. 959–968. Springer, Heidelberg (2001). https://doi.org/10.1007/3-540-45545-0_108

15. Chakrabarty, T., Trivedi, A., Muresan, S.: Implicit premise generation with discourse-aware commonsense knowledge models (2021)

16. Chen, W.F., Wachsmuth, H., Al-Khatib, K., Stein, B.: Learning to flip the bias of news headlines. In: Proceedings of the 11th International Conference on Natural Language Generation, pp. 79–88. Association for Computational Linguistics, Tilburg University, The Netherlands (2018)

17. Cherumanal, S.P., Spina, D., Scholer, F., Croft, W.B.: Evaluating Fairness in Argument Retrieval. In: Proceedings of the 30th ACM International Conference on Information & Knowledge Management, pp. 3363–3367 (2021)

18. El Baff, R., Wachsmuth, H., Al Khatib, K., Stede, M., Stein, B.: Computational argumentation synthesis as a language modeling task. In: Proceedings of the 12th International Conference on Natural Language Generation, pp. 54–64 (2019)

19. Erkan, G., Radev, D.R.: LexRank: graph-based lexical centrality as salience in text summarization. J. Artif. Intell. Res. **22**, 457–479 (2004)

20. Farag, Y., et al.: Opening up minds with argumentative dialogues. In: Findings of EMNLP (Empirical Methods in Natural Language Processing) (2022). In-Press

21. Gretz, S., Bilu, Y., Cohen-Karlik, E., Slonim, N.: The workweek is the best time to start a family–a study of GPT-2 based claim generation. arXiv preprint arXiv:2010.06185 (2020)

22. Gretz, S., et al.: A large-scale dataset for argument quality ranking: Construction and analysis. In: Proceedings of the AAAI Conference on Artificial Intelligence, vol. 34, pp. 7805–7813 (2020)

23. Habernal, I., Wachsmuth, H., Gurevych, I., Stein, B.: The argument reasoning comprehension task: Identification and reconstruction of implicit warrants. arXiv preprint arXiv:1708.01425 (2017)

24. Hidey, C., McKeown, K.: Fixed that for you: generating contrastive claims with semantic edits. In: Proceedings of the 2019 Conference of the North American Chapter of the Association for Computational Linguistics: Human Language Technologies, Volume 1 (Long and Short Papers), pp. 1756–1767. Association for Computational Linguistics, Minneapolis (2019)

25. Hua, X., Hu, Z., Wang, L.: Argument generation with retrieval, planning, and realization. arXiv preprint arXiv:1906.03717 (2019)

26. Hua, X., Wang, L.: Neural argument generation augmented with externally retrieved evidence (2018)

27. Hua, X., Wang, L.: Sentence-level content planning and style specification for neural text generation (2019)

28. Jo, Y., Bang, S., Manzoor, E., Hovy, E., Reed, C.: Detecting attackable sentences in arguments. arXiv preprint arXiv:2010.02660 (2020)

29. Lauscher, A., Wachsmuth, H., Gurevych, I., Glavaš, G.: Scientia potentia Est— on the role of knowledge in computational argumentation. Trans. Assoc. Comput. Linguist. **10**, 1392–1422 (2022)

30. Lawrence, J., Reed, C.: Argument mining: a survey. Comput. Linguist. **45**(4), 765–818 (2020)

31. Le, D.T., Nguyen, C.T., Nguyen, K.A.: Dave the debater: a retrieval-based and generative argumentative dialogue agent. In: Proceedings of the 5th Workshop on Argument Mining, pp. 121–130. Association for Computational Linguistics, Brussels (2018)

32. Levy, R., Bilu, Y., Hershcovich, D., Aharoni, E., Slonim, N.: Context dependent claim detection. In: Proceedings of COLING 2014, the 25th International Conference on Computational Linguistics: Technical Papers, pp. 1489–1500. Dublin City University and Association for Computational Linguistics, Dublin (2014)

33. Lipton, P.: Inference to the best explanation. A Companion to the Philosophy of Science, pp. 184–193 (2017)

34. Marro, S., Cabrio, E., Villata, S.: Graph embeddings for argumentation quality assessment. In: EMNLP 2022-Conference on Empirical Methods in Natural Language Processing (2022)

35. Pasumarthi, R.K., et al.: TF-ranking: scalable tensorflow library for learning-to-rank. In: Proceedings of the 25th ACM SIGKDD International Conference on Knowledge Discovery & Data Mining, pp. 2970–2978 (2019)
36. Prakken, H.: A persuasive chatbot using a crowd-sourced argument graph and concerns. Comput. Models Argument **326**, 9 (2020)
37. Radford, A., Narasimhan, K., Salimans, T., Sutskever, I.: Improving language understanding by generative pre-training, p. 12 (2018)
38. Rinott, R., Dankin, L., Alzate, C., Khapra, M.M., Aharoni, E., Slonim, N.: Show me your evidence-an automatic method for context dependent evidence detection. In: Proceedings of the 2015 Conference on Empirical Methods in Natural Language Processing, pp. 440–450 (2015)
39. Sathe, A., Ather, S., Le, T.M., Perry, N., Park, J.: Automated fact-checking of claims from Wikipedia. In: Proceedings of the Twelfth Language Resources and Evaluation Conference, pp. 6874–6882. European Language Resources Association, Marseille (2020)
40. Sato, M., et al.: End-to-end argument generation system in debating. In: Proceedings of ACL-IJCNLP 2015 System Demonstrations, pp. 109–114. Association for Computational Linguistics and The Asian Federation of Natural Language Processing, Beijing (2015)
41. Saveleva, E., Petukhova, V., Mosbach, M., Klakow, D.: Graph-based argument quality assessment. In: Proceedings of the International Conference on Recent Advances in Natural Language Processing (RANLP 2021), pp. 1268–1280 (2021)
42. Stab, C., Gurevych, I.: Recognizing insufficiently supported arguments in argumentative essays. In: Proceedings of the 15th Conference of the European Chapter of the Association for Computational Linguistics: Volume 1, Long Papers, pp. 980–990 (2017)
43. Tekiroglu, S.S., Chung, Y.L., Guerini, M.: Generating counter narratives against online hate speech: data and strategies. arXiv preprint arXiv:2004.04216 (2020)
44. Wachsmuth, H., et al.: Computational argumentation quality assessment in natural language. In: Proceedings of the 15th Conference of the European Chapter of the Association for Computational Linguistics: Volume 1, Long Papers, pp. 176–187. Association for Computational Linguistics, Valencia (2017)
45. Wachsmuth, H., Stede, M., El Baff, R., Al Khatib, K., Skeppstedt, M., Stein, B.: Argumentation synthesis following rhetorical strategies. In: Proceedings of the 27th International Conference on Computational Linguistics, pp. 3753–3765 (2018)
46. Wachsmuth, H., Syed, S., Stein, B.: Retrieval of the best counterargument without prior topic knowledge. In: Proceedings of the 56th Annual Meeting of the Association for Computational Linguistics (Volume 1: Long Papers), pp. 241–251. Association for Computational Linguistics, Melbourne (2018)
47. Wang, L., Ling, W.: Neural network-based abstract generation for opinions and arguments. arXiv preprint arXiv:1606.02785 (2016)
48. Woods, B., Adamson, D., Miel, S., Mayfield, E.: Formative essay feedback using predictive scoring models. In: Proceedings of the 23rd ACM SIGKDD International Conference on Knowledge Discovery and Data Mining, pp. 2071–2080. ACM, Halifax (2017)
49. Zukerman, I., McConachy, R., George, S.: Using argumentation strategies in automated argument generation. In: INLG 2000 Proceedings of the First International Conference on Natural Language Generation, pp. 55–62 (2000)

Novel Benchmark Data Set for Automatic Error Detection and Correction

Corina Masanti[1(✉)] [iD], Hans-Friedrich Witschel[2] [iD], and Kaspar Riesen[1,2] [iD]

[1] Institute of Computer Science, University of Bern, 3012 Bern, Switzerland
{corina.masanti,kaspar.riesen}@unibe.ch
[2] Institute for Informations Systems, University of Applied Sciences and Arts
Northwestern Switzerland, 4600 Olten, Switzerland
hans-friedrich.witschel@fhnw.ch

Abstract. The present paper introduces a novel benchmark data set for automatic error detection as well as error correction in text documents based on language models or other techniques. The data set contains a large number of sentences from various domains annotated with various types of errors (orthographic, grammatical, punctuation, and typography errors). The paper presents the method used to collect and annotate the documents, provides statistical analyses of the data set's properties and evaluates two preliminary baseline models for automatic error detection on a specific benchmark task. The results show, on the one hand, the effectiveness of the proposed data set for the evaluation of automatic error detection systems. On the other hand, these initial analyses also reveal that the data set contains challenging cases that are difficult to detect. Finally, the paper discusses potential applications of the proposed data set in the development and research of error detection and error correction systems.

Keywords: Error Detection · Error Correction · Benchmark Data Set · Document Analysis

1 Introduction

Current solutions for fully automated error correction often do not meet the requirements of professional proofreading services. This is particularly true in multilingual scenarios as it is often the case in Switzerland, where documents typically appear in three of the four[1] official Swiss languages (viz. German, French, Italian) as well as in English. This means that, especially in the professional field, several reviewers still proofread and annotate documents manually.

---

[1] The fourth official language of the country is Rhaeto-Romanic and is used relatively rarely.

Supported by Innosuisse project 101.128 IP-ICT: A PROSE - Advanced PROofreading SErvices and Rotstift AG.

E. Métais et al. (Eds.): NLDB 2023, LNCS 13913, pp. 511–521, 2023.
https://doi.org/10.1007/978-3-031-35320-8_38

With the recent advent of powerful and large-scale language models as well as deep-learning methods in document analysis, a universally applicable proofreading framework seems within reach. However, to date there are – at least in part – unresolved challenges for automated proofreading. This comprises, for instance, the detection of so-called real-word errors, the compliance with language-specific typesetting rules or company-specific spelling guidelines, as well as ensuring the use of gender-neutral language. Other areas that require further research and better solutions are the automatic detection of subjective language or the recognition of erroneous information (e.g. wrong dates or addresses).

One of the major challenges in the research of automatic proofreading systems is the lack of training data, which hinders scientific progress and maturity of software solutions. In other words, the availability of high-quality and comprehensive data sets with erroneous documents (whereby these errors should also be correctly annotated or corrected) is the crucial basis for pushing the frontiers of current knowledge in this particular field. A widely used solution to this problem is to generate artificial errors in correct sentences [1]. This can be done automatically, for instance, by algorithms that introduce grammatical mistakes, use wrong punctuation, or substitute one or two characters of a word. However, without a sufficiently large number of examples of real errors, automated error generation will not cover the broad range of possible human errors and artificial data sets are thus ill-suited to address the above mentioned challenges.

Major contribution of the present paper is the introduction of a novel large-scale and multilingual database of text documents. Actually, we present and provide a unique set of more than 50,000 documents that include several hundred thousand sentences in total. The text documents are exclusively written by native speakers of the respective language and are thus of linguistically fairly high quality. For each text document two versions are available – the original and the corrected version before and after proofreading by professional editors. That is, the corrections are made exclusively by human experts in proofreading. The main purpose of the novel data set is to enable the research of existing and novel techniques that automatically detect errors and correct text documents.

The remainder of this paper is organized as follows. Next, in Sect. 2, we briefly review the related work which is important for our research project. Eventually, in Sect. 3, we thoroughly describe the novel data set and the corresponding benchmark tasks. In Sect. 4 diverse preliminary results of two existing error detection models are provided. Finally, in Sect. 5, we draw conclusions and outline possible future research activities.

2   Related Work

The problem of automatic error detection and error correction in text documents has been extensively studied in the field of natural language processing [2]. Various approaches have been proposed to address this problem, and this section provides a brief overview of some of the most relevant works.

When it comes to error detection in text documents, dictionaries play an important role. Non-word errors may be detected by comparing all words in a text to dictionary entries. Obviously, this task is complicated by out-of-dictionary words which are uncommon real words, rare proper names (e.g. product or brand names), or words taken from other languages [3]. Detection of real-word errors is more challenging. Usually, a model of context is used to identify words that do not fit into a given linguistic context [4]. Often, this is achieved by using language models which capture the probability of words appearing in the context of other words [5]. The trigram-based model, for instance, is a popular approach that is often applied in this context [6,7]. In [8], real-word errors are detected using the Google Web 1T 3-gram data set in conjunction with a modified version of the Longest Common Subsequence string matching algorithm.

Another approach to error detection is based on statistical methods. In [9], for instance, two state-of-the-art approaches to grammatical error correction, viz. machine learned classification and machine based translation, are researched. In [10], the authors propose to train a compositional model for error detection that calculates the probability of each token in a sentence being correct or incorrect. To this end, the full sentence is used as context and the N best hypotheses, generated by statistical machine translation systems, are re-ranked.

Recently, with the advent of deep learning models, neural network-based approaches have also been proposed for error detection. In [11], for instance, a study using neural machine translation for error correction is presented. This system applies the so-called encoder-decoder mechanism proposed by [12]. Encoders read and encode entire source sentences into vectors, while decoders output translations by predicting the next words based on the encoded vectors and all the previously predicted words. In [13], it is proposed to use a multilayer convolutional encoder-decoder neural network for error correction. The network is initialized with embeddings that make use of character N-gram information.

With the availability of large-scale language models such as BERT or GPT even more sophisticated context modeling is possible [14]. Many of these approaches, for instance [15], tackle spell checking and correction simultaneously by treating spelling correction as a sequence labeling or "translation" task (translating an incorrect into a correct sentence). In [16], the authors also examine language models in grammatical error correction and show that it is entirely possible to build a simple system that only requires minimal annotated data (about 1,000 sentences). However, this particular system addresses only a small selection of error types. Moreover, since this approach relies on language-specific confusion sets created both manually and automatically, increasing the range of errors requires additional work. In [17], the authors explore the potential of more sophisticated language models in error correction and show that transformer architectures achieve consistently high performance rates.

3   Novel Data Set and Benchmark Tasks

A challenge for sophisticated methods of unrestricted error detection and error correction is their dependence on rather large quantities of labeled data, i.e., pairs of correct and incorrect sentences [18]. Several English data sets have become popular for training and evaluating error detection and error correction models, mostly as a result of shared tasks [19]. One such data set is the NUS Corpus of Learner English (NUCLE) [20], which consists of approximately 1,400 essays written by mainly Asian undergraduate students at the National University of Singapore annotated by professional English teachers. The NUCLE data set represents a specific genre of English which makes the models prone to overfitting and not being able to generalize well for other English levels and abilities. To address this gap, the BEA 2019 task [21] introduced a new annotated data set, the Cambridge English Write & Improve (W&I) and LOCNESS corpus, which is intended to represent a much broader range of English proficiency and levels than previous corpora. The W&I+LOCNESS test set contains 350 essays (4,477 sentences) on about 50 topics written by 334 authors around the world (including native English speakers).

Vast majority of efforts in spell checking focus on English, but for resource-scarce languages the research base is somewhat sparse [22]. A potential solution for languages less represented than English can be to generate artificial training data [18]. However, this relies on another resource, namely word or letter confusion sets, containing pairs of often confused words such as "accept" and "except". In [23], this problem is addressed by constructing generators introducing random insertions, deletions, replacements, or swappings of single characters within a randomly chosen word. Another problem that arises when creating such artificial training data is that one needs a large data set with error-free sentences in the first place. Wikipedia (or similar) can be easily used for this purpose (although a text that can be edited by anyone is likely to contain at least some errors).

The novel data set of text documents presented in the present paper for the first time comes from a professional Swiss proofreading company that has various clients, which in turn come from many different industries, including pharmaceutical companies, banks, insurance companies, wholesalers, retailers, communication agencies, advertising agencies, and others. The novel corpus represents a variety of different documents, including annual reports, letters, documentations, legal documents, advertisements, presentation slides, social media posts, newsletters, websites, magazine articles, and many others.

Since Switzerland has multiple national languages, many documents include a translation for each region of Switzerland. Thus, the language of the documents includes German, French, Italian, and English, with German being the language most used in the documents.

The corpus consists of both PDF and Word documents collected between 2019 and 2022, making it a large and unique collection of around 50,000 documents. In the present paper we focus on the Word documents only[2], containing a total of 142,449 sentences, where about 20% of the sentences are actually corrected by the editors. Remember, that these corrections are exclusively made by human experts in proofreading. The experts focus on orthography, grammar, punctuation as well as typography.

---

[2] Due to several technical problems currently arising on the PDF documents.

An interesting feature of the new data set is that it includes a variety of non-trivial errors, such as errors in the context of quotation marks, apostrophes, dashes, hyphens, real-word errors, misspelled brands and product names, missing or wrong punctuation marks, incorrect use of gender-neutral language, and lacking consistency (e.g. in terms of handling certain compounds in German, where both joining into one word or separating via hyphen are generally possible, but should be applied consistently).

For illustration purposes, we give three examples of corrected partial sentences[3] that can be found in the novel data set.

Example 1. Removing a hyphen between two nouns.
Brunch-Angeboten → *Brunchangeboten*

Example 2. Replacing a dash with a comma.
Keine leichte Aufgabe - hat eine [..] → *Keine leichte Aufgabe, hat eine* [..]

Example 3. Replacing a word with a more suitable expression.
[..] *mit einer Schiebetüre verbunden.* → [..] *mit einer Schiebetüre versehen.*

We propose two specific tasks on the novel data set. The first task consists of assigning a binary label to each sentence that encodes whether the sentence is correct (0) or not (1). The models and the experimental evaluation presented in Sect. 4 actually address this problem. The second, more difficult task, is not only to detect, but to directly correct those words inside a sentence that are incorrect. For the first task, classification models can be applied, while the second task requires models that can not only analyze and classify text inputs but can also produce well-formed sentences.

For both tasks, the 142,449 sentences are randomly shuffled and split into a training and test set (another option would be to randomly shuffle the document texts instead of the sentences). We define and provide two different splits, viz. a 0.6/0.4 and a 0.9/0.1 split for training and testing, respectively. Both sets for training and testing have a proportion of about 20% corrected sentences.

The cleaned (and possibly extended) version of the data set will be made publicly available on the Git repository of our research group[4].

4 Preliminary Experimental Evaluation

In the present paper, we experimentally investigate only the first task defined in Sect. 3, which concerns the detection of incorrect sentences in a data set of multilingual text documents. Two suitable models for this task are evaluated and compared with each other in the present paper in order to provide a first benchmark result for future research activities.

The first model employed is the Multilingual Text-to-Text Transfer Transformer (mT5) [24]. The model mT5 is based on the transformer architecture and

---

[3] All examples are in the German language.
[4] https://github.com/Pattern-Recognition-Group-UniBe.

is originally intended for translation tasks. The model is pre-trained on a massive multilingual corpus, enabling it to perform translation across a wide range of languages (about 100 languages, including low-resource languages). The model (actually, a multilingual variant of T5 [25]) can be fine-tuned for specific tasks – in our specific case for error detection. The original model solves text-to-text tasks. In the present case, however, we first let the model output the corrected sequence, and if the produced output is identical to the input sequence, we classify the sentence as correct, and otherwise as incorrect. For the experimental evaluation, we use the pre-trained base model of mT5 with both the encoder and decoder consisting of 12 blocks, attention mechanisms with 12 heads, and a hidden size of 768. The number of parameters is around 580M.

The second model used in the experimental evaluation is the Bidirectional Encoder Representations from Transformers (BERT) [26]. Originally, BERT was trained on two unsupervised tasks, masked language modeling and next sequence prediction. For our experimental evaluation, we use multilingual BERT (mBERT), which is a variant of BERT trained in 104 different languages. Actually, mBERT is well suited for sequence classification, and we can directly tune the model to predict the grammatical correctness of an input sentence. In the experimental evaluation, we use the pre-trained case-sensitive base model of mBERT with 12 transformer blocks, a hidden size of 768, and 12 self-attention heads. It has a total of around 110M parameters.

Preliminary evaluations show that the two models agree in their decision in about 65% of the sentences. Hence, we decide to combine the two models mT5 and mBERT in two different ways. First, we label a sentence as incorrect if, and only if, both mT5 and mBERT label the sentence as incorrect (we term this combined model as mT5 && mBERT). Second, we label a sentence as incorrect if either mT5 or mBERT detects that the sentence is incorrect (referred to as mT5 || mBERT).

Table 1. Overview of the performance metrics precision (P), recall (R), F1, and F0.5 measure for mT5 and mBERT as well as two combinations on the test set of the novel data set. The highest values for each metric are highlighted in bold. Prior to the evaluation, the models are fine-tuned on the training set of the same data set. We present results on two different training and test splits (0.6/0.4 and 0.9/0.1).

Model	0.6/0.4 Split				0.9/0.1 Split			
	P	R	F1	F0.5	P	R	F1	F0.5
mT5 [24]	0.32	0.65	0.43	0.35	0.33	0.66	0.44	0.36
mBERT [26]	0.71	0.48	**0.57**	**0.68**	0.72	0.54	**0.62**	**0.68**
mT5 && mBERT	**0.78**	0.40	0.52	0.65	**0.77**	0.44	0.56	0.67
mT5 || mBERT	0.33	**0.74**	0.46	0.38	0.35	**0.76**	0.47	0.39

In Table 1 we show the precision (P), the recall (R), the F1, and the F0.5 measure achieved by all models on the novel data sets (for both training-test splits). It is clearly observable that mT5 achieves higher recall values than mBERT, and vice versa mBERT achieves higher precision values than mT5. Moreover, we observe that the combination of the two models using a logical and (mT5 && mBERT), reaches the highest precision value, whereas the combination with a logical or (mT5 || mBERT) achieves the highest recall value. For all configurations, there is an increase in the F1 and F0.5 values for the 0.9/0.1 split, as can be expected. However, the increase is minor, which calls for additional investigation. We assume that the precision, recall, F1, and F0.5 values achieved through fine-tuning of the mT5 model as well as training of the mBERT model represent current lower bounds for the accuracy of future models and configurations.

Considering the relatively low values for both precision and recall, the question naturally arises as to how the underlying errors manifest themselves. For this reason, we conduct a qualitative analysis, in which we manually examine some erroneous example outputs of the mT5 model. In Table 2, we give ten example sentences and comments, which are labeled as

- false positive (i.e., correct sentences that are mistakenly corrected by the model)
- false negative (i.e., incorrect sentences that are mistakenly *not* corrected by the model)

With regard to this early qualitative assessment we conclude that there are several difficulties in the data set not adequately addressed yet by mT5 and mBERT. For instance, not all sequences marked as erroneous are objectively incorrect. With a higher proficiency level in a language, there are more possibilities for phrasing a sentence. The third false negative example in Table 2 showcases, for instance, that a sentence can be grammatically correct, but the readability could be improved depending on the context. Also, in the first false positive example, we see that the sentence is not grammatically wrong when we remove the word *However*, but we decrease the overall quality of the text. In addition, there is also human limitation. There is a possibility that not every error will be captured in the end by the human proofreaders. For example, one could argue that *industry-driven* can be preferred over *industry driven* (see the third false positive example).

Table 2. Qualitative analysis of false positive and false negative predictions of mT5. For the false positive and false negative examples, the sequence the model changed in the original sentence and the sequence that should be changed are both shown in italics, respectively (S) and described in the comment (C).

Case	Sentence (S) and Comment (C)
False Positives	**S:** *However,* the same conditions apply [..]
	C: The model removed the word *However.*
	S: [..] *Und* wir versprechen Ihnen, [..]
	C: The model removed the word *Und*
	S: [..] through its *industry driven* approach, [..]
	C: The model changed *industry driven* to *industry-driven*
	S: *IT:* Che fare dei soldi ricevuti in regalo?
	C: The model removed the language identifier *IT*
False Negatives	**S:** [..] Schweizer Nationalbank und der *europäischen* Zentralbank [..]
	C: The model missed capitalizing the word *europäischen*
	S: [..] , die den Weg auf den Südbalkon *freimachen*
	C: The model missed replacing the word *freimachen* with *freigeben*
	S: Die stilvollen *zwei* Nasszellen [..]
	C: The model missed removing the word *zwei*
	S: [..] über den App- oder Play Store
	C: The model missed removing the dash

5   Conclusions and Future Work

In this paper, we present a novel large-scale data set of text documents with several hundred thousand sentences in total in conjunction with high-quality corrections made by professional proofreaders. The text documents come from many different industries (banks, insurance companies, wholesalers, etc.) and represent various types of texts (annual reports, letters, documentation, etc.). The languages of the documents include German, French, Italian, and English. Preliminary experimental evaluations show that although language models have proved to be effective in such tasks and seem to be the most promising candidates for more in-depth analyses, they do not automatically produce perfect error detection. This means that with the two models evaluated (including their combination) we find either low values for recall or for precision, and we have to conclude that these systems are not yet ready to be a real aid for professional proofreaders. In a qualitative evaluation, it turns out that the errors we deal with are not simple orthographical or grammatical errors but of a more complex form, such as contextual misspellings (or not even errors in the grammatical sense but rather stylistic language issues). In summary, we observe that our novel data set reveals some unresolved challenges for automatic error detection systems.

For future work, we see several rewarding avenues to be pursued. First, it is our goal to further improve the language models by thoroughly optimizing the parametrization in validation experiments. Moreover, it would also be interesting to see how models with different architectures perform in our novel task and if more elaborated combinations of them turn out to be beneficial. In addition, we intend to explore strategies involving the identification of languages present in documents, followed by the use of dedicated monolingual models for each identified language, as opposed to multilingual models. Furthermore, we want to research methods to tackle the second task defined in the present paper (error correction rather than error detection). Last but not least, another objective could be to use the data set to design algorithms for automated error generation in order to produce an even larger variety of errors.

References

1. Rei, M., Felice, M., Yuan, Z., Briscoe, T.: Artificial error generation with machine translation and syntactic patterns. CoRR, abs/1707.05236 (2017)
2. Bryant, C., Yuan, Z., Qorib, M.R., Cao, H., Ng, H.T., Briscoe, T.: Grammatical error correction: a survey of the state of the art (2022)
3. Hládek, D., Staš, J., Pleva, M.: Survey of automatic spelling correction. Electronics 9(10), 1670 (2020)
4. Pirinen, T.A., Lindén, K.: State-of-the-art in weighted finite-state spell-checking. In: Gelbukh, A. (ed.) CICLing 2014, Part II. LNCS, vol. 8404, pp. 519–532. Springer, Heidelberg (2014). https://doi.org/10.1007/978-3-642-54903-8_43
5. Ali, M., Khalid, S., Rana, M.I., Azhar, F.: A probabilistic framework for short text classification. In: IEEE 8th Annual Computing and Communication Workshop and Conference, CCWC 2018, Las Vegas, NV, USA, 8–10 January 2018, pp. 742–747. IEEE (2018)
6. Wilcox-O'Hearn, A., Hirst, G., Budanitsky, A.: Real-word spelling correction with trigrams: a reconsideration of the mays, Damerau, and Mercer model. In: Gelbukh, A. (ed.) CICLing 2008. LNCS, vol. 4919, pp. 605–616. Springer, Heidelberg (2008). https://doi.org/10.1007/978-3-540-78135-6_52
7. Fossati, D., Di Eugenio, B.: A mixed trigrams approach for context sensitive spell checking. In: Gelbukh, A. (ed.) CICLing 2007. LNCS, vol. 4394, pp. 623–633. Springer, Heidelberg (2007). https://doi.org/10.1007/978-3-540-70939-8_55
8. Islam, A., Inkpen, D.: Real-word spelling correction using google web 1t 3-grams. In: Proceedings of the 2009 Conference on Empirical Methods in Natural Language Processing, EMNLP 2009, 6–7 August 2009, Singapore, A meeting of SIGDAT, a Special Interest Group of the ACL, pp. 1241–1249. ACL (2009)
9. Rozovskaya, A., Roth, D.: Grammatical error correction: machine translation and classifiers. In: Proceedings of the 54th Annual Meeting of the Association for Computational Linguistics, ACL 2016, 7–12 August 2016, Berlin, Germany, Volume 1: Long Papers. The Association for Computer Linguistics (2016)

10. Yannakoudakis, H., Rei, M., Andersen, Ø.E., Yuan, Z.: Neural sequence-labelling models for grammatical error correction. In: Palmer, M., Hwa, R., Riedel, S. (eds.) Proceedings of the 2017 Conference on Empirical Methods in Natural Language Processing, EMNLP 2017, Copenhagen, Denmark, 9–11 September 2017, pp. 2795–2806. Association for Computational Linguistics (2017)
11. Yuan, Z., Briscoe, T.: Grammatical error correction using neural machine translation. In: Knight, K., Nenkova, A., Rambow, O. (eds.) NAACL HLT 2016, The 2016 Conference of the North American Chapter of the Association for Computational Linguistics: Human Language Technologies, San Diego California, USA, 12–17 June 2016, pp. 380–386. The Association for Computational Linguistics (2016)
12. Cho, K., et al.: Learning phrase representations using RNN encoder-decoder for statistical machine translation. In: Moschitti, A., Pang, B., Daelemans, W. (eds.) Proceedings of the 2014 Conference on Empirical Methods in Natural Language Processing, EMNLP 2014, 25–29 October 2014, Doha, Qatar, A meeting of SIGDAT, a Special Interest Group of the ACL, pp. 1724–1734. ACL (2014)
13. Chollampatt, S., Ng, H.T.: A multilayer convolutional encoder-decoder neural network for grammatical error correction. In: McIlraith, S.A., Weinberger, K.Q. (eds.) Proceedings of the Thirty-Second AAAI Conference on Artificial Intelligence, (AAAI-18), the 30th innovative Applications of Artificial Intelligence (IAAI-18), and the 8th AAAI Symposium on Educational Advances in Artificial Intelligence (EAAI-18), New Orleans, Louisiana, USA, 2–7 February 2018, pp. 5755–5762. AAAI Press (2018)
14. Zhang, S., Huang, H., Liu, J., Li, H.: Spelling error correction with soft-masked BERT. CoRR, abs/2005.07421 (2020)
15. Moslem, Y., Haque, R., Way, A.: Adaptive machine translation with large language models. CoRR, abs/2301.13294 (2023)
16. Bryant, C., Briscoe, T.: Language model based grammatical error correction without annotated training data. In: Proceedings of the Thirteenth Workshop on Innovative Use of NLP for Building Educational Applications, pp. 247–253, New Orleans, Louisiana. Association for Computational Linguistics (2018)
17. Alikaniotis, D., Raheja, V.: The unreasonable effectiveness of transformer language models in grammatical error correction. CoRR, abs/1906.01733 (2019)
18. Tan, M., Chen, D., Li, Z., Wang, P.: Spelling error correction with BERT based on character-phonetic. In: 2020 IEEE 6th International Conference on Computer and Communications (ICCC), pp. 1146–1150. IEEE (2020)
19. Bryant, C., Yuan, Z., Qorib, M.R., Cao, H., Ng, H.T., Briscoe, T.: Grammatical error correction: a survey of the state of the art. CoRR, abs/2211.05166 (2022)
20. Dahlmeier, D., Ng, H.T., Wu, S.M.: Building a large annotated corpus of learner English: the NUS corpus of learner English. In: Tetreault, J.R., Burstein, J., Leacock, C. (eds.) Proceedings of the Eighth Workshop on Innovative Use of NLP for Building Educational Applications, BEA@NAACL-HLT 2013, 13 June 2013, Atlanta, Georgia, USA, pp. 22–31. The Association for Computer Linguistics (2013)
21. Bryant, C., Felice, M., Andersen, Ø.E., Briscoe, T.: The BEA-2019 shared task on grammatical error correction. In: Yannakoudakis, H., Kochmar, E., Leacock, C., Madnani, N., Pilán, I., Zesch, T. (eds.) Proceedings of the Fourteenth Workshop on Innovative Use of NLP for Building Educational Applications, BEA@ACL 2019, Florence, Italy, 2 August 2019, pp. 52–75. Association for Computational Linguistics (2019)

22. Etoori, P., Chinnakotla, M., Mamidi, R.: Automatic spelling correction for resource-scarce languages using deep learning. In: Shwartz, V., Tabassum, J., Voigt, R., Che, W., de Marneffe, M.-C., Nissim, M. (eds.) Proceedings of ACL 2018, Melbourne, Australia, 15–20 July 2018, Student Research Workshop, pp. 146–152. Association for Computational Linguistics (2018)

23. Näther, M.: An in-depth comparison of 14 spelling correction tools on a common benchmark. In: Calzolari, N., et al. (eds.) Proceedings of The 12th Language Resources and Evaluation Conference, LREC 2020, Marseille, France, 11–16 May 2020, pp. 1849–1857. European Language Resources Association (2020)

24. Xue, L., et al.: mT5: a massively multilingual pre-trained text-to-text transformer. In: Toutanova, K., et al. (eds.) Proceedings of the 2021 Conference of the North American Chapter of the Association for Computational Linguistics: Human Language Technologies, NAACL-HLT 2021, Online, 6–11 June 2021, pp. 483–498. Association for Computational Linguistics (2021)

25. Raffel, C., et al.: Exploring the limits of transfer learning with a unified text-to-text transformer. J. Mach. Learn. Res. **21**, 140:1–140:67 (2020)

26. Devlin, J., Chang, M.-W., Lee, K., Toutanova, K.: BERT: pre-training of deep bidirectional transformers for language understanding. CoRR, abs/1810.04805 (2018)

Weakly-Supervised Multimodal Learning for Predicting the Gender of Twitter Users

Haruka Hirota, Natthawut Kertkeidkachorn[✉], and Kiyoaki Shirai

Japan Advanced Institute of Science and Technology, Ishikawa, Japan
{s2110142,natt,kshirai}@jaist.ac.jp

Abstract. Social media platforms, e.g. Twitter, are significant sources of information, with various users posting vast amounts of content every day. Analyzing such content has the potential to offer valuable insights for commercial and research purposes. To gain a comprehensive understanding of the information, it is crucial to consider the demographics of users, with gender being a particularly important factor. Nevertheless, the gender of Twitter's users is not usually available. Predicting the gender of Twitter's users from tweet data becomes more challenging. In this paper, we introduce a weakly supervised method to automatically build the supervision data. The experimental result show that our weak supervision component could generate well-annotated data automatically with an accuracy rate exceeding 85%. Furthermore, we conduct a comparative analysis of various multimodal learning architectures to predict the gender of Twitter users using weak supervision data. In the study, five multimodal learning architectures: 1) Early Fusion, 2) Late Fusion, 3) Dense Fusion, 4) Caption Fusion, and 5) Ensemble Fusion, are proposed. The experimental results on the evaluation data indicate that Caption Fusion outperforms the other multimodal learning architectures and baselines.

Keywords: Gender Prediction · Multimodal Learning · Deep Learning · Transformer-based Models · Tweet Data

1 Introduction

Twitter has become a significant communication platform that generates a vast amount of data for both commercial and research purposes [12]. Since the content on Twitter is created by various users, understanding the characteristics of users, such as their gender, is crucial for gaining insights into content, user behavior, and preferences. This understanding can be particularly valuable for companies and service providers seeking to improve their products and services [1]. Nevertheless, since the gender is often not included in user profiles, it can be challenging to accurately analyze differences in trends and opinions between men and women.

Several studies [6,7,9,11,13] have investigated gender prediction for Twitter data. The studies show that multimodal learning approaches, where texts and

E. Métais et al. (Eds.): NLDB 2023, LNCS 13913, pp. 522–532, 2023.
https://doi.org/10.1007/978-3-031-35320-8_39

images of tweets are incorporated, could improve the accuracy of gender prediction. Although many multimodal learning approaches have been studied so far, most of them rely on the existing annotated data for supervision. Obtaining annotated data for model training typically involves self-annotation or crowdsourcing methods, which is time-consuming.

To address this issue, we introduce a weakly supervised method for generating annotated supervision data to train the gender prediction model. Furthermore, we propose five multimodal learning architectures: 1) Early Fusion, 2) Late Fusion, 3) Dense Fusion, 4) Caption Fusion and 5) Ensemble Fusion, for the gender prediction task. To evaluate the effectiveness of our approach, we conducted empirical experiments and compared them with various baselines.

The rest of the paper is organized as follows. In Sect. 2, we discuss the related work. The problem definition of the task is given in Sect. 3. Section 4 presents the methodology used for gender prediction. In Sect. 5, we describe the experiments and results. Finally, we conclude our work in Sect. 6.

2 Related Work

Several studies have been conducted on estimating the gender of Twitter users. Sakaki et al. improved the accuracy of gender estimation by using images of tweets in addition to the text of tweets [11]. In their approach, representations for images and text were learned separately and then combined to predict the gender. Ma et al. showed that images of tweets were effective in estimating the gender of users [7]. They constructed a dataset with 10 different labels for the type of subject of the image corresponding to the gender of the user who posted it. Then they trained a model on this dataset to classify the subject of the image and a model to predict the gender of users. Liu et al. compared the performance of classical machine learning models and deep learning models and found that Bidirectional Encoder Representations from Transformers (BERT) gave the best results for gender estimation [6]. Wang et al. trained a classifier that estimates gender based on profile images, user names, user screen names, and self description text and could achieve a high accuracy rate for gender prediction [13]. Apart from the studies mentioned above, the Author Profiling Shared Tasks (PAN at CLEF) [9,10] have been introduced, which involves gender prediction from Twitter data. Numerous systems have been developed through this shared task.

Based on our review above, we found that many studies utilized self-annotation, crowdsourcing, or publicly available datasets to train their models. However, constructing these datasets can be both expensive and time-consuming. While the study [5] has employed weak supervision to extract user profiles from Twitter, their focus has primarily been on obtaining information such as job status, educational background, and marital status - all of which are usually included in the user's profile and therefore easier to obtain. In contrast, the gender is typically not provided in the profile, making it more challenging to obtain the gender label.

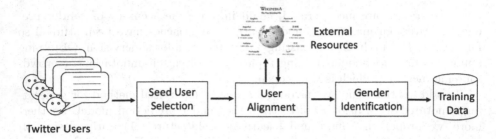

Fig. 1. The flow of Weak Supervision for generating annotations for the gender of Twitter users.

3   Problem Definition

The gender prediction on Twitter is a task to predict the gender of Twitter users by using historical tweets. We can formally define this problem as follows: Given the set of n users $U = \{U_1, U_2, U_3, ..., U_n\}$ and the m historical tweets of the $i\text{-}th$ user $U_i = \{U_{i,1}, U_{i,2}, U_{i,3}, ..., U_{i,m}\}$, the goal is to predict gender of U_i as $F(U_i) \rightarrow \{male, female\}$. A tweet could include both text and images. Note that, while a user profile could aid in predicting gender, our study merely focuses on analyzing the user's tweets.

4   Methodology

In our study, there are three components: 1) Weak Supervision, 2) Multimodal Learning, and 3) Classification. The Weak Supervision component generates supervision data, which is then utilized by the Multimodal Learning component to train a model capable of estimating gender scores. Finally, the Classification component determines the gender of the Twitter user by aggregating the gender scores. We provide detailed information on each of these components below.

4.1   Weak Supervision

Weak Supervision is used to automatically generate annotations for the gender of Twitter users, which can be used to train gender prediction models. As shown in Fig. 1, Weak Supervision consists of three steps: 1) Seed User Selection, 2) User Alignment, and 3) Gender Identification. The details of each step are explained below:

Seed User Selection is the process of selecting users who are reliable and have the potential to be annotated the gender easily. The selection of user accounts plays an important role in achieving high-quality annotation data for training. On Twitter, many users are not real, such as spare accounts or bots. Additionally, automatic labeling of the gender for unknown users might be difficult since it is challenging to obtain their information from external resources. In Seed User Selection, users are selected based on the number of followers. We assume that the more followers a user has, the more famous they are, and the easier it is to obtain their information from external resources. Therefore, we aim to select the users with many followers as seed users.

User Alignment is the process of aligning seed users with external resources to enhance the information relating to Twitter users. This process is essential because Twitter does not provide users with gender information. Aligning the users with the reliable external resource, particularly Wikipedia, aims to obtain the information of their gender. In User Alignment, we use a search engine to find the user on Wikipedia. Here a user is supposed to be a celebrity and there is his/her article on Wikipedia. If we can find the user's image on Wikipedia, we align the user to that image. However, if we cannot find the user's image on Wikipedia, we utilize Google Image Search and retrieve the top five images from the search results as the images representing the user. Note that we aim to use an image of users to identify their gender because gender information is not provided on Wikipedia.

Gender Identification is the process of classifying the gender of users based on their aligned images. During Gender Identification, an existing face recognition system is applied to classify the gender of users. If a user can be matched with a Wikipedia image during the User Alignment process, we identify their gender using that image alone. This is because Wikipedia images are considered as the reliable reference. However, if a user cannot be matched with a Wikipedia image, we use the top five images from Google Image Search and classify each one. The results are then voted on to determine the user's gender.

4.2 MultiModal Learning

The multimodal learning component aims to learn a model capable of predicting the gender score for each tweet post. The gender score is a value of [0,1]. The score closer to 1 represents male, and closer to 0 represents female. In our approach, we aim to investigate and compare various multimodal learning architectures for the gender prediction task. Therefore, we have proposed five multimodal learning models: 1) Early Fusion, 2) Late Fusion, 3) Dense Fusion, 4) Caption Fusion and 5) Ensemble Fusion, for predicting the gender of a tweet, as shown in Fig. 2. The Early Fusion, Late Fusion, and Dense Fusion models jointly learn representations from raw texts and raw images. The Caption Fusion model converts images into the description and combines the texts with the description of the images. The Ensemble Fusion model combines the Early Fusion model with a pretrained language model.

The representation of the text of a tweet, denoted as r_{txt}, is computed by $r_{txt} = PLM(U_{i,j}^{text})$, where $U_{i,j}^{text}$ is the text part of the j-th tweet of the user U_i, and $PLM(\cdot)$ is a pretrained language model. The representation of the image of a tweet, denoted as r_{img}, is defined as $r_{img} = PVM(U_{i,j}^{image})$, where $U_{i,j}^{image}$

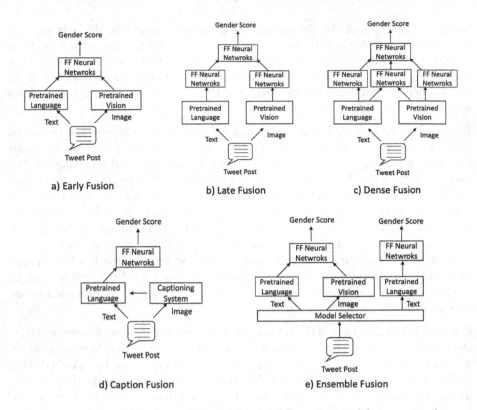

Fig. 2. The architectures of four Multimodal Learning models in our study

is the image part of the *j-th* tweet of the user U_i, and $PVM(\cdot)$ is a pretrained vision model. The details of each model are as follows.

Early Fusion is a model that combines the representations of text r_{txt} and the representations of image r_{img} by using a feed-forward neural network, as shown in Fig. 2 a). The Early Fusion model is defined as follows:

$$\hat{y}_{i,j} = \sigma(W \cdot [r_{txt}; r_{img}] + b), \tag{1}$$

where $\sigma(\cdot)$ is the softmax function, W and b are trainable parameters of the feed-forward neural network.

Late Fusion is designed to pass r_{txt} and r_{img} through separate feed-forward neural networks before combining them with another feed forward neural network, as shown in Fig. 2 b). The gender score of the Late Fusion model is calculated as follows:

$$\hat{y}_{i,j} = \sigma(W \cdot [FF(r_{txt}); FF(r_{img})] + b), \tag{2}$$

where $FF(\cdot)$ is a feed-forward neural network.

Dense Fusion combines both the Early Fusion model and the Late Fusion model, as depicted in Fig. 2 c). The Dense Fusion model is defined as follows:

$$\hat{y}_{i,j} = \sigma(W \cdot [FF(r_{txt}); FF(r_{txt}; r_{img}); FF(r_{img})] + b) \tag{3}$$

Caption Fusion is designed to convert the image into a text description, which is then concatenated with the text and fed into a pretrained language model to predict the gender score. The model is shown in Fig. 2 d). The Caption Fusion model can be calculated using the following equations:

$$r_{twt} = PLM(U_{i,j}^{text} \langle sep \rangle CPT(U_{i,j}^{image})) \tag{4}$$

$$\hat{y}_{i,j} = \sigma(W \cdot r_{twt} + b), \tag{5}$$

where $CPT(\cdot)$ is a captioning system used to convert images into text and $\langle sep \rangle$ is the special token used to separate text and image description in the pretrained language model.

Ensemble Fusion is designed to utilize either the Early Fusion model or the pretrained language model, depending on the input tweet. Typically, a tweet may contain either text only or both a text and an image. In the Caption Fusion model, if the tweet does not include an image, the text description of the image from the captioning system cannot be obtained, and we simply disregard the output of the captioning system. However, the Early Fusion, Late Fusion, and Dense Fusion models require an image as part of their architecture. When an image is absent from a tweet, we replace its representation with a zero vector ($\vec{0}$). This substitution can potentially impact the effectiveness of the model. To address this issue, we introduce the Ensemble Fusion model, which is trained separately on tweets that contain either text and image or text only. In the Ensemble Fusion model, the Model Selector module is responsible for determining which model to use in order to predict the gender score for a given tweet. The Model Selector module chooses the Early Fusion model when a tweet contains both text and image, and selects the pretrained language model when the tweet contains only text. The Ensemble Fusion model is defined as follows.

$$\hat{y}_{i,j} = \begin{cases} \sigma(W \cdot [r_{txt}; r_{img}] + b), & \text{if an image in } U_{i,j} \\ \sigma(W \cdot [r_{txt}] + b), & \text{otherwise} \end{cases} \tag{6}$$

In the multimodal learning component, the five models are used to train for predicting the gender score for each tweet. To optimize the five models, the cross-entropy function is applied as follows

$$L = -\sum_{i=1}^{n} \sum_{j=1}^{m} y_{i,j} \cdot log(\hat{y}_{i,j}), \tag{7}$$

where $y_{i,j}$ is the gender label obtained from the weak supervision component, $\hat{y}_{i,j}$ is the gender prediction score from the Early Fusion model, the Late Fusion model, the Dense Fusion model, the Caption Fusion model, or the Ensemble Fusion Model.

4.3 Classification

The Classification component is responsible for identifying the gender of Twitter users. Through the Multimodal Learning models, we can predict the gender score for each tweet. However, users typically have many historical tweets, making it necessary to aggregate the gender scores of these tweets to determine the user's gender. We employ two aggregation methods: 1) average aggregation, and 2) stereotype aggregation. The average aggregation method simply calculates the mean gender score for historical tweets.

$$S_i = \frac{1}{m} \sum_{j=1}^{m} \hat{y}_{i,j}, \tag{8}$$

where m is a number of tweets for the user U_i.

The stereotype aggregation method selects 20% of a user's tweets - 10% with scores closest to 1 (male) and 10% closest to 0 (female) - and then calculates their mean. This process filters out unreliable scores, as those close to 0.5 are difficult to interpret whether the user is male or female. We define it as follows:

$$S_i = \frac{1}{|High(U_i)| + |Low(U_i)|} \sum_{j \in High(U_i) \cup Low(U_i)} \hat{y}_{i,j}, \tag{9}$$

where $High(U_i)$ and $Low(U_i)$ are sets of the indices of the tweets of the user U_i with the 10% highest and lowest gender scores, respectively.

5   Experiments and Results

5.1 Evaluation Data

To assess the effectiveness of our approach, it's crucial to have a dataset that's been manually labeled since the weak supervision data could contain wrong gender labels assigned through the automation process. For this reason, we manually labeled a smaller group of users to create the evaluation dataset. Our study is focused on estimating the gender of ordinary users. Consequently, we randomly select 500 users with fewer than 1,000 followers. We then ask three experts to annotate the latest 20 tweets and the profiles of Twitter users. There are 3 categories in the annotation process: "Male", "Female", and "Unknown". the Fleiss' kappa coefficient [4] is calculated to determine the level of agreement among the annotators. We obtained the coefficient of 0.747, indicating that the gender labels were assigned with a relatively high level of agreement.

In order to create a high-quality evaluation dataset, we only included users who were assigned the same label by two or more annotators, with "unknown" users being excluded from the dataset. Our evaluation dataset was comprised of 459 users, consisting of 286 males and 173 females.

5.2   Implementation

For the weak supervision component, the top 5,000 users from the public follower ranking list[1] are selected as the seed users. We then utilize Face++[2] to automatically annotate images associated with users. Face++ was chosen as the annotation tool due to its claim of achieving high accuracy in gender annotation for human images.

In the multimodal learning component, the pre-trained language model is Bidirectional Encoder Representations from Transformers (BERT) [2]. Given that our tweet data is in Japanese, we utilize bert-base-japanese[3]. The pre-trained vision model is Vision Transformers[4] [3]. In the Caption Fusion model, we adopt the Clip model, as the captioning system, from the study [8]. To enable the English caption to be applied to Japanese BERT, we use a Translation service to translate the caption into Japanese[5].

The output data from the weak supervision component is split into three parts: training, validation, and test, with a ratio of 8:1:1. The training data is utilized to train the model, whereas the validation data is used for the hyperparameter selection. The test data is used to evaluate the models.

5.3   Experimental Setup

This study comprises two experiments. Experiment 1 assesses the effectiveness of the weak supervision component, while Experiment 2 investigates the effectiveness of our multimodal learning approach for the gender prediction task.

In Experiment 1, we evaluate the Weak Supervision component by selecting 200 users from both the most popular and least popular users in our user pool. The annotator is then tasked with verifying the accuracy of the labels in the weak supervision data. Our report on this experiment includes the number of users that are misclassified, including those that are mistakenly labeled as male-to-female, female-to-male, and non-human accounts. Additionally, we present the total error rate obtained from the experiment.

Experiment 2 aims to evaluate the effectiveness of our multimodal learning models by conducting the gender prediction task. To this end, we employ two test datasets: 1) Weak Supervision Test Set and 2) Evaluation Data. The Weak Supervision Test Set is generated from Weak Supervision, with 10% of the data reserved for testing, as outlined in Subsect. 5.2. On the other hand, the Evaluation Data is a human-created dataset, as described in Subsect. 5.1. In this experiment, we use accuracy as the evaluation metric.

---

[1] https://meyou.jp/ranking/follower_allcat.
[2] https://www.faceplusplus.com.
[3] https://huggingface.co/cl-tohoku/bert-base-japanese.
[4] https://pytorch.org/vision/main/models/vision_transformer.html.
[5] https://pypi.org/project/googletrans/.

Table 1. Statistical Error Report of Weak Supervision Data

	A Number of Error Cases	
	Top Famous Users	Least Famous Users
Miss Match Male To Female	11	7
Miss Match Female To Male	0	0
None Human Account	2	5
Total Error Rate	13.5%	12.5%

5.4   Baselines

In Experiment 2, we have selected three baselines for comparison: Text Only, Image Only, and Sakaki et al. approach [11]. The Text Only model only takes the text component of tweets into account, and we train it using Japanese BERT. The Image Only model, on the other hand, only analyzes the image portion of tweets, and we train it using Vision Transformers. As for Sakaki et al.'s approach, its architecture is similar to Early Fusion, but instead of concatenating text and image representations, they calculate the average of both representations.

5.5   Experimental Results

In Experiment 1, we check the annotations of 200 top famous users and 200 least famous users from our list. We found that out of 200 users, 96 are labeled by our weak supervision component for each of top famous users and least famous users. However, some users are left unannotated because such users could not be aligned to Wikipedia. The error report of the weak supervision component's annotation is presented in Table 1. Upon analyzing the results, we found that the weak supervision component's errors occurred due to mismatches from male to female and non-human accounts. Non-human accounts refer to users that represent an organization/company rather than an individual. The false alignment appears because some organizations have the same name as an individual. Also, Table 1 presents the results, revealing that the weak supervision component generated data with an incorrect rate of less than 15%. This means that more than 85% of the weak supervision data are labeled correctly.

Table 2 presents the findings of Experiment 2, revealing that the Ensemble Fusion model utilizing the stereotype classifier achieves superior performance on the weak supervision test set. On the other hand, the Caption Fusion model with the average classifier demonstrates the best performance on the evaluation data. As for the aggregation technique, the average aggregation proves to be more effective than the stereotype aggregation, with the exception of the Late Fusion model on both test data and the Ensemble Fusion model on the weak supervision test set. This suggests that even tweets having middle scores can aid in determining gender in the majority of the models.

After analyzing the Text Only results, we found that it perform well on the weak supervision test data. However, its performance significantly drops

Table 2. Accuracy on predicting the gender of Twitter users.

Model	Weak Supervision Test Set		Evaluation Data	
	Average	Stereotype	Average	Stereotype
Text Only	0.852	0.845	0.667	0.624
Image Only	0.774	0.762	0.758	0.754
Baseline [11]	0.858	0.817	0.791	0.782
Early Fusion	0.791	0.786	0.739	0.721
Late Fusion	0.608	0.561	0.617	0.725
Dense Fusion	0.582	0.672	0.732	0.708
Caption Fusion	0.855	0.823	**0.813**	0.754
Ensemble Fusion	0.881	**0.893**	0.791	0.782

when tested on the evaluation data. This indicates that the text characteristics generated from famous users in the weak supervision data are not similar to those produced by ordinary users. On the other hand, Image Only yields comparable results on both the weak supervision test set and evaluation data, implying that images are robust features for gender classification. This finding further supports the idea of using a multimodal learning approach, involving both text and images, for the gender prediction task on Twitter.

When comparing the Baseline, Early Fusion, and Ensemble Fusion models, all three are based on the Early Fusion architecture. Nevertheless, the Early Fusion model lacks a mechanism for handling situations where an image in the tweet is missing, and instead represents the image as a zero vector. On the other hand, the Baseline model uses the average representation of both text and image. In cases where the image is absent, the model relies solely on the text representation, which is similar to our Ensemble Fusion model. Although our study suggests that images are crucial, it is still necessary to address how the model should function when the image is missing.

Of the three approaches - Early Fusion, Late Fusion, and Dense Fusion - the results indicate that Early Fusion performed the best on both test datasets. This suggests that building a complex network may not be necessary for the gender prediction task.

Despite the training data from the weak supervision component achieving around 85% accuracy, the best model achieved an accuracy of 81.3% on the evaluation data. Therefore, weakly supervised multimodal learning is a very promising.

6   Conclusion

This paper presented a novel approach to predicting the gender of Twitter users using weakly supervised multimodal learning. Our approach leveraged weak supervision to generate sufficient training data for prediction models. We also proposed five multimodal learning models, including Early Fusion, Late Fusion, Dense Fusion, Caption Fusion, and Ensemble Fusion. In Experiment 1, we showed that we could automatically generate supervision data with over 85% accuracy. Moreover, we demonstrated that we could successfully train multimodal learning models using this weak supervision data. Our experimental results indicated that the Caption Fusion model outperformed other models and baselines on the evaluation data. In the future, we plan to explore the user profile to enhance the prediction performance further.

References

1. Argamon, S., Koppel, M., Pennebaker, J.W., Schler, J.: Automatically profiling the author of an anonymous text. Commun. ACM **52**(2), 119–123 (2009)
2. Devlin, J., Chang, M.W., Lee, K., Toutanova, K.: BERT: Pre-training of deep bidirectional transformers for language understanding. In: Proceedings of the 2019 Conference of the North American Chapter of the Association for Computational Linguistics: Human Language Technologies, pp. 4171–4186 (2019)
3. Dosovitskiy, A., et al.: An image is worth 16x16 words: Transformers for image recognition at scale. arXiv preprint arXiv:2010.11929 (2020)
4. Fleiss, J.L.: Measuring nominal scale agreement among many raters. Psychol. Bull. **76**(5), 378 (1971)
5. Li, J., Ritter, A., Hovy, E.: Weakly supervised user profile extraction from twitter. In: Proceedings of the 52nd Annual Meeting of the Association for Computational Linguistics, pp. 165–174 (2014)
6. Liu, Y., Singh, L., Mneimneh, Z.: A comparative analysis of classic and deep learning models for inferring gender and age of twitter users. In: Proceedings of the 2nd International Conference on Deep Learning Theory and Applications (2021)
7. Ma, X., Tsuboshita, Y., Kato, N.: Gender estimation for SNS user profiling using automatic image annotation. In: 2014 IEEE International Conference on Multimedia and Expo Workshops (ICMEW), pp. 1–6. IEEE (2014)
8. Mokady, R., Hertz, A., Bermano, A.H.: Clipcap: clip prefix for image captioning. arXiv preprint arXiv:2111.09734 (2021)
9. Rangel, F., Rosso, P., Montes-y Gómez, M., Potthast, M., Stein, B.: Overview of the 6th author profiling task at pan 2018: multimodal gender identification in twitter. Working notes papers of the CLEF (2018)
10. Rangel, F., Rosso, P., Potthast, M., Stein, B.: Overview of the 5th author profiling task at pan 2017: Gender and language variety identification in twitter. Working notes papers of the CLEF (2017)
11. Sakaki, S., Miura, Y., Ma, X., Hattori, K., Ohkuma, T.: Twitter user gender inference using combined analysis of text and image processing. In: Proceedings of the Third Workshop on Vision and Language, pp. 54–61 (2014)
12. Suman, C., Naman, A., Saha, S., Bhattacharyya, P.: A multimodal author profiling system for tweets. IEEE Trans. Comput. Soc. Syst. **8**(6), 1407–1416 (2021)
13. Wang, Z., et al.: Demographic inference and representative population estimates from multilingual social media data. In: Proceedings of the World Wide Web conference, pp. 2056–2067 (2019)

Cross-Domain Toxic Spans Detection

Stefan F. Schouten$^{(\boxtimes)}$, Baran Barbarestani, Wondimagegnhue Tufa,
Piek Vossen, and Ilia Markov

Vrije Universiteit Amsterdam,
De Boelelaan 1105, 1081 HV Amsterdam, The Netherlands
{s.f.schouten,b.barbarestani,w.t.tufa,p.t.j.m.vossen,i.markov}@vu.nl

Abstract. Given the dynamic nature of toxic language use, automated
methods for detecting toxic spans are likely to encounter distributional shift. To explore this phenomenon, we evaluate three approaches
for detecting toxic spans under cross-domain conditions: lexicon-based,
rationale extraction, and fine-tuned language models. Our findings indicate that a simple method using off-the-shelf lexicons performs best in
the cross-domain setup. The cross-domain error analysis suggests that
(1) rationale extraction methods are prone to false negatives, while (2)
language models, despite performing best for the in-domain case, recall
fewer explicitly toxic words than lexicons and are prone to certain types
of false positives. Our code is publicly available at: https://github.com/
sfschouten/toxic-cross-domain.

1 Introduction

The rise of social media over the past decade and a half and the accompanying
increase in exposure to toxic language has motivated much research into the
automated detection of such language [6,13]. Online toxic language use is highly
dynamic and often specific to particular communities. To deal with shifts in use
of toxic language over time and to handle particular communities being underrepresented in the training data, methods for toxic language detection should
generalize outside the original data distribution. Generalization for message-level
toxic language detection was previously investigated by evaluating methods in a
cross-domain setup [22]. This has provided valuable insights into how well methods trained on data from one domain perform on data from other domains. In
this work, we investigate the *detection of toxic spans* [14] in a cross-domain setup.
In contrast to detecting overall toxicity, detecting spans aids the explainability of
such systems and supports moderators in deciding on appropriate interventions
sensitive to the dynamics within specific communities.

We address the following research question: how well do current methods for
toxic spans detection perform in a cross-domain setting? Our first contribution
answers this question quantitatively: we evaluate three kinds of methods using
the same metrics on the same datasets, reporting in-domain and cross-domain
performance. Two experimental settings are considered: one where the overall
toxicity of the texts is considered known a priori, and another where a binary

E. Métais et al. (Eds.): NLDB 2023, LNCS 13913, pp. 533–545, 2023.
https://doi.org/10.1007/978-3-031-35320-8_40

toxicity classifier is used to infer the overall toxicity. The second contribution is an in-depth error analysis of the best performing methods where we investigate and group incorrect predictions by type.

Our experimental results indicate that off-the-shelf lexicons of toxic language outperform all other methods in a cross-domain setup, whether the binary toxicity is assumed to be known or inferred. The error analysis suggests that language models recall fewer explicitly toxic words than lexicons, and that they are prone to particular types of false positives, such as incorrectly predicting the target of the toxicity as a part of the toxic span.

2   Related Work

The task of toxic spans detection originated as a shared task at SemEval 2021 [14]. From the submissions, Pavlopoulos et al. [14] identified multiple interesting approaches, three of which are described in the following paragraphs.

Lexicon-based approaches were widely used for message-level toxicity classification. They are based on word-matching techniques, which do not take context into account and miss censored or altered swear words. Despite this, and although these methods are unsupervised, they still achieve fairly good results [6]. When lexicons were used for toxic spans detection, several approaches constructed them from (span-annotated) toxic data [14]. The lexicon-based approaches performed well, with F1 scores of up to 64.98% attained by Zhu et al. [24]. Using a simple statistical strategy, Zhu et al. built their lexicon from the shared task's training data (see Subsect. 3.2). We include their method for constructing lexicons in our experiments and explore its effectiveness in a cross-domain setting.

Rationale extraction techniques use Explainable Artificial Intelligence (XAI) methods to attribute a toxicity classifier's decision to its inputs. Performing the detection of toxic spans using XAI approaches assumes that the inputs that are most important to a toxicity classifier also comprise the toxic spans we aim to detect. A big benefit is that XAI approaches are generally unsupervised and do not require much data [15]. Different XAI methods have been used, including model-specific attention-based methods [15,18], but also model-agnostic methods such as SHAP [15] and LIME [3]. We include the rationale extraction approach in our experiments and evaluate rationales from four XAI methods under cross-domain conditions.

Fine-tuned language models (LMs) formed the most popular category among the shared task submissions [14]. Both the winner and the runner-up of the shared task were based on ensembles of fine-tuned LMs [12,24]. Both submissions used LMs fine-tuned for sequence labeling with the BIO (Beginning, Inside, Outside) scheme, but Zhu et al. [24] also used an LM fine-tuned for span boundary detection. Others participants, such as Chhablani et al. [4], used models designed for extractive question answering. We also include a fine-tuned LM in our experiments, investigating how well it performs in a cross-domain setting.

Recently, Ranasinghe & Zampieri [16] used the dataset from the SemEval shared task to train a model with multi-lingual embeddings, evaluating on

Danish and Greek datasets. They also evaluated their model off-domain for document-level toxicity detection, whereas we evaluate cross-domain toxic span detection. Previous work has also investigated *message-level* toxicity classifiers under cross-domain conditions, reporting significant drops in performance [8,10,13]. On the message-level task pre-trained language models show better generalization and ability to deal with domain shift. However, combining them with either external resources such as lexicons [13] or with feature-engineered approaches [8] can improve cross-domain prediction performance further. Pamungkas et al. [13] note that previous works have investigated two types of domains: topic domains (e.g., racism vs. sexism), and platform domains (e.g., Twitter vs. Facebook). While there may be differences in the topic distributions of our domains, our primary focus is on toxic spans detection across platform domains.

To the best of our knowledge, we are the first to evaluate methods for the detection of toxic spans under cross-domain conditions. By doing so, we shed light on which approaches are best suited to handle shifts to out-of-domain data.

3   Methodology

This section describes in detail the methods for toxic spans detection we include in our experiments, and how we evaluate them.

3.1   Evaluation

Our evaluation metric is based on that used in SemEval-2021 Task 5, where Pavlopoulos et al. [14] define the following metric:

$$F_1^+(\mathcal{Y}, \mathcal{T}) = \begin{cases} F_1(\mathcal{Y}, \mathcal{T}) & |\mathcal{T}| > 0 \\ 1 & |\mathcal{T}| = |\mathcal{Y}| = 0 \\ 0 & otherwise \end{cases} \qquad (1)$$

Where $\mathcal{Y}$, $\mathcal{T}$ correspond respectively to the predicted and ground truth sets of toxic character offsets, and with:

$$F_1(\mathcal{Y}, \mathcal{T}) = \frac{2 \cdot P(\mathcal{Y}, \mathcal{T}) \cdot R(\mathcal{Y}, \mathcal{T})}{P(\mathcal{Y}, \mathcal{T}) + R(\mathcal{Y}, \mathcal{T})}, P(\mathcal{Y}, \mathcal{T}) = \frac{|\mathcal{Y} \cap \mathcal{T}|}{|\mathcal{Y}|}, R(\mathcal{Y}, \mathcal{T}) = \frac{|\mathcal{Y} \cap \mathcal{T}|}{|\mathcal{T}|}. \qquad (2)$$

They introduce this modified F_1 score to handle texts that do not include span annotations. We further use it to evaluate performance on non-toxic texts, which we include in our experimentation (see Sect. 4). We use the same metric, but report the macro (instead of micro) average between toxic and non-toxic samples. We do so because the chosen datasets differ in ratio of toxic to non-toxic (see Table 1). By using macro averages we can compare results across datasets.

We investigate each method in two settings. The first setting assumes that we know for each text if it is toxic or not, we call this setting 'ToxicOracle'. This demonstrates the ability of each method to identify toxic spans separately from their ability to identify overall toxicity. The second setting 'ToxicInferred' makes no such assumption. Instead, it includes a binary toxicity classifier to predict whether texts are toxic before predicting the actual toxic spans. The errors made in the first stage are propagated to the second stage by not predicting any spans whenever the binary classifier predicts the text as non-toxic.

3.2   Methods for Toxic Spans Detection

We perform toxic spans detection using three distinct approaches chosen based on the results of SemEval 2021 task [14].

Lexicons. We use two varieties of lexicons: pre-existing lexicons of toxic language and lexicons constructed from toxic spans detection training data. For the latter we use the methodology proposed by Zhu et al. [24]: we quantify the toxicity of a word as the frequency with which it occurs in a toxic span relative to its overall frequency. The lexicon is constructed by only including words with a toxicity score higher than a certain threshold.

Rationales. We extract rationales from a model (in our case, BERT [5]) trained on binary toxicity classification (*toxic* vs. *non-toxic*) using various eXplainable AI (XAI) methods. The XAI methods we use attribute the decision of a model to its inputs. The result is a score for each input indicating its importance relative to the other inputs. To obtain the toxic spans we threshold these importance scores, thereby predicting that the toxic parts of the input are those parts which were most important to the binary toxicity classifier.

LMs. We fine-tune an LM (BERT) for token classification using BIO labels.

4   Experimental Details

Our main experimental contribution is the systematic evaluation of methods for the prediction of toxic spans in a cross-domain setting. Each of our methods is evaluated both under in-domain and cross-domain conditions.

4.1   Datasets

Our experiments are carried out with two datasets annotated for toxic spans. Their similarities and differences are described below.

SemEval-2021 Task 5 [14]. This shared task introduced a dataset of toxic samples harvested from the Civil Comments dataset, re-annotating a portion for toxic spans. In the campaign, annotators were asked to "Extract the toxic word sequences (spans) of the comment [...], by highlighting each such span". The inter-annotator agreement was "moderate", with the lowest observed Cohen's Kappa being 0.55.

Table 1. Dataset statistics. Columns 'Train', 'Dev', and 'Test' show the distribution of toxic (Toxic) and non-toxic (¬Toxic) spans. The rows show the fraction of data that has spans (Span) and the fraction that does not (No span). The last column shows the average percentage of each sample's text that is part of a toxic span.

		Train		Dev		Test		Span-%
		Toxic	¬Toxic	Toxic	¬Toxic	Toxic	¬Toxic	
SemEval	Span	93.9%	-	93.8%	-	80.3%	-	13.2%
	No span	6.1%	-	6.2%	-	19.7%	-	-
HateXplain	Span	57.6%	-	57.4%	-	57.5%	-	15.7%
	No span	1.8%	40.6%	2.0%	40.6%	1.9%	40.6%	-

HateXplain [11]. This dataset consists of posts from the social media platforms Twitter and Gab. Besides the message-level toxicity annotations, the annotators were also asked to "highlight the rationales that could justify the final class." No inter-annotator agreement is reported for the span annotations.

In Table 1, one can see that both datasets have toxic samples annotated with toxic spans. However, the SemEval data does not include any non-toxic samples. Furthermore, both datasets have some toxic samples without any spans (6.1% and 1.8%, respectively). For both datasets this could either indicate that the annotators disagreed on which characters/tokens were toxic (final annotation was decided by a majority vote) or that the annotators agreed that, despite the sample being toxic, there is no specific span that is responsible for the toxicity of the message (implicit toxicity).

In order to perform the evaluation in the 'ToxicInferred' setting, we train a binary toxicity classifier. To make this possible on the SemEval dataset, we supplemented the data with non-toxic samples from the same Civil Comments data that the original dataset is based on. In line with the requirements used for collecting the SemEval data, we take comments that were marked not toxic by a majority of at least three raters. We randomly sample from the eligible comments until we reach a 50/50 balance between toxic and non-toxic messages.

4.2   Implementation Details

We use BERT-base [5] in the following three cases. After fine-tuning for binary toxicity classification we use it (1) as the model to which we apply rationale extraction and (2) for the binary toxicity predictions that are required for the 'ToxicityInferred' setting. Finally, we also fine-tune BERT directly for toxic spans detection, including a variant with a final Conditional Random Fields (CRF) layer [7]. We choose BERT because Zhu et al. [24] used it to obtain state-of-the-art performance in the Semeval 2021 shared task [14].

4.3   Hyper-parameter Search

We first evaluate each combination of hyper-parameters using the same dataset for training and evaluation (in-domain). The training and evaluation are done on the canonical training and development splits, respectively. To perform the hyper-parameter tuning, we select the set of hyper-parameter values with the best in-domain performance. These are then used to evaluate on the test splits of both the same dataset (in-domain) and cross-domain dataset.

Method-Agnostic. We include one hyper-parameter that influences the way in which the predicted spans are evaluated, determining how close together different spans are allowed to be. This process merges any two spans that are at most n characters apart, which may be beneficial for each of the methods, since none of them predicts white space between tokens as toxic (the lexicons just match the words, while the other two methods use BERT tokenization which removes white space characters). The grid-search values are $n \in \{0, 1, 9\,999\}$. A value of $9\,999$ is added to join all spans together, never allowing more than one span.

Lexicons. We evaluate both constructed and existing lexicons. The existing lexicons we use are HurtLex [2] and the lexicon published by Wiegand et al. [23]. Both lexicons come in two differently sized variants: 'conservative' and 'inclusive' for HurtLex, and 'base' and 'expanded' for Wiegand et al. [23]. We refer to these as Hurtlex-c, Hurtlex-i, Wiegand-b, and Wiegand-e. The constructed lexicons have method-specific hyper-parameters. The first is the threshold θ that sets the minimum toxicity score required for a word to enter the lexicon (see Subsect. 3.2). The second is the minimum number of occurrences of words in the dataset (min_occ). We thereby exclude words that occur so infrequently that we cannot accurately measure their toxicity. Values included in the search are: $\{0, 0.05, \ldots, 1\}$ for the value of θ, and $\{1, 3, 5, 7, 11\}$ for the value of the minimum number of occurrences.

Rationales. We include the following four input attribution methods in our experiments: Saliency [19], Integrated Gradients [21], DeepLIFT [20], and LIME [17]. Each method works by generating scores that indicate the relative importance of the input tokens. Following Pluciński & Klimczak [15], we rescale the scores to sum up to 1. The threshold that the score must exceed in order to be predicted as toxic is a hyper-parameter that we tune. Values included in the search for the threshold are $\{-0.05, -0.025, \ldots, 0.5\}$.

LMs. The hyper-parameters specific to the language models such as learning rate, dropout, etc. are left to their default values[1].

---

[1] See https://huggingface.co/bert-base-cased/blob/main/config.json.

Table 2. Results for setting 'ToxicOracle' after hyper-parameter tuning for F_1^+ on the Toxic part of each dataset. The metric columns from left to right are: F_1^+, Precision, and Recall on the Toxic part of the datasets; the F_1^+ score on the non-toxic part of the datasets ($\neg$Toxic); and, the macro average (harmonic mean) of the F_1^+ scores between the toxic and non-toxic parts of the dataset. The last two of which are in gray to emphasize that in this setting these metrics are not optimized and/or tuned for. For both tables the overall highest scores are in bold, the best scores of the second best method are underlined.

(a) In-domain results for the SemEval and HateXplain datasets.

		Toxic			$\neg$Toxic	Macro	Toxic			$\neg$Toxic	Macro
		F_1^+	Prec.	Rec.	F_1^+	F_1^+	F_1^+	Prec.	Rec.	F_1^+	F_1^+
				HateXplain					SemEval		
Lexicons	Constr.	64.7	74.4	69.6	12.4	20.8	59.8	59.5	84.5	59.0	59.4
	HurtLex-c	36.4	47.2	39.5	14.2	20.4	42.9	40.4	72.2	20.0	27.3
	HurtLex-i	40.3	39.5	56.5	2.7	5.0	34.9	29.0	76.6	6.3	10.6
	Wiegand-b	47.4	68.2	48.4	37.5	41.8	36.1	44.7	42.1	58.3	44.6
	Wiegand-e	44.9	56.3	50.4	15.7	23.3	46.1	44.2	73.7	21.9	29.7
Rationales	Saliency	44.1	50.1	61.7	5.5	9.8	53.6	57.5	73.4	26.8	35.7
	Int. Grad.	54.0	69.9	57.1	7.0	12.4	57.6	60.2	77.0	20.4	30.1
	DeepLIFT	27.3	22.7	70.0	4.9	8.2	33.7	33.4	54.3	9.2	14.5
	LIME	40.6	46.6	46.1	0.3	0.5	45.9	48.1	63.1	52.0	48.7
LMs	BERT	**74.9**	**82.3**	**80.4**	12.3	21.1	**64.4**	**64.7**	**87.4**	51.0	56.9
	BERT+CRF	73.5	80.8	79.3	12.1	20.9	64.1	64.5	86.7	50.4	56.4

(b) Cross-domain results for the SemEval and HateXplain datasets. Column title $X \rightarrow Y$ indicates trained on X, evaluated on Y.

		SemEval $\rightarrow$ HateXplain					HateXplain $\rightarrow$ SemEval				
Lexicons	Constr.	24.6	49.7	23.1	45.0	31.8	13.6	16.7	9.1	46.5	21.0
	HurtLex-c	36.4	47.2	39.5	14.2	20.4	42.9	40.4	72.2	20.0	27.3
	HurtLex-i	40.3	39.5	**56.5**	2.7	5.0	34.9	29.0	**76.6**	6.3	10.6
	Wiegand-b	**47.4**	**68.2**	48.4	37.5	41.8	36.1	**44.7**	42.1	58.3	44.6
	Wiegand-e	44.9	56.3	50.4	15.7	23.3	**46.1**	44.2	73.7	21.9	29.7
Rationales	Saliency	39.0	53.8	41.2	6.8	11.5	33.2	28.3	63.8	28.7	30.8
	Int. Grad.	34.2	44.0	37.6	2.7	5.0	35.0	33.1	61.1	12.8	18.7
	DeepLIFT	27.2	33.6	34.6	3.1	5.5	17.5	13.9	63.5	11.7	14.0
	LIME	23.5	34.4	24.8	8.2	12.1	17.6	15.4	32.4	0.9	1.6
LMs	BERT	42.7	56.7	45.9	16.8	24.1	25.7	31.5	31.8	60.5	36.0
	BERT+CRF	42.8	57.6	46.1	18.5	25.9	27.5	29.3	40.6	27.7	27.6

Table 3. Results for the 'ToxicInferred' setting after hyper-parameter tuning for Macro F_1^+. The metric columns from left to right are: F_1^+, Precision, and Recall on the Toxic part of the datasets; the F_1^+ score on the non-toxic part of the datasets (¬Toxic); and, the macro average (harmonic mean) of the F_1^+ scores between the toxic and non-toxic parts of the dataset. In both tables, the overall highest scores are in bold, the best scores of the second best method are underlined.

(a) In-domain results for the SemEval and HateXplain datasets.

		Toxic			¬Toxic	Macro	Toxic			¬Toxic	Macro
		F_1^+	Prec.	Rec.	F_1^+	F_1^+	F_1^+	Prec.	Rec.	F_1^+	F_1^+
				HateXplain					SemEval		
Lexicons	Constr.	53.3	81.1	53.2	82.0	64.6	60.5	61.9	81.2	95.8	74.2
	HurtLex-c	30.8	48.4	31.8	82.6	44.8	43.7	41.2	70.6	95.2	59.9
	HurtLex-i	33.8	40.9	45.7	81.5	47.7	35.7	29.4	74.2	94.8	51.9
	Wiegand-b	42.9	72.3	42.9	**84.5**	56.9	37.0	45.9	41.4	**97.0**	53.6
	Wiegand-e	41.2	61.1	44.7	82.2	54.9	46.7	45.1	71.9	95.3	62.7
Rationales	Saliency	36.0	53.3	46.8	82.7	50.1	53.5	58.4	70.4	94.7	68.4
	Int. Grad.	46.7	80.3	45.1	81.3	59.4	57.9	61.7	74.4	94.7	71.9
	DeepLIFT	21.6	21.5	54.8	81.7	34.1	34.4	33.8	52.2	94.8	50.5
	LIME	37.4	59.1	37.5	81.3	51.2	47.1	49.8	61.8	94.6	62.8
LMs	BERT	**59.5**	**84.9**	**61.7**	81.5	**68.7**	**63.9**	**65.6**	**84.1**	94.8	**76.4**
	BERT+CRF	58.6	83.6	61.1	81.7	68.3	63.6	65.4	83.3	94.9	76.1

(b) Cross-domain results for the SemEval and HateXplain datasets. Column title $X \rightarrow Y$ indicates trained on X, evaluated on Y.

		SemEval → HateXplain					HateXplain → SemEval				
Lexicons	Constr.	14.3	43.6	11.1	**64.2**	23.4	17.2	18.2	2.6	97.7	29.3
	HurtLex-c	29.5	51.2	30.8	51.9	37.6	23.1	34.2	20.0	96.4	37.3
	HurtLex-i	30.6	41.8	**40.6**	48.6	37.5	21.3	25.3	**21.6**	96.1	34.9
	Wiegand-b	**34.5**	**66.6**	34.4	62.0	**44.3**	22.7	**39.2**	13.2	**97.8**	36.8
	Wiegand-e	31.8	56.0	34.3	54.2	40.1	**23.4**	35.2	19.9	96.4	**37.6**
Rationales	Saliency	27.3	53.6	27.0	49.5	35.2	21.1	28.2	15.8	96.4	34.6
	Int. Grad.	25.4	47.7	24.4	48.3	33.3	22.4	34.7	15.3	96.0	36.3
	DeepLIFT	19.7	34.3	22.7	49.0	28.1	16.5	11.5	19.3	96.0	28.1
	LIME	20.1	40.7	19.2	49.0	28.5	19.8	23.9	13.6	96.0	32.9
LMs	BERT	31.6	55.7	33.3	51.3	39.1	20.3	27.0	11.8	96.4	33.5
	BERT+CRF	32.1	56.7	33.8	51.7	39.6	20.1	25.9	13.1	96.2	33.2

5   Results

In this section, we present the results of our experiments. We first report the in-domain performance of the span detection methods. Then we report the cross-domain performance and the relative drop compared to the in-domain results.

In-Domain. Performance of the methods can be seen in Table 2a for the 'ToxicOracle' setting, and in Table 3a for the 'ToxicInferred' setting. We observe similar patterns in both settings. For example, it is clear that in both cases in-domain performance is highest for the fine-tuned LMs, which matches results obtained in the shared task [14]. The second best scores are achieved with the lexicons constructed from span-annotated training data. Existing lexicons do worse and are outperformed by the rationale extraction using Integrated Gradients.

When comparing our results (Table 2a) to those obtained by Zhu et al. [24], we see that our fine-tuned LMs and lexicon underperform theirs by several points (64.4 vs. 69.44 for the LMs and 59.8 vs. 65.0 for the lexicon). This could be because we did not clean the training data as they did or due to minor differences in training setup and lexicon construction.

Cross-Domain. The performance of the methods under cross-domain conditions can be seen in Table 2b for the 'ToxicOracle' setting and in Table 3b for the 'ToxicInferred' setting. Contrary to the in-domain results, the fine-tuned LMs are outperformed by the Wiegand et al. [23] lexicons in all cases.

We calculate the ratio of cross-domain performance to in-domain performance (as measured by Toxic and Macro F_1^+ scores for the 'ToxicOracle' and 'ToxicInferred' settings, respectively). The performance of the constructed lexicons drops dramatically (to 34% of the in-domain scores on average) resulting in them being ranked last in the cross-domain setup. The LMs retain more of their performance, but still drop to (on average) 50% The rationale extraction methods keep 62% of their original performance on average. Since the existing lexicons are not related to any domain, they do not lose any performance in the 'ToxicOracle' setting. In the 'ToxicInferred' setting the drop is small for 'SemEval → HateXplain' (retaining 86%) while losing substantial performance for 'HateXplain → SemEval' (keeping only 56%). The only reason these lexicons could perform worse in this setting is due to cross-domain application of the binary toxicity classifier, suggesting that the classifier transfers much better in one direction than the other.

6   Error Analysis

We analyse and compare the types of errors made by each of the methods. We take inspiration from van Aken et al. [1] who perform a detailed error analysis where they classify errors by their type. We analyse prediction errors made by the best performing variant of each method. By selecting the best methods we analyse the best case scenario for each approach. The errors are sampled such that we have guaranteed representation for every combination of high and low precision and recall. We sample 75 errors for each method on each dataset (225 per dataset, 450 total). We identify a number of error classes, where each contains either false negatives (FN) or false positives (FP). Four classes and three aggregations can be seen with their prevalence for each method and dataset in Table 4.

Doubtful Labels. Likely due to the subjective nature of this task, the number of errors classified as having a doubtful label was quite high. In total, 40.9% of the sampled HateXplain errors, and 23.5% of the sampled SemEval errors had a doubtful label. This is in line with analyses done for message-level detection [9].

False Negatives. The language model has the lowest false negative rate for HateXplain, but for the SemEval dataset the lexicon-based span prediction has the lowest false negative rate. The FN-explicit class indicates what proportion of false negatives involved explicitly toxic words (e.g., "nonsensical aussie **retarded** babbles"). The class was applied to any prediction that involved not predicting a word despite it being explicitly toxic. On both datasets, these kinds of errors were most common for the rationale extraction method, and least common for the lexicon-based predictions. The latter was expected since these lexicons are created specifically to cover explicitly toxic words. We also tracked what we call subword errors, which are span predictions that do not cover a word entirely. The FN-subword-toxic class was applied to any erroneous spans from which a morphologically relevant part was missing. For example: "...what **stupid**ity and arrogance ..." (predicted span in bold). These errors were most prevalent among the lexicon-based predictions. This is due to the lexicons being applied by finding exact matches without taking into account affixes.

False Positives. The overall false positive rate is the lowest for the rationale extraction method on both datasets, and was high for the lexicons and LMs. A high false positive rate for LMs is in line with previous findings on message-level toxicity detection [8]. For the lexicon the high rate can be explained by the high rate of FP-subword-toxic errors. That class tracks false positives where one of the spans is an explicitly toxic word, but inside a non-toxic word, for example, the words 'ho' and 'lame' being marked in: "...that I some**ho**w b**lame** him ...". This happens often for the lexicon predictions, because it looks for any matches with the lexicon's entries. We also included FP-target, which is a false positive of a target group, for example: "... **republican** you are not welcome here ...". This error type is quite rare, but more common for the fine-tuned LMs.

Table 4. The results of the error analysis, showing the prevalence of each class (rows) for every method on each dataset (columns). Last three rows show aggregates, with percentage of errors that had any of the subword classes, false negative classes, or false positive classes.

	SemEval → HateXplain			HateXplain → SemEval		
	Lexicon (Wiegand-b)	Rationale (Saliency)	LM (BERT)	Lexicon (Wiegand-e)	Rationale (Int. Grad.)	LM (BERT)
FN-explicit	19.6%	36.5%	21.4%	1.7%	37.3%	32.3%
FN-subword-morph	34.5%	4.9%	0.0%	11.9%	4.0%	0.0%
FP-subword-toxic	5.5%	2.1%	0.8%	31.1%	0.9%	3.6%
FP-target	0.0%	3.1%	5.5%	0.7%	0.6%	2.2%
-subword-	16.7%	16.3%	2.5%	66.5%	10.2%	12.0%
FN-*	59.9%	56.5%	48.1%	23.6%	60.4%	52.6%
FP-*	32.5%	22.3%	48.2%	76.8%	25.9%	60.9%

7 Conclusion and Discussion

We have evaluated three kinds of methods for toxic spans predictions in a cross-domain setting. Our results show that the performance of the fine-tuned LMs suffers greatly when applied to out-of-domain data, thereby making off-the-shelf lexicons of toxic language the best performing option. This suggests that fine-tuned LMs do not handle domain shift that may occur from changes in the use of toxic language or the relative prominence of communities in the data. This differs from what was observed for the message-level task, where LMs showed better generalization capabilities. The cross-domain error analysis showed that language models are more likely to produce false positives (excluding subword false positives). This means that tokens that are toxic in the training data are not toxic in the test data across domains, where the learned lexical representations do not transfer and are also not corrected in context by the models. In some cases, we also found that targets of toxic language were falsely included in the predicted spans. On the other hand, the spans predicted by language models also miss more explicit toxicity than those predicted with lexicons, although rationale extraction misses even more still.

Limitations of this work include: (a) the fine-tuning approach being evaluated with BERT and no other LM; (b) the absence of attention-based XAI methods among those selected for the rationale extraction approach; and (c) having no more than two span-annotated datasets for the cross-domain evaluation.

In future work, we will focus on improving cross-domain performance by combining approaches explored in this work within an ensemble strategy, since our error analysis suggests that the methods make different types of errors.

Acknowledgements. This research was supported by Huawei Finland through the DreamsLab project. All content represented the opinions of the authors, which were not necessarily shared or endorsed by their respective employers and/or sponsors.

References

1. van Aken, B., Risch, J., Krestel, R., Löser, A.: Challenges for toxic comment classification: an in-depth error analysis. In: Proceedings of ALW2, pp. 33–42 (2018). https://doi.org/10.18653/v1/W18-5105
2. Bassignana, E., Basile, V., Patti, V.: Hurtlex: a multilingual lexicon of words to hurt. In: Cabrio, E., Mazzei, A., Tamburini, F. (eds.) Proceedings of CLiC-it 2018, pp. 51–56 (2018). https://doi.org/10.4000/books.aaccademia.3085
3. Benlahbib, A., Alami, A., Alami, H.: LISAC FSDM USMBA at SemEval-2021 task 5: tackling toxic spans detection challenge with supervised SpanBERT-based model and unsupervised LIME-based model. In: Proceedings of SemEval-2021, pp. 865–869 (2021). https://doi.org/10.18653/v1/2021.semeval-1.116
4. Chhablani, G., Sharma, A., Pandey, H., Bhartia, Y., Suthaharan, S.: NLRG at SemEval-2021 task 5: toxic spans detection leveraging BERT-based token classification and span prediction techniques. In: Proceedings of SemEval-2021, pp. 233–242 (2021). https://doi.org/10.18653/v1/2021.semeval-1.27
5. Devlin, J., Chang, M.W., Lee, K., Toutanova, K.: BERT: pre-training of deep bidirectional transformers for language understanding. In: Proceedings of NAACL-HLT2019 (Long and Short Papers), vol. 1, pp. 4171–4186 (2019). https://doi.org/10.18653/v1/N19-1423
6. Fortuna, P., Nunes, S.: A survey on automatic detection of hate speech in text. ACM Comput. Surv. **51**(4), 85:1–85:30 (2018). https://doi.org/10.1145/3232676
7. Lafferty, J.D., McCallum, A., Pereira, F.C.N.: Conditional random fields: probabilistic models for segmenting and labeling sequence data. In: Proceedings of ICML 2001, pp. 282–289 (2001)
8. Markov, I., Daelemans, W.: Improving cross-domain hate speech detection by reducing the false positive rate. In: Proceedings of NLP4IF 2021, pp. 17–22 (2021). https://doi.org/10.18653/v1/2021.nlp4if-1.3
9. Markov, I., Gevers, I., Daelemans, W.: An ensemble approach for Dutch cross-domain hate speech detection. In: Rosso, P., Basile, V., Martínez, R., Métais, E., Meziane, F. (eds.) NLDB 2022. LNCS, vol. 13286, pp. 3–15. Springer, Cham (2022). https://doi.org/10.1007/978-3-031-08473-7_1
10. Markov, I., Ljubešić, N., Fišer, D., Daelemans, W.: Exploring stylometric and emotion-based features for multilingual cross-domain hate speech detection. In: Proceedings of WASSA2021, pp. 149–159 (2021)
11. Mathew, B., Saha, P., Yimam, S.M., Biemann, C., Goyal, P., Mukherjee, A.: HateXplain: a benchmark dataset for explainable hate speech detection. In: Proceedings of the AAAI Conference on Artificial Intelligence, vol. 35, pp. 14867–14875 (2021). https://doi.org/10.1609/aaai.v35i17.17745. Number: 17
12. Nguyen, V.A., Nguyen, T.M., Quang Dao, H., Huu Pham, Q.: S-NLP at SemEval-2021 task 5: an analysis of dual networks for sequence tagging. In: Proceedings of SemEval-2021, pp. 888–897 (2021). https://doi.org/10.18653/v1/2021.semeval-1.120
13. Pamungkas, E.W., Basile, V., Patti, V.: Towards multidomain and multilingual abusive language detection: a survey. Pers. Ubiquit. Comput. **27**(1), 17–43 (2021). https://doi.org/10.1007/s00779-021-01609-1

14. Pavlopoulos, J., Sorensen, J., Laugier, L., Androutsopoulos, I.: SemEval-2021 task 5: toxic spans detection. In: Proceedings of SemEval-2021, pp. 59–69 (2021). https://doi.org/10.18653/v1/2021.semeval-1.6
15. Pluciński, K., Klimczak, H.: GHOST at SemEval-2021 task 5: is explanation all you need? In: Proceedings of SemEval-2021, pp. 852–859 (2021). https://doi.org/10.18653/v1/2021.semeval-1.114
16. Ranasinghe, T., Zampieri, M.: MUDES: multilingual detection of offensive spans. In: Proceedings of NAACL-HLT2021: Demonstrations, pp. 144–152 (2021). https://doi.org/10.18653/v1/2021.naacl-demos.17
17. Ribeiro, M., Singh, S., Guestrin, C.: "Why should I trust you?": explaining the predictions of any classifier. In: Proceedings of NAACL-HLT2016: Demonstrations, pp. 97–101 (2016). https://doi.org/10.18653/v1/N16-3020
18. Rusert, J.: NLP_UIOWA at Semeval-2021 task 5: transferring toxic sets to tag toxic spans. In: Proceedings of SemEval-2021, pp. 881–887 (2021). https://doi.org/10.18653/v1/2021.semeval-1.119
19. Shrikumar, A., Greenside, P., Kundaje, A.: Learning important features through propagating activation differences. In: Proceedings of ICML 2017, pp. 3145–3153 (2017). ISSN 2640-3498
20. Simonyan, K., Vedaldi, A., Zisserman, A.: Deep inside convolutional networks: visualising image classification models and saliency maps. In: ICLR (2014)
21. Sundararajan, M., Taly, A., Yan, Q.: Axiomatic attribution for deep networks. In: Proceedings of ICML 2017, pp. 3319–3328 (2017). ISSN 2640-3498
22. Wiegand, M., Ruppenhofer, J., Kleinbauer, T.: Detection of abusive language: the problem of biased datasets. In: Proceedings of NAACL-HLT2019 (Long and Short Papers), vol. 1, pp. 602–608 (2019). https://doi.org/10.18653/v1/N19-1060
23. Wiegand, M., Ruppenhofer, J., Schmidt, A., Greenberg, C.: Inducing a lexicon of abusive words - a feature-based approach. In: Proceedings of NAACL-HLT2018 (Long Papers), vol. 1, pp. 1046–1056 (2018). https://doi.org/10.18653/v1/N18-1095
24. Zhu, Q., et al.: HITSZ-HLT at SemEval-2021 task 5: ensemble sequence labeling and span boundary detection for toxic span detection. In: Proceedings of SemEval-2021, pp. 521–526 (2021). https://doi.org/10.18653/v1/2021.semeval-1.63

How Shall a Machine Call a Thing?

Federico Torrielli[✉], Amon Rapp, and Luigi Di Caro

Department of Computer Science, University of Torino, Turin, Italy
{federico.torrielli,amon.rapp,luigi.dicaro}@unito.it

Abstract. This paper aims to investigate the feasibility of utilising Large Language Models (LLMs) and Latent Diffusion Models (LDMs) for automatically categorising word basicness and concreteness, i.e. two well-known aspects of language having significant relevance on tasks such as text simplification. To achieve this, we propose two distinct approaches: i) a generative Transformer-based LLM, and ii) a image+text multi-modal pipeline, referred to as *stableKnowledge*, which utilises a LDM to map terms to the image level. The evaluation results indicate that while the LLM approach is particularly well-suited for recognising word basicness, *stableKnowledge* outperforms the former when the task shifts to measuring concreteness.

Keywords: Large Language Models · Latent Diffusion Models · Language Basicness · Language Concreteness · Text Simplification

1 Introduction

Human communication and reasoning rely on lexemes and linguistic expressions that are arranged in hierarchical structures [30]. In this context, researchers in psycholinguistics have identified the concept of *basic level* of language, which refers to the level of inclusiveness that is most efficient for human cognition, as it strikes a balance between information richness and cognitive economy [8]. Basic terms are usually culturally common, salient, or frequently used. Moreover, a variety of studies have consistently found that concrete concepts are easier to identify, recall [23], and understand [33] than abstract ones, supporting the notion that concreteness enhances linguistic processing [36].

The importance of studying and automatically detecting both *basicness* and *concreteness* aspects of a language has a significant impact on several tasks and applications, both of passive and transformative types such as *i)* text complexity analysis [12], *ii)* Word Sense Disambiguation [13], *iii)* Text Simplification [2], *iv)* Machine Translation [19] and others [7,14]. Moreover, automatic tools and novel lexical resources may impact on the education context and/or support the treatment of disorders such as Dyslexia [39].

In this paper, we propose two different approaches built on top of the recent advancement in Natural Language Understanding (NLU) and Computer Vision (CV) technologies, in the specific context of Second Language Acquisition (SLA). SLA [9] regards language learners (LLs), i.e., adults with a complete process of

E. Métais et al. (Eds.): NLDB 2023, LNCS 13913, pp. 546–557, 2023.
https://doi.org/10.1007/978-3-031-35320-8_41

linguistic (and cognitive) development dealing with the learning of an additional language. While there exists a significant overlap between the two scenarios, LLs are not learning to name new concepts, but rather to assimilate new terms for something they already know how to lexicalise in a native language.

In the context of text simplification, one of the main applications of basic terms, Second Language Acquisition (SLA) holds significant importance. The necessity for simplified texts primarily stems from second language learners' efforts to assimilate new terms for concepts they can already express in their native language, making text simplification particularly relevant to this group. In contrast, native speakers typically possess a more comprehensive understanding of their language, making text simplification less interesting for them. Focusing on SLA in our proposed approaches is thus essential to address second language learners' needs and enhance text simplification as an effective learning tool.

One approach leverages state-of-the-art technology in natural language understanding (NLU), specifically, Transformer-based models known as Large Language Models (LLMs). The hypothesis is that, given their adeptness at processing textual data, they would excel at distinguishing between basic and advanced terminology. The second method involves a multi-modal pipeline that incorporates both text and image processing. The underlying assumption is that abstract concepts are more difficult to represent visually than concrete concepts [17]. Therefore, by first generating synthetic images for abstract and concrete concepts and then attempting to recreate their textual descriptions (using artificially-generated text), this AI pipeline would likely struggle to reconstruct the abstract concepts.

Given these premises, our contribution is thus four-fold:

1. A novel notion of *basicness* for lexical items, inspired by the existing literature on concreteness [35] and realised through an agreement score over a large-scale annotation involving 10 different annotators;
2. A novel resource of *basic*-vs-*advanced* lexicon for the English language (as direct outcome of the previous contribution), composed of 500 open-domain words which includes and extends current basic word lists;
3. A text-based and a multi-modal text+image approach for automatically capturing basicness and concreteness of words by leveraging current state-of-the-art neural architectures in the fields of NLU and CV;
4. An extensive experimentation that both *i)* validates the quality of the novel resource by means of human judgements and *ii)* demonstrates our hypotheses on the effectiveness of the proposed approaches.

The rest of the paper is organised as follows. Section 2 reports notions and principles related to BL and the state of the art in the context of text- and image automatic generation. Section 3 describes the extraction of basic and advanced concepts and the human-in-the-loop creation of a ground truth. Then, Sect. 4 details the technological pipeline with the obtained results, while Sect. 5 concludes the paper with future research directions. Our work materials and the datasets are available at the following link: https://github.com/federicotorrielli/stableKnowledge.

2   Related Work

The idea of identifying basic terms in a language dates back to Rosch et al. in 1976, followed by a large literature proposing an extensive set of names, principles and examples. Then, after the work by Rosch, many measures and detection strategies for BL have been proposed along the years, continuously summarised in specific surveys over time, e.g. in [10] or in the most recent literature on the topic [5]. At the same time, another historical niche in the literature is represented by the work on concept *concreteness*, originated by [25] and later often linked with the ease of processing concrete words in the human mind [35].

Apart from the conceptualisation of basic level (BL, from now on) and concreteness, a number of computational approaches for their automatic detection have been proposed along the year. For example, [22] proposed a set of 52 rules to identify basic level words, working on different characteristics such as the number of characters, prefixes, minimal frequency in SemCor [21] and others. In [11], the authors started from a new set of 518 lemmas belonging to three categories (hand tool, edible fruits and musical instruments) which have been first labelled as basic or not by three annotators. Then, they utilised lexical, structural and frequency-based features to feed standard classification algorithms such as Support Vector Machines and Decision Trees, obtaining an average Cohen's k score of 0.61 with the annotators. More recently, [6] implemented the Rosch's principle of *cue validity* on similar features as in [22], but also employing Distributional Semantics methods and neural architectures (BART [15]), achieving an overall classification accuracy of 75%. Conversely, fewer efforts have been spent on computational methods for concreteness automatic assessment, often leaning towards the creation of dictionaries [4]. However, the utilisation of Large Language Models (LLMs) and Latent Diffusion Models (LDMs) have not been explored in both tasks so far. In this field, generative models like GPT3 [26], BLOOMZ [32] and OPT [41] are considered state-of-the-art for various Language Modeling [34] tasks. These are models based on the Transformer architecture [37], pre-trained on massive text collections that achieve impressive results when generating text. In addition to LLMs, LDMs are increasingly being used for natural language representation tasks, in addition to their traditional use in image synthesis. Examples of such models include DALL-E 2 [27], Stable Diffusion [29] and Imagen [31].

3   A Benchmark for *Basic* vs *Advanced*

While in literature there is a certain agreement over the existence of a basic lexicon, no unique definition actually exists. On the contrary, several notions, principles and frequently-occurring properties have been reported over time. Apart from the proposals of basic lexicons pioneered by Ogden [24] and the many frequency-based vocabularies available, a significant gap within BL-related studies is represented by their weak link to the conceptual level. Indeed, while it is generally assumed to identify and collect basic level *concepts* or categories, all the reported experiments have been mostly made at the conceptual level or through vague guidelines involving both the lexical and the conceptual areas. In this contribution, we instead manifestly focus on the lexical level, proposing an experimentation with second language learners to empirically grasp an inventory of basic level terms for the English language. In this section, we detail the components of our first contribution, i.e., the creation of a *basicness*-based ground truth.

3.1 Extraction of Seed Words

In this study, we propose a Transformer-based pipeline for the extraction of basic and advanced words from text. The pipeline is applied to a corpus of literature sources and raw, noisy data from the Internet to create a dataset of 500 seed words. The performance of the pipeline is evaluated by comparing its results to the judgements of ten human annotators who are second language learners.

The first step of the pipeline involves the creation of a corpus of probable basic words (and associated synsets) by extracting them from literature sources and Internet data. A generative Large Language Model is then employed to filter them through the use of a specific Language Model-based prompt. Next, each term is mapped to its corresponding WordNet synset [20] for a subsequent phase of advanced (i.e., non basic) term extraction. The final annotation dataset, consisting of 500 total lemmas, was then obtained through a last selection process. All these phases are detailed in the following paragraphs.

(a) Basic raw list extraction. The extraction of basic words from the sources follows simple but clear rules: they must be nouns, not redundant, and easy to learn for a non-English speaker. This was achieved by selecting nouns from basic English word lists such as Ogden's [24] and from language-learning subreddits on Reddit[1]. Then, we used SemCor [21] to map the previously selected nouns into synsets using frequency disambiguation[2]. The resulting basicness raw list is composed of more then 5000 terms, which has been used to test the proposed approaches.

(b) Basic word selection. To select a subset of basic words that could be employed in the manual annotation phase, we employed a state-of-the-art LLM, i.e. *OPT-6.7b* [41]. In particular, we hypothesised that a LLM, trained on textual data, would excel in distinguishing between basic and advanced terminology. Our findings confirmed this hypothesis. Since this is a generative transformer model, it was instructed to give a *"yes/no"* output at the prompt *"Is this a simple, basic and short English word that is used in everyday language?"*, followed by standard examples mentioned in the literature [5]. Through prompt engineering, we tested several possible prompts, obtaining almost overlapping results.

(c) Advanced word extraction. For the identification of advanced terms, we instead proceeded in accordance with the existing approaches (e.g. [11]), i.e., by

---

[1] https://www.reddit.com.

[2] For each synset, we selected the noun from its *lemma names* with the highest frequency in SemCor.

exploring downwards the WordNet sense hierarchy from the selected word list of point (b). A synset for an advanced term is evaluated using four key factors: *i)* lemma-frequency relative to text occurrence, calculated using SemCor; *ii)* limited path distance from the original (basic) synset, measured using path similarity using *nltk* [3]; *iii)* absence of shared words with the hypernym; and *iv)* the absence of basic synsets within the advanced list. With more details:

- *(i)* **significant SemCor frequency:** we look for a hyponym that is rare, but only to a certain extent. An example could be the difference between *"Granny Smith"* and *"Cox's Orange Pippin"* - both are apples, but one is more commonly used in texts than the other;
- *(ii)* **path distance:** since we are traversing WordNet, we used Path Distance to evaluate the similarity instead of a non-native algorithm. The optimal distance from the original basic concept was calculated to be 0.63 through fine-tuning of the results. This condition is necessary since we seek a worthy similarity distance from the basic concept - a good hyponym for *"apple"* must still be an apple;
- *(iii)* **no sharing words between the synset and the hyponym.** This was done to prevent less interesting advanced terms, e.g. as with *"state"* and its hyponym *"American state"*, which is probably not the best advanced counterpart among all its hyponyms;
- *(iv)* **no basic words in the advanced list:** we avoided cases where hyponyms can be lexicalised through basic words, e.g., the hyponym of *"ocean"* is *"deep"* which is also a candidate basic word.

We further considered an alternative advanced word extraction method, by direct employing the LLM prompting strategy (thus by asking *OPT* to extract the advanced words). However, the motivation behind pursuing the approach described at this point (c) stemmed from the previous literature claiming that advanced-level words are more frequently identified as hyponyms of a set of selected basic words [11].

(d) Dataset fine-tuning. To prepare the dataset for an annotation scenario, a subset of terms was carefully chosen from the resulting list, with a focus on removing any potentially harmful words. This subset was generated by sorting the seed words according to their SemCor frequency and selecting 500 terms, comprising 250 *OPT-basic* and 250 *OPT-advanced* terms. The resulting set was then shuffled. Our dataset of 500 words then underwent human classification (Sect. 3.2) to establish a gold standard "super-annotator" and subsequently assessed against the latter's judgement (Sect. 3.4).

3.2   Setting of the Human-Based Annotation

In [11], annotators had been asked to mark basic words extracted from the hyponyms of three WordNet synsets[3]. In this contribution, we tried to reshape the experiment without limiting the semantic coverage of the candidate words.

---

[3] *hand tool.*01, *edible fruit.*01 and *musical instrument.*01.

Regarding the methodology and the annotation process through the web interface, we ensured that the scope, method of annotation, and definition of basic words were clearly outlined on the first page of our annotation platform. To aid the annotators in their task, we provided examples of basic and advanced terms on the second page, organised into categories. These examples were presented without definitions or descriptions to avoid any potential bias. Additionally, we included a video that explained the task and provided examples of high-quality annotations from the literature. On the annotation page, we focused on individual words rather than concepts, synsets, or definitions. This approach allowed annotators to indicate whether a word was hard to evaluate, providing valuable feedback for our research.

3.3   Inter-annotation Agreement

We conducted an annotation task on the resulting dataset, recruiting 10 gender-balanced language-learner annotators. These were chosen for their English level (from B1 to C1 in the *CEFR* spectrum) and with different work and study backgrounds. By focusing on individual words and developing a new set of guidelines (see Sect. 3.2), we were able to achieve a Cohen's κ of 0.70 (with a Krippendorff's alpha of 0.71). The highest value of κ between each pair of annotators was 0.89, while the lowest was 0.66. To further evaluate the reliability of our annotation task along the entire process, we calculated the annotators agreement with a sliding window of 130 words, obtaining the stable sequential values of 0.6834, 0.6255, 0.6268 and 0.7879.

The annotation task revealed other interesting insights, e.g., the amount of time spent by annotators evaluating a single word[4] rather than specific words that appeared difficult to evaluate, like compound nouns (e.g., *"vitamin pill"*), words borrowed from other languages(e.g., *"avenue"*) and short words that were abstract or conceptually complex, (e.g., *"kin"*).

One aspect of the annotation is that it demonstrated the existence of a *basicness* scale. For example, only a small subset of the whole word list has been annotated as basic or advanced by all annotators with perfect agreement. We could call these words *most basic* and *most advanced* respectively. On the contrary, we identified a *gray area* of $21 + 14$ (for basic) and $14 + 21$ (for advanced) terms for which the panel is split 5 to 5. Unsurprisingly, more than 50% of the lexical items falling in this space were marked as *hard* to classify. In Table 1 we summarised different agreements on the annotation, from the mentioned *gray area* cases in the first row to the *most basic/most advanced* cases at the bottom.

3.4   Benchmark Dataset Evaluation

A key step in evaluating the validity of our proposed method was to assess the agreement between human annotators and the list generated with the *OPT*

---

[4] The results are depicted in this image, which shows that they spent an average of 1.4s on a single word, with 0.9s spent on *OPT*-basic words and 2.0 on the *OPT*-advanced ones.

Table 1. Our basic vs. advanced agreement distribution over the ten annotators. To make an example (marked in **bold**), 48 advanced words have been classified with a high agreement of 9-vs-1 annotators split.

Annotators split	n. of basic	n. of adv	total
low agreement			
ооооо vs ооооо	35	35	132
оооооо vs оооо	35	27	
medium agreement			
ооооооо vs ооо	48	43	203
оооооооо vs оо	52	60	
high agreement			
оооооооо vs о	35	48	165
оооооооооо	**41**	**41**	

method (Sect. 3.1). To this end, we created a baseline *"super-annotator"* by applying majority voting to the basic/advanced annotations. We then compared this newly *super-annotator* annotation with our original *OPT* list and obtained an agreement of $\kappa = 0.63$, with a Precision/Recall/F scores of $0.82/0.81/0.82$. This finding suggests that *(i)* large generative language models can effectively differentiate between basic and advanced terms using simple queries, improving the current state of the art by around six percentage F-score points with respect to [6] for the English language, and *(ii)* the LLM demonstrates a strong alignment with the agreement among humans of $\kappa = 0.7$, as reported in Sect. 3.3 and that could be considered as an asymptotic maximum limit for our task [38].

4   Multi-modal Text+Image Pipeline

In the previous section we focused on the *basicness* aspect of language, providing *i)* a novel benchmark dataset for future and possibly different research objectives and *ii)* demonstrating the capability of a state-of-the-art LLM in classifying basic language. Our second and parallel intent regards language concreteness, a similar and significantly overlapping aspect that, however, has been often faced separately in the current literature. In fact, on the concreteness aspect, different research efforts already carried to benchmark datasets and graded scores for word lists. One of the most employed consists of 4293 nouns in the MRC Psycholinguistic Database [40], where each noun is accompanied by a concreteness score ranging from 0 to 700. By directly testing the LLM-based *OPT* model on the abstract/concrete classification task, and using the best performing concreteness threshold of 380, we reached a very low Cohen's κ of 0.27. This demonstrates that even the most powerful language models are not capable of capturing the hidden different shape behind language concreteness, as opposed to basicness.

Thus, as a further contribution, we introduce a second method operating at the image level with the goal of exploring a more complete and multi-modal perspective by taking advantage of the latest state-of-the-art image synthesis models in conjunction with LLMs. To the best of our knowledge, this is the first time that such an approach has been proposed and implemented for this task.

4.1 The Multi-modal Pipeline

In this section, we introduce the pipeline architecture providing an overview of its various components, leveraging state-of-the-art techniques in Natural Language Processing and Computer Vision to enable accurate classification of a wide range of visual and linguistic data. The pipeline is composed of three parts:

- **Image generation step:** given the lemmas, we produce images[5] using Stable Diffusion, a latent diffusion model (LDM) introduced in [29] (see Sect. 4.1);
- **Interrogation step:** from the images, we extract definitions using BLIP [16], a unified model for vision-language understanding and generation (see Sect. 4.1);
- **Evaluation step:** to evaluate the similarity between the description produced by the interrogation step and the lemmas in input we used Sentence Transformers [28] embeddings, enabling the use of similarity measures (see Sect. 4.1).

(a) Image generation using Stable Diffusion. The image generation process uses Stable Diffusion 1.5 [29]. In order to maximise performance while simultaneously reducing our carbon footprint, we *i)* enabled the cuDNN auto-tuner for faster convolution, *ii)* utilised the highly performant DPM Solver [18] for efficient model sampling, and *iii)* employed attention slicing, which allows for the computation to be performed in steps rather than all at once[6]. We then generated 5 images per prompt using 30 inference steps and a guidance scale of 7.5. Furthermore, we employ negative prompts [1], such as *"writing, letters, handwriting, words"* to avoid visual clutter resulting from the model attempting to resemble text in the generated images.

(b) BLIP Interrogator module. After generating five images for each lemma, we converted them to RGB format and used them as input for the Interrogator module. This module utilises the BLIP large captioning model [16]. Finally, we generated captions using nucleus sampling and a maximum generation length of 20. The synthetic text generation approach utilised in BLIP has been shown to produce results that are comparable to those generated by humans, as demonstrated in various state-of-the-art experiments [16].

(c) Evaluating embeddings using SBERT. The final step involved evaluating the quality of the captions we generated by comparing them to the original lemmas. To accomplish this, we utilised SBERT [28] to produce embeddings where to apply cosine similarity, thus having a quantitative evaluation measure on the generated captions. To further refine our analysis, we experimented with both the mean and the maximum similarity value across all five captions.

---

[5] In-depth examples of the outputs can be examined in the following link: https://github.com/federicotorrielli/stableKnowledge/tree/master/appendix_b.pdf.
[6] The total GPU hours required for image generation, captioning and evaluation was approximately 12 h using a single consumer grade NVIDIA 2080Ti.

4.2   Language vs Vision Technologies: An Evaluation of the Two Approaches on Basicness and Concreteness

By pairing the results on concreteness classification with the LLM-based approach, the *stableKnowledge* pipeline demonstrated superior performance, achieving a Cohen's κ of **0.57** (more than the double) with a concreteness threshold of 520 and a cosine similarity threshold of 0.3564, as detailed in Table 2. On the contrary, the LLM-based method outperformed the LDM-based pipeline *stableKnowledge* in classifying language basicness, as shown in Table 3. Thus, our initial hypotheses are fully verified by the experiments.

Furthermore, it is worth to outline some relation between the two separate dimensions of basicness and concreteness. By looking at the accuracy values in Tables 2 and 3, *OPT* experiences a significant drop in performance uniquely on the abstract concepts. Contrarily, it performs at best with basic, advanced but also concrete expressions.

Table 2. Accuracy scores of *OPT* and *stableKnowledge* on the abstract/concrete task.

	OPT model ($k = 0.27$)			stableKnowledge ($k = 0.57$)		
	Precision	Recall	F1	Precision	Recall	F1
abstract	0.63	0.40	0.49	**0.77**	**0.85**	**0.81**
concrete	0.70	**0.85**	**0.77**	0.82	0.72	0.76

Table 3. Accuracy scores of *OPT* and *stableKnowledge* on the basic/advanced task.

	OPT model ($k = 0.63$)			stableKnowledge ($k = 0.21$)		
	Precision	Recall	F1	Precision	Recall	F1
basic	**0.82**	**0.81**	**0.82**	0.61	0.59	0.60
advanced	**0.81**	**0.82**	**0.82**	0.59	0.61	0.60

5   Conclusion and Future Work

In this paper, we aimed to build upon the existing literature and techniques related to the classification of the basic nature of a language by developing a novel notion of *basicness*, i.e. a graded representation obtained through human-in-the-loop experiments, taking inspiration from the existing works on *concreteness*. First, we generated a novel candidate word list integrating existing principles and resources, which resulted to overcome the current state of the art in terms of its open-domain and balanced qualities. Then, we proposed a human-in-the-loop methodology for the realisation of the basicness idea through a 10-annotators panel, reaching the highest human agreement scores as compared with the current literature, up to 0.89 of Fleiss' k. Finally, we experimented with the current state-of-the-art approaches in Natural Language Understanding and in Computer Vision on the automatic classification of both basicness and concreteness, establishing new standards on the topic and highlighting the power of generative models on the two tasks. Future work includes *i)* applying the presented approaches to other language-oriented tasks, *ii)* examining the psycholinguistic implications of *basicness* and *iii)* experimenting with models hyperparameters.

References

1. Negprompt   (2023).   https://github.com/AUTOMATIC1111/stable-diffusion-webui/wiki/Negative-prompt
2. Al-Thanyyan, S.S., Azmi, A.M.: Automated text simplification: a survey. ACM Comput. Surv. (CSUR) **54**(2), 1–36 (2021)
3. Bird, S., Loper, E.: NLTK: the natural language toolkit. In: Proceedings of the ACL Interactive Poster and Demonstration Sessions, Barcelona, Spain, pp. 214–217. Association for Computational Linguistics (2004)
4. Brysbaert, M., Warriner, A.B., Kuperman, V.: Concreteness ratings for 40 thousand generally known English word lemmas. Behav. Res. Methods **46**, 904–911 (2014)
5. Castellanos, A., Tremblay, M.C., et al.: Basic classes in conceptual modeling: theory and practical guidelines. J. Assoc. Inf. Syst. **21**(4), 3 (2020)
6. Chen, Y., Teufel, S.: Synthetic textual features for the large-scale detection of basic-level categories in English and Mandarin. In: Proceedings of the 2021 Conference on Empirical Methods in Natural Language Processing, Punta Cana, Dominican Republic, pp. 8294–8305. Association for Computational Linguistics, Online (2021)
7. Di Caro, L., Ruggeri, A.: Unveiling middle-level concepts through frequency trajectories and peaks analysis. In: Proceedings of the 34th ACM/SIGAPP Symposium on Applied Computing, pp. 1035–1042 (2019)
8. Finton, D.J.: Cognitive economy and the role of* representation in on-line learning. The University of Wisconsin-Madison (2002)
9. Gass, S.M., Behney, J., et al.: Second Language Acquisition: An Introductory Course. Routledge (2020)
10. Hajibayova, L.: Basic-level categories: a review. J. Inf. Sci. **39**(5), 676–687 (2013)
11. Hollink, L., Bilgin, A., van Ossenbruggen, J.: Predicting the basic level in a hierarchy of concepts. In: Garoufallou, E., Ovalle-Perandones, M.-A. (eds.) MTSR 2020. CCIS, vol. 1355, pp. 22–34. Springer, Cham (2021). https://doi.org/10.1007/978-3-030-71903-6_3
12. Jensen, K.T.: Indicators of text complexity. In: Mees, I.M., Alves, F., Göpferich, S. (eds.), pp. 61–80 (2009)
13. Lacerra, C., Bevilacqua, M., et al.: CSI: a coarse sense inventory for 85% word sense disambiguation. In: Proceedings of the AAAI Conference on Artificial Intelligence, vol. 34, pp. 8123–8130 (2020)
14. Leone, V., Siragusa, G., Di Caro, L., Navigli, R.: Building semantic grams of human knowledge. In: Proceedings of the Twelfth Language Resources and Evaluation Conference, pp. 2991–3000 (2020)
15. Lewis, M., Liu, Y., et al.: Bart: denoising sequence-to-sequence pre-training for natural language generation, translation, and comprehension. arXiv preprint arXiv:1910.13461 (2019)

16. Li, J., Li, D., et al.: Blip: bootstrapping language-image pre-training for unified vision-language understanding and generation (2022)
17. Löhr, G.: What are abstract concepts? On lexical ambiguity and concreteness ratings. Rev. Philos. Psychol. **13**(3), 549–566 (2022)
18. Lu, C., Zhou, Y., et al.: DPM-solver: a fast ode solver for diffusion probabilistic model sampling in around 10 steps (2022)
19. Marchisio, K., Guo, J., et al.: Controlling the reading level of machine translation output. In: Proceedings of Machine Translation Summit XVII: Research Track, pp. 193–203 (2019)
20. Miller, G.A.: Wordnet: a lexical database for English. Commun. ACM **38**(11), 39–41 (1995)
21. Miller, G.A., Chodorow, M., et al.: Using a semantic concordance for sense identification. In: Human Language Technology: Proceedings of a Workshop held at Plainsboro, New Jersey, 8–11 March 1994 (1994)
22. Mills, C., Bond, F., et al.: Automatic identification of basic-level categories. In: Proceedings of the 9th Global Wordnet Conference, pp. 298–305 (2018)
23. Nelson, D.L., Schreiber, T.A.: Word concreteness and word structure as independent determinants of recall. J. Mem. Lang. **31**(2), 237–260 (1992)
24. Ogden, C.K.: Basic English: a general introduction with rules and grammar (1930)
25. Paivio, A.: Abstractness, imagery, and meaningfulness in paired-associate learning. J. Verbal Learn. Verbal Behav. **4**(1), 32–38 (1965)
26. Radford, A., Kim, J.W., et al.: Learning transferable visual models from natural language supervision. In: ICML (2021)
27. Ramesh, A., Dhariwal, P., et al.: Hierarchical text-conditional image generation with clip latents. arXiv abs/2204.06125 (2022)
28. Reimers, N., Gurevych, I.: Sentence-BERT: sentence embeddings using Siamese BERT-networks. In: Proceedings of the 2019 Conference on Empirical Methods in Natural Language Processing. Association for Computational Linguistics (2019)
29. Rombach, R., Blattmann, A., et al.: High-resolution image synthesis with latent diffusion models (2021)
30. Rosch, E., Mervis, C.B., et al.: Basic objects in natural categories. Cogn. Psychol. **8**(3), 382–439 (1976)
31. Saharia, C., Chan, W., et al.: Photorealistic text-to-image diffusion models with deep language understanding. arXiv abs/2205.11487 (2022)
32. Scao, T.L., Fan, A., et al.: Bloom: a 176b-parameter open-access multilingual language model. arXiv abs/2211.05100 (2022)
33. Schwanenflugel, P.J., Shoben, E.J.: Differential context effects in the comprehension of abstract and concrete verbal materials. J. Exp. Psychol. Learn. Mem. Cogn. **9**(1), 82 (1983)
34. Shannon, C.E.: A mathematical theory of communication. Bell Syst. Tech. J. **27**, 623–656 (1948)
35. Solovyev, V.: Concreteness/abstractness concept: state of the art. In: Velichkovsky, B.M., Balaban, P.M., Ushakov, V.L. (eds.) Intercognsci 2020. AISC, vol. 1358, pp. 275–283. Springer, Cham (2021). https://doi.org/10.1007/978-3-030-71637-0_33
36. Strain, E., Patterson, K., et al.: Semantic effects in single-word naming. J. Exp. Psychol. Learn. Mem. Cogn. **21**(5), 1140 (1995)
37. Vaswani, A., Shazeer, N.M., et al.: Attention is all you need. arXiv abs/1706.03762 (2017)
38. Warrens, M.J.: Five ways to look at Cohen's kappa. J. Psychol. Psychother. **5**(4), 1 (2015)

39. Washburn, E.K., Joshi, R.M., et al.: Teacher knowledge of basic language concepts and dyslexia. Dyslexia **17**(2), 165–183 (2011)
40. Wilson, M.: MRC psycholinguistic database: machine-usable dictionary, version 2.00. Behav. Res. Methods Instrum. Comput. **20**(1), 6–10 (1988)
41. Zhang, S., Roller, S., et al.: OPT: open pre-trained transformer language models (2022)

Detecting Artificially Generated Academic Text: The Importance of Mimicking Human Utilization of Large Language Models

Vijini Liyanage[(✉)][iD] and Davide Buscaldi[iD]

LIPN, Université Sorbonne Paris Nord, CNRS UMR 7030,
99 av. Jean-Baptiste Clément, 93430 Villetaneuse, France
{liyanage,davide.buscaldi}@lipn.univ-paris13.fr

Abstract. The advent of Large Language Models (LLMs) has led to a surge in Natural Language Generation (NLG), aiding humans in composing text for various tasks. However, there is a risk of these models being misused. For instance, detecting artificially generated text from original text is a concern in academia. Current research works on detection do not attempt to replicate how humans would use these models. In our work, we address this issue by leveraging data generated by mimicking how humans would use LLMs in composing academic works. Our study examines the detectability of the generated text using DetectGPT and GLTR, and we utilize state-of-the-art classification models like SciBERT, RoBERTa, DEBERTa, XLNet, and ELECTRA. Our experiments show that the generated text is difficult to detect using existing models when created using a LLM fine-tuned on the remainder of a paper. This highlights the importance of using realistic and challenging datasets in future research aimed at detecting artificially generated text.

Keywords: Automatic text generation · Detection · Academic text

1 Introduction

Current Natural Language Generation (NLG) models are competent enough to replace humans in composing text. For instance the latest model GPT4 (ChatGPT plus) is a breakthrough introduced by OpenAI, which is capable of generating astounding responses for its users. Starting from ordinary-level problems raised by the general public to advanced-level concerns put up by professionals, ChatGPT which was GPT4's predecessor has already been able to deliver satisfying solutions. While these novel technologies can undoubtedly be helpful, they can also be used maliciously. In academia, specifically, it is essential to check the authenticity of texts and determine whether these tools can be considered lawful writing support or instead computer-assisted plagiarism. As a result, it is crucial to develop mechanisms that can help to distinguish between text generated by

E. Métais et al. (Eds.): NLDB 2023, LNCS 13913, pp. 558–565, 2023.
https://doi.org/10.1007/978-3-031-35320-8_42

humans and that generated by machines. Various researchers have paid attention to the detectability of machine-generated text from human-written text [2,9]. Nevertheless, not much research has focused on detecting automatically generated academic text.

DAGPap22 [4] is a shared task targeted at detecting automatically generated academic text. Their dataset consists of abstracts generated using summarization and generative models. By utilizing an ensemble of the three models SciBERT, RoBERTa and DeBERTa, Glazkova and Glazkov., 2022 [3] have gained an F1 score of 99.24% on DAGPap22 data. SynSciPass [8] is another latest approach that facilitates the detection of automatically generated scientific content by providing labels for the type of technology adapted for generation. They also used the SciBERT model for detection and obtained an F1 score of 98.3% for DAGPap22 data. Rodriguez et al.,2022 [7] experimented cross-domain applicability of detectors. In their work, they have studied the detectability of tampered (created by a mix of original and generated paragraphs) research papers using BERT-based models and reported accuracies ranging from 86 to 95% across the domains, depending on the configurations.

Although the aforementioned research has obtained higher results in terms of the detectability of academic text, their considered datasets aren't composed in a manner that a human would possibly employ NLG models in composing a research article. In this work, we experiment detection of automatically generated corpora using several SOTA deep classification models and analyze how the detectability of artificially generated data is influenced by the method adopted in composing them. The paper is organized as follows. Section 2 provides details of the datasets we utilized in our work. Section 3 delivers explanations of our experiments and the corresponding results. And Sect. 4 concludes the paper.

2   Corpus Creation

For our experiments, we utilized five main corpora:

- GPT wiki intro data [1];
- Dataset published by DAGPap22 [4];
- Benchmark dataset by Liyanage et al., 2022 [5];
- A dataset of fully generated articles using a fine-tuned GPT2;
- A dataset of abstracts generated using a pre-trained GPT2 (without fine-tuning).

"GPT wiki intro" is a dataset composed of human written Wikipedia introductions and GPT(Curie) generated introductions. For the generation, the first seven words of the original introduction are fed to the model as the seed text. In this task, they have considered 150k different topics from various domains (including academia). For our experiments, we extracted 500 original introductions and their respective 500 generated introductions from the original dataset.

DAGPap22's original data is comprised of excerpts extracted from "Microprocessors and microsystems (MICPRO)" journal and abstracts copied from papers related to UN's Sustainable Development Goals[1]. Its fake (generated) content are composed of abstracts generated by GPT, GPT-neo and GPT3 models (The initial sentence of each original abstract is chosen as the prompt), summarized abstracts produced by Longformer Encoder-Decoder (LED) text summarization model (aforementioned original papers were used as the inputs), abstracts paraphrased with Spinbot[2] and excerpts that are taken from retracted papers of the MICPRO journal. Altogether their training set contains 5327 records in which around 69% is fake.

Liyanage et al., 2022 corpus contains two datasets, one is composed of fully generated papers and the other is a hybrid one that contains abstracts which are constructed by replacing several sentences of original abstracts with generated sentences. Since the former is created in a similar way a human would try to compose a paper, we chose it for our experiments. It was generated by a fine-tuned GPT-2 model and the model was fine-tuned with original papers extracted from ArXiv[3]. The first 50 words of each chosen original paper were fed to the model as the seed text. This seed represents an important lead for the generation process, therefore the generated articles contain a lot of content from the respective original paper.

To address the aforementioned issue, we tried to introduce more randomness in the models' output. In language models, one way to introduce more randomness is to increase the temperature τ of the softmax that is used to determine the probabilities of the following token w:

$$\frac{\exp\left(\frac{h^T e_w}{\tau}\right)}{\sum_{w_i \in V} \exp\left(\frac{h^T e_{w_i}}{\tau}\right)} \tag{1}$$

where h^T are the outputs of a hidden layer in the LM, and e_w are embeddings of the w token in the vocabulary V. Since increasing the temperature increases the probability of generating more variations in the text with respect to the original, we built a new dataset of fake articles by increasing the temperature of the model to 0.9 instead of the original temperature of 0.7). For this generation process, we followed the same steps applied for the aforementioned research. We leveraged BLEU and ROUGE scores to measure the novelty of the generated articles when compared with the original ones and the respective results are provided under Sect. 3.

Moreover, we built another dataset of abstracts using OpenAI's pre-trained GPT-2 English model without fine-tuning. This dataset corresponds to the way most of the previous works have introduced the generated data in their detection experiments. The GPT-2 model that we used has 24 layers, 1024-hidden states, 16-heads and 345M parameters. The temperature of the model at this generation was set to 0.7. The model has been pre-trained on abstracts from the Arxiv-NLP domain. To prevent the model from repeating the output tokens starting from

---

[1] https://sdgs.un.org/2030agenda.

[2] https://spinbot.com.

[3] https://arxiv.org.

the beginning, we had to set the early stopping feature of the model to true, which makes the generated abstracts shorter in length than the original abstract lengths. Furthermore, when examining the generated abstracts, we could see that they contain sentences that can be factually incorrect. This is expected since the model is not fine-tuned. All the produced data are available at the following URL: https://github.com/vijini/Detection-of-Automatically-Generated-Academic-Text.git.

3 Evaluation and Results

3.1 Experiments with GLTR

Since GLTR [2] is a visualization tool to support humans in distinguishing artificially generated text, we leveraged it to examine the detectability of the various corpora. Figure 1 shows visualizations provided by GLTR for a few excerpts extracted from several datasets. Here, in green it represents text that belongs to the 10 most probable tokens produced by GPT-2, which means they are very likely to be automatically generated. Likewise, the tool shows tokens belonging to the 100 most probable ones in yellow, top 1,000 in red and in violet those who fall outside the 1,000 most probable tokens. Therefore, according to GLTR, the excerpt produced by the pre-trained model is highly distinguishable from the original one. On the contrary, the other two excerpts which were generated by fine-tuned models have similar visualizations to the original text.

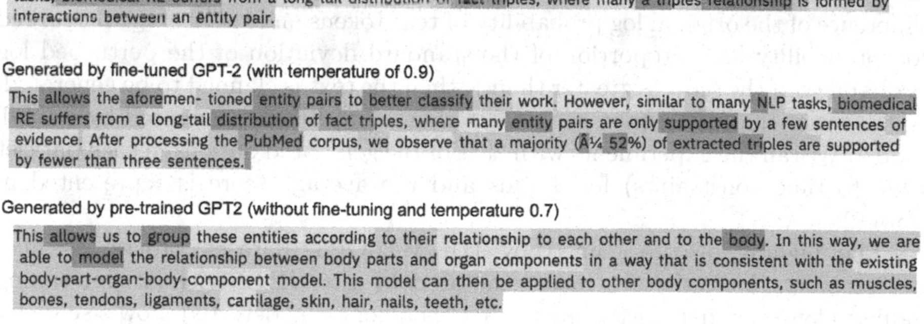

Original content

This allows us to place the aforemen- tioned sentences into the same MIL bag based on their entity type, creating a heterogeneous bag of entity pairs that express the same relationship. With this reformulation, bags containing a single duplicated sentence are reduced by half. AMIL produces better overall performance for biomedical RE with significant performance gains for "rare" triples.

Generated by fine-tuned GPT-2 (with temperature of 0.7)

This allows the entity pair to automatically generate labels to train deep-learning models. However, similar to many NLP tasks, biomedical RE suffers from a long-tail distribution of fact triples, where many a triples relationship is formed by interactions between an entity pair.

Generated by fine-tuned GPT-2 (with temperature of 0.9)

This allows the aforemen- tioned entity pairs to better classify their work. However, similar to many NLP tasks, biomedical RE suffers from a long-tail distribution of fact triples, where many entity pairs are only supported by a few sentences of evidence. After processing the PubMed corpus, we observe that a majority (Ä¼ 52%) of extracted triples are supported by fewer than three sentences.

Generated by pre-trained GPT2 (without fine-tuning and temperature 0.7)

This allows us to group these entities according to their relationship to each other and to the body. In this way, we are able to model the relationship between body parts and organ components in a way that is consistent with the existing body-part-organ-body-component model. This model can then be applied to other body components, such as muscles, bones, tendons, ligaments, cartilage, skin, hair, nails, teeth, etc.

Fig. 1. GLTR Outputs for Excerpts of Corpora.

3.2   BLEU and ROUGE Scores

BLEU and ROUGE are n-gram based scores that measure the naturalness of the generated text when compared with the respective original text. We computed them on our data which were generated by the fine-tuned GPT2 (with 0.9 temperature) and compared the results against the corresponding scores provided by liyanage et al., 2022 to examine the influence of the increase in temperature parameter of the generation model on the creativity of its outputs. The associated Unigram Level BLEU (U-BLEU), Sentence Level BLEU (S-BLEU) and Rouge-L scores are demonstrated in Table 1. It can be seen that the scores are decreased when the model temperature is increased. This is justifiable since the more the randomness is the more the differences in the generated text in comparison to the original. Moreover, there is a significant decrease of scores in data produced by the pre-trained model, manifesting the fact that when a generation model is not fine-tuned, it tends to output more random (out of the context) content.

Table 1. Average BLEU and ROUGE Scores

Corpus	U-BLEU	S-BLEU	Rouge-L
Fine-tuned GPT-2(temp = 0.7)	0.867	0.809	0.853
Fine-tuned GPT-2(temp = 0.9)	0.858	0.766	0.834
GPT-2 without fine-tuning(temp = 0.7)	0.467	0.356	0.533

3.3   DetectGPT Results

Since the majority of our considered data are generated using GPT models, we leveraged the latest DetectGPT [6] to check the detectability of our generated data. DetectGPT calculates a Z-score which is computed by considering the difference of the original log probability of text tokens and the average perturbed log probability as a proportion of the standard deviation of the perturbed log probability. If the score is greater than 1, then the text is claimed to be generated, if it is lower than 0.25, then the text is claimed to be not generated by a GPT model. We ran the experiments with 20% of the generated data from each dataset (due to time constraints) for 3 runs and the average score is represented in Table 2.

The highest z-score gained by the WikiGPT dataset proves its high detectability. Also, the abstracts generated by the GPT2 without fine-tuning gained a low score demonstrating the likelihood of being detected. Low z-score for DAGPap22 data, states that they are not generated by a GPT model (although some of its data are generated so). This might be due to the reason that the generated text in DAGPap22 dataset is produced by several other models in addition to GPT models, thus making the average Z-score slightly lower than

0.25. Surprisingly the two other datasets which are generated using fine-tuned GPT2 are recognized as not containing data generated by a GPT model. Therefore, it is important to note that when a GPT model is fine-tuned, the generated data is difficult to be distinguished by DetectGPT itself.

Table 2. Z-scores Produced by DetectGPT

Model	WikiGPT	DAGPap22	Fine-tuned GPT2 (0.7)	Fine-tuned GPT2 (0.9)	GPT2 without finetuning (0.7)
Z-score	1.747	0.240	-0.351	-0.192	0.911

3.4 Classification Results

We considered detection as a binary classification task for which we employed several advanced deep classification models to experiment detectability of the considered corpora. Table 3 shows an overview of the models that are utilized in this task. The datasets were split into 60:20:20 for training, testing and validation. All the models were trained for 3 epochs and the average F1 scores are presented in Table 4.

Overall WikiGPT data, DAGPap22 data, and the dataset which was generated by GPT2 without fine-tuning have better F1 scores than the other two datasets which are generated using a fine-tuned GPT2 model. This means that the generated data of the latter are difficult to distinguish from the original content, owing to the fact that when the model is fine-tuned with original data, the model is capable of generating text that looks similar to the original (as exhibited in Fig. 1). SciBERT delivers the highest classification results for the fine-tuned data since SciBERT is pre-trained on vast amounts of scientific domain corpora.

Table 3. Hyper Parameter of the Classification Models

Model	Vocab (K)	Hidden Size	Layers	Batch Size	Parameters(M)
SciBERT$_{base}$	30	768	12	16	110
RoBERTa$_{large}$	50	1024	16	16	355
DeBERTa$_{large}$	50	1024	24	16	350
Electra$_{base}$	30	768	12	16	110
XLNet$_{base}$	32	768	12	16	110

Table 4. F1 Scores Produced by Models on Classification Task

Model	WikiGPT	DAGPap22	Fine-tuned GPT2 (0.7)	Fine-tuned GPT2 (0.9)	GPT2 without finetuning (0.7)
SciBERT	92.97	95.02	84.65	79.16	94.99
RoBERTa	97.00	96.87	67.83	33.33	84.85
DeBERTa	98.50	97.17	67.03	48.13	95.00
Electra$_{base}$	81.95	96.64	56.16	48.13	95.00
XLNet$_{base}$	84.12	95.67	56.36	59.60	97.50

4   Conclusions and Future Work

This research work is focused on analyzing the detectability of automatically generated academic content. In this task, we have taken into account data generated in a manner that replicates how humans leverage an LLM in composing scientific articles. To examine the detectability of generated text, we employed tools such as GLTR and models such as DetectGPT, SciBERT, DeBERTa, RoBERTa, ELECTRA, and XLNet. The results we obtained prove that when text is generated using a fine-tuned model over part of already available content –such as in the case of completing an existing text rather than creating a new one– the generated text fragments are quite difficult to detect, even using tools and methods that are able to identify generated text when it is produced by a non-finetuned model. Therefore, our experiments prove the importance of utilizing realistic and challenging datasets in future research aimed at detecting artificially generated text, especially if the scenario is a tampering one. In future work, we plan to further analyze classification errors to understand and improve the detection task. Moreover, we plan to take advantage of knowledge bases to find inconsistencies between the original and generated content so that they can be utilized to build better detectors.

References

1. Bhat, A.: GPT-wiki-intro (revision 0e458f5). https://huggingface.co/datasets/aadityaubhat/GPT-wiki-intro
2. Gehrmann, S., Strobelt, H., Rush, A.M.: GLTR: statistical detection and visualization of generated text. In: Proceedings of the 57th Annual Meeting of the Association for Computational Linguistics: System Demonstrations, pp. 111–116 (2019)
3. Glazkova, A., Glazkov, M.: Detecting generated scientific papers using an ensemble of transformer models. In: Proceedings of the Third Workshop on Scholarly Document Processing, pp. 223–228 (2022)
4. Kashnitsky, Y., Herrmannova, D., de Waard, A., Tsatsaronis, G., Fennell, C., Labbé, C.: Overview of the DAGPap22 shared task on detecting automatically generated scientific papers. In: Third Workshop on Scholarly Document Processing (2022)
5. Liyanage, V., Buscaldi, D., Nazarenko, A.: A benchmark corpus for the detection of automatically generated text in academic publications. In: Proceedings of the Thirteenth Language Resources and Evaluation Conference, pp. 4692–4700 (2022)

6. Mitchell, E., Lee, Y., Khazatsky, A., Manning, C.D., Finn, C.: DetectGPT: zero-shot machine-generated text detection using probability curvature. arXiv preprint arXiv:2301.11305 (2023)
7. Rodriguez, J., Hay, T., Gros, D., Shamsi, Z., Srinivasan, R.: Cross-domain detection of GPT-2-generated technical text. In: Proceedings of the 2022 Conference of the North American Chapter of the Association for Computational Linguistics: Human Language Technologies, pp. 1213–1233 (2022)
8. Rosati, D.: SynSciPass: detecting appropriate uses of scientific text generation. In: Proceedings of the Third Workshop on Scholarly Document Processing, pp. 214–222 (2022)
9. Zellers, R., et al.: Defending against neural fake news. In: Advances in Neural Information Processing Systems, vol. 32 (2019)

Leveraging Small-BERT and Bio-BERT for Abbreviation Identification in Scientific Text

Piyush Miglani[1], Pranav Vatsal[2], and Raksha Sharma[1(✉)] 🆔

[1] Indian Institute of Technology Roorkee, Roorkee, India
pmiglani@ce.iitr.ac.in, raksha.sharma@cs.iitr.ac.in
[2] Indian Institute of Technology, Kharagpur, Kharagpur, India
vatsalpranav@iitkgp.ac.in

Abstract. Abbreviations are short forms of phrases that aid in the communication of long sentences in texts and are an essential part of the writing process. Abbreviations save a lot of time and space in writing scientific documents such as research articles, papers, clinical notes, *etc.* However, it is challenging to identify or map abbreviations to the complete form in scientific documents due to the vast and dynamic range of rules for forming an abbreviation. On the other hand, a massive increase in scientific papers over the Web has raised the need for an automatic abbreviation identification system by many folds. Thus, this paper proposes an LSTM-based deep learning system that encodes the target word and its context sentence using two different forms of pre-trained BERT embeddings (Small BERT and Bio BERT). The proposed system classifies whether the target word is an abbreviation or not. We experimented with two scientific datasets, *viz., MeDal* and *SciAI*, for the abbreviation detection task. We built abbreviation detection systems with two different settings, 1. having a lowercase module and 2. no explicit lowercase module. We observe that retaining the actual case of the letters in the abbreviation is crucial for abbreviation detection. Our system results in an F1-score of 90.04% on the SciAI dataset and 85.68% on the MeDal dataset for the abbreviation detection task. To observe the domain-specific behavior of the abbreviations, we also performed cross-domain evaluation (trained on MeDal, tested on SciAI, and vice versa). We obtained an F1-score of 76.50% on SciAI data and 62.72% on MeDal data in the cross-domain settings. We compared our system with six other statistical systems for the abbreviation detection task. Results show that our system is able to outperform other models by a significant margin.

Keywords: Abbreviation Detection · Deep Learning · MeDal dataset · SciAI dataset · Small BERT and Bio BERT embeddings · Neural Network Architecture · LSTM · Lower case preprocessing

---

P. Miglani and P. Vatsal—The first two authors have contributed equally in the paper.

E. Métais et al. (Eds.): NLDB 2023, LNCS 13913, pp. 566–576, 2023.
https://doi.org/10.1007/978-3-031-35320-8_43

1   Introduction

An abbreviation of a word or phrase is the shortened form of the word or phrase, which is used to save space and time while representing the word at several occurrences to avoid repeating words and phrases or to adhere to standard practice [2]. Abbreviation detection is particularly useful in language technology applications such as information retrieval [1], information extraction [7], Named Entity Recognition (NER), and anaphora resolution. According to Yu et al. (2002b) [14], the inclusion of abbreviations in the Information Retrieval (IR) systems enhances the number of relevant documents retrieved. In addition, Friedman et al. (2001) [15] report that not addressing abbreviations is a major cause of the drop in performance in many NLP applications.

Because of the inconsistent and arbitrary styling, with many conceivable variations, abbreviating identification is challenging. According to Liu et al. (2001) [15], there are seven different types of abbreviations (mentioned in Table 1) that are generally used in the biomedical domain, mainly found from the UMLS (Unified Medical Language System). Some abbreviations are created by leaving out all except the initial few letters of a word; these abbreviations commonly end in a period: *Oct.* for October, *univ.* for university, and *cont.* for continued. Other abbreviations are made by leaving out letters in the middle of a word and usually ending in a period: *govt.* for government, *Dr.* for the doctor, and *atty.* for an attorney. The names of states in the United States are abbreviated with two capitalized letters, such as *AR* for Arkansas, *ME* for Maine, and *TX* for Texas.

Acronyms are abbreviations formed from the initial letters of an expanded phrase and usually do not include periods. For Example-*PR* stands for public relations, *CEO* stands for the chief executive officer, and *BTW* is for, by the way. *FEMA* (Federal Emergency Management Agency) and *NATO* (North Atlantic Treaty Organization) are two acronyms that are pronounced like words. Although some argue that all acronyms that are not pronounced as words, such as *EPA* (Environmental Protection Agency), are called *initialism*, the term acronym is used to describe both.

On the other hand, the number of biomedical abbreviations is continuously increasing due to the explosion of biomedical knowledge in all diverse fields. The vast and dynamic range of rules in different domains for abbreviation formation makes abbreviation identification a very challenging task. Abbreviation identification in the biomedical domain has its peculiarities. For Example, the prevalence of abbreviations in most clinical reports, such as admission notes, differ from those in the literature because they rarely appear with their extended counterparts in clinical reports, making identification more difficult. As a result, techniques based on abbreviation-definition patterns that work in the literature don't work in the medical record. On the other hand, abbreviations can often be confusing in the biomedical domain. For Example, *RA* could be *right atrium* or *rheumatoid arthritis*.

In this paper, we present an LSTM-based deep learning approach using two different types of pre-trained Bidirectional Encoder Representations from Transformers (BERT) models for abbreviation detection in scientific text documents.

We have reported results on two scientific datasets, *viz.*, 1. biomedical dataset, that is, MeDal [24], and 2. SciAI [22] dataset, which deals with general scientific text. We conducted experiments with two different settings; in the first case, we trained the model on the lower-cased pre-processed dataset, and in the second case, we trained the model without lower-casing the dataset. We observed that the second setting produced significantly better results, supporting the idea that abbreviations are case-sensitive. Hence, we have reported results without lowering the case in this paper. We received an F1-score of 90.04% on SciAI and 85.68% on the MeDal dataset. To observe the dominance of the domain, we performed cross-domain experiments (trained on MeDal, predicted on SciAI, and vice versa). We obtained an F1-score of 76.50% on SciAI data and 62.72% on MeDal data in the cross-domain settings. Furthermore, results (Sect. 6) show that our system outperformed the state-of-the-art model [22] for the abbreviation detection task.

Table 1. Different types of Abbreviations used along with an example of each.

S.No.	Types of Abbreviations	Example
1	Truncating the end	"adm" for administration or administrator
2	First letter initialization	"AAA" for abdominal aortic aneurysm
3	Opening letter initialization	"HeLa" for Henrietta Lacks
4	Syllabic initialization	"BZD" for benzodiazepine
5	Initialization of a combination	"e-mail" for electronic mail
6	Initialization by substitution	"ASD I" for Primum atrial septal defect
7	Chemical Abbreviations	"CXCR4" for chemokine receptor fusine

The rest of the paper is organized as follows. Section 2 provides the related work. Section 3 describes the dataset used. Section 4 elaborates the use of BERT model in our approach. Section 5 describes our approach. Section 6 presents the results and Sect. 7 concludes the paper.

2   Related Work

Typically acronym definitions are discovered by employing a variety of patterns to locate candidates in the context of the acronyms and a set of rules to choose the most likely choice. Patterns and rules are manually defined or learned either in supervised manner [17] or unsupervised manner [9]. Schwartz and Hearst (2002) [19] concentrate their efforts on locating and extracting abbreviations from medical papers by identifying *short form* and *long-form* pairs. They suggested that while many abbreviations in the biomedical sector follow a predictable pattern in which the first letter of each word is a letter from the short form, this is not always the case. As a result, they provide a simple and quick approach with high recall and precision for locating those combinations utilizing string operations. This ensures that the acronym letters appear in the long-form in the correct order. The biomedical field has done a lot of study on acronym resolution and disambiguation [6, 18, 23].

Several alternative ways and resources have been presented over the last two decades to address the two sub-tasks for acronyms. These methods range from rule-based methods for abbreviation identification and feature-based models for abbreviation disambiguation (*i.e.*, SVM and Naive Bayes) [17–19, 27] to the more recent deep learning methods [3, 4, 8, 11, 12, 25].

On the one hand, traditional feature-based models for abbreviation identification are limited in their capacity to capture situations effectively and thus fall behind in terms of accuracy compared to machine learning models [10, 16]. However, several current deep learning models for abbreviation identification cannot successfully encode the lengthy relationships between words in sentences. They mostly rely on either language models or sentence encoders (e.g., LSTMs) to capture contextual information which does not keep a long term memory of the context of the words [22, 26]. In this paper, we show use of the Bidirectional Encoder Representations from Transformers (BERT) vector embeddings which is capable of maintaining memory bidirectionally and thus resulted in better performance. We observe a precision of 90.41% and recall of 81.42% when tested on MeDal data and precision of 88.91% and recall of 90.17% when tested on SciAI data, which outperformed the precision of 88.58% and recall of 86.93% by Pouran et al., (2020) [22] for the abbreviation detection task.

3   Datasets

We used two separate datasets in this work. The first is the MeDal dataset [24], which is related to the Bio-medical field, and the second is the SciAi Abbreviation Identification dataset [22], which is associated with the general scientific domain.

3.1   MeDal Dataset

MeDAL [24] (Medical Dataset for Abbreviation Disambiguation for Natural Language Understanding) is an important medical text dataset collected for abbreviation disambiguation and developed for pre-training in natural language understanding in the medical domain. Its data production process, particularly, is influenced by the reverse substitution technique [6, 20]. There are 14, 393, 619 articles in the MeDAL dataset, with an average of three abbreviations per item. The MeDAL dataset is made up of abstracts from PubMed that were published in the 2019 annual baseline. PubMed is a scientific search engine that indexes papers in the biomedical field. The PubMed corpus contains 18, 374, 626 valid abstracts, with an average of 80 words per abstract.

Our system transforms the MeDal dataset into a more suitable format for the training of the abbreviation detection task. It labels all abbreviation words and their context sentences (4 words before and 4 words after the abbreviation) as *one* (1) and then randomly adds normal words (words that are not abbreviations) along with their context sentences and label them as *zero* (0). For example, in the sentence *the full form of ATP is Adenosine triphosphate, and it functions as the energy currency for cells. It allows the cell to store energy briefly and transport it within the cell to support endergonic chemical reactions*; the abbreviation word is *ATP*. The transformed representation is as follows.

- Format: (Word $$ context sentence $$ label)
- Example-1: *ATP* $$ the full form of *ATP* is Adenosine triphosphate and $$ *1*
- Example-2: *transport* $$ store energy briefly and *transport* it within the cell $$ *0*.
- Example-3: *endergonic* $$ the cell to support *endergonic* chemical reactions $$ *0*.

3.2 SciAI Dataset

The SciAI dataset [22] (scientific acronym identification) contains $17,560$ phrases annotated for acronym identification. Each sentence is tagged for short and long-form acronym boundaries in BIO format. The SciAI data was split into train and test in a ratio of 9:1. To build this dataset, developers used an arXiv corpus of $6,786$ publications, identified potential phrases in these papers that were likely to contain acronyms, and recruited Amazon Mechanical Turk users to gold label the sentences. The candidate sentences had consecutive (or almost consecutive) word sequences. The concatenation of the first few characters from these words could spell out another word in the document with at least 50% capital letters. To annotate the dataset, people were asked to identify abbreviations manually. They were asked to find all short-form acronyms in the sentence, even if the acronym's long-form did not appear in the statement. We used the same train-test split of the SciAi dataset in this paper to report the results.

4   BERT for Abbreviation Detection

In this paper, we have used sentence embeddings and two different types of word embeddings. We used small BERT [21] embeddings both as sentence embedding (on the context sentence) and word embeddings (on the target word to be checked for abbreviation). We also used Bio-BERT embeddings on the target word so that our model can be used for medical and general scientific datasets with high precision.

4.1   Small BERT Embeddings

The regular BERT formula (containing model architecture and training aim) works over various model sizes.[1] The smaller BERT models are designed for

---

[1] Small-BERT embedding is available as a pre-trained embedding on TensorFlow hub at https://tfhub.dev/tensorflow/small_bert/bert_en_uncased_L-2_H-128_A-2/2.

situations when computational resources are limited. They can be fine-tuned in the same way as the original BERT models. They work best in information distillation, where the fine-tuning labels are created by a larger, more accurate architecture. It uses $L = 2$ hidden layers (*i.e.*, Transformer blocks), a hidden size of $H = 128$, and $A = 2$ attention heads. Small BERT is pre-trained for the English language on Wikipedia and Books Corpus. Text is normalized in the *uncased* manner; that is, the text is lower-cased before being tokenized into word fragments, and any accent indicators are removed. Random input masking has been applied to word fragments independently for training (as in the original BERT [5]).

4.2 Bio BERT Embeddings

To make the BERT model more suitable in the medical domain, Bio BERT leverages the BERT architecture and trains it from scratch on the MED-LINE/PubMed dataset. Hence, this is a BERT-based architecture that modifies the initial training and export strategy based on newer learning that increases accuracy over the original BERT base checkpoint. It provides more examples during training with larger batch sizes and always uses the maximum sequence length. The Bio BERT generates examples with unique masks so that an exact example is not repeated during training, using contiguous *ngram* masking. It also replaces the pooling layers with an identity matrix after training, which has been observed to be more stable during downstream tasks.[2]

5 Approach

5.1 Data Preparation

The MeDal data contains about three abbreviations per sentence. To prepare the dataset for training, we used these abbreviations and their context sentence (4 words before and after). We also used other words (non-abbreviations) and their context. As the number of abbreviations in a sentence is much less than in other words, we undersampled the dataset by selecting approximately ten normal words per abbreviation along with their context sentence. The selection of normal words was completely random, with no filter applied. We took 22k sentences from the MeDal dataset and assigned the first 20k sentences as a training set and the rest 2k as the test set. For SciAI, we took the same training and test set as Pouran et al. (2020) [22], which is in the ratio of 9:1.

5.2 Abbreviation Identification

We fed the target word (w) and its context sentence (s) as input to the model (as shown in Fig. 1) for classifying whether the target word is an abbreviation

---

[2] Bio-BERT embeddings are available as pretrained embeddings on TensorFlow hub at https://tfhub.dev/google/experts/bert/pubmed/2.

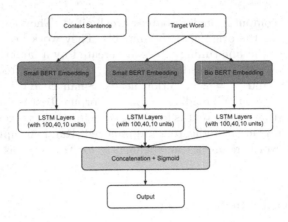

Fig. 1. Schematic Diagram of our model architecture

or not. Then the target word (w) was passed through the encoder of two models
E1 (Small BERT) and *E2* (Bio BERT) and obtained $e1 = E1(w)$ and $e2 = E2(w)$ as encoded output. The embedding models used are pretrained models.
The context sentence (s) was passed through Small BERT ($E3$) and obtained
$e3 = E3(s)$ as encoded output. Three LSTM models ($L1$, $L2$, $L3$) were setup,
and each contained triple-layered LSTM with 100, 40, and 10 units in the first,
second, and third layers, respectively. Then the embeddings $e1$, $e2$, $e3$ were fed
through $L1$, $L2$, $L3$ and $o1$, $o2$, $o3$ were obtained as outputs where $o1 = L1(e1)$,
$o2 = L2(e2)$, $o3 = L3(e3)$. Further, the outputs were concatenated and obtained
$C = concatenation(o1, o2, o3)$ and then C was passed through a sigmoid output
activation, which makes the prediction. The pseudocode of the overall approach
is given in Algorithm 1.

Algorithm 1. Proposed approach for abbreviation identification

---

$w \leftarrow$ *target word $s \leftarrow$ context sentence*
$E1 \leftarrow$ *First Small Bert Encoder $E2 \leftarrow$ Bio Bert Encoder $E3 \leftarrow$ Second Small Bert Encoder*
$e1 = E1(w)$ $e2 = E2(w)$ $e3 = E3(s)$ ▷ e1,e2,e3 are embedding representations
$L1$ $L2$ $L3$ $\leftarrow$ *three triple layered stacked LSTM architectures*
$o1 = L1(e1)$ $o2 = L2(e2)$ $o3 = L3(e3)$
$C = concatenation(o1, o2, o3)$
$Output = Sigmoid(C)$

We performed two different operations on the above-mentioned architecture
framework and named the models as *model_lower* and *model_nolower*, respectively. In the first operation, we took the model_lower. We trained it on a subset of
lower-cased preprocessed training data for five epochs, using adam optimizer and
binary cross-entropy as the loss function. In the second operation, we took the

model_no lower and trained it on the same subset of the MeDal dataset without being lowercased for five epochs, using adam optimizer and binary cross-entropy as loss function. We observed that the *model_nolower* performed significantly better than the *model_lower*. Hence, the preprocessing step of converting data to lowercase in the case of the abbreviation detection task is misleading the classifier. However, lower casing boosts the performance of many NLP tasks, such as sentiment analysis and machine translation; it is noticeable that the abbreviations and acronyms are case-sensitive. In this paper, we use two different types of datasets, *viz.*, SciAI, and MeDal representing different domains. We report in-domain and cross-domain results using the SciAI and MeDal datasets, keeping the letter case in the result section.

6   Results

We evaluate our approach on two publicly available datasets, *viz.*, SciAI and MeDal representing other domains. SciAI [22] represents the scientific domain, and MeDal [24] represents the medical domain. We report in-domain as well as cross-domain results using the two datasets. SciAI is a popularly used dataset in literature for abbreviation detection. We compared our abbreviation detection system with six other statistical models from the literature on the SciAI dataset. Table 2 shows the precision, recall, and F1 score obtained on the SciAI dataset. The first three methods are rule-based approaches, *viz.*, NOA [3], ADE [13] and UAD [4]. The next two models, BIOADI [10] and LNCRF [16], use a feature-based approach to define a set of features and feed it to the machine learning algorithms. LSTM-CRF is the state-of-the-art approach by Pouran et al., (2020) [22] for the abbreviation detection task. Our system produced precision and a

Table 2. Accuracy on the SciAI dataset by various models

S.No.	Model	Precision	Recall	F1 Score
1	NOA [3]	80.28	19.97	31.98
2	ADE [13]	79.23	86.42	82.67
3	UAD [4]	86.14	**91.48**	88.73
4	BIOADI [10]	83.20	87.31	85.20
5	LNCRF [16]	85.10	90.42	87.68
6	LSTM-CRF [22]	88.58	86.93	87.75
7	Our Model	**88.91**	90.17	**89.54**

Table 3. Accuracy in cross domain setup by our approach

Train	Test	Precision	Recall	F1 Score
MeDal	SciAI	79.63	73.62	76.50
SciAI	MeDal	89.95	48.14	62.72

recall of 88.91% and 90.17% (F1-score = 89.54%), respectively. Table 2 shows that our model outperformed the LSTM-CRF model reported by Pouran et al., (2020) [22] along with the other five approaches. In addition, we observed the performance of our approach with the MeDal dataset, which is a biomedical dataset. It gives a precision of 90.41% and recall of 81.41% (F1-score = 85.6%) on the MeDal dataset.

Further, we also performed cross-domain evaluation by training on MeDal Dataset and testing on SciAI dataset, next training on SciAI and testing on MeDal dataset. Table 3 shows that both the domains have domain specific features, hence the cross-domain performance is not as good as in-domain (Table 2) results.

7 Conclusion

Abbreviations enhance the readability and writability of text; hence they have a significant role in scientific writing. However, the identification of abbreviations is crucial to perform several language-processing tasks. This paper presents an approach to identify abbreviations from scientific text automatically. Our model leverages the Small-BERT and the Bio-BERT embeddings with a deep neural framework to capture the abbreviations. We also confirmed that the abbreviation detection task is case-sensitive. We report in-domain and cross-domain results on two publicly available datasets for the abbreviation identification task. Results show that our model can outperform the various baseline and state-of-the-art approaches for the abbreviation detection task. The automatic abbreviation detection model proposed in this paper can assist many-high level natural language processing tasks, such as machine translation, summarization, *etc.*

References

1. Byrd, R.J., Ravin, Y., Prager, J.: Lexical assistance at the information-retrieval user interface. IBM TJ Watson Research Center (1994)
2. Chang, J.T., Schütze, H.: Abbreviations in biomedical text. In: Text Mining for Biology and Biomedicine, pp. 99–119 (2006)
3. Charbonnier, J., Wartena, C.: Using word embeddings for unsupervised acronym disambiguation (2018)
4. Ciosici, M.R., Sommer, T., Assent, I.: Unsupervised abbreviation disambiguation. arXiv preprint arXiv:1904.00929 (2019)
5. Devlin, J., Chang, M.W., Lee, K., Toutanova, K.: BERT: pre-training of deep bidirectional transformers for language understanding. arXiv preprint arXiv:1810.04805 (2018)
6. Finley, G.P., Pakhomov, S.V., McEwan, R., Melton, G.B.: Towards comprehensive clinical abbreviation disambiguation using machine-labeled training data. In: AMIA Annual Symposium Proceedings, vol. 2016, p. 560. American Medical Informatics Association (2016)
7. Grigonyte, G.: Building and Evaluating Domain Ontologies: NLP Contributions. Logos Verlag, Berlin (2010)

8. Jin, Q., Liu, J., Lu, X.: Deep contextualized biomedical abbreviation expansion. arXiv preprint arXiv:1906.03360 (2019)
9. Kirchhoff, K., Turner, A.M.: Unsupervised resolution of acronyms and abbreviations in nursing notes using document-level context models. In: Proceedings of the Seventh International Workshop on Health Text Mining and Information Analysis, pp. 52–60 (2016)
10. Kuo, C.J., Ling, M.H., Lin, K.T., Hsu, C.N.: BIOADI: a machine learning approach to identifying abbreviations and definitions in biological literature. In: BMC Bioinformatics, vol. 10, pp. 1–10. BioMed Central (2009)
11. Li, C., Ji, L., Yan, J.: Acronym disambiguation using word embedding. In: Proceedings of the AAAI Conference on Artificial Intelligence, vol. 29 (2015)
12. Li, I., et al.: A neural topic-attention model for medical term abbreviation disambiguation. arXiv preprint arXiv:1910.14076 (2019)
13. Li, Y., Zhao, B., Fuxman, A., Tao, F.: Guess me if you can: acronym disambiguation for enterprises. In: Proceedings of the 56th Annual Meeting of the Association for Computational Linguistics (Volume 1: Long Papers), pp. 1308–1317 (2018)
14. Liu, H., Aronson, A.R., Friedman, C.: A study of abbreviations in MEDLINE abstracts. In: Proceedings of the AMIA Symposium, p. 464. American Medical Informatics Association (2002)
15. Liu, H., Lussier, Y.A., Friedman, C.: A study of abbreviations in the UMLS. In: Proceedings of the AMIA Symposium, p. 393. American Medical Informatics Association (2001)
16. Liu, J., Liu, C., Huang, Y.: Multi-granularity sequence labeling model for acronym expansion identification. Inf. Sci. **378**, 462–474 (2017)
17. Nadeau, D., Turney, P.D.: A supervised learning approach to acronym identification. In: Kégl, B., Lapalme, G. (eds.) AI 2005. LNCS (LNAI), vol. 3501, pp. 319–329. Springer, Heidelberg (2005). https://doi.org/10.1007/11424918_34
18. Okazaki, N., Ananiadou, S.: Building an abbreviation dictionary using a term recognition approach. Bioinformatics **22**(24), 3089–3095 (2006)
19. Schwartz, A.S., Hearst, M.A.: A simple algorithm for identifying abbreviation definitions in biomedical text. In: Biocomputing 2003, pp. 451–462. World Scientific (2002)
20. Skreta, M., Arbabi, A., Wang, J., Brudno, M.: Training without training data: improving the generalizability of automated medical abbreviation disambiguation. In: Machine Learning for Health Workshop, pp. 233–245. PMLR (2020)
21. Turc, I., Chang, M.W., Lee, K., Toutanova, K.: Well-read students learn better: on the importance of pre-training compact models. arXiv preprint arXiv:1908.08962 (2019)
22. Veyseh, A.P.B., Dernoncourt, F., Tran, Q.H., Nguyen, T.H.: What does this acronym mean? introducing a new dataset for acronym identification and disambiguation. arXiv preprint arXiv:2010.14678 (2020)
23. Vo, T.N.C., Cao, T.H., Ho, T.B.: Abbreviation identification in clinical notes with level-wise feature engineering and supervised learning. In: Ohwada, H., Yoshida, K. (eds.) PKAW 2016. LNCS (LNAI), vol. 9806, pp. 3–17. Springer, Cham (2016). https://doi.org/10.1007/978-3-319-42706-5_1
24. Wen, Z., Lu, X.H., Reddy, S.: MeDAL: medical abbreviation disambiguation dataset for natural language understanding pretraining. arXiv preprint arXiv:2012.13978 (2020)
25. Wu, Y., Xu, J., Zhang, Y., Xu, H.: Clinical abbreviation disambiguation using neural word embeddings. In: Proceedings of BioNLP 2015, pp. 171–176 (2015)

576   P. Miglani et al.

26. Yeganova, L., Comeau, D.C., Wilbur, W.J.: Identifying abbreviation definitions machine learning with naturally labeled data. In: 2010 Ninth International Conference on Machine Learning and Applications, pp. 499–505. IEEE (2010)
27. Yu, H., Kim, W., Hatzivassiloglou, V., Wilbur, W.J.: Using MEDLINE as a knowledge source for disambiguating abbreviations and acronyms in full-text biomedical journal articles. J. Biomed. Inform. 40(2), 150–159 (2007)

RoBERTweet: A BERT Language Model for Romanian Tweets

Iulian-Marius Tăiatu[1], Andrei-Marius Avram[1(✉)], Dumitru-Clementin Cercel[1], and Florin Pop[1,2]

[1] Faculty of Automatic Control and Computers, University Politehnica of Bucharest, Bucharest, Romania
{iulian.taiatu,andrei_marius.avram}@stud.acs.upb.ro,
{dumitru.cercel,florin.pop}@upb.ro
[2] National Institute for Research and Development in Informatics - ICI Bucharest, Bucharest, Romania

Abstract. Developing natural language processing (NLP) systems for social media analysis remains an important topic in artificial intelligence research. This article introduces RoBERTweet, the first Transformer architecture trained on Romanian tweets. Our RoBERTweet comes in two versions, following the base and large architectures of BERT. The corpus used for pre-training the models represents a novelty for the Romanian NLP community and consists of all tweets collected from 2008 to 2022. Experiments show that RoBERTweet models outperform the previous general-domain Romanian and multilingual language models on three NLP tasks with tweet inputs: emotion detection, sexist language identification, and named entity recognition. We make our models (https://huggingface.co/Iulian277/ro-bert-tweet) and the newly created corpus (https://huggingface.co/datasets/Iulian277/romanian-tweets) of Romanian tweets freely available.

Keywords: BERT · Twitter · Corpus · Romanian Language

1 Introduction

Over the past several years, there has been a substantial surge in interest and enthusiasm related to natural language processing (NLP) techniques for various social media-related tasks. These techniques may include but are not limited to training NLP models for purposes such as sentiment analysis, identifying offensive or sexist language, performing part-of-speech (POS) tagging, or conducting named entity recognition (NER). Nguyen et al. [19] have presented a BERT [6] language model specifically developed for analyzing English tweets. Concretely, their model has been trained on a large corpus of 850 million English tweets and has yielded impressive results in several NLP tasks relevant to Twitter text analysis, such as POS tagging, NER, and text classification (i.e., irony detection and sentiment analysis).

I.-M. Tăiatu and A.-M. Avram—Equal contribution.

Various other BERT models designed to analyze tweets have been developed, with each model focusing on a different language. For example, Guo et al. [9] have designed and trained a BERT model to analyze French tweets. Similarly, Koto et al. [13] have presented their own BERT model optimized to analyze Indonesian tweets, while Pérez et al. [22] have created a BERT model that is capable of handling Spanish tweets. Additionally, Zhang et al. [29] have introduced a highly sophisticated multi-lingual BERT model trained on a massive dataset of over 7 billion tweets in more than 100 languages.

This paper presents two versions of language models for the Romanian language that were pre-trained on a novel corpus of Romanian tweets. In short, we summarized our main contributions as follows:

- We collect and release a novel corpus of Romanian tweets from 2008 to 2022, consisting of 65M unique tweets. It is a significant contribution to the field, as no such resource existed for the Romanian language.
- We conduct a comprehensive set of experiments based on this newly-created corpus, further demonstrating the usefulness of our dataset and pre-trained models.
- We develop the first language models pre-trained on the tweet domain for the Romanian language under the name RoBERTweet-base and RoBERTweet-large. These models can be utilized with the Transformer library [27], and we expect them to provide strong baselines for future research and applications related to Romanian tweet NLP tasks.
- We obtain state-of-the-art (SOTA) results on three existing Romanian tweet tasks: emotion detection (ED), named entity recognition, and sexist language identification (SLI).

2   Related Work

The English BERT language model was pre-trained on two large datasets, Book-Corpus and English Wikipedia, using two prediction tasks, masked language model (MLM) and next sentence prediction (NSP). After pre-training, BERT was fine-tuned on several target datasets where it learned to make inferences on specific tasks such as NER, question answering, or natural language inference, obtaining state-of-the-art results on the General Language Understanding Evaluation (GLUE) benchmark [26]. Since BERT was introduced, this mechanism of first pre-training a language model on a large corpus and then fine-tuning the resulting model on specific tasks has become ubiquitous in NLP. Thus, many researchers have flocked to this area, developing larger and more complex language models.

One important iteration in this direction is the Robustely Optimized BERT (RoBERTa) model [15], which argues that the BERT model is sub-optimized. Therefore, RoBERTa pre-trained the architecture on a larger corpus with a larger batch size, applied the dynamic MLM, and removed the NSP task, achieving state-of-the-art performance on the GLUE benchmark. A Lite version of BERT (ALBERT) [14] is another important architecture introduced in the literature that addressed the issue associated with many parameters of BERT and solved it by proposing a cross-layer parameter sharing and an embedding parameter factorization technique. To achieve better results, the Efficiently Learning an Encoder that Classifies Token Replacement Accurately (ELECTRA) [4] applied a replace token detection (RTD) task in pre-training instead of employing MLM.

The first Romanian BERT models (i.e., BERT-base-cased-ro and BERT-base-uncased-ro) were developed by Dumitrescu et al. [7]. The models were trained on a general-domain corpus collected from diverse sources such as OPUS [25], Wikipedia dumps[1], and OSCAR [24], totalling over 15.2 GB of text data. Since then, various BERT-like models have been introduced in the research literature, including other general variants of the Romanian BERT (i.e., RoBERT-small, RoBERT-base, and RoBERT-large) [18], the distilled versions of Romanian BERTs (i.e., Distil-BERT-base-ro, Distil-RoBERT-base, and DistilMulti-BERT-base-ro) [1], the "judiciar"[2] BERT (i.e., jurBERT-base and jurBERT-large) [17] trained on legal data, and A Lite Romanian BERT (ALR-BERT) [20], a monolingual language model that follows the ALBERT architecture.

3 RoBERTweet

3.1 Dataset

Figure 1 depicts the dataset generation pipeline. We crawl Romanian tweets over an extensive period from 2008 to 2022 using the *snscrape* package[3]. When sending the query, we set the *RO* flag to ensure the corpus contains only Romanian text. We also employ the language identification component of *fastText* [11] and the *langdetect* library[4] to further filter out non-Romanian tweets. These are crucial steps because of pre-processing is not handled accordingly, the resulting corpus would contain text in other languages that introduce noise and uncertainty to the model predictions while also potentially increasing the number of [UNK] tokens.

The following pre-processing steps are inspired by the existing approach of Nguyen et al. [19]. For each tweet, we employ the normalization technique to convert user mentions, URL links, and hashtags into special tokens, namely USER, HTTPURL, and HASHTAG. We further exclude tweets shorter than five or longer than 256 words and filter out the tweets that contain more than three mentions, three hashtags, three URLs, or three emojis, as they are considered irrelevant or spam and may add noise to the training procedure. In addition, to increase the language understanding and make the model stronger for future downstream tasks (e.g., emotion detection), we translate each emoji with its corresponding text. This is done using the *emoji* package[5].

---

[1] https://github.com/dumitrescustefan/wiki-ro.
[2] "Judiciar" is the Romanian equivalent to the English "criminal record".
[3] https://github.com/JustAnotherArchivist/snscrape.
[4] https://pypi.org/project/langdetect.
[5] https://pypi.org/project/emoji.

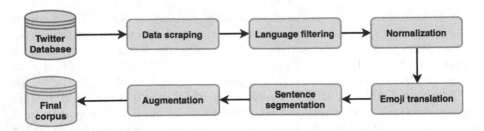

Fig. 1. RoBERTweet training corpus pre-processing pipeline.

We also use the *sentencizer* component from *spaCy*[6] to split the tweets into sentences. This observation is necessary for the NSP task, which is part of the pre-training objective of the BERT model. After each sentence of a tweet, we introduce a new line, and after the last sentence of a tweet, we introduce two blank lines, thus delimiting two tweets.

After performing all these data cleaning and normalization steps, we obtained a 5GB corpus containing 65M tweets, which we open-sourced and made publicly available. Finally, we convert the uncompressed text files to *tfrecords* using the script that creates the pre-training data[7]. We augment the dataset using a dupe factor of 10, meaning that each tweet is randomly masked ten times using different seeds. Thus, we generate a tenfold increase in the size of our pre-training corpus, effectively performing a form of data augmentation.

3.2 Methodology

In this study, the developed RoBERTweet models use a cased tokenizer and have the same architecture as BERT-base and BERT-large. The pre-training procedure is also the same, which involves using MLM and NSP objectives. The MLM objective selects 15% of the tokens for possible replacement, with 80% of those selected being replaced by the special [MASK] token, 10% remaining unchanged, and 10% replaced by random tokens from the vocabulary. The NSP objective involves pairing 50% of the input sentences with the real subsequent sentence as the second sentence. In contrast, in the other 50% of cases, a random sentence from the corpus is selected as the second sentence.

The weights are randomly initialized, and training is initiated from scratch. The base version (i.e., RoBERTweet-base) uses 12 layers, 768 hidden dimensions, and 12 attention heads, resulting in 110M parameters. In comparison, the large version (i.e., RoBERTweet-large) has 24 layers, 1024 hidden dimensions, and 16 attention heads, resulting in 345M parameters. Inspired by Zampieri et al. [28], we depict in Table 1 more details regarding the architecture of our RoBERTweet models compared to the other available Romanian BERT models.

---

[6] https://spacy.io/api/sentencizer.
[7] https://github.com/google-research/bert.

Table 1. Comparison of our RoBERTweet models and the other Romanian BERT models available in the literature regarding their training data size, number of layers, number of hidden units on each layer, number of heads, vocabulary dimension, and number of parameters.

Model	Train Size	Layers	Hidden	Heads	Vocab	Params
BERT-base-cased-ro [7]	15.2 GB	12	768	12	50K	124M
BERT-base-uncased-ro [7]	15.2 GB	12	768	12	50K	124M
RoBERT-small [18]	12.6 GB	12	256	8	38K	19M
RoBERT-base [18]	12.6 GB	12	768	12	38K	114M
RoBERT-large [18]	12.6 GB	24	1024	16	38K	341M
Distil-BERT-base-ro [1]	25.3 GB	6	768	12	50K	81M
Distil-RoBERT-base [1]	25.3 GB	6	768	12	38K	72M
DistilMulti-BERT-base-ro [1]	25.3 GB	6	768	12	50K	81M
jurBERT-base [17]	160 GB	12	768	12	33K	111M
jurBERT-large [17]	160 GB	24	1024	16	33K	81M
ALR-BERT [20]	15.2 GB	12	768	12	50K	81M
RoBERTweet-base (ours)	5 GB	6	768	12	51K	110M
RoBERTweet-large (ours)	5 GB	6	768	12	51K	345M

In language modeling, the vocabulary plays a critical role in model performance. Generally speaking, the better the tokenization of sentences (i.e., the fewer pieces each word is broken into), the better the model is expected to perform. In this study, the vocabulary used for the models is an extension of the BERT-base-ro vocabulary, created by adding the special tweet tokens resulting from preprocessing (i.e., USER, HTTPURL, and HASHTAG) and the most frequent 25% of emojis found in the tweets. The resulting vocabulary contained 51K tokens, an increment of 1K tokens compared to the vocabulary used by BERT-base-ro.

Each RoBERTweet variant was trained using a v2-8 Tensor Processing Unit (TPU), requiring approximately three weeks each. The RoBERTweet models were trained using a batch size of 2048 and a total of 3M steps. However, the pre-training process was stopped after 1.5M steps since the model ceased to make any progress. We employed the Adam optimizer [12], together with a linear scheduler. The first 30K steps (i.e., 1% of the total steps) are used for warming up the learning rate.

4 Experiments and Results

Since our RoBERTweet models are the first pre-trained language models for Romanian tweets, we compare them with the Romanian general-domain BERT language models[8]: BERT-base-cased-ro, BERT-base-uncased-ro, RoBERT-small,

---

[8] We were not able to load the ALR-BERT model from the HuggingFace repository (available at https://huggingface.co/dragosnicolae555/ALR_BERT), so we did not include its results in our evaluation.

RoBERT-base, RoBERT-large, DistilMulti-BERT-base-ro, Distil-BERT-base-ro, and Distil-RoBERT-base. Subsequently, we fine-tune and analyze the results of our RoBERTweet models and the other general-domain BERT language models on three Twitter-related NLP tasks: emotion detection, sexist language identification, and named entity recognition.

4.1 Emotion Detection

The ED task is a supervised classification task that aims to predict the emotion of a given text. To perform this task, we use the second version of the Romanian emotion dataset (REDv2) [2], a helpful resource designed for detecting emotions in Romanian tweets. It is an extension of the REDv1 dataset [3] and consists of 5,449 multi-label annotated tweets with seven types of emotions: anger, fear, happiness, sadness, surprise, trust, and neutral. We present the results of the evaluated models treating this task as either classification or regression.

Following the methodology proposed by Devlin et al. [6], we append a linear prediction layer on top of the mean output of the pre-trained language model and include a dropout rate of 10% for regularization. For the fine-tuning process, we utilize the AdamW optimizer [16] with a fixed learning rate of 2e-5 and a batch size of 16. To prevent overfitting, we implement early stopping, which stops the training procedure when no performance improvement happens on the validation set in 3 consecutive epochs. We compute accuracy (Acc), the Hamming loss (Ham), the F1-score (F1), and the mean squared error (MSE) score on the test set for each model.

The classification and regression results for ED are depicted in Table 2. Except for MSE, the highest scores were obtained by RoBERTweet-large, achieving a Hamming loss of 0.085, an accuracy of 58.6%, and an F1-score of 69.6% when the ED task was treated as classification, and a Hamming loss of 0.088, an accuracy of 57.6%, and an F1-score of 70.0% when the ED task was treated as regression. It outperforms its general domain counter-part, RoBERT-large, on all these metrics, improving the classification Hamming loss by 0.003, accuracy by 0.8%, and F1-score by 0.5%, as well as the regression Hamming loss by 0.007, accuracy by 2.4%, and F1-score by 1.3%.

The lowest MSE scores were obtained by Distil-RoBERT-base, with a 6.85 MSE for classification ED and 6.41 MSE for regression ED. To the best of our knowledge, we do not have a clear justification of why this model specifically performed so well on this metric, and a detailed analysis would be outside the scope of this paper. Our only observations are: (1) the classification MSE scores have a high variance ranging from 6.85 to 26.79 with no consistent pattern in the results, and (2) the MSE regression scores are lower than the classification MSE scores. These two observations are expected since, compared to regression, we do not try to minimize the MSE loss in classification directly.

Table 2. Emotion detection scores in the classification and regression setting. The baseline models in the paper that introduced the dataset are depicted in italics.

Model	Classification				Regression			
	Ham	Acc	F1	MSE	Ham	Acc	F1	MSE
BERT-base-cased-ro [2]	0.104	0.541	0.668	26.74	0.970	0.542	0.670	10.06
XLM-RoBERTa [2]	0.121	0.504	0.619	18.40	0.104	0.522	0.649	9.56
BERT-base-cased-ro [7]	0.105	0.549	0.675	20.87	0.098	0.541	0.664	10.33
BERT-base-uncased-ro [7]	0.097	0.547	0.669	9.83	0.097	0.546	0.679	9.92
RoBERT-small [18]	0.106	0.524	0.642	9.93	0.102	0.529	0.645	7.62
RoBERT-base [18]	0.106	0.550	0.666	26.79	0.094	0.566	0.684	9.67
RoBERT-large [18]	0.098	0.578	0.691	18.49	0.095	0.552	0.687	9.50
Distil-BERT-base-ro [1]	0.113	0.502	0.623	14.47	0.106	0.488	0.627	8.81
Distil-RoBERT-base [1]	0.101	0.550	0.659	**6.85**	0.096	0.570	0.653	**6.41**
DistilMulti-BERT-base-ro [1]	0.107	0.552	0.661	15.55	0.105	0.550	0.648	7.82
RoBERTweet-base (ours)	0.102	0.556	0.677	22.60	0.096	0.557	0.673	9.92
RoBERTweet-large (ours)	**0.095**	**0.586**	**0.696**	24.43	**0.088**	**0.576**	**0.700**	9.67

4.2 Sexist Language Identification

The CoRoSeOf corpus [10] is a manually annotated resource that aims to identify the sexist and offensive language in Romanian tweets. The dataset contains approximately 40K tweets and five labels: sexist direct, sexist descriptive, sexist reporting, non-sexist offensive, and non-sexist non-offensive. Using these labels, two evaluation tasks were derived from this dataset: binary classification, where a model has to predict whether a tweet is a sexist or non-sexist, and three-way classification, where a model has to predict the kind of sexism in a tweet identified as such (i.e., direct, descriptive, and reporting).

For this experiment, we adopt the same fine-tuning strategy as in the previous task, but our target is to maximize the F1-score in this task. We compute the precision, recall, and F1-scores of our RoBERTweet variants and compare them with the scores achieved by the other general-domain Romanian BERT models available in the literature. In addition, we outline the results of the Support Vector Machine (SVM) [5] baseline model introduced in the dataset paper [10].

Table 3 depicts our binary and three-way classification task results. The highest F1-scores for both binary and three-way SLI were obtained by RoBERTweet-large with 85.5% and 78.0%, respectively. It outperformed the second best model, RoBERT-large[9], by 1.2% and 0.3% on the binary and three-way SLI, respectively. RoBERTweet-base also performed well on this task, achieving a higher F1-score than all the other base and smaller Romanian models on binary SLI. However, the same does not hold on the three-way SLI classification, and it fell behind BERT-base-cased-ro, BERT-base-uncased-ro, and RoBERTweet-base on this subtask.

---

[9] Distil-RoBERT-base achieves the same F1-score on three-way SLI as RoBERTweet-large.

Table 3. Sexist language identification results for both the binary and three-way classification tasks. The baseline models in the paper that introduced the dataset are depicted in italics.

Model	Binary			Three-way		
	P	R	F1	P	R	F1
SVM [10]	0.830	0.832	0.831	0.693	0.700	0.716
BERT-base-cased-ro [7]	0.844	0.812	0.836	0.821	0.753	0.778
BERT-base-uncased-ro [7]	0.846	0.814	0.829	0.878	0.732	0.771
RoBERT-small [18]	0.855	0.811	0.831	0.840	0.662	0.677
RoBERT-base [18]	0.849	0.784	0.812	0.812	0.710	0.736
RoBERT-large [18]	0.853	0.833	0.842	**0.894**	0.740	0.777
Distil-BERT-base-ro [1]	0.828	0.795	0.810	0.730	0.654	0.673
Distil-RoBERT-base [1]	0.855	0.753	0.793	0.795	**0.763**	0.777
DistilMulti-BERT-base-ro [1]	0.860	0.747	0.790	0.708	0.610	0.655
RoBERTweet-base (ours)	**0.866**	0.821	0.841	0.798	0.724	0.749
RoBERTweet-large (ours)	0.837	**0.878**	**0.855**	0.823	0.754	**0.780**

4.3 Named Entity Recognition

Păiș et al. [21] have constructed a NER dataset from microblogging texts sourced from social media platforms (i.e., Twitter, Reddit, and Gab). The dataset contains high-quality annotations for nine entity types as follows: persons (PER), locations (LOC), organizations (ORG), time expressions (TM), legal references (LEG), disorders (DIS), chemicals (CHM), medical devices (MD), and anatomical parts (ANT). A total of 7,800 messages have been manually annotated in the dataset, which in turn contains 11K annotations. We use this dataset to train our models to perform NER on Romanian microblogging.

Fine-tuning follows the supervised token classification method proposed by Devlin et al. in [6]. Specifically, we employ a fully-connected layer on top of the embeddings produced by BERT that correspond to the first subword token of each word. The models are trained using the AdamW optimizer with a fixed learning rate of 2e−5 and a batch size of 16, to which we add the weight decay. We compute performance scores for each entity class and the overall F1-score. The baselines used for comparison are those reported in the literature [21] and consist of three systems: Neuroner CoRoLa, Neuroner MB, and Neuroner CoRoLa + MB.

Table 4 depicts our results of the evaluated models on NER. The highest F1-score was obtained by the RoBERTweet-base model with 74.43%, RoBERTweet-large occupying the second place with an F1-score of 74.26%. An interesting result of this evaluation is that except for the LOC entity, RoBERTweet-base and RoBERTweet-large do not obtain the best F1-score on individual entities. However, the two models get the first two best average F1-scores. This may indicate that general language models pay too much attention to certain entities due to their lack of domain-specific knowledge. In contrast, the performance

Table 4. NER performance for each entity class and the overall F1-score. The baseline models in the paper that introduced the dataset are depicted in italics.

Model	ANT	CHM	DIS	LEG	LOC	MD	ORG	PER	TM	Total
Neuroner CoRoLa [21]	42.96	60.47	75.47	45.71	77.69	72.73	66.21	84.14	63.96	72.03
Neuroner MB [21]	22.54	58.82	71.43	47.37	81.27	61.54	65.95	80.95	63.64	71.26
Neuroner CoRoLa + MB [21]	21.43	**82.87**	73.47	36.36	81.21	**66.67**	62.00	83.51	61.50	70.75
BERT-base-cased-ro [7]	50.01	58.42	74.61	47.61	83.43	66.66	**71.19**	84.17	64.02	74.14
BERT-base-uncased-ro [7]	**61.11**	60.21	79.59	43.24	82.22	46.15	69.19	85.57	61.89	74.16
RoBERT-small [18]	38.85	58.82	74.14	32.65	79.38	18.18	67.09	79.04	59.91	69.54
RoBERT-base [18]	50.21	66.39	76.35	**54.00**	82.55	41.28	69.44	**85.70**	63.40	74.14
RoBERT-large [18]	55.20	63.01	**80.73**	47.38	82.42	60.03	69.91	85.04	**66.62**	74.22
Distil-BERT-base-ro [1]	42.85	60.21	70.46	47.61	77.02	30.76	63.17	75.28	62.97	68.51
Distil-RoBERT-base [1]	36.11	53.33	68.65	40.90	75.00	30.76	60.37	75.52	60.30	66.31
DistilMulti-BERT-base-ro [1]	41.77	33.45	46.61	51.22	72.22	60.03	44.77	72.47	56.91	65.69
RoBERTweet-base (ours)	45.33	69.66	77.94	50.00	**83.84**	57.14	70.29	83.31	64.90	**74.43**
RoBERTweet-large (ours)	44.73	65.90	76.09	51.28	82.80	61.53	71.08	85.43	62.97	74.26

of domain-specific language models is more evenly distributed between entities. However, further analysis is necessary to confirm this observation for other domains, models, and languages, which would be outside the scope of this paper.

5 Conclusions

In this work, we presented the first pre-trained language models for Romanian tweets on a large scale: RoBERTweet-base and RoBERTweet-large, together with the novel corpus on which they were trained. This corpus comprises 65M Romanian tweets which have been carefully filtered and normalized. Our experimental results demonstrated the usefulness of both RoBERTweet variants by outperforming the baselines, while also showing superior performance compared to the previous SOTA Romanian BERT models on three downstream Twitter NLP tasks: emotion detection, sexual language identification, and named entity recognition.

Possible future work directions of this paper involve creating new kinds of Romanian language models using our novel dataset, such as GPT-2 [23] for tweet generation. In addition, we intend to add the results obtained by our RoBERTweet models in LiRO [8], a Romanian benchmark for NLP models.

Acknowledgements. This research has been funded by the University Politehnica of Bucharest through the PubArt program. We gratefully acknowledge the support of the TensorFlow Research Cloud program (https://sites.research.google/trc) for generously providing us access to Cloud TPUs, which enabled us to carry out our extensive pre-training experiments.

References

1. Avram, A.M., et al.: Distilling the knowledge of Romanian BERTs using multiple teachers. In: Proceedings of the Thirteenth Language Resources and Evaluation Conference, Marseille, France, pp. 374–384. European Language Resources Association (2022)
2. Ciobotaru, A., Constantinescu, M.V., Dinu, L.P., Dumitrescu, S.: RED v2: enhancing red dataset for multi-label emotion detection. In: Proceedings of the Thirteenth Language Resources and Evaluation Conference, pp. 1392–1399 (2022)
3. Ciobotaru, A., Dinu, L.P.: RED: a novel dataset for Romanian emotion detection from tweets. In: Proceedings of the International Conference on Recent Advances in Natural Language Processing (RANLP 2021), pp. 291–300 (2021)
4. Clark, K., Luong, M.T., Le, Q.V., Manning, C.D.: ELECTRA: pre-training text encoders as discriminators rather than generators. arXiv preprint arXiv:2003.10555 (2020)
5. Cortes, C., Vapnik, V.: Support-vector networks. Mach. Learn. **20**, 273–297 (1995)
6. Devlin, J., Chang, M.W., Lee, K., Toutanova, K.: BERT: pre-training of deep bidirectional transformers for language understanding. In: Proceedings of the 2019 Conference of the North American Chapter of the Association for Computational Linguistics: Human Language Technologies, Volume 1 (Long and Short Papers), pp. 4171–4186 (2019)
7. Dumitrescu, S., Avram, A.M., Pyysalo, S.: The birth of Romanian BERT. In: Findings of the Association for Computational Linguistics: EMNLP 2020, pp. 4324–4328 (2020)
8. Dumitrescu, S.D., et al.: LiRo: benchmark and leaderboard for Romanian language tasks. In: Thirty-Fifth Conference on Neural Information Processing Systems Datasets and Benchmarks Track (Round 1) (2021)
9. Guo, Y., Rennard, V., Xypolopoulos, C., Vazirgiannis, M.: BERTweetFR: domain adaptation of pre-trained language models for French tweets. In: Proceedings of the Seventh Workshop on Noisy User-generated Text (W-NUT 2021), pp. 445–450 (2021)
10. Hoefels, D.C., Çöltekin, Ç., Mădroane, I.D.: CoRoSeOf-an annotated corpus of Romanian sexist and offensive tweets. In: Proceedings of the Thirteenth Language Resources and Evaluation Conference, pp. 2269–2281 (2022)
11. Joulin, A., Grave, É., Bojanowski, P., Mikolov, T.: Bag of tricks for efficient text classification. In: Proceedings of the 15th Conference of the European Chapter of the Association for Computational Linguistics: Volume 2, Short Papers, pp. 427–431 (2017)
12. Kingma, D.P., Ba, J.: Adam: a method for stochastic optimization. In: Proceedings of the 3rd International Conference on Learning Representations. In: ICLR 2015 (2015)
13. Koto, F., Lau, J.H., Baldwin, T.: IndoBERTweet: a pretrained language model for Indonesian twitter with effective domain-specific vocabulary initialization. In: Proceedings of the 2021 Conference on Empirical Methods in Natural Language Processing, pp. 10660–10668 (2021)
14. Lan, Z., Chen, M., Goodman, S., Gimpel, K., Sharma, P., Soricut, R.: ALBERT: a lite BERT for self-supervised learning of language representations. arXiv preprint arXiv:1909.11942 (2019)
15. Liu, Y., et al.: RoBERTa: a robustly optimized BERT pretraining approach. arXiv preprint arXiv:1907.11692 (2019)

16. Loshchilov, I., Hutter, F.: Decoupled weight decay regularization. In: International Conference on Learning Representations (2019)
17. Masala, M., et al.: jurBERT: a Romanian BERT model for legal judgement prediction. In: Proceedings of the Natural Legal Language Processing Workshop 2021, pp. 86–94 (2021)
18. Masala, M., Ruseti, S., Dascalu, M.: RoBERT-a Romanian BERT model. In: Proceedings of the 28th International Conference on Computational Linguistics, pp. 6626–6637 (2020)
19. Nguyen, D.Q., Vu, T., Nguyen, A.T.: BERTweet: a pre-trained language model for English tweets. In: Proceedings of the 2020 Conference on Empirical Methods in Natural Language Processing: System Demonstrations, pp. 9–14 (2020)
20. Nicolae, D.C., Yadav, R.K., Tufiş, D.: A lite Romanian BERT: ALR-BERT. Computers 11(4), 57 (2022)
21. Păiş, V., Mititelu, V.B., Irimia, E., Mitrofan, M., Gasan, C.L., Micu, R.: Romanian micro-blogging named entity recognition including health-related entities. In: Proceedings of The Seventh Workshop on Social Media Mining for Health Applications, Workshop & Shared Task, pp. 190–196 (2022)
22. Pérez, J.M., Furman, D.A., Alemany, L.A., Luque, F.M.: RoBERTuito: a pre-trained language model for social media text in Spanish. In: Proceedings of the Thirteenth Language Resources and Evaluation Conference, pp. 7235–7243 (2022)
23. Radford, A., Wu, J., Child, R., Luan, D., Amodei, D., Sutskever, I., et al.: Language models are unsupervised multitask learners. OpenAI Blog 1(8), 9 (2019)
24. Suárez, P.J.O., Sagot, B., Romary, L.: Asynchronous pipeline for processing huge corpora on medium to low resource infrastructures. In: 7th Workshop on the Challenges in the Management of Large Corpora (CMLC-7). Leibniz-Institut für Deutsche Sprache (2019)
25. Tiedemann, J.: Parallel data, tools and interfaces in opus. In: Proceedings of the Eighth International Conference on Language Resources and Evaluation (LREC 2012), pp. 2214–2218 (2012)
26. Wang, A., Singh, A., Michael, J., Hill, F., Levy, O., Bowman, S.: GLUE: a multi-task benchmark and analysis platform for natural language understanding. In: Proceedings of the 2018 EMNLP Workshop BlackboxNLP: Analyzing and Interpreting Neural Networks for NLP, pp. 353–355 (2018)
27. Wolf, T., et al.: Transformers: state-of-the-art natural language processing. In: Proceedings of the 2020 Conference on Empirical Methods in Natural Language Processing: System Demonstrations, pp. 38–45 (2020)
28. Zampieri, M., et al.: Language variety identification with true labels. arXiv preprint arXiv:2303.01490 (2023)
29. Zhang, X., et al.: TwHIN-BERT: a socially-enriched pre-trained language model for multilingual tweet representations. arXiv preprint arXiv:2209.07562 (2022)

Evaluating the Effect of Letter Case on Named Entity Recognition Performance

Tuan An Dao[1]([✉])(iD) and Akiko Aizawa[1,2](iD)

[1] The University of Tokyo, Tokyo, Japan
dtan@g.ecc.u-tokyo.ac.jp, aizawa@nii.ac.jp
[2] National Institute of Informatics, Tokyo, Japan

Abstract. Letter case information can impact named entity recognition (NER) by affecting the way entities are represented in the text. For instance, if proper nouns are capitalized, NER models can utilize this information to identify named entities. Although studies have analyzed the performance drop of NER models without capitalization information, it is not clear how different letter-case scenarios affect the NER performance for different types of data and domains. In this study, we examine the impact of different letter-case features on NER and investigate their effectiveness in improving NER system performance and robustness. The analysis of the effect of different letter-case scenarios on NER performance is performed for one domain and across multiple domains. The experimental results demonstrate that capitalization errors significantly affect the NER performance in both in- and cross-domain evaluation. The case-insensitive (BERT-base-uncased) model is more robust to inconsistencies in capitalization that may occur in noisy text data, whereas the case-sensitive (BERT-base-cased) model performs better on well-written text that provides clear case information. However, when the case-sensitive model is required in the application, we propose a simple data augmentation heuristic based on a letter case that improves the model's robustness against capitalization errors commonly observed in user-generated text. Overall, our findings suggest that changing the style of the source domain to match that of the target domain can lead to better domain adaptation for NER and that the choice of the BERT model should consider the nature of the text data being analyzed. Our code and data for reproducing this work are available at https://github.com/daotuanan/Letter-case-NER.

Keywords: named entity recognition · letter case · robustness

1 Introduction

Named entity recognition (NER) is a sub-task of information extraction, the goal of which is to classify text spans into redefined categories [1]. Letter case information can impact NER by affecting the way entities are represented in the

E. Métais et al. (Eds.): NLDB 2023, LNCS 13913, pp. 588–598, 2023.
https://doi.org/10.1007/978-3-031-35320-8_45

text. In general, the capitalization of proper names is a convention for most languages that use the Latin alphabet (e.g. English, French, German, and so on). This capitalization acts as a clue for NER models to identify entities. However, NER models need to be able to handle variations in capitalization, such as all uppercase or all lowercase text, as well as inconsistent capitalization, to accurately recognize entities. NER models need to be trained on a diverse corpus of text to be robust to different writing styles and capitalization conventions.

In traditional NER systems, statistical approaches were used to train classifiers based on features such as capitalization patterns, the context of the entity, and the words contained within the entity [2–4]. In a recent study, the problem of performing NER in languages where capitalization is not used was addressed by systematically analyzing solutions to lowercased text in English [5]. The results of the study demonstrated that model performance drops significantly in scenarios where capitalization is not used, such as in noisy web text or machine translation outputs. It has been shown that NER models are vulnerable to adversarial attacks related to letter-case, with significant drops in performance for all models compared to their performance on the original datasets [6]. Simple data augmentation that combines the training set's original sentences, lower-cased sentences, and upper-cased sentences may improve the models' generalizability and robustness against the noisy text [7]. However, there is a lack of a comprehensive study that evaluates the effectiveness of different capitalization features and their combinations in improving the performance of NER systems. Although there have been studies that analyze the performance drop of NER models without capitalization information [6,7], it is not clear how different letter-case scenarios affect NER performance for different types of data and domains. Therefore, a comprehensive study that systematically evaluates different capitalization features and their combinations and investigates their impact on the performance and robustness of NER systems could fill this knowledge gap.

In this paper, we explore the following research question: "How do different letter-case scenarios and their combinations affect the performance and robustness of NER systems in one domain or across different domains". The results demonstrated that capitalization errors significantly affect the performance of both in- and cross-domain evaluation. The best performance is achieved when the letter case of the testing data is similar to that of the training data. Moreover, BERT models process lower-cased entities better than upper-cased ones. In the case of popular pretrained language models (BERT [8], BioBERT [9]), we have to train two different versions: cased and uncased models. This pretraining process is time-consuming and resource-intensive, which limits the scalability of these models. We want to answer the question "Which version is better for NER task?" so that we can choose the model that is suitable for the downstream applications. Our experimental results indicate that the BERT-base-uncased model is more robust to inconsistencies in capitalization that may occur in noisy text data, whereas the BERT-base-cased model performs better on the well-written text that provides clear case information. Therefore, there is a need for techniques that can improve the performance of cased models against capitalization errors in noisy text data. In this paper, we propose an augmentation technique that can enhance the robustness of the BERT-cased model against capitalization errors commonly observed in user-generated text. Our experimental results reveal that the proposed technique can improve the performance of the BERT-cased model, reducing the need for training both cased and uncased models.

2   Methodology

2.1   NER Model

Pre-training of deep bidirectional transformers (BERT) [8] is prevalent owing to its easily applicable pipeline: (1) pre-training on extensive corpora and (2) fine-tuning the model for only a few epochs with the downstream tasks. Although it requires only a few epochs for fine-tuning, the BERT model exhibits state-of-the-art or comparable performance in various tasks, including text classification and NER [8]. There are some advanced pretrained models for NER problems, such as FLAIR [10] and Electra [11]. However, owing to the BERT model's high performance and popularity, we decided to use it in our analysis. We implement our NER models, based on BERT, with the Transformer library of Hugging Face [12]. We used two BERT variants: BERT-base-cased and BERT-base-uncased models pre-trained on English Wikipedia and BooksCorpus as our base model. We fine-tuned the model for three epochs using the batch size of 32, the learning rate of $5e - 05$, and the random seed set at 42. The other hyper-parameters are set by default. Figure 1 shows the architecture of BERT-based models used in our experiments.

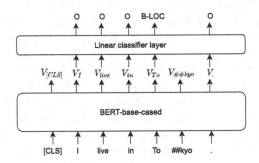

Fig. 1. BERT-based NER model.

2.2   Data Augmentation Based on Letter-Case for NER

Data augmentation helps extend training data by applying transformations that do not change the label of the original data [13]. For NER, the intuition to use data augmentation is model generalized because the letter case of the augmented version better matches the target domain when data augmentation is applied for domain adaptation. For instance, named entities in tweets could appear without letter-case information "I love la la land," but with a letter-case for a domain such as news the form, "I live in Tokyo" is standard. Two common strategies are used to improve robustness to capitalization errors in natural language processing. The first is to ignore capitalization information by using case-agnostic models or lower-casing every input in deep learning models. The second is to explicitly correct capitalization by using another model trained for this purpose, called "truecasing". Both methods have the limitation of discarding orthographic information in the target text, which can lead to degradation of performance on well-formed text. Simple data augmentation that combines the training set's original sentences, lower-cased sentences, and upper-cased sentences may improve the models' generalizability and robustness against noisy text [7]. This simple rule-based method can be seen as transformations 1 and 2 in Table 1, which are sentence-level transformations. In this study, we explore the entity-level transformations that apply lowercase, uppercase, or capitalize only the first character of the named entities. Table 1 lists examples of all transformations used in this study. Transformations can be combined to extend the training dataset. The final training data is concatenated from the original training and the augmented training sets (with one or multiple transformations). Because these transformations preserve labels, the original label is assigned to the augmented versions of the data. To create a large and diverse training set that better represents the target domain with more inconsistencies of letter case, we choose our augmentation by combining all of the transformations in Table 1.

Table 1. Examples of different transformations based on letter-case.

ID	Label	Level	O	O	O	B-LOC	O
0	Original		I	live	in	Tokyo	.
1	Lower-cased	Sentence	i	live	in	tokyo	.
2	Upper-cased	Sentence	I	LIVE	IN	TOKYO	.
3	Lower-cased	Entity	I	live	in	tokyo	.
4	Upper-cased	Entity	I	live	in	TOKYO	.
5	Capitalize first char	Entity	I	live	in	Tokyo	.

3 Experiment

3.1 Experiment Settings

For evaluation, following the CoNLL 2003 shared task [14], we use the classic entity-level precision (P), recall (R), and F1-score metrics to compare the models. Regarding the total performance, we use the micro average for all metrics. For true-casing, we use the framework truecase[1] inspired by the previous work [15].

---

[1] https://pypi.org/project/truecase/.

3.2   Benchmark Datasets

We use the CoNLL 2003 dataset [14] for in-domain evaluation and the PLONER dataset [16] for cross-domain evaluation.

3.2.1   CoNLL 2003

To explore the effect of letter case on NER performance in one domain, we use the standard dataset CoNLL 2003 [14], which has been widely used for NER. Owing to this popularity, we can compare our results with several previous studies that also used this dataset. This corpus comprises 1393 news stories from Reuters from August 1996 to August 1997. The CoNLL03 contains four types of entities: PER (person), LOC (location), ORG (organization), and MISC (miscellaneous).

3.2.2   PLONER

Following a previous study [16], the PLONER dataset is used to evaluate cross-domain generalization. The dataset contains texts from various sources and domains, making it suitable for evaluating the robustness and generalizability of NER models across different domains and text types. This is a combination of CoNLL03 [17] (news domain), WNUT16 [18] (tweet domain), and OntoNotes 5.0 [19] (various domains). The PLONER dataset contains three types of entities: PER (person), LOC (location), ORG (organization).

3.3   Experiment Scenarios for Letter-Case

To simulate a scenario where the model is trained on data containing named entities that are not capitalized, which could occur in text that has been automatically transcribed or extracted from unstructured sources such as social media posts or online articles, we compare different settings of data for the models. The settings are as follows: Original (orig.): The sentence is the original CoNLL03 dataset without any modifications; Truecase (tc): The sentence is truecased using the truecaser; LowerSent (loS): The sentence is converted to a lowercase sentence; UpperSent (upS): The sentence is converted to an uppercase sentence; LowerEnt (loE): The entities (such as person, location, and organization names) in the data are converted to lowercase while the remainder of the sentence is unchanged; UpperEnt (upE): The entities in the data are converted to uppercase while the remainder of the sentence is unchanged; RandomSent (rS): Each word in the sentence can change its letter case randomly with a probability of 0.5; and RandomEnt (rE): Entities in the sentence can change its letter case randomly with a probability of 0.5.

4   Result

4.1   Effect of Letter Case for NER in One Domain

In this experiment, we focus on in-domain evaluation for the standard NER dataset (CoNLL03) to explore the effect of casing on NER performance in one domain. In the first part, we explore the effect of different training and testing scenarios on the normal NER (BERT-base-cased) model. We use the BERT-base-cased model [8] because the BERT-base-uncased model will lowercase the input data, thus we can't access the effect of various letter-case scenarios on NER performance. After that, we compare two versions of the BERT models, the BERT-base-cased and BERT-base-uncased, and analyze the effect of different test scenarios on these models.

Table 2. Performance (F1-scores) of different models on the CoNLL03 dataset under different training and testing data scenarios. The rows represent the training data scenarios, while columns represent the testing data scenarios. The last column shows the average F1 score of the model for all testing scenarios. The results in bold are the highest among the same version of test data.

(a) Performance (F1-scores) of BERT-base-cased model on the CoNLL03 dataset under different scenarios for the training and testing data.

Train Data	Test Data								AVG
	orig.	tc	loS	upS	loE	upE	rS	rE	
orig.	**90.43**	80.07	24.61	42.11	24.30	55.25	27.07	40.58	48.05
tc	85.79	**88.94**	60.24	29.79	59.81	45.61	24.53	41.10	54.48
loS	54.16	55.53	**85.15**	32.76	83.26	46.65	20.83	47.56	53.24
upS	56.11	50.32	48.17	**75.45**	48.42	73.98	**44.40**	**60.33**	**57.15**
loE	4.09	10.70	78.94	0.07	**85.80**	0.10	11.00	25.34	27.01
upE	26.35	9.60	0.84	52.52	0.89	**85.10**	27.13	49.83	31.53
loS + upS [7]	90.47	86.52	86.73	79.02	85.34	83.98	44.51	73.45	78.75
Our AUG	90.42	87.15	**87.21**	**79.97**	**86.88**	**87.35**	**48.54**	**78.36**	**80.73**

(b) Performance (F1-scores) of BERT-base-cased and BERT-base-uncased on the CoNLL03 dataset under different testing data scenarios.

Bert Model	Test Data								AVG
	orig.	tc	loS	upS	loE	upE	rS	rE	
BERT-cased	**90.43**	80.07	24.61	42.11	24.3	55.25	27.07	40.58	48.05
BERT-uncased	89.81	**89.81**	**89.81**	**89.81**	**89.81**	**89.81**	**89.81**	**89.81**	**89.81**

Abbreviations: orig. = original, tc = truecase, loS = lowerSent, upS = upperSent, loE = lowerEnt, upE = upperEnt, rS = randomSent, rE = randomEnt, AUG = Data Augmentation.

4.1.1   NER Performance

The performance (F1-score) of **BERT-base-cased** model on CoNLL03 with different scenarios for training and testing data is summarized in Table 2a. The results demonstrate that the model's performance varies significantly depending on the training and testing letter case. When the training and testing data are the same, the model achieves the highest F1-score (90.43% for the original). When the testing data is from different scenarios (lowercase sentences, uppercase

Table 3. Average F1 scores of the BERT-base-cased model trained on the original data and tested on different test scenarios of the PLONER dataset subdomains. The last column shows the average F1 score of the model across all subdomains.

Test data	CoNLL03	OnBC	OnBN	OnMZ	OnNW	OnWB	WNUT16	AVG
Original	73.56	78.21	78.86	78.38	71.20	67.50	57.08	72.11
lowerSent	25.83	22.03	27.13	41.63	34.90	26.78	14.13	27.49
upperSent	23.61	14.03	14.46	12.96	1.84	0.60	12.91	11.49

Table 4. Performance (F1-score) of different BERT models on original test data on the PLONER

Model	CoNLL03	OnBC	OnBN	OnMZ	OnNW	OnWB	WNUT16	AVG
BERT-cased	**73.56**	**78.21**	**78.86**	78.38	71.20	67.50	**57.08**	72.11
BERT-uncased	50.17	54.06	51.40	60.28	51. 56	46.08	39.89	50.78
BERT-cased+ AUG	72.74	76.32	77.43	**80.41**	**71.29**	**70.99**	56.50	**72.24**

sentences, lowercase entities, uppercase entities, random sentences, and random entities), the model's performance decreases significantly. It can be observed that the highest F1 scores are achieved when the letter case settings of the training and testing data are the same. Additionally, the table includes the results of two different data augmentation methods: lowercase sentence (loS) + uppercase sentence (upS) from previous work [7] and our proposed augmentation (AUG). We observe that the data augmentation technique (AUG) has significantly improved the performance of the model in most scenarios. Moreover, our proposed method outperforms the loS + upS method from previous work in terms of the average F1-score (80.73% vs. 78.75%) which indicates the effectiveness of entity-level transformations. The average F1-score of the model trained on the augmented data is the highest among all scenarios, indicating that data augmentation has helped the model learn more generalizable patterns.

4.1.2   Comparison of the BERT-Cased and BERT-Uncased

In Table 2a, we use the BERT-base-cased model to analyze the effect of letter-case information on NER performance. However, there are two versions of the BERT models: BERT-base-cased and BERT-base-uncased. BERT-base-uncased is the version that does not rely on letter-case information. Previous studies have revealed that current NER models suffer significant performance losses (up to 40% in terms of F1-score) when missing letter-case information [6,7]. Thus, we can expect the NER performance of the BERT-base-uncased model to be much worse than that of the BERT-base-cased model. The performance of the BERT-base-cased model and the BERT-base-uncased model on the CoNLL03 dataset are compared in Table 2b. Contrary to our expectations and the result of previous studies, with the original testing data, there is no significant reduction in the performance of the BERT-base-uncased compared to that of the BERT-base-cased model. Moreover, the performance of the BERT-base-uncased model appeared to be unaffected by the removal of letter-case information. The BERT-base-uncased model outperforms the BERT-base-cased model in most scenarios. This is surprising considering the previous study showing that letter-case information is important for NER performance. It is possible that the BERT-base-uncased model is able to capture semantic information that compensates for the loss of letter-case information. These results further support the idea that the BERT-base-uncased model is more robust than the BERT-base-cased model when handling letter-case noise from input text at inference time.

4.2   Effect of Letter Case for NER Across Domains

Similar to the in-domain evaluation (see Sect. 4.1), the objective of this experiment was to explore the effect of letter-case, but for cross-domain settings, on the PLONER dataset.

4.2.1   NER Performance

The average F1 scores of the BERT-base-cased model on different test scenarios (original, lowerSent, upperSent) are listed in Table 3. Overall, the performance is highest for the original data, lower for the lower-cased data, and lowest for the upper-case data. This evidence suggests that letter-case information is crucial for cross-domain transfer. The significant drop in performance on the lowerSent and upperSent scenarios highlights the model's sensitivity to changes in letter case. Moreover, it is much harder to train models on the original data to detect uppercase entities than lower-case ones. This is consistent with the results of the in-domain evaluation.

BERT-base-cased test on the original test data (see Table 5a): the diagonal elements are the highest because the model has learned the specific patterns and characteristics of the named entities in that particular subdomain during training. In contrast, the off-diagonal elements represent the performance of the model when tested on a subdomain that it was not specifically trained on. This can be more challenging because named entities in different subdomains may have different patterns and characteristics, making it more difficult for the model to recognize them accurately. The highest F1-score is 90.50, which is achieved when the model is trained on the CoNLL03 subdomain and tested on the same subdomain; however, on average, training on OnBN provides the best generalizability (76.80%). The lowest F1-score is 50.83% (tested on the WNUT16 subdomain), indicating that WNUT16 is extremely different (tweets) from other subdomains (news). The average F1 score across all subdomains is 72.11.

BERT-base-cased test on original test data with data augmentation on training data (see Table 5b): similar to Table 5a, the diagonal elements are the highest. The results suggest that the BERT-base-cased model still performs relatively well on the off-diagonal elements, indicating that it is able to generalize to some extent across different subdomains of the PLONER dataset. When looking at the improvement with data augmentation compared to the original training data

Table 5. Performance (F1-score) of the original testing data on PLONER of the BERT-base-cased model with and without data augmentation. The AVG row shows the average F1 score of the model tested on one subdomain. The AVG column shows the average F1 score of the model trained on one subdomain and tested on all subdomains. The bold value is the highest when testing the same test set (same column).

(a) BERT-base-cased without data augmentation.

train \ test	CoNLL03	OnBC	OnBN	OnMZ	OnNW	OnWB	WNUT16	AVG
CoNLL03	**90.50**	72.89	72.95	74.89	61.29	60.84	56.49	69.98
OnBC	71.68	**87.51**	83.72	80.33	72.66	72.32	51.82	74.29
OnBN	74.46	85.65	**89.74**	81.45	77.04	72.50	56.79	76.80
OnMZ	71.03	77.25	77.26	**90.07**	77.54	60.41	51.15	72.10
OnNW	69.63	79.63	80.29	82.40	**84.87**	70.05	52.67	74.22
OnWB	63.25	80.24	80.02	79.20	74.21	**77.09**	57.25	73.04
WNUT16	74.34	64.28	68.03	60.34	50.83	59.29	**73.39**	64.36
AVG	73.56	78.21	78.86	78.38	71.20	67.50	57.08	72.11

(b) BERT-base-cased with data augmentation.

train \ test	CoNLL03	OnBC	OnBN	OnMZ	OnNW	OnWB	WNUT16	AVG
CoNLL03	**93.82**	69.71	71.83	73.92	58.12	62.3	57.37	69.58
OnBC	68.79	**88.6**	82.15	82.6	77.13	73.58	50.58	74.78
OnBN	74.21	81.94	**90.73**	83.21	76.66	74.69	55.75	76.74
OnMZ	68.82	71.58	75.26	**90.95**	77.89	68.32	49.81	71.80
OnNW	62.29	75.05	77.28	82.03	**87.78**	72.35	47.84	72.09
OnWB	63.15	77.61	79.34	80.4	73.72	**82.49**	57.92	73.52
WNUT16	78.09	69.74	65.41	69.78	47.74	63.17	**76.24**	67.17
AVG	72.74	76.32	77.43	80.41	71.29	70.99	56.50	72.24

(c) Improvement of augmented training data over the original training data.

train \ test	CoNLL03	OnBC	OnBN	OnMZ	OnNW	OnWB	WNUT16	AVG
CoNLL03	3.32	-3.18	-1.12	-0.97	-3.17	1.46	0.88	-0.40
OnBC	-2.89	1.09	-1.57	2.27	4.47	1.26	-1.24	0.48
OnBN	-0.25	-3.71	1.00	1.76	-0.38	2.19	-1.04	-0.06
OnMZ	-2.21	-5.67	-2.00	0.88	0.35	7.91	-1.34	-0.30
OnNW	-7.34	-4.58	-3.01	-0.37	3.91	2.30	-4.83	-1.99
OnWB	-0.10	-2.63	-0.68	1.20	-0.49	5.40	0.67	0.48
WNUT16	3.75	5.46	-2.62	9.44	-3.09	3.88	2.85	2.81
AVG	-0.82	-1.89	1.43	2.03	0.23	3.49	-0.58	0.15

(see Table 5c), the results indicate that data augmentation improves the performance of the model on most of the target datasets, with an average improvement of 0.15%. The largest improvements are observed for training on the WNUT16 (2.81%), OnWB (0.48%), and OnBC datasets (0.48%). However, there are some target datasets where the performance decreases after data augmentation, such as the OnBC (-1.89%), CoNLL03 (-0.82%), and WNUT16 datasets (-0.58%).

4.2.2 Comparison of BERT-Cased and BERT-Uncased for Cross-Domain NER

Similar to Sect. 4.1.2, we intend to compare the BERT-base-cased (see Table 5a) and BERT-base-uncased models across domains using the PLONER dataset as described in Sect. 3.2. Table 4 compares the NER performance obtained from the two BERT models and BERT-base-cased with augmentation in the PLONER test set. The performance of the BERT-base-cased model outperforms that of the BERT-base-uncased model in all sub-domains of the PLONER dataset. These results suggest that the cased model is better for transferring entity information across domains and that letter-case information is crucial for cross-domain transfer. Our augmentation (BERT-cased +AUG) slightly outperforms BERT-cased model for average results indicating the effectiveness of the data augmentation for cross-domain transfer.

5 Conclusion

This study investigated how changing the name regularity of entities improves domain adaptation for NER. Overall, letter cases significantly affect the performance of NER models in both in- and cross-domain transfers. The best performance was achieved when the letter case of the testing data was similar to that of the training data. The experimental results indicate the robustness of the BERT-base-uncased over the BERT-base-cased model when handling noisy text data. In contrast, the BERT-base-cased model is more effective when transferring NER output across domains. For well-written text such as Wikipedia or news, letter case information gives the case sensitive model (BERT-cased) an advantage for pure performance. However, the case-insensitive model (BERT-uncased) can explore other linguistic features in addition to letter case, which makes it more robust to inconsistencies in capitalization that may occur in noisy text data. If the case sensitive model is required in the application, our proposed augmentation technique improves the robustness of the BERT-cased model against the capitalization errors commonly observed in user-generated text. These findings may lead to better domain adaptation for NER by changing the style of the source domain to match the target domain.

Acknowledgement. This work was partly supported by JSPS KAKENHI Grant Number 22K19818; JST SPRING, Grant Number JPMJSP2108; and JST, AIP Trilateral AI Research, Grant Number JPMJCR20G9, Japan.

References

1. Grishman, R., Sundheim, B.: Design of the MUC-6 evaluation. In: Proceedings of the MUC, pp. 1–11. Association for Computational Linguistics (1995)
2. Malouf, R.: Markov models for language-independent named entity recognition. In: Proceedings of the CoNLL (2002)
3. Collobert, R., Weston, J.: A unified architecture for natural language processing: deep neural networks with multitask learning. In: Proceedings of the IMLS, pp. 160–167 (2008)
4. Collobert, R., Weston, J., Bottou, L., Karlen, M., Kavukcuoglu, K., Kuksa, P.: Natural language processing (almost) from scratch. J. Mach. Learn. Res. **12**, 2493–2537 (2011)
5. Mayhew, S., Tsygankova, T., Roth, D.: NER and POS when nothing is capitalized. In: Proceedings of the EMNLP-IJCNLP, pp. 6256–6261 (2019)
6. Das, S., Paik, J.: Resilience of named entity recognition models under adversarial attack. In: Proceedings of the DADC, pp. 1–6 (2022)
7. Bodapati, S., Yun, H., Al-Onaizan, Y.: Robustness to capitalization errors in named entity recognition. In: Proceedings of the W-NUT, pp. 237–242 (2019)
8. Devlin, J., Chang, M.-W., Lee, K., Toutanova, K.: BERT: pre-training of deep bidirectional transformers for language understanding. In: Proceedings of the ACL, pp. 4171–4186 (2019)
9. Lee, J., et al.: BioBERT: a pre-trained biomedical language representation model for biomedical text mining. Bioinformatics **36**(4), 1234–1240 (2020)
10. Akbik, A., Blythe, D., Vollgraf, R.: Contextual string embeddings for sequence labeling. In: Proceedings of the COLING, pp. 1638–1649 (2018)
11. Clark, K., Luong, M.-T., Le, Q.V., Manning, C.D.: ELECTRA: pre-training text encoders as discriminators rather than generators. arXiv preprint arXiv:2003.10555 (2020)
12. Wolf, T., et al.: Transformers: state-of-the-art natural language processing. In: Proceedings of the EMNLP, pp. 38–45. Association for Computational Linguistics (2020)
13. Simard, P.Y., Steinkraus, D., Platt, J.C., et al.: Best practices for convolutional neural networks applied to visual document analysis. In: ICDAR, vol. 3 (2003)
14. Sang, E.T.K., Meulder, F.D.: Introduction to the CoNLL-2003 shared task: language-independent named entity recognition. In: Proceedings of the HLT-NAACL, pp. 142–147 (2003)
15. Lita, L.V., Ittycheriah, A., Roukos, S., Kambhatla, N.: Truecasing. In: Proceedings of the ACL, pp. 152–159 (2003)
16. Jinlan, F., Liu, P., Zhang, Q.: Rethinking generalization of neural models: a named entity recognition case study. In: Proceedings of the AAAI, vol. 34, pp. 7732–7739 (2020)
17. Tjong Kim Sang, E.F., De Meulder, F.: Introduction to the CoNLL-2003 shared task: Language-independent named entity recognition. In: Proceedings of the HLT-NAACL, pp. 142–147. Association for Computational Linguistics (2003)
18. Strauss, B., Toma, B., Ritter, A., De Marneffe, M.C., Xu, W.: Results of the WNUT16 named entity recognition shared task. In: Proceedings of the WNUT, pp. 138–144 (2016)
19. Weischedel, R., et al.: Ontonotes release 4.0. LDC2011T03 (2011)

Author Index

© The Editor(s) (if applicable) and The Author(s), under exclusive license
to Springer Nature Switzerland AG 2023
E. Métais et al. (Eds.): NLDB 2023, LNCS 13913, pp. 599–600, 2023.
https://doi.org/10.1007/978-3-031-35320-8

Printed in the United States
by Baker & Taylor Publisher Services